JEWISH LEADERS
(1750-1940)

EDITED BY

LEO JUNG 1892-

NEW YORK

BLOCH PUBLISHING COMPANY

5714-1953

PRINTED IN UNITED STATES OF AMERICA

DEDICATED TO THE SACRED MEMORY OF
AUGUSTA Le VINE

PREFACE

I

ALMOST *100 years ago, Isaac Reggio emphasized the fact that the neglect of the Mitsvoth Maassiyoth (the so-called customs and ceremonial laws) would lead to religious anemia, communal assimilation and ultimately to national destruction. The history of our people since has shown how true his statement was. Dissidents of all sorts have chosen the Mitsvoth Maassiyoth as their favorite target of attack, with devastating results to Judaism and Jewry alike.*

The term assimilation has been used to describe the tendency of some Jews to become like their West European neighbors, to shed their religious characteristics, water down and eventually lose their religious heritage. It was identified originally with the salons of Jewish women in Germany—during the 18th and 19th centuries— in which everything but Jewish topics was welcome; then, with exclusive Jewish clubs and their frantic attempts to prove themselves 110% Teutonic or American; with similar eccentricities in France, England and elsewhere. The impact of the New Israel and the Hitler horror have driven this type of assimilation from practically every Jewish community. It leads a precarious existence in the "American Council for Judaism" which is un-American, un-Jewish, and has no counsel of significance to offer.

But there is another kind of assimilation no less harmful, and at present both powerful and widespread. That is irreligious radicalism, imported from Eastern Europe. In Russia, the church was corrupt; it acquiesced shamefully in the state's religious and economic oppression. Even pogroms received the church's approbation. How often did a Russian priest bless the murderous Cossacks on their way to massacre peaceful Jewish folks, or machinegun orderly crowds of protesting citizens, all in the name of "the Czar and the Holy Church." Revolutionaries in the Russian empire, with more fervor than wisdom, then proceeded to identify all religion with Russia's corruption. No wonder that they postulated that the

v

interests of religion and of the common people are incompatible. Similarly many Jewish working men thought that Judaism had no message for them. A great deal of the Israeli anti-religious sentiment stems from this tragic mistake. This anti-religious assimilation prevents cooperation of the whole people in the upbuilding of the country and causes unnecessary tension. This is both deplorable and baseless. The Torah, the prophets and the rabbis were all labor-minded; collective bargaining, a national labor board, the right to a job, the protection of the laborer, are all imbedded in the legislation of the Torah. Indeed even some secularist circles have already recognized that the scheme of Jewish life has great survival-value for the Jewish people; that the Sabbath has kept the Jew more than the Jew has kept the Sabbath; that the Mitsvoth have done more for our people than our people have done for the Mitsvoth. When the members of the Histadruth in Israel will have emancipated themselves from the misconceptions and false slogans of Eastern Europe's radicalism, the moment will have arrived for their rediscovery of the faith of our people as the source of national encouragement, individual ennoblement and universal good.

These two forms of assimilation have come closer to each other in some modern deviations, especially in a Godless nationalism which endeavors to enthrone a secularist Jewish culture in the place of the Faith of our Fathers; and a contentless reform Judaism which starves people's emotions whilst keeping their intellect dissatisfied. Unfortunately, for the last hundred and fifty years, Torah-true Jewry has suffered not only from the handicaps of Ghetto life before emancipation but also from the enormous burdens of carrying the double program of Jewish life and secular citizenship since then. Until Hitler's hell-hounds destroyed one third of the Jewish people, the majority of Jews were Torah-true. The relations between them and their more or less assimilated brethren were not always pleasant, and are thus reflected in the words and deeds of some of our leaders during that period. In word and deed, reform rabbis and lay leaders have gone to incredible extremes. Their excesses were described, deplored, and denounced by rabbis Meldola de Sola in a famous monograph, Dr. Joseph H. Hertz in "Affirmations of Judaism", by Elisha Friedman in "Israel of Tomorrow" and by others.

*One of the consequences was a Judaism with a much reduced
God or a profession of faith in God with a much reduced Judaism,
a combination of reform and nationalism—one lost in pale theology,
the other in impotent "liberalism." Opportunists in another camp
are riding the crests of whatever transient waves come rushing
towards them. At the present moment much of the iconoclastic
thunder has died down and some centripetal effort is observable in
the camp of reform. The gap between them and Torah-true Jews
has not been bridged because the foundations of Jewish life are still
being officially and almost universally violated by reform Jewry.*

*What is now indicated is, indeed, not name-calling but a clear
appreciation of the solid facts and a determination of Torah-true
Jewry to invest all its efforts in the upbuilding of Judaism, both
in America and in Israel. No argument against rootless, bootless
reform, no evidence as to their destruction of Jewish religious life,
no matter how eloquent, will basically help the situation. Nor may
our private appreciation of fine personalities among reform brethren
or their achievements in the field of organized philanthropy dull
the acuity of our conviction that reform spells the dissolution of the
Jewish problem. Even recent discussion of a reform Shulhan Arukh
does not justify cautious optimism. Their violation of Jewish marriage law has wrought havoc with Jewish family life, the reduction
of Shabbath and Yom Tov to a minimum have brought about a
wide-spread hereditary religious anemia. Only the Nazi nightmare
and the restoration of Israel have for the moment halted and perchance in some manner helped to reverse the process of disintegration.*

*As for the Torah-true leaders whose life and works this book
describes, they labored painfully, slowly, but with a clear purpose,
to achieve the combination of loyalty to the Din Torah with efficiency of method. They were willing to apply Jewish law to modern times by application of precedent or principle to new conditions
but not to adapt it in accordance with any intellectual or social
fashion. The esthetical and ethical expression of our Torah has
been a timeless postulate of Halakhah though often rendered nu-
gatory by the cruel emergencies of Jewish life.*

*In our days we face problems which call for tremendous courage
and vision. This volume I hope will convey at least some picture of*

the bold pioneering in which the Torah-true leaders engaged. From Alkalai who almost two generations before Herzl travelled through two continents summoning Jewry to the paramount duty of the restoration of Israel, to Samson Raphael Hirsch, great scholar, thinker, leader, who espoused the positive elements of the 19th century culture; from J. Reines and M. Z. Jung who pioneered in high school education, to Sarah Schenierer who led the foundation of what was the largest network of girls' schools in Eastern and Central Europe—there is a heartening record of an awareness of modern problems, of bold grappling with difficult situations, of selfless dedication to the new task.

The great rabbis—the heads of Yeshivoth and Kehilloth all over the Diaspora—made their major contribution through spreading knowledge of the Torah, as a philosophy and programme of life, around which the whole of the people could rally. They endowed their students and communities with sufficient learning, intellectual conviction, and courage to carry the teaching of Moses and the prophets into every clime and century. It was through these rabbis that the passion for enlightenment, for righteousness, for a dynamic interest in the under-privileged, penetrated the home and heart of the Jews. It was they who, utterly impervious to political and social pressure, kept stressing the glory of Zion and Jerusalem and who prepared among all Jews, religious and non-religious, the renaissance of the Jewish people in the Holy Land.

Torah-true Jewry has its problems: Ghetto imperfections, lack of organization, often lamentable unawareness of contemporary problems, insufficient preoccupation with proper approaches. As reform Jews rejected the obligations to Jewish law, they simultaneously discarded heavy obligations and proper anchorage; hence their headlong flight into all sorts of theological and practical absurdities. Torah-true Jewry in competition with the social glory and overwhelming opulence of reform could not offer so easy a Gan Eden. Salvation on easy terms which the Reform Temple appeared to offer (minus the sacrifices, the inconveniences and the steady purpose of Jewish life) should have proved very attractive to the average immigrant, burdened with a hundred problems. Yet it failed to capture more than a small fraction of our people.

As for the conservative movement, it is, because of the extreme elasticity of its doctrines, practically dependent upon the personal vagaries of the individual. Being more subtle than outright reform, it is more alluring to the uninitiated and more difficult to overcome. In one of its further departures it may be at least as destructive as reform, because it borders on a non-theistic concept of the Jewish religion.

The time has come for both calm appraisal and firm determination. Organizationally, Torah-true Jewry in the U. S. A. has made tremendous strides, to which Yeshiva University, two dozen other Yeshivoth, a hundred and fifty Jewish Day Schools, the revived Union of Orthodox Jewish Congregations, and the Rabbinical Council of America bear eloquent testimony. There has been some improvement of personal observance but not enough to justify a rosy optimism. To move towards a renaissance of Torah-true Judaism in our country and therefore elsewhere, we need a new heart and a fresh spirit, and a goodly portion of wisdom above learning, and courage—above power. For an unbarbered program of Jewish life and for the Din Torah as its basis, we need the unceasing attention of the laity and far-sighted creative legislative activity of the Torah authorities in Israel and in the Golah. As the latter will rise to the occasion, and act in accordance with the prerogatives and tasks the Torah has allotted to them, they will inspire the laity and especially the youth to abiding participation in Jewish work.

Let us hope that reform will continue its tendency of turning Jews back towards Judaism, that conservative Jews will learn how to conserve the Jewish tradition and that Torah-true Jewry will move towards the height of Judaism. The ultimate decision of our youth depends not on theoretical foundations but on community and individual patterns of Torah-true effort and presentation. The philosophy of Torah-true Judaism is at least as attractive to the thoughtful as that of its dissenting branches. Our gravest theological problems are faced equally by other groups. To encourage the average Jew to assume or continue the burdens of Torah-true life, a well-thought out presentation of its survival and serenity values is vital.

At Yeshiva University in our country, at Jews' College in England and elsewhere, a missionary movement of Judaism by Jews among Jews appears indicated.

The introduction exemplifies one of the relevant Halakhic attitudes. From the Rav of Liady to the Hafets Hayyim the rabbis offered both clear teaching and luminous examples of ethical conduct. The twenty-five chapters of this book convey a sense of Torah-true leadership through the last 190 years. A chapter each on Rabbi Samuel Mohilever and on "The Vilna Gaon as Scientist" had been promised by a Mizrachi leader and a Jewish scientist respectively, but unfortunately, in spite of repeated pledges, the MSS have, as yet, not arrived.

LEO JUNG

Tammuz 5173
June 1953

CONTENTS

VOLUME VI

INTRODUCTION

THE RABBIS AND THE ETHICS OF BUSINESS

By Leo Jung

THE RABBIS AND THE ETHICS OF BUSINESS

INTRODUCTION

KEDUSHAH

PRINCIPLES BEHIND THE LAWS

THE LAWS

BUYERS AND SELLERS

FAIR PRICES

WEIGHTS AND MEASURES

FRAUD AND REPENTANCE

RABBIS, LAW AND JUSTICE

DYNAMIC JUSTICE

EARLY PRECEDENTS

LATER APPLICATIONS

THE WHITE COCK

JUST WAGES AND FAIR DEALING

SUMMARY

INTRODUCTION

The standards which govern men's lives have been accepted on at least two grounds. They come to us as laws, principles or attitudes from a recognized higher authority, divine or human. Or else, their practical nature has commended them to conscience and common sense.

The higher a man's culture, the more he is apt to judge his own and other creeds or groups by the measures they have devised to make ideals concrete, to help their adherents reach higher levels of conduct. But even in primitive societies, men and women were conscious of basic principles governing their dealings with their fellow men. A common denominator of all societies has been the universal appreciation of the virtue of fairness and the need to limit greed.

This article attempts to give a picture of the contributions of Jewish life and law (as developed and interpreted through the centuries) to today's general code of practical ethics. The magnitude of these contributions can best be understood if we first examine an underlying and unique concept, first developed by the ancient Jews—the concept of *Kedushah.*

KEDUSHAH

Kedushah is a Hebrew word meaning "holiness." It is the keyword to Judaism. All teachings and judgments of Jewish scholars stem from it.

Kedushah connects man with God and sets the pattern for man's conduct according to *Torah,* God's precepts. It is an attitude based on righteousness and it embodies reverence and mercy as well. It is expressed in the conduct of an individual or a nation. It has no catechized form; *Kedushah* is the theme, the means and end of every hour of the day, for every age and sex, for private and public life.

All prayers and ceremonies are but formal expressions of *Kedushah* and represent a form of intensified communion with God. *Kedushah* amounts to a total program for a noble, wise and generous life. In business, it means honesty; on the field of sports,

5

fair play. At home, it means honest and decent relations between husband and wife, mutual consideration between parents and children.

Kedushah offers the concept of a God who is mighty—but not only for reasons of power or infiniteness or independence. God is holy because of His righteousness. He is the God of mercy, the Father who understands human frailty. He is the Judge with whom no specious pleading will avail. He is the God of righteousness and the man who is righteous is closest to Him.

The Jewish code of ethics draws its source and strength from *Kedushah.*

PRINCIPLES BEHIND THE LAWS

In Biblical times, up to the age of Solomon, the majority of Hebrews were either farmers or shepherds. The very name for merchant in Hebrew was Canaanite, or foreigner. But, before settling in Palestine, the Jews had seen and suffered from much injustice, oppression and fraud at the hands of strangers. Therefore, even in the Code of Moses, we find many principles governing trade laws and admonitions against *Ona'ah,* a word meaning oppression, fraud, and deceit. The Mosaic law was practical to the extreme—it was designed to protect the common people's food and health against the predatory instinct of would-be monopolists and greedy merchants.

All early law was based on the principle of fairness with its corollary of reciprocity. In many a country in which the Jews travelled, the Roman principle of Caveat Emptor prevailed: The purchaser had to be on his guard at the moment of sale because any error or fraud later discovered could not be legally corrected. By the same token, in the legal climate of Rome, a person at the exchange booth or banker's table had to count his change at the moment, for the transaction was considered complete once he left the table and no refund was obligatory. According to the laws of antiquity it was generally understood that the finder of an object may keep it.

Jewish law in all cases was much different. The finder of an object that had any marks of identification on it had to proclaim it on three public occasions. An overcharge in a commercial transaction was collectable by the victim as a refund. A refund after a fraudulent transaction was mandatory.

A problem frequently appeared in the case of transactions between a Jew and a Gentile, in a country or district where both codes prevailed. On the basis of reciprocity, which governs all fair laws, a Jew was not legally obliged to return an overcharge to a Gentile when such overcharge would not be returnable by the Gentile had the Jew been victimized. The same was true with regard to return of lost property. In many a country it would not occur to the finder to proclaim or restore an article lost by a Jew because the law of the country did not protect the loser.

Jewish law, however, knows two levels: a legal one which it shares with all civilized codes, and the moral one which is characteristically its own. The Rabbis insisted that one should "go beyond the law," that one should act on moral grounds even when there was no legal obligation to help one's neighbor. The principle involved is called *Kiddush ha-Shem,* the sanctification of the name of God. In order to sanctify the name of God by their conduct, Jews were taught to ignore the benefit of the law and act so generously and nobly that the non-Jew might benefit and thus magnify and glorify the Name of God. This is the purpose, the rabbis explained, for which the Jew was chosen: to be a *"Kingdom of Priests,"* not for privilege, but for service.

Conversely, a mean attitude, a violation of general moral principles, leads to the desecration of the Name of God *(Hillul ha-Shem).* That is the worst offense possible for a Jew. The desecration of the Name of God in public is one of those grave sins for which it is very difficult to atone.

Jewish law considers righteousness in small things as well as in big things as so vital that it actually determines in detail how much the tailor or shoemaker may retain from material one has given him for making a suit or a pair of shoes. It considers as real "oppression" even the harsh or inconsiderate word towards someone in a position economically or socially inferior. It frowns upon a visit to a store or shop unless one intends to make a purchase. All these offenses constitute sins not only against one's neighbor but against God. They are a touchstone of the Jews' loyalty to the faith of his fathers.

THE LAWS

BUYERS AND SELLERS

The laws against oppression protect the seller as well as the buyer. If, by error, the seller had sold something more than one-sixth below its value, the transaction would be considered retroactively invalid; the purchaser would have to restore the merchandise and collect the money he had paid for it.

Since the laws against oppression are meant to prevent abuse of people's merchandise and their vital necessities, they do not apply to luxuries. If a man paid too much to a dealer in jewelry or any object not required for the normal needs of life, the laws of Ona'ah would not apply.

These laws applied to Jews and non-Jews resident in Israel or under the jurisdiction of the Jewish court of justice elsewhere. The only exceptions applied to members of a caravan. The principle of inter-territoriality protected the foreign trader from interference by local law. Caravans were important in antiquity because they offered the only chance for an exchange of goods. Caravan members, therefore, enjoyed rights denied to the resident alien and the citizen. They were usually subject to courts of law specially established to judge them in accord with the law of the country from which they came. This was meant to assure the application of some principles of righteousness without imposing Jewish law upon the non-Jews.

Thus, the non-Jew in Israel enjoyed certain privileges denied to the native. On the basis of reciprocity, since the non-Jew was not obliged to heed the laws of oppression, legally it would be unfair to impose upon the Jew a responsibility not shared by the alien trader. But for the sake of *Kiddush ha-Shem* it was rendered obligatory for the Jew to ge beyond legal or technical protection for the sake of the non-Jew.

The term "Sons of Noah" is pertinent here. Any non-Jew arriving in Israel was offered opportunity for equality before the law and the protection of the community in time of trouble if he accepted upon himself the seven principles included in the laws of the "Sons of Noah." Six of them were negative and one positive. The negative ones included the prohibition of cruelty to animals, blasphemy, theft or robbery, homicide, immorality and idolatry.

The positive principle the non-Jew had to accept was the furtherance of justice in all ways possible. The non-Jew accepting these
seven principles is considered "among the righteous of the nations
of the world and has a share in the world to come, even as an
Israelite."

FAIR PRICES

Kedushah was in evidence in the early laws. In antiquity,
there were no rigid standards of price. A buyer's consent was taken
for granted to allow a definite margin between the real value of
merchandise and the seller's profit. Jewish law considered a net
profit of one-sixth above the real value of an item to be excessive—
the overcharge had to be returned. If the profit was more than
one-sixth, the transaction was considered invalid and both merchandise and money had to be returned.

This rule applied in every case of oppression or fraud. Rabbi
Judah the Prince, editor of the Mishnah (the first code of Jewish
law, about 175 C. E.), held that the person who had been deceived
should have the upper hand and could ask for the return of his
money, making the whole transaction invalid. Or else, he could
demand the return of the overcharge and keep the merchandise.

This conformed to the rules against *Ona'ah* (oppression).
The only exceptions had to do with the sale of an object by a
layman, not a merchant, who attributed subjective value to an
article for reasons of sentiment. Conversely, the buyer, knowing
the seller's position, was presumed to ignore the real value in an
attempt to help him.

WEIGHTS AND MEASURES

In the opinion of the Jewish authorities, a man using scales,
or any measure, performed the function of a judge. Even as a
dishonest or careless judge is despised, so a man careless or deliberately fraudulent in the use of weights and measures is an abomination. He "makes the land unclean, profanes the name of God,
causes the Divine Presence to depart, causes Israel to die by the
sword and to be exiled from its country." A man committing
fraud "commits the abomination of idolatry," with all the terrible
consequences ensuing.

Commenting on the verse *"Ye shall do no unrighteousness in meteyard* (land measurement), *in weight, or in measure,"* the Rabbis say that, "Divine Law forbids the use of one cord in summer and another in winter. When brothers divide a land left by legacy, one's portion must not be measured off in summer and another's in winter, because the measuring cord expands in summer and shrinks in winter. The words *'in weight'* prohibit the steeping of weights in salt; and the words *'in measure'* teach that one must not allow the liquid to foam, because when the foam subsides, the measure is found to be short."

Faulty weights are not to be kept in a home, not only because they are presumptive evidence of transgression or temptation to wrong-doing but because every person should avoid keeping anything evil under his roof.

The kind of weights used in trade are considered most important. Weights, the laws said, must not be made either of tin, lead, or *gasistron* (a fusion of different metals) or of any other kind of metal since wear and tear in constant use would reduce their weight. Thus they must be made of stone or glass.

FRAUD AND REPENTANCE

Defrauding one's neighbor is considered worse than committing an act of immorality. Genuine repentance might bring divine forgiveness for an act of immorality. But in matters of false weights, it may be impossible to discover and make restitution to all the customers defrauded. Even the most sincere effort to return illicit gains would fail because of the improbability that one would be able to remember all transactions and return the proper amounts. The only advice the Talmud could offer to the repentant sinner is that after a generous estimate of all the unlawful gain, he should restore whatever he could to the persons he knows to have been victimized by himself and devote the rest of his unrighteous gain to the public welfare. In such manner perchance all his defrauded customers might reap some direct or indirect benefit.

What fundamentally matters is a man's attitude, according to the writings of the ancient sages. Man cannot abolish every kind of wrong-doing. But he must try. Rabbi Yohanan Ben Zakkai, for example, expressed his dilemma concerning the sharp practices of trades. "Woe to me if I should speak of them; woe to me if I should not speak. Should I speak of them, knaves may learn from the discussion. Should I keep silent about them, the scoundrels might think that the scholars are unacquainted with their practices, and they will endeavor to deceive still more."

Ultimately Rabbi Yohanan did decide to speak of these practices in an attempt to stop them. He based his decision on the text of Hosea: *"For the ways of the Lord are right, the just do walk in them, and the transgressors stumble therein."*

RABBIS, LAW AND JUSTICE

DYNAMIC JUSTICE

Rabbis were often called upon to give interpretations of the laws. Their decisions or enactments enjoyed absolute authority within the city, district, or province in which they were promulgated. This right was invoked particularly against monopolists, and other abusers of the people's physical and spiritual needs.

EARLY PRECEDENTS

One classic case is reported in the Mishnah of Kerithoth. Jewish women were required to offer two doves as a sacrifice after each confinement. They gave these at an appointed time of the year. But frequently, they did not go to Jerusalem—where the sacrifices were given—for intervals of several years. When they did get there, they had to give several pairs of doves—a pair for each confinement.

The seasonal demand for doves was, therefore, high. At one time, in Jerusalem, they cost two golden denarim—many times more than the non-seasonal price. Rabbi Simeon Ben Gamliel said "By the Temple! I shall not to sleep this night until they cost but one silver *denar* (one twenty-fifth of a golden *denar*)." He went to the house of study and taught: "If a woman suffered five miscarriages or five issues that were not in doubt, she need bring but one offering, and she may then be considered ritually clean; she is not obliged to offer the other four offerings (usually due after each birth or miscarriage)."

By the end of the same day, a pair of doves cost only one quarter of a silver *denar* each.

Rabbi Simeon Ben Gamliel acted on the principle, described in the Talmud (Berakhoth 54a): "When the moment has come to strike a blow for God (to prevent oppression or any other wrong-doing), one may—as a one-time emergency matter—cancel one of the teachings of His *Torah*."

Since the poor could not afford the fancy prices of the wicked profiteers, the fear was justified that they might enter the Sanctuary in their state of ritual uncleanliness and eat of the holy food with the grave consequences implied. This *hora'ath sha'ah* (emergency decision) took care especially of the poor, protecting both their little money and their religious conformity.

Rabbi Simeon Ben Gamliel was a great grandson of Hillel and president of the *Sanhedrin* from 50 to 70 C. E. Recognized as the greatest judicial authority of his time, he was exemplary in discernment and energy. He called for full rebellion against the brutal Romans and urged his people to extraordinary effort. Rabbi Simeon became one of the famous ten victims of the Romans and was executed by them at the time of the destruction of the Temple. He fought the battles of righteousness to his last day. He made full use of the powers entrusted to him by Jewish law to punish profiteers and other abusers of the religious scruples of the people.

In his name are recorded the admonitions, *I found nothing better for a man than silence. Not learning is the main thing, but doing.* In political matters as in those of social righteousness he eschewed long sermons and acted on behalf of justice.

Samuel, a pupil of the great Rabbi Judah the Prince (editor of the Mishnah), followed Rabbi Simeon and extended some of his interpretations. Samuel was one of the most brilliant personalities of Jewish history. He mastered Latin and Greek, medicine, astronomy, the lore of calendars and, above all, the whole field of Biblical and Rabbinic literature. Fifteen hundred teachings are reported in his name. Countless students sat at his feet. He was called the Judge of the Diaspora. Recognizing the evolutionary character of the law, and the demands imposed by new conditions, he made many brilliant and ingenious interpretations in order to further justice. He was a bold social reformer whose sympathies were with the common people. He understood not only their needs but also their ways. From his father, Abba, who had sold his corn at harvest cheaply to prevent any rise in price, he had inherited a hatred for hoarders. Samuel warned against selfish disregard of the common good for one's own enrichment. "Let no man withdraw from the community," he said, "but let him identify his good with that of the common man." Samuel battled without compromise against every form of commercial oppression.

There have always been some persons who looked upon other people's ideals as a good source of their own profit. They appreciated the scruples of the religious, but only because they knew that these scruples would yield them additional income, fair or unfair.

One of Samuel's notable cases concerned these opportunists. The law of the Torah prohibits the use on Passover of every type of *hamets* (leavened food). With its emphasis on consistency, the Torah prohibits even the use of utensils which have absorbed leaven.

Rab, a colleague of Samuel's, had said, "Pots in which leaven is cooked—and which absorbed and retained some of it—must be broken on Passover."

The sellers of new pots saw a chance to enrich themselves during the Passover season when the demand for fresh pots would be great; the harassed housewife would have been forced to pay unreasonable prices. But Samuel told these merchants, "Unless you charge an equitable price for your pots, I shall decide in accordance with Rabbi Simeon who permits the use of such pots after Passover. Then people will not break their pots before Passover—as Rab suggested—and you will find yourselves abundantly overstocked." As Chief Justice and leading Rabbi of his day, Samuel had the power, in times of emergency, to ignore local law in order to uphold justice and fair prices.

There was a buyer's market on the pot exchange that year and for a long time to come!

Samuel's courageous righteousness inspired his disciples in every age or clime. A similar situation took place concerning the ceremony of Succoth. A cluster of four plants—palm-branch, citron, myrtle and willow of the brook—is waved in every direction during this holiday, symbolizing God's omnipresence. The law insists that the plants in the cluster must be beautiful, for an emphasis on the esthetic element (*hadar*) in worship is always preached in the Talmud.

There was a division of opinion as to whether *all* the myrtle twigs in the cluster had to be whole to satisfy the demand for beauty in the service, or whether *one whole* twig would be sufficient. Samuel again found eager profiteers raising the price of myrtle twigs. He said to the merchants, "Sell at a normal price, or I shall decide like Rabbi Tarfon that even broken myrtles are valid for the ceremonies." That lesson was not lost: Florists had to keep their prices reasonable and their customers benefited.

"Agreeing to Disagree"

Samuel's great friend and collaborator, with whom he agreed on many things and agreed to disagree on others, was Rab, whose works are recounted in the Babylonian Talmud. Rab believed in free trade. He thought that the law of supply and demand in itself would take care of profiteers, that the people would shun their stores. The supreme civil authority in Babylonia was in the hands of the Exilarch who had appointed *agoranomoi* (market commissioners). Rab was one of them. He punished storekeepers who kept fraudulent weights or measures. But Rab was not interested in examining prices.

The Exilarch did not share Rab's optimism and had him arrested for dereliction of duty. Rab's argument that high prices would destroy the clientele of the storekeeper and force him to be decent did not impress the Exilarch. Another colleague, Qarna, also differed with Rab. Rab argued with Qarna, "The agoranomoi, according to the sages, were meant to supervise only measures, not prices," and instructed Qarna to go forth and tell them not to meddle with prices, but to make sure only that weights and measures be in order.

Rab based his conclusion on the fact that the Torah said *"Thou shalt not have in thy house diverse measures."*

But Qarna felt bound to differ. He taught that the job of the market commissioner includes both. He held that one may not deceive by false weights and measures, that one may not oppress by excessive prices, and that one type of fraud needed the same control as the other.

Rashi, the revered expounder of the Bible and Talmud, more than seven hundred years later, discussed the differences of opinion between Rab and Qarna. Writing in the eleventh century he said: "There are some merchants who buy up commodities cheaply, then corner the market and raise prices." Rab's fine faith that high prices would automatically defeat the get-rich quick scheme of the profiteers, is shattered by the facts. There are goods which can be cornered to the hurt of the common people, resulting in high profits to the monopolists. Hence, Qarna would not accept Rab's generous teaching.

The agoranomoi themselves were not always above suspicion, but the problem was so complex that the Exilarch had appointed Rab as their head. Rab felt that the responsibility for interfering with free trade was too great for any single man to shoulder. That accounts for his emphasis on fraud perpetrated by defective weights and measures. On the other hand, he could readily see the consequences of hoarding and took every precaution against them.

Rab and Samuel agreed on many things. Neither would see any good in asceticism, which they interpreted as a sterile withdrawal from the world. The task of religion, according to both, was to bring to the market places the message of God, of righteousness and equity. Both condemned hoarders of food, usurers, manipulators of fraudulent weights, and profiteers. Nevertheless, in this case, the decision of the rabbis went against both and sustained the opinion of Qarna. So did Maimonides in later years. And so did Rabbi Joseph Karo (Hoshen Mishpat 239) who said that the Jewish court of justice is obliged to appoint inspectors to prevent profiteering, especially in food stuffs, and to punish severely those convicted of transgression. As a matter of fact, price-fixing committees to curb profiteering were eventually authorized to be established in every city with authority to punish those who acted against their rules.

Later Applications

In 1648, thousands of Jews were in flight from the savage butchery of Chmielnitzky, a Cossack headman who rebelled against the Polish overlords and revealed his "heroism" in unparalleled sadistic orgies against defenseless Jews.

It was a year fateful in the history of Europe. The Thirty Years' War was about to be concluded, and organized religions were to dedicate themselves no more to the indiscriminate slaughter of the various non-conformist denominations, but, it was hoped, to humane reconstruction.

In that year, Rabbi Menahem Mendel Krochmal was appointed chief rabbi of Moravia. A native of Cracow and a disciple of the great Rabbi Joel Serkes, he had held earlier positions in the country and took his seat in Nikolsburg. In 1652 he presided at a synod at which the famed Three Hundred and Ten Statutes were enacted, among them that every community of tax-paying members is obliged to appoint a rabbi who should lecture on talmudical subjects. Menahem Mendel was a renowned scholar whose collection of responsa *"Tsemah Tsedek"* ("The Branch of Righteousness") reveals great learning and incisive brilliance of mind. But his character was greater than his learning.

Among the refugee scholars was one Sabbatai Cohen who applied for the vacant position of local rabbi in Holleschau. The president of that community inquired of Menahem Mendel, his country's chief rabbi, as to the qualifications of Rabbi Sabbatai. By accident, the latter's teacher, a renowned halakhic authority, visited the chief rabbi at that moment, and when the latter showed him the note of inquiry, he said, with more enthusiasm than wisdom: "Rabbi Sabbatai is so excellent a disciple of mine that you would be justified in offering him your own position and accepting the Holleschau rabbinate for yourself."

The gentle Menahem Mendel conveyed this advice literally to that community. As a result, Rabbi Sabbatai Cohen received a unanimous call to the important position in Holleschau. But the same self-effacing rabbi Menahem Mendel manifested no timidity when espousing the cause of the poor, nor did he hesitate to take drastic action on their behalf!

In the 44th responsum of the "Tsemah Tsedek," Menahem Mendel opposed a too literal interpretation of municipal statutes and insisted that changes are lawful as long as the general spirit of the enactment is not violated. In such matters, "The criterion is the intent of the founding fathers and not the wording of any particular authority." He also stresses the significance of service of

Jewry to the whole country as against narrow local interests, calling all selfish localism highly improper.

Menahem Mendel discusses this in the 28th chapter of "Tsemah Tsedek." The chapter deals with the time-hallowed custom of the Jews of honoring the Sabbath by a special dish of fish.

The local fishmongers, well aware of the fact that Jews were anxious to buy fish for the Sabbath meal, even though the prices were high, decided to increase their profits. Community remonstrances with the profiteers proved unsuccessful and the question arose as to whether it would not be proper to make an emergency decision (*hora'ath sha'ah*) on the principle of abiding vigilance to protect a basic matter (*lemigdar miltha*). The court of justice and the executive of the community could avail themselves of such authority to protect decency, the needs of the poor, and the morality of the city. When all pleas to the profiteers proved unavailing, it was decided to break the iron ring of monopoly by declaring all fish prohibited for a period of two months.

Another problem then arose: Did the community have a right to use the device of prohibition, in view of the fact that it might interfere with proper observance of the Sabbath and with the enjoyment of the holiday by the faithful.

Menahem Mendel endorsed the principle of the decision. He said that it was justified because his major concern was not so much with the rich who would buy the fish no matter how expensive, but with the poor who, because of the high prices, would be prevented from celebrating the holiday and relaxing for its duration from the burdens and tensions of the workaday week.

Undoubtedly, this decree taught a powerful lesson to the fish interests and prevented them from ever again abusing the scruples of the faithful for the satisfaction of their greed.

The White Cock

Rabbi Joel Serkes was a renowned Polish rabbi who died in Cracow in 1640. In his commentary on Tur Orah Hayyim, he referred to *kapparoth*, a custom in which on the eve of Yom Kippur a cock would be waved three times around the head of a penitent while appropriate verses from Psalm CVII and Job

XXXIII were recited. The cock was white, a symbol of purity which the sinner hoped to attain through God's forgiveness. The cock was then given to the poor or slaughtered and its value distributed amongst the needy.

Somewhat reminiscent of the sacrifice in the Temple, this custom was severely condemned by some rabbis as a revival of a sacrificial service prohibited since the Temple's destruction. It was condemned by others because it suggested vicarious atonement, foreign to Jewish thinking. But the people clung to this ceremony, and it has persisted among many Jews to this day.

White cocks were preferred for the ceremony and some enterprising merchants excessively raised the price of the fowl on the days before the Day of Atonement. Rabbi Serkes, therefore, abolished the custom of buying white cocks for this occasion because of the high prices demanded. Indeed, he felt that the whole custom might belong to the customs of the Amorites (heathen natives of Palestine), which Jews should shun.

But the most interesting and fascinating of all these decisions comes from the Court of Rabbi Hayyim Halberstam of Sandz, famed leader of 19th century Hassidism and a great authority on rabbinic law. In his country, machinery was used for the baking of *matsoth* for the first time during his lifetime. The new process was subjected to much ecclesiastical scrutiny. Many rabbis found machine production safer from the ritual point of view, faster and generally more satisfactory. Rabbi Halberstam, however, declared that matsoth produced by machine were absolutely out of accord with Jewish law . . . (*hamets gamur*) and prohibited their use during Passover. There was much controversy, and most of the authorities disagreed with Rabbi Halberstam. But Rabbi Shalom Mordecai ha-Kohen of Brezan in Poland, a world-famous scholar, was one of the few who agreed with him.

There were two baffling aspects to this situation.

1. Rabbi Halberstam insisted on his point of view, utterly impervious to the fact that the majority of the authorities opposed him. Talmudic principle universally calls for acceptance of the majority view in disputed cases. A well-known legend in the Talmud tells of a stubborn scholar who resorted to every possible stratagem to upset the general rule in one particular case, only to

lose his battle repeatedly and finally. That legend and its solid teaching were known to Rabbi Halberstam. Yet he insisted on the acceptance of his opinion by "all living in the sphere of his influence."

2. More amazing is the fact that Rabbi Shalom Mordecai ha-Kohen, who endorsed him in the local battle, rendered an opposite decision in answer to a question from America. In that case, he permitted the use of machine-made matsoth and insisted only that the manufacturer use the most punctilious methods for assuring the preparation of the matsoth in strict accord with Jewish law.

Both aspects become clear through a study of the local situation. A great number of Jewish families living in Rabbi Halberstam's district derived their livelihood from home-made matsoth. All these families would have suffered if wholesale machine production had been approved. The rabbi appreciated the benefits of the industrial revolution, but in order to protect the livelihood of these people, Rabbi Halberstam availed himself of the authority vested in every rabbi to enact a law to protect his community, such laws being valid only in his city or district. The case of the poor Jews of Sandz, bereft of economic opportunity, was utterly different from that of American Jewry, who had many opportunities for employment. Rabbi Shalom Mordecai, therefore, was consistent in siding with his colleague in the matter concerning the Jews *in his district,* and giving a contrary decision in another area, knowing that this rule was not meant to apply to a community over which Rabbi Halberstam had no special authority and where the motive for his enactment did not exist.

Just Wages and Fair Dealing

The greatest twentieth century teacher of Judaism was the universally revered Rabbi Israel Meir ha-Kohen of Radin, the author of many books of moral instruction, most famous among them "Hafets Hayyim" (Lover of Life). The last part of another book (on "The Love of Kindness"), deals with labor law. This excerpt reveals the normal climate of Jewish social ethics:

"If one plans to engage his fellowman in any kind of work for which he is to receive payment, let him arrange for a defi-

nite price or wage in advance. For otherwise he is most likely
to become an oppressor, by denying the wage demanded by the
hired man, unless he chooses to be over-generous with his money
to escape all doubt of having wronged the worker. Most of
us depend upon our fellow men to perform hundreds of actions
for us, and it happens frequently that after such work is performed, disputes arise between employer and employee with
regard to payment due. When they finally part with each other,
each of them is convinced that the other had robbed him. Each
is willing to engage in endless strife, but he does not forgive
the other the wrong he feels to have been perpetrated against
himself. In some cases they protract their quarrel. As far as
Jewish law is concerned, the place (local standard and custom)
decides the proper payment as well as the time when the work
is being done. Even if he kept back only one penny of what
is due to the worker, the employer on that account would be
considered a robber, 'withholding the hired man's wages.' Who
is able to know exactly what the local standard or custom is?
And particularly with regard to any kind of work that he
may impose upon the other? Of necessity, then, if he wished
to do what is right, he would be obliged to give the working
man whatever he demands. And that, too, is very difficult.
Hence, anyone who wishes to fulfill God's wish in this manner,
to do what is proper, let him settle with him in advance what
payment he should receive and thus obviate any doubt."

Rabbi Israel Meir ha-Kohen eked out a very frugal living,
travelling from place to place and selling his books among the Jews
of Poland and Lithuania. One day he was left a little legacy by
a relative and the chance of remaining in his native townlet seemed
too good to resist.

He established himself in the grocery business. His assistant suffered from the rabbi's exceeding scrupulousness and inces-
sant worry about the perfect state of the scales, the absolute
assurance of painstaking service to the customers and the avoid-
ance of any advertising—even by word of mouth—that might not
be in complete agreement with the facts. Every customer had to
be informed about the slightest imperfections of any commodity the
store offered for sale, and the rabbi himself would go out of his
way to warn the would-be purchaser of possible flaws. To his
amazement, Rabbi Israel Meir discovered that his business was
prospering and he became conscience-stricken about the harm being

done to his competitors. He felt sure that his reputation rather than the quality of his goods drew so many customers to his establishment. He felt that he had really become an unfair competitor. All his efforts to persuade purchasers to patronize his competitors too proved a failure. Finally, Rabbi Israel Meir decided that "this oppression" must stop. He closed his shop.

In "Hafets Hayyim" he described the grave consequences of the "evil tongue", i.e., careless or malicious unfavorable comment on anyone's character, habits, or ability. Rabbi Israel Meir said again and again that even if the reports were substantiated, it was wrong to spread them unless some immediate social good would result. Otherwise, any unfavorable comment is a sin against God and man. Were one genuinely interested in promoting good and fighting evil, then one should approach the dishonest or careless man oneself, speak to his heart, reproach him gently and understandingly so as to bring him back to the right path. Character assassination is a heinous offense, classed by the Talmud with murder and immorality. But, adds the sage, spreading evil rumors about a man's product or merchandise is also a grave sin against the Law of the Torah, and none who ever revered God dare commit it.

Jewish law prohibits not only usury, but the taking of any interest whatsoever. However, to be able to remain active in modern business life, investment in someone else's enterprise is permitted, provided the investor shares both profit and loss, and provided that if one of the partners alone works, he is recompensed for his service. Our neighbor's emergency, financial, social or political, must never be used for personal aggrandisement or enrichment. Instead it calls for the translation into solid co-operation of the principle of brotherhood and social responsibility.

In accordance with the law of the *Torah,* any non-Jew in the state of Israel, although he does not engage in the forms of Jewish religious life, as long as he is a law-abiding citizen, is entitled to this dynamic brotherhood, and his emergency should, according to this paragraph of Jewish law, evoke automatic community help. In the words of the Talmud: It is a duty to provide for the non-Jewish poor even as for the Jewish poor, to heal the non-Jewish sick even as the Jewish sick. It is obligatory to provide a burial space for the non-Jewish dead, found unattended, as it is a duty to provide it for the Jewish dead.

Zion, said the prophet, *can be redeemed only by righteousness;* the world, great and small, can be built up only by kindness. Righteous profit is in accord with the timeless teaching of His Book; ill-begotten gains will plague the gainer, and land him in unending trouble.

SUMMARY

Judaism pledges its adherents neither to socialism nor to capitalism. Socialism borrowed from Judaism its emphasis on responsibility for the fellow-man's welfare and for the creation of a society in which every human will receive essential protection and security. Capitalism borrowed from the Hebrew Bible the emphasis on a man's rights to the rewards of his honest labor limited only by the common good. If any *ism* attaches to Judaism, it would be *Tsedekism,* the rule of Tsedek, which means righteousness, fair play, and human compassion. The same Tsedek insists on full integrity in connection with commercial affairs—from weights and measures to the limitation of profits—to the prevention of abuse in times of scarcity. But above the level of Tsedek is that of *Kiddush ha-Shem* which warns each man that he must remain conscious of the obligation to do everything that will enhance reverence for God by man, to avoid any action that may reflect upon the Divine Law-giver. Just as righteous conduct integrates the individual Jew in that historic task of his people, so does unrighteous conduct —especially in relation with non-Jews—make him a pariah. It is only by living these fundamentals of goodness, expressing them in private and business life, that all men can reach peace, security and survival.

BIBLIOGRAPHY

1. Talmud Bavli.

2. Talmud Yerushalmi.

3. Maimonides, Mishneh Torah.

4. Joseph Karo, Shulhan Arukh, Hoshen Mishpat.

5. M. Findling, Tehukat ha-Avodah, Jerusalem, 1945.

6. Ch.Ch. Medini, Sdei Hemed, V.

7. M. Amiel, Ha-Tsedek ha-Sotsiali.

8. M. Bloch, Ethik der Halakhah.

9. M. Bloch, Mos. Talmudisches Polizeirecht.

10. D. Hoffmann, Shulhan Arukh.

11. E. Munk, Nichtjuden im Jued. Religionsrecht.

12. H. Gold, Judengemeinden Maehrens.

13. Frank Schechter, Study in Comparative Trade Morals.

ELIYAHU OF VILNA

by M. M. Yoshor

ELIYAHU OF VILNA

By M. M. Yoshor

I

The Glory of Vilna

For nearly three centuries the city of Vilna (metropolis of Lithuania) was a leading center of Jewish learning. Her scholars enjoyed prestige and her rabbis were revered throughout the diaspora. Jews everywhere looked to Vilna for inspiration and guidance. They turned to her authorities for decisions in matters of law. Students from many countries flocked there, to satisfy their thirst for knowledge at the feet of her distinguished masters.

The Jewish settlement in Vilna had its inception in the fourteenth century. Records show that by the second half of the sixteenth century Vilna already had a flourishing Jewish community. Its first rabbi was[1] Abraham Seigel, at the dawn of the seventeenth century. He was followed by Menahem Manus Hayes (ca. 1616-1636),[2] whose contemporaries referred to him as *Rosh Yeshivah* (Academy Head) and Rabbi of Vilna, and described him as the *Meor ha-Golah,* (Light of the Diaspora).[3] After him came Feibush Ashkenazi (ca. 1637-1645),[4] who soon left for Jerusalem to assume leadership of the Ashenazic community in the Holy Land. As his successor Vilna chose the renowned Rabbi Mosheh ben Isaac Judah Lima (ca. 1648-1655).[5]

Rabbi Lima initiated in Vilna a school of expounders of the Shulhan Arukh.[6] His own work *Helkath Mehokek* (The Legis-

---

[1]*Ir Vilna,* H. M. Steinschneider.

[2]ibid; *Kiryah Neemanah,* S. J. Finn.

[3]*Ethan ha-Ezrahi,* R. Abraham Rapaport, Lemberg, 1636.

[4]R. Feibush was a brilliant Rav and great Paskan (decider of ritual questions). See *Ir Vilna* and *Kiryah Neemanah.*

[5]R. Mosheh Lima studied at the Yeshivah of Cracow under R. Joshuah ben Joseph. At the age of twenty he became Chief Rabbi of Slonim and head of its Yeshivah. From Vilna he moved to Brisk, where he served as rabbi until his death in 1657 at the age of 53. His *Helkath Mehokek* was first published by his sons, Raphael and Lima, in Cracow, in 1670.

[6]*Shulhan Arukh* (The Set Table) is the classic code of Judaism, a systematic arrangement of the immense material of Talmudic law. It is

27

lator's Portion) is recognized as an essential commentary on the section of the Shulhan Arukh dealing with marriage and divorce (*Even ha-Ezer*). He presided over a *Beth Din* (rabbinical court), all of whose members were men of great distinction. Together they laid the groundwork for the vast expository literature that buttressed the authority of the *Shulhan Arukh*. Drawing on the immense store of their erudition, they elucidated the terse code, showing the way for its continuous applicability, and enhancing its practical effectiveness for the people.

Four men stood out in Rabbi Lima's Beth Din. Chief among them was young Sabbatai ben Meir ha-Kohen (d. 1663). He was called "fountainhead of wisdom." At the age of twenty-four he published his monumental *Sifthei Kohen,* a commentary on Yoreh Deah, the second section of the Shulhan Arukh. He proceeded with *Gevurath Anashim,* a commentary on the third section (*Even ha-Ezer*), *and Sifthei Kohen,* a commentary on the fourth section (*Hoshen Mishpat*). He also wrote liturgical poetry of merit. Usually he is known as the "Shakh," after the first two Hebrew letters of his *Sifthei Kohen.*

Others were: Rabbi Aaron Samuel Kaidenover (d. 1686),[a] Rabbi Hillel ben Hertz (d. 1690,[b] Rabbi Ephraim Cohen (d. 1678)[c] and Rabbi Moshe Rivkes (d. 1671).[d]

These scholars made Vilna famous. In 1654 Rabbi Sabbatai ha-Kohen requested the Council of Four Lands in Lublin to admit

divided into four sections. (a) *Orah Hayyim* ("The Way of Life") contains the laws of ritual and prayer; of Sabbath and festivals. (b) *Yoreh Deah* ("Teacher of knowledge") deals with the Dietary laws, Family Purity, with the laws concerning the duties towards parents and teachers, and also with agricultural laws and those of mourning and burial. (c) *Even ha-Ezer* ("Stone of Help") contains the laws of marriage and divorce. (d) *Hoshen Mishpat* ("The Breastplate of Judgment") comprises civil and criminal laws.

[a]Known as the "Mharshak," he wrote *Birkhath Zevah* on one of the Talmudic orders and the super-commentary *Tifereth Shemuel* on the halakhic decisions of the Rosh (Rabbenu Asher).

[b]He wrote *Beth Hillel* on all four sections of the Shulhan Arukh, but only the portions dealing with the second and third sections were ever published.

[c]He wrote *Shaarei Ephraim,* a collection of responsa covering the entire range of the Shulhan Arukh.

[d]He is the author of *Be'er ha-Golah,* an extensive work of annotations on the Shulhan Arukh.

his beloved community as a member of the Council and her rabbi, Moshe Lima, as a member of its Supreme Rabbinical School.[7]   In support of his argument he stated that there were in Vilna more than three hundred scholars, each one of them ordained and fit to fill the office of rabbi in any large community.[8]

To be a son of Vilna conferred prestige on the scholar.   No wonder that her sons who chanced to wander from her environs to occupy high positions elsewhere would proudly add to their other titles: "a native of Vilna."

It is sad to record that this flourishing community was ruthlessly uprooted by the Cossacks in their onslaught in 1655.   Vilna was burned and about thirty thousand of her Jews, who had failed to escape in time, were brutally murdered.   Few of her banished scholars ever returned.   One of the few who did, Rabbi Moshe Rivkes, described the travail of exile:

> "I was driven from my home on the twenty-fourth day of Tammuz 1655, and took nothing along save the staff in my right hand, my tefillin and a luah (Jewish religious calendar).   Dark thoughts entered my mind: 'Who knows where I may be cast forth!' Alas! My home full of all good I had forsaken, my possessions I had abandoned, particularly my treasured books, many of which were inherited from my father of blessed memory. . . . I reached Amsterdam. . . . There I made my work on the *Shulhan Arukh* ready for print."

The cruel treatment that Rabbi Moshe had suffered at the hands of some Christians did not embitter him against all of them. In his unusually concise *Be'er ha-Golah* he expatiates on the gravity of deceiving a gentile.   It is not only morally wrong, but self-destructive.

> "I wish I could impress on coming generations what my eyes have witnessed.   Some individuals who apparently had waxed rich from deceiving Gentiles, in the end forfeited all that they had accumulated.   On the other hand, those who were honest in their dealings with Gentiles— in doubtful cases

---

[7] *Kiryah Neemanah; Aliyoth Eliyahu.*
[8] Ir Vilna. *The Vaad Arba Aratsoth* (Council of Four Lands) was the governing body of Polish, including Lithuanian, Jewry from 1580 to 1764.   The latter, in the second half of the seventeenth century, organized its own independent council.   Thereafter, Vilna joined the Lithuanian Council of Provinces.

they even returned a substantial amount to honor His Holy
Name—prospered greatly."

When Rabbi Moshe returned to the reconstructed Vilna, the
Jewish residents sought to draft him as rabbi. Unlike his colleagues who had yielded to the requests of various communities,
Rabbi Rivkes determined not to accept the call, but to remain a
layman.[9] The post went to Rabbi Nahman of Ludmir, a man of
great learning and piety but whose tenure was brief.

Before his death, Rabbi Nahman urged his *Ba'alei Batim* (community heads) to choose as his successor an obscure shopkeeper.
The new rabbi was to be Moshe Kramer. (The surname Kramer
denoted "shopkeeper" or "merchant."). The leaders of the community were baffled by Rabbi Nahman's recommendation. Rabbi
Moshe Kramer's record had not attracted any particular attention.
Like countless other scholars in Vilna, he engaged strenuously
in the study of Torah, while his wife carried the yoke of *parnas-
sah* (earning a livelihood). Nor was Rabbi Moshe Kramer less
surprised when approached by the committee with the offer of the
position. Humbly he protested that he was not fit. Informed of
the expressed will of the late Rabbi Nahman, he yielded, but
on condition that he would serve without remuneration and that
his wife should be allowed to continue with the grocery shop.

(Later it developed that too many customers came to the shop,
wishing to do honor to the new rabbi. Thereupon Rabbi Moshe
instructed his wife to keep the shop open only part of the day,
and as soon as the earnings were enough for the bare necessities
until the coming Sabbath, she was to close for the rest of the
week.)[10]

The "grocer" was endowed with talents of leadership. He
diffused the knowledge of Torah in his community. He defended
Jewish dignity successfully before the secular authorities, and on one
occasion saved his people from the plot of the shameless blood
libel. He was acclaimed one of the greatest Talmudists of his
time. It was said of him, "At his fountains the entire Diaspora
quenched its thirst."[11]

[9]*Kiryah Neemanah; Aliyoth Eliyahu.*
[10]*Das Wort, Vilna, 1935.*
[11]Introduction to *Biurei* ha-GRA; *Kiryah Neemanah.*

His son, Rabbi Elijah Hassid, was a member of the rabbinical
court, and an active leader, whose wife was the daughter of Rabbi
Pethahiah, son of Rabbi Moshe Rivkes. The union of these two
families—Rivkes and Kramer—brought its greatest asset to Vilna.
For the son of Rabbi Elijah Hassid was Rabbi Issakhar Ber, and
the latter's son was Rabbi Shlome Zelman.

On the first day of Passover, in the year 1720, Treina, the
wife of Rabbi Shlome Zelman, gave birth to their first child.
It was a boy. Rabbi Shlome thought of his grandfather, and
named the boy Elijah.

II

THE YOUNG ELIJAH

The child was a prodigy; that was manifest from a very early
age—an intellect of gigantic potentiality, of phenomenal ingenuity.
His mature questions and answers amazed his elders, and made
them conscious of an insufficiency in their own stores of knowledge.
His exceptionally keen and analytical mind, his singular clarity
of thought, coupled with his quick powers of perception and fabulous memory, made the lad the cherished companion of hoary
scholars.

According to his biographers, he had so far advanced by the
age of six as to be able to study Bible and Talmud by himself.
When Elijah was only six and a half, they report, he delivered a
lengthy discourse on halakhah in the great synagogue of Vilna.
That evening—accompanied by his father—he visited the chief
rabbi, Joshua Heshel (d. 1749), who, to test the child, queried:
Could young Elijah prepare a similar discourse now, entirely by
himself, without the help of his father? The rabbi chose a topic,
and gave the child an hour to prepare. To the amazement of
all, before the hour was up the boy said that he was ready to discourse. They listened to him with wonder. The chief rabbi of
Brisk (Brest), Rabbi Abraham Katzenellenbogen, happened to be
present, and he was so impressed that he implored Rabbi Shlome
Zelman to entrust his son to him. Rabbi Shlome Zelman agreed.
Elijah was taken by Rabbi Abraham to the small Lithuanian town

of Kaidan, and turned over to Rabbi David Katzenellenbogen—
Rabbi Abraham's father. A tutor, Rabbi Moshe Margolit, was pro-
cured, under whose guidance Elijah studied for several months.[12]
Afterwards, he found he could "learn" by himself, and sometimes
his comprehension was so swift as to make it impossible for others to
keep up. Whilst boys of his age were laboring through *Humash*
(the Pentateuch), Elijah could navigate through the vast sea of
Talmud. He knew even the obscure inlets of Kabbalah.

No Talmudic problem was too difficult for him to tackle. He
could rapidly unravel the most complicated problem, plumb it to
its depth, and illumine all its subtleties. Though endowed by
nature with an extraordinary mind, Elijah never permitted himself
to grow smug and indolent. Illustrious descent did not lead him to
think too well of himself. He refused to subsist on the merits of
his progenitors.

[12]Ibid; *Aliyoth Eliyahu.* R. Moshe ben Shimeon Margolit, author of
Pnei Mosheh and Mareh ha-Panim on T. *Yerushalmi.* According to *Enc.
le-Toldoth Gedolei Israel* (by Mordecai Margolioth, Jerusalem 1950), he
was born between 1710-1720. He was a young lad (neither a rabbi nor
Rosh Yeshivah in Kaidan as supposed by Ginzberg) when Rabbi Katzenellenbogen chose him as a senior companion of the seven-year-old Eliyahu.
(b. 1720). Their companionship lasted but three months (Aliyoth
Eliyahu). Doctor Ginzberg's questioning of the probability of that companionship seems questionable. (See his *Students, Scholars and Saints*—p.
274: "The statement, however, that the Gaon at the age of seven studied
there (in Kaidan) under R. Moses Margolit, the famous author of the commentary *Pnei Mosheh* on the Talmud Yerushalmi (died at Brody 12 Tebeth
5541 . . .) is based solely on Lewin's authority (*Aliyoth Eliyahu*), which is
open to question").

In his introduction to his commentary on the *Yerushalmi,* Prof. Ginzberg continues to doubt whether Margolit ever studied with Eliyahu.
"Margolit had never been Eliyahu's teacher, for Eliyahu in his many
works never refers to him nor does he ever mention him."

It is amazing how Dr. Ginzberg (who himself suggests that Margolit
must have died at the age of seventy) fails to realize that the latter was
but a lad when R. David Katzenellenbogen had chosen him as senior
companion to Eliyahu. The latter greatly excelled Margolit, and found no
advantage in continuing his studies with him. They parted after three
months' studying together. There was thus no good reason for Elijah ever
to refer to Margolit, as he never considered him his teacher.

The early interest of Moshe Margolit in the T. Yerushalmi perhaps did
impress young Eliyahu. So also might have been the former's interest
in science as a help to a proper understanding of the Torah. There is
an undeniable record that Margolit later took a course in botany at the
University of Frankfurt a.M. in order to facilitate his understanding
of the first section of the Palestinian Talmud, *Zeraim.* Also, Ginzberg sur-
mises that Rabbi Margolit was about seventy years old at his demise in
1781. According to our figures, he may have been not older than 56-61.

Elijah must have remembered his great grandfather's witty stricture on ancestor worship. Old Rabbi Moshe Kramer had changed *ovoth* to *avoth* in the Scriptural injunction, *Al tifnu el ha-Ovoth,"* "Turn ye not unto ghosts," so that the meaning of the passage was altered to "Turn ye not unto the ancestors."[13] Elijah determined to obtain everything through *yegiah,* strenuous effort, to strive only for the fruit of his personal exertion. He disliked gratuities in any form, whether material or spiritual. Wisdom self-acquired through travail Elijah regarded as the greatest boon in life. As the Talmud said, "A man prefers one measure of his own to nine measures given him by others."

> "His (Rabbi Elijah's) soul showed satisfaction only . . . in what he obtained by painful labor. . . . His soul desired no gifts. He rejected offers from itinerant preachers (maggidim), masters of hidden lore and princes of the Torah, to transmit to him—without any effort or exertion—founts of sagacity, secrets and mysteries of the most sublime regions."[14]

The older he grew, the more he intensified his studies. In accord with his self-imposed regimen, he committed to memory the Talmudim and cognate rabbinic literature, as well as all of the Scriptures, along with their vast exegesis.

Convinced that ignorance of secular learning was a hindrance to a proper understanding of the Torah, Elijah included secular matters in his program; he studied philosophy, history, astronomy, mathematics and anatomy. He abstained from the study of medicine, because he feared that its practice would disturb his absorption in Torah. He had to forego botany, being unable to get used to the harsh life of Lithuanian peasantry, among whom he would have had to study it.

Erudition did not affect Elijah's outlook on the mitsvoth. The end of all his knowledge was their devout performance. He had an acute sense of what was ethically proper and what was not. Once the very young Elijah refused to play on the seesaw with the other youngsters, and explained to his surprised mother that he could

---

[13]Introduction to *Sifra di-Tseniutha* (The Book of Concealment) by R. Hayyim Volozhin.
[14]*Aliyoth Eliyahu.*

not allow himself to be pushed up and thereby cause someone else
to be pushed down!

At eighteen he married a girl from Kaiden, Hannah, daughter
of Rabbi Judah. No doubt, a great deal of Elijah's success was
due to his felicitous choice of Hannah. She proved selfless in her
devotion to him. In many instances she was the only one who had
access to the secret retreats he chose for devout meditation. She
brought him food, and told him the news of the community. He
gave her his full confidence, and she, an exceptional Tsidkanith
(pious woman), gave him full empathy.

III

In Exile

Such understanding was vital when, at the age of twenty,
Elijah decided to leave his wife and home in Vilna, to wander
away in self-exile. He had taken stock and concluded that his
store of knowledge was inadequate; in his seclusion he had missed
the touch of reality. He must gain a fuller comprehension of
Judaism by viewing Jewish life in its various aspects. He must
gain an insight into the customs and traditions of various peoples.

As a matter of fact, Jewish saints for generations used to
impose exile on themselves. It served as a corrective of a too regular and agreeable life, facilitated their efforts to obtain penance for
sin, and enabled them to partake of the suffering of the "Shekhinah
in exile," and thereby arouse the mercy of Heaven towards the
termination of Israel's Galuth.

For eight years Elijah wandered in an impoverished state
through the kingdoms and provinces of Europe. For a while he
served as a tutor to Jewish children in an isolated village.

There are fabulous but unverified stories about Elijah helping
perplexed scholars arrive at solutions and formulae. According to
one, a professor accosted him in Berlin and beseeched his aid on
an abstruse astronomical problem, and Elijah obliged him with a
sketch on a scrap of paper which opened the professor's eyes.[15]

[15]*Aliyoth Eliyahu.*

Whatever the primary motives for Elijah's *"goluth aprichten,"* Providence employed it as a means to further its own objective. The pilgrim-genius wished to hide his personality, to wrap his talents in incognito, but Providence contrived to expose his greatness and to promulgate his name far and wide. As a result of eight years of wandering his reputation was not diminished, but, on the contrary, was immensely increased. "When a flask of balsam is sealed and stored away, its fragrance is not perceptible, but opened and moved about, its sweet odor becomes widely diffused."[16] What the Midrash had said in praise of Father Abraham, applied also to Elijah of Vilna.

He returned as a recognized authority in the Law. Rabbis from all over Europe turned to him with their halakhic difficulties.

Again and again townspeople urged him to become the rabbi of Vilna, but he refused. He would not even accept membership in the Rabbinical Board, but his opinion was sought on all important questions. Only on rare occasions would he publicly assert his great, though unofficial, authority. As a rule, he preferred his status as a layman.

IV

THE LIGHT OF VILNA

Elijah settled in Vilna for the rest of his life. He trod a humble path. Like his father, he was maintained by a weekly stipend from the *Kehillah* (community). The money came from a legacy left to the *Kehillah* by Elijah's great-great-grandfather (Rabbi Moshe Rivkes), to help any descendant who devoted himself entirely to Torah.

The *Kehillah* used to send the weekly stipend to Elijah through its *"Shammes"* (beadle). Once the *Shammes* greedily decided to keep the allowance, knowing that Elijah would not inform against him. Elijah and his family suffered for some time, but said nothing. Later, on his death-bed, the *Shammes* confessed.[17]

[16]Genesis R. LIX, I.
[17]*Aliyoth Eliyahu; Kiryah Neemanah.*

Scholars soon acclaimed Elijah as the *Gaon* (Talmudic scholar par excellence), while the people called him the *Hassid* (saint). These titles gradually took the place of his personal name.

Yet he upheld the prestige of the local rabbinate by submitting to its decisions even when they did not accord with his own view.

In 1755, when Elijah was thirty-five, he was asked by the sixty-five-year-old Rabbi Jonathan Eybeschuetz (1690-1764) to render an opinion concerning his controversy with Rabbi Jacob Emden (1697-1776). Rabbi Eybeschuetz discloses what prompted him to turn to Elijah of Vilna.

> "For I have heard that among the learned men of that city there is one singularly distinguished as a saint, a holy and pure person, a light unto Israel, who embraces the knowledge of all sciences, and wisdom and understanding, also possessing ten measures of mystic lore— the eminent Rabbi Elijah whose renown is spread in all the countries of Poland. In Lissa and Berlin, where he passed by (during his exile), many great things were attributed to him."[18]

A characteristic illustration of Elijah's extreme modesty is his reply to Rabbi Eybeschuetz:

> "I wish I had wings like a dove. I would then fly to restore peace and quench the strange fire of dissension. But who am I that people should listen to me? If they ignore the instructions of their rabbis, heads of holy congregations, how will they listen to the voice of an unknown person who lacks the virtue of age?"[19]

V

CONTEMPORARY DILEMMAS

The eighteenth century found East European Jewry in a state of despair. The humanism heralded by the Renaissance and Refor-

[18]*Das Wort,* Vilna, 1935.

[19]*Luhoth ha-Eduth,* Prague, IV. 73; *Aliyoth Eliyahu* p. 55. R. Jonathan Eybeschuetz, a famous rabbinic scholar, was at that time Chief Rabbi of the three combined communities; Altona, Hamburg and Wandsbeck. His bitter controversy with R. Jacob Emden had to do with the amulets Eybeschuetz issued as charms, which Emden branded as containing reference to Sabbataism.

mation failed to improve the lot of the Jew in Eastern Europe. Poland ceased to be friendly to the Jews. The Jesuits incited the Christian populace against their Jewish neighbors. Riot and bloodshed frequently resulted. The wounds left by the savagery of the Cossacks were slow to heal. Disillusionment had followed the messianic stir created by the impostor Sabbatai Tsevi. In most of the Jewish communities in Eastern Europe learning was on the decline and the people looked to mysticism for rays of hope to penetrate the gloom. Messianic longings swayed their imagination. They yearned for someone who would be near to them, understand them, heal their wounds and restore their crushed spirits.

That man came in the person of Rabbi Israel Baal Shem Tov (Master of the Good Name, 1700-1760). He brought cheer into the humble dwellings and happiness to the depressed hearts. He banished moroseness. He denounced repining and self-affliction. He taught that God should be served with joy, and that asceticism might be the root of evil.

He gave birth to a new movement, *Hassidism,* which assigned the pre-eminent place in Judaism not to learning but to sentiment. It valued not the light that illumined, but the warmth that set aglow. Above the attainment of holy knowledge, it placed the achievement of religious exultation.

As Hassidism extended its foothold in the Eastern community, there arose an antagonist movement, the *Haskalah* ("Enlightenment"). The Haskalists took an adverse view of the Hassidim and their anti-rationalistic tendency.

The Haskalah in Eastern Europe had emanated from the West. It was introduced in Germany by the philosopher Moses Mendelssohn (1729-1786), who was acclaimed a modern Socrates. Historians place Mendelssohn in the forefront of those who inspired the *Aufklaerung* (enlightenment) of eighteenth-century Germany,[20] a movement which proclaimed freedom of thought combined with contempt for authority and tradition. The incentive came from the Voltairian philosophy of realism and rationalism.

Mendelssohn carried a version of the *Aufklaerung* to his brethren of the *Judengasse*. Although he personally was scrupu-

[20]Ibid.

lous in his adherence to traditional practice, his devotion lacked the fervor which would inspire emulation in others. He placed excessive reliance on speculation. The minds of his followers turned to criticism of Judaism and their loyalty to the faith was shattered.

The Haskalists in Eastern Europe adopted the Mendelssohnian innovation, and exerted their utmost energies to impose it on their co-religionists. By loosening their ties with their ancestral heritage, they became susceptible to the blandishments of Christian society. Hassidism with its outpouring of emotion, its ecstasy of worship, became the chief target of the Haskalists; they considered it their bitterest enemy, a monstrous obstruction on their road to emancipation. Little did they know that the hidden motive of the *Judenemanzipation* was not the Jews' redemption from millennial bondage, but *Emancipation from Judaism*. The French formula "To the Jew (we grant) nothing, to the human being everything" had, at any rate, the asset of candor. But the ghetto-weary modernists saw only the beckoning promise of "equality, fraternity, liberty," and many rushed ultimately headlong into apostasy. Meantime they denounced the Hassidim as fanatics who would envelop the Jews in a heavy cloud of superstition.

In their nascent forms, Hassidism and the Haskalah presented a serious threat to the integrity of Judaism. Too much exultation (bordering on hilarity) in Hassidism and too much rationalism (bordering on atheism) in Haskalah—either extreme undermined the Jewish tradition. Yet both movements contained kernels of moderation that might grow into benefits.

On the shoulders of Elijah of Vilna fell the burden of anticipating both of these extremes. Providence seems to have designated him to stem on the one hand mystical romanticism and overflowing emotionalism, and on the other, frigid reasoning and rigorous intellectualism. He saved Judaism from being crushed between the two.

To Elijah, harmony between heart and mind constituted the criterion of true religion. It was as important to serve God through knowledge as through faith. Faith and reason ought to function in harmony as auxiliaries. The more the amazing phenomena of nature are unfolded, the more baffled stands man—abashed by secrets that this reasoning cannot fathom, and overawed by divine omnipotence.

"It is not possible to understand the fundamentals of creation, how all segments are closely tied and arranged in a wonderful manner, unless we infer the unity of the Creator and of reality." Elijah perceived the grandeur of the universe in this very unity of its diverse appearance. As the source of divine wisdom, the Torah manifests this same unity: "the mitsvoth are interwoven and supplement each other as though they were one mitsvah . . . one truth." The Torah and the cosmos represent a unity.[21]

Elijah's writings cover the entire range of Scripture, Talmud and Kabbalah. He also wrote on algebra, trigonometry, astronomy and grammar. He encouraged the translation of Euclid into Hebrew,[22] and examined the historical works of Josephus rendered into Hebrew. But his favoring of secular study does not place him in the camp of the Haskalah, which aimed at the substitution of reason for faith.

He was, on the contrary, a severe critic of those who relied too much on speculation.[23] He did not spare even the revered Maimonides for having interpreted certain passages of Scripture or Talmud in a philosophical manner, ignoring the simple meaning (peshat).

The Gaon of Vilna would rather see a Jew adhere to the tenets of Torah in simple faith than have him condition his religious observance on continuous rational satisfaction. Since Judaism is an eternal religion, its verities cannot hinge on the changing fashions of the mind.

[21]Jewish Encyclopedia.

[22]His disciple Barukh of Shklov translated Euclid's Geometry into Hebrew. Barukh was a student of natural sciences. He had a laboratory for his experiments, maintained for him by the patron of learning Joshua Zeitlin who was a faithful follower of the Gaon of Vilna. In his introduction to his Hebrew Euclid, Barukh quotes his master Elijah; "If a man is deficient in sciences, he will be deficient a hundredfold in the knowledge of the Torah for both—Torah and science—go together." He was also urged by his master to translate into Hebrew other secular works on sciences.

[23]In *Avnei Eliyahu* (on Psalm XIX) commenting upon the passage *"The Torah of the Lord is perfect, restoring the soul,"* Elijah says: "Only if we accept the teaching of the Torah in toto, in accord with the truth of prophecy and faith, only if we avoid the error of adulterating its words with the speculations of the Greeks, is the Torah refreshing and invigorating to the soul."

"At the point where philosophy ends," said Elijah, "thence upward begins the wisdom of Kabbalah."[24] But he was imbued with traditional theism; he shunned the error of pantheism which he suspected in the vague phraseology of early Hassidism.

Elijah loved life. He valued every second, for to him it abounded with spiritual opportunities. On his deathbed he lamented, "How hard to forsake this world in which with a few groschen, spent on *tsitsith* (fringes), one fulfills a mitsvah and gains immeasurable reward."

In spite of his all-out opposition to Hassidism, it would be wrong to ascribe to Elijah the advocacy of asceticism as a way of life. The rigorous habits that he imposed on himself, he persistently discouraged in others.

With remarkable modernity, he deprecates the notion that any force or faculty of human life is unholy and should be suppressed. Commenting on the passage, *"The saint doeth good to his soul, but he that troubleth his flesh is cruel,"* he said, "Man's desires should be purified and idealized, but not done away with." He remonstrated with his disciple, Rabbi Zalman of Volozhin, for wasting himself in fasts and vigils. There were better paths to saintliness. He regretted the asceticism of his own youth. Rabbi Zalman answered that he, too, would like to have something to regret.

The Gaon, whose supposed austerity the Hassidim resented, included gladness of heart in his teaching.

> "Only through rejoicing can a man reach perfection in the performance of a mitsvah. 'The Shekhinah,' say the rabbis, 'rests only on him who finds delight in a meritorious deed.' Commenting on the Psalmist's exhortation, *'Serve the Lord with gladness, Come before His presence with singing,'* they said, 'Man ought to feel cheered by the privilege to serve God and to occupy himself with the divine commandments.' As Solomon has it, *'Draw me to Thee, we will run after Thee. The King has brought us into his chambers; we will be glad and rejoice in Thee.'* This suggests that the further man is

[24]*Biur ha-GRA* on *Yoreh Deah* 179, 13. *Ma'aloth ha-Su'am* p. 24; *Orhoth Hayyim* by R. Hayyim of Volozhin. It is related that a zealot once complained to Elijah against someone who organized a group to study Maimonides' "Guide of the Perplexed'. The Gaon answered: "It is the work of the *Rambam* and nobody should ever dare prevent its study."

permitted to penetrate the secret chambers of knowledge, the greater will be his joy and the more will his heart exult within him."[25]

Such an interpretation of Judaism hardly differed from that of the Hassidim. Had not Israel Baal Shem Tov also urged his disciple, Rabbi Jacob Joseph, to abandon his too-frequent fasting, saying it was a device of Satan to confuse man in his effort to serve God?[26] Had not other Hassidic leaders declared, "God loves the man who serves Him cheerfully, rather than the man who, consumed by grief, makes himself wretched with self-imposed suffering," and that "the custom of self-imposed torture causes darkness and confusion to the mind and has nothing in common with true piety."[27]

VI

THE FOCAL POINT

A Hassidic regime of joy, though excessively practiced, would not have aroused Elijah of Vilna to extreme ire. There had to be a more profound reason for the mild Gaon's wrath.

Indeed it was something of fundamental consequence. He viewed the rapidly-spreading movement of Hassidism as a serious threat to the very existence of Judaism, because early Hassidim attempted serious innovations in the Shulhan Arukh.

Rabbi Joseph Karo (1488-1575) had codified Jewish law brilliantly.[28] His conciseness and lucidity of style made his work comprehensive and readily serviceable. Indeed, one could take from the Shulhan Arukh as from a "prepared table" of food. Rabbi Karo, as a Sephardi, had followed almost exclusively the authorities and customs of the Sephardic group. Rabbi Moses Isserles (1525-1572) covered the "Prepared Table" (*Shulhan Arukh*) with his Ashkenazic "Tablecloth" (*Mappah*). That sup-

---

[25]*Avnei Eliyahu,* Psalm XIX, 9.
[26]*Shivhei ha-Besht,* p. 30; *Midrash Rivesh* Tov. 11.
[27]Introduction to *Saint and Sage,* by M. M. Yoshor.
[28]It was an abridgement of the Four Rows (Arbaah Turim) by R. Jacob ben Asher, with additions found in his own commentary Beth Yoseph (House of Joseph) on that work.

plement recorded the practices of the Ashkenazim, so that the code could now be consulted by all the Jews.

If Rabbi Joseph Karo named his code "The Prepared Table" (*Shulhan Arukh*) and Rabbi Moses Isserles called his supplement "The Tablecloth" (Mappah), the appropriate title for Rabbi Elijah's commentary would have been "The Table Lamp," inasmuch as it sheds light on each law and custom in all its ramifications. But, in deference to his humble character, it was named simply, "The Commentary of the Gaon, Rabbi Elijah" (*Biur ha-GRA.*)

Elijah considered the *Shulhan Arukh* the quintessence of Judaism. To him it represented the gist of Talmudic halakhah. In his commentary he traced every statement, every decision, every custom and tradition to its mainspring—the Talmud. It was not this or that author of post-Talmudic fame, whether Sephardic or Ashkenazic, that carried weight with him. He valued rather the inferences they drew from the Talmudic source.

Rabbi Yehudah Leib and Rabbi Avraham, the sons of Elijah, explain the intention of their late father in their introduction to his commentary. It was to show that the laws of the Shulhan Arukh stemmed ultimately from divine revelation.

"If you will open your eyes, my brother (the reader), and thoroughly examine this work from beginning to end, following one chapter after another, and if you seek to learn the truth, you will perceive a certain, straight-line principle.

"Our great-grandfather, the illustrious Rabbi Moshe Rivkes, in his *Be'er ha-Golah* confined himself primarily to a disclosure of the sources of laws and opinions as derived from the *Beth Joseph* (Rabbi Karo's magnum opus on the Turim).

"Yet our eminent father, the Gaon of blessed memory, reached out far beyond. In his commentary he proved that the source and origin of each word in the *Shulhan Arukh* was either the Babylonian or the Palestinian Talmud, or *Rashi* or *Tosafoth*. Such a revelation even Rabbi Joseph Karo in his *Beth Joseph* had not envisaged, nor did any of the early commentators. Our eminent father actually inaugurated a new method. All the laws and customs now assume a new face; they are shown to stem from one shepherd (Moses) and from one God."

Elijah's intimate knowledge of Kabbalistic lore prompted him to declare that there was no contradiction between the Zohar and the Talmud; that only he who lacks a perfect understanding of either the Talmud or the Zohar would fail to see their essential agreement.[29]

By tracing it back to its ancient origin, he demonstrated that the Shulhan Arukh was not an arbitrary system of legalisms devoid of spiritual content. It was rather a life-giving force covering the entire theater of human action, and having for its primary objectives the creation of an equilibrium among the inner forces of man, allowing outlet to all his faculties, enhancing his mercy and his forbearance. The Code defined right conduct in terms of progressive morality, always raising the standard and never lowering it. At its heart lay the peace and well-being of society.

To Elijah, the Shulhan Arukh constituted a wonderful unifying power for a people dispersed, keeping persons of all strata together. He read the Biblical verse, *"And all the people answered together and said, 'All that the Lord hath spoken we shall do,'"* with emphasis on *"all the people"* and *"together."*[30] It meant that the Torah provided for an ethical unity of the people; there must be no splitting into segments.

It was now about two hundred years since the Shulhan Arukh had seen the light (1555). The Code had weathered the initial disapproval of some scholars. But several events had since weakened the authority of both Shulhan Arukh and rabbis. The Sabbatai Tsevi heresy, a century before, had devastated the Jewish communities and the psychic scars were still visible. In 1764, the weakened Polish government abolished the Jews' Council of Four Lands that since 1580 had maintained their religious autonomy. From 1772 to 1795 Poland herself was being dismembered by her rapacious neighbors. There was serious confusion among the Jews. Now, more than ever, the moral power of the Shulhan Arukh had to be reasserted. Now, more than ever, no schism in Jewry could be countenanced.

[29]Introduction to *Sifra di-Tseniutha,* by R. Hayyim Volozhin; *Aliyoth Eliyahu.*
[30]Ex. XIX, 8.

The Hassidim seemed to have seized the opportunity to fill
the vacuum. With the Council dissolved, they moved in to capture the leadership of the Jewish community. Hassidism fanned
out from the small towns and villages where it had been born,
conquered most of the Ukraine, Volhynia and Podolia provinces
and a large part of Poland proper, and attempted to storm Lithuania. As an escape from the turbulence of the time, the Jewish
masses went over eagerly to the new movement which lifted them
from austerity and lured them into the region of the mysterious
and the supernatural. Talmud? It was no longer the supreme
authority; they set the Zohar in its place. *Shulhan Arukh?* It
might now be disregarded when, in their view, it contradicted the
mystic teaching.

How then could Elijah remain indifferent to a general aban-
donment of established tradition when he heard of families split
into factions, of separate houses of worship, of divided communities? How could he remain mild when tidings were brought
of changed orders of prayer, of laxness in the performance of
mitsvoth, of disrespect for study, of disparagement of rabbis and
scholarship? He set his signature to the severe manifesto against
the Hassidim: "New ideas are being disseminated which our fathers
had not surmised . . . sects and parties have chosen new customs
that are alien to us and in disconformity with our hallowed traditions. They have adopted improper statutes which set them apart
from the whole people of Israel."[31]

Hassidism stopped short at the gates of Vilna. It was like an
out-of-control vehicle that, responding to efficient control, braked
now to a slower speed. The Gaon's pronouncement, valorous and
uncompromising, had stayed its momentum.

There would be no schism. Shocked into self-examination, the
Hassidic Jews revised their diffuse intents and altered their aspirations; they set their movement within the framework of the Shulhan
Arukh. They acknowledged the propriety of a more intensive
study of Talmud and Halakhah.

But they vilified Elijah. In his time and for years thereafter,
only a few Hassidim understood that his firmness had checked the

[31]*Toledoth ha-Hassiduth,* by S. Dubnov.

schismatic tide, diverting it into safe channels. A Hassidic leader of uncommon perception, Rabbi Menahem Mendel Shnayersohn, admitted the debt:

"Hassidim failed to appreciate the great benefit and aid that the Gaon of Vilna lent to their cause. They ought to realize that, but for the Gaon's strong opposition, the Hassidic Movement would have been in danger of drifting into the wrong direction. There was good reason for believing that the new path blazed for us by our fathers would not be visible clearly enough to prevent a misstep. The Hassidim might have overdone their acceptance of the teachings of Kabbalah as the guiding standard. Overpowered by a glowing ecstasy and exceeding zeal, they might have weakened in their loyalty to the Torah and to the Shulhan Arukh's precepts.

"Fortunately the Gaon arose and by his opposition prevented Hassidism from developing into a sect; kept it within the sphere of ancient Judaism . . . .As a result of that opposition my grandfather (Rabbi Shneur Zalman of Liady) was persuaded by his teacher, Rabbi Ber of Meseritz, ca. 1710-1772, to compile a reworking of the *Shulhan Arukh,* thus influencing his followers to pursue a way of life in accord with the requirements of the authoritative code."[32]

Rabbi Shneur Zalman hoped that his efforts to introduce a rational-halakhic approach among the Hassidim would win Elijah away from his anathema.

The Talmud and the *Shulhan Arukh* are fortresses around a city which is the Jewish soul. He repulsed attacks against the fortresses, he strengthened the walls themselves, and he trained new defenders for the walls.

The allegory is apt: Elijah repulsed the proto-Hassidim; his seventy books gave strength; and the disciples he set up assured continuity.

VII

MEN ABOVE BOOKS

After his fortieth year, Elijah devoted most of his attention to the raising of these disciples. He had completed his magnum

---

[32]*Mekor Barukh,* III, 20/I, by R. Barukh Epstein.

opus—*Be'urei ha-GRA,* but he did not publish it, or any of his other works, perhaps because he wished to concentrate his attention on his students. Perhaps this great genius regarded it as futile to consign everything to books. In the second half of his life he determined to inscribe his knowledge on the tablets of men's hearts.

He surrounded himself with a number of disciples of brilliant minds and genuine piety. They would be living Shulhan Arukhs! They would supersede the books!

They became messengers disseminating their master's teachings. To them, he was like an overflowing fountain from which each drank according to his capacity. He warned them against wasting their precious time in pilpul (dialectic excesses). He taught them to adopt clear and straight thinking and painstakingly to search for truth. He lent them his corrected texts of the great books of halakhic literature, the result of years of sifting the Talmud. He showed that very frequently such corrections changed the interpretation of the passage. He toppled many beautiful casuistic structures built on the foundation of erroneous texts. He thus opened to his disciples a new frontier: critical examination of the text.

He insisted not only on proper intellectual training, but also on the cultivation of moral faculties. He believed that in order for the Torah to have its divine effect, the heart must be clean; otherwise, Torah learning would be an injurious craft.

> "The Torah is to the soul as rain to the soil. Rain, in descending upon the earth, causes different kinds of plants to grow, both nourishing and poisonous. Similarly the Torah helps the good toward perfection, while it also increases impurity in the hearts of those who were originally wicked."

The teacher, he felt, ought to concentrate his primary, though not entire, attention on his most distinguished pupils. *"Be thou diligent to know the state (literally the 'face') of thy flocks, and look well to thy herds."*[33] He noted that "be thou diligent" referred to the flocks, the best; while "look well to" referred to the herds, the less distinguished.

[33]Proverbs XXVII, 23.

Outstanding among his flock was Rabbi Hayyim of Volozhin (1749-1821). Thoroughly imbued with the master's charge, he returned, in 1803, to his home town to found his Yeshivah, which for a time he kept up entirely out of his own funds. There were academic innovations; students had to meet high standards of admission; the maintenance of indigent students was no longer a haphazard affair. Above all, the new Yeshivah embodied the Gaon's method. There was to be no hairsplitting subtlety; straightforward clarity would rule. Attention would be paid to Elijah's corrections of the text. Until its dissolution by the Russian government in 1892, the Volozhin school ranked supreme among the Yeshivoth of the world. The best students of other Yeshivoth regarded Volozhin as a kind of institute of advanced studies, admission to which was a great distinction.

Under the direct influence of the Gaon was also Rabbi Abraham Danzig (1748-1820). Whilst Rabbi Hayyim took care of the needs of the intellectuals, Rabbi Abraham took care of the needs of the people. He popularized the Shulhan Arukh, citing the Gaon's opinions. Rabbi Abraham, originally a merchant, was later prevailed upon to accept an appointment to the rabbinical court of Vilna. He had enjoyed a close attachment with the master. Through marriage he formed a connection with Rabbi Judah Leib, the son of Elijah, and he proudly mentions the relationship in the introduction to his work.[34]

He called one book "Man's Life" (*Hayyei Adam*), and the other "Man's Wisdom" (*Hokhmath Adam*). They summarized the laws contained in the first two sections of the Shulhan Arukh. As a practical man of business he emphasized the pertinent everyday laws, wrote of them in simple language, and avoided dryness through his lively ethical explanations and homespun allusions. He included a digest of the enormous amount of halakhic material that had accumulated since the appearance of the Shulhan Arukh.

Rabbi Danzig thus helped to consummate the goal of the Vilna school of exponents of the Shulhan Arukh; he made its contents accessible to the people. His works attained an extraordinary popularity, far beyond his expectation. Not only the less educated —the bar mitsvah lad and the burdened layman—consulted his

---

[34]Introduction to second edition of *Hayyei Adam*.

works; rabbis and serious students relied on "Hayyei Adam" for quick reference and for review. As the handbook for the observant, it came to be used as a text for both individual and group study.

* * * *

Elijah of Vilna posthumously inspired an emigration to the Holy Land, far in advance of Herzl. It was the Gaon's unfulfilled dream to go to Palestine. Once he started out, but for some unknown reason turned back and never again attempted the journey.

The Vilna *aliyah* (emigration) began in 1808 and brought hundreds to Palestine, reinforcing the depleted population. Six of the Gaon's disciples headed the movement, and they found the time propitious.[35]

Czarist Russia had fastened her iron grip on Lithuania. In the nearby Grand Duchy of Warsaw, formed in 1807 under Napoleonic aegis, little was done to ameliorate the lot of the Jews. In Western Europe emancipation spelled promise rather than reality. The Sanhedrin, so dramatically convoked by Napolean, paid a tribute of assimilatory concessions to the emperor. All these troubles aroused an inner reaction in the Jews, stirring in many a desire to be done with the Exile and to start anew in the Land.

The first Vilna settlers, about seventy in number, reached the Land in 1808 and established themselves in Safed. In all Palestine they found only one hundred fifty Jewish families.

They and subsequent groups of Vilna settlers were administered by the brilliant Rabbi Israel of Shklov (1770-1830). He was a foremost Talmudist who knew how to organize trips and raise funds. He journeyed to Europe frequently to get money for the emigrations, and was often helped by his elder colleague, Rabbi Hayyim Volozhin.

Between 1832 and 1836, Rabbi Israel worked on a valuable contribution to the halakhic literature of the Vilna school. Little had been done hitherto to arrange the Laws pertaining to the Land.

[35]They were R. Abraham Dayan of Shklov, R. Hayyim Katz of Pokroy, R. Isaac of Haslawitz, R. Israel of Shklov, R. Menahem Mendel of Shklov and R. Saadia of Vilna. They were instrumental in founding most of the sacred institutions of the Old Yishuv and were thus the forerunners of the New. It was they who led in the founding of the New Jerusalem outside the Walls of the ancient city.

These laws were regarded as a dead letter, at least until the Redemption occurred in His good time. Elijah had to revive the study of the Palestinian Talmud; fortunately his commentary had illumined its difficulties.

Now, thanks to Elijah's disciples, a resettlement had begun. With the aid of his master's *Biur,* Rabbi Israel constructed a miniature *Shulhan Arukh* that covered the halakhah of the Land. He called his work "The Edge of the Table" (*Peath ha-Shulhan*), that is, the edge of "The Prepared Table" (*Shulhan Arukh*).

On the day that Rabbi Israel of Shklov handed the first copies of the book to the new settlers it might truly have been said that Elijah of Vilna had gone up to the Land of Israel.

* * * *

It is 1885. Nahum Sokolow, the journalist, visits Vilna. He comes from Warsaw, where he edits the Hebrew daily *Ha-Tsefirah.* In Warsaw he stands at the center of a pulsating religious life, pietistic and scholarly. Yet he is amazed to find in Vilna that ordinary workmen are learned. He is astounded to find a carpenter in one synagogue elucidating the Mishnah in scholarly fashion. In another synagogue, he sees a blacksmith teaching adults the weekly portion, citing profound theological thinkers such as Nahmanides and Gersonides. In amazement he turns to his companions, the famous Samuel Joseph Finn, a native of Vilna, and asks, "Where did the Jews of Vilna get their teachers? Does Vilna have greater educators and more able instructors than other Jewish communities, than Warsaw or Lemberg?"

Finn answers, "Not teachers, but a teacher. Vilna had the Gaon."

Later Sokolow commented on the incident: "Although nearly ninety years had passed since the Gaon had departed, his influence on the people was as tremendous as if he were still the active teacher of the carpenters, tailors, blacksmiths and cobblers of Vilna.

There is a well-known legend: Once Elijah, while passing through a crowd of playing children, noticed that they were pointing to him and exclaiming, *"Der Vilner Gaon! Der Vilner Gaon!"* He stopped and said to the children; "If you only will it (*"will nor"*), you, too, will become Geonim."

This was an oversimplification. No amount of dedicated study would make men into Elijahs of Vilna. There was only one. He was the extraordinary exception that hardly ever recurs. A sage of our era was heard to remark, "Only once in four or five centuries does Providence favor us with such a great soul as the Gaon of Vilna."

SHNEYUR ZALMAN OF LIADY

By Charles B. Chavel

SHNEYUR ZALMAN OF LIADY

By Charles B. Chavel

I

Rabbi Shneyur Zalman of Liady, author of the *Tanya* and one of the greatest luminaries in the galaxy of our religious leaders, sprang out of the very centers of the Jewish world of his time.

There were two centers of spiritual activity in the world of Shneyur Zalman's youth: Vilna in Lithuania, and Mezeritsch in Volhynia. Vilna was the home of Rabbi Elijah, the towering personality, the incomparable scholar, the saintly man who consecrated every moment of his life to the study and observance of the word of God—the Gaon whose beacon lights still illumine today the high seas of Torah! Mezeritsch was the center of Rabbi Dov Ber, popularly known as the Maggid (Preacher), successor to the Besht (Rabbi Israel Baal Shem Tov), who was the founder of Hassidism, the God-intoxicated teacher who kindled the flame of faith in the hearts of the masses of Israel, the saintly man whose beacon lights still illumine the paths of millions of our brethren in their daily lives! Vilna and Mezeritsch! Towards the middle of the eighteenth century there was rivalry rising between them. One was the acknowledged capital of Torah, the other the heart of Worship. One was the home of historic tradition as embodied in the Torah and Mitsvah ideals of Israel, the other was the center of Hassidism, the movement which deepened Israel's spirit, and opened new vistas of moral and philosophic thought. It is to the glory of Rabbi Shneyur Zalman that before his span of sixty-five years of life was over, he not only carried on the struggle for Hassidism from beginning to an enduring end, but also succeeded in uniting in himself the noblest elements of both Vilna and Mezeritsch.

Shneyur Zalman was born on the eighteenth day of Elul in the year 5508 (1748)[1] in Lozna, White Russia, a small city near

[1]See Dubnow, Toledoth ha-Hassiduth, p. 225, note, where he quotes a record of Lozna to this effect, and not as usually stated (e.g. Teitlebaum, *ha-RAV mi-Liady,* 1, p. 1) that his birth took place in 5507 (1747).

the border between the districts of Mohilev and Vitebsk, then part
of the kingdom of Poland. His father, Baruch, a descendent of
the famous Maharal of Prague,[2] was in comfortable circumstances.
Not much is known about his devout mother, Rebeccah.

Trained in the traditional paths of Jewish education which
included the study of the Bible, Talmud and Codes, Shneyur Zalman's erudition was recognized when he was still a youth. Upon
his reaching religious majority, the Jewish leaders inscribed his
name in glowing terms upon the community records.

At the age of 20, Shneyur Zalman was already married. At
that time, utterly dissatisfied with his spiritual accomplishments,
he decided to turn to some great personality for light and guidance. But where was he to go—to Vilna, or to Mezeritsch?
At last he made the decision: "A little knowledge of the Torah,"
he said, "I have already acquired, but of the principles of true
Worship I have yet learned nothing. I shall go to Mezeritsch."[3] In
that decision lay the seed of Hassidism's growth.

When Shneyur Zalman reached Mezeritsch, Rabbi Israel Baal
Shem Tov had been dead some ten years. Thus he never met the
Besht face to face, a matter which he deeply regretted all his life,
but he found in the Maggid such an excellent master of the truth
and beauty of pristine Hassidism, that he later called himself the
spiritual grandson of the Besht.

Shneyur Zalman was warmly welcomed by everyone in
Mezeritsch, and the Maggid especially befriended him in every
possible way. He asked him to instruct his son Abraham, known
as *Avraham ha-Malakh,* (Abraham the Angel), in Talmud and
Codes; he, in exchange, was to initiate him into Hassidic lore.[4]
Later Shneyur Zalman was to join the Maggid's select group of
disciples whom he instructed in the deeper aspects of Hassidism,
which the Besht had taught him. This inner group of disciples
consisted of the future leading spirits of the movement, who carried
its torch to the far-flung Jewish communities of Eastern Europe.

[2]Teitlebaum, 1, p. 2; Beth Rabbi, p. 108. However, see ibidem, 1, pp.
250-252, where he throws doubt upon this tradition. That Shneyur Zalman's father was a learned man is established beyond question (Ibid.,
p. 2.).
[3]Quoted in Dubnow, p. 225, from an old Lonza Jewish city record.
[4]Beth Rabbi, p. 123.

To this circle belonged Elimelekh of Lezyansk, who blazed the trail in the Polish communities; Levi Yitzhak of Barditchev, leader of the movement in Volhynia; Menahem Mendel of Vitebsk, who founded the Hassidic community in the Holy Land; and Nahum of Tschernobel, leader of the Hassidim in the Ukraine. Of all his pupils, Shneyur Zalman was most dear to the Maggid, who recognized his scholarship and urged him to compose a new code of Jewish Law—Israel's *modus vivendi*. On this project young Shneyur Zalman set out immediately, writing some parts while still under the Maggid's tutelage, and compiling the rest of the work later on. It is called the *Rav's Shulhan Arukh,* a classic among the works of the Jewish masters. Appraising Shneyur Zalman's profound insight into every question, Rabbinic or Hassidic, the Maggid wrote in his testament: "Our dear Zalman's immediate grasp of any problem is a minor prophecy in itself."[5]

The teachings which emanated from Mezeritsch changed the spiritual countenance of East-European Jewish life. At first the movement gained adherents only among the rank and file of the people. But when such distinguished personalities as Menahem of Vitebsk, Levi Yitzhak and Shneyur Zalman joined it, and Hassidism gathered powerful momentum in its sweep throughout eastern Europe, its opponents, the *Mithnaggedim,* became deeply perturbed, and were compelled to act.

For an understanding of the great career of both Hassidism and our hero, a sketch of the highlights of popular Hassidism is prerequisite. A profound presentation of Hassidic thought, the *Tanya,* which we shall examine later on, undoubtedly evidences the popular appeal of Hassidism which won the hearts of the people.

The first principle that Hassidism taught was the absolute nearness of the Divine Presence to the material world, especially to man. Jewish sacred literature had voiced this doctrine throughout the ages, yet it was left to the Besht to infuse it with real vitality and pragmatic meaning: God is everywhere. There is no place devoid of Him. The universe in its various manifestations is but the outward embodiment of the Infinite Glory of the Divine

[5]Baal ha-Tanya, p. 16. The Rav as a rule sided with the *Mahmirim,* i.e., those who adopt the stricter opinion in the interpretation of Jewish law, especially in connection with the observance of Sabbath and Passover.

Majesty, and does not exist independent of His Province. The sum total of the forces at work throughout the universe, known as nature, derives its existence solely from the Almighty. God's presence permeates every phenomenon and is responsible not only for its creation but also for its continued existence and operation.

The nearness of God to the world surrounding man entails the principle of *Simhah* (Joy): Man must banish all melancholiness and be ever joyful in the presence of the Almighty. "For how can one enter within the King's gate wearing sackcloth?" To be despondent in God's presence is to show distrust of His justice and wisdom. The devout Jew must ever be happy. Since hope and joy are akin to each other, he is characterized not only by his joyful disposition under all circumstances, but also by his hopeful outlook on life.

For having taught these doctrines, Hassidism deserves the undying gratitude of the Jewish people. The Talmud speaks about a man who earned his reward in the World to Come because he brought smiles and temporary happiness to some poor people in the market place.[6] How much greater were the accomplishments of the Besht and his disciples, who kindled the flame of a new awareness of God in the hearts of legions of Jews, inspiring them with enduring joy and hope!

However, there was one aspect of Hassidic teaching which made it susceptible to criticism. This was the Besht's overemphasis of the doctrine that joyful prayer is a chief mode of the true worship of God. In this doctrine, tending to equalize the unlearned with the learned, the Mithnaggedim saw a potential source of danger to Israel's lifeline, the study of the Torah. History has shown that this charge was unfounded. During two hundred years of its history, Hassidism has brought its devotees nearer to their Father in Heaven through both Worship *and* Torah. Yet the leaders of eighteenth-century Judaism had reason to be alarmed by the victorious sweep of this movement. The wounds inflicted upon Israel by the deceptions of Sabbattai Tsevi and Jacob Frank had hardly been healed and the nation's guides considered it a sacred duty to stay on

[6]Taanith 22 a.

the alert against any new doctrine which again might undermine
the welfare of the Jews.

A few days after Passover of 5532 (1772),[7] the Mithnaggedim,
with the consent of the Gaon of Vilna, excommunicated the fol--
lowers of the new movement. Unless the Hassidim abandoned
their ways, which set them apart from the rest of the people, they
would be regarded as dissidents from the Jewish faith, and all contact with them would be prohibited. As one might have anticipated,
persecution in itself did not deflect the Hassidim from the path of
their convictions. But when some nine months later (19th of Kislev,
5538), the Maggid of Mezeritsch passed away, this town, the capital of Hassidism, quickly declined, and unity in Hassidic ranks almost disappeared. His outstanding disciples spread throughout
Eastern Europe to found centers of their own. Shneyur Zalman,
out of his deep respect for the Maggid, stayed at first with his son,
"Abraham the Angel," but later joined the group which gathered
around Menahem of Vitebsk. When urged to head a group of his
own, he said: "In the midst of my people I dwell." However, in
spite of his determination to remain in obscurity, the following
events threw him into the midst of the conflict:

In 5537 (1777), Rabbi Menahem of Vitebsk and his followers
embarked on a plan to leave for the Holy Land, to found there a
Hassidic community which would be free from persecution. Before
leaving Europe, they deemed it advisable in the interest of peace to
proceed first to Vilna, to intercede with the Gaon and convince him
of the positive values of Hassidism. As their representatives they
chose Menahem, the leader of the group, and Shneyur Zalman,
both his disciple and colleague. In Vilna, the two emissaries were
accorded little recognition. Twice they appeared before the Gaon's
study, but each time they were refused admission. Twenty years
later, in a letter to his followers in Vilna, Shneyur Zalman recalled
the incident in the following words:

> "Immediately we set out towards the saintly Gaon's home
> to discuss the whole matter with him in order that all misunder-
> standings might be removed. I myself took part in this mission,
> as well as our saintly master, the deceased Rabbi (Menahem)
> Mendel. But twice the Gaon locked the door against us. When

[7]Dubnow, p. 116.

the leaders of the community approached him, saying: 'Our master, their chief spokesman has come to discuss the matter with you, and when he will be convinced of his mistakes, as undoubtedly he will be, peace will be restored in Israel,' he gave them evasive replies. When they commenced to beseech him, he left the city and stayed away until we left for home."[8]

The delegation left Vilna broken-hearted but undefeated in spirit. It is indicative of Shneyur Zalman's nobility of character that not one bitter word against the Gaon ever passed his lips. On the contrary, in his writings to his followers, he pleaded with them to judge the Gaon's action as having been motivated by a sincere desire to defend the truth.[9]

A second group was to proceed to Shklov, a city of prominent rabbis and leaders, to conduct an open disputation with the *Mithnaggedim*. But this debate never materialized.[10]

Having failed in their peace-mission, Menahem and his followers decided to go through with their plan of settling in the Holy Land. In the month of Adar 5537 (1777), some 300 souls, Shneyur Zalman among them, set out on the journey. Many Hassidic leaders accompanied them part of the way. At Mohilev (Podolia), they urged Shneyur Zalman to remain in Europe to lead the Hassidim in his country. After much thought he accepted for a brief time the Rabbinical post of his native city. It is related that when he first saw thousands of people streaming to his home for guidance and instruction, he became overwhelmed with the

[8]Beth Rabbi, p. 40.
This letter is found in Teitlebaum, 1, pp. 218-221, and in Kahane, *Toledoth ha-Mekubbalim*, 11, pp. 150-152.
Teitlebaum 1, pp. 43-44 suggests that Shneyur Zalman's role in the delegation was to convince the Gaon that among the Hassidim there was also great scholarship.
[9]Kahane 11, p. 109, finds the reason for the Gaon's refusal to enter into a discussion with the delegation, in his knowing that they could defend their position on the basis of Kabbalistic literature. The Gaon too was a student and follower of the Kabbalah; however, since he held that not all Kabbalistic writings were authentic, he found it inadvisable to enter into a debate with people who believed in the authenticity of the *entire* Kabbalistic literature. Kahane's theory is well supported in the latter half of the letter quoted above, where in refuting the Gaon's charges against certain Hassidic doctrines, the Rav states that by rejecting the authenticity of certain works containing the teachings of Rabbi Isaac Luria, the Gaon has disqualified himself from rendering an expert opinion in the matter.
[10]Referred to in the same letter quoted above.

responsibility of the task. At that moment, his wife, ever a source
of courage and comfort, remarked: "After all, these people have
not come to demand new Torah from you. They are merely seeking to hear from you the teachings of your great master, the Maggid
of Mezeritsch." When he heard these words, his mind was relieved, and he consented to don the mantle of leadership.[11] However, though his master Rabbi Menahem was away in the Holy
Land, out of his deep respect for the latter, Shneyur Zalman did
not officially consent to become the head of the movement until
the former passed away in 1778. At that time Shneyur Zalman or,
as he was now known throughout Israel, the *Rav* (the teacher, the
master) was already acknowledged as the head of the Hassidim
in his century, and the leading thinker of the movement.

Soon his influence extended all over Eastern Europe. He
welded into one brotherhood the numerous and widely different
Hassidic groups, by strengthening their hands, by keeping in constant touch with them, and by letters which were to become
classics in Hassidic literature and thought. To avoid friction with
their opponents, he urged them to establish synagogues of their own.
He counselled many adherents to turn to the pursuit of agriculture.[12] He insisted that a regular contribution be made by every
group towards the upkeep of the Palestine community.[13] He
showed partiality to no one. When a rich man once asked him
for a blessing, he replied: "You have stated the things you need,
but you have not mentioned why we need you."[14] He guided his
followers in the path of truth blazed by his masters. He ennobled
their spirit through his classic work, the *Tanya.* Many of his
ordinances are now accepted throughout Israel. He adopted the
prayer ritual of the famous sixteenth-century Kabbalist Rabbi
Isaac Luria, and rewrote it, under the name of *Nussah Sefarad,*

[11]Beth Rabbi, p. 109. A few years after his assumption of leadership
Shneyur Zalman's followers numbered some 100,000 (Teitlebaum, 1, p. 50).

[12]This idea of the Rav was later elaborated by his successor, his son
Rabbi Dov Ber, who wrote a letter to his followers in which he urged them
to learn all forms of manual labor, and especially agriculture (Beth Rabbi,
11, pp. 5-6, notes; Teitlebaum, 1, p. 125, n. 3). The Rav also urged his
followers to engage in trades which are above reproach, as well as to practice frugality, and never to be ostentatious (Teitlebaum, 1, p. 126).

[13]*Tanya,* "The Holy Epistle," ch. 21.

[14]Baal ha-Tanya, p. 18.

for use by his followers.[15] Two sets of *Tefillin* (in accord with the instructions of both Rashi and Rabbenu Tam) were to be donned daily by everyone. On Hol ha-Moed, mid-festival days, the *Tefillin* were not to be donned. He provided for the establishment of warm ritual immersion pools. He ordained that all knives used in the ritual slaughtering of cattle and fowl should not only be sharp but also polished, sparkling clean. This was a far-reaching ordinance, for the Rav's insistence that only with a polished knife can *Shehitah* be permitted, compelled the Hassidim to engage separate slaughterers.[16] Under his leadership, which encompassed every aspect of life, the movement went from strength to strength.

Hassidism's rapid progress in north-eastern Europe re-galvanized the opposition to action. Once again the little foxes that gnaw at the vines when they are in bloom, became busy. The misconduct of some individual Hassidim was described as typical of the whole group.[17] Reports that Hassidim violated the law were maliciously fabricated, and their names were linked even with followers of the notorious Sabbatai Tsevi.[18] A new wave of persecution of Hassidim began, culminating in the re-affirmation in Vilna, in the summer of 1781, of the original ban against them. From Vilna, the edict of excommunication spread to all leading communities in Poland and White Russia.[19] A tragic situation

[15]The Rav's adoption of the *Minhag ha-Ari,* the ritual established by Rabbi Isaac Luria, accounts for the fact that Hassidim are averse to the reciting of special *piyutim* on the Sabbath and Festivals. It was Luria's theory, based upon mystic reasons, that only prayers composed by the Men of the Great Assembly and the Sages of the Talmud should be recited. This opinion, quoted by the Rav in his Prayer Book, spread among all Hassidim (Beth Rabbi, p. 172). It is also of interest to add that wherever there was a difference of opinion between the Halakhah and Kabbalah regarding a certain law, the Rav in his *Shulhan Arukh* followed the decision of the Kabbalists. (See Teitlebaum, 1, p. 13, n. 3).

[16]Beth Rabbi, pp. 31-32.

[17]Dubnow, pp. 228-230.

[18]A notorious example was that of witnesses testifying that they saw Hassidim eating on the ninth of Ab. However, they failed to add that that year this day occurred on the Sabbath (and in consequence the fast was postponed to Sunday, the tenth)! (Baal ha-Tanya, p. 21). By charging the Hassidim with eating on the Ninth of Ab, the accusers also aimed to stigmatize the Hassidim as being followers of Sabbatai Tsevi, the pseudo-Messiah of Turkey, who had ordained the day as a holiday (Ibid.).

[19]Beth Rabbi, p. 35. The chief instigator of the present, and all subsequent, persecutions against the Hassidim was one Avigdor, chief Rabbi of Pinsk, whose position was threatened by the unprecedented growth of the Hassidic community in that city. (Teitlebaum, 1, pp. 34-38, 66-68, 90-102, also p. 23, n. 3.).

resulted. Families were torn apart by strife. Husbands were separated from their wives. Fathers, whose children had entered the
ranks of Hassidim, observed the week of mourning over them, as
if they had died!

In those trying days, it was the far-sighted leadership of the
Rav which saved the movement from extinction. With word and
deed he strengthened the feeble hands of the persecuted. When, in
1784, community leaders gathered in Mohilev to discuss plans of
pursuing their anti-Hassidic policies and demanded of the Rav that
he appear before them, he refused and instead dispatched one of his
most stinging letters in which he rebuked them bitterly for hound-
ing innocent people. As a result, the persecution in White Russia
subsided for some time.[20]

In 5556-1796, the year which marked the publication of the
Tanya, the storm broke out again. This time the *Mithnaggedim*
were enraged over stories spread by some irresponsible Hassidim to
the effect that the Gaon in his old age was admitting the truth of
Hassidism. To fortify their position, the *Mithnaggedim* called the
Gaon's attention to certain objectionable passages in Hassidic literature. Certain Hassidic works were publicly burnt in Vilna.[21] The
Gaon in a letter to all communities urged them to resume their fight
against the movement. At this point, pressure was brought to
bear upon the Rav to proceed to Vilna in order to convince the
Gaon that there was nothing in Hassidism that was foreign to
our faith. But remembering his former experiences in that city,
the Rav refused, and instead addressed a letter to his followers in
Vilna, in which he answered all charges, and proposed an open
debate between the proponents of the two factions.

The Rav's letter reached Vilna in the last days of the Gaon.
On the third of the Mid-festival days of Succoth, in the year 5557-
1797, the Gaon of Vilna passed away. All Israel, in spite of the
holiday, was thrown into deep mourning. When, however, some
of the fanatical Hassidim in the city proceeded with the regular

[20]Dubnow, pp. 161-164. (The letter is found in Teitlebaum, 1, pp. 223-
230). However, historians are not in accord as to the time of this letter.
See Teitlebaum, 1, p. 62, n. 1, who places it in 1797, while the author of
Beth Rabbi holds that it was written after the death of the Gaon.

[21]Beth Rabbi, p. 40, and cf. Dubnow. p. 243, n. 1. Which Hassidic
works were burnt? Was it only the "Testament of the Besht," or also
the *Toledoth Yaakov Yosef* (see Beth Rabbi, p. 40, n. 2; Dubnow, p. 253, n.

festival celebrations, the community swore to avenge the desecration of the Gaon's name.[22]

Some leaders of the Mithnaggedim informed the Russian Government[23] that the Rav, as head of the Hassidim, was organizing an independent form of rule; that in directing funds to Palestine he was helping a foreign government, seeking to win its favor, and finally, that he had established laws which were against the principles of the Torah. As a result of this charge, the Rav was carried off in chains to the government prison in St. Petersburg, precisely a year after the passing of the Gaon.[24]

The Rav's followers immediately came to his rescue. Funds for his release, as well as for the upkeep of his family, were gathered in all the Hassidic communities. It appears from stories current about his fifty-three days of imprisonment that the Rav was not treated harshly.[25] At the trial, he answered all questions to the satisfaction of his judges. To the question of whether he was a follower of the Besht, although this might have endangered his life, he answered emphatically in the affirmative. In the end, the government, convinced of his innocence, released him on the nineteenth day of Kislev, the *Yahrzeit* of the *Maggid*.[26]

The joy of the Hassidim knew no bounds. To this day they celebrate the nineteenth day of Kislev as the Rav's day of liberation. At this time, the magnanimity of the Rav's character again became

2). The contention that the *Tanya* too was put to the flames (Baal ha-Tanya, p. 22) is not correct, although it is certain that the Gaon objected to certain teachings therein (see Beth Rabbi, p. 40; Teitlebaum, 1, pp. 55-56, n. 3). As to the specific doctrines of Hassidism to which the Gaon objected, see Final Note at end of this paper.

[22]Dubnow, p. 255, n. 1.

[23]Under the terms of the final division of the kingdom of Poland in 1794, the majority of the Jews of Poland fell under the rule of the Czars.

[24]Teitlebaum, 1, pp. 72-74; Baal ha-Tanya, p. 25.

[25]According to one story, a high official of the Russian government, who was well versed in the Bible, visited the Rav in his prison cell, and asked him the following question: Scripture states that after Adam had sinned in eating of the forbidden fruit, God asked him, "Where art thou?". "Did God not know," the Russian dignitary asked him, "where Adam was?" Thereupon the Rav asked him whether he believed that the Bible contains revealed eternal truth. Upon being assured that he did, the Rav told him that God's question was directed not only to one specific individual but to men of all times. Whenever man sins, God calls him to repentance in these words: "Where art thou? See to what depths thou hast sunk." The officer was deeply impressed (Baal ha-Tanya, p. 27).

[26]Beth Rabbi, p. 65.

manifest. For in a letter to his followers, in which he informed them of his freedom, he warned them against stirring up the envy and defiance of their opponents.[27]

Two years later, new accusations were trumped up against the Rav, and he was again taken to St. Petersburg for questioning. But this time too he disposed of all accusations, and on the 12th day of March, 1801, the day of Alexander the First's ascension to the throne of Russia, he was given his freedom.[28] Shortly after his return to his home, the Rav transferred his residence from Lozna to Liady. Ever since he has been known as Rabbi Shneyur Zalman of Liady.

Now a new period of growth and development began for Hassidism. The Rav decided to visit many of the outstanding rabbis of the opposition. Upon becoming acquainted with his greatness in Torah and piety, many of them became reconciled to the new movement, some even joining its ranks. The influence of the Rav both as the leading thinker of Hassidim and as an outstanding Torah authority, was now felt throughout Israel. Thus Rabbi Shneyur Zalman of Liady succeeded in harmonizing the two conflicting ideals of eighteenth-century Judaism: Torah and Hassidism. The noblest traditions of Vilna and Mezeritsch were at last united in one personality!

The closing years of his life were marred by two problems: One was an inner struggle within the ranks of Hassidism centering around a certain Rabbi Abraham Kolisher, a youthful companion of the Rav, and successor to Rabbi Menahem as leader of the Palestine Hassidic community. Following the publication of the *Tanya,* Kolisher raised a protest against the Rav's rationalistic tendency of interpreting Hassidism. The issue was soon brought to a head by many Hassidic authorities, with the famous Rabbi Levi Yitzhak of Barditchev siding with the Rav. The controversy lasted for a number of years; it did not subside until the passing of Rabbi Abraham in Tiberias, in the year 1810.[29]

[27]Tanya, The Holy Epistle, ch. 2.
[28]Beth Rabbi, p. 76.
[29]Dubnow, pp. 335-337, Beth Rabbi, pp. 81-86. Involved in this struggle was also a certain misunderstanding about the collection and distribution of funds for the Palestine Hassidic community. See the Rav's letter to Rabbi Abraham Kolisker published in Teitlebaum, 1, pp. 231-238.

The cataclysmic events of the Napoleonic wars produced the other problem. When Russia and France were interlocked in mortal combat, Hassidic authorities became divided on the question of loyalty. Some leaders, remembering the constant persecution of Jews by the Russians, favored Napoleon, who symbolized the ideals of the French Revolution, whilst others preferred the Russian czars, under whose dominion at least religion was assured of existence. The Rav preached and demanded support for the Russian cause. Hence, as the armies of Napoleon proceeded to Moscow, he was forced to leave his home and seek refuge behind the Russian lines. After Napoleon's defeat at Moscow, the Rav on his way home became ill. He was taken to a little village, where, within a few days, on the twenty-fourth of Teveth, 5573 (1813), he breathed his last.

It is reported that in the last moments of his life he asked his grandson, who was near his bedside, whether he saw the ceiling of the room. The young man did not understand the meaning of the question. Thereupon Rabbi Shneyur Zalman said: "I see nothing at present but the Infinite Light stretching high above me, far into the endless spaces of heaven."[30]

Thus, after a stormy life, Rabbi Shneyur Zalman of Liady reached the end of his earthly journey.[31]

---

[30]Beth Rabbi, p. 91. His body was interred in the city of Hoditz, Poltava (Ibid).

[31]The Rav left three sons and three daughters. He was succeeded by his oldest son, Rabbi Dov Ber, (1774-1826), who transferred the seat of the Habad movement from Liady to the city of Lubavitsch, and since then the followers of the *Tanya*, or of Habad, have been known as Lubavitsher Hassidim. Rabbi Dov Ber was succeeded by the son of one of the Rav's daughters, Deborah Leah, Rabbi Menahem Mendel (1789-1866), who became famous for his authorship of the *Tsemah Tsedek*, a collection of responsa on Jewish law. The latter was succeeded by his son Rabbi Samuel (1834-1883), who in turn was followed by his son Rabbi Shalom Dov Ber, (1861-1920), whose son Rabbi Yosef Yitzhak (1880-1949), the recognized head of all Lubavitsher Hassidim, recently departed this world. (See Kuntras *Torath ha-Hassiduth*, containing a section dealing with the genealogy of Hassidic teachers, pp. 25-32, Brooklyn, published by Otsar ha-Hassidim Lubavitsch). The new leader of the Habad movement is Rabbi Menahem Schneirson, son-in-law of the sainted last rabbi.

II

Some of the Major Foundations of the Tanya

The writing of the *Tanya*[1] was inspired by the verse, *"For the word is very near to thee, in thy mouth, and in thy heart, that thou mayest do it"* (Deuteronomy 30, 14). It was the aim of the Rav to indicate to his followers that true worship of God is indeed very near to all Israel.

He devoted twenty years of life to the composition of this work.[2] He toiled hard to present his views in as concise and brief a form as possible, so that there should not be one superfluous word or letter in the whole book.

Parts of the *Tanya* first appeared in manuscript form among his disciples, who had written down their master's discourses. As hundreds of these manuscripts soon made their appearance, the Rav realized that it would be best for him to assume formal authorship of the work. Thus was born the *Tanya,* which (with its recent issue in Tel Aviv) has been reprinted some thirty-six times,[3] the text being carefully preserved, almost like that of the Holy Scriptures.

The *Tanya* consists of the following four divisions: "Selected Sayings," containing fifty-three chapters (which, Hassidim discovered, correspond to the Rav's fifty-three days of imprisonment); "The Gate of the Unity and Faith," and "The Epistle on Repentance," each containing twelve chapters; and "The Holy Epistle" and "Final Manuscript," consisting of thirty-four chapters.[4]

---

[1]Beside the *Tanya,* three other main works contain the thoughts and teachings of the Rav: *Torah Or,* containing his discourses on the books of Genesis and Exodus, and on the holidays of Hanukah and Purim; *Likkutei Torah,* containing his discourses on the books of Leviticus, Numbers, and Deuteronomy, on the High Holidays, and the Festival of Succoth; *Béurei ha-Zohar,* explanations of the Zohar which the Rav delivered to a select group of disciples. However, since the *Tanya* is the only work which issued from the pen of the Rav, while the other works were compiled by his sons, although partly checked by the Rav, we have confined our analysis to his teachings as found in the *Tanya.*

[2]Baal ha-Tanya, p. 38.

[3]Ibid.

[4]When the *Tanya* first appeared in the year 1796 it contained only the first two parts. "Selected Sayings," and "The Gate of the Unity and Faith." Although the work was published anonymously, it gained im-

The *Tanya,* meaning "It has been taught," derives its title from the first word of its opening quotation from the Talmud: "It has been taught that (before a person is born) they adjure him (in heaven): 'Be righteous, and do not be wicked. Even if the whole world tell you that you are righteous, regard yourself still as wicked'!"[5] It is this teaching of the Sages that the Rav uses as a starting point to unfold his thoughts. He raises first the following questions: Have we not been taught in "The Ethics of the Fathers" that one should never regard himself as wicked?[6] Moreover, if a person judges himself to be wicked, will it not hamper his joyful worship of God?[7] To solve these problems, the Rav undertakes an analysis of the soul.

The soul of every Israelite consists of two major parts. First is the animal soul, residing in the blood of the person and centered in the left opening of the heart, which circulates the blood throughout the body.[8] This animal soul is the core and substance of man's vitality and of his attributes of character, both good and bad. Among the bad attributes are anger, conceit, love of pleasure, pride, scorn, laziness, and melancholiness. The good attributes include compassion, and the devotion to deeds of loving-kindness. All attributes of the human character are derived from the forbidden fruit of the Tree of Knowledge which gave man his pleasurable and painful states of consciousness.[9]

The second part is the divine soul, which is centered in the mind of man as well as in the right opening of his heart, which is free of blood. The divine soul is the source of man's vital powers of thought, speech and deed. These three powers find their highest expression in the observance of the *TARYAG Mitsvoth* (the 613 Commandments of the Torah).[10]

mediate wide popularity, because its authorship was known to all Hassidim. It was republished in the year 1799. In 1806 the Rav prepared a new edition of the work, adding "The Epistle on Repentance." In the year 1814, shortly after the death of the Rav, the Tanya appeared in its present form.

[5]Niddah 30 b.
[6]Aboth 2, 13.
[7]Tanya, "Selected Sayings," ch. 1.
[8]Ibid. ch. 9.
[9]Ibid. ch. 1.
[10]The numerical value of these four Hebrew letters (tav, resh, yod, gimel) is 400 + 200 + 10 + 3, or 613.

Through deed, man fulfills the commandments; through speech, he studies the law and its interpretation, and through thought he penetrates the mysteries. Even though the Torah is concerned with earthly matters, its study is equal to the comprehension of the Divine Majesty, for "there is no difference whether one embraces Him in many garments or in one."[11]

The study of the Torah is the food of the divine soul. For just as bread provides nourishment for the body, so does the Torah prepare nutriment for assimilation into the system of the divine soul. It is the means by which man keeps in touch with the Infinite. Hence the Sages have said that the study of the Torah equals all other commandments. For, while all the Mitsvoth are the manifestations of the Divine Will, the Torah is also the means by which man keeps in contact with the Divine. If in meditating the words of the Torah man also gives verbal expression to his thoughts, speech reaches the summit of its function, acting as the Embracing Light which unites God and man.[12]

The two faculties of the soul, the animal and the divine, are in perpetual conflict, each seeking to conquer man and bring him into complete subjection.[13] If man succeeds in utterly destroying the evil in the left opening of the heart, supplanting it with the unbounded love of God, he is termed "an absolutely righteous man" (*tsaddik ve-tov lo*). For, in having transformed evil into good, he has reached the apex of moral development. However, if he succeeds only in repressing his evil feelings and impulses, bringing them only into moral subjection by the superior force of the good in him, he is called "a relatively righteous man" (*tsaddik ve-ra lo*).[14] Similarly, "an absolutely wicked man" (*rasha ve-ra lo*) is one who has uprooted from the right opening of his heart all inclinations to goodness and repentance, while "the relatively wicked man" (*rasha ve-tov lo*) is he who has permitted the evil in him merely to repress his good feelings and impulses.[15]

[11]Ibid. ch. 2.
[12]Ibid. ch. 5.
[13]Ibid. ch. 9.
[14]Ibid. ch. 10.
[15]Ibid. ch. 11.

The average man (the *beinoni*) is he who is able to rise to the heights of absolute righteousness only on certain occasions in his daily life, such as when reciting the *Shema* and the *Shemoneh Esreh* (the Eighteen Benedictions recited silently), but who immediately after that again lapses into the state of relative righteousness. The *beinoni* reaches the summit of human existence, absolute righteousness, but is unable to maintain that position.[16]

It is with this Average Man that the author of the *Tanya* is chiefly concerned, suggesting ways and means of training himself to hold on to those precious moments of absolute righteousness. From this standpoint we may understand the subtitle of the first part of the *Tanya*: "Selected Sayings, known as the Book of the Average Man."

This feature of the Tanya is a remarkably high tribute to Hassidism. That a religious classic should be concerned chiefly with the problem of perpetuating these sacred moments of absolute righteousness in the life of the religious man, is unique in all world literature. That such a discussion could have captured the imagination of countless people, who studied and pondered its words, and sought to put them into practice in their daily lives, makes one thrill at the Biblical passage: *"And who is like Thy people Israel, a nation unique in the world?"* (I Chron., XVII, 21).

To return now to the *Tanya* and the statement of the Sages, that before a person is born, he is adjured: "Be righteous, and do not be wicked. Even if the whole world should tell you that you are righteous" (meaning, that you have already reached the state of absolute righteousness, where it will hardly ever be possible for you to commit evil) "still regard yourself as wicked." That is to say, you should only consider yourself, even under the best of circumstances, as having reached the state of the *beinoni,* the Average Man, for whom the committing of evil is quite possible. The *beinoni* may be likened to a person who is asleep, but likely to wake at any moment. Similarly, when the Average Man is engaged in the process of reciting the *Shema* and the Prayers, the evil in the left opening of his heart lies dormant, for he is aflame with the love of God, but thereafter the evil may be reawakened.[17]

16Ibid. ch. 12.
17Ibid. ch. 13.

Some of the greatest Sages of the Talmud considered themselves as being only in the class of the *beinoni,* even though they devoted their entire lives to the study of the Torah.[18]

The saying in "The Ethics of the Fathers" that a person should never regard himself as wicked, is meant to teach us that one should never regard himself as "an absolutely wicked man," for in so doing he will lose confidence in himself altogether.

Seeking to reach the summit of absolute righteousness, a man will find it helpful to advance on the three-rung ladder of HABAD, which stands for *Hokhmah* (Wisdom), *Binah* (Understanding), and *Deah* (Knowledge). Knowledge and Understanding are the lower rungs of the ladder, because they represent the things which man actually knows and comprehends. The highest rung is Wisdom, from which Knowledge and Understanding receive their spiritual nourishment. Wisdom may be likened to a spring of water; Understanding is the stream which carries the water down; and Knowledge is the water which man actually drinks. But higher than these three rungs is *Emunah,* simple faith, which is accessible to all, the educated as well as the uneducated. It is for this reason that ordinary people are sometimes ready to suffer death for the sanctification of the Divine Unity, although they possess little knowledge about the Divine.[19]

In the perpetual struggle waged on the battlefield of man's heart, it is of the utmost importance to remember that a joyful disposition is a great help in bringing about the victory of good over evil. Even when man ponders about his sins, and becomes dejected because of them, his sad thoughts must immediately give way to the recognition that because *God's tender mercies are over all His creatures,* He in that instant has already forgiven his sins, and that therefore man must demonstrate his thankfulness by joyful worship.[20]

---

[18]Ibid. ch. 13.

[19]Ibid. chs. 18-19. In view of the fact that the Rav himself states in his introduction to *Tanya* that he gathered its teachings from other Hassidic writings, a matter which is verified by examination of earlier Hassidic works, it is, strictly speaking, not correct to credit the Rav with being the creator of the Habad concept. However, he was beyond doubt its greatest expositor and formulator (see Teitlebaum II, p. 6, n. 1).

[20]Ibid. ch. 26.

Humility before every person is another exceedingly helpful
virtue. Even when confronted by a sinner, one should realize
that if the conditions of the two persons were studied and compared, it would be found that one's own failure to accomplish
worthwhile things is greater than that of the sinner, for the latter
must struggle against both his natural inclinations and his environment.[21]

Just as it is important to set aside regular hours for daily
prayer and study, so should one make the meditation on the Divine
a regular daily effort.[22] "For the heart and core of Knowledge
is not merely to know the Majesty of God from hearsay, from
authors and books, but to deepen one's own thought of the Divine,
so concentrating on Him mind and heart that one will ever
passionately cleave to Him."[23]

"The Gate of the Unity and Faith" constitutes the theological
part of the Tanya. Here the author seeks to shed light on a
statement in the Zohar, the Bible of Jewish mysticism, that the
reciting of the verse Shema Yisrael . . . constitutes an expression
of the Higher Unity, while the reciting of "Blessed be the Name
whose glorious Kingdom is for ever and ever" forms an expression
of the Lower Unity. In his interpretation, the Rav makes the
following points:

Man is utterly incapable of understanding the nature and
essence of the Creator. Even when we state, "It is impossible for
any being to conceive His wisdom and essence," we are, strictly
speaking, making an incorrect statement. For the word "conceive" implies the possibility that the object to be conceived is either
conceivable or inconceivable. To apply this term to God, whose
Infinity is far above our minds, is as preposterous as to say that a
certain profound principle of science is not subject to the sense of
smell.[24]

The impenetrable mystery and unfathomable essence of the
Creator is embraced within the terms of the Shema Yisrael, where

[21]Ibid. ch. 30.
[22]Ibid. ch. 41.
[23]Ibid. ch. 42.
[24]"The Gate of the Unity and Faith," ch. 9.

the unique Unity of the Divine Sovereign is affirmed. This is what the Zohar means by the Higher Unity.

However, since the term "sovereign" necessitates the existence of some realm over which He exercises his sovereignty (for there can be no king without a kingdom), the existence of the finite universe and of Israel is necessary. Hence the statement, "Blessed be the Name whose glorious *kingdom* is for ever and ever." Note the word *kingdom,* for it points to the earthly, finite, material world, where God's manifestation can be described as the Lower Unity. Here we have the deeper meaning of the first two statements of the *Shema*: the verse *Shema Yisrael* affirming our faith in the principle of the Higher Unity, and the statement "Blessed be the Name whose glorious kingdom is for ever and ever" expressing our belief in the Lower Unity as made manifest in this world.[25]

"The Epistle on Repentance" is highlighted by the following teachings: According to Scriptures, repentance seems to entail the abandoning of the sinful way of life, confession being part of this process; it does not entail fasting in expiation of the sin committed.[26]

However, this applies only to obtaining forgiveness for the sin proper. But to regain one's former status of fellowship with the Divine, some higher expression of man's willingness to come near Him is necessary. When the Holy Temple was still in existence, the sacrifices served this purpose. At present, fasting takes their place.[27]

The distribution of charity is another step towards regaining one's fellowship with the Creator. The Sages ruled that one should not distribute more than a fifth of his wealth for charity. This does not apply here, since this form of charity entails the redemption of one's soul. If people spend all their wealth for the purpose of regaining their physical health, should they not spend more than a fifth for the healing of their soul?[28]

[25]Ibid. ch. 7.
[26]"The Epistle on Repentance," ch. 1.
[27]Ibid. ch. 2.
[28]Ibid. ch. 3.

Just as in the case of the Unity of God, so is there in contrition a Lower and Higher form of Repentance. Lower Repentance consists of the heart pleading to God for mercy, and attempting to uproot the source of evil responsible for the sin committed.[29] Higher Repentance consists of the joyful spirit, manifest in moments of prayer, when we study the Torah or engage in deeds of loving-kindness. Complete Repentance is the harmony between the contrite heart and the joyful spirit. The pious men of old were able to shift easily from a state of Lower to Higher Repentance. But at present, when a man's spirit is at a low ebb, it is best to go through the process of Lower Repentance at midnight, during the service of *Hatsoth*,[30] and through that of Higher Repentance during the reciting of the prayers.[31]

Although the reciting of the daily prayers partakes of the nature of Higher Repentance, the Sabbath Services stand on a still higher plane, making the weekday Services by comparison a form of Lower Repentance.[32]

The Rav beautifully illustrates the Divine attribute of forgiveness in connection with his explanation of the blessing: "Blessed art Thou, O Lord, who art gracious in being abundant to pardon." If a person has sinned against his fellowman and obtained his pardon, he will find it more difficult to secure his goodwill after having committed the same sin a second or third time. But with the Holy One, blessed be He, it is not so. For since His attribute of forgiveness stems from His mercy, His mercy being infinite, His forgiveness is also infinite. Hence it makes no difference whether a person committed a sin once, or a thousand times. The gate of repentance is always open. This is the deeper meaning of the phrase *"abundant in pardoning."*[33]

The concluding part of the *Tanya,* "The Holy Epistle," consists of a number of communications sent by the author to his friends and disciples on important occasions. These letters cover

[29]Ibid. ch. 7.
[30]Midnight Prayer Service instituted by Kabbalists in commemoration of the Destruction of the Temple, and the exile of the Divine Majesty.
[31]Ibid. ch. 10.
[32]Ibid.
[33]Ibid. ch. 11.

a variety of themes. In one document he congratulates them on having completed the study of the Talmud, encourages them to continue that work, and urges them to recite the prayers slowly and carefully.[34]

The importance of charity is stressed at great length. The statement of the Sages that the study of Torah is equal to the practice of deeds of loving-kindness, was true only in ancient times, when they made the study of the Torah their chief occupation. *But today, nothing equals charity.*[35] Having once been informed that some of his disciples were not zealous in the practice of this all-important Mitsvah, the Rav chastised them in a letter because of the great sin they were committing, and appealed to them to be ever-ready to help the cause of the unfortunates in their community.[36] He urged them especially to set aside weekly contributions for the support of the Palestine community.[37]

As to the manner of distributing charity, the Rav recommended giving it in smaller portions on several occasions rather than the whole sum at one time, for the habitual practice of giving charity purifies the soul.[38] In one letter he complains of his followers who turn to him for counsel and advice in earthly matters. His mission, he claims, is only to help them find the path of truth, the way of the Torah.[39]

This section of the *Tanya* also contains two of his letters of condolence, one to the Hassidic community in Palestine upon the death of Rabbi Menahem, and the other to Levi Yitzhak of Barditchev, his relative by marriage, upon hearing of the death of his son.[40]

A closing section, known as *Kuntras Aharon,* "The Final Manuscript," consists of the Rav's passionate plea to his followers on a number of important matters. He urges them not only to devote more time to the reciting of the prayers, but also to reciting them in unison. He urges the study of the whole Talmud

[34]"The Holy Epistle," ch. 1.
[35]Ibid. ch. 9.
[36]Ibid. ch. 16.
[37]Ibid. ch. 21.
[38]Ibid.
[39]Ibid. ch. 22.
[40]Ibid. chs. 27, 28.

every year by each community, arranging for the apportionment of various tractates among its members. They should read at least once a week Psalm 119, which is dedicated to the greatness of the Torah. Above all, they should be strict in the observance of the Sabbath, both in cessation from all manner of work, and as regards greater devotion of heart during the reciting of the Sabbath Services.

The influence of the *Tanya* has extended far beyond the limits of the Rav's followers, or even of Hassidim in general. In the course of 150 years since its publication, the *Tanya* has gained for itself an honored place among the classics of Jewish religious literature.[41]

Hassidim conferred their highest tribute upon Rabbi Shneyur Zalman by giving him the title of *Rav,* the master. Thus, just as Rabbi Elijah of Vilna is known throughout the Jewish world as the Gaon, so is the Rabbi of Liady known as The Rav. As we study the teachings and thoughts of these two men, we overlook completely their mutual struggles and differences. For in the higher world of Jewish spirituality there are many mansions, or as the Sages of the Talmud have put it, "The utterances of both men are the words of the Living God."

[41]All factions in Israel, Mithnaggedim as well as Hassidim, liberal thinkers as well as mystics, are now united in acclaiming the work a masterpiece of religious literature (See Teitlebaum I, pp. 254-257; II, p. 5, n. 2).

The *Tanya's* crowning victory may be seen in the fact that the work exerted a positive and constructive influence upon the *Nefesh ha-Hayyim,* a philosophic-mystic work of Rabbi Hayyim Volozhin, the Gaon's most celebrated disciple (See Teitlebaum II, pp. 90-94).

FINAL NOTE

What was the specific theological doctrine of Hassidism to which the Gaon took exception? While a detailed discussion of this subject is outside of the scope of this essay, a brief word of explanation is necessary.

Jewish mystic thought had been deeply concerned with the problem of where there was place for the universe to materialize at creation, if God was omnipresent even prior to creation?

To meet this problem, sixteenth-century Rabbi Isaac Luria, the master thinker of Kabbalah, advanced the doctrine of *Tsimtsum* (self-concentration). According to this teaching, God confined Himself—or better, concentrated His Essence, shrank it, so to speak—thereby making place for the material world and everything in it. This process of *Tsimtsum* underwent an infinite number of gradations until the world came into its present form.

Once the doctrine of *Tsimtsum* was well established in Kabbalistic literature, a controversy arose as to the proper interpretation thereof. One school of thought held that it was to be taken literally, that is to say, God in the process of *Tsimtsum* had actually removed Himself from the sphere allotted to the universe, retaining His connection with it only through the exercise of His Providence over it. The Scriptural declaration, *"The whole earth is full of His glory"* (Isa. VI, 3) according to this school of thought, is to be understood thus: By exercising His Providence over the universe, and everything that goes on in it, God's glory is made manifest everywhere. This was the Gaon's interpretation of *Tsimtsum,* well supported by a long line of authoritative opinion. By upholding the literal meaning of the doctrine, the followers of this school of thought simplified all theological problems. By His Self-Concentration God removed Himself from the universe, retaining His Connection with it through the exercise of His Providence.

However, to the pining, mystic soul of the Besht, the founder of Hassidism, this interpretation of *Tsimtsum* was highly unsatisfactory. How could we ever think that God has utterly removed Himself from the universe? Quoting ancient sources, the Besht was convinced that such a view is untenable. Instead, he taught, we must understand the doctrines of *Tsimtsum* only in a figurative sense. God, *as it were,* concentrated Himself and made a place for the universe, but actually He is still in the universe as before creation. The doctrine of *Tsimtsum* is merely a helpful instrument—a poetic figure of speech—to enable us to penetrate somewhat the mysteries of the impenetrable. *"The whole earth is full of His glory"* is therefore to be understood in the sense that God is actually found in the universe. In fact, He is to be found even in the lowliest of places, that is, even where man sins and rebels against Him; "there is no place devoid of His Divine Presence." (Be-Midbar Rabbah, XII, 4. See Tanya, Likkutei; XXII and Iggereth ha-Rav I, 218.)

Behind this controversy was a clash of two *Weltanschauungen.* To the Gaon, the supreme master of *Halakhah,* the universe was an open book; God created it, gave it independent existence, and still watches over it in His Providence. The Hassidic teaching that God's essence pervades even sin was to the Gaon a great sacrilege. This explains why in his call to war against the Hassidim the Gaon specifically singled out for criticism the Hassidic interpretation of verses referring to God's glory in the world, as well as Hassidism's tendency to find the Divine "in every tree and stone" (see ha-Rav mi-Liady I, 56).

The Besht, on the other hand, was primarily a poetic religious thinker. To him the utter removal of the Divine from the universe was an absolute impossibility. Hence his figurative interpretation of *Tsimtsum,* which forms one of the major foundations of Hassidic thought.

That the final word in such a profound controversy cannot be said is obvious. However, it is certainly significant that in his *Nefesh ha-Hayyim* (chapter 3), Rabbi Hayyim Volozhin, the Gaon's most outstanding disciple, accepted the exposition of *Tsimtsum* found in the Tanya, although he does not mention the Rav or his work by name!

Bibliography

(1) M. Teitlebaum, Ha-Rav mi-Liady, Warsaw, 1914.

(2) H. M. Heilman, Beth Rabbi (a collection of all relevant material).

(3) D. Zeira, Baal ha-Tanya, Tel Aviv, 1945.

(4) Tanya, Habad World Organization, Tel Aviv.

(5) H. I. Bunim, Mishnath Habad, Warsaw, 1936.

(6) S. Dubrow, Toledoth ha-Hassiduth, Tel Aviv, 1931.

(7) D. Kahane, Toledoth ha-Mekubalim, ha-Shabbethaim ve-ha-Hassidim.

(8) Shneyur Zalman, Sefer Hassiduth, Tel Aviv, 1947.

(9) S. A. Horodetzky, Ha-Hassiduth ve-ha-Hassidim, 4 vols., Berlin, 1923.

(10) Jewish Encyclopedia, XI, pp. 299-300, article by Isaac Broyde.

(11) Jacob S. Minkin, The Romance of Hassidism, chs. VIII-IX, New York, 1935.

EZEKIEL LANDAU

By Solomon Wind

EZEKIEL LANDAU (1713-93)

By Solomon Wind

Life and Learning

Ezekiel Landau was born on the 18th of Heshvan, 5474 (Oct. 1713), in the city of Opatow, Poland. His father, Yehudah, was a scholarly community leader who represented his district in the "Council of the Four Lands" which settled legal and social problems of the Jewish community of Poland and Lithuania. The Landau family had resided in Central Europe since the 16th century and had produced many scholars and leaders. They proudly traced their descent from Rashi, the famous commentator of Bible and Talmud.

Landau was from early youth a brilliant and diligent student in all fields of learning. His prime interest was the Talmud as the source and basis of the interpretation of Jewish law. At the age of thirteen he left home for Brody, at that time the center of Talmudic scholarship. At the age of twenty, he was appointed a judge of one of the four courts of that city. There he commenced a long career as teacher and celebrated commentator of Rabbinic law, embracing every phase of life. Eager students flocked to his lectures, and many rabbis and community leaders addressed their problems to him. At the age of thirty he was elected rabbi of the city of Yampol, Poland, and ten years later, rabbi of Prague, where he continued his activities on an ever-widening scale for the rest of his life. The incumbency of the rabbinate of Prague, was primarily of a local character, but because of the importance of that city in world affairs, it conferred upon Landau the title of chief rabbi of the Austrian Empire, and ultimately also recognition as the official spokesman for world Jewry.

Vigor and Asceticism

Landau was well endowed both physically and intellectually; his tall stature, robust health, boundless energy and imposing

79

countenance, no less than his mental and moral greatness, commanded respectful attention. Throughout his life his major interests were literary.* In the morning he taught as many as four classes various parts of the Talmud and Codes; he presided in the afternoon at court sessions, and took part in community administration. Late evenings found him in his library editing his responsa and answering other correspondence, his powers unaffected by the constant pressure of routine tasks. Always he would rise before dawn, study, teach and work for the major part of the day and night. He would deny himself physical comfort but did not preach abstinence to others. From the 17th of Tammuz to the 1st of Ab, the fortnight of semi-mourning in the Jewish calendar, he would abstain from meat and fish. From the 1st to the 9th of Ab, the period of more intensive mourning, he subsisted on dry bread sprinkled with ashes in profound grief over the destruction of the Temple. His asceticism, however, did not diminish his vigor; he remained in full possession of his faculties until his last days.

THE MYSTIC CURRENTS.

The century knew two mystic movements: (1) Sabbatianism, aimed at the overthrow of traditional Judaism, initiated by the

---

*SCHOLARLY WORKS.

Landau enriched rabbinic literature with the following works:

1. Tselah—a page-by-page commentary on the tractates Pessahim, Betsah and Berakhoth.

2. Tselah on Seder Moed—containing brief comments on all the tractates in that order of the Talmud.

3. Doresh le-Tsiyon—containing thirteen elaborate discourses on six major disputes between Abbaye and Rabba.

4. Shulhan ha-Tahor—a volume of corrections of errata in various editions of the codes due to copyists' errors and printers' devils.

5. Dagul me-Revavah—containing brief comments on the Four Codes.

6. "Noda bi-Yhuda"—his major work, containing responsa to current problems solved in the light of Talmudic principles, and reflecting the social, economic and religious conditions of the time.

7. Ahavath Tsiyon and Derushei ha-Tselah—two volumes of sermons delivered during his Prague period, expositions of the Jewish ethical doctrines with practical methods for their application.

pseudo-Messiah Sabbatai Tsevi (1626-76) and (2) Hassidism, dedicated to religious revival among the Jews.

In the middle of the 17th century (1648-9), the Chmielnitzky massacre had devastated the Jewish community in Poland and its horrors were interpreted by contemporay mystics as an indication that the exile was about to end and the redemption to begin. Sabbatai Tsevi, a famed mystic and ascetic, seemed to give fulfillment to the hopes of his fellow-Jews and was almost universally acclaimed Messiah and Redeemer. But the Messiah turned out to be a weakling and a traitor. In the supreme moment, when he was to take possession of Palestine for the Jewish people and don the royal crown, he embraced Mohammedanism (1666) to escape the Caliph's threat of the death penalty. His conversion threw the Jewish people into an abyss of despair and left in its wake a disheartened and confused generation. Nevertheless, in the 18th century the Sabbatian movement re-emerged to defy traditional Judaism openly. The yearning for redemption, never absent from the heart of Jewry, was given a new impetus. Unlike the Kabbalists of yore who endeavored to bring about redemption by a rigorous asceticism, the Sabbatians flagrantly advocated the abolition of the traditional law and moral restraint, themselves indulging in uninhibited pleasures of the flesh. They buttressed their lawlessness by the doctrine of reincarnation proclaiming that Sabbatai Tsevi, their former leader, had been reincarnated to perform miracles. They were lucky enough to secure the protection of the local governments which viewed them as the vanguard of Christianity amongst the Jews. The Sabbatians' extreme wing, the Frankists, forced rabbis to engage them in public debates in which the Talmud was slanderously attacked, and they succeeded in having it publicly burned by decree of local government (1759). These Frankists ultimately embraced Christianity (1760) and enjoyed special government protection.

THE EIBESCHUETZ-EMDEN CONTROVERSY.

This deplorable intra-mural strife served as evidence of both the turbulence of the times and of the serious inroads Sabbatianism had made in Jewish life. Rabbi Jonathan Eibeschuetz (1690-1764), a renowned Talmudic authority and a highly ethical personality, formerly rabbi of Prague (Bohemia) and Metz (France), accepted in 1750 a call to the distinguished rabbinate of the three free and independent cities in Europe—Altona, Hamburg, Wandsbeck—commonly designated by their initial letters as *AHW*.

Hardly had he settled down to his tasks when he was accused of being a secret adherent of the Sabbatian sect. This charge was levelled by a famous resident of Altona, Rabbi Jacob Emden (whose father, Tsevi Ashkenazi, rabbi of Altona, was one of the determined opponents of Sabbatai Tsevi in the 17th century), and was based on evidence found in mystic amulets, which Eibeschuetz, while rabbi in Metz, had issued to ailing persons. This accusation spread rapidly like wildfire throughout the Jewish diaspora and divided the house of Israel into two hostile camps. Everyone was either for or against Eibeschuetz. Conciliation seemed an impossibility. That scholar, indeed, defended himself. He claimed that he had always condemned and banned the Sabbatian sect, and published a book *"Luhoth ha-Eduth"* (Tablets of Testimony), in which he collected character testimony on his behalf from famous rabbis on the continent, including the Gaon of Vilna. But the vigorous opposition, headed by rabbis Emden and Falk (author of the "Penei Yehoshua"), demanded a public trial before a rabbinic court and, on their own authority, designated such a rabbinic court before which Eibeschuetz was to vindicate himself in person within a definite time, or face the penalty of a major ban.

Landau's Iggereth ha-Shalom.

At this crucial moment Rabbi Landau was consulted for his opinion. He acted promptly and impartially. In Sivan 5512 (June 1752) he issued his "Iggereth ha-Shalom" (Letter of Conciliation) in which he offered a practical plan for the settling of this controversy. He defended Eibeschuetz as a man of learning and saintly character, and counselled that he henceforth refrain from issuing other amulets and withdraw permanently from circulation those already issued. At the same time he forbade under the penalty of excommunication any attacks on Rabbi Eibeschuetz's character.

Landau's proposal proved acceptable to the majority of the Jewish communities; the fury abated, a semblance of peace appeared and the proposed major ban on Eibeschuetz, which would have constituted a great tragedy, was averted. Yet the few irreconcilable enemies of Eibeschuetz were displeased with the turn of events and relentlessly continued their attack on him. Emden and Falk charged that Landau, too, was a "secret admirer of the accursed sect" and interpreted his mediation as a clever and selfish maneuver whereby he might be considered favorably for the rabbinate of Prague where Eibeschuetz had many admirers.

Landau's Personal Attitude to Eibeschuetz.

The problem of Eibeschuetz's and Landau's attitude toward Sabbatianism and each other is still a matter of dispute among some scholars. But whilst Landau was zealous in defending his colleague's honor against public attack, he seemed gradually to lose faith in him. Thus, in his second year in Prague, he ostracized a hazan for making vile statements about Eibeschuetz and re-admitted him to his post only upon due repentance and upon the receipt of Eibeschuetz's personal pardon. He indeed defended him in numerous public speeches and especially in his eulogy in 1764. Yet in his heart of hearts he may have begun to suspect him of leanings toward the Sabbatian sect, particularly when, in spite of Landau's request, Eibeschuetz failed or refused to restrain his renegade son, Wolf, from active leadership in that sect. Landau's correspondence reveals that thereupon he severed all relations with Eibeschuetz and viewed the malfeasance of the son as having the tacit consent of the father.

Landau's Effective War on Sabbatianism.

Throughout his life, Landau was an implacable foe of Sabbatianism. Every Yom Kippur eve he pronounced the ban on its adherents and stated that he would never consider the sincerity of their repentance. He forbade intermarriage with them and availed himself of every opportunity to discredit them in the eyes of the public and the government. He advised against a premature study of the Kabbalah and the Zohar, since they were claimed by the sect to be the mainspring of its doctrine. His vehement and insistent antagonism toward the sect finally induced the emperors Joseph II and Franz Joseph II to issue successively decrees forbidding the importation of Kabbalistic literature into the Austrian empire.

LANDAU'S ATTITUDE TOWARD HASSIDISM.

Hassidism, a quasi-mystic movement in defense of the traditional pattern of Judaism, was initiated in the 18th century by Israel Baal Shem Tov (1700-60) to challenge a growing schism in Jewry. Its emphasis on joyous worship and its democratic impulse drew on classic Jewish doctrine. The prevailing tendency towards abstract learning increasingly raised high barriers between the scholar and the layman and resulted in sterile knowledge and perfunctory piety. Hassidism sought to re-establish Jewish unity by conferring equal status on all Jews irrespective of intellectual attainments, and by encouraging a happy spirit in the study of Torah and the performance of Mitsvoth, ascribing equal importance to sincere intention and to actual attainments.

Under normal circumstances, this movement, like a fresh and vigorous mountain breeze, would have been highly welcome in Jewry, but, in the exigencies of the times, it was viewed with alarm by the rabbinate. Its possible kinship with the Sabbatian sect (Hassidism in some measure derived its doctrine from Kabbalistic literature and especially from the Zohar, the mystic commentary to the Pentateuch) aroused keen suspicion. Landau was an outspoken antagonist and caustic critic of the Hassidic movement. He derided its tendency to concentrate on hidden meanings of the law, to resort to mystic prayers as a means of arousing special attention; he criticized the curious habits of the Hassidim, their frequent indulgence in convivialism and above all questioned the reputed role of the Tsaddik as intermediary between God and His people.

Hassidic legend, however, has Landau change his view in favor of the movement: A disciple of the Baal Shem Tov alerted him to the value of its doctrine and to its essential harmony with the traditional view of life, and thereafter Landau became an admirer of the movement and a student of its literature.

THE TREND FOR SECULARIZATION: THE HASKALAH MOVEMENT.

Jewry in Western Europe was pre-occupied with Haskalah—the movement for secular learning—which had as its main objective the obtaining of citizenship for Jews in the countries of their sojourn. Up to this time the scope of a decent livelihood for the Jews was very limited indeed. With very few exceptions all economic activity was guild or government-controlled. The Jew therefore lived on the periphery of the general economy and was utterly dependent on the few privileges granted him. Secularization, it was argued, would lead to citizenship, to equal economic and civic rights and to respectable independence. Haskalah leaders therefore aimed to train the Jewish youth in wordly studies and professions. The movement gained momentum with the appearance in 1788 of Mendelssohn's German translation of the Bible, which opened an avenue into general literature and wordly ideas.

The German translation of the Bible, first intended for the education of Mendelssohn's children and later for the Jewish public, had two aims: the objective understanding of the text, its content, grammar and rhetoric, and the popularization of the German language, which was accomplished by rendering the German translation in Hebrew characters. The ultimate goal therefore was an appreciation and understanding of both languages, especially the German, which would introduce the reader to German literature and to secular knowledge and thus help him to adapt himself to the social and economic life of the country.

It was this latter tendency and not secular knowledge per se that the orthodox rabbinate feared. It was felt that the Bible after serving as a handmaid to secular learning would be completely neglected and that secular learning, at that time replete with heretical doctrines, would eventually predominate. The youth adrift from spiritual mooring, and immersed in idle philosophic speculation in matters of faith, would be lost to Jewry. Mendelssohn's German translation, therefore, as well as his commentary, was considered heretical and both were banned.

Landau's attitude toward Haskalah, at its inception, was one of watchful waiting. He himself was conversant with secular knowledge and encouraged his sons and students to follow his example. His oldest son, Samuel, knew the works of the French philosopher Montesquieu, his grandson Moses published a lexicon of Hebrew words and their German equivalents, and many of his students attended lectures on science, particularly mathematics, at the universities. Yet he felt that secular learning needs both guidance and restraint either because of the dangers of over-secularization, or because of its tendency then towards heretical doctrines.

Mendelssohn and Haskalah.

Because of his love for all learning, Landau always maintained an attitude of deference towards Moses Mendelssohn. He styled him a complete scholar and considered his German translation of the Bible and its Hebrew commentary as based upon the standard Jewish commentaries. Indeed, upon Mendelssohn's request, he sent him a digest of the responsa in which he had examined some philological and grammatical portions of the Bible. With Landau's consent, they were later incorporated in the "Tikkunei Soferim"—the supplement to the German translation of the Bible. Landau defended the sage of Berlin against harsh criticism on the part of his colleagues and withheld his consent from the proposed ban of the German translation and Hebrew commentary.

His policy of watchful waiting, however, suddenly changed into a vigorous attack on the Haskalah Movement. In 1781, Joseph II, the Austrian Emperor, issued an Edict of Toleration aiming at the amelioration of conditions amongst Jews within his Empire and providing among other things for a system of compulsory secular education. The Haskalah leaders were delighted, and one of them, Naftali Wessely, circulated a pamphlet "Divrei Shalom ve-Emeth" (Words of Peace and Truth) in which he pleaded with the Jewish people to cooperate with the beneficent aims of the government.

Wessely was a versatile scholar, held in great esteem by his contemporaries. Eibeschuetz had praised his halakhic work "Torath Kohanim," Landau had given a glowing approval to his "Yein Levanon," a commentary on the Ethics of our Fathers; there he also spoke hopefully of Wessely's subsequent literary labors but with a cautious proviso—that all his works remain based on Torah and tradition. Mendelssohn engaged Wessely's talents in the German translation and the Hebrew commentary to the Bible.

However, when in his "Divrei Shalom ve-Emeth," Wessely sarcastically criticized the current Jewish educational system and in the spirit of the "New Education" of the emperor urged the adoption of a curriculum in which secular studies could predominate, and the study of Talmud be at best restricted to a gifted few, the heretical tendencies of both Wessely and Haskalah became the target of rabbinic scorn and condemnation. Landau was particularly vehement in his denunciation. He branded his propaganda pamphlet as "Divrei Shav" (Words of Falsehood) and wrote: "Unfortunately, I see an inversion of values: a wicked man (Wessely) dares declare that secular learning is better than Torah. I too am in favor of secular training and am thankful for our government's interest in the education of our children. In Biblical times we were criticized when we did not know how to speak the languages of the nations. Daniel and his colleagues were ordered by the Persian king to study Persian. Language and secular studies are important for our daily occupations. But Torah is vital, the root of Torah is Faith and not loose philosophical inquiry. When one studies language in books that are primarily intended not for the study of language but for idle speculation in matters of faith, he is led into disbelief. These books deny Providence and darken faith with muddled thinking."

THE COURSE OF THE NEW EDUCATION.

Traditional Jewry fought the New Education in vain. The government established secular schools in every community and attendance was made compulsory in spite of the "Jesuit of Prague"—as Landau was styled by the Austrian Emperor. Yeshivoth and religious schools had to adjust their programs in accord with the government regulation that all children must attend its schools during the major part of the day. These schools, however, taught heretical doctrines instead of factual knowledge, and the government, itself religiously minded, began to view them with disfavor and soon closed many of them. Even Haskalah leaders, particularly Wessely, voiced their bitter disappointment in these schools. Many Jewish communities now organized their own institutions, offering a combined program of Torah and secular studies, but the main emphasis remained on Torah.

PATRIOTISM.

Landau had arrived at Prague on the eve of the Seven Years' War (1756-64), when the government, in its official policy, was hostile to the Jews and was planning a series of harsh measures against them. He helped greatly to dissipate the atmosphere of distrust and thus avert the application of these discriminatory measures. When the city was besieged, he mobilized all Jewish assistance for the government, such as fortification of the walls, extinguishing of fires, raising of sufficient taxes both for the government and the Jewish community, and prevention of profiteering and of hoarding the necessities of life. He proclaimed a major ban on all violators and traitors. He ordered daily prayers in the synagogue on behalf of the government and assigned ten people to fast daily for the duration. By his actions and his spirit, he helped to bring about victory and to gain the confidence of the government in its Jewish subjects. When Queen Maria Theresa visited Prague at the end of the War, she acknowledged her indebtedness to Landau and the Jewish community. At the official reception tendered her, she accepted publicly the blessings of Landau in the name of his correligionists, acknowledging her appreciation of their consistent loyalty.

When the Queen in 1767 became seriously ill, Landau summoned all Jewish sympathy in her behalf. He ordered prayers in all synagogues, proclaimed a general fast day for the entire Jewish community, and upon her recuperation arranged for a festive celebration with widespread distribution of charity to all needy people.

A PROPOSED AUTONOMOUS JEWISH GOVERNMENT.

Landau's patriotic service gained for him and for the Jewish community the esteem of the government. By way of compensation, the latter planned the creation of a vast Jewish autonomous government within the provinces annexed from Poland, Galicia and Podolia. The *"Judenverordnung"* of 1772 provided that this government be administered in accordance with Jewish law, independent of the local government and solely responsible to the royal crown in Vienna. Landau was invited to be its chief administrator and was most eager to secure this position, but he yielded to the pleadings of his community who urged him to remain with them in Prague.

EMANCIPATION AND ITS PROBLEMS.

The project for Jewish autonomy was eventually abandoned, and the government proceeded on its own to solve the Jewish problem by emancipation. It granted citizenship and equal economic rights to all Jews within the Austrian empire (the very purpose of Haskalah, incidentally), and demanded in return a partial secularization of Jewish life and implicit obedience to the state law of the empire. This last provision was originally intended to refer to civil matters only, but later on, by the supplementary edict of 1783, included the religio-social life in the realm of marriage and divorce. The state law was to regulate all walks of life, and the Jewish Court was divested of all authority. The enforcement of this act meant not only a violation of religious liberty hitherto enjoyed by all Jews on the continent, but tended, moreover, to disrupt the foundations of the Jewish family.

Of historical significance was Landau's intervention at this moment. The Jewish community was in combined uproar and trepidation. The challenge called for a mind both erudite and judicious, for an argument impressive and objective. Landau rose to the occasion and prepared a memorandum in which he managed to condense a great mass of Jewish marriage laws into 11 paragraphs, comparing the government's statutes with them point by point and arguing that where the state law differed with Jewish law, the latter should prevail in order that religious liberty be safeguarded and the Jewish family protected. Landau's learning, forcefulness and dignity finally carried the day. The emperor accepted his recommendations, and a great danger to Jewish family life was averted.

Emancipation, that is, the granting of citizenship and equal rights to Jews, brought in its wake another problem—compulsory military service.

THE DREAD OF COMPULSORY MILITARY SERVICE.

Military service, a concomitant feature of emancipation, was novel in Jewish life, because Jews had never served in any of the armies on the continent. They naturally abhorred war, and patriotic sentiments had not as yet struck deep roots. Military service also involved the possible desecration of the Sabbath, violation of the dietary laws and other religious precepts. It was therefore viewed with alarm and was deemed by some to be tantamount to *Kareth*—a complete severance from the Jewish historic stem. Landau, however, rose to the needs of the hour. On the day of the departure of the recruits for military training, Landau came to the army barracks and, in the presence of army officers and state dignitaries, addressed the Jewish contingent. He stressed the need for patriotic service which would redound to Jewry's honor and help alleviate the lot of Jews in countries where they were still oppressed, he urged cooperation with army officials and non-Jewish comrades, he promised in the name of the government that Jewish recruits would not be forced to violate the Sabbath or the dietary laws, he pleaded for daily prayers, at least for the reading of the Shema when time was pressing, and concluded by blessing all the recruits. At the end, he gave to each Jewish recruit a package containing tsitsith, tefillin, a siddur, and some money. Landau's unexpected presence and his warm-hearted address dissipated all fears and inspired patriotic fervor in all hearts.

In 1789, the year of general conscription, Joseph II scored a victory over his enemies, which was celebrated in all synagogues with great enthusiasm. Landau praised the wise benevolence of the emperor, the freedom and abundance which prevailed in his realm, and asserted that his conquests had been divinely ordained so that freedom and the blessings of good government could reach other peoples still oppressed.

THE RABBINATE OF PRAGUE.

Prague, the most important city of Bohemia, had for centuries been a center of Talmudic learning and rabbinic authority. In the 18th century it became the center of political and social unrest, with unavoidable repercussions in the hitherto secluded Jewish community. Landau entered his post in a period of veritable storm and stress and had to exert his tremendous energy and influence in steering Jewish life into the grooved channels of tradition.

ANTI-JEWISH SENTIMENT.

There was in the first place a prevalent anti-Jewish sentiment on the part of the government and the general populace—a legacy of the War of Succession in the middle of the century. In the early 18th century, Eibeschuetz had been active in the rabbinate of Prague as lecturer and preacher and was considered a logical candidate for the chief rabbinate. During the War of Succession, when the city was in the possession of the French (1740-43), Eibeschuetz suddenly left under a safe conduct pass to accept a post in Metz, France. His move was interpreted by the Austrian authorities as an act of disloyalty and reflected unfavorably upon the entire Jewish population of Bohemia. As soon as Bohemia was re-annexed to the Austrian Empire (1744), a decree of exile was issued to all Jews, and although the Jews managed to acquit themselves of the false charges brought against them, and were successful in having the decree rescinded, it left its deep imprint in the form of discriminatory measures: a decree limiting the size of the Jewish family, and others restricting the areas of Jewish settlement and reducing their means of subsistence. The economic and social crisis was followed by a general breakdown of morale and brought despair to the Jews of Bohemia. Eibeschuetz in France had to appeal to all his Jewish communities and even to the Papal authorities in Rome to come to the rescue of his suffering correligionists in Bohemia.

THE QUESTION OF A SUCCESSOR.

In 1751, Rabbi Arye Leib, of the Ashkenazic community of Amsterdam, a brother-in-law of Jacob Emden, was considered as a candidate but later rejected because of his involvement in the Eibeschuetz-Emden controversy, which, it was feared, would keep contention alive and endanger the peace of the community. In 1752 Landau was elected chief rabbi; his "Letter of Conciliation" had given him great prestige. He had been acclaimed for the impartiality he had shown in the affair. A Kethav Rabbanuth was immediately dispatched to him at Yampol, praising his scholarship and personality, and outlining his duties: he was to be the chief rabbi of the city, a lecturer at the Yeshivah, the preacher in the synagogues and the president of the Jewish court. He would ordain rabbis and issue titles of honor to worthy and scholarly members of the community.

SOME INHERENT DIFFICULTIES.

In spite of the renown that Landau enjoyed he encountered many difficulties. The problems of transition inherent in the century caused a cleavage in the community, bringing to the fore two contradictory views regarding the Jewish polity. Senior rabbis and scholarly laymen considered Landau too young for the post. They continually tried to discredit him and prove him ignorant of many parts of the Talmud and the Codes. The younger and restless elements clamoring for change considered him too old and set in his ways. They resorted to mockery and effrontery, remarking derisively that the Torah of Yampol was not applicable to modern times. Once at a public lecture, Ephraim Wehli, a rich merchant and reputed master of Maimonides' Code, cited a difficult passage of the Code and asked Landau to explain it. Landau found it inexplicable and struggled with great difficulty to make it plausible. At home Landau rapidly reviewed all the four parts of the Maimonides Codes and did not find the passage there. He later remarked to his examiner that he must have had access to a fifth volume of the Code, and the latter retorted that a rabbi who cannot immediately detect a spurious passage is not fit to hold office. The situtation therefore required courage and determination. Landau had to exercise tact and resourcefulness to calm the opposition and to gain a friendly following.

The Seven Years' War and its aftermath threw other grievous problems into the lap of the rabbinate. As a result of the war, the Jewish community had become impoverished and the non-Jewish population was somehow and without reason incensed against them. Thus Landau having once saved a gentile boy from distress, the latter felt very grateful and years later, as a government official, helped to save the Jewish community by secretly informing Landau of a plot to kill many of the Jews of Prague.

According to custom the Jews ate only bread baked by non-Jews on the day following Passover. Some non-Jewish bakeries therefore were induced to poison the bread sold to the Jews. Landau speedily called for a special assembly of all Jews on the afternoon of the last day of Passover, informing his congregants that that year a mistake had occurred in the calendar and Passover had started a day too soon. Hence the following day was legally the last day of Passover and all must abstain from the eating of Hamets. There was much tension at this time and a menacing moral breakdown. Landau pleaded for firm loyalty to ethical standards, emphasizing that economic crises are but challenges to righteous living and would certainly disappear with the vigorous exertion of inherent energies.

AUSTERITY.

However, not content merely with noble utterances, the rabbinate adopted an austerity program which was to provide all needy people with the necessities of life. This to some extent stemmed the rising tide of envy and hatred on the part of the non-Jewish community. A rabbinic ordinance provided for a rigid economy in food and apparel and forbade all luxuries. For religious and festive occasions, it limited the number of guests to be invited, prescribed simplicity in dress, reduced the menu to one or two simple courses and ruled out most entertainment.*

TORAH LIFE AS CURE.

These measures, though helpful, proved insufficient to remedy the situation. In the third year of his office Landau complained of unscrupulous business practices and the disregard of the law of Torah when it conflicted with self-interest. He was disturbed also by mounting government taxes and pending anti-

---

*An application for an increase in the number of guests and courses on the menu was granted only upon the payment of a corresponding sum of money to the community chest. On paying a very high annual tax to the community one was allowed to prepare a feast in accordance with his own desires, but was advised to exercise moderation in food, dress and entertainment. A vigilance committee enforced these regulations and meted out fines to the violators.

Jewish legislation, some of which meant possible expulsion of the Jews from certain communities. The crisis, which might have created a spirit of unity, instead had rent the community apart, stirring up distrust, hatred and scepticism, resulting in a series of heretical doctrines which ascribed all existence to a blind materialistic force and which as such sanctioned the law of might and the pursuit of selfishness without any moral restraint.

Landau believed that in the constant study of the Torah lay the cure for all physical and spiritual ills. The Torah, he said, imparts a spiritual outlook on life in the face of which all heresy fades into nothingness. Torah as an activating principle makes manifest the inward worth of the people, giving happiness and contentment to all. He therefore mobilized all Jewish resources for a Torah-life. He established a huge educational fund for the instruction of the youth and for the dignified maintenance of poor scholars. He urged all parents to keep their children in the house of learning until they master the rudiments of the Torah and he pleaded with adults to study the Torah daily—particularly on the Sabbath.

THE JEWISH COURT.

The administration of the Jewish court was a major function of the rabbinate. The court exercised wide powers, both legislative and executive, and its decisions were honored by the state judiciary. It was thus the basis of Jewish self-government, drawing its authority from the Talmud. Landau became so renowned as both jurist and judge that his decisions were sought by rabbinic courts all over the continent. The Responsa, "Noda biYhuda", his major life work, cover a variety of problems touching on religious and family life, charity, education, business and civic problems, and relations of the Jewish community with the government.

PERSONAL CHARACTERISTICS AND ATTITUDES:

Master of all learning.

Although the Talmud constituted his major interest, Landau was equally proficient in many other fields of learning. He was master of the Scriptures and of their major commentaries and had a thorough knowledge of Hebrew grammar. The latter helped him in the establishment of the correct literal and metaphorical meaning of Hebrew roots and idioms.*

He was well versed in philosophic and Kabbalistic literature; the latter found expression in his sermons and in the exposition and analysis of difficult Aggadic passages in the Talmud as bearing on such topics as suffering of the righteous, reward and punishment, the nature of the hereafter and of the resurrection, etc. He was well acquainted with the natural and social sciences and often employed the former in the clarification of certain halakhoth—particularly of a medical nature—and the latter in the elucidation of historical and chronological data. His knowledge of the German language was useful to him in his many activities connected with the Jewish community and the government.

Champion of Truth.

Landau was an ardent and consistent worshipper of truth, especially in the field of halakhah, no matter how formidable his opponent or untoward the circumstances. He defied the proud lay leaders and the impressive rabbinate of Frankfurt am Main when they interfered in a matter outside their jurisdiction. By way of reprisal they publicly burned Landau's responsa on this subject and proclaimed in their communal register that Landau and his descendants up to the third generation were to be barred from holding public office in their city. When a mediaeval authority had made rulings more stringent than the Talmud, Landau, after thorough study of the matter, did not fear to differ with him. He remarked therefore with reference to the Sefer ha-Hassidim of

---

*Thus he asserts that the verb "bara" (create) besides its literal meaning also connotes the idea of "creatio ex nihilo" and that its association in the Bible with the word "nefesh" (soul) predicates the preexistence of the soul. Similarly the word "shekhinah" (Divine Presence) carries the connotation of an activating principle as a direct emanation from God. This concept adds special significance to the Aggadic passage "Ha-Shekhinah shorah be-Yisrael" (the divine Presence dwells in the midst of Israel)—When Israel is in spiritual accord with God then His Providence with concomitant bounty is centered on him and its overflow reaches the rest of the world; when sin intervenes a severance is caused and the process becomes reversed: the main bounty is centered on the world and only a bare overflow reaches Israel.

Rabbi Yehudah ha-Hassid, (a 13th century Tosafist), that Talmudic scholars who lived after the Talmud must accept Talmudic principles unqualifiedly, and that their decisions, when stricter than the Talmud's, had validity only for their relatives and descendants. Custom (minhag) might prevail only in situations where the Talmud was non-committal. The Midrashic and narrative portions of the Talmud, though integral parts of it, were not intended to set the norm for minimal conduct, but rather raise it to ever loftier heights. Their teachings can therefore not be considered as legally binding.

His Friendliness.

Landau was fatherly and friendly to all people, particularly to his pupils whose careers he diligently followed, encouraging them to become thorough scholars of the Talmud and enjoy sending their halakhic responsa abroad. He was highly charitable and diverted most of his income to the needy, particularly to poor scholars. He loved people and believed in their innate goodness which he ever endeavored to encourage. It was his conviction that man never voluntarily deviates from the right path. He constantly praised the exercise of all virtue and piety, extended every consolation to the grieved and depressed and often mollified the rigor of the law in their behalf. Penitents were welcomed back without the ascetic ritual prescribed by the moralists. To Landau repentance consisted of sincere regret and continued study of Torah.

His Modesty.

Landau was very modest and never imposed his views upon others. In rendering halakhic decisions he requested that they be accepted only if two or three contemporary rabbinic authorities concurred. "It is enough that may words be listened to attentively, none should hold them infallible." The increasing recognition of his authority he ascribed only in small part to his diligence and mostly to his father's character and to the special grace of God: "My father raised me in an atmosphere of learning. He possessed scholarship and prestige. People would solicit his advice and favor. I am honored because of him. People have sought my instruction from my early youth. There is no special wisdom in me; there are far greater scholars living in obscurity, of whom no one makes inquiries, whilst I rise to find hundreds of people knocking at my door. God was indeed wonderful to me all these years because of the merit of my father."

Appreciation of Womanhood.

Landau was well aware of the merit of the Jewish woman and described her in glowing terms. Very happily married, he was ever appreciative of the steadying influence of his wife in his activities. His devotion to her was revealed in the touching obituary: "In her youth she remained alone in the house for six days of the week to enable me to devote myself to study; she stood by me faithfully in old age. All these 58 years she attended me like a mother, calming my temper with fine understanding, and always on guard to spare me grief, to remove causes of discontent between my congregants and myself. She was always a God-fearing, charitable woman."

Admonition.

Landau could be very severe when violation of principle was involved; he was then moved both to righteous indignation and instant activity. He would excuse human frailties in his pupils but was very strict when he detected presumption. He rebuked young rabbis for hasty and immature decisions and even suspended some of them from rabbinic functions pending their realization of the errors committed. He criticized scholars for exacting fees for halakhic decisions and performance of religious functions. He was equally harsh with those whose halakhic decisions were affected by personal motives. He deemed undue criticism of Talmudic authorities tantamount to disrespect for the Torah. In all admonition he was conciliatory at first but vigorous and implacable when his accomodating attitude was not reciprocated.

A Disciple's Tribute:

Rabbi Eliezer Flekeles, his devoted disciple and his successor in Prague, summed up his personality in the following words: "My master taught Torah for 60 years (20 years in Brody and

Yampol, and 40 years in Prague) and trained thousands of pupils, many of whom are rabbis, judges and leaders in Israel. He was a most gifted speaker, whose fervor prevented many from sin and induced them to repentance and a life of virtue. He replied in his own handwriting to those who wrote to him from all parts of the world, and never stopped studying until his last days. He was a gifted author and the acclaimed sage and saint of his generation. He served every righteous cause faithfully and unselfishly at great personal sacrifice. He loved peace and fostered it in all communities and among scholars. He was loved and respected for his courageous and devoted leadership. He enjoyed robust health and rare intellectual vigor which enabled him to work with increasing zeal and capacity in many fields of endeavor."

AKIBA EGER

By Harold I. Leiman

AKIBA EGER

By Harold I. Leiman

Two conquerors were born in the same decade. Both were short in stature and of pale complexion, both were unique in creativity and originality; both were possessed of indefatigable energy. But here their likenesses end, for they were opposites in character. The one was egoistic, the other altruistic; the one was immoral and unscrupulous, the other ethical and kind; the one's ambition was to make humanity serve him, the other's to serve humanity; the one almost conquered the world, the other conquered only himself; the one became the hero of Western civilization, the other a hero of Torah civilization; the one was a Man of Destiny, the other a Man of Torah; the one was—Napoleon Bonaparte, the other—Akiba Eger.

The average person is likely to picture Rabbi Akiba Eger in his mind as the Tsaddik (righteous, pious man). But to the scholar, he is Akiba Eger, the Gaon; he is the Posek ha-Dor (Supreme authority on Jewish Law), to whom all the scholars of his generation turned for enlightenment in Halakhic problems. For scholars, he remains *the* head of the Yeshivah, not only for his time but for all times. His chief contribution was in the method of logical analysis, precision, and depth. He practically banished the then popular "pilpul (sharp dialectics) for pilpul's sake," and stressed only the search for truth. Open any volume of the Talmud and turn to any page, and you are likely to find at least one comment (in the *Gilayon* of Rabbi Eger) which no diligent student can afford to miss. Although he was thorough and prompt in responding to the overwhelming number of questions sent to him, he continued his lectures at the Yeshivah without interruption. In fact, he was ready to relinquish the rabbinate, so that he could have more time for the study of Torah. For himself, he was strict in his interpretation of the law, lest his action might lead to the slightest *Hillul ha-Shem* (Desecration of the Divine Name); for others, he was lenient. Because of his vast knowledge, and the confidence which comes from keen understanding, he was able to render decisions on Halakhic problems which, because of their complexity, many of his contemporaries avoided. Few indeed have made such a revolution in method as Rabbi Akiba Eger; few indeed hold such an ideal position in the eyes of every student of Talmudics. The learned have felt with the ancient Tanna, that "when Rabbi Akiba died, the glory of Torah was lost."

Yet neither the average person nor the scholar knows the true nature of Rabbi Eger, for he was both Gaon and Hassid. He synthesized the scholarship of the *mithnaggeddim* (opponents of Hassidism) and the piety of the Hassidim; both were integrated in his personality. In his everyday living there was reflected the logic and circumspection of the scholar; in his Halakhic decisions, the consideration and modesty of the saint. He was the Man of Torah. His originality, creativeness, and profundity recalled Rabbi Akiba of old; his humility was reminiscent of Moses, our Teacher.

As we approach the great, an electric vibrancy runs through us. We are blinded by their radiant personalities, and it is only with much difficulty that we can look up to, and catch a glimpse of them on their high level. Our attempts to appraise them correctly, of necessity, fall short of the goal. Nevertheless it would be unpardonable to fail to transmit that which is known and recorded.

Life and Times

In the last half of the eighteenth century, Poland was the power vacuum she is today. The benevolent despots Frederick the Great of Prussia, Maria Theresa and her son Joseph II of Austria, and Catherine the Great of Russia, developed spheres of influence in Poland, and finally partitioned it. Until it became part of the German Empire, the southwestern portion of Poland shifted alternately between Prussian and Polish rule. As the territory, so did the people vacillate between progressive western and backward eastern European culture. It was inevitable that this borderline status should have its effect on the Jewish population. Many saw in the Prussian rule greater opportunity for freedom. They felt that a change in dress and appearance, reform in religion, and a little "enlightenment" would afford them a passport into the

Gentile world. Others were prepared to take the radical step and assimilate. At first there were few renegades; later there followed a reform movement guided by militant leadership. Jewish Orthodoxy was thus threatened from within and without and required an authority it could turn to for guidance and protection. Into these turbulent times, Akiba Eger was born, in the small town of Eisenstadt (Hungary), in the winter of 1761.

Akiba was descended from a long line of scholars. His father was Rabbi Moshe Günz, great grandson of Rabbi Abraham Brode; his mother was Gittel Eger, daughter of the old Rabbi Akiba Eger for whom Akiba had been named; his uncle, Rabbi Wolf Eger, was head of the Yeshivah at Breslau.

Even as a child, Akiba amazed his teachers with his remarkable depth of understanding. At the age of twelve, he had thoroughly mastered several treatises of the Talmud and had written an original commentary on the tractate Hullin.

Rabbi Wolf Eger corresponded regularly with Rabbi Moshe Günz. Their letters always contained brief inquiries as to the health of each other's family, followed by lengthy Talmudic discussions. One dealt with a problem which defied solution. "Even the great Rabbis of Breslau could find no answer to this question," wrote Rabbi Wolf. The problem challenged Rabbi Moshe and he read it to his son, Akiba. How great was his amazement when the twelve-year-old youngster casually offered a satisfactory answer! The father immediately wrote to Rabbi Wolf, who presented the solution to the sages of Breslau in the name of Akiba. The latter were overjoyed and urged that Rabbi Wolf bring the boy to the Yeshivah at Breslau, so that they might find delight in his company.

In Breslau, under the watchful eye of Rabbi Wolf, Akiba excelled in his studies. His phenomenal memory, amazing comprehension, analytical mind, and unquenchable love for study and research, all contributed to the renown of the young genius. At the age of eighteen, he married and went to live at the home of his father-in-law, Rabbi Isaac Margolis, in the town of Lissa. He was provided with a beautiful home and a well-equipped library where he spent his days and nights in study. From far and wide many disciples came to listen to his Talmudic discourses. He had two sons and two daughters. The younger son was the later famous Shlomo Eger; the younger daughter became the wife of Rabbi Moses Sofer.

Early in 1791, a fire destroyed hundreds of Jewish homes in Lissa, among them the home of Rabbi Eger. Reluctant as he was to assume rabbinic office, he felt that he could no longer be a burden to his father-in-law, who had lost most of his wealth in the conflagration, and he accepted his first rabbinate in the town of Maerkisch Friedland. Here Rabbi Eger achieved fame through his Yeshivah, to which students from distant cities came to study, and whither inquiries were directed from many foreign countries.

When, in the winter of 1797, his wife passed away, Rabbi Akiba Eger was profoundly grief-stricken. His friends urged him to remarry soon, but he wrote:

> "——how can I forget my wife and all she has done for me? She has raised my children and instilled in them the fear of the Almighty. Whatever Torah I have learned, I have her to thank for. She cared for me in my feeble health, and, as I have recently discovered, she hid from me financial embarrassments and worries so that I would not be disturbed in my studies. Many times I have had discussions with her on interesting religious problems, until the late hours of the evening. My suffering is great; joy has left me. May her soul rest in peace, and may her virtues incline heaven in our favor forever and ever."

Rabbi Akiba Eger led the Kehillah of Maerkisch Friedland for almost twenty-four years. Yet he was never content to remain in the rabbinate, and was particularly unhappy over the fact that, in spite of all his urging, the people of the town did not make any serious attempt to prepare their children for the Yeshivah. Once, but for the insistent pleadings of his mother, he would have given up his post. The largest Jewish communities, Vilna among them, asked him to become their leader. After writing to his son-in-law, Rabbi Moshe Sofer, to pray for him "that he may have strength to lead a large Kehillah", Rabbi Akiba Eger accepted the Rabbinate of Posen in 1816, and remained in that position for the last twenty-two years of his life.

Posen had been the seat of the greatest Geonim in Germany. However, it was also a cradle of "enlightenment" and reform.

Even before Rabbi Eger's coming, the "enlightened" Jewish leaders tried to limit his activities. But they were unsuccessful. His dynamic personality and his determination to guard traditional Judaism could not be restrained. When the government forbade the study of Talmud, Rabbi Akiba Eger wrote a lengthy memorandum defending it, and asked his disciple, Rabbi Solomon Plessner, to translate all statements by Gentile scholars about the contributions of the Talmud to modern civilization and collect them in a special volume. The government, much impressed by the memorandum and the book, rescinded the order. Rabbi Eger carried on open warfare against all who attempted to introduce innovations into the Prayer Book. He forbade the use of any language but the traditional Hebrew in public prayer; he interdicted any omission or change of form.

In Posen, his Yeshivah flourished. Many of the great Jewish leaders of the next generation studied under his guidance. Inquiries were sent to him from all Jewish communities, including Tiflis in Asia and Tangiers in Africa. He was considered the authority on all Jewish matters, even in the eyes of the government.

Each Thursday was examination day, when children of the Talmud Torah were brought before him to be tested on matters they had studied during the week. Thus he kept close vigilance on their progress in the Talmud Torah. For Rabbi Eger believed that the most important duty of the Rabbi was the inculcation of Torah in the minds of the youth.

In spite of his small stature, he made an indelible impression upon all who came in contact with him. It was his concern for the welfare of all that called forth universal respect. He was possessed of that modesty which is characteristic of only the truly great. He greeted everybody with a smile; he spoke deferentially even to young children. He would not permit even his disciples to serve him. If, in the middle of a lecture in the Yeshivah, he needed a book, he would climb up the ladder and get it himself. He was careful never to hurt the feelings of an individual. On one occasion, when it became his unpleasant duty to admonish a young man, he performed it reluctantly. When, fifteen years later, Rabbi Eger leraned of his address, he sent the former student a note asking to be forgiven.

To his children, who were preparing to publish his Responsa, he wrote:

"No doubt you will find that many of those who wrote to me had studied in my Yeshivah. Please do not refer to them as pupils, for I have never called a person a pupil. How, indeed, can I know who has learnt more from whom? Please ignore also the flattering salutations in the letters addressed to me. I have always had the desire to stop this annoying practice. Therefore please omit the adjectives. I despise them, and they can only serve to embarrass me in the world to come."

It was his custom, on his travels, to pay his respects to the local Rabbi. So when he came to Nikolsburg he visited Rabbi Mordecai Benet. The latter invited him to deliver an Halakhic lecture from the pulpit, on the Sabbath. Rabbi Akiba Eger was developing his topic brilliantly when Rabbi Mordecai interrupted him with a question which seemed to upset his whole Halakhic argument. For a moment Rabbi Akiba Eger paused; then he descended from the pulpit, vanquished. Rabbi Mordecai was grieved that he had so embarrased his distinguished colleague, and after the services he visited him to beg his forgiveness. Rabbi Akiba Eger smilingly disclosed that he knew the answer to his question.

"But then why didn't you tell me in the synagogue that I was in error?" asked Rabbi Mordecai.

"I did not want to belittle you in the eyes of your congregants. After all, you are their leader; they look up to you. I am only a passer-by; my reputation is inconsequential."

Rabbi Mordecai was greatly impressed, and would not let his personal pride stand in the way of truth. He called together all the scholars of the city and related the true facts to them so that all might know the real greatness of the visitor.

And when Rabbi Eger visited Lomza he found the local Rabbi Benjamin Diskin depressed because of a Talmid Hakham who had vowed never to leave the Beth ha-Midrash. He was especially disturbed because the people of the city could not bring him food on the Sabbath, since Lomza had no Eruv.* Rabbi Eger

*A symbolic object establishing city continuity, by which the carrying of objects throughout that city is permitted on the Sabbath.

said, "If he cannot come to us, let us visit him in the Beth ha-Midrash."

When they entered, the scholar was taken aback. Summoning his courage, he rushed over and said nervously, "Why did you come here? After all, it is not proper that such Rabbis should go to such trouble for the sake of a wretched soul like myself."

"Had you known that we would come to you, would you have made your vow?" asked Rabbi Akiba Eger.

"No, of course not. I would never think of inconveniencing you so."

"Your vow is annulled, annulled, annulled" said Rabbi Eger. "Annulled, annulled, annulled"! repeated the crowd.

Yet in spite of his soft-spoken manner and his unique modesty, he was adamant in upholding law and tradition. Even his love for his best friend did not prevent him from denying a rabbinate to the latter's son, whom he considered unfit for the position. But within the realm of the law he granted maximum leniency, and the human element was given precedence above all other considerations. Even the length of his responses was adapted to the nature of his correspondent:

"Often you will find that I have gone into lengthy discussions of theory, not directly concerned with the law. Know that I was motivated by the knowledge that my correspondent was a man who had undergone many trials and much suffering. Therefore I have lengthened my reply so that he may have greater pleasure and forget his troubles in the delight of the discussion."

His considerateness was extended to all. One winter he travelled all night to perform a Mitsvah. On the way, a heavy rain came down, and the hind wheel of the carriage skidded into a ditch. The driver alighted, jumped into the water of the ditch, and raised the wagon to the roadway. When he returned to his seat, Rabbi Eger offered him a pair of dry socks to replace his wet ones. The driver was profundly impressed by this thoughtfulness. Yet he was puzzled, because he knew that the Rabbi's baggage was locked in back of the wagon.

In the morning, when Rabbi Eger alighted from the carriage, the driver noted that he was barefooted. "But Rabbi", he said, "how—" The Rabbi smiled: "You didn't think that I would permit you to drive out there in wet socks while my feet were dry."

He always found time to be careful and considerate, although he was kept busy from early morning till late at night. A government official, who wished to visit him, wrote to ask when he had some free time. "I have no *free* time," replied the Rabbi, "but I always try to be courteous to my visitors."

Often he was characterized as a man from another world. Actually he had a keen sensitivity for the neat and beautiful. When his children notified him that they intended to publish his Responsa, he wrote:

> "Take care to use good paper, dark ink, and beautiful lettering, for, to my mind, the soul is enraptured, the mind relieved, and the attention aroused, when one studies from a book that is beautiful and meticulously arranged."

Nor was he lacking in a sense of humor. When the local government official complained to him that the Kehillah was exacting too large a fee for the burial of a miserly usurer, he replied, "Our Sages tell us that usurers will not rise at the resurrection, and this is a special fee for *permanent* burial". The government official was much pleased, and the case was closed.

In all his busy moments he did not neglect to write letters of comfort and congratulation to his friends. He even addressed an inspiring letter to a youngster entering upon his Bar Mitsvah day.

But it was his great learning, wedded to exceeding modesty, that fascinated all who knew him. Little wonder that his loyal friend, Rabbi Jacob of Lissa, amazed after one of his profound Talmudic discussions with him, remarked, "How can he be so modest, when I know that he knows that I know that he knows?"

LOVE OF TORAH

Rabbi Eger's love for Torah was insatiable. His method of study was intensive, penetrating, and analytical. As he studied, he wrote critical comments for his personal use, never intended for publication. Fortunately, his children edited and published them. They remain guideposts for all Jewish scholars. Simultaneously, they reveal the greatness of the master. One senses in his comments the precision of a mind which weighs each word and examines each passage with infinite care. It seems as though every word and every concept in the Torah, the Talmud, and all the commentaries, are brought to bear on the particular passage under study. His explanations clarify and classify; they leave no doubt.

His *Kushyoth* (questions as to difficulties in the text or subject matter of the Talmud), equally clear, frequently defy solution. When he ends one with the comment, "It warrants further study", there is some chance for the student to discover a solution. But when, in his modest manner, he says, "It warrants profound study," the problem is practically inexplicable.

His major works, most of them published posthumously, are:

1. Notes on the Talmud *(Haggahoth al ha-Shass)* later known as *Gilyon ha-Shass.*

2. Notes on the Mishnah *(Haggahoth al ha-Mishnah),* later known as *Tosefoth R. A. Eger.*

3. Responsa (Teshuvoth).

4. *Drush ve-Hiddush.*

5. Notes on the Four Parts of the Shulhan Arukh *(Haggahoth al Shulhan Arukh).*

These works reveal him not only as analyst and teacher, but also as the master of both rational and mystic lore.

The quality of his Difficult Questions (Kushyoth) became so famous that it offered a challenge to the best Talmudic minds, and many great scholars dedicated their books to their solution.

Although only 450 of his responsa were published, Rabbi Eger had written close to one thousand. In a busy life such as he led, this was a feat attributable only to his superior intellect.

Rabbi Hayyim, the great Rosh-Yeshivah of Volozhin and disciple of the Gaon of Vilna, spent many months in the preparation of a monograph on a difficult Halakhic problem. Because of the complexity of the issues involved, he hesitated to publish his conclusions before they were corroborated by another authority. He therefore dispatched a messenger with instructions to leave the document with Rabbi Eger for at least one month so that he could have ample time for criticism and comment. Immediately upon receipt, Rabbi Akiba glanced at the work and asked the messenger to return in a few hours, when he handed him his lengthy commentary and criticism. Rabbi Hayyim, who as disciple of the Gaon of Vilna had become accustomed to genius, expressed his profound amazement at the greatness of Rabbi Eger.

In technical matters, such as anatomical problems, he consulted the proper authorities before arriving at Halakhic decisions. Thus we find him (Resp. I, 61) writing to a professor at Frankfort for clarification on the conflicting opinions of local medical authorities.

He had the highest respect for the law of the land and considered himself a loyal citizen of the country. He forbade the conversion of Gentiles in countries where this was prohibited by the government. Thus, after expressing his approval of the decision of a Rabbi not to convert a Gentile, he writes:

"Indeed, it is the duty of every Rabbi to urge his congregants to obey the laws of the land. I have done so many times in my sermons, and have brought evidence from the Bible and the Talmud to show that it is obligatory upon every Jew to obey the laws of the land. More so, is it the duty of the Rabbi to lead in this direction so that the others may follow." (Resp. I, 41)

On the other hand, where a government ruling actually forced transgression of religious practice, he was the first to protest. He held that it was in the interest of government to strengthen religion, to see that all people were God-fearing and religious. Invariably, he succeeded through this argument in convincing government officials of the ill effects of their rulings and of the necessity to modify or rescind them.

Although the world acclaimed his profound scholarship, he felt uncomfortable in the cloak of the rabbinate. At one time he was concerned over the possibility that some of the townspeople might contribute to the salary of the rabbi against their will. At another time, annoyed by the many responsibilities and time-consuming obligations of the rabbi, he wrote:

"Nevertheless, my aim always was to leave the rabbinate. After all, a rabbi is responsible for all the transgressions of his congregants. And who am I to lash them with my tongue? True, many have been rabbis before me—many have crossed stormy seas and many will; that does not make the sea safer nor the water calmer. I have concluded that we can get along with less dainty foods and less costly clothing. We can live contentedly with the poor. Is it sensible to sacrifice one's spiritual self so that the physical self might be happy?"

His Modes of Worship

Study of Torah was indeed his mode of worship; it was his way of expressing love for God. From his fifteenth year, he had suffered chronic stomach trouble. The pain was agonizing; yet he never permitted it to interfere with his study. Because of his unwillingness to give up his strenuous mode of life, even medical men despaired of bringing him relief. Authentic tradition has it that when the doctors told him that he might not live much longer if he continued his intensive study of Torah, he replied, "If I study Torah, I *may* not live much longer; if I discontinue my study of Torah, I *shall* not live much longer; doubt must not prevail against certainty!"

On a typical day, he would rise at four in the morning and study the Mishnah. After *Shaharith* (morning prayer) he taught the Talmud to the laity, concluding with a brief sermon. Then followed a small breakfast and the study of the Bible. From ten to twelve, he lectured at the Yeshivah. Lunch was followed by a "rest" period in which he reviewed the latest publications. Now his sons and his closest disciples came in for a discussion of the morning lecture. Then he sat down to receive people who brought their lawsuits before him and to render decisions on communal and private problems. Because they knew of his piety and integrity, even non-Jews brought their problems to him.

Minhah (the afternoon prayer) was followed by a lecture on Shulhan Arukh; at *Maariv* (evening services) he offered prayers for the sick of his city, and, in compliance with frequent requests, for those of distant cities. From eight to ten in the evening, he wrote replies to questions addressed to him from Jewish communities in every part of the globe.

Rabbi Nahman Bratzlav once remarked that he never knew a man to achieve greatness, who did not isolate himself regularly so that he could subject himself to self-criticism, self-analysis, and repentance before God. Rabbi Akiba secluded himself every tenth day in a room in the synagogue and spent the day in this exercise. Though every moment of his day was spent in holiness, one tenth of his mature life was spent in the holy of holies.

His Love for the Underdog

Akiba Eger did not wait for the opportunity to perform kind deeds, but went out to seek them. He pursued that Mitsvah with all his heart, all his soul, and all his power. His sympathy for his fellow man knew no bounds; his words of encouragement to the poor and the suffering brought them hope and strength.

He visited the sick, always bringing little gifts. The psychological effect on the patient was immediate; he knew that somebody cared; he was honored that the rabbi had come to see him. Often, in order to comfort the critically ill, Rabbi Akiba Eger would spend the night at their bedside. To the poor, he gave of his own meagre income; frequently he visited, and wrote to, their relatives in their behalf. He was an active member in every organization to help the poor.

When an epidemic of puerperal fever took the lives of many mothers, Rabbi Eger appealed to the more fortunate mothers to take the orphans into their homes and to raise them. Once a week, he would personally visit each home to see that the children were properly cared for. He inspected the rooms, bedding, and clothing, to assure himself that the surroundings were sanitary.

Through his many visits to patients, Rabbi Eger became expert in the care of the sick and in preventive hygiene. The cholera epidemic which engulfed Europe, in 1831, found him prepared. He issued proclamations which listed precautions to be taken by the populace. He forbade the gathering of crowds in close quarters; he raised funds in order to clothe the poor. He advised on diet, sanitation, and mental hygiene. Thus he saved hundreds of lives. He was cited for distinguished service and loyalty by Emperor Friedrich Wilhelm III, who wrote to him personally.

It is no accident that the only authentic gem in homiletics attributed to Rabbi Eger is his interpretation of the verse in Psalm

XLIX: *"They leave* (ve-azevu) *to others their wealth."* Here he gives the stem of "ve-azevu" the meaning it has in another passage. Accordingly the verse will mean:

"The help that people give to others is their only wealth."

In this sense of "ve-azevu", he died a "wealthy" man indeed, on the thirteenth of Tishri, 1838, at the age of seventy-seven. His will stipulated that his epitaph should contain no words of praise but the following:

"Here lies Rabbi Akiba Eger, servant to the servants of God."

But the people of Posen could not forego a minor addition, altering the epitaph to read:

"Here lies *our rabbi,* Rabbi Akiba Eger, servant to the servants of God."

BIBLIOGRAPHY

Eger, A., and Eger, S., *Toledoth Rabbenu Eger,* Berlin, 1862.

Kämpf, S. J., *Biographie des Rabbi Akiba Eger,* Lissa, 1838.

Lewyson, S., *Vollständige Biographie des Rabbi Akiba Eger,* Posen, 1878.

Ovadiah, A., *Rabbi Akiba Eger, Jerusalem,* 1938.

Sofer, S., *Hut ha-Meshulash,* Drohobycz, 1908.

. . . . , *Igroth Soferim,* Vienna, 1929.

Wreschner, L., *Rabbi Akiba Eger—der letzte Gaon in Deutschland,* Frankfurt, 1906.

. . . . , *Rabbi Akiba Eger—Eine volkstümliche Biographie,* Frankfurt.

MOSES SOFER

By S. Ehrmann

MOSES SOFER

By S. Ehrmann

The personality of Rabbi Moses Sofer can be evaluated only at a proper distance. More than a century after his demise, that distance may not yet have been reached, because our appreciation of him is still too subjective. His writings are being used in hundreds of cases as sources of decisions in Jewish law and doctrine.

I

YOUTH AND FORMATIVE YEARS

The 7th day of Tishri 1762 fell upon Friday. In Frankfort-on-the-Main it was customary to start the Sabbath very early. That afternoon Mrs. Rezel Sofer, wife of the Torah-scribe Rabbi Samuel Sofer, sent a messenger to Rabbi Abraham Abish requesting him to postpone the Sabbath eve prayers, because she was about to give birth to a child and would fain do so before the Sabbath, thus avoiding a "desecration" of the Holy Day.

Deeply moved, Rabbi Abish gave the necessary instructions. A child of such a mother, he told his colleagues, was sure to be endowed with deep religious sensitivity. Shortly before Sabbath, Moses Sofer was born.

The Sofer (Schreiber) family tree, reaching back to Rashi, reveals a number of outstanding Talmudic scholars, among them Rabbi Simeon, author of the *Yalkut Shimeoni,* and Rabbi Samuel, author of the Commentary *Kos Yeshuoth* on the order *Nezikin.*

From his earliest childhood Mosheh showed unusual intelligence and application. This induced his father to dispense with tutors and to assume personal responsibility for his religious education. Rabbi Nathan Adler, one of the great Talmudists, who later on, as Moshe's teacher, played a vital part in his life, had recommended this step. In his seventh year, the little student was able to celebrate his completion of the Talmudic tractate of Betsah.

117

(Sixty years later, when he celebrated with his pupils the completion of the same volume, he electrified the audience by reciting the speech which he had delivered on the first occasion).

Adequately prepared by his father for his advanced Yeshivah studies, the youth, shortly after his Bar-Mitsvah celebration, was sent to nearby Mainz, where Rabbi T. Scherer and his son instructed him also in secular subjects, especially mathematics, natural sciences and history. Later on these studies proved invaluable for his responsa.

In the proper execution of Hebrew documents of divorce (gittin) most scrupulous attention must be given to the minutiae of names of persons and locations. Languages and dialects undergo continued changes affecting personal names. Geographical boundaries are revised and reflected in the names of town and districts. In some decisions had to be included comments about weights and measures relevant to religious purposes.

Other responsa, with their amazingly accurate definitions of human and animal pathology, reveal the depth and width of Rabbi Sofer's studies commenced in Mainz.

From Mainz he returned to Frankfort, to the Yeshivah of Rabbi Adler and the courses of Rabbi Pinehas Horowitz, the teachers to whom he remained profoundly attached throughout his life, and who, he felt, guided his decisions. Soon after his return, with his parents' consent, he made his home with Rabbi Adler.

At the age of fifteen Mosheh was able to celebrate the extraordinary accomplishment of his completion of the whole Talmud. To prevent any possible smugness, his teachers bade him observe a three days' fast, interrupted only by a daily evening meal. When, soon thereafter, Rabbi Adler received a call to Boskowitz (Moravia), Mosheh jointed him. Rabbi Adler ranked not only as a great teacher of the Talmud, but as one of the outstanding scholars of mystic lore (Zohar and Kabbalah). He found Mosheh, despite his youth, mature enough for profound study in that field, too.

II

YEARS OF TRAVEL

The fame of the Frankfort Bahur's genius travelled fast throughout Moravia and its neighboring countries. Many rabbinical positions were offered to him, but he refused them all, because as yet he wanted to learn only, not to teach.

In 1796, Rabbi Adler, on his return to Frankfort, advised his disciple to accept the call to the important community of Prosnitz (Moravia). There he faced the hard task of opposing the Frankists, the followers of the Pseudo-Messiah Sabbatai Tsevi, who were spreading their pernicious teaching. In 1796 Moses Sofer established his first Yeshivah and commenced evening lectures for the community. But he refused the title of Rabbi and indeed counselled the community to appoint a more experienced scholar to the pulpit. He left when Rabbi Wolf Boskowitz was given the post. The latter's father (author of the *Mahatsith ha-Shekel*), on assuming that position, wrote his son: "You will find in Prosnitz the Bahur from Frankfort. Maintain brotherly relations with him; do as he tells you and see that your students be taught at least one Shiur (course) by him."

The major reason why Rabbi Sofer refused to become a rabbi was his unmarried state. Soon after his arrival in Prosnitz he married the daughter of the late Rabbi Moses Terwitz of that city. Her brother took care of their financial needs so that Rabbi Moses could dedicate himself solely to the study of Torah. Thus is described his routine: From Saturday night to Sunday eve he studied without interruption. After the evening prayers he retired until 11 P. M., then partook of a small meal and continued the same routine until Monday night; he slept only once in forty eight hours. To keep awake he would soak his feet in cold water Thus he continued for two years. Then he accepted the position of rabbi of the Dresnitz community. Five years later came the call to Mattersdorf (Burgenland). On the way to his new pulpit he stopped at Pressburg and visited the world-renowned patriarch, Rabbi Samuel Tusmenitz. Even then the community recognized the full potentialities of their future spiritual leader. Rabbi Samuel remained deeply impressed by the young man who had met him for a prolonged discussion, and the latter was deeply moved by the respect the Pressburg community showed to their spiritual leader.

Rabbi Mosheh assumed his new post in 1798. He was joined by a large group of his students from Dresnitz who formed the nucleus of the Yeshivah in Mattersdorf, soon to become famous throughout the country.

In 1803, the Gaon Samuel, Rabbi of Pressburg, passed away. For three years his pulpit remained unoccupied. A number of great rabbis were considered for his position, for only a world-renowned figure could fill that place. A powerful group in the community wanted the Rabbi of Mattersdorf to be invited. To avoid invidious impressions or rumors as to the reasons why the other candidates were rejected, it was decided to choose the rabbi by lot. The winner was Rabbi Moses Sofer. A deputation of the community brought the decision to Mattersdorf; at length he decided to accept that post because of the far greater field of action that Pressburg afforded.

III

In the Fall of 1806 Rabbi Moses Sofer reached Pressburg, and his very first sermon won him the heart of the community.

To promote adult education, he selected scholars to hold classes for businessmen in the evenings and on Saturdays. Besides his Yeshivah work, he wanted also to create an atmosphere of Torah in his community. This would eventually result in a sustained and generous interest in the welfare of Torah scholars. The number of students in the Yeshivah of Pressburg soon grew to several hundred. The young men in the community would attend the Yeshivah for two or three years, and other students from far and near flocked to Pressburg because there, they heard, personalities were developed, deeply rooted in love of Torah and loyal Jewishness, no matter what profession they ultimately chose to follow.

The Yeshivah became famous for its original methods of teaching as well as for its teacher-student relations. Rabbi Sofer knew how to bring the most involved subject-matter down to the intellectual level of his students. Like a student, he proceeded slowly and patiently until he was convinced that every one of his listeners was able to follow. Weekly and final examinations covered all subjects. In spite of his own keeness of mind, Rabbi Moses Sofer was opposed to mere intellectual brilliance and artificial dialectics (pilpul). He would often present to his more advanced students two interpretations of an especially difficult passage of

Maimonides, one full of scintillating cleverness which he later proved to be spurious, the other, simple and true. He put every one of his lectures (Shiurim) in a form which would make even the most difficult passages easy to comprehend.

Every Friday night, he repeated with his advanced students the study of the week. In the month of Elul, during the Yeshivah vacation, the rabbi went over the enormous material of the Babylonian and Palestinian Talmuds in order to correct any lapses of his own memory. At the beginning of any session in the Yeshivah he would recite a passage from Bahya's classic, *"The Duties of the Heart."* He urged his students to study cognate works. He started each term with a lecture on an ethical theme.

He was not only their teacher but acted like a father towards his students, treating them with both firmness and tender regard. He planned assiduously for their material and spiritual future, and they in turn looked upon him with reverence and love. Towards each other, the students felt like brothers, cherishing their attachment long after they had left the Yeshivah.

The following episode conveys a sense of his extraordinary humaneness. Rabbi Moses Sofer had announced to his students that the subject of his lecture would be certain a passage from Taharoth. One of the older students, who had heard that same lecture a few years earlier, recited it to his friends in the very words and manner he claimed the rabbi was going to deliver it. The following day the rabbi delivered in the packed classroom a lecture literally identical with the student's performance. The unusual hilarity that followed aroused the rabbi's curiosity. Upon learning its cause he at once stopped and left the room muttering "Impudence."

The consternation among his students grew worse when, at the beginning of next day's lecture, he asked his former student to step forward, and said to him: "Against my better judgment, I became angry with you yesterday. That's why I interrupted the Shiur, for, according to our sages, the Shekhinah departs from one who is angry, and in such a mood one is unable to study. Now I must ask for your forgiveness in the presence of the men who heard my harsh word!" The rabbi delivered the lecture again, in a new and most fascinating manner.

Another facet of his character is revealed in one of his poems (Shirei ha-Kodesh): "We are children of our father Abraham who stated: 'I am but dust and ashes;' disciples of our teacher Moses who exclaimed: 'What are we but God's servants'; and descendants of King David who said, 'I am a worm.' Whom should we follow: those great teachers ,or Jeroboam who, in his pride, knew only to ask: 'Who will be the leader,' and he meant himself."

It was because of this humility that, all urging notwithstanding, he refused to publish even one line during his lifetime. "Almost every author," he would say, "feels proud upon reading his name in print. Such pride ignores the teachings of the Fathers: 'A name made great, is a name destroyed.' Similarly was the writing down of the oral tradition permitted only when it served God's honor but not one's own!" Fortunately he did write down his novellae (Comments on Torah) and responsa to countless inquiries from far and near. After his death, between 1841 and 1861, the latter were published in six volumes. Other books include homiletical and exegetical material.

A Memorial Volume ("Sefer ha-Zikkaron") describes events during the Napoleonic Wars against Austria, when the French Army wrought havoc with the life of the Pressburg Jewish community. It deals with the flight to the countryside and other experiences until the armistice. That volume contains also a number of speeches through which the rabbi endeavored to give courage and strength to his grievously harassed community. The Rabbinical Council of Pressburg had to act in cases between Jews, involving some semi-legal and illegal traffic in arms. R. M. S. was summoned to appear before the French court because he had failed to notify the French authorities of such deals. But his personality and his bearing convinced the authorities of his complete innocence.

Because of the War, the State of Austria declared itself in bankruptcy in 1811, and the official currency was devaluated to one-fifth its original value. This brought forth a flood of inquiries addressed to Rabbi Sofer, concerning the payment of debts, alimony and other obligations.

His answers to every type of question throughout thirty-six years of his rabbinate in Pressburg may offer the key to his spiritual effectiveness.

IV

His Responsa

Even a superficial study of these volumes explains the universal fame of the author throughout the Jewish World. Questions came from the Austro-Hungarian monarchy, from Germany, Italy, Holland, Switzerland, and Palestine. They deal with the whole range of Jewish life and lore, from questions as to the essence of Judaism down to minutiae of law and custom and proper copying of Torah scrolls. We also find questions about civil rights, community and family laws and difficult passages in the Talmud. There is a well-known passage in Berakhoth to the effect that the face of a man who depends on others, will change color. The rabbi offers another interpretation of *"shenitsrakh la-beriyoth,"* to wit: a person whose decision and counsel is wanted by many must have great patience and infinite capacity for adjustment. He will be pale with the exertion, and red with occasional tension.

"Talmudic learning is not enough. A judge must also be familiar with other fields of human knowledge for a proper application of the laws of the Torah to the complexity of everyday problems." Unconsciously, the rabbi described himself.

Many of his answers show his general knowledge, which made him familiar also with problems outside the Jewish realm. As a Torah-scholar he was fully aware of his own limitations. Asked how he was able to give immediate written replies to the most difficult questions, and out of thousands of questions only twice had to admit an error, he explained that since his eighteenth year, with the exception of Tisha be-Av, he never let a day go by without studying the Torah by himself or with his students. Even on the eve of Yom ha-Kippurim he was in the habit of holding a Shiur. The nights, spent with only a minimum of rest, with his feet immersed in cold water, to prevent himself from falling asleep, enabled him in later years to draw out from his phenomenal memory instantaneously the right answer to any question. He interpreted wittily the verse of the Psalms *"Kehitsim beyad ha-Gibbor ken b'ne ha-Neoorim"* to mean: "As arrows in the hand of the hero, so are the children (results) of nights spent awake," *Neoorim* meaning both "youth" and "wakefulness,"

V

THE HOLY LAND

Soon after he became Rabbi of Pressburg, R. M. S. was named Nassi (head) of all the Kolelim (Graduate Talmudic Academies of Palestine). All their grave problems were brought before him. In his diffidence he would thus preface his decision: "My opinion comes from the darkness of the Galuth. I trust that the light of Erets Yisrael's great rabbis will bring about the right solution."

His decision about *Mitsvath Yishuv Erets Yisrael* (the obligation to rebuild and settle in the Holy Land) is very significant. Some people had frowned upon working the soil or the pursuing of a trade as interfering with Torah study. But Rabbi Sofer declared that productive work in Palestine was a great Mitsvah. "Just as little as one could refuse to put on Tefillin in the Golah, on the ground that it would cause an interruption in one's studies, so little could one on the same pretext ignore the Biblical command to cultivate the soil of our Homeland."

He further emphasized the outstanding importance of Jerusalem above all other cities in Israel, and labored to discover the reason why settlers preferred Safed and Tiberias, despite the fact that conditions had at the time made life in Jerusalem less difficult. He pointed to the teaching of Moses Nahmanides, who advised some of his students who were returning to Israel to settle in Jerusalem. For the same reason he felt that the Holy City was to be favored in any distribution of money sent to the Yishuv. He was somewhat skeptical about the new custom of lighting bonfires on Lag bo-Omer in honor of Rabbi Simeon bar Yohai,, for "Since the beginning of the Galuth even days mentioned in the Megillath Taanith had lost their festive character, and it is not up to us to start any new Minhagim."

VI

THE LAW OF THE COUNTRY

Rabbi Moses Sofer not only endorsed the right of the Jews to entrust relevant documents to non-Jewish courts, but declared it incumbent upon the members of the Beth Din to make declarations before a non-Jewish tribunal in order to bring about governmental action—but only in cases where the incorruptibility of the authorities concerned was beyond doubt. With great indignation did he condemn any attempts by Jews to mislead non-Jewish officials through circumlocution or perjury. He declared currency inflation caused by the government binding for all transactions among Jews, including those involving community or charitable institutions. The currency rate established by the State was to serve as basis in the repayment of debts contracted under an earlier rate of exchange. The only exception was the silver payment involved in the Pidyon ha-Ben (the ceremony of the Redemption of the First-born).

Whosoever bribes a judge, whether Jewish or non-Jewish, violates the prohibition: *"Thou shalt not put a stumbling block before the blind."* In the course of this responsum, R. M. S. cited an earlier decision of Rabbi Joel Bacharach (author of *"Havvoth Yair"*, 17th century). Pfalzgraf (Count) Karl Ludwig had bitterly complained about the Jews bribing non-Jewish judges in any litigation between themselves and Christians. Rabbi Bacharach replied: "The Judge's intense Anti-Semitism normally made him decide against the Jew, no matter how much he was in the right. Thus the bribe succeeded in achieving impartiality, and this made a fair trial possible. From the point of view of the Torah a bribe could not be justified, yet the Jews felt they were not doing wrong as they were merely attempting to secure justice". R. M. S. remarks apropos that it is forbidden to make a non-Jew transgress any of the seven Noahide laws, one of them being a fair application of justice.

An interesting responsum concerned a hired maid who had deposited a pair of golden earrings with her employer as a pledge against leaving his employ before the proper time. She disappeared, and could not be found; the earrings therefore could not be returned. R. M. S. decided that since public announcement of a found object is mandatory according to the Talmud, the employer was obliged in this case to search for the maid through newspaper advertisements so that the earrings might be returned to her. If the maid has not called for the earrings within a reason-

able period of time, they should be deposited with the community
for future surrender to the maid or her representative.

VII

COMMUNITY OFFICIALS

Rabbi Sofer insisted on the autonomous right of the community
to choose its spiritual leader: "A rabbi, no matter how great a
scholar, if installed by the State without or against the wishes
of his community, lacks all authority." Although the laws of the
State are generally binding upon its Jewish citizens, the rabbi
must inform the authorities that he is not willing to assume his
position without the approval of his community, thus preventing
non-Jewish authorities from imposing upon the Jews. Rabbi
Sofer buttressed his decision by this quotation from Rabbi Meir
of Rothenberg:

> "In solemn session, we determined to forbid anyone, on
> penalty of excommunication, to accept a position of authority
> over his fellow-citizens solely with help of a king, judge, or
> other non-Jewish power. Such office would breed tyranny in
> all matters, secular or religious. Only by a majority vote
> of the community and on the basis of personal merit, may such
> a position be awarded. Anyone who acts against our decision
> shall be excommunicated from all Israel, from his own students
> as well as from the students of his students. His bread and
> wine shall be considered forbidden to fellow-Jews, and as com-
> ing from heathens; his books shall remain unread. Those who
> follow our decision shall be blessed."

The other signatories are 150 other rabbis. Rabbi Sofer recommends that the community negotiate with the rabbi foisted upon
them by non-Jewish authorities rather than with the latter, that
they read to him Rabbi Rothenberg's decision and seek a peaceful
solution by offering the applicant, if he be worthy, a seat in the
local Beth Din, as a compromise.

Characteristically, Rabbi Sofer would erase all names from
copies of his decisions, or substitute "John Doe" in all cases involving the wrongdoing of an individual or community.

In a responsum about the rabbi's emolument, R.M.S. considered himself perchance incapable of an impartial decision, as

he himself was the recipient of a salary. However, on the basis of law and precedent, he held that every Jew is required to study and teach as far as possible without compensation. But he is also obliged to take care of his family. He must not refuse a pupil merely because teaching him might interfere with his own studies. He could refuse to teach one if thereby his own income might suffer. For such work he could demand compensation. On the other hand, every community should employ a person whose time and energies would be available for teaching and handing down decisions to any member of the community at any time. Compensation for such work is to be determined by the financial position of the rabbi. In case of inflation the community must increase his salary regardless of the sum stipulated in the original contract.

An extremely difficult and embarrassing question concerned a rabbi who in theory and practice had violated the Torah and refused to account for his actions to any outside council of rabbis. Very painstakingly R.M.S. examined the credibility of the witnesses and established beyond doubt that the rabbi in question, in spite of repeated warnings, had committed grave errors in matters of divorce. When the accused rabbi heard about Rabbi Moses Sofer's decision that the community should relieve him of his post, he visited R.M.S. in the hope of affecting a settlement. The discussion only strengthened Rabbi Sofer in his conviction. Nevertheless he made an exact summary of the discussion and transmitted it to the community.

A shohet, in a penitent mood during a dangerous illness, confessed that repeatedly and deliberately he had declared trefah meat kosher. The question arose as to how he should expiate his offenses, whether he should be held responsible for replacing all utensils involved, and whether, after recuperation, he should be permitted to perform Shehitah again. R.M.S. decided that he was unwilling to impose fasting and other self-castigation; that indemnification should not be imposed, but everything should be done to help him do Teshuvah (come back to God). However, for some time to come, he should be permitted to act as Shohet only in the presence of a second, learned and responsible, colleague.

After a rabbi had been elected, a compromising letter revealed that his relatives had influenced the election by buying votes. Rabbi

Sofer declared the election void, even though the number of the votes bought had not determined the outcome. If the rabbi himself had been aware of what his relatives were doing, he could no more be a candidate for any other rabbinical position, until he repented and mended his ways. The members of the community who had accepted bribes must be excluded from the new election, even though they had returned them. Electors serve as judges, and a bribe offered to them is as reprehensible as one offered to a judge. Incidentally, Rabbi Sofer condemns the opening of any letter addressed to someone else. Such offense comes under the ban imposed by Rabbi Gershon, The Light of the Diaspora (11th cent.), and re-endorsed in the responsa of Rabbi Meir of Rothenberg.

VIII

Youth Problems

May a child perform work on the Sabbath, even if it involves merely carrying an object? He answered emphatically "No," especially since Maimonides is very definite about the importance of Sabbath-observance from early age. Exception could be made only in the case of carrying a prayerbook to the synagogue, because attendance at worship constitutes *Hinukh* (religious training).

A minor, mentally incurable, may be put into a non-Jewish institution even if this involves his partaking of non-Kosher food.

Must one live up to the wishes of a testator who imposed upon a youth the obligation to study Torah out of his tome-town? "Yes," said Rabbi Sofer, "It is an advantage for a student to sit at the feet of many scholars. Out-of-town students have the additional advantage of being free from home distraction."

IX

Differences In Minhagim (Customs)

With the spread of Hassidism, the problem arose in Hungary as to whether the prevailing Ashkenazic ritual should be replaced by the Sephardic one, based on the Siddur of Rabbi Isaac Luria.

Disciples of the latter did not hesitate to assert that only prayers
of that ritual would be granted. R.M.S. emphatically opposed
that opinion and forbade his congregation to change its minhag.
He quoted his Frankfort teachers who, although personally using
the Luria Siddur, did not encourage their community to do so.
Each minhag has its own justification, each one reflects its special
tradition. The responsum includes reminiscences of his stay in
Mayence, where he visited the house in which Rabbi Amnon, the
author of *"Nethaneh Tokef"*, had lived, and the grave of Rabbi
Amram, an early editor of the Siddur. He quotes fascinating
precedents from the writings of Rabbi Asher and Nahmanides.

As to performing marriage ceremonies under the open sky, he
bases the various minhagim in this connection on the differences
among Eastern and Western European Jews.

Among other interesting subjects dealt with, are unilateral
contracts of rabbis; protection of authors against plagiarism; laws
concerning suicide, etc. Noteworthy is a brilliant dissertation on
the principles of the Jewish law of acquisition. Rabbi Sofer
proves that originally natural law was recognized in Israel, the
Torah superseding it only in special cases; in all others the original
principle retains its validity. On this basis, a number of otherwise
insolvable difficulties involving the acquisition of property find an
amazingly simple solution.

X

CHAMPION OF THE FAITH

In any century or climate R.M.S. would be recognized as
a great man. But the significance of his providential role in the
19th century can be comprehended only by one who has studied the
life of Central European Jewry in that period. The declaration
of human rights enunciated by the French Revolution brought
about the emancipation of Jews and, as its corollary, their assimilation. Commonly, the beginning of Jewish assimilation in Western
Europe is blamed on Moses Mendelssohn and his followers. The
former, indeed, through his Bible translation, unintentionally made
the Jewish assimilation movement possible. He was succeeded by

Geiger, Jakobsohn and other leaders of Jewish reform who gained tremendous influence among Jews and characterized the classical rabbis as products of medieval ignorance. That schism tore families apart, communities were split, child education was channelled into new spheres, and fashioned after prevailing non-Jewish cults. Jewish family life lost the purity and holiness which had preserved it through two millennia of exile. Reform is one of the greatest spiritual tragedies of Jewish history, from whose consequences we are suffering to this day. Normally, assimilation takes one away from one's traditions. Reform anchored assimilation in Judaism itself. From the beginning of the 19th century, Reform insisted on being recognized as a legitimate school of thought in Judaism and demanded this legitimization from religious Jews.

On Yom Kippur, 1818, for the first time, in the Synagogue of Hamburg the prayers were sung with organ accompaniment, with the text of the Siddur, of course, emasculated, and the choir mixed. The Dayanim of Hamburg called on all the great rabbis of Germany, Poland, France, Italy, Bohemia, Moravia and Hungary, among them also Rabbi Moshe Sofer, for a statement about the new Temple. As one man, they all condemned this attempt on the life of Judaism. Reform leaders were searching for an authoritative rabbinical body to come to their aid. Germany found only a future convert to Christianity, Rabbi Eliezer Liebermann, to defend their movement. This Liebermann found a fellow-traveller in Rabbi Aaron Chorin of Arad, who became the spokesman for the Reform Movement in Hungary and in a book tried to justify Reform not as a schism but as based on Talmud and Shulhan Arukh. Moses Sofer and others rose to denounce these falsifications. In numerous pamphlets and publications, R.M.S. revealed their weakness and self-contradictions. The Rabbi of Pressburg condemned the three main innovations of Reform: the organ, the substitution of the German for the Hebrew language in worship, and the omission of all prayers relating to the redemption of the Jewish people, as incompatible with our tradition. He declared: "There have always been a few who left the fold and either found their way back or disappeared. The latter are like unto dead leaves dropping from a tree without harming it. But when these apostasies occur in groups, as was the case with

Sadducees and Karaites, the breach becomes irreperable. We are facing such group defection in our time. The leaders of this movement have split from us. We must record all the facts of this split so that our ranks may remain unaffected by any contamination."

On another occasion he used this illustration: "A king's child lay deathly ill of a contagious disease. A world-renowned physician, in spite of utmost efforts, saw no hope. At dawn, the amazed king met the doctor in front of the sick-room, his sword drawn. 'What is the meaning of this?' demanded the king. The doctor replied: 'As long as there was any hope, I did my utmost to bring about recovery. Now that all hope is lost, my sword at the threshold is to prevent the spread of contagion.'"

Germany had no Moses Sofer, hence apostasy made great progress and caused tremendous devastation. Only towards the middle of the century did Samson R. Hirsch and Ezriel Hildesheimer arise to defend our heritage, and inspire many followers. They spent themselves in the presentation of true Judaism, in defensive work, and in efforts to win back individual souls. The battle of words had to be waged in German, for only few remained interested in Hebrew or capable of understanding the original language of the Torah. In Austria and Hungary the untiring efforts of Rabbi Sofer met the crisis with much greater success. Like a dam, he prevented every invasion. He trained thousands of his students to preserve traditional Judaism in Hungary and adjacent countries.

XI

EMANCIPATION, ROYAL DIGNITARIES, AND OTHER PROBLEMS

When the Congress of Vienna brought emancipation to the Jews of Austria and Hungary, all Jewish communities held special thanksgiving services. In his address on that occasion, R.M.S. told this story: "A young prince, for disciplinary reasons, was banished by his father to a village in a far-away land. There he was to share the frugal life of the villagers. After a number of years, the father took pity upon his son and gave instructions to have a palace built for him in the village, and to provide him with servants and comforts befitting his rank. At first, the prince was overjoyed. Yet soon he declared: 'If my father had any intention of calling me home, he would not have bettered my lot in exile. I see now clearly that my days of banishment will last for a long time.' Similarly, the rabbi explained, our hearts at first were overjoyed and thankful that our country had finally granted us equality as citizens. Yet our joy is dampened by the knowledge that our heavenly Father does not deem us worthy at this time to return to our own Palace, in our own country on which the Shekhinah rests."

In the year 1821 the Austrian authorities called on the Rabbinate of Pressburg for a decision regarding the terms of a divorce to be granted by a baptized Jew to his unbaptized wife. In his opinion, written in German, R.M.S. says: "With regard to the question addressed to me by his Royal Highness and by his Majesty's Chancellery as to whether a form different from the one commonly used for divorce decrees between Jewish marriage partners could be introduced in the case of one who has been converted and who may find its normal provisions disturbing in the exercise of his new religion, the undersigned humbly declares: The document of divorce used in the dissolution of a Jewish marriage is prescribed verbatim in the Talmud as well as in the Jewish Code, together with all formalities attached to its presentation. The laws involved contain not a single passage from which one might deduce that a difference obtains between a divorce in which both partners are conforming Jews and a divorce in which one of them has been converted to Christianity. Therefore the undersigned holds, according to the precepts of his religion and his own conviction, that a marriage between Jews, even if one partner at a later date was converted, cannot be considered dissolved until such time as the husband has presented to the wife, either himself or through a lawfully authorized person, a document of divorce executed according to the precepts of Jewish law. Therefore, no substitute is possible.

Pressburg, on the 8th Day of November, 1821.
Moshe Schreiber, Chief Rabbi.

XII

His Character

The secret of the practical effectiveness of the great rabbi can be found not only in his universally recognized mastery of Torah knowledge, but especially in the strength of his character, ethical impregnability, humility and love of humanity. Although a stalwart opponent of the reform movement, he never stooped to personal attacks in writing or by word of mouth. Again and again he impressed upon his students the duty of preventing strife and litigation in their communities and, when this proves unavoidable, they must try to secure peace at once. In his commentary on Deuteronomy (XX, 10) he admonishes every rabbi, even in his fight for Torah, to adhere to the Jewish principle of warfare of calling first for peace. Only after every such effort has failed may one engage in war. Where truth or any other good cause was concerned, he knew of no intimidation, remaining unimpressed by position, wealth or influence. Of rocklike strength and dauntless honesty, he could be exceedingly soft and sensitive where the needy or helpless were involved. Of his earnings, he contributed to the poor not only the legal tithe, but twice that amount, the normal maximum within Jewish law. When the community heard that he was depriving his own family in order to help others, they decided to put at his personal disposal any amount he would require. Rabbi Moses refused the offer.

Together with Chief Rabbi Mordecai Baneth, he would visit the health resort of Baden. Unable once to find lodgings with Jews, they had to take quarters with a non-Jew, who, feeling greatly honored by their presence, refused to accept payment. The two decided to compensate him thus: Rabbi Baneth would bring him food at the end of every week. R.M.S. decided to do so every day, so that should a fatal accident befall him during the week, he would not owe him anything.

Another vacation R.M.S. spent at the home of a pious but ignorant Jew. He was baffled to hear of his landlord spreading the rumor that Rabbi Moses belonged to the reform rabbis. The good man at last explained: He had based his opinion on the fact that the rabbi had failed to make kiddush over the wine at the third Shabbath meal, as he himself was in the habit of doing. Rabbi Sofer delighted in such simplicity and told his pupils: "I was always afraid of the day when rabbis, unworthy of their profession, would lead our people astray; if they succeeded, God forbid, there might be no one to uphold Torah. Now, however, I have seen zeal for Torah in the souls of even simple laymen. Although I am the Rabbi of Pressburg, known as a Torah-scholar, this humble man is not afraid to stand up against me, if he, even erroneously, believes that I am violating a Jewish Minhag. Such sentiment assures us that Torah will not be forgotten in Israel."

Like his great teacher, Rabbi Nathan Adler, R. M. S. exercised the function of a Mohel without accepting any remuneration. In his *Mohelbook* he lists 735 children whom he had inducted into the bond of Abraham. The last entry, on the 23rd of Tammuz 1835, concerned his youngest son Joseph (called Jospe).

This son was born to his second wife, Sarah, daughter of Rabbi Akiba Eger. This union strengthened the spiritual bond between the two princes of the Torah. Rabbi Sofer had been in constant contact with Rabbi Eger, not only with regard to the solution of Talmudic problems and difficult cases, but especially in the battle against reform. The correspondence between the two great rabbis represents for the student one of the most interesting parts of R. M. S.'s work. In his later years Rabbi Eger would send those seeking his advice to the Gaon of Pressburg.

Rabbi Sofer's marriage to Sarah Eger was blessed with three sons and seven daughters. The oldest son, Rabbi Samuel Benjamin Schreiber, succeeded him in Pressburg. His second son, Simon, was called to the pulpit of Krakau in the year 1860, and in 1879 was elected a member of the Austrian Parliament, where he represented the Jewish people. His native wit is preserved in this anecdote: Rabbi Simon, on more than one occasion, had voted with the liberal bloc in the Parliament. When, on the occasion of a visit to the Emperor, the latter questioned him in amazement: "How can you, a Jewish rabbi, vote with the *left*?" The courageous man replied: "This, your Majesty, is because we Jews have *no rights.*" (Emancipation, like the mills of democracy, was grinding more slowly than finely.)

The daughters married well-known scholars; one of them became the wife of Rabbi Samuel Spitzer, the leader of Torah-true Judaism and founder of the Schiff Synagogue in Vienna.

Thirty years after the passing away of the Hatham Sofer, his life's work, continued by his son's successors and disciples, was crowned through the establishment, by government decree, of autonomous orthodoxy. R. M. S. had prepared the theoretical blueprint for this consummation.

On the fifth day of March, Parliament decided that orthodox communities had the right to constitute themselves an independent orthodox central chancellery. Its focal points were Pressburg and Budapest, joined by 150 lesser communities. When, after a bitter struggle, the independence of orthodoxy was established in Germany, its geratest leader, S. R. Hirsch, was able to take Hungary as his example. He leaned heavily upon R. M. S.'s opinion about the definite need for absolute separation.

In the winter of 1821 the community of Fuerth (Bavaria) approached the rabbi with an urgent request to accept the rabbinate there, not only to lend the glamor of his name to that Kehillah, famous for its learning and practice of Torah, but primarily to became the defender of the faith against the terrific onslaught of the reform movement.

Spokesman for the community was Rabbi Wolf Hamburg, the well-known editor of *"Simlath Binyamin."* Rabbi Sofer, who had spiritually always felt part of German Jewry, was not opposed to heeding the call. Whilst he was wondering as to whether he would be able to maintain the Yeshivah in Fuerth in a manner similar to the one in Pressburg, the latter community, its president, trustees and rank and file, implored him to remain with them.

The decisive moment came when the greatly respected Hirsch Jaffee insisted in moving words that whilst the rabbi might be able to save German Jewry, most of his accomplishments in Hungary would be lost by his departure. Rabbi Sofer accepted that argument and decided to stay in Pressburg.

During his lifetime he was honored by the establishment of a school in Safed (Palestine), which bears the name *Yeshivath Hatham Sofer.* When, in 1837, an earthquake killed 200 people

and destroyed most of the buildings in that city, his eloquent call
to European Jewry for help resulted in sufficient funds to enable
the survivors to rebuild their homes and start a new life.

XIII

HIS LAST WILL

At the age of seventy-four, R. M. S. wrote his last will for
family and community. In this testament, republished many times,
he implores his children to pursue their lives as in their father's
home, without any deviation, and to beware of pride. Economic
problems should not trouble them too much. They are not to be
burdened by material needs. God, who had helped them until
now, would never fail them. In moving terms, he thanks his
community for their aid in expanding the Yeshivah and for having
maintained its thousands of students. He begs them not to leave
his pulpit vacant too long after his death, but to select as soon as
possible a Gaon distinguished by his desire to teach, by financial
integrity, by a deep sense of honor, and by popularity. No changes
are to be made in either Beth ha-Midrash or Beth ha-Knesseth
(synagogue). He blesses the whole comunity and each one of
its members, adjuring them to follow the way of the Lord. His
final word to his family: "May the tree not be felled nor the
source run dry," closes the document.

His wish was granted. The spirit of their forefathers was
maintained by his descendants, who for three generations graced
the pulpit of Pressburg. After the defeat of Germany in 1945,
the great-grandson of R. M. S., the Rav of Pressburg, moved to
the Holy Land, where he re-established the Yeshivah and assumed
the leadership of the remnants of his community.

XIV

HIS LAST DAYS

The Succoth spirit of 1840 was greatly dimmed by the grave
sickness of the renowned rabbi. In spite of physical agony, he
insisted on celebrating the holidays with his family and pupils.
The night of *Hoshanah Rabbah* he spent studying in his Succah.

He then attended morning services, but had to leave because of excruciating pain. He no longer was able to leave his home. He worried constantly about the payment of salaries to those in his employ, even after his doctors had pronounced his condition grave. The specialist called from Vienna confirmed the unfavorable diagnosis of his Pressburg colleagues. From that moment on the synagogue never remained empty. Day and night prayers rose to heaven for the beloved leader. One of the community representatives spoke thus to the disciples: "Friends, do you know for whom we are praying? For one who is the greatest of our time, unequaled in Torah, wisdom and strength of character." On Simhath Torah, services were held in the sickroom and, as usual, the rabbi was "called up" as Hathan Torah. At the words *"Va-yamoth Mosheh"* ("And Moses died"), he was the only one to remain calm, while the rest of the congregation burst into tears. The festival passed and the doctors declared that he could live only for a day or two. Nevertheless, he mustered enough strength and lucidity of thought to deliver a Talmudic lecture to the students surrounding him. He said farewell to the members of his community who visited his bedside, quoting blessings from the last address of Moses our Teacher. Thursday, on the morning of the 25th of Tishri, the Torah was read to him again. When he removed his Tefillin, he presented them to his "house bahur",* saying: "I will not need them tomorrow." He then proceeded to explain the saying of Rabbi Joshuah Ben Hananya (quoted on page 53a of Tractate Succoth): "We saw no sleep in our eyes because of the joy at the ceremony of Drawing Water." "Why," asked Rabbi Sofer, "this irrational expression, instead of 'We failed to sleep?' There is a good reason for it," he continued: "Besides a physical state of sleep there is one of mental inertia. That is the dormancy of our spiritual power. This state is different from natural sleep because one remains conscious of it. One can see this sleep with one's own eyes." Hence the passage must be interpreted to mean: Even during the great celebration of the Drawing of Water, the great men did not while their time away even for a moment. Every minute of their day was filled with thought and work. Consciously or unconsciously, R. M. S. in these last few words described himself.

*(A favorite student privileged to board with the rabbi.)

He then proceeded in a clear voice to recite the last prayer. The first two repetitions of the Shema were uttered by the multitude who filled the hospital and the streets outside. The third repetition could no longer be heard, yet his lips continued to move for awhile, until the great soul escaped the prison of its body and returned to its heavenly creator.

Thus the earthly career of this master of Torah had come to an end. The pledge of loyalty and battle for God which his family and community made at his grave, was fulfilled. Torah-true Hungary became a pillar of traditional Judaism wherever its members settled in the wide world. Rabbi Sofer's ideals, even a century after his death, directed the autonomous organization of the Torah-true members of our people.

On the borderline between the East and the West, this Jewish champion and thinker built bridges between the Ghetto and the life without, through which he helped save the heritage of Israel.

His example should inspire this generation for our task: to bring modern life into ever-closer touch with the word of God and His direction.

MENAHEM MORGENSTERN OF KOTZK

By Joshua Finkel

MENAHEM MORGENSTERN OF KOTZK

By Joshua Finkel

Menahem Mendel Morgenstern, commonly known as the Kotzker Rabbi, was born in Gorey, Poland, in 1787. He was a scion of learned and respected families on both his father's and mother's side, but he was humble in his bearing, noble in spirit, unstained by arrogance of family pride. Always seeking a middle way, peacemaking, not standing on his dignity, his unconscious embodiment of the ideal "noblesse oblige" proclaimed him the true aristocrat. "Of two contenders, he is of superior lineage, who first stops wrangling," according to the Talmud (Kiddushin 71 b.)

His first education, as a matter of course, he received in the *hadarim* of Gorey. At a tender age he exhibited such great intellectual power and such zeal for learning that his native town could no longer contain him. He was therefore sent to neighboring Zamoshtsh where he continued his studies in the Yeshivah of Rabbi Joseph Hochgelernter. The latter was one of the great educators and eminent Talmudists of his day, distinguishing himself in Halakhah and Aggadah alike. He must have made a deep impression on the young arrival and undoubtedly inspired him to broaden his scholastic pursuits.

It was perhaps fortunate for the young student that the district of Lublin fell, at that period, under Austrian sway. Under the new law, the study of German became compulsory and thus the secular culture of the day became for him an open book. Forced to learn a trade also in compliance with the new law, he chose pharmacy, although he never had occasion to practice it.

In 1807 Menahem Mendel married Glickel Nei of Tomashov, and in accordance with the custom of the day, he went to live in his father-in-law's house. From there he made his first pilgrimage to the "Seer" (Hozeh) of Lublin, who accorded him the signal honor of making him a member of his exclusive minyan. This meant so much to him that in later years he told his son-in-law

141

(the Rabbi of Sochatchov), that for many years he had to struggle to keep from being too puffed up over being thus preferred.

However, he was not destined to become the follower of the Lubliner "Seer." Instead he became the devoted pupil of the *Yud ha-Kadosh,* R. Jacob Isaac of Pshisha. The *Yud* died in 1814. Thereupon the Kotzker rabbi became an adherent of R. Simhah Bunim of Pshisha.

R. Simhah Bunim it was who gave a new direction to Hassidism. He endeavored to modify its emotionalism and ecstasy by an intellectual orientation, notably by the intensive study of the Talmud and the works of the Maharal of Prag. He definitely abandoned the study of Kabbalah. This daring departure he defended on the ground that "nowadays one can no longer feel competent to discuss it." Another basic principle of his Hassidism was *"to walk humbly with thy Lord!"* (Micah VI, 8), i.e., one must draw the veil over one's piety so as to make it not only unostentatious but completely private. His ideology was on the whole greatly influenced by the works of the Maharal. R. Bunim's active interest extended also to the sphere of practical world affairs. He advocated the purchase of Palestine from the Turkish government, and was thus a harbinger of political Zionism. Upon the latter phase of his activities we shall have occasion to comment below.

To these trends of Rabbi Bunim's teachings, the Kotzker fell spiritual heir. After the death of R. Bunim, a group of his followers chose the Kotzker as their leader. Gradually many hassidim flocked to his banner, among them the versatile scholar, R. Isaac Meir of Ger, who later came to be famous as author of the *Hiddushei ha-Rim.*

Menahem Mendel wielded his hassidic sceptre in Tomashov. His hassidim were not satisfied with merely spending a Sabbath or two at his table, but made his house their second home. There were some who were willing to neglect their families and become the constant companions of the "Rebbe." The rabbi reminded them of their duties to wife and children.

The number of his adherents was not great to begin with and, as a matter of fact, he was not eager to increase his flock. He envisaged an élite of about two to three hundred disciples, each as great and simple as the Besht, each capable of wearing a cabbage leaf instead of a skull-cap on his head and a belt made of straw instead of silk, and each exclaiming withal, *"Unto the Lord belongeth the earth and the fullness thereof."*

However, in the midst of this rich spiritual realm, Menahem Mendel's material poverty was conspicuous. In one of his letters at that period of his life he remarked to his correspondent that he would write more often, if he could afford the cost of postage stamps. But even at that, he aroused the jealousy of the burghers of Tomashov, by his singular gift of inspiring and maintaining the attachment of a distinguished following. With his peace-loving nature, he decided to leave Tomashov, and upon the advice of one of his pupils, took up his abode in Kotzk. Here his fortune turned. The name "Kotzk" began to spread far and wide. Kotzker *shtiblech* (rooms of worship and study) opened everywhere, and were frequented by citizens who ranked high in learning and society.

In 1817 the Kotzker lost his wife, Glickel, who had borne him a son. A year later he married Haya Lifshitz, the Gerer's sister-in-law, who bore him two sons and two daughters. She proved an understanding companion and a worthy successor to Glickel.

But his horizon did not continue unclouded. An able and distinguished follower of his, R. Mordecai Joseph, forsook him and established himself as Rebbe in Tomashov, to which town he attracted a number of hassidim. It was a grievous experience to the Kotzker. Mordecai Joseph succeeded in rallying even a goodly number of the Kotzker followers to him. Did this mean that the Kotzker's personality had lost its old magnetism or that his teachings failed to stand the test of time? Neither was the case. Why then did his influence wane? Because his manner was aloof, and lacked warmth. His doctrine struck fire in the hearts of his listeners, but his retiring manner was often mistaken for coldness. Moreover, this became accentuated with age, until it made almost a recluse of him. It gave anxiety to friends and encouragement to idle tongues.

An old Kotzker hassid describes his experience and that of many of his confreres during their last journeyings to the Rebbe, in the following manner:

"Kotzk defies description. The journey thither was difficult. We even lacked the means of transportation. So a company of us proceeded on foot with flaming enthusiasm and determination that fused all our desires into a single wish: to reach Kotzk and salute the Rebbe. At this happy thought our feet became nimble and our steps ethereal as those of the pilgrims journeying to Jerusalem of old. But upon reaching Kotzk, our fond expectations turned into bitter disappointment. The Rebbe was incommunicative. In the last years of his life he used to seclude himself for long stretches of time during which he received no one. Everyone was overwhelmed with grief and walked about with contrite heart. We came to blame ourselves and made a high resolve to unearth our hidden sins, which, we imagined, stood like a wall between the Rebbe and ourselves. For what else could have prevented him from seeing his flock? At long last God was merciful to us and we were privileged to shake the hand of the Rebbe when departing. The Rabbi transfixed us with his penetrating gaze, and we shrank into nothing before his imposing presence. We left his chamber united in spiritual joy and straightway proceeded to celebrate the occasion with a fitting *Seudah*."

The Kotzker died in 1859. At his funeral the Gerer eulogized him as follows: "The world is not aware of its loss. There is no one to grasp the quality of his genius and the degree of his holiness. *The Tsaddik perisheth and no man layeth it to heart.*" (Isa. 57, 1). Worse than that, there is no one to lay the words of the Tsaddik to our hearts."

Below are a number of the Kotzker's precepts, pithy sayings, and instructive anecdotes. Their salient features are terseness and incisiveness, but upon closer examination of their implications one discovers that the author was a profound thinker and an adroit judge of human nature. Moreover, if hassidic Rebbes were to be counted among the poets, the Kotzker would be their Heine. Like him he possessed rare discernment and the ability of galling his adversary to the quick. For soul-searching depth he certainly had no peer among any of the hassidic leaders at all times.

The first topic herein noted is Zionism. How did it happen that the Kotzker was the harbinger of definite and unmistakable Zionist sentiments and ideas? The story is a long one, but we may put it in a nutshell: He did not forge the chain of these ideas, but he was a strong link in it.

APPENDIX

(A) ZION

Since the Kotzker's utterances are pregnant with meaning and rich in implication and allusion, every one of them calls for some comment.   Moreover, throughout hassidic literature one finds statements partially resembling those of the Kotzker. These should be adequately discussed and evaluated with a view to determining influence, or originality of thought.   But to do justice to such a broad inquiry one would have to go far afield and treat of a diversity of topics which the limitations of the present paper do not warrant.   However, a few of these topics have been chosen for discussion.   It is to be hoped that the reader will realize that the brief sayings of the Kotzker really merit thought.

(1) In the *Kuzari,* Rabbi Judah ha-Levi recounts the glories of Palestine and the virtues of living there: "All roads lead to Palestine, but none from it." "It is better to dwell in the Holy Land, even in a town mostly inhabited by heathens, than abroad in a town chiefly inhabited by Israelites; for he who dwells outside the Holy Land *is compared to him who has no God.*" "To be buried in Palestine is like being buried beneath the altar." These statements, of course, are culled from the Talmud, and need therefore no endorsement from R. Judah ha-Levi. But the great poet has given them the proper setting and prominence in his philosophic work in order to revive his people's lagging interest in their duty of settling in Palestine. The roads to the Holy Land were infested by plunderers and crusaders and all sorts of brigands. The dangerous trip was avoided. The exalted patriot felt it therefore his holy duty to impress upon his brethren the paramount importance of *Mitsvath Yishuv Erets Yisrael* (the commandment to settle in the Holy Land) and to inspire them to fulfill it in spite of lurking danger.

But all these exhortations are addressed to individuals rather than to the nation as a whole. Only solitary pilgrims or families are visualized by R. Judah ha-Levi as journeying to Palestine to be rewarded there with individual bliss. The diaspora or a segment of it, proceeding thither to undergo a collective spiritual rebirth, is not contemplated by the poet. Neither are political elements involved in his call nor, of course, is the regaining of statehood on the part of the Jews thought of by him.

Not so David Kimhi. He comments on Ps. CXLVI, 3: *"Victory is from the Lord,* but He brings it about through the instrumentality of man. And just as He ended the Babylonian exile through the intervention of Cyrus the Great, so will He cause the future redemption by moving the hearts of kings to release the Jews from their lands, as is written, *"And they shall bring all your brethren out of all nations for an offering unto the Lord"* (Isa. LXVI, 20). Here the point of view as well as the scale of action are altogether different. The instrumentality here, though brought to pass by divine means, is entirely political, and it benefits not small groups of individuals but the nation as a whole. The implication is that the Jews who will be allowed by the kings to return to Palestine will establish there *a state of their own* even as in the days of Cyrus the Great.

Similar sentiments have been expressed by other Jewish scholars in the Middle Ages. To quote but three of them:

R. Ezra, the teacher of Nahmanides: *"With the permission of the kings of the nations and with their assistance the Jews will re-establish themselves in Palestine, as it is written, 'And they will bring all your brethren out of all nations . . . to My holy mountain Jerusalem'* (Isa. LXVI, 20). And the Jewish state will continue there forever without interruption."

R. Raphael Molkho: "In the end of days, God will give the inhabitants of Jerusalem one heart, and the city will be desired by all, and many will wish to dwell therein. And when Palestine will have been populated by the Jews, the Holy One, blessed be He, will bring to pass Israel's redemption."

Joseph ibn Kaspi gave the fullest expression to this political idea. In his collection of essays, entitled *Tam ha-Kesef,* he discusses the vicissitudes of empires and foreshadows a philosophy of history much like that of Hegel, viz., that the history of the world is a scene of judgment where one people, to the exclusion of all others, holds the sceptre for a while, until God causes another to rise in its place. Kaspi rightly remarks that this *Weltanschauung* had already been adumbrated in the description of the four beasts in Daniel VII, and explicitly stated in Jer. XXVII, 5-7: *"And I give it* (My great power) *unto whom it seemeth right unto me. And now have I given all these lands into the hand of Nebuchadnezzar . . . and all the nations shall serve him . . . until the time of his own land come."*

Pursuant to this philosophical theory, Joseph ibn Kaspi thus continues: "This land of Palestine we have taken from the Canaanites, for so did God will. The sons of the first beast (the Babylonians, Dan. VII) have taken it from us. The sons of the second beast (the Persians) have taken it from them and returned it to us. The sons of the third beast (the Romans) have again deprived us of it. Afterwards the sons of the fourth beast (the Moslems) have taken it from the sons of the third beast. Often did the French king attempt to conquer it, but did not succeed. He is even now making preparations to invade it, and who knows whether he will accomplish his design. But whatever the result, whether Palestine remains in the hands of the Moslems or succumbs to the Christians, are there no more 'beasts'? Are there no more rises and falls of kingdoms? . . . Indeed why should not God bring things to pass now as He did in the time of Cyrus, the second 'beast,' who made a proclamation throughout his kingdom: *'Whosover there is among you of all His people—the Lord his God be with him—let him go up' (II Chron. XXXVI, 23).* . . . . Is it not possible that God should give us a leader, who, like Moses of old, would plead our cause before the king of Egypt or of Tartary; and these rulers should, as a consequence, grant Palestine to the Jews and allow their Jewish subjects to emigrate thither? Or perhaps a king might arise that will wrest Palestine from the Egyptian ruler, called commonly al-Sultan, making known unto all that we are to return to the Land?"

In view of the above quotations, the Kotzker's remarks in connection with Palestine should not strike us as unique or without precursors in Jewish literature. As a matter of fact, some events in the non-Jewish world of his time undoubtedly prompted his Zionist reflections.

R. Bunim of Pshisha, his teacher, had proposed that Moses Montefiore and other Jewish notables buy Palestine from the Turkish government for the Jewish people. This idea too had a powerful stimulus. Napoleon Bonaparte, in 1799, issued an appeal to the Asiatic and African Jews to enlist in his army, promising "to give them the Holy Land" and "restore ancient Jerusalem to its pristine splendor." It seems that Napoleon's intentions were sincere, for although he regarded the Jews in Europe as only a religious minority, he considered those of Asia and Africa as a nation having indisputable historical claims on Palestine. That the French Jews were mentally prepared for Napoleon's call follows from a letter addressed by a representative French Jew to his co-religionists in 1798, one year before the Bonaparte proclamation. The letter truly foreshadows a Zionist program: "We are more than six millions of people scattered over the face of the earth. . . . Let us employ the means that are in our power to restore us to our country. The moment is propitious, and it is our duty to profit by it."

Indicative of the spirit of the time is also the opinion expressed on this subect by James Bicheno, an English minister and school-master of Newburg, in his pamphlet entitled "Restoration of the Jews, the Crisis of all Nations," (London, 1800). He claims that all portents that accompanied the world war by which humanity was then being ravaged pointed to the early restoration of the Jews to Palestine. More than that, M. Margoliouth in his "Pilgrimage to the Land of My Fathers," reports that in the first half of the 19th century, a Christian gentleman, Mr. Cribbace by name, advocated that the *English* people purchase Palestine for the purpose of reinstating the Jews there as a nation.

The next topic that deserves detailed discussion is that relating to psychoanalysis. In one of his brilliant insights into human behavior and its intricacies, the Kotzker seems to have been quite original. A special study of this topic has appeared elsewhere. The salient features are reproduced in the sequel.

(B) FREUD

No passage as yet has been found in world literature to bear out the precise analysis of Freud in regard to the latent dream content. This is, by and large, true of all major propositions of Freud. However, the theory of repression seems to be the exception to the rule. Says Freud: "The theory of repression I certainly worked out independently. I knew of no influence that directed me in any way to it, and I long considered this to be original until O. Rank showed us a passage in Schopenhauer, where the philosopher is struggling for an explanation for insanity. What he states there concerning the striving against the acceptance of a painful piece of reality agrees so completely with the content of my theory of repression, that once again I must be grateful to my not being well read, for the possibility of making a discovery." The passage to which Freud is referring to is found in Schopenhauer's *"Die Welt als Wille und Vorstellung,"* and was quoted by Otto Rank, a pupil of Freud, in the "Zentralblatt fuer Psychoanalyse" in 1911. I am reproducing only as much of it as is sufficient for our purpose. "The exposition of the origin of madness given in the text will become more comprehensible, if it is remembered how unwillingly we think of things which powerfully injure our interests, wound our pride, or interfere with our wishes; how easily, on the other hand, we unconsciously break away or sneak off from them again; how, on the contrary, agreeable events come into our minds of their own accord, and, if driven way, constantly creep in again, so that we dwell on them for hours together. In that resistance of the will to allowing what is contrary to it to come under the examination of the intellect, lies the place at which madness can break in upon the mind."

If Freud himself considers the above passage as superbly Freudian in spirit, any further corroboration to that effect would be utterly superfluous, except perhaps the regret that Schopenhauer had not substituted for "intellect" and "madness" the corresponding psychoanalytic terms, "the conscious" and "neurosis." The identity of the two theories would then be complete in both form and content.

But the matter does not end here. Yeuschsohn records a statement of the Kotzker which, to all intents and purposes, is as fully Freudian as that of Schopenhauer, and it touches upon the same subject, repression. Once a neighboring rabbi approached him to endorse the candidature of one of the former's hassidim for a rabbinical position in Biala. The Kotzker accused his colleague of favoritism, a policy to be shunned especially when choosing a spiritual head for a community. The Rabbi assured the Kotzker that he was actuated by no bias. However, the latter persisted in his opinion. Soon thereafter, Biala made its choice and the man elected was not that rabbi's protege.

At a later meeting with the rabbi, the Kotzker asked him: "Now tell me the truth! Were you not prejudiced at the time?" "Why do you ask me this," retorted the Rabbi, "If you did not believe me then, you will not believe me now." Replied the Kotzker: "When Eliezer repeats to Rebecca's relatives the question he had asked of Abraham, viz.: *'Peradventure the woman will not go after me?'* (Genesis XXIV, 39) the immortal sage Rashi comments: "Peradventure," *oolie,* is here written without a *waw,* hence it may also read *ailie,* "unto me." Eliezer, having a daughter of his own, has thus subtly suggested to Abraham her availability for Isaac.' Hence, Eliezer had an ulterior motive. (But similarly, *oolie* in the original question (Genesis XXIV, 5) should also have been written without a *waw,* all the more so since the homiletical interpretation would best have fitted the situation in which Eliezer could have hoped for Abraham's favorable reaction to his question). We may parry this stricture with the fact that often, while in pursuit of selfish ends, one is unconscious of them and thinks himself quite irreproachable. It is only after one's self-seeking ambitions have proved abortive that one becomes aware of them, in retrospect. Thus, only after having sensed in Rebecca's home the success of his official mission and the unattainability of his secret hope, Eliezer realized that when he had originally talked to his master, he had been trying to feather his own nest."

Indeed, Schopenhauer's remark as to our disinclination to think of things which hurt our sense of pride or loyalty must also serve as the basis for the Kotzker's characterization of the state of mind of Eliezer, when Abraham instructed him to arrange for the match with his relatives in Mesopotamia. The Kotzker presupposes that it would have been a moral shock to Eliezer to regard himself capable of betraying Abraham's trust, even in thought. *"Every way of a man is right in his own eyes."* (Prov. XXI, 2). One of the ways to facilitate this illusion is to blot out conveniently from the mind what is painful to it. However, when Eliezer's private hopes were shattered, he was in a position to face the situation squarely. He no longer feared his pangs of conscience, for his master's cause was now safe. The repression mechanism has now lost its protective significance and has consequently lifted the veil of secrecy. To be sure, it would have been embarrassing for Eliezer to reflect even on a past culpability, but the mental uneasiness thus created would not be potent enough to force the memory out of consciousness.

(The foregoing discussion is based upon my article "A Psychoanalytic Prefiguration in Hasidic Literaure" in the Bernard Revel Memorial Volume, "Eidenu," New York, 1942).

*　*　*　*

We append a selection of topics, lightly touched upon by the Kotzker but nevertheless very interesting and significant food for thought.

1. "Where does God live? Wherever He is admitted" (Religious Philosophy, 1) is not merely to say that God is found in the hearts of men. The latter is an old and commonplace adage, while the Kotzker's remark has a ring of originality and is quite far-reaching in its implications. Not only does it find God in the hearts of men, but it makes Him take up His abode there by the grace of His creatures. This is quite a picturesque and hyperbolic presentation of the doctrine of free will.

2. "I thank Thee" etc. (Religious Philosophy, 2). It is to be regretted that the Kotzker did not enlarge upon this statement. As it stands, it seems to be tinged with pantheistic forebodings. More than that, it portends kinship with the final stage in the spiritual life of the Mohammedan mystic (Sufi), viz. the goal of union with ultimate Reality. At the end of his journey, the Sufi passes away from himself into everlasting life in God. It is the culmination of the simplifying process by which the soul is gradually separated from all that is foreign to it in order to attain union with the supernatural. Of course, the Kotzker has not given unequivocal expression to this doctrine, but he seems to have vaguely suggested it. At any rate, he was not original in this mystical belief among Jews. Similar ideas had been entertained

before him. It is said of the Lubliner "Seer" that he recited his prayers in trembling and trepidation. R. Meir of Premyshlan used to say of him: "He who wishes to fathom the full significance of *and Isaac trembled very exceedingly'* (Gen. 33), let him observe R. Jacob Isaac (the "Seer") in prayer . . . From this state of exultation he passed on to that of 'pining away of the soul.' " Needless to say that this hassidic ecstasy is quite independent of its Islamic counterpart.

3. In Religious Philosophy 14, the Kotzker presents his views on the fundamental and intrinsic significance of the Mitsvoth. Already in his time the Reform movement, as well as a number of assimilationist and rationalist movements, had begun to attack openly the tenets of traditional Judaism. Their chief target, of course, were the *Mitsvoth Maassiyoth.* The Kotzker does not attempt to disprove the contention of his opponents in a direct or specific manner. In fact, he puts forward his theory as if it were a spontaneous inspiration and not a stand necessitated by the inroads of the German *Aufklaerung* movement upon orthodox Judaism. It is also true that the Kotzker's argument is mystical and metaphysical. But how much more realistic have the rationalists proved to be? Their revolt against beliefs and institutions untried by human reason has not stood the test of time. Neither society nor the individual are activated by rational considerations alone. Rationalism is not tantamount to truth, nor is rational truth ultimate truth. And what is equally important: rationalism has not enriched our lives nor has it made us happy. The Kotzker, on the other hand, views things *sub specie aeternitatis* and by giving levers to the Mitsvoth he has given wings to the truth.

4. "There is holiness in works and there is holiness in thought" (Religious Philosophy, 17). Because of its very brevity, the statement is open to more than one interpretation. A partial elucidation of this statement may possibly be found in the "Histories of the Anchorites." "One of the brethren asked Abba Poemen, saying: 'My body is feeble, and I cannot lead an ascetic life.' Abba Poemen said unto him: 'Canst thou lead the ascetic life *in thy thought,* and not permit it to go with deceit to thy neighbor. . . . If thou art not now able, by reason of weakness, to toil in the labors of

the body as thou didst formerly, toil in *the labors of the soul,*
that is to say, the ruling of the thoughts, which is the ruling of
the mind; if thou art unable to fast from meats, fast from evil
thoughts; and if thou art no longer able, through the weakness of
the body, to stand up and to recite as many Psalms as formerly,
make thy mind to stand up before our Lord, and pray before Him
vigilantly with the prayer which is secret and pure."

(C) Religious Philosophy

1. Where does God live? Wherever He is admitted.

2. Commenting on the Morning Prayer: "I thank Thee
(eternal King for having restored my soul to me in mercy)": Who
is the "I" and who is the "Thee"?

3. *"And they said unto Moses: 'Speak thou with us, and we
will hear: but let not God speak with us, lest we die.' And Moses
said unto the people: 'Fear not; for God is come to prove you,
and that His fear may be before you, that ye sin not.'"* (Exod.
XX, 16-17).
Moses told Israel that fear of the Lord is not to be connected
with fear of death ("least we die") but with fear of sin ("that
ye sin not").

4. The Gerer once said to Alexandrer: "Just as there was
thunder and lightning when the Torah was received on Mount
Sinai, so is there thunder and lightning now when the Torah is
being received in Tomashov (from the Kotzker)".

5. The difference between a Mithnagged (opponent of Hassidism) and a Hassid is that the former fears the *Shulhan Arukh* and
the latter fears the Lord.

6. *"Because thou didst not serve God with joyfulness . . .
therefore shalt thou serve thine enemy"* etc. (Deut XXVIII, 47).
How can the absence of the incidental factor of joy make one
liable to the terrible punishments enumerated in Deut. XXVIII?
It can do so because serving God without joy is the conventional
service, the worship out of habit which does not contemplate God.
Once this deterioration sets in, every mishap is possible, and we

may easily slip into sin. Indeed, one may discover by self-analysis, that one's not having served God with joy ultimately gave rise to many of one's misdeeds.

7. Once on Simhath Torah night, the Kotzker opened the door of his chamber leading to the Beth ha-Midrash and asked all present there: "What is the cause of this joyous celebration?" No one dared answer him. Then he continued: "We know that we are finishing the Torah at present, but we also know that we have hardly begun its study. Because of our deep realization of this exalted paradox we are rejoicing in the Torah."

8. *"Seest thou a man swift in his work? Before kings he may place himself"* (Prov. XXII, 29).

On first thought one might surmise that a Mitzvah is to be fulfilled advisedly and with deliberation. But on second consideration one realizes that this is true only of the preparatory stage of the Mitsvah, i. e. its planning; the Mitsvah itself must be performed rapidly and with alacrity. Similarly the architect must work on his blueprints slowly and carefully, but once his well-laid plans are crystalized they can be executed swiftly and efficiently. Hence it is written *"swift in his work" (mahir bi-melakhto),* not *"swift to undertake his work"* (mahir limelakhto).

9. A grandchild of Rabbi Akiba Eger once asked the Kotzker how he would justify before his renowned grandfather his practice of overstepping the time limit of the morning prayer. Surely before him he would have to defend his action on the basis of Halakha, not on grounds of Hassidism. To this the Kotzker retorted: Maimonides states that the artisan's preliminary sharpening of his tools, even if it takes a whole day, should be credited to him as a regular work by his employer.

10. The Kotzker once remarked to the Rebbe of Alexander that he would do without food, if it were not necessary for him to come in contact with people, for the study of the Torah in itself imbued him with sufficient vitality. He asked the Alexanderer whether he felt likewise.

11. Countless are the miracles that are being wrought for Israel in the exile, but no one perceives and recognizes them, as it

is said *"To Him who doeth great miracles—alone,"* i.e. only God knows them. They are inscribed in Heaven and will someday grow into a volume there.

12. Authors are in the habit of writing introductions to their works. There is a well-known adage: "A book without an introduction is like a body without a soul." God, too, has written an introduction to his work (The Torah), and that is "proper conduct," as is evinced from Lev. Rabbah IX, 3: "The duty of proper conduct (derekh erets) preceded the Torah by twenty-six generations." (The duty of derekh-erets commenced with Adam, while the Torah was not given until the days of Moses.).

13. Noticing his son-in-law glancing at Bedrisi's *Behinoth Olam,* the Kotzker remarked that Bedrisi's belittling of the present world was needless admonition. The intellect knows this anyway. But how can our flesh discover it? By studying the Talmud assiduously and devotedly.

14. Once Friday night after Kiddush, the Kotzker took his seat at the table. A change came over his face; he briskly stretched out his hands, washed, and, having made the benediction over the bread, quoted Exod. XXIV, 7: *"All that the Lord hath spoken we will do and obey."* Then he proceeded to expatiate: There are scientists and philosophers who make inquiries concerning the nature of God, but can grasp no more than their intellectual capacity will allow. Jews, however, have levers—the commandments, whereby they can attain divine knowledge exceeding the reach of their natural endowments and may even equal the angels in power of comprehension. This is the signification of *"we will do and obey."* If we will do, if we will acquire the means of action and make use of the levers, i.e., the Mitsvoth, we will then obey—*nishma,* literally "hear," i.e., hear the music of the spheres, climb the scale of perfection and reach the highest degrees of enlightenment.

15. One should continue in contemplation until he becomes oblivious of himself and feels as if he ceased to exist and that *only* God exists.

16. "It is all one whether a man offers much or little, if only he direct his mind towards Heaven" (Menahot 13, 11).

It follows that he who offers much must also direct his mind towards Heaven.

17. There is holiness in works and there is holiness in thought.

(D) PSYCHOLOGICAL

18. The Kotzker once said: "I have no time to trace my lineage. The Koznitzer Maggid used to say: 'If I were sure that I am the offspring of Abraham, Isaac and Jacob (some Tannaim expressed doubt on this point; see Kiddushin 71b.), I would give my hat a debonair tilt and would, for sheer abandon, dance a *kozatzke* in the middle of the market-place. But, after all, I cannot help feeling that I *am* a descendent of Abraham, Isaac and Jacob, (and must therefore observe decorum).' "

19. *"And the people trembled and stood far off . . . but Moses drew near unto the thick darkness where God was"* (Exod. XX, 15-18).

No matter how much one may "shake" during prayer, he may still stand far removed from God. It is the inner emotion that counts. Moses approached the divine presence without any outward sign of excitation.

20. The Kotzker once intimated to his brother-in-law, Rabbi Isaac Meir of Ger, his misgivings about the validity of his marriage to the latter's sister-in-law: No doubt, she must have thought that she was marrying a Rabbi (in the ordinary sense), and I am not a Rabbi. To this R. Isaac Meir replied that it really made no difference to her whether he was actually a rabbi or not. What mattered to her was the fact that he was considered as such. And—significantly added Rabbi Isaac Meir—the world will never regard and designate you as the Rabbi of Kotzk.

21. The Kotzker used to say that he did not really belong to his generation but to a period preceding the destruction of the first temple, and that his belated appearance in this world was for the sole purpose of expounding the distinction between holiness and profanity.

22. The Rabbi of Sohatchov had a watch of which he was very fond because by means of it he could accurately apportion his time between study and prayer. But after awhile its works broke down. The Sohatchover prayed to God and the watch began to move again. It then occurred to him to apply the same procedure to his Talmudic studies; so whenever he grappled with a difficult topic he implored God to facilitate his understanding of it. The Kotzker's conviction, however, was that an intricate Talmudic argument could only be grasped by a pure intellectual effort. He therefore expressed his fear lest the Sohatchover's misapplication of prayer injure his intellectual powers.

23. *"Create unto me a clean heart, O God"* (Ps. LI, 12).

This means that there are also hearts that are unclean, and that the Psalmist himself is aware of his shortcomings and implores God to supply his deficiencies. It follows, therefore, that he who thinks that he is perfect is decidedly impure.

24. The Holy One, blessed be He, said to Israel: "My sons, present to me an opening of repentance no bigger than the eye of a needle, and I will widen it into openings through which wagons and carriages can pass." (Shir ha-Shirim Rabba to v. 2 of ch. 5).

This does not mean that man generally does or is somehow encouraged to be less repentant than he is capable of being. One must repent to the full extent of the consciousness of his guilt. What the Midrash wants to convey is that the self-healing powers which heaven, by way of reward, subsequently adds to the awakened conscience are ever so much greater than those it originally possessed.

25. There is an evil force (*Kelippoth*) that impels man to engage in the study of the Torah with muddled reasoning and clouded perception. One must be on his guard against it.

26. When the Gerer was offered a Rabbinic position in Kutno, he consulted the Kotzker about this matter. The latter advised him not to leave Warsaw. "What does Warsaw benefit from me?" asked the Gerer. "Even if its people should do no more than pass by the house you live in, they would be amply rewarded," rejoined the Kotzker.

27. *"And we were in our own sight as grasshoppers, and so we were in their sight"* (Numb. XIII, 33).

"And we were in our own sight as grasshoppers" is indeed an apprehension that may have seriously dejected the spirit of the spies, but *"and so we were in their sight"* is a speculative figment that should not have merited their immediate concern.

28. "Wherein did the spies sin? Did they not bring back a true report, as evidenced from Numb. XIV, 17-29? However, the word Emeth ("truth") does not mean literal truth, but the very core of truth. The most that can be said of a man who adheres to formal truth is that he is not a liar, but it cannot be said of him that he is a man of truth. A seeker after truth is he who, when confronted with a situation that on the surface seems to be at variance with the will of God, is not dismayed by appearances, but fearlessly pursues the investigation of the truth to its utmost limits. Indeed, the ten spies sinned in that they refused to fathom the true meaning of the words of God, as did Joshua and Caleb.

29. No matter where one's fate has driven him, to Kotzk he must come to set his soul aright.

30. A hassid once complained to the Kotzker of his constant sufferings and tribulations. Thereupon the latter pointed out to him, by way of illustration, the law that states that the gulping down of the bitter herbs falls short of the obligation of eating them on Passover night. To fulfill one's duty, one must thoroughly chew them before he swallows them. Only he who digests well his bitter experiences may truly claim that he had tasted them.

31. Once a hassid sought his advice in regard to a matrimonial match and pressed him for an immediate answer. The Kotzker replied: Do you really think that whenever presented with a problem, the Rebbe forthwith ascends to heaven, opens a book there, turns to page so and so and finds the correct answer immediately? How brazen would such conduct be on the part of a Rebbe! The actual process is altogether different, and this is how it may roughly be described. When the Rebbe is approached with a problem, he reacts to it like an ordinary mortal: He be-

comes conceited and thinks that he was called upon to solve it because he is a sage and a pundit. But pride *blunts* the powers of the intellect, and the Rebbe must now make a serious effort to *conquer* the advance of self-flattery. Having thus coaxed himself into humility, he must next feel sure that his rendered opinion is in accordance with justice in general and the Torah in particular. Having satisfied all these conditions, the Rebbe's advice is likely to prove beneficial.

32. As is well known, R. Makhir, the author of the book *Avkath Rokhel,* was extravagant in recounting in it the horrors that will befall mankind before the coming of the Messiah. The Kotzker remarked: The author of *Avkath Rokhel* is under obligation to do the will of God, but God is not obligated to do the will of the author of *Avkath Rokhel.*

33. Once he said to a group of youths: I wish you did not sin, not so much because sin is objectionable, but rather that you could not find time for it.

34. Pride in a man chiefly rears its head after his carnal passions have begun to decline.

35. The greatest affliction for the body is the observance of the Torah.

36. "If *that* ugly one (the tempter) meets you, drag him to the house of study" (Kiddushin 30b).

Why is the tempter referred to as "that ugly one" rather than "the ugly one"? Because there is also "an ugly one" in the house of study against whom one must be on guard.

37. In order to rid a certain town of the ravages of an epidemic, the Kotzker advised its Rabbi to hold a scholarly disquisition in the synagogue for that purpose.

38. One should eat in his youth and sleep in his grave, but as for sadness there is no time or place for it.

39. A hassid without a belt is like a barrel without a hoop.

40. *"And all the people perceived the thunderings"* (when the Torah was given) (Exod. XXX, 15).

The masses perceive only the external aspect of things.

41. "When Solomon instituted *erubin* and the washing of the hands, a Heavenly Voice came forth and declared: '*My son, if thy heart be wise, my heart shall be glad, even mine*' " (Prov. XXII, 15).

This statement in Shabbat 14b is interpreted by the Kotzker as follows: *Erubin* really means "mingling," i. e. mingling with the world, whereas "washing of the hands" betokens washing one's hands of the world and being severed from it. To integrate one's personality one must reconcile these two conflicting forces within himself. It is easy for a *batlan,* whiling away his time before the Beth ha-Midrash stove, to renounce worldly affairs, but it was not so easy for Solomon, who headed an empire. But Solomon, while richly enjoying the pleasures of this world, nevertheless did not become contaminated by their impurities. To effect such a felicitous union of seemingly irreconcilable tendencies one must be endowed with great wisdom. This is the purport of the statement in Shabbat 14b, which is an unmistakable allusion to Solomon's consummate skill in the art of living.

SAMSON RAPHAEL HIRSCH

By Isaac Breuer

SAMSON RAPHAEL HIRSCH

By Isaac Breuer

"Thou hast beset me behind and before and laid Thine hand upon me!" (Ps. CXXXIX, 5).

In this one sentence, the royal psalmist, looking back upon his own life, cast light upon the secret of every great historical personality. His sphere of influence moves within the completely imaginary space of time between the past which is no more and the future which has not yet come; and it is only God's receptive, protective and supporting hand which causes his influence to loosen up the rigidity of the past and to give creative impetus to the formless future.

I

A great personality, placed between past and future, can be appraised historically only in connection with past and future and not merely as an individual. It is not even important what idea he has of himself or what his contemporaries think of him. Important is only that part of his achievement, caught in God's directing hand, which converts it into a historic one, reviving in a certain sense the historical past and anticipating the historical future. Every great personality is a guide to history—unravelling the twisted paths of the past and at the same time pointing the way into virgin land.

If this is true of all great personalities, it is particularly true of the great personalities of the Jewish people. If history is understood as the absolute oblivion of the fictitious present in favour of the past and the future, then the Jewish, more than any other people, is the people of history. It is only unhistoric man who lives in the present. Other nations may seclude themselves from history and dwell comfortably in their present, but for the Jewish people in the last two thousand years the present has signi-

fied only—Galuth. How has the Jewish people managed to bear
two thousand years of Galuth? Only because it is so completely
the people of history, the people of the history of God's word;
and because the word of God has declared the Galuth to be
nought but a transition from the happy past to a happier future.

Countless are the Jewish men who have devoted the whole
strength of their lives to this divine message. Every true thought
of theirs is stored up in God's protecting hand, for they have
enriched the history of the divine word. But only very few
personalities have been divinely appointed in the Galuth, not
only to enrich the history of God's word but further to give
that history a new impulse summoning the past to new life and
announcing the future and thus creating new links between
past and future, destined, in the end, to bring the redemption
of the Jewish people nearer to fulfillment.

Rabbi Samson Raphael Hirsch of blessed memory was such an
intrinsically historic personality constrained between past and
future, but by special divine privilege empowered to envisage the
past as a living future and the future as a living reality, and thus
to point out to the Jewish people the way to the past which is
likewise the way to the future.

II

Every great historic personality is a revolutionary figure. By
virtue of his historical mission he stands out in some measure
from his contemporaries; the more significant the mission, the
more pronounced the distinction which is inherited by his followers until the mission is achieved, when the revolutionary becomes
accepted. But, with the Jewish people, revolution takes a course
different from that which it takes in other nations.

Every national revolution involves a breach of law. The law
of the nations is not everlasting; it is a product of the prevailing
opinion on the forms of human relationships. These opinions
change quicker than the law, once fixed, can change, so that
gradually a cleavage arises between the opinions and the law.
If this cleavage is not closed or at least narrowed in time by suitable adjustment of the law, there will develop an ever-increasing
tension between the law as it is and the law which represents cur-

rent opinions; this will finally lead to an upheaval which will bring about a change of law by more or less pronounced force.

But the law of the Jewish people is not the expression of public opinion on human relationships but rather the expression of God's command with regard to His relationship to the Jewish nation. There is no such thing as revolution against the Torah just as there can be no revolution against the law of nature. Jewish history is the history of the people of God's word, and every revolt against God's word is a breach of law and cannot be legitimized by any fact or any lapse of time. How then can revolutionaries figure in the Jewish nation without being branded as breakers of the law in the history of God's word?

From the days of Jeroboam I, down to Geiger and Philippson, the Jewish nation has had enough revolutionaries. Jewish history, as the history of God's word, commemorates them as absolute law-breakers, sinful men who led on many others to sin. But does Jewish history recognize any legitimate revolutionaries?

It does. These are the few great historical personalities, selected by God to give new and powerful impetus to His word. But Jewish revolutionaries, within the history of God's word, exert an influence quite different from that of the revolutionaries of the other nations of the earth. When, in the course of time, the conditions of human relationship undergo considerable change, the revolutionaries of the other nations turn against the law which is no longer in accord with these conditions; they break it down with iron fists and put up new laws in its place.

But the revolutionaries of the law-abiding Jewish people do not turn against God's law but against conditions. When, in the course of time, the conditions of Judeo-human relations suffer such essential alteration that they threaten to go beyond the all-embracing dominion of God's word, the legitimate revolutionaries arise and break the tension between God's word and prevailing conditions; they do so not by any refutation of God's word but by mastering, with incomparable energy, the new conditions. In complete rupture with prevailing opinion they vindicate the sovereignty of God's word over the new tendencies which they mould, reform, adjust and even break up if necessary, until they fit into the Torah, affording new fuel for the eternal divine flame. God's word, ever sovereign, ever immutable, bestows on its legitimate revolutionary the strength of youth with which He has endowed him to reveal a new message for the new conditions. No revolutionary of God's word has arisen who has not likewise enriched the history of God's word.

Such revolutionaries were, for instance, the founders of Hassidism. Such a revolutionary was also Rabbi Hirsch of blessed memory.

The sainted Rav of Aschaffenburg once drew a parallel between Hassidism and Rabbi Hirsch. They found themselves in what was fundamentally the same situation. These revolutionaries of the divine precept in both cases adapted the new conditions to the ancient word of God.

III

The close of the eighteenth and the opening of the nineteenth centuries brought astonishing new facts to light. The renaissance of individuality and the boundless right of the individual had already been proclaimed. But it was the French Revolution and its forerunners which spread the political and cultural ideal of liberalism among the masses. The individual threw off the fetters of custom and recognized solely— for purposes of orientation—the issues of a humanity which had little historical connection in thought or feeling. In the realm of economics, liberalism initiated the rule of capitalism, which invested the fight for existence with hitherto undreamt-of urgency and made earning a living the main object of life. For the first time, science was invested with the right of free research, making human intellect the supreme law-giver of the universe. At the same time, the ghetto walls in Western Europe collapsed to the thrust of liberalism and the new tendencies swept unrestrained over the *Judengasse*.

Each of these new tendencies presented a dangerous antagonism to the divine precept. According to the latter, the personality of the individual is not a gift but a responsibility; humanity is only the first step towards the higher concept of the subservience to God of the individual as well as the nations. Capitalism as life's directive is absolute idolatry; science with the human mind

ruling it, is primarily a means to human domination of the earth—
but in no way is it, unguided, the final source of truth.

No one realized the conflict between the new tendencies and
the divine precept better than Moses Mendelssohn. But this
same Moses was neither a legitimate nor an illegitimate revolutionary. He was only a puny evolutionary who valiantly assisted
in spreading the new tendencies among his people in the secret
hope that the divine precept would gradually adapt itself to them.
The road leads straight from him to the illegitimate revolutionaries
of Reform who broke the divine precept in order to make it
adaptable to the new conditions.

With sure instinct the old rabbis sensed the conflict. They did
not hesitate for one moment to renounce the worldly advantages of
an emancipation if it was to be won only at the expense of the
divine precept. But not only did they cling with the whole
strength of their love to the divine precept itself, but also, with
the tragic persistence of despair, to the old conditions now fading
away with frightening inevitability, which in centuries of practice
had become absolutely adapted to the divine precept and its
demands; thus they intensified unbearably the tension between the
divine precept and the unrestrained invasion of the new conditions
until the man in the street completely identified the divine precept
with the old way of life—until the decline of the latter almost
brought about the decline of the divine precept itself. It was then
that Rabbi Hirsch stood forth as the legitimate revolutionary of
the divine precept.

IV

Rabbi Hirsch is usually regarded as the representative and protagonist of a theoretical principle. Much has been written and said
in recent times about *Torah im Derekh Erets.** People who
shunned the leap into orthodoxy for fear of losing their sight and
their hearing and who nevertheless failed to use their ears to
listen sufficiently to the voice of the Torah or their eyes to read

---

*The original meaning is undoubtedly, "*Torah together with a wordly
occupation* (Torah and Work)" or "Torah and the Way of the Land, the
Way of Life." But it has also been interpreted as "The combination of
Judaism and Modern (Western) Culture." The Fall of Western culture
provoked a revolt against the combination.—Ed.

of the writings of Rabbi Hirsch, yet had the courage to accuse him pedantically of having somewhat misrepresented the term Derekh Erets in a well-known Mishnah. Discussion of this principle never ceases even in more informed circles and persists deep down into the ranks of orthodoxy, a continuous source of the most serious misunderstandings.

The fact that Rabbi Hirsch himself never actually set forth any thorough presentation or justification of the theory, nor even developed the theoretical aspect of his principles in any of the works he intended for posterity, should give us food for thought. We can only determine his purpose from the whole tendency of his writings, from the force of his educative actions, and the general aspect of the life he led in the sight of the world.

Revolutionaries are never theoreticians, least of all the legitimate revolutionaries of the divine precept. The more unflinching their determination not to sacrifice a tittle of that precept, the more energetic their rally to action. For the revolutionary act is not formed on the spur of the divine precept but on that of the actual facts; and it is not theory but history which offers the only possible justification of this act.

The greatness of Rabbi Hirsch lies not in his pronouncement of a new or a resurrected doctrine, but in his almost prophetic historical vision which has been magnificently confirmed long after his death, actually in our own days and will continue to be so in the days to come; his greatness lies in the immeasurable reverence and love he had for God, in the supreme trust he had in our wise teachers who gave him courage and strength not only to withstand the terrible dangers which his historical perception entailed, but also, despite the danger, to make this historical perception the pivot of his thought and action. It was in this way that he became the guiding hand of the Jewish people pointing out the right road of historical development.

Rabbi Hirsch's fight was not for balance and not for reconcilement, not for synthesis and certainly not for parallel power, but for domination—for the true and absolute domination of the divine precept over the new tendencies. The divine precept can countenance no collateral rule and certainly no toleration. Like a true revolutionary he seized on the liberal-minded individual, on

the liberal ideal of humanity, the liberal capitalistic money-earn-
ing profession and finally on the human mind revelling in the
liberal doctrine and led them all to the flaming fire of the Torah
that they might find in it purification, and if needs be, destruction.
He broke the almost unendurable tension between the divine
precept and the new era which had fallen upon West-European
Jewry. As a true revolutionary of the divine precept descending
into the arena of the new era armed with the divine precept itself,
he broke it up into its component parts, forming and moulding
them, until they were ready to be brought to the fire as worthy
fuel of the divine precept. The historical achievement of his life
for his contemporaries was the proclamation of the dominion of
the Torah over the new era.

Rabbi Hirsch's epigones quoted the principle "Torah im
Derekh Erets" more frequently than the master himself. As for
him, he drew on it mainly for the obvious confirmation of the
fact—so important if the Torah is to become the law of life for
the people—that the aim and end of the Torah should not be
confined to the house of learning, but that it should be brought
into contact with and applied to the prevailing conditions of life.
The Torah is ever-enduring and immutable; but Derekh Erets is
ever-changing and mutable. The revolutionary aspect of Rabbi
Hirsch's life teaching is not the coordination of Torah and Derekh
Erets; the Torah has at all times been intimately connected with
the life for which it has had to constitute the law   There has never
been a time when Derekh Erets has not been regarded as the
province in which the Torah asserts itself. It is the prerequisite
of the Torah; it is only because of the existence of Derekh Erets
that man needs a Torah to prevail over it. Derekh Erets is indeed
no invention of Hirsch's nor can he claim to have originated the
idea that there exists an interrelation between Torah and the prevailing Derekh Erets. What was revolutionary about Rabbi
Hirsch was the incomparable courage he displayed in detecting the
dwindling of one Derekh Erets, and in grasping a new one with
giant's strength, dragging it up to the throne of judgment which is
the Torah. He was revolutionary in that he prevailed over the
supreme power of a centuries-old custom which conceived of the
Torah only in connection with a definite kind of Derekh Erets;

he was revolutionary in that with the foresight of a genius he freed the Torah from the strangling hold of an outlived Derekh Erets and affirmed a new, vital and prevailing Derekh Erets to be a possible setting for the Torah; at the same time imposing on this new setting the absolute and supreme domination of the Torah with a strictness which should actually have precluded any misunderstanding as to the true nature of his revolutionary act.

The key to the understanding of the historical importance of Rabbi Hirsch is not to be sought in his relation to the so-called *hitsoniuth* (outside world, practical advantages, socio-political realities)—a problem nearly as old as the history of the Jewish nation itself. Traffic with hitsoniuth for its own sake was absolutely condemned by him.

Revolutionary as his action was, it seemed to him all the less to be in need of a far-fetched halakhic justification. He found in the eternity of the divine precept his absolute conviction that it could in no way be bound to a *definite* Derekh Erets, for that had come into being in the course of time and was therefore variable. On the other hand he also interdicted any doubt as to whether the divine precept was equal to the new Derekh Erets. In the strength of this conviction he assumed the right of letting the old Derekh Erets go and of accepting the new one as the object of the supremacy of the Torah. But his attitude to the new Derekh Erets—the way in which he brought it into relation with the primacy of Torah—signified ultimately the introduction of a new form of the Jewish way of life, the deepest significance of which is only to be grasped from the historic approach of Rabbi Hirsch. His own contemporaries were scarcely in a position to realize this significance. We of today should be able to do so; the greatest significance of Rabbi Hirsch's achievement was the reconducting of the Jewish people into its own history—the aim of which is no other than the reestablishment of the Divine State.

V

Only once did Rabbi Hirsch refer, ex cathedra as it were, to the historical vision to which he dedicated himself for the duration of his life.

He must have had this historic vision in early life, for the reference occurs in the "19 Letters." Woe to our youth if these "Letters" no longer convey their message! Woe to our youth if their only response to the glow which emanates from these papers is a contemptuous criticism of their style!

The earlier centuries of the Galuth had no connection apparent to the human eye with Jewish national history, the immutable aim of which has always been the re-establishment of the Divine State (*"Gottesstaat"*) round the sanctuary of the law on Zion, as the centre according to the Divine promise. The Divine State—that is the spread of the rule of the Torah over the complexity of humanity itself which finds its highest expression of development in the national state, in the relation of the Temple-crowned Zion to Jerusalem, the seat of human intercourse. Zion and Jerusalem —the supreme Torah and the supremely dominated Derekh Erets. But the Derekh Erets of the early times of the Galuth, even of the last century before Rabbi Hirsch, bore little resemblance to the Derekh Erets of Jerusalem past and future. The Torah could exert its influence only over a very small section of human activity. No one has shown a deeper understanding of our dead ancestors in the ghetto than Rabbi Hirsch and no one has honoured their memory in more moving terms. He regarded their era as the era of triumph for the Torah that pervaded even the life of the pariah with sunshine and joy and bestowed upon him the deepest piety and a halo of scholarship. True, Jewish national history as such appeared at a standstill; its whole essence seemed to be summed up in suffering and waiting. It was an epoch of absolute passivity in Jewish national history.

And now Rabbi Hirsch saw the walls of the ghetto falling, the spirit of humanity and justice growing stronger and stronger among the nations—the lasting merit indeed of the liberalism of the French Revolution. He saw a new Derekh Erets growing up among the Jews of Western Europe which, although it added great complications, also immeasurably enriched the scope of their life. He was filled with the vision of ancient Zion sovereign over Jerusalem—of the coming Zion sovereign over Jerusalem; and out of such a past and such a future he conceived the image of the new Jewish individual facing the new epoch of Jewish na-

tional history—deriving strength for future action from the re-
suscitated national past, and able in the many-sidedness of the
new Derekh Erets under the sole rule of the Divine precept,
as citizen of the coming Divine State, to lay Jerusalem at the feet
of Zion.   The history of the Jewish nation in the Galuth is
the history of the divine precept in the Galuth; it is the history
of the future Divine State, projected as an actuality in every
present.   If a national Jew is one who is conscious of being
a citizen of the Divine State and who consciously devotes his
life work to its furtherance, then Rabbi Hirsch may be said to
be the first National Jew of modern times.   Long before Theodore
Herzl dreamt his false dream of the *Judenstaat,* Rabbi Hirsch
proclaimed the eternally true vision of the Divine State.   It was
solely with a view to this future Divine State, with Zion dominat-
ing Yerushalayim, that he joyfully set himself the immense task of
overcoming the new Derekh Erets through the immutable divine
precept.   This new Derekh Erets was for him in truth that of
the future Erets Yisrael.   To build up the Jewish nation for the
future Erets Yisrael; to win over for it the great devotees of the
Torah who are versed in the manifold aspects of life, in order
to mould them in the form of the Torah; to foster in businessmen, physicians, scientists, in all the intellectual forces, supreme
loyalty to the Torah; all this was the most profound historical
meaning of Rabbi Hirsch's life work for the future.

His greatest work—the commentary on the Pentateuch—is
completely under the banner of the coming Divine State.   Thus the
way he outlines the part played by the divine precept in the creation;
his description of the magnificent concept of the Sabbath in its
universal-human sanctity; the way he then goes deep into universal-
human history, seeing in Adam's catastrophe the free choice of one
of the two possible historical trends; the way he traces the beginnings of civilization, finding in them the origins of the three
cultural developments which mark the history of humanity in
the lives of Noah's sons after the flood, and interpreting the
prophetic words of the father as divining genius; the way he
conceives the building of the tower of Babel, regarding it as the
establishing of usurped state sovereignty, by which the divine precept is withdrawn from universal history only to set up against the

assumed sovereignty of the states, the Torah state of Divine
sovereignty through the call of the patriarchs; how he then proceeds
to describe with great insight the characteristics of the patriarchs,
conveying a lucid picture of the way God establishes and cares for
the eternal nation; how with incomparable fervour, he describes
the characteristic traits of the civil law of the Divine State,
bringing into actual prominence only those of its institutions
which most Zionist and liberal assimilationists would like to
ignore—the sanctuary and its appurtenances, the sacrificial service,
the doctrine of purity and impurity; how he interprets the right
of the individual and the social law of the Divine State (the
latter almost as a program for the imminent upbuilding of the
nation in Erets Yisrael); and how finally, after describing the
journeys in the desert with their manifold episodes, he cites
the parting words of our teacher Moses at the end of which he
joins him in the hymn of rejoicing over the eternity of the Jewish
nation and the eternity of the divine precept within the Jewish
nation. For anyone who has read, studied and re-studied this
imperishable work, Rabbi Hirsch must appear indeed as the great
guide of the Jewish nation in its national history, as the great
proclaimer of that Divine State of the future as the goal of this
national history, as the great exhorter of the Jewish nation to
return in its active national history to the upbuilding of the Jewish
people in order to prepare the nation for its reunion with the
Jewish land in the Divine State.

Indeed God laid upon Rabbi Hirsch the hand which steers history—the hand which comprehends, preserves and fashions anew.

VI

To come back to the Jewish national history of the development
of the Divine State; to come back to the manifold aspects of the
modern Derekh Erets dominated by the preparedness of the Jewish
people for a Jerusalem paying homage to Zion. Back to Jewish
national history with the universal glorification of God's name in
every nook and corner of the earth, as ordained by the divine
precept! Has evolution since the death of Rabbi Hirsch out-

stripped his conception or has it not rather invested it with more burning actuality than ever before?

With what disastrous blindness is the Jewish world smitten, even right down to the ranks of the orthodox!

Only fools could believe that the great revolutionary, who freed the divine precept from the strangling hold of a moribund Derekh Erets, performed this heroic task only to fetter the divine precept, for better or worse and for all eternity, with another Derekh Erets such as the German one of his own generation. Only fools could believe that Rabbi Hirsch chose the German Derekh Erets of his own generation for its own sake and that he presented it to a certain extent as the second absolute beside the absolute of the divine precept. He who thinks thus and who preaches thus, must have made Rabbi Hirsch's acquaintance in a very draughty corner. This voice is indeed not that of Rabbi Hirsch but of his own chronic hoarseness. The great achievement of Rabbi Hirsch for his contemporaries was just this emancipation of the divine precept from a centuries-old Derekh Erets and his claim that the eternally immutable divine precept must be ready to face any Derekh Erets which Providence produces in the course of history and imposes on the body of the Jewish people. Anyone who views the latest events in Germany as marking the collapse of Rabbi Hirsch's philosophy has not the faintest idea of his historical importance!

The essential point is this: Was Rabbi Hirsch right to drop the Derekh Erets of the Western Europe of the former century and thus bring the new Derekh Erets face to face with the divine precept? Was he right in inaugurating a new epoch of Jewish Galuth history, summoning us to return to the dynamic national history of the divine precept and the Divine State, and undertake the tremendous task of preparing the Jewish national body for the coming Divine State? Shaken to our depths, we of today can answer the question. The direct progress towards the Divine State prophetically foreseen by Rabbi Hirsch—the last opposition of the future Zion and the future Jerusalem, likewise prophetically foretold by Rabbi Hirsch, together with the inevitable insignificance of the Jewish people in the historical tribune of the nations, where God's name is supposed to be publicly glorified—in infinite tribulation we of today have seen all these things come to pass as a terrifying reality! Sooner than Rabbi Hirsch himself foresaw, the time has come when the modern Derekh Erets, powerfully proclaimed in the name of the divine precept by Rabbi Hirsch, has been revealed as the Derekh Erets of Erets Yisrael. At that time, there were in Germany the merest beginnings of the upbuilding of the Jewish nation for the coming Zion-dominated Jerusalem. And already in our own time in Erets Yisrael the strife between the divine precept of Zion and the rapidly growing realities of life in Jerusalem is being waged. Scarcely were the eyes of the great teacher closed when his rally to the Divine State was closely followed by the rally to the Jewish state; it is indeed only through this rally to the Jewish state in its diametric opposition to the rally to the Divine State that the full significance of Rabbi Hirsch's achievement has been revealed to us, his followers. After the rally to the meta-historic, came the rally to the pseudo-historic—the legitimate revolutionary followed by the illegitimate. Either an ascent to the meta-historical or a descent to the national-historical: there is no third way. At last our Galuth history has been converted from an epic to a drama. It goes forward and can not be halted. If Rabbi Hirsch prevails, the Divine State will wave the palm of victory over the Zion-dominated Jerusalem. If Rabbi Hirsch should not prevail—the Divine State will only be achieved as an act of grace. There is no third way. Providence has not vouchsafed us the leisure required for the gradual grooming of the Jewish people in the Galuth to meet the needs of the coming Divine State, such as Rabbi Hirsch himself hoped for. Lacking insight into the meta-historic nature of the Jewish people and completely absorbed in his purely political ethos, Herzl unfurled the flag of a Jerusalem completely separated from the traditional sanctuary of Zion. Long before there was a Jewish national Derekh Erets impregnated with and dominated by the divine precept, long before our people were ready to be Zion's Jerusalem, Hirsch's shrill summons of a return to Jerusalem had rung out. If Providence has provided this summons with historic results, if it has brought into being the national home at least in the form of a trial start, it has therewith set the Jewish people a task of such immeasurable magnitude that we would have to despair of its achievement had not Providence given us Rabbi Hirsch before Herzl! Rabbi Hirsch alone can prevail over Herzl.

Our Zionist opponents sense this with the sure instinct which only an opponent has. The divine precept confined to the precincts of the Beth ha-Midrash, limited in its influence to the miserable Derekh Erets of past centuries, which often only exists because it has not strength enough to die—presents no danger for them. Not so the divine precept of the Beth ha-Midrash extending a ruler's hand over a national life which harmoniously releases human powers—the divine precept of Zion—streaming powerfully through the animated streets of Jerusalem! Alas, Rabbi Hirsch's historic vision does not penetrate their minds, because spiritually they are totally and incurably assimilated. Foolish is the belief that it is sufficient to speak and to write Hebrew in order to ward off assimilation; all too frequently do the notorious asses' ears of European thought and approach betray the lion's skin of "Ivrith." The real danger for secular Zionism is a Judaism which consciously re-invigorates itself through Rabbi Hirsch.

Divine State or Jewish state—this overwhelming either-or which drags us all willy-nilly into the vortex of history, which from the historical viewpoint proves Herzl, in the sense of an antinomy, to be the greatest abettor of Rabbi Hirsch, bestows on Rabbi Hirsch, as the guide of our latest historic advance, the most incredible actuality. It was the essence of his spirit that through the agency of Agudath Yisrael saved the orthodox masses. It is the essence of his spirit which will build up Jerusalem for Zion.

We face a great task—the translation into Hebrew of Rabbi Hirsch's writings so that he may be able to speak directly to the Jewish people, especially to the people of the future Jerusalem. This translation will prove Rabbi Hirsch to be the powerful Jewish link between the Jewish past and the Jewish future. Just as in former times Rabbi Hirsch ennobled the German language with his writings, so the translation of his work will permeate modern "Ivrith" with its sanctity. And just as once the writing of Rabbi Hirsch in its German version saved the Jewry of Western

Europe and exerted and still exerts an incredible influence far
into the East, so may his writings in their Hebrew dress proclaim
his victory in Erets Yisrael and help to bring about the formation
here of the coming Divine State of Erets Yisrael as—Erets Tsevi!
(Tsevi meaning both "glory" and "Hirsch").

SELIGMANN BAER BAMBERGER

By M. L. Bamberger

SELIGMANN BAER BAMBERGER

By M. L. Bamberger

I

The first half of the nineteenth century saw the so-called "Reform" Movement rather firmly established within German Jewry.[1] In the large Kehilloth, such as Berlin, Hamburg, Frankfurt, Breslau, the orthodox elements were on the defensive, losing more and more ground, desperately struggling not to be overcome by the rapid advance of those who were fanatically bent on destroying Jewry and Judaism or, at least, fundamentally changing them both, by assimilation and secularization. If there was to be any hope for the survival of the Jewish way of life, two developments had to be stopped quickly: the disappearance of traditional institutions and of Traditionalism as the leading power in the Kehilloth, and the growth of individual faithlessness to Torah in theory and practice, going hand in hand with a vast decrease of Torah-study.

As so often in Jewish history, the imminent danger brought to the forefront great leaders, men deeply rooted in *Torah and Yirath Shamayim* (Reverence), who combined the clear insight into the requirements of the hour with intellectual equipment and enthusiasm for translating conviction into action. They proved able to stop the religious downfall, to bolt the door before the stormy advance of the Reform and even to reconquer lost positions. Convinced of the eternal truth of what they were teaching, they inspired confidence in the ideals of the Torah and defended them successfully against the spirit of the "New Era" which had upset the religious balance of so many. Their activities were chiefly directed towards the strengthening of their own

[1]As sources were used: Nathan Bamberger, *Rabbiner Seligmann Baer Bamberger,* Wuerzburg 1897 (appendix to Annual Report 1896/7 of the Isr. Lehrerbildungsanstalt zu Wuerzburg).
M. Auerbach, *Seligmann Baer,* in "Jeschurun," 1928, pp. 524, 538; the works of S. B. Bamberger himself, and the other literature mentioned in this article.

ranks. They recreated the spiritual foundation of traditional
Judaism, they spread Torah-knowledge and Torah-observance, and
established urgently needed institutions.

At that time, there still existed in Bavaria, the southern part
of Germany, a strong bulwark of orthodox Judaism, especially in
the province of Unterfranken. The followers of Reform tried,
not always unsuccessfully, to gain the upper hand in the larger
Kehilloth of Bavaria, such as Munich, Fuerth, and Wuerzburg.
The majority of the Jews, however, lived in the smaller towns
and in the villages, and there, in a tranquil atmosphere, remained
faithful to the old tradition. Here were still to be found many
Baalei-battim (laymen) who possessed a profound knowledge of
Torah, here were still alive simple, deeply rooted *Yirath Shamayim*
and complete adherence to the spirit and letter of the Shulhan
Arukh; here lived still a great number of personalities of the old
type, sincere, strong, and unbroken in spirit. In such surroundings stood the cradle of Seligmann Baer Bamberger, the "Wuerzburger Rav," who was destined to become one of the great leaders
of German Orthodoxy in the middle of the nineteenth century.

Bamberger was born on the 5th of Heshvan 5568—(the 6th
of November 1807), in the village of Wiesenbronn. His father,
Simhah, by profession a small business man, a modest and deeply
religious man, was generally beloved for his honesty and humaneness. His mother, Judith, was a daughter of the great Talmudist, R. Moses Loeb Hatzfeld, the "Medinah Rav" (district rabbi)
of Heidingfeld, where at that time a flourishing Jewish community provided the seat for the Province-Rabbinate of Unterfranken.[2] His parents had little ambition in material matters.
They had no greater desire than to see their son grow up a
Talmid Hakham. His secular education he received in the village
school, but from his earliest youth, most of the time of the bright
boy was devoted to the study of Torah and Talmud, especially
under the guidance of the learned local Rabbi, R. Gerson Levi.
At the age of fifteen, his parents sent him to the Talmudical
High School in Fuerth, gladly undergoing great financial hardship in order to enable their son to devote himself for years ex-

[2]This was afterwards, under Rabbi Abraham Bing, transferred to
Wuerzburg, and later on subdivided into other rabbinates.

clusively to Talmudical studies. This Yeshivah, then one of the
most famous places of learning in Germany, had Rabbi Wolf
Hamburger as its head, one the greatest Talmudists of his time
and a fearless fighter for the old Jewish ideals. Among its
teachers was the famous Dayan of the Kehillah, Rabbi Yehudah
Loeb Halberstadt. The highly-gifted and noble-minded pupil
soon became the favourite of his teachers and Haverim (comrades).
Five years of very intensive learning laid the foundation for a
vast, profound, and systematic knowledge of Talmud and Posekim
(jurisconsults, great rabbis). When at the age of twenty he left
the Yeshivah, he received the *Hatarath-Horaah* (rabbinic diploma)
from Rabbi Hamburger, and returned to Wiesenbronn. A most
creative period began now in the life of the young man, decisive
for the development of his personality.

Bamberger had not the slightest wish to use his learning as
"a spade wherewith to dig." He opened a small shop, satisfied
with the absolute minimum necessary for his livelihood. Two
years later, he married Kela, a daughter of the Rabbi of Fulda,
Rabbi Seckel Wormser,[3] and found in her a companion who relieved
him of his financial worries as much as she could. His chief occupation, every free minute of the day, and during a great part of
the night, remained his Talmudical studies.

There are stories about how dear "learning" was to him.[4]
The fame of this great young scholar soon spread far. Even
then letters reached him asking for his opinion about Talmudical
and halakhic questions. Pupils gathered round him, especially

---

[3]The wife of Rabbi Seckel Wormser was a granddaughter of Rabbi
David Strauss in Fuerth, and on her father's side a near relative of
Rabbi Nathan Adler in Frankfurt, the teacher of the Hatham Sofer and
of Rabbi Abraham Bing.

[4]Once he was sitting in his shop, completely absorbed in a difficult Talmudical subject, when a customer entered. Unwilling to interrupt his
studies, he asked if there was not some other shop in the place, and went
on learning. Another time he was offered a partnership which would
guarantee him a certain income, but would keep him away from home for
a few days. His wife wanted him to seize this opportunity of improving
their difficult financial circumstances, but he asked her if she would give
him this advice if he would be prevented from learning a whole year.
"Certainly not!" was her answer. "No more can I sacrifice a few days'
learning. Rather would I live in poverty than to keep away from learning
even for a short time."

such as wanted to prepare themselves for a rabbinical career.[5] At this time he wrote his first talmudical book, *Nahalei Devash,* but did not publish it until twenty-seven years later.[6] The approbations to this work show how the young scholar met with the enthusiastic appreciation of the *Gedolei ha-Dor* (rabbinic authorities).

In the quiet of Wiesenbronn, Bamberger became a great scholar and teacher, perhaps the last outstanding Talmudist reared exclusively in a German-Jewish milieu. In another respect, too, he showed even then the qualities of the future leader of Orthodoxy. He possessed an uncompromising vigor and will to stand up for genuine Judaism. In 1836, an assembly of leaders and delegates of the Jewish congregations was convened by the Bavarian Government to discuss the claims of the "Reform Party" to declare antiquated some of the fundamental Jewish beliefs and laws.

The opponents had placed high hopes on this meeting, but due to Bamberger's convincing arguments it ended with victory for the orthodox and a crushing defeat for the reformers.

More and more the attention of Orthodox Jewry was turning to Bamberger. In December 1837, the ailing Chief Rabbi Bing of Wuerzburg sent him unexpectedly a Rabbinical Diploma *(Hatarath Horaah)* and directed his congregations to Bamberger in case he should be prevented from giving religious decisions and performing rabbinical functions.

When in August 1838, Rabbi Abraham Bing retired, Bamberger appeared to be his predestined successor. Wuerzburg was not only the seat of a large rabbinate, comprising many towns and villages, but as a University town, it attracted many students, for whom the guidance of a strong rabbinic personality was essential. A bitter fight for the rabbinate was to be expected, and Bamberger, as the greatest hope of Orthodoxy, was urged to apply for the position. After nearly two years, during which the followers of Reform used every argument and even threats, to prevent Bamberger's appointment, he was elected. In April 1840, he began a career which was to inaugurate a new era for Jewry of Bavaria and

[5]Amongst them were Chief Rabbi Stern of Hamburg, and Rabbi Seligmann Fromm of Frankfurt, who later became his son-in-law.
[6]First edition, Altona, 5613.

beyond its frontiers. Bamberger's work, originally devoted to his own rabbinate, grew beyond his district and assumed great importance.

He was a rabbi of the old type, inspired by the one passion of studying and teaching Torah. But he was well aware of what the times required from a leader of Orthodoxy. In the agitation before the election, the chief weapons of his opponents were his alleged insufficient mastery of the German language and inadequate secular education. Having never intended to become a rabbi, he had not found it necessary to acquire more than the minimum of secular knowledge. But now, being placed in such a responsible position, he recognized that if he was to succeed in preserving the sacred heritage, he had to be the equal in modern education of those who hoped to bring orthodoxy into discredit. In a very short time he acquired considerable secular knowledge, mastered Greek and Latin and of course the German language, in which he delivered his sermons. Surely all this was not for him an aim in itself. Unlike some of his great contemporaries and friends, he refused on principle to let secular knowledge form part of his "Weltanschauung." Yet he decided on these studies out of his conscientiousness about the task set for him by Providence.

The same consideration applied to his care for the secular education of our youth. He understood that they could not be imbued with the right spirit by attending all-day general schools, receiving some religious instruction only in the late afternoon. The greatest enemy of *Yirath Shamayim* is *Am ha-Aratsuth* (ignorance). He therefore opened an elementary Jewish school in 1855. "Jewish children should get their education in a Jewish school, combining secular and religious education, but no more time than necessary should be taken away from Torah-learning. The aim and spirit of secular education must be such as will not endanger our *Emunah* (faith)."

Another very important achievement had to do with the more than thirty religious schools in his rabbinate, all of which he inspected at least once a year. He was confronted with the problem of finding teachers with sufficient Jewish background to bring up a youth strong in character and conviction and advanced in knowledge. He was grieved to find that the religious knowledge of the ordinary *Baal-ha-Bayith* (layman) was rapidly decreasing. Whence would come teachers able to transmit the tradition? The government, too, had asked for proposals with regard to the profession of Jewish teachers. In consultation with other rabbis, Bamberger found the remedy in the establishment of a teachers' seminary which would provide in harmonious combination Jewish and secular education on a traditional basis. He applied himself to the task with extraordinary initiative and devotion. He did all the preliminary work both for the internal organization and for procuring very considerable financial backing. In 1864, he opened in Wuerzburg the *"Juedische Lehrerbildungsanstalt"* (Seminary for the Education of Jewish Teachers) which, to the end of his life, remained under his special care and almost daily supervision. Its importance for German Jewry was soon recognized and during its seventy-five years of existence it became a powerful reservoir, providing many communities and schools with highly-qualified religious teachers for both Jewish and secular subjects.

II

In the domain of literature, we find some of Bamberger's best-known works dealing with Mitsvoth which the great leader of a large rabbinate saw neglected or improperly observed through ignorance. This great Talmudist refrained from publishing works which would show his "pilpulistic" acuteness, but gave first place to Sefarim (volumes, books) necessary for practical Jewish life. His first published book, *"Melekhet Shamayim"* *(Heavenly Work)* contains all of the laws connected with the writing of *Sifrei Torah, Tefillin and Mezuzoth.* In the preface, he expresses his anxiety that Soferim (scribes of these ritual articles) might no longer be able to gain, by their own studies of the sources, the necessary thorough knowledge of the many difficult regulations. It is a masterly work based on Talmud and the vast literature of Rishonim and Aharonim, (authorities from the 11th to the 19th centuries), in which the author decides between divergent opinions and modestly offers his own wherever necessary. In the main part, called *"Hokhmah"* (wisdom), he arranges systematically and in precise language the Dinim (laws) ; in the second, *"Binah"* (understanding), he adds a detailed discussion of the processes by which he reached the decisions recorded in the book. It proved to be an excellent handbook for Soferim; it was equally appreciated by the learned world.

His second Sefer *"Amirah le-Veith Yaakov"*[7] (Talks to the House of Jacob) Bamberger addressed to the Jewish wife. He became well aware of the perils, both of ignorance and ill-will, threatening the purity of married life. Where should the Jewish wife find reliable instruction in the laws on which the holiness and integrity of family life depend? It could no more be left to the mothers' teaching. The safest way seemed to be to make available a book easy to understand, succinct and sufficient. The great scholar did not deem it below his dignity to write such a popular guide. Indeed, who but an authority could undertake this task? Bamberger wrote this work about the laws of *"Niddah, Hallah, and the Lighting of the Festival Lights"* with an appendix about the kashering of meat in Hebrew letters but German language. In the preface he speaks earnest and fatherly words about the holiness of these duties entrusted to the Jewish woman. The book appeared in many editions in the lifetime of Bamberger and afterwards,[8] and without exaggeration, it may be described as a continual source of blessing for the preservation of *"Taharath ha-Mishpahah"* (the purity of family life).

His next work, too, grew from interest in laws of practical importance. He had observed with great concern the gradual disappearance of the type of Shohatim equipped for their holy profession with an intimate knowledge of the relevant parts of the Talmud and Posekim, and the lack of compilations which give the necessary Dinim (laws) in a concise and fully reliable way. So he decided to provide the Shohet with a Sefer, describing the Dinim in plain language and systematic arrangement. His *Moreh le-Zovehim*[9] became the standard work for generations of Shohatim.

---

[7] First edition, Fuerth, 5618.

[8] In 5670, his grandson, Rabbi Seckel Bamberger of Bad Kissingen, published it in German letters, as changed conditions had made this necessary, and also in this form it saw many editions. Lately, in 5708, the son of the above, Rabbi Simhah Bamberger, published in Erets Yisrael a Hebrew translation, which edition found the very warm appreciation of the Gedolim of the Holy Land. A translation into English is in preparation.

[9] First edition, Fuerth, 5623.

The principal part, *Halakhah Sedurah,* gives in clear and exact manner the whole of the relevant Halakhoth without indication of the extensive study of all the sources on which they are based. The notes, *Tosefeth Halakhah,* supply material for profounder acquaintance with more difficult questions, especially such which the first part leaves undecided and open to authoritative decisions.

III

The rabbi of Wuerzburg was a gaon in the true sense of the word. Soon after he occupied the seat of the rabbinate, disciples began to gather, to sit at his feet, and Wuerzburg became again a center of Torah-study, one of the last great Yeshivoth in Germany. Besides his manifold activities, he found the time to give two daily lectures. In these lectures he showed his mastery of the matter, his comprehensive *Lamdanuth,* a natural dialectic keenness, yet he always endeavored to lead his pupils from the Talmud to the final decision of the Shulhan Arukh. Even as in his Sefarim, he purposely restricted "Pilpul" in order to achieve practical results from "learning." Many rabbis and leaders of Orthodoxy came forth from his Yeshivah. Through his disciples, he kept up for generations Torah-knowledge and loyalty to our tradition throughout Central and Western Europe. His Yeshivah was also of great importance for the Jewish students at the University, who received from him the antidote against assimilatory tendencies stemming from modern knowledge, hazardous to youth unfortified by a sound knowledge of Torah.

IV

The list of the literary works of Bamberger is not exhausted by those already described. To his son's *Shaarei Simhah*[10] (Rabbi Simhah's edition of a manuscript in Paris of the *"Halakhoth of Rabbi Isaac ben Rabbi Jacob ibn Gayath"*), Bamberger contributed vital comments in addition to correcting errors in the manuscript, revealing the sources of ibn Gayath's halakhic explanations, and comparing the manuscript with quotations of ibn Gayath's opinions by other Rishonim (authorities before 1500).

[10]First part Fuerth 5621, second part Fuerth 5622.

The fruit of his early years in Wiesenbronn was his *Nahalei Devash* (Rivers of Honey) on the laws of Halitsah. In spite of warm approbations by the Gedolim (authoriteis) of that time, such as Rabbi Wolf Hamburger in Fuerth and Rabbi Mendel Kargan, he postponed its publication. The more pressing needs of the day urged the rabbi of Wuerzburg to write and publish first works of daily practical importance. For more than twenty-seven years the *Nahalei Devash* remained unpublished, but was worked on again and again, corrected and supplemented, to appear finally in 5627.[11]

It was hailed by the rabbinical authorities as a standard work on the subject. At the end of this work, a few Responsa are added, some already demonstrating his interest in the problem of the *al Tikrei* (Changes for special purposes, in Massoretic Readings), to which his last work, *Kore be-Emeth,* (The Reader of the True Text) was devoted.[12] Modern critics who dared lay hands on the holiness of the Bible by amending its text, tried to justify their method by reference to the *al Tikrei* explanations. Bamberger refutes the attempts to find in the *al Tikrei* critical considerations of the Tannaim and Amoraim. In the preface he points out how the inclinations toward Bible criticism are utterly contrary to the spirit of our rabbis. With great originality and fine exegetical insight he shows that the *al Tikrei* explanations were never meant to be a correction of the text. Very often they are based on a double meaning of the word in question, excluding a more obvious one in favor of another which really represents the true meaning of the word in the context. Even more often *al Tikrei* indicates by the resemblance of two words in sound or meaning that a certain idea or lesson is expressed in this sentence of the Bible. Whilst his main interest was devoted to halakhic and talmudical problems, Bamberger was equally master of Biblical grammar and exegesis, putting at their service his great knowledge of Talmud and Midrashim.

Bamberger was also instrumental in providing an edition of the Pentateuch with short comments, correct in text and translation. The "Orthodoxe Israelitische Bibelanstalt" which he together with

[11]Ed. Frankfurt.
[12]The first part on the *al Tikrei in the Talmud* was published in 5631 (Frankfurt), the second part on the *al Tikrei in the Midrashim* in 5635 (Mainz).

some other rabbis had founded, made this cheap edition of the Pentateuch available for the Jewish public and thus counteracted the intentions of Bible-critical circles.

V

Outstanding was Bamberger as an expert on matters Halakhic. From everywhere legal and ritual questions came before him for decision. Together with Rabbi Jacob Ettlinger of Altona,[13] he was the undisputed halakhic authority for German Jewry in the middle of the nineteenth century, for affairs of individual as well as of general importance.[14] It was not only his scholarship and practical experience but especially his extreme conscientiousness which made the questioner sure that even the seemingly small problem was answered with great care. His reputation in this regard stood very high. His Halakhic correspondence included great contemporary authorities, living abroad, as, e.g., Rabbi Solomon Kluger in Brody, and the Beth-Din of Pressburg. He left many volumes of Responsa but expressed the wish that they should not be published, because in his modesty he feared that the decisions might not always be reliable, having often had to answer questions in a very short time. What posterity thought of him is shown by the fact that Geonim like Rabbi J. E. Spektor of Kovno,[15] Rabbi N. Z. J. Berlin of Wolosin,[16] and Rabbi J. J. Diskin,[17] decided in Responsa to his son Rabbi M. K. Bamberger in Bad Kissingen that nevertheless these Responsa ought to be published[18] and that all the

---

[13]Died in 1870.

[14]For instance, the threatening abolition of the second day of Yomtov in Italy.

[15]See preface to *Zekher Simhah,* p. VIII, note 4.

[16]See Responsa *Meshiv Davar* I, 24.

[17]See Responsa *Netiah shel Simhah,* preface, note.

[18]Rabbi Seckel Bamberger of Bad Kissingen, grandson of the Wuerzburger "Rav", published (Deva 5688) *Netiah shel Simhah*: Responsa of S. B. Bamberger to his son M. L. Bamberger. In another work published by Rabbi Seckel Bamberger, Zekher Simhah (Frankfurt 5685), containing responsa of his father Rabbi Simhah of Aschaffenburg, Bamberger's oldest son, he added some related Responsa of his grandfather, also in the notes to *Zikhron Avraham* (Pressburg 5652), likewise published by Rabbi Seckel Bamberger. Some other books contain Responsa of S. B. Bamberger, such as *Binyan Tsion* of Rabbi Jakob Ettlinger and the rabbinical periodical *Shomer Tsion ha-Neeman* edited by Rabbi Jakob Ettlinger.

See also the works of two of Bamberger's sons, Nathan (his successor) and Solomon of Sennheim.

publishers had to do to comply with his wish was to preface the Responsa with Bamberger's note asking that his decisions be accepted only after careful consideration.[18a]

VI

SEPARATIST PROBLEMS

The reputation of Bamberger as a Halakhic authority involved him, in the last years of his life, in a controversy of utmost importance and of far-reaching consequences. In 1872, four hundred rabbanim of Germany, Hungary and Russia, amongst them Bamberger, rendered their opinion that the orthodox members of the Kehillah (The General Jewish Community) in Vienna were forbidden to remain in it, since its administration had introduced reforms contrary to the Torah. By the Prussian *"Austrittgesetz"* of 28th of July, 1876, Orthodoxy succeeded after a long struggle in procuring the right to withdraw from the official Kehillah. Rabbi S. R. Hirsch of Frankfort now declared it obligatory for the members of his own congregation to give up membership in the general Kehillah. When asked for his opinion, Bamberger agreed, deciding (in 1877) that the minor concessions which the administration of the general Kehillah had offered were insufficient. Alarmed by the threat that many orthodox members would now act according to the decision of their rabbinical leaders, the administration of the general Kehillah saw itself forced to grant more adequate concessions which constituted a decided change of attitude. They agreed to provide the orthodox members with all necessary institutions which were to be placed under the exclusive and independent jurisdiction of Orthodoxy. The orthodox members would also be exempted from all taxes and imposts which went towards the

It should be mentioned in this connection that five of the six sons of S. B. Bamberger were well-known Rabbanim (besides those mentioned above, his son Rabbi Seckel was Dayan in Frankfort), and his three daughters were married to Talmidei Hahhamin, Rabbi Unna, and the rabbanim E. Adler in Kitzingen, and S. Fromm in Frankfort. A great number of his grandsons continued the tradition and were rabbanim in different parts of Germany. With regard to the unpublished works of S. B. Bamberger, an irreparable loss occurred when some of the most comprehensive manuscripts of the last years of his life were destroyed during the tragic events of recent years.

[18a]R. J. E. Spektor refers to the precedents of the *Shakh* and *Peri Megadim*.

maintenance of religious and educational institutions of anti-traditional character. Again approached by members of the orthodox Kehilla to exercise his personal influence on such orthodox members as had not yet withdrawn, Bamberger refused, as his effort might have the opposite effect, since the changed conditions might change their decision. Urged, nevertheless, to come, he reluctantly agreed, and indeed there he came to the conclusion that the concessions were of such a radical character that it was no longer imperative to withdraw from the general Kehillah. The publicity given to the matter by a misleading report in a newspaper of Bamberger's decision, forced him to answer that his decision was subject to certain indispensable conditions (see above). S. R. Hirsch now, in defense of his opinion, addressed an "Open Letter" to Bamberger to which the latter replied in an "Open Answer." The second "Open Letter" of S. R. Hirsch, Bamberger refused to answer. Deeply concerned about the peace within the ranks of orthodoxy, he also prohibited the publication of replies by some of his pupils and followers.[19]

The decision of Bamberger, that sharpest opponent of any kind of reform, was entirely free from any compromise. He was guided exclusively by the absolute authority of the Din (Law), as he saw it. The argument that by remaining in a Kehillah, not entirely based on the Torah, the orthodox members admitted the existence of two legal, equally justified parties within Jewry, was not accepted by him. On the contrary, he saw in such a Kehillah only a loose connection of individuals for certain, mainly social, purposes, and never regarded the administration of such a body as the legal representation of a Jewish Kehillah. The real Kehillah was the union of the orthodox members with their orthodox institutions and their own administration, though, as individuals, they remained within the framework of the general "Kehillah." Bamberger's opinion has very often been misunderstood and misrepresented by followers as well as by opponents. The following points clearly show his attitude:

---

[19]That Bamberger adhered to his decision is shown by some later private correspondence with Hungarian Gedolim (not published).

See also Resp. Zekher Simhah 230, where Bamberger suggested that the dispute be submitted to the judgment of an impartial Beth-Din, but the other side refused.

He decided that if certain conditions stipulated by him were fulfilled, there was no religious duty to withdraw.

He never went back on his earlier decision that if these conditions were not fulfilled it was a religious duty to withdraw.

He was never against withdrawal, even if these concessions were made.

His decision never justified Reform and Liberalism in considering themselves as legal within Judaism.

The two points of view in the *"Austrittsfrage"* had important consequences for the development of orthodoxy. The "Austritt" (withdrawal party) had the great merit of creating independent bulwarks of orthodox life but had to be content with losing all direct influence on those outside their ranks. The adherents of the "Nicht-Austritt" (non-withdrawal party), by not severing all ties, on the one hand, risked becoming adversely influenced by the anti-Torah views of the followers of Reform, but on the other hand, could maintain their influence on many who would otherwise have been driven towards assimilation and faithlessness to tradition. Retrospectively, it may be said that Providence needed both ways for the preservation of Traditionalism as a consistent and influential factor within Jewry.

VII

HIS CHARACTER

It seems unnecessary to mention that with Rav Bamberger, as with all real Talmidei Hakhamim, *Lamdanuth* (Learning) and *Yirath Shamayim* (Reverence) went hand in hand. Indeed all accounts transmitted by pupils and contemporaries speak of his exceptional piety. An air of saintliness surrounded him and was felt in his words and deeds. Even a small Minhag was sure of his most careful observance. Of his considerateness and moral sensitiveness, two examples shall suffice.

In those times a small toll had to be paid when crossing a bridge. He insisted on getting a receipt from the non-Jewish collector. He was afraid he might induce the collector not to deliver the toll to its owner. The collector would be guilty of keeping money that was not his own, and he himself would be guilty of causing dishonesty. When sending a letter by a private messenger and not by mail, he used to destroy a postage stamp, as the monopoly of forwarding mail was held by the state. He possessed wonderful ethical qualities (Middoth). He was consistent and strict, but even his opponents recognized that all his deeds and words resulted from conviction and conscientiousness and were never meant to hurt. His manner in dealing with poor and troubled people showed a heart full of love and humanity.[20] He not only cared for such individuals, but also created institutions for their benefit. Thus he suggested the building of a Jewish Hospital in Wuerzburg. His loving care was directed to the Talmidei Hakhamim and the poor of *Erets Yisrael,* and he did much for their support and relief. Together with others he worked for the establishment in 1873 of a Jewish Hospital in Jerusalem. He collected very considerable sums for this purpose and, as a first step, a Jewish physician was appointed there. He did not live to see the fulfillment of the project which, many years later, was achieved by the opening of the Shaarei Tsedek Hospital in Jerusalem. It is certain that the boundless love and reverence of his pupils and friends and the very great esteem in which he was held by everybody, even by opponents, were as much due to his qualities of heart as to his intellectual achievements.

The "Wuerzburger Rav" died suddenly in the Synagogue of Wuerzburg on the second day of Sukkoth 1879, in the midst of the Reading of the Law. The whole of German Jewry mourned with his Kehillah for the irreplaceable loss of a man who had put his

---

[20]Significant is a story of a poor man who came to him in the midst of a Talmudical lecture complaining that he needed shoes. He interrupted the lecture and fetched him some of his own. When his pupils remarked that these shoes were his best, bought only a short time before, he simply replied, "Torn shoes the poor man has himself. I should only give him the best."— A poor widow from a neighboring village told him of her dire proverty. He advised her to move to Wuerzburg where he would care for her, and did so to the end of her life. When he heard that she had died, he was very grieved that he was now deprived of this Mitsvah.—Proverbial was his selflessness. Once he was offered by an admirer a great amount of money as a present. Although he was himself in poor circumstances, he refused to accept it, advising the donor to give it to his own needy relatives. Even in Wiesenbronn he never took any fees from his pupils, and even managed to support with his own very modest means those who were in need. One of his sons was engaged to a girl of a very wealthy family; when before the marriage they suddenly lost their fortune, he remarked that only now was he really pleased with the engagement.

seal on the life of Orthodoxy in the middle of the nineteenth century.

The "Wuerzburger Rav" of blessed memory is recognized as one of the few great personalities by whose influence *Torah* and *Yirath Shamayim* were preserved in German Jewry down to our own day.

ISRAEL SALANTER

By Joseph Elias

ISRAEL SALANTER

By Joseph Elias

"It is worthwhile to give one's life for the saving of *one* soul
in Israel." This remark of Rabbi Israel Salanter's may well be
taken as the *motif* of his own life. An unending battle takes place
in history between the spirit of divine holiness and that of selfish
desire. It must be fought out in the heart of every individual and
in the life of every community. In a time of crisis Rabbi Israel
assumed leadership, to save his own soul and that of his age.

I

THE SETTING

When he appeared on the scene of history, nineteenth century
Lithuanian Jewry was in the throes of a profound religious
upheaval: the spiritual well-springs of Jewish life threatened
to run dry. There was the aggressive *Haskalah* movement
which aimed to reshape traditional Jewish life in the spirit
of modern "enlightenment". But the spread of the *Haskalah*
was largely due to a fatal weakness which had appeared in the
life of traditional Jewry itself: Torah-observance still flourished
but with many of its adherents it threatened to become a matter
of habit and convention, without sufficient regard for the spiritual
content of the Law. Whilst there existed in many towns societies
devoted to the study of the *"Menorath ha-Maor"* and other
ethical works, unthinking observance nevertheless represented a
growing evil.

This problem, to be sure, was not a new one. The Torah
presents to the Jew the ideal of human perfection, attained through
his attachment to, and loving service of, God. But man is not
a purely rational being. His insight and conduct are colored by
deep-seated instincts; the this-wordly elements in his nature tend
to divert him from loyalty to his ideals, to short-sighted self-

assertion. Hence the Torah imposed a system of laws "to purify His creatures," to enable them to gain control over their nature and to put it at the service of God. Yet there has always been the danger that Law-observance would become mechanical, perfunctory, and that it would therefore fail to bring about the truly perfect service of God.

The power of man's natural instincts is such that it is apt to threaten our spiritual aspirations at the very moment at which they seem to triumph. Our innate selfish tendencies, the archenemies of our divine mission, are not necessarily checkmated by our observance of the laws. There can be no true perfection without these; yet they may be turned into unthinking habits or, even worse, become tools of our selfishness. Piety can become a source of spiritual pride, Torah-study a quest for scholarly prestige, and Law-observance a matter of showing off. The visit to the synagogue can easily be turned into a social event, as we know so well, and charity into a tool of social ambition. Even where our intentions are of the very best, we may fail; a kind act may flow from unjustifiable weakness, and a good deed may often hide a better one left undone. Such dangers must not of course be taken as justifying disregard of the Law; on the contrary, they represent a warning to us never to relax in our striving for perfection, for at the very moment at which it seems within our grasp, it may slip away from us.

Indeed, the Torah has warned us again and again to be on guard against this danger. It has exhorted us always to see in the Law the means to our perfection and to make every observance a conscious act of divine service. This conception, like a golden thread, runs through all the books of the Bible; the Sages of the Talmud constantly emphasized the "duties of the heart," and in the course of the centuries a vast ethical literature sprang up, which ever stressed the need for thoughtful observance and was industriously studied at all times. The modern age with its intellectual and social distractions greatly aggravated the problem. Thus it became vitally necessary for the future of European Jewry, to point out the spiritual wealth inherent in the traditional observances.

This problem was particularly acute in Poland. Here, seventeenth century persecution had undermined the spiritual and material development of the Jewish community; and here, too, a solution was offered: Hassidism. It pointed out the proud meaning of man's divine service; in fulfilling the Law he not only redeemed himself but lifted up the entire universe to God. Hassidism inspired a great upsurge of religious enthusiasm among the Jewish masses which, under the leadership of the *Tsaddikim*, inspired joyful divine service. However, Hassidism did not appeal to the staid and restrained Lithuanian Jew.

"Whilst running after a *Mitsvah*, one can do a great deal of harm," Rabbi Israel Salanter used to say. With his penetrating insight into human nature he pointed out that the Hassidic teachings could turn even the drinking of whiskey into an act of divine service, but that, on the other hand, fasting could be devoid of religious spirit. Deep-rooted evil impulses obstruct and vitiate man's most noble aspirations; they are responsible for the "sickness" from which, as he realized, his age so bitterly suffered. It was his historic role to find a remedy for it.

II

THE BIRTH OF AN IDEA

Rabbi Israel was born on the third of November (sixth day of Heshvan) 1810, in the small Lithuanian town of Zhagory, where his father, Rabbi Wolf Lipkin, a distinguished Talmudic scholar, at that time served as rabbi. According to the custom of the period, he married at an exceedingly early age and went to live with his wife's parents in Salant (hence his byname, Salanter), devoting himself with the greatest zeal to the study of the Torah. Even then he attracted attention by the brilliance of his mind and the purity of his character.

He was inspired by intense dedication to the teachings of the Torah, impatient of any manner of compromise or self-deception. Thus, before long, he came to question the current form of Talmudic dialectics *(Pilpul):* Did it not tempt the student to indulge in mental acrobatics and to display mental agility? He decided to limit himself to straightforward logical exploration of the plain meaning of the texts. Yet after only a short while, it occurred to him that perhaps his new way of study was prompted by too proud a reliance on the power of his mind to uncover the truth; perhaps one might approach it more closely by the loving exploration of all the nooks and crannies of the Law. And without hesitation, young Israel turned back to *Pilpul,* though he remained ever watchful of its dangers.

This had taught him a lesson which he was to remember throughout his life: that even our most meritorious actions, such as the study of the Torah, can be inspired and misdirected by impure motives, unless we succeed in gaining control over the selfish instincts which influence us. There was need, then, for constant watchfulness; the true servant of God had to lay bare and to eradicate all the hidden weaknesses of his nature if he was to attain to perfection. Yet how could this be done? It was in quest of an answer to this problem that young Israel came to attach himself to Rabbi Zundel.

Rabbi Zundel of Salant was a strange man, or so it seemed to the good people of Salant. He had no fixed occupation, but would live from hand to mouth, ever absorbed in study and contemplation. Yet Rabbi Zundel did not think of himself as in any way out of the ordinary. He considered himself a plain Jew who was trying to take the teachings of the Torah seriously. His task in life was the wholehearted service of God and the mending of any weakness of his that might stand in the way of his goal; the satisfaction of his material needs, in contrast, was only a very subordinate means to the end of a good life, to be taken care of incidentally, as circumstances permitted.

He would go out and walk for long hours through the fields and forests surrounding Salant, reciting Biblical and Talmudic passages which were to implant in his heart the love and fear of God. On one of these walks he noted Rabbi Israel stealthily following him. He turned to him, and said: "Israel, study *Mussar** and you will fear God!" As Rabbi Israel told his disciples in later years, these words hit him like a bolt of lightning. They revealed to him, in an instant, the vast gap between what he was and what he should be. The shock which they gave him tore him away from all the petty concerns of every day towards the supreme purpose of man's life, the wholehearted service of God. In this

Mussar may be translated as "moral exhortation and discipline".

moment, Rabbi Israel found the answer to his deepest longing, a way to the perfect realization of the divine will. This, he now understood, could not be reached by the mere study of moralistic books; only a profound emotional experience, such as he had gone through, was capable of changing human nature. It alone could overcome man's selfish instincts and make effective the sacred ideals to which we otherwise pay only lip service. Through such experience, one could attain to the pure understanding of the Torah and to its devoted observance, untouched by outside considerations.

This was the foundation upon which Rabbi Israel came to build the philosophy of *Mussar*. He wrote no systematic exposition of it; but it stands clearly revealed in his essays, letters, and talks which have come down to us. It is necessary to emphasize that *Mussar* did not offer a new "world-outlook" or a new ideal of Jewish living. Its sole goal was the perfect service of God, through which man becomes a partner in the divine work of creation, leading the universe to ultimate perfection and redemption and, through his labors, achieving these himself. This was what Judaism had always taught; and it had also stressed that this goal could be attained only if man restrained his obstructing selfish urges by efforts for his spiritual self-improvement. The main "textbooks" of *Mussar* stemmed from earlier centuries, as, e.g., the *"Path of the Righteous"* by Rabbi Mosheh Hayyim Luzzatto, or the *"Gates of Repentance"* by Rabbenu Jonah Gerondi. They emphasized what Rabbi Israel called the "science of the world", the understanding, in the light of the Torah, of the nature of the world and of man, and, in particular, of one's own nature, with all its weaknesses and potentialities. This knowledge they viewed as the indispensable basis for the proper planning of one's life.

However, mere knowledge is not powerful enough to shape man's conduct. It was the discovery of this fact that led Rabbi Israel to make this contribution to the Jewish science of self-improvement: not the seeking of a new *goal* of life but a new *method* of attaining the old one. He sought to find a form of *Mussar* study that would stir up the individual and make a profound impression upon him, not once only (for then its effects would wear off, as Rabbi Israel came to realize), but again and again, until the teachings of the Torah would become his second nature.

For the pious Jew, Rabbi Israel stressed that the mere study of
the requirements of the Law represented a powerful moral challenge; hence he demanded regular study of the laws, particularly
of those dealing with the proper conduct towards one's fellow-
beings and with the love and fear of God. He urged that we should
at all times reflect on these subjects and seek a deeper understanding
of them. But all this, and all *Mussar* study in general, had to be
invested with emotional intensity *(Hithpaaluth)*. How could
this be achieved? The life of Rabbi Israel came to be entirely devoted to this quest for the proper form of Mussar study. His
success ensured the rise of the *Mussar* movement.

III

IDEA AND REALIZATION

Rabbi Israel, it must be emphasized, did not at first intend
to found a movement. He merely sought to find for himself a
path to the more perfect service of God. Yet before long he
realized that aiding the community was a vital part of his quest
for self-perfection. Thus he came to gather around himself a
circle of people willing to study Mussar with him. Soon we see
him travel around the country; wherever he found an audience,
he spoke of Mussar, the royal road to God.

Contemporaries have described him as a masterly speaker. His
Talmudic discourses earned him general admiration; yet his sermons, the outpouring of his great passion, did not achieve their end:
They did not make converts. Rabbi Israel did not "preach" in
the customary manner; he rather asked his listeners to think with
him, to consider the greatness of man and our failure to live up to
it. He would stress how the entire meaning of our existence is
summed up in service to God and, in contrast to the trivialities of
our daily life, how little attention we give to it. To recognize our
failure before God, to be frightened by it, this was to Rabbi Israel
the vital first step towards our redemption; and it required Mussar
to make us take this step. Yet to his audience his demand seemed
so obvious that they immediately forgot all about it; they saw in
his words only another moral exhortation, whereas he had meant
to offer them a radical challenge to their way of life.

Thus disappointed, Rabbi Israel gladly accepted a call to become the head of the Meilis Yeshivah in Vilna; here, in the center of Lithuanian Jewry, he hoped to find real understanding at last. Indeed, in the Meilis Yeshivah, and later in a Yeshivah which he himself founded, he attracted a few loyal followers. Among the townspeople, too, there were such as understood him and eagerly listened to his Mussar talks. At his suggestion, old Mussar treatises were reprinted for the benefit of his disciples. The opponents of his teachings he subdued by the power of his personality.

As a rule, Rabbi Israel went to extraordinary lengths to hide his saintliness and learning; but he never shirked responsibility and, when the moment demanded it, he assumed communal leadership. During a disastrous cholera epidemic he instructed the Jews of Vilna to eat on Yom Kippur and, when they hesitated, he himself set an example by partaking publicly of food. Attacked for this, he invited the leaders of the community to a Talmudic discourse, which never touched on the subject at issue but established his authority beyond further challenge. On other occasions, when violation of the Law was involved, he could be just as forthright in condemning the transgression. He knew that someone had to make sacrifices for the community, even at the cost of his retiring personality.

Despite all the recognition that he received, Rabbi Israel was not satisfied. He had not yet succeeded in finding the institutional form which *Mussar* needed in order to become a real force in communal life. However, a new chance offered itself when he was suddenly forced to move to Kovno in order to escape the unwelcome attentions of the *Haskalah* (which, with the assistance of the Russian government, aimed to enlist him in its assimilationist crusade). In Kovno, after 1849, Rabbi Israel continued his efforts to gain adherents for *Mussar,* and for them he created what came to be called a *"Mussar-klaus"* (conventicle), a small meeting place where people could come to study *Mussar.*

In a short while, such conventicles, founded by loyal followers of Rabbi Israel, sprang up in other localities, too. Finally *Mussar* seemed to have found its proper institutional expression. These small, darkish rooms, sparsely furnished, provided an ideal setting for *Mussar* study. From the bustle of the outside world, people could escape to them, to pore over some moral treatise and be absorbed in self-analysis and self-improvement.

In these books they did not look for novel ideas, but rather for the eternal verities by which the Jew lives: the need to cleave to God, the duty to erase one's shortcomings. As these immortal thoughts would be recited over and over again, in the sad and mournful chant of the *Mussar* student, they would strike a chord in his heart; they would probe into the depths of his personality and prepare him for a passionate longing for divine redemption, for the ascent to a higher life.

The *Mussar-klaus,* it turned out, did indeed make possible the *"study of Mussar with intensity,"* which Rabbi Israel demanded. Yet it did not, and could not, provide the proper foundation for the *Mussar* movement. It was dedicated to the man of the street, the businessman or artisan, in quest of the good life. But as these experienced the challenge of Mussar, an intense conflict developed in them. They were "finished" individuals, part and parcel of established society, who found it well-nigh impossible to apply the radical consequences of their *Mussar* studies in their practical life, with all its petty conventions and pretenses. The result, all too often, was frustration, rather than redemption.

For twenty years Rabbi Israel failed to find a way out. With all the profound intensity of which he was capable, he strove for a solution. At one time he tried again to appeal to the community at large, in sermons and through a shortlived Torah-journal, *Tevunah* (1861); at another time he attempted to popularize the teachings of Judaism in general, through a Talmudical dictionary and similar projects. He used to withdraw into isolation, to correct what he considered his own weaknesses, which, he felt, were responsible for his failure. At other times, he travelled all over Europe, founding religious congregations, teaching the younger generation what Judaism demanded of them. In 1857, he was afflicted by a nervous disease which caused him unspeakable suffering until his death; yet this only intensified his passionate efforts for the future of Jewish life. And indeed only one of all his projects proved successful—the *Mussar Yeshivah.*

This was, in a way, the logical outgrowth of Rabbi Israel's experiences. If "finished" people cannot be made over any more, unfinished ones must be worked on. All through the years a circle of younger disciples of Rabbi Israel had existed in Kovno. In 1877 he obtained the funds to establish a proper institution, a *"Kolel"*, in which a few students, relieved of material worries, lived and studied together, dedicated to a life of Mussar. This was a revolutionary plan, for until then Yeshivoth had been essentially devoted to the dissemination of knowledge, whilst the new institution aimed to go beyond that and create strong Jewish personalities, capable of going out into Jewish life and shaping it according to the radical demands of *Mussar*.

IV

RABBI ISRAEL: SAINT AND LEADER

In 1880, at the age of seventy, Rabbi Israel set out on one more errand in the divine service. He went to Paris, to bring direly needed spiritual leadership to the Russian-Jewish colony there. Shortly after his return, on the twenty-fifth day of Shevat, 1883, he passed away in Koenigsberg, believing himself a failure and unaware of the fact that the Kovno *Kolel,* then still young and small, was the first of a large number of Yeshivoth that would, in time, carry the Mussar idea across the world. This was the tragic note in Rabbi Israel's heroic life; until the last he was convinced that, because of his personal shortcomings, he had been unworthy of success in his mission.

Needless to say, the picture of Rabbi Israel which emerges from the accounts of his contemporaries completely contradicts his own appraisal of himself. The most remarkable feature of his personality, as they describe it, is the way in which he realized in his own person the ideal he always proclaimed: the complete reshaping of one's nature in accordance with the teachings of the Torah. Every moment of his time was given to them, so much so that, in order to prevent unpleasant incidents, his Prussian passport carried the official annotation: "always absorbed in philosophical thoughts" (immer in philosophischen Gedanken versunken). He warned against man's tendency to note the faults of neighbors and to be lenient towards himself. He himself was, indeed, as kind towards others as he was strict towards himself.

Innumerable are the stories and sayings which his circle preserved about him. There was, for instance, his complete rejection of material comforts and possessions. He did not believe in asceticism, but he saw no need for money and felt that it would only distract him from his infinitely more important spiritual interests. Thus, when he died, he left not even one *Kopeke* behind. On the other hand, he showed the most intense concern for the well-being of all those with whom he came in contact; whenever any money came into his hands, it speedily found its way to the poor among his disciples.

But the greatness of his personality, his saintliness and wisdom (two qualities which cannot truly exist apart from one another), are most clearly revealed in the towering stature of his disciples, and in the impression he made on other leaders of contemporary Jewry. His contacts ranged from the Gerer and Lubavitcher Hassidic "Rebbes" to Rabbi Samson Raphael Hirsch and Dr. Ezriel Hildesheimer. These associations bear eloquent testimony to his deep understanding of the crisis which traditional Jewry faced in the modern age. As he once remarked: "In former times a person sinned only when possessed by a spirit of madness; today, however, a man will only do good deeds when possessed by a spirit of sanctity." It was to the quickening of this spirit that his life and work were devoted.

V

THE MUSSAR MOVEMENT

When Rabbi Israel died, the future of *Mussar* still appeared to be in doubt; a few years later it actually appeared doomed. The *Kolel* in Kovno, and similar groups in other localities, had developed under the watchful patronage of the local communities. Such a public set-up bred tensions which, before long, flared up in bitter controversy. This seemed to seal the fate of *Mussar*. Yet in reality it strengthened it; the *Mussar Yeshivoth*, by the force of circumstances, withdrew into complete privacy which ensured their undisturbed and most fruitful development.

The carefully selected student body devoted most of its time to the traditional talmudic studies; in addition, the spiritual leader of the Yeshivah delivered periodic Mussar talks, such as Rabbi Israel had first introduced. These talks moulded the character of the Yeshivah and the lives of its students. They were not conventional lectures but intense addresses, meant to affect the listeners deeply and to create in them the longing for a life of self-improvement. The various Yeshivoth that came into existence at Slobodka, Kelm, Telshi, Radun, to mention a few, developed diverse ways of evoking this response. Rabbi Israel had done so by speaking of the fear of God; but he had emphasized that what mattered was not the method, but only whether the desired result was attained. Thus in Slobodka they talked about the deeper meaning of sin, whilst Radun emphasized quiet absorption in the profundities of the Law.

Each Yeshivah in its way, however, gave to its students a compelling personal experience, which taught them to *live Mussar,* and to go out into the world to labor in its spirit. Despite an occasional failure, the Mussar Yeshivah, as a whole, was tremendously successful as a training ground for Jewish personalities. It is remarkable that today, when the European Yeshivoth lie in ashes, the Mussar idea has been carried across the oceans by its followers and whilst its great exponents of the last generation are no longer with us, their words are now being disseminated more widely in print than ever before. The seeds which Rabbi Israel Salanter so devotedly planted, have in truth borne splendid fruit.

His work and achievement, it must be added, have often been belittled because their true nature was little understood. Professor Louis Ginzberg declared that "the story of the short-lived Mussar movement is the biography of Rabbi Israel Salanter"; and he added that "Rabbi Israel did not have a comprehensive original philosophy of Judaism and did not even leave behind him any major works." S. Rosenfeld saw in Mussar an un-Jewish asceticism, and declared that the Mussar controversy after Rabbi Israel's death sounded the death-knell of the movement. Rabbi J. Weinberg described it as a moralistic movement which never attracted a considerable number of adherents and dated its demise from the rise of the various Yeshivoth and their different approaches.

But Mussar has survived all these obituaries. This should occasion no surprise, if we recall what it really set out to do. Mussar,
as Rabbi Israel Salanter conceived it, never aimed to represent a
new *philosophy,* but only to point out a new approach to Law-
observance, a new *method* of attaining to the perfect service of
God. Rabbi Israel realized that only a powerful spiritual experience can lead to this, and the Mussar Yeshivah has given effective
institutional expression to this conception of his. The withdrawal of the Yeshivoth from the public eye, the lack of a systematic exposition of Mussar, the different ways of producing the
Mussar experience in the various Yeshivoth, none of these factors
affected the essence of Rabbi Israel's great teachings. Not even the
relatively small number of *Mussarniks* allows us to pass lightly
over them; they have left their imprint upon the spiritual development of modern Jewry, and they still hold a message for us.

SELECT BIBLIOGRAPHY

(only readily available titles are listed)

1. Classics of the *Mussar* movement:

    Or Yisrael, a collection of letters and essays of Rabbi Israel
    Salanter, edited with an introduction to *Mussar* ideology and
    a biographical essay, by Rabbi Isaac Blaser, a disciple of
    Rabbi Israel (Reprinted, Munich, 1947).

    Madregath ha-Adam, by Rabbi Joseph Hurwitz, another dis-
    ciple of Rabbi Israel and founder of the Yeshivah of Novo-
    radek (Reprinted, New York, 1946).

    Hever Maamarim, a collection of *Mussar* talks, by Rabbi
    Yeruhem Levovitz, later *Mashgiah* of the Yeshivah of Mir
    (Vilna, 1939).

2. Recent works on the *Mussar* movement:

    Tenuath ha-Mussar, by Rabbi Dov Katz; volume 1 (Tel-
    Aviv, 1946) offers the latest and most detailed treatment
    of the history of *Mussar* to the death of Rabbi Israel, as well
    as a full bibliography.

Mussar, by Ezriel Carlebach (in the *Jahrbuecher der Juedisch-Literarischen Gesellschaft,* Vol. XX, Hamburg, 1930), a brilliant analysis of the phychological foundations of *Mussar;* deals also with the later history of the movement.

Rabbi Israel Salanter and the Mussar Movement, by Rabbi Kopul Rosen (London, 1943), valuable for refuting some current misinterpretations of *Mussar,* such as those of L. Ginzberg and S. Rosenfeld.

Movements in Contemporary Judaism (New York, 1948), by the author of this essay, contains in Chapter III a review of Rabbi Israel's work against the historic background of Jewish spiritual life.

EZRIEL (ISRAEL) HILDESHEIMER

By Isaac Unna

EZRIEL (ISRAEL) HILDESHEIMER

By Isaac Unna

I

During the first half of the nineteenth century, Judaism in Germany was dominated by reform tendencies. Though Moses Mendelssohn himself still adhered to the Jewish law, the spirit of "enlightenment" and assimilation which was spread by his followers undermined tradition and replaced it by individualism and an indiscriminate reform-mania. The French Revolution having brought equality to the Jews in France and in the countries under her influence, attempts were made to attain emancipation in Germany as well. Through a reform of the Jewish religion it was believed possible to remove entirely the barriers between Jews and non-Jews. Such reform was to consist chiefly in introducing more aesthetic synagogue services and in imitating the forms of the Church. The elimination of the national element from the Hebrew prayers and from Jewish life was intended to serve as evidence of the Jews' sincere patriotism.

The most radical protagonist of reform was Abraham Geiger. His aim, in his own words, was "to strive towards the recognition of a progressive historical development within Judaism, to place into relief its permanent content and the significance of its influence within the history of the world, aiming to dignify representation of its spiritual content, and to strengthen its vital principle with a view to overcoming all obsolete, temporary forms." To him tradition was nothing but the principle of continuous progress and of evolution conditioned by the times, and therefore every period had not only the right but even the obligation to bring religion into harmony with its own mode of thinking and its particular religious consciousness. The essence of Judaism he believed to be contained in the teachings of the prophets, whereas the "ceremonies" were a product of the times and had to be adhered to only so long as they corresponded to the religious spirit of each epoch. Geiger's collaborators went even farther in their hostility towards

215

the religious law which is based on tradition. They did not shrink from declaring as irrelevant the most important institutions of Judaism such a circumcision, etc. But even the representative of "moderate reform," Zacharias Frankel, found himself in opposition to traditional Judaism. In his view, too, the Halakhah was a product of evolution and owned its origin to the spiritual work, first of the Soferim and then of the Tannaim, who set up the rules of interpretation (*Middoth*) and by the application of these rules derived the oral law from the Torah. The expression *Halakhah le-Mosheh mi-Sinai* (Law given to Moses on Sinai), often used in the Talmud, according to him, was not to be taken literally, but to be understood to mean that these traditions were "as clear as if they had been handed down from Sinai." This conception, too, deprived the religious law of its authoritative character and gave free hand to any reformist tendency.

Wherever the reform party gained influence, they waged a bitter fight against traditional Judaism, whose adherents were branded as clericalists and obscurantists. The study of the Talmud was prohibited. Talmud schools were closed down and the students driven out of town. Obstacles were put in the way of observing the religious law, and important institutions such as the Mikveh, etc. were left to fall into decay.

The resistance of orthodox Jewry to these attacks could not be effective, because most of its representatives lacked the general education that would have enabled them to expose the reformers' lack of system, of logic and of historical understanding. Moreover, the rabbis of the old school distrusted polemics, fearing, not without justification, that they would lead to loose thinking. They opposed even the slightest deviation from old customs and the abolition of obvious abuses. When on the occasion of the founding of the "Temple" in Hamburg and the publication of its new prayer-book, a congregation for the first time openly renounced important principles of the Jewish faith, the outstanding authorities of their times, Rabbi Moshe Sofer and Rabbi Akiba Eger, together with many others, did issue a strong protest. But as their declarations were written in Hebrew, they could reach only a small fraction of the public.

The first signs of a reversal of public opinion came with the appearance of Rabbi Samson Raphael Hirsch who, in his "Nine-

teen Letters" and "Horev" sounded the tocsin for a whole, un-
divided Judaism and showed the possibility of its synthesis with
a spirit of genuine scientific thinking. There were two others besides him to whom we owe the preservation and the renascence of
traditional Judaism in Germany: Dr. M. Lehmann, the founder
of the "Israelit" (who, through his activity in the field of journalism and fiction, exercised a strong influence especially on the
youth), and Rabbi Israel or Ezriel Hildesheimer.

II

Ezriel Hildesheimer was born at Halberstadt, Germany, on
the 27th of Iyar, 5580 (May 20th, 1820). Though not one of the
oldest Jewish communities in Germany (only in the course of the
thirteenth century does its name appear in the chronicles), it seems
to have even then enjoyed considerable reputation. Towards the
end of the seventeenth century, a man by the name of Issakhar
Bermann, also called Berend Lehmann, lived at Halberstadt
and distinguished himself as a *"Shtadlan"*, i.e., spokesman for his
fellow-Jews, and also as a scholar. He founded the so-called
"Klaus" which to our own days was a centre of Torah study.
More important even was the founding of *"Hakhsharath Tsevi"*
by Hirsch Koslin, a school primarily for children from the
poorer classes, where they received thorough instruction not only in
the Torah, but also—a novelty in those days—in such subjects of
general knowledge as would enable them to get on in life. This
school, run on the lines of traditional Judaism, was of the most
beneficial influence on the spirit of the community. One of its
students was Ezriel Hildesheimer. His father, Rabbi Loeb, a
pupil of R. Pinchas Horowitz (author of *Haflaah,* a classic in rabbinic lore), and his mother, Golde, also a descendant of a well-
known family of scholars, gave him a basic Torah education.
At the age of twelve Ezriel lost his father who had introduced
him to the study of the Talmud, and his elder brother, Abraham,
then took charge of his education. For advanced study Ezriel, later
on, went to Altona to attend the Yeshivah of Rabbi Jacob Ettlinger,
one of the greatest authorities on the Talmud in his time, and also
possessed of general culture. Ettlinger adhered to the German
method of Talmud study, which, by logical and methodical re-

search, tried to arrive at full mastery of the text in order to render the right halakhic decision. On the other hand, R. Jacob Cohn, teacher at the Klaus, who had studied under Hatham Sofer, (Rabbi Moses Sofer), was rather inclined to follow the Hungarian method which preferred the Pilpul. Thus Ezriel Hildesheimer had an opportunity of getting acquainted with both methods, and thanks to his fine mental endowment and untiring diligence, he derived great benefit from both scholars. In Altona, the Beth-Din (the Chief Rabbi's court) still retained the right of jurisdiction in civil cases, and thus Hildesheimer had the opportunity of perfecting his knowledge of *Hoshen Mishpat* (the civil-law part of the Shulhan Arukh.). He was greatly inspired by R. Jacob Ettlinger's work as head master of the school in which Bible and Talmud and also the subjects of general knowledge were taught. Through his periodical, *"The True Guardian of Zion"* ("Shomer Tsiyon ha-Neëman"), Jacob Ettlinger had created for orthodox Jewry an organ which was of a high journalistic and scientific standard and served at the time as a powerful defense against reform. In addition to his activity within his congregation, R. Jacob Ettlinger devoted his attention also to general questions of Judaism, especially in the field of *Gemiluth Hassadim* (Organized Charity), and Erets Yisrael was the centre of his interest. Thus his years in Altona proved very important for Hildesheimer's development, especially as he had the opportunity at the same time to attend in Hamburg the lectures on the Kuzari by the brilliant Hakham Bernays, who combined Talmudic knowledge with profound philosophic erudition. Having acquired great learning, Hildesheimer returned to Halberstadt, where he obtained at the Domgymnasium the "certificate of maturity" which enabled him to enroll at a university. Unworried about financial means for his studies because of his betrothal to Henriette Hirsch, the sister of Joseph Hirsch, owner of the renowned metal firm, Hildesheimer proceeded to the Berlin university, to devote himself to the study of Semitics and to attend lectures in philosophy, mathematics and astronomy. But even there he spent the greater part of his time on the study of Talmud, and was especially thrilled with the courses at the Beth ha-Midrash, given by Michael Landsberger. Berlin was at that time the chief seat of the Reform.

The leaders of the Jewish community looked down with contempt on orthodox Jewry and its representatives; Jewish students too were completely indifferent to tradition. Here Hildesheimer had already an opportunity of preparing himself for his future fight for the restoration of the honour of the Torah and the respect due its representatives. With dignity and determination he fought for the cause of traditional Judaism, assisted by congenial friends, above all by Wolf Feilchenfeld, the future Rabbi of Posen, and Hirsch Plato, later the head of the Teachers Training College founded in Duesseldorf and then transferred to Cologne. At the university of Halle, Hildesheimer perfected his knowledge of Semitic languages and obtained the doctorate on his thesis: "On the Right Way of Interpreting the Bible." Back in Halberstadt, he married his fiancee, with whom he had all the time remained in correspondence and had thus laid the foundation of that spiritual unity which was soon to make his house a centre for young men to whom Limmud Torah was the chief aim of their education, but who also aspired to acquire secular knowledge. He took an active part in the administration of the community and assisted its leaders with advice and help. Inclinations towards reform which in Halberstadt, too, tended to spread, were opposed by him with determination and, together with other energetic men, he succeeded in maintaining the strictly religious character of the congregation. At the same time he continued his scientific activity and among other things published in the *"Literaturblatt des Orients"* an essay: "Material fuer das Studium der Septuaginta," which shows both his familiarity with the Greek language and his scientific mind. In 1851 he was offered the post of Rabbi of the community at Eisenstadt, Hungary, which he accepted on condition that he be allowed to establish a college for rabbis.

III

It was a difficult task that Hildesheimer had undertaken. Right from the start he encountered fierce opposition from two sides: The Hassidic section was suspicious of a rabbi who possessed university training, fearing that religious training coupled with secular subjects would prejudice the students against the study of the Talmud, and that the poison of "enlightenment" would estrange the Ba-hurim (youthful students) from tradition. The reform parties, on the other hand, saw in the educated Orthodox rabbi a dangerous adversary and tried to cast on him the suspicion of obscurantism. Hildesheimer was not diverted from his course. He was resolved to prove that general studies may very well go with a thorough knowledge of the Talmud and consistently faithful adherence to tradition. During the founding of the Yeshivah, his gift of organization and enormous capacity for work became very evident. According to a well-planned syllabus, he imparted to a steadily increasing number of pupils a thorough knowledge of Talmud and *Posekim,* (jurisconsults, halakhic authorities) ; he also taught them German, classical languages and mathematics. All this he did practically single-handed, being rarely assisted in this task. He knew how to put general knowledge to the serv-ice of Talmudic study. Thus he used mathematics for elucida-tion of relevant passages of the Talmud (Erubin, Kilayim, Mid-doth) and Greek and Latin for the explanation of the foreign elements in the Hebrew and Aramaic languages. But it was especially the affectionate relation between himself and his stu-dents that contributed in no small measure to his success. With his wife, he took fatherly care of his students who, on their part, were attached to him with rare love and veneration. They not only received instruction from him but were also encouraged to do scien-tific work on their own. In the annual reports of the Rabbinical College, we find not only works from Hildesheimer's own pen such as, e.g., a paper on the measures, coins and weights mentioned in the Talmud, but also essays by his pupils, as, e.g., research on Saadia's introduction to his Commentary on the Psalms, by Jacob Cohn of Altona, later rabbi of Kattowitz. Besides his work for the Yeshivah, Hildesheimer had also to attend to the needs of the community, to supervise the religious institutions, to exercise, with the help of the Dayanim, judicial functions and to work for the charitable organizations.

Hildesheimer's successful activity in the Yeshivah should have convinced even his opponents of the soundness of his ideas ; at any rate those rabbis who maintained an objective judgment had to admit that he was inspired by the purest of motives.

R. Moshe Schick, much venerated even in Hassidic circles for his erudition as well as for his truly pious life, speaks of Hildesheimer as a *Tsaddik* (righteous and pious man). But the majority of the Hungarian orthodox Jews, in their complete lack of understanding of the demands of the time, led a campaign against the Rabbinical School and looked upon the German Rabbi with suspicion. Indeed, Hildesheimer was deeply hurt by the opposition of men who in reality ought to have been his supporters. But he did not turn from the road he had recognized as the right one. The short-sightedness of his opponents became evident both in the course of preparations for the Hungarian Jewish Congress, convened by the government with the object of regulating the status of the Hungarian Jewish communities, and also during the sessions of that congress (1868-1869). The Congress was entirely dominated by the reform party, the preparations were made without even consulting a single orthodox rabbi, and it was due only to the efforts of Rabbi Hildesheimer that some rabbis were later admitted as delegates. The proceedings centered round the question of the Seminary and the status of the rabbinate within the community. Owing to the determined opposition of the ultra-orthodox rabbis, Hildesheimer could not win over the Congress to his view, that they agree to the founding of a seminary on orthodox lines. The result was that a Seminary in Budapest was founded, remaining entirely under the influence of the reform party. The Congress itself led to that deep split which divided Hungarian Jewry literally into two denominations. Hildesheimer now tried another way to carry out his plan, viz., to found an orthodox rabbinical college in Hungary. He submitted to the Rabbinical Assembly in Hungary a motion to introduce the instruction of general subjects at the Pressburg Yeshivah. This proposal even gained the support of the Rabbi of Pressburg, the head of the Yeshivah, but it could not overcome the opposition within Hassidic circles.

IV

The futility of his efforts in this field may have largely contributed to his decision to leave the scene of his activities. As far back as in 1867, negotiations had been proceeding between the board of the Beth ha-Midrash in Berlin and Hildesheimer, with the object of engaging him as a teacher. That institute was then under the direction of R. Elchanan Rosenstein and R. Michael Landsberg. Its programme, comprising only Talmudic subjects, was to be enlarged by the addition of scientific subjects, like exegesis of the Scriptures, history, etc., in order to offer the students the possibility of a thorough training on a traditional basis. The head of the Rabbinical school at Eisenstadt was regarded as the suitable man for this task. Rabbi Hildesheimer was inclined to follow the call because he hoped to work in Germany with better success. At first the negotiations did not lead to a definite result because of obstacles raised by the praesidium of the Berlin Community, which probably planned the founding of a rabbinical college with reform tendencies. But when R. Elhanan Rosenstein died in January, 1869, and Hildesheimer was invited to become his successor as the co-rector of the Beth ha-Midrash, he decided to leave Eisenstadt and to go to Berlin, whither many of his pupils followed him.

Berlin, at that time, was entirely dominated by the reform party. With the death of Michael Sachs, the highly cultured and fearless representative of orthodox Jewry, the last obstacle was removed from the way of extreme reformism, and the Board of the Jewish Community—a body which is sufficiently characterized by the words of one of its members: "Over here orthodox Jewry is destined to die"—now summoned Abraham Geiger, the most unscrupulous protagonist of reform, from Frankfurt to Berlin. Now the time had come for the orthodox to look for a leader, and they found him in Ezriel Hildesheimer. Two hundred men, filled with enthusiasm for their Jewish faith, gathered round him to form an orthodox congregation, because they believed that his energy, his optimism, and his indomitable perseverance would bring about the revival of observant Judaism. His work in Berlin became the climax of his activity. His aim was at first the continuance of his activity at Eisenstadt within a larger framework. At the same time, the foundation of the congregation of Adath Yisrael offered him the possibility of work in another direction. Realizing the necessity of religious instruction of the young, he established, a few weeks after his assumption of office, the religious school of

Adath Yisrael. In this he was actively supported by Nathan Deutschlaender, one of the students who had followed him from Eisenstadt. That school, which provided its pupils with a wide range of Biblical and Talmudic knowledge, has done very much for the religious education of large sections of Berlin Jewry. It has re-awakened and preserved in them the enthusiasm for tradition and the respect for its representatives.

Much more important and more far-reaching in its consequences was the foundation of the Rabbinical College. At first it had been planned to take up again the project of attaching a rabbinical college to the Beth ha-Midrash on the Eisenstadt model. The plan of the re-organization of the Beth ha-Midrash and of the new course of studies was already completed. The two rabbis of the Beth ha-Midrash, Hildesheimer and Zomber, were to take charge of Talmudic subjects, David Cassel of the non-Talmudic subjects. But the institute never started work, partly due to external influences, which brought about the failure of the project, and partly to Hildesheimer's own refusal to participate. He demanded a college entirely in his charge, which he could fill with his spirit and for which he could bear the whole responsibility. The founding of such a college had become an urgent necessity, since, shortly before, the *"Hochschule fuer die Wissenschaft des Judentums"* had been started, with a tutorial staff comprising men like Abraham Geiger and Steinthal, who maintained a completely negative attitude towards tradition. If the future of Orthodox Jewry was to be assured, an institute had to be founded for the training of rabbis who should have Talmudic knowledge and scientific training, but who, above all, would be men of character. The personality of Hildesheimer, his profound learning, the purity of his character and his determination, were a guarantee that an institute in his charge would fulfill these requirements. Hildesheimer now approached several rabbis and outstanding laymen with his plan, and he had surprising success. A central committee of prominent orthodox personalities from all over the country was formed and a prospectus issued which gave an outline of the principles and of the syllabus of the new institute. It was intended to create for the Torah an abode in the most comprehensive sense, a Yeshivah which was to admit students from all walks of life, but which was to give special training to future rabbis. That training was to comprise not only Talmud and Codes, but also exegesis of the Scriptures, philosophy of religion, Jewish history, homiletics and pedagogics. Diligent work was required to overcome the difficulties and to clear up misunderstandings within and outside their own camp. There were, on the one hand, representatives of the Breslau Seminary under Zacharias Frankel to whom the emphasis laid on the strictly orthodox character of the new foundation appeared to be directed against their own institute. On the other hand, there were within the German orthodoxy, among the circles around Rabbi Hirsch, a good many who viewed the plan with suspicion because they feared that the attention devoted to general scientific subjects would prejudice an intensive study of the Talmud. This apprehension was unfounded in view of the personality of Hildesheimer and his activity in Hungary. At last, the combined efforts and the indefatigable perseverance of Hildesheimer and his collaborators succeeded in removing all obstacles, and on the 1st of Marheshvan, 5634 (October 22, 1873), the Rabbinical College of Orthodox Jewry in Berlin was solemnly opened. From all parts of Germany delegates arrived, the government was represented, and a large audience listened to Hildesheimer describing the nature and the significance of this new achievement of orthodox Jewry. In the College, science would find its place also, but the chief object would be to impart to the students a profound and comprehensive knowledge of the Torah, which was to enable them to carry on the historic task of Israel, to spread Torah in the communities which would choose them as their leaders and to strengthen and preserve loyalty to tradition.

For a quarter of a century, Hildesheimer himself remained at the head of the College, and his great success was chiefly due to his venerable, and at the same time lovable, personality. His zeal and the fire of his enthusiasm did not fail to have their effect on his pupils and to awaken in them the love for learning. The abundance of his knowledge in all spheres of Talmudic and post-Talmudic literature, combined with rare pedagogic ability, with patience that knew also to draw the weaker ones towards him, made him a leader whose teaching produced an abiding impression.

The success of the college was to no small extent due also to the activity of Hildesheimer's collaborators whom he chose with intuition. There was, above all, David Hoffmann, who, in addition to his comprehensive and profound knowledge of the Talmud, devoted himself to the exegesis of the Pentateuch and led it along new paths. In his *"Instanzen"* he successfully refuted the Graff-Wellhausen theory of the composition of the Pentateuch, at the time prevailing in the scientific world and penetrating also into Jewish circles. On the basis of the sources, Hoffmann, disproved conclusively the critical theories. His commentary on Leviticus and Deuteronomy deals with questions of Bible criticism and shows how the traditional conception of the Biblical word may very well be reconciled with the modern scientific outlook.

Of the other teachers, Abraham Berliner considerably enriched general Jewish history and the history of Jewish literature by his energetic activity as collector and research worker, whilst Jacob Barth was recognized in the scientific world as an authority in the field of Semitic languages. His research work on the Hebrew grammar and Lexicon, his papers on Isaiah and Job, appeared under the auspices of the College and indicated the way of approach to the Bible text by philological methods, on a Jewish basis, opposed to all conjectures and hypotheses. The College had solved in an outstanding way its task of training men who were equipped with the necessary knowledge and imbued with the courage of their convictions and the love of tradition, to qualify them as leaders in their communities. In their communities, his disciples exercised great care that the heritage of the forefathers be preserved and that Torah learning and a Jewish sense of duty be implanted in the young generation. In congregations where the spirit was not homogeneous, they knew how to counteract destructive tendencies, to win respect for traditional Jewry and to secure it its rightful position. Many of them, by their scientific work, have brought honor to orthodox Jewry and have destroyed the prejudice of the incompatibility of scientific study and loyalty towards tradition.

Hildesheimer's founding of the Rabbinical College is an achievement which has proved to be a real blessing to traditional Jewry. True to the Mishnaic principle *ve-Haamidu Talmidim Harbeh* ("Raise many disciples"), he saw in the direction and the development of his institution the most important task of his life, and devoted to it all his energy. Nor did he neglect his congregation, the Adath Yisrael. The latter was at first only a private congregation, intended to serve as a bulwark against the arbitrariness and destructiveness of reform, and to create—if only in a small circle—new religious life on the basis of the holy tradition. But when it seceded from the main body of the community, it possessed already all the institutions of a congregation, created by Hildesheimer in an exemplary form: Kashruth institutions, Shehitah, Mikveh, and Hevrah Kadisha. The *Austritt* (secession) itself had been made possible by the decree on secession of 1876. It had become a necessity through the attitude of the liberals who saw "progress" in the abolition of venerated institutions and in the negation of the aspirations of the Jewish people. If a man of such conciliatory spirit and loving heart as Rabbi Hildesheimer decided to take that step, it was clear that only bitter necessity forced him to do so. Under the circumstances it was the only means to maintain the authority of tradition and thus to save the honor of Judaism. In Hungary the idea of secession had been realized in the extreme and had even led to a complete split of Jewry. In Germany it was Rabbi Hirsch who propagated the idea, and Hildesheimer, together with him, had obtained the decree on secession. But he never considered secession the ideal; on the contrary, as far as possible (e.g., in the field of social relief), he maintained unity, for the idea of the "Klal," the feeling of solidarity with all Israel, was one of the outstanding features of his character and is reflected everywhere in his activity. The secession had its beneficial effect on the "liberals" as well. It brought about a more tolerant attitude on their part, and more respect for the conservative minorities within the large communities.

In his congregation, just as in his Yeshivah, Hildesheimer was the tutor and the leader. He often gave lectures and preached sermons, and while he was not a brilliant orator, his great learning and his profound knowledge of Judaism lent to his sermons a wealth of ideas which did not fail to impress his listeners.

V

We have so far chiefly described Hildesheimer's work for the preservation and dissemination of the Torah, and indeed this was the centre of his activity, as he put it on the occasion of the opening of the Rabbinical College: "The work of training students in Jewish knowledge and their education in faithfulness to the Jewish law form the centre of gravity of my vocation, in comparison with which I consider every other activity of second importance." His pupils were not only the students of the Yeshivah and the members of his congregation; his teaching found its way to the masses of Jewry as well, for he was also considered an authority in the field of Halakhah and was recognized as such even by the great scholars of Eastern Europe. His comprehensive knowledge is also revealed in his writings. In one College publication, he deals with the chapters on astronomy in *Hilkhoth Kiddush ha-Hodesh* of the *Rambam;* in another, with the layout of the Herodian Temple according to the description of Flavius Josephus. Of special importance is a work of his old age, his edition of the MS of the 8th century compendium, *Halakhot Gedoloth,* discovered in the Vatican. Mention should also be made of many of his pamphlets written against Reform, and of numerous articles in periodicals on local questions of the moment or on general Jewish problems. But no less important was his activity in the field of *Gemiluth Hessed.* Apart from his fabulous generosity and his untiring care of Talmidei Hakhamin, he was always at the head of every fund-raising campaign for the benefit of needy coreligionists, even in the most distant countries. His readiness to help was not charity in the usual sense, it was rather based on the idea that the Jews of the various countries are organs of the body of one nation and therefore any pain inflicted on any part affects the whole of the body of the people. Hence each part must help all other parts. The saying *"Kol Yisrael arevin zeh lazeh"* (all Israelites are responsible for one another) was given ample application by him. In this way, he succeeded in bridging the gulf between Eastern and Western Jewry, which was very wide in the Germany of those days. By his indefatigable activity on behalf of the *Falashas,* in the organization of assistance for the refugees from the pogroms in Russia and in innumerable other causes, he showed what a single energetic individual full of ardent love for his people can achieve. Nor was his charity limited to fellow Jews. He was an active member of public societies for the relief of the poor, and during the war between Germany and France he extended his care to the wounded soldiers in the hospitals and to their destitute dependents.

His love for Erets Yisrael and his efforts for its settlement deserve special mention. Even during his term of office in Eisenstadt he was one of the most successful Gabbaim and, according to his own statement, he was able to remit to the Kolel* of Austria-Hungary in Jerusalem an average annual subsidy of 18,000, and in emergency years even 19,000, Austrian Gulden, very considerable sums in those days. But gradually he gained the conviction that the method of *"Halukkah"*, in which the decisive factor was not the merit and the need of the individual, but often quite different considerations, was not the right method and that he could no longer be responsible for it. However, the principles of distribution of the funds became a matter of controversy of which he himself said, "He who tries to intervene stirs up a hornets' nest of the worst kind under the sun." As he left Eisenstadt, his association with the Hungarian Kolel came to an end, and he had nothing to do with it any more. In Germany, too, his work for Palestine took up a large part of his far-reaching and untiring activity. He devoted his special interest to the education of the young, but here, too, any attempt at improvement and introduction of the teaching of general knowledge encountered the most embittered opposition of the hassidic extremists. What he envisaged he expressed in the following words: "A radiant picture of Jerusalem stands as an ideal before my eyes even before it will please the Heavenly Father to fulfill the messianic words and to establish the real ideal of Yerushalayim: an upright, loyal young generation, of which one may be justly proud, brought up in Palestine, imbued with deep and real religious feeling, and equipped with the indispensable secular knowledge. By their

*The Jewish population in Palestine was divided into the so-called Kolelim, according to their countries of origin. These Kolelim received subsidies from their correligionists in the respective countries.

peace-loving and blameless conduct they are to uphold the honour of Jerusalem. The average individual shall have a sound knowledge of Bible and Talmud, and the majority, according to capacity and inclination, should penetrate deep into the Jewish Scriptures; they should earn their living by their own toil, by craftsmanship or trade which is properly learnt and honestly exercised. Such a young generation is the high ideal towards which all friends of Zion and Jerusalem strive with all the fibres of their being." This was also the underlying idea of the founding of the *"Lemaan Tsiyon"* (For the sake of Zion) society among whose various objects was the assistance of artisans by means of loans. Of great importance was also the erection of dwellings for Jewish pilgrims and poor people, which was initiated as early as 1858 by Hildesheimer, together with R. Jacob Ettlinger, the rabbi of Altona, and his own brother-in-law, Joseph Hirsch of Halberstadt. As a consequence of the increased immigration there was a scarcity of apartments. From funds raised in Austria-Hungary, Germany and Holland, a plot of 13000 sq. pic was purchased in one of the most beautiful and healthful parts of the city, opposite the Mt. of Olives. On the plot small dwellings were built. In the year 1882, after the pogroms in Russia, committees were set up everywhere to handle the emigration of Jews from Russia, and when in Berlin a joint consultation took place on the countries of destination of these emigrants, *Hildesheimer was the only one who advocated Palestine as a possible destination,* whereas the other delegates almost unanimously proposed to direct the masses of the emigrants to America. Even then he had recognized what has now become a generally accepted view, that only Palestine can be a safe and permanent homeland for the Jewish people.

VI

We have tried to give a description of the work of Ezriel Hildesheimer and to throw into relief his nature and his character. But his qualities, love of the Torah, deep piety, and a loving kind heart that felt sympathy with all who suffered, were not separate traits; they all merged in his unique and harmonious personality. In the "Israelit" (V, 1860) a disciple describes this teacher in the following words: "Do you want, dear reader, to get an idea of this man? Then take all the virtues that adorn a man, a Jew: genuine piety, boundless love for mankind, strict honesty, infinite enthusiasm for our holy religion, untiring energy, superhuman assiduity, disinterestedness, together with amazing erudition in philosophy, in the exact sciences, in classical and modern languages and particularly in specifically Jewish studies, in Talmud and Posekim. Dear reader, take all these excellent qualities and many others, and then picture to yourself the man whom all his pupils adore, for whom all who know him have the greatest admiration—the man who gathers round him seventy pupils and teaches them Torah day and night, who has been a benefactor to thousands, who feeds many hungry people and procures maintenance and medicines for many sick people and whose *Gemiluth Hessed* never fails. In spite of all this he possessed singular modesty and never boasted in any way of his devoted work for the Jewish cause. His whole nature bore the stamp of the prophet's demand *"Hatsnea lekheth im Elohekha"* (to walk humbly with thy God). As we speak of his activity and his achievements, we must not forget to mention his wife, who stood by his side as a true *ezer kenegdo* (helpmate) and who, full of understanding and energy, assisted him in his work. The general admiration which he enjoyed found its expression on the occasion of his 70th birthday which I, too, had the privilege of attending. Numerous pupils came to visit him, many of them from great distances. Many educational and charitable institutions, and especially his congregation and the College, competed in paying homage to him. In the last years of his life signs of old age showed themselves even in this indefatigable worker, who during all his life had never allowed himself to rest. But it was still given to him to witness the further development of his work and to live long enough to see the celebration of the 25th Jubilee of his College. On the 4th of Tammuz 5659 (1899), he closed his eyes. At his funeral it became again evident how deeply his personality had impressed all that knew him, far beyond the circle of his friends. In the funeral orations, expression was given to the feelings of the loss sustained by the passing away of a man of unique qualities, who had been a leader and a guide to his people. His spirit lived on in his pupils and in his sons, one of whom, Hirsch Hildesheimer, distinguished himself by his extensive activity in the defense of anti-Semitic attacks, and in particular in the defense of the Shehitah, when the danger of its suppression threatened. His other son, Meier Hildesheimer, was a worthy successor of his father in the field of charity.

Rabbi Ezriel Hildesheimer belonged to the men who will always live on in the memory of the Jewish people, and to whom apply the words:

> *"And they that be wise shall shine as the brightness of the firmament; and they that turn many to righteousness, as the stars for ever and ever"* (Daniel 12, 3).

ELIE BENAMOZEGH

By Josue Jehouda

ELIE BENAMOZEGH

By Josue Jehouda

I

In 1895 a Catholic from Lyon, Aimé Pallière, appealed to the Rabbi of Livorno, asking him to instruct him in Judaism. Contrary to all his expectations, the Rabbi strongly urged him to remain within the faith of his birth. "And," he wrote him, "Christianity, as seen in the Jewish tradition, presents the universal aspects of Monotheism, equally acceptable to the Gentile. This rather unknown Christianity is based upon an accord with Noah and is called Noahism." That is why, when Aimé Pallière, a Catholic by birth, approached Rabbi Benamozegh asking what to do in order to be a convert to Judaism, the Rabbi answered, "In order to be our brother, in the sense that you want it, there is no need for you to embrace Judaism in the manner that you understand it. I mean by that, that it is not necessary for you to submit to the limitations of our law. We Jews are carrying within ourselves the form of Religion predestined ultimately for the whole human race, the one and only faith to which the Gentiles will also become subject and through which they will be saved by the grace of God, as were our Patriarchs before the Law was established."

Rabbi Benamozegh explained to the Catholic, who was all prepared to become converted to Judaism (and who became more and more surprised to see the lack of enthusiasm on the part of the Rabbi), that there is no reason whatsoever for a Christian to be converted in order to become acceptable in the Jewish order of the world. Judaism sees a distinction between Jew and Gentile, he writes to his disciple. The former, as priests of humanity, are subjected to the priestly rules of Judaism. The latter, as the laymen of humanity, are subject only to the one, ancient and eternal, universal religion, in whose service the Jews have been placed. Christianity, however, has given birth to the most regrettable confusion. "But without any doubt," adds the Rabbi, "any layman has the right to become a priest; it is up to the individual to embrace the Jewish faith if he so desires, as long as he is fully aware that he is not required to do so."

II

The religion called *Noahism,* as taught by the rabbi to his disciple, is at the same time unchangeable and progressive. It is based upon the agreement between Providence and Noah and embraces all of humanity. It contains seven basic principles conformity with which would obtain for the non-Jewish immigrant to ancient or modern Palestine: (1) equality before the law, (2) the Jewish community's help in time of trouble, ("The non-Jew accepting these principles for his conduct must be fed when poor, cured when sick, and provided with free burial if found dead and unattended"), and, above all, (3) a status of acceptance, for he would be considered a righteous non-Jew and "The righteous people among the nations of the world have a share in the world to come, even as the Jews." Of these seven principles, one, the promotion of justice, is positive; and six are negative: He must promise to abstain from cruelty to animals, blasphemy, theft, murder, idolatry and immorality. This religion, meant for the Gentile, escaped the attention of many sages. "That fact," the rabbi continues placidly, "does not make it less of an incontestable truth. It is the ultimate key to all difficulties in history and especially in the relations among the different biblical religions." Further on the rabbi notes: "The Nazarene was in the right and deserves every praise, when he freed the Gentiles from the obligations of the Mosaic Law. But his disciples erred when, in later years, they demanded the very same freedom for the Israelites."

The *Minim* whom the ancient sages mention were the ancient Christians. Of all the laws, they respected only the Decalogue. The Decalogue has served the theologians of the new faith as a basis for establishing a rather arbitrary distinction between the moral and ceremonial laws of Judaism. It is not true, as Christian theology with incredible assurance affirms, that the Decalogues contain only moral laws. The banishment of images, the interdiction of pronouncing God's name in vain, most of all the institution of the Sabbath, do not belong to the realm of moral laws. It is false to say that civil, political and ceremonial laws were given to Moses gradually as the need arose. With a few rare exceptions, no occasion ever gave rise to these laws. In most cases there was no necessity to apply them for years to come; some were never applied, for lack of opportunity. It is not true that Moses placed only the two tablets of the command-ments in the Ark. The book of the Law, which Moses wrote in his last days, was placed side by side with the commandments. The tab-lets themselves contain commandments which could never be called moral laws. It is not true that only the Decalogue was inscribed on a stone altar when the Jews entered Palestine; the law in its entirety—all the commandments—was also recorded thereon. If the ten commandments were more solemnly proclaimed, if they were transmitted with more elaborate ceremonies, it is, as our sages so wisely said, because they envisage the Law in its entirety, be-cause they are made up of general principles from which all other commandments are deductible. And if, on the other hand, the prophets had most often chosen for discussion such topics as justice, charity, morality, it is because their contemporaries tended to observe the ceremonial part of Judaism, while they failed to live up to the model of virtue which Hebraism demands."

III

Hyacinthe Loyson, the great Christian who attempted in vain to reform Catholicism, reproaches the Jews "for having remained silent too long." There can be no doubt that prejudices and hatred on the part of the Christian world forced Israel into this self-effacing attitude. But since the Jews have had freedom of self-expression it became necessary for them to propagate their monotheistic and universal teachings. Loyson exclaims, "How are we to understand Christianity as long as Judaism, its source of origin, remains repudiated? Jews have to furnish reasons for their steady objections to our interpretation of the role and teachings of Chrisitanity. Christian theology, be it Catholic, Protestant or Orthodox, considers the Ancient Testament as but the forerunner of the New." But the independent exegesis, and more particularly the critics of the Gospels, have completely shattered these fundamental ideas. The certainty that Monotheism is the universal religion, predestined for the human race, can be deduced from tradition. In the time of the Messiah, the credo of the Jewish religion will unite all nations of the world: There will be one God, Father of all mankind, and one family of brothers united in their adoration of the divine Father.

This universal facet of Jewish doctrine, developed with serene confidence by Rabbi Benamozegh, has not been sufficiently expounded. But this much we know: The world has repudiated the view of Ernest Renan that Judaism is a religion without dogmas and without God; or that of Werner Sombart, who claimed that the Jewish religion was materialistic, averse to anything mysterious and eschewing any enthusiasm for that which is divine in the tangible world. But it is impossible to undo *all* the damage which these "scientific" stupidities have caused Israel through the centuries. Advocates of this singular shortsightedness which predominated in regard to the religion of Israel will profit by consulting the work of Paul Vulliaud. This thinker of Catholic origin devoted his lifework to showing how these different theories, one more grotesque than the other, and widely disseminated to hurt Israel, should be evaluated. As to the real shortcomings of Jewish people we seem to agree with Jean Izoulet, another Catholic thinker, "There can be no doubt that the Jewish people, like any other people, has its faults and vices, even greater ones, if it is true that vices run in proportion to virtues, and abysses in proportion to summits. But it is not through this that Israel has succeeded. It is not because of . . . but in spite of. . . ." It is only through the possession and application, throughout centuries, of the highest wisdom as well as philosophical and political virtues! Let us therefore deduce with Izoulet that "the spiritual law of Israel must no longer be underestimated."

IV

In order to convert heathens to monotheism, a mission abandoned by Israel for almost two thousand years, Christianity cloaked Jewish ethics with a pagan myth. That is one reason why the monotheistic doctrine, thus imprisoned in an "in adjecto" contradiction, in spite of all theological subtleties, does not succeed in balancing the social and individual spheres, morals and politics, the old and new aspirations. From this lack of balance stems the religious crisis which, in our present-day-civilization, represents the almost constant revolution and international disorder so menacing to peace on earth. Deprived of justice, Christian Society is incapable of organizing itself in peacetime. Unknowingly, Benamozegh brings proof, far in advance, that, after two thousand years of Christianity, extermination camps were still possible! For Christian charity disdained its natural companion—justice.

Christianity, having thrust away the spiritual law of Israel, thus empties itself of all meaning. If it wants to live in accord with itself, it must free the individual from all coercion of this law. But a society, void of all legal limitations, falls into depravity of morals and heresies become unavoidable. Going even further, Christianity, having rejected the laws of Moses, is forced to adopt heathen laws. From this stems its fundamental dualism, both chronic and tragic. Incapable of establishing a homogeneous society, Christianity denies the blessings of this world which it considers evil. Hence its conception of the present world as a valley of tears; hence its fundamental pessimism; hence particularly its fatalistic passivity which borders on *imprévoyance* and which is often confused with blind confidence in God. Therefore also that resigned disdain towards world events, towards blessings and curses, towards the past, present and future, in short, towards history. Belief in a better humanity which clearly emerges in Judaism, where industry, work and the good things of life are so actively stressed, are forced into second place in Christianity, as it is primarily concerned with salvation of the soul and with the hereafter. In Judaism work is considered like a cult; idleness is condemned. And it is this affirmation of life on earth which makes Judaism appear to be a materialistic religion.

V

The views of Rabbi Benamozegh, who drank of the purest Jewish tradition with regard to Israel's vocation, in this respect parallel the views of the Catholic writer, Saint-Yves d'Alveydre. The latter sees in the vocation of Israel a constant example for Humanity: "Like the falcon in the clouds," he writes, "that little people is never more alive than when it is in the thrusts of tempests which swallow heavy vessels. It rediscovers its wings and gains all its virile and vibrant energies, all its strength, all the force of its original institutions; it cunningly rides on the breezes of the storm, while great political bodies are engulfed, while they stupidly throw themselves upon each other. That which would destroy any other human group tends to revive this one and restore to it its original form."

The great achievement of Benamozegh lies in his having clarified, several centuries after the rise of Kabbalah, the original meaning which can be traced to it, but abandoned by Jewish thinkers as dangerous because of its close resemblance to the teachings of Christianity.

"I have always taken care," says he, "not to succumb to the temptation of despising the Kabbalah out of hatred for Christianity. The followers of Kabbalah have every right to deplore the strange suspicion which Christianity has cast upon their doctrines. Indeed, if we were to reject everything in our lore which bears close resemblance to other religions, good-bye to Judaism." With incontestable scientific ability the Rabbi of Livorno has shown that "it is this struggle between Israel and Christianity, lasting for centuries, which retards the coming of permanent peace between nations." He has formulated a spiritual solution to the Jewish problems which the sociologist Izoulet, starting from the positivism of Auguste Comte, and without ever having known Benamozegh's work, offers in his own way:

VI

"The vocation of Israel primarily lies in its function of keeping the tradition of universal monotheism alive. The seed of this tradition is found in the Pentateuch and the flower in the works of the Kabbalah. Thus the tradition of Israel remained alive for thousands of years. However, in our time, the 'Science of Judaism' elaborated upon by the disciples of Mendelssohn has rejected the authority of the Kabbalah and has thus hurt the very root of Jewish religion. It is only because of this fact that materialistic and atheistic science was able to usurp the place of knowledge transmitted by tradition. Jewish thinkers themselves believed that Science was destined to dethrone religion. When Max Nordau at the end of the last century denounces conventional hypocrisy, he does so in the name of modern science as opposed to religion. While attacking conventional falsities, he strikes unintentionally at the deep roots of Israel, which is as much a science as a religion and which, in the course of its long existence, has stood up against much more terrible onslaughts than those of materialistic science whose cause so many Jewish thinkers have espoused, unaware all the time how far they have gone astray from the true path of Jewish world outlook.

VII

Offspring of a family from Fez, Elie Benamozegh was born in 1823 in Livorno. In that town he held, for almost fifty years, the position of Rabbi-Preacher. His Moroccan origin indicates Sephardic ancestry. Because of the writings of Munk and of his successors, we nowadays know better than ever the vast literary output of Spanish Jewry at the rise of the Middle Ages. On the other hand, we are much less familiar with the source material of the Semitic genius of the Kabbalah, which represents the esoteric trend of Hebraism. Benamozegh is a commentator well-versed in the Kabbalistic doctrine, transmitted from generation to generation down to our days. Under the tutelage of Rabbi Coriat, Benamozegh at an early age became initiated in Jewish science. Later on, through self-education, he assimilated European culture. As he advanced in his studies, both sacred and profane, new problems arose which he attempted to solve with full independence of spirit. His culture was subjected to the scrutiny of a piercing mind. His information accumulated to such a point that his writings became flooded with quotations. All this he culled from original sources, enlightened by a wealth of details which hold our constant attention. Not looking for anything in particular, he is only anxious to contribute his share to the re-establishment of truth as transmitted through Jewish tradition for the good of Humanity.

But, precisely because he was looked upon as fallen under the spell of the Kabbalah, he became a lone wolf among his correligionists. He became discredited even before his works became known. The Intelligentsia, devoted to the science of Israel, remained hostile to the Kabbalah. To their liberal rationalism and to their mnemotechnical methods, they added contempt for any mysticism, even a healthy one, which they considered destructive to Jewish fate. They barred Benamozegh from being recognized, thus depriving Judaism of the wonderful contribution of that silenced thinker who one day was to be called *"The Plato of Italian Judaism,"* and of whom Pallière said "My master is not only a scientist, he is also a man of God." His isolated disciples in Italy were unable to provide the audience due him. As his disciple, Dante Lattes, sadly notes, Benamozegh found during his lifetime "a weak generation, incapable of understanding him."

The exclusively materialistic and rational ideas which had emanated from Germany served as a pattern for the Jewish reform movement in all countries. The reformists tried to impose their authority with a show of ponderous erudition. They placed their own thinkers, like Mendelssohn or Solomon Maimon, on dusty shelves, managed to ignore a philosopher of the stature of Nahman Krochmal, and hardly ever mentioned Benamozegh.

Thus, in spite of the ardent praise of Pallière for his revered teacher, Benamozegh has until this day failed to inspire a single detailed documentary study in Jewish literature. When the Jewish writers do not ignore him completely, they are satisfied with a few superficial remarks. With the exception of his Italian disciples, only Jacob Gordin has attempted, in a short, hardly known study, to place Benamozegh in relation to other modern Jewish thinkers, by giving him the great place he deserves. In his erudite writings about the Jewish Kabbalah, the Catholic author, Paul Vulliaud, mentions Benamozegh frequently, at times praising him to high heaven, and at times shooting at him ironical arrows, according to his habit, only to conclude finally: "The Rabbi of Livorno has been, it is true, a superior intelligence in contemporary Judaism." This admission on the part of a writer as exacting as Paul Vulliaud represents a solemn approbation which should not be ignored.

On the other hand, Jean de Menasche, the Jewish writer converted to Catholicism, has attempted to formulate the ideas of Benamozegh, but notwithstanding his sympathy for the Rabbi, his neo-thomistic conception of life prevents him from paying him tribute, and his attacks against Benamozegh's attitude towards Christianity rest on erroneous premises.

A general appraisal of the work of the genial rabbi will be possible only when his hitherto inedited works have been published. At this moment the recent republication of his volume "Jewish and Christian Morality", which first appeared in 1867, then in 1925, but which went scarcely noticed, although it received the prize of the Alliance Israelite Universelle, at last has permitted Benamozegh to be introduced to the general public.

VIII

The publication of this volume marks a turning point in the history of occidental thought. For the work of Benamozegh, drawing from three primary sources of Judaism, namely the Bible, Rabbinic literature and the Kabbalah, holds the key to the modern religious problem whose solution is impossible without the help of Jewish monotheism. The literary world, at last, has an opportunity to find a valid answer to the religious crisis facing humanity in our time, with the help of this modest, self-effacing and retiring rabbi, hidden away in a lost corner of Italy. Thus, forty years after his death, our rabbi finally obtains an audience befitting his all-embracing genius.

Benamozegh, no doubt, should be placed among the great masters of modern Jewish thought, who are still waiting for complete recognition by the Jewish and non-Jewish world. The main contribution of this "genial Rabbi," as Guglielmo Ferrero in the "Jewish Revue of Geneva" of July 1934 called him, is considerable.

Thus he writes: "Not before 1931, by this I mean, not until the moment that Mr. Josue Jehouda brought the volume 'Jewish and Christian Morality' to my attention, had I heard the name of its author; I did not even realize that Livorno had for years the honor of counting among its residents a man of such outstanding genius and an author of so great a doctrine of life. It is a book which impressed me. Yea, it is a satirical work which, somehow, by its wit and purpose, if not by its composition and style, reminds one of Pascal's *Provincial Letters*. It seems to me that nobody desiring to understand the cause of all contradictions which beset the present day occidental world could remain indifferent to the greatness and depth of the historical views upon which Benamozegh bases his arguments. No other book has made me feel and understand, I should say, the community of distant origins, i.e., the deep-rooted spiritual affinities of Judaism and Christianity in face of all that which, in our present day civilization, stems from Greco-Roman culture. If the Christian method was strongly influenced by Greek metaphysics, Christian morality is the result of the long labors of the Jewish spirit alone. This conclusion emerges irresistibly out of these brilliant pages; many are the enigmas in the history of Christianity which become illuminated by the glow of these ideas."

The great accomplishment of Benamozegh lies in his having placed Israel in relation to Christianity, and Christianity in relation to Israel. This double historico-philosophical illumination was never attempted with so much intellectual vigor and moral frankness by any thinker before Benamozegh. For understandable reasons, Jewish literature remains mute in regard to the position of Israel towards the Christian schism; it is a subject which Jewish authors dare not approach with a light heart. However, in order to understand the trend of universal history, the spiritual struggle occurring at all times and continuing in our days under the most diverse forms, in spite of forever changing habits, it is indispensable to set the ideological conflict which separates Israel from Christianity, in its proper perspective.

Yet this new defense of Israel against Chrisitanity was achieved only at the end of the 19th century, and with the help of Benamozegh's work. The hour has come when his authoritative contribution is available to our generation, stricken but purified by unparallelled trials. In this decisive hour when all fundamental values of our culture are being challenged, the volume of "Jewish and Christian Morality" has had certain repercussions among the cultured public, more than ever frightened and lost. This volume offers an objective analysis of the cause of the present day crisis, based not on theological arguments valid only for those who have faith, but upon objective and logical reasoning.

For only by minute comparison of the ancient Jewish texts and the Gospels can it be clearly shown that the origin of our present-day crisis goes back to the birth of Christianity. With rare perspicacity, Benamozegh lays bare the original cause of the religious conflict which, for more than two thousand years, has divided Jews and Christians. The field, encumbered by the tangled maze of petty dogmatic disputes, is at long last cleared. The real cause for the lack of political balance in the world, which afflicts civilized people with revolutions and wars, appears to be discovered. The vicissitudes of Christian origins permit us to take a stand in regard to the conflict between Israel and Christianity. It is at last possible to construct, upon the purified basis of monotheistic doctrine, a solid bridge between Judaism and Christianity. Scorning all apologies, Benamozegh, despite his occasional satirical tone, seeks most of all a basis for an understanding between Christian and Jew. He brings us the tools necessary for a reconciliation between the mother religion and her two recalcitrant daughters, Christianity and Islam. The peace of tomorrow depends upon their spiritual understanding.

As the successor of Salvador, Benamozegh aspires to reestablish the lost basis for a universal religion. This basis he correctly finds in the Jewish esoterism, called the Kabbalah.

As a thinker, endowed with a central vision, he projects full light upon the universal facet of the doctrine of Israel, a doctrine which, for almost two thousand years, has been totally eclipsed by Christianity, but which, under the name of Noahism, has been preserved by Jewish tradition. Benamozegh also reestablishes several authentic rules of the spiritual world, without which no harmonious expansion of individual, social or political life is possible. He also offers us the elements indispensable for formulating a final answer to the empty enigmas. His answer is all the more plausible and objective, because it brings reason and faith together. In their separation lies the primary cause for the spiritual weakness of civilized humanity. Thence also stems the failure of Christianity to recognize the true spirit of the Jewish Messiah, which Christianity borrowed and propagated throughout the heathen world.

IX

Benamozegh sheds new light upon the origins and formation of Christianity to the satisfaction of every unbiased spirit and dispels, at the same time, the so-called mystery of Israel. Its enigma of thousands of years is beginning to be solved. The spiritual world becomes a source of unending joy and a tangible reality for everyone concerned. That is why a final answer to the enigma of Israel contains, ipso facto, a solution for the religious crisis of civilized humanity. This solution must culminate in an indispensable accord between faith and reason, which will put an end to the atheistic materialism which leads to political imperialism and mocking scepticism. Faith, mystified and isolated from life, must be based upon a permanent and rational basis, from which neither the supernatural nor revelation is to be excluded. This renewed faith based upon reason will bring us the indispensable agreement between Israel and the world, which is the best assurance for peace among nations. From this agreement, based upon a spiritual foundation rather than the shifting balance of unpredictable economic forces, will be born the new civilization longed for by all men of good will, conscious of their responsibilities.

MARCUS HOROVITZ

By Isaac Unna

MARCUS HOROVITZ

By Isaac Unna

When Rabbi Marcus Horovitz died in 1910, the city of Frankfort-on-the-Main was a center of Jewish life. Today, not only are its synagogues burnt down, its houses of learning destroyed, its hospitals and orphanages obliterated, the wonderful social and cultural institutions of that Jewish community wiped out, but the town itself is but a ghost of its previous splendor. It is not for the first time in history that centers of Jewish life have become victims of fanatical fury and devastation. But what the spiritual heroes of the Jewish people have created has remained a potent source of good, all the powers of darkness notwithstanding.

The seed which Rabbi Horovitz sowed, too, will not be lost. His personality will continue to be felt, his disciples carrying on his teachings; his writings will endure as a monument of his spirit and his work. In his personality there is revealed a harmonious integrity—in the original sense of the word—and therefore he knew how to unite people, gathering around him men of different opinions and influencing them. He was an outstanding scholar of Rabbinics and also a man of great general culture; but these two elements did not clash; they existed side by side in him and complemented each other. His knowledge of secular subjects served him in rendering decisions concerning the *Halakhah* (Jewish Law), while the great rabbis of the Talmud served as models in his social relations. One of his outstanding traits was his desire to create *Kiddush ha-Shem* whenever possible, and to maintain, within and without the fold, the honor and reputation of Torah and of Judaism. He had started to work toward this end in the small communities to which he first ministered, but only in Frankfort did his personality blossom forth in its full beauty. His acceptance of the position of Rabbi in that outstanding community was in itself a considerable risk, for he had to count with

249

the opposition of the right and of the left. He came in conflict
with the separatist group of Rabbi S. R. Hirsch, who had declared
it the duty of loyal Jews to withdraw from the general Jewish community, and who considered his acceptance of a pulpit therein a
hostile act. In the community itself, only a short time before, the
"Liberals" had violently opposed the orthodox element, and
categorically refused any concessions. Finally the "liberal"
president consented to some of the orthodox practices only
out of fear that he might lose the bulk of his members; deep down
in its heart his group remained opposed to the new order which
justified withdrawal from a congregation any of whose central
institutions was not conducted in accord with Jewish law and
custom. Only the self-confidence of Rabbi Horovitz and his
determination to maintain his stand against everybody, enabled
him to assume the difficult task. After a few years he was acknowledged as a leader. The Orthodox community had to recognize
him as an outstanding *Talmid Hakham,* who as a spiritual leader
never strayed from the requirements of orthodox Judaism and
who created exemplary religious institutions. In the general
community, he was recognized as a man of outstanding culture
and great charm, but one who would never accept any compromise in matters of Jewish law. When early in the 1880's
I lived in Frankfort as a disciple of Rabbi Horovitz, Dr. Heinrich
Heinemann, his friend and collaborator, once in the course of a
discussion said to me: "If Rabbi Horovitz had come in conflict
with his Board ten years ago, his position might have been endangered. If today, however, such a conflict should arise, the
Board would have to resign." The extraordinary influence which
he was able to achieve in a comparatively short period of time
was due, to a great extent, to the power of his personality and
to the grace of his social contacts. He has been called a great
diplomat. If diplomacy implies a psychological understanding
and the art of handling people, he should indeed be called a
diplomat. It was because of these qualities that he commanded
respect and admiration in all circles, orthodox, liberal, and
assimilatory, and was able to succeed in far-reaching charitable
endeavors. Only his intimates knew how widely spread these
activities were, what vast amounts went through his hands for
the support of the needy. The religious school established by

him was in its beginning entirely financed by private donations. The society for the support of orphans in Palestine and the society "Lemaan Tsion" owe, to a great extent, their prosperous development to him. To many a hapless individual, too, did he extend a helping hand. Just one example out of many: In 1892, the ritual libel trial against the butcher Buschoff took place in Cleve. Buschoff was acquitted, but the excitement among the population, caused by anti-Semitic rabble-rousers, made it impossible for him to remain in Xanten. He needed money to finance his emigration to America. On Thursday night his acquittal was made known in Frankfort, and on Friday afternoon, Rabbi Horovitz had already 15,000 marks for this purpose at his disposal. His prestige in the public eye was greatly due to the fact that in everything concerning Judaism and its ritual, he met the most exacting esthetic requirements.

Respect for the Sanctuary, to his mind, should manifest itself not only in the Synagogue and during Services. He was, for instance, very strict about maintaining order and dignity during religious judiciary functions, such as divorces. This attitude, together with his noble bearing, won him respect and influence in non-Jewish circles, too. He was a member of Frankfort's educational commission, the first rabbi indeed to conduct classes in Jewish subjects at the high school ("Gymnasium")! At his funeral the representative of the city expressed the sorrow of all its inhabitants at the passing of a man who was "always gentle in his philosophy of life, always princely in his thinking." The introduction of Jewish religious education in the Public Schools was due to his initiative. He often was invited to serve as expert before the court. In Germany, as elsewhere, rabbis, out of unjustified sympathy, were often induced to give recommendations to unworthy persons. During a trial against a man who possessed such a document, the judge exclaimed to Rabbi Horovitz: "I have never seen one of your recommendations in the hands of an unworthy man."

Besides his work on behalf of his flock, he developed an extensive field of activity beyond its borders. In all affairs of German and World Jewry, in rabbinic associations, in the Bnai Brith movement, in the Hilfsverein der Deutschen Juden, and above all, in the work for Erets Yisrael, he played an important part.

He had all the qualities of a real *Talmid Hakham,* deriving his powers from his deep attachment to Torah and tradition, and what satisfied him most was studying and teaching. The quality of sympathetic understanding which he manifested in his intercourse with all people, showed itself especially to his pupils. He was interested in every question put to him, in every comment, however wide of the mark. He was never known to utter a sarcastic remark, nor did one ever have the impression that the teacher felt superior to his disciples. For two years I was fortunate enough to be able to attend his private classes (*shiurim*). He was never absent, even when under great pressure of work, and I will always recall with gratitude the love he showed me, just one of his students, during that time.

In his Talmudical lectures he always stressed the clear exposition of basic terms. Although familiar with the complicated paths of Talmudic dialectics (*Pilpul*), he was not interested in shining through ingenious interpretation, but desired to introduce his disciples to the profundities of Talmudic thought, through the exploration of its basic elements, and unfold before them, as it were, the inner nature of things. Whether it was a question of civil law or a purely ritual matter, he always attempted through this basic method to throw light on the whole Talmudic discussion. He attached great importance to an examination of the Biblical passages which the Talmud quoted as the basis of the law in question, and to their context, in order to acquire an understanding of the problem involved: "We must look up the verse" he often used to say, when meeting with a difficulty in the deductions of the Talmud. Through this method he was often able to achieve amazing clarification. In his *shiurim* (lectures) he would occasionally venture into dialectics, but even then he would never lose sight of his major quest, viz., to understand all matters under consideration in their true perspective.

HIS RESPONSA

In his Responsa, dealing with decisions affecting practical life, one discerns only straightforward logic and simple deduction from precedent and principle. To him applies what in his book on "Frankfort Rabbis" he states about the *shiurim* of Rabbi Mass:

"Whenever the discussion of purely theoretical questions threatened to stray from the realm of strict logic, his warning that the question might have important repercussions in religious practice was sufficient to calm all spirits. Thus mere hairsplitting was revealed as futile, and the natural, common sense, explanation won the day."

His Responsa deserve special attention and recognition; in two parts, chronologically widely apart, they were published under the name *"Matteh Levi"*. The first appeared in 5651 (1891) as a belated contribution in honor of the 70th birthday of Rabbi Ezriel Hildesheimer. It contains an index of names culled from the old *Gittin* (documents of divorce); the entire procedure of *Get* and *Halitsah* in the German language; and, the final section, a number of responsa.

The second part was published in 5693 (1933) from the author's literary remains by his son, Dr. Jacob Horovitz, a noted rabbi and fine scholar.

Marcus Horovitz was recognized, together with David Hoffmann, as the leading Talmudical authorities in Germany. Of the many questions addressed to him, those pertaining to the sections *Orah Hayyim* and *Yoreh Deah* of the *Shulhan Arukh* are collected here. In addition, a number of interesting problems related to modern mechanics are contained in this volume. There is ample material for an appreciation of the author's approach to decisions of legal questions. The presentation of the responsa is clear and transparent; the problem is stated, and its different aspects are discussed with reference to sources and previous authorities. Yet, such wide search notwithstanding, the author always remains close to the subject, never losing himself in by-paths, which would prevent a full comprehension of the issue. In the responsa, as in his *shiurim,* the author often refers to relevant Biblical passages for elucidation (as, e.g., in Responsa 1 and 2 of vol. I). The aim to present everything related to the commandments of the Torah in a beautiful and attractive form, and to maintain the respect for Torah and Judaism in the eyes of the outside world, is manifested in his legal decisions. Thus, in one of his responsa, an ordinance of Rabbi Horovitz in his own community is mentioned. It happened that the veterinarians in the slaughter house, while permitting the sale of the flesh of an animal, confiscated, on hygienic grounds, its lungs. In such a case, the *shohatim* (slaughter-ers) were forbidden to declare the meat kosher without having first obtained the consent of a rabbi. This was done in order to prevent the impression that Jewish law was laxer in its sanitary requirements than the non-Jewish authorities.

In general the author is opposed to unnecessary stringency. However, Rabbi Horovitz was inclined to be stricter in questions involving the partnership of non-Jews in Jewish business, arranged for the purpose of keeping the business running on the Sabbath. He offers two reasons: first, that most of those who desire such joint business enterprise are doing it only for the purpose of cir-cumventing the law, so as not to lose "the Sabbath profits"; and secondly, because such practice would result in rendering it im-possible for young Jews, who want to observe the Sabbath, to obtain any positions. Places of business which were open on the Sabbath would prefer to hire those willing to work on that day.

He always speaks with profound respect for earlier authorities. At one point he says: "I am of the opinion that wherever later authorities argue in derogatory manner and self-assured tone against the opinions of those who came before them, they are wrong" (vol. I, resp. 11). However he arrives at his decisions on his own and (as he says himself in Responsum 32 of vol. II): "Without looking at what others do, without timidity and without any personal motive."

Other interesting problems dealt with in the responsa follow: An extremely pious man desired that, after his death, in accordance with the commandment of the Torah, a double share of his estate go to his first-born son. As the law of the Torah applies only to the capital at hand, but not to loans, and other not immediately avail-able assets, the author examined the question as to which part of the estate is subject to that law, and whether, for instance, shares, bonds, and coins are exempt (vol. I, resp. 12).

In another case the government of a State wanted to issue a law according to which the butchers should expedite the death of the animal immediately after ritual slaughter with the knife, through a blow on the head. The rabbi's answer was in the negative (vol. II, resp. 21).

In another responsum the question is discussed as to whether Jews may contribute towards the building of a church. After an interesting discourse on the position of Christianity with regard to pure monotheism, and on the opinions of other authorities, the author decides to allow it. In No. 54 the question is discussed when, and under what conditions, it is permissible to circumcise the child born to a Jew from a non-Jewish mother.

Yet not only practical halakhic questions, but also absorbing theoretical problems are mentioned in the responsa. We may mention a correspondence with outstanding authorities, such as Rabbis Samuel Mohilever (vol. II, resp. 26), Isaac Elhanan (vol. I, resp. 13, vol. II, resp. 54, 55), Solomon ha-Kohen of Vilna (vol. I, resp. 23, 60), Isaac ha-Levi (vol. II, resp. 18), and R. N. Rabinowitz, author of *Dikdukei Soferim* (vol. I, resp. 9). They all speak with the greatest admiration of Rabbi Horovitz and of his comprehensive knowledge of Torah.

"The History of the Rabbis of Frankfort"

The mastery of the sainted rabbi in the field of the Talmud shows itself also in his presentation of the history of the Frankfort rabbis. In reading this work, we are led to the conclusion that, in order to assess justly and fully these luminaries of rabbinical literature, a masterly and deep knowledge of the whole field of culture in which they lived and worked is essential. Here are described not only the outward conditions of the time in which these men worked; not only are the persecutions from which Jewry suffered presented in full. The author is not satisfied, like other historians, with touching but lightly on the institutions and the inner life of the community. He takes great pains to offer us a complete picture. His thoroughness and his keen eye are evident here. From chance remarks and stray notes of contemporaries he often derives valuable information. His greatest art lies in his ability to portray the great spiritual leaders of the Frankfort community, in their studies and teachings, their individual traits and scholarly approaches.

Many a layman seems to think that the rabbinical authors were lacking in such things as method and style; they are "just Talmudists, all of one type." (Even the historian Graetz, in describing the great Polish scholars of the 16th and 17th century, advances the opinion that not only is the life of each of these rabbis practically indistinguishable from those of his colleagues, but that their stream of thought and manner of expression are also of a monotonous sameness. It was he who characterized the life work of R. Sabbatai Cohen by saying that he "made new comments on old items", a remark which in itself proves Graetz's utter lack of understanding of rabbinical literature). Yet even the connoisseur, who knows that there is a difference in style and method between earlier and later scholars, is often unable to tell where this difference lies. But herein lies the new and original contribution in the historical presentation of Rabbi Horovitz. He describes these differences with admirable exactness and empathy, and succeeds in presenting every one of these masters of the Talmud as a literary personality. A study of his characterization of the writings of Rabbi Jacob Joshua Falk in the third volume of the "Frankfort Rabbis" is not only a treat for those familiar with these writings, but even the outsider catches a glimpse of the peculiar and special methods of research of this great savant of Talmudic lore.

His descriptions of regular discussions in the House of Learning, and his semi-annual lectures, have a singular attraction. We admire not only the lucid presentation of the difficult material, but also the occasionally almost three-dimensional clarity of description. The whole work is permeated with a deeply gratifying aura of tender love. To this historian, these scholars are not petrified figures of gray antiquity; he feels a close spiritual kinship with them, and recognizes them as intellectual and ethical heroes of our people, who were able to draw out of their life-element, the Torah, not only instruction but also an ideal philosophy of life. Add to this a gracious trait of local patriotism, which knew how to discover the most attractive aspects of the institutions and leaders of Frankfort. The "Frankfurter Rabbinen" covers only a small segment of Jewish history; yet in presentation and conception, the book may serve as pattern for works of truly Jewish history.

German Jewry of the past two generations was not as poor in Torah-scholars as some would make it appear. Rabbis like Jacob Ettlinger, Seligman Baer Bamberger, Ezriel Hildesheimer,

and David Hoffmann were the equals of the great scholars of the
East and were recognized by them as such. Rabbi Horovitz takes
his place among them. What essentially characterizes his personality, as indicated above, is that he knew how to unite harmoniously
knowledge of Torah with general culture, and deep-seated Jewish
feeling with worldly grace. In the final period of the history of
German Judaism he will always occupy a place of honor.

MARCUS HOROVITZ

By Isaac Heinemann

MARCUS HOROVITZ

By Isaac Heinemann

As great paintings can be appreciated only from a distance, so can the stature of great men be understood only in the perspective of time. We may estimate the power of their personalities during their lifetime, but only many years after their death can we measure the effects of their life's work upon their own generation. Indeed the labors of great men are to the end that their children's children may reap the fruits of their toil. Like our Father Abraham, they walk not only *with God* but *"before God"* (*lifnei ha-Elokim*), for they prepare the road of the future.

Last Purim commemorated the one-hundredth anniversary of the birth of Rabbi Marcus Horovitz, the "Ramah". Thirty-four years have passed since his death.[1] His two volumes of responsa, the *Matteh Levi*,[2] testify to his mastery of the field of Halakhah, while the impressive work on "The Rabbis of Frankfort"[3] displays his keen historical ability. His merits as rabbi, teacher, and organizer were attested to by his students and friends at the time of his death. But despite the stirring eulogies and the brilliant articles about him,[4] his conception of Judaism, which underlay his many-sided personality and manifold accomplishments, remained largely unknown. Perhaps it was not possible to discover his philosophy until a profound change had occurred in the entire

---

[1]He was born in a small Hungarian village near Tokai, and received his major education at the Yeshivah of Eisenstadt, as a disciple of Rabbi Ezriel Hildesheimer, on whose advice he acquired his doctorate degree. After serving a few smaller congregations of Eastern Germany, he was invited to serve as Chief Rabbi of Frankfort-on-the-Main. There he led that portion of the Orthodox group which refused to separate itself from the Jewish community, as S. R. Hirsch had decreed. In Frankfort, he established three synagogues, a Yeshivah, two grammar schools and two youth organizations.

[2]The first volume was published in 1881. The second was published posthumously by his son, the late Rabbi Jacob Horovitz.

[3]"The Rabbis of Frankfort" is at present out of print, but an English translation of the work may soon be available.—*Frankfurter Rabbinen, Beilagen zu den Jahresberichten der isr. Religionsschule* (1882-85).

[4]In the "Juedisches Lexikon" and "Encyclopaedia Judaica" may be found many of his essays and the names of the various organizations to which he dedicated his energies.

Weltanschauung of Germany Jewry. It was towards this very change that Rabbi Horovitz's life work was aimed.

When the "Ramah" began his work, a significant segment of German Jewry considered itself solely a religious fellow- ship, not unlike that of Christians or Mohammedans. Apart from religion, they recognized no differences between Jew and non-Jew. From this disavowal of the national aspect of Juda- ism stemmed two hopes: that anti-Semitism would inevitably disappear[5] "just as religious wars had disappeared"; and that it might be possible to dampen the spirit of revolt which had seized the youth who, thirsty for European culture, refused to be satis- fied with the "four cubits of Halakhah." Through the introduction of formal decorum into the religious services and the removal of everything which to them seemed to smack of superstition, they hoped to bridge the gap between world culture and Jewish tradition and to "improve" Judaism in the process.

But from this abridged version of Judaism arose the danger of division. For if all Jews are brothers only by virtue of their abstract faith, how could Orthodox Jews be brothers with those who rejected traditional Judaism, denying not only the *Oral Torah,* but, in most cases, the *Written Torah* as well? Similar dif- ferences in religious thinking prevailed also among Protestants, but they did not cause a rift in their central body; nor was this Protestant unity due merely to the necessity for inner peace and cohesion, but to ideological reasons as well. But the extremists in the two Jewish camps argued that the division between the traditional and non-traditional Jews was no less final than that between Catholics and Protestants, requiring the formation, there- fore, of new organizations.

The reformers, who represented the majority of Jews in the larger German cities, extended their efforts to undermine tradi- tional Judaism. After Rabbi Horovitz had been called to Frank- fort, a Reform monthly commented: "Would that the black clouds, that have arisen to darken our community, might dis-

[5]Their opinions were very enlightening; as for example the words of as great a scholar as Guedemann, who wrote in a German paper (1918—p.62): "The Jews have waited until they no longer are in danger of being burnt or banished, so they have the patience to wait until they may become officers and ministers."

appear"! And when the *B'nai Brith* movement began to spread in Germany and such an outstanding orthodox personality as Rabbi Hildesheimer joined its ranks, one of the leading reform rabbis wrote: "The basis of B'nai Brith is that of a purified Judaism, and all who attempt to graft branches of Orthodoxy onto its trunk labor in vain."[6]

On the other side, the heads of the orthodox congregations in Germany demanded complete separation of every loyal Jew from any community supporting a reform congregation—even if the community were willing, at the same time, to respect the rights and privileges of its orthodox members. For, in their opinion, any community which did not unequivocally accept the laws of the Torah as binding ceased being a Jewish community. Some Orthodox leaders further asserted that the faithful must not even participate in a charitable group, the complete orthodoxy of which was open to question. Indeed, Rabbi S. R. Hirsch wrote: "An orthodox Jew must not consider joining a B'nai Brith group, for it threatens traditional Judaism."[7] This attitude on both sides spelled imminent peril to the religious strength of the Jewish people and to the timeless ties of love and brotherhood which bound them together.

When Rabbi Hirsch attempted to find legal justification for devout Jews separating themselves from their community organizations, practically all of his orthodox friends stood by his side, including the Ramah's great guide and teacher, Rabbi Ezriel Hildesheimer. Only Rabbi Marcus Horovitz, then a young man of thirty, refused to accept the decision of his beloved teacher and fought separation with all the power at his disposal. The Ramah based his life's work upon the recognition that, in all communal matters, people with diverse religious convictions but with a united sense of responsibility for the greater community of Israel, must labor together. An ardent worker for all communal causes, he served as a member of the executive in both the Union

[6]See Moretzky, "Geschichte des Ordens Bnei Brith" (1882-1907, p. 69, p. 114). The suspicion of jealousy on the part of the reform group did not cease even after Rabbi Horovitz's arrival in the Community. Thus he organized *"Beth ha-Sefer leDath"* solely through the contributions of private individuals in order that the communal assembly would have no control over his leadership.

[7]Moretzky, Page 113.

of Rabbis and the *Hilfsverein der deutschen Juden*. He was chairman of the Society *Lema'an Tsiyon* and *Tomhei Yethomin shel Erets Yisrael*. He participated in the B'nai B'rith (the Frankfort lodge was later named after him) and the society *Yedidei Safruth Yisrael*, but would accept no formal office. He was influential in the society *Kol Yisrael Haverim* and in various Jewish youth movements. Of course, he founded organizations specifically for traditional Jewry in order better to meet the particular problems facing them, such as the Union of Orthodox Rabbis and the youth organization *Tifereth Bahurim*. That he established a Yeshivah and several Jewish religious schools, it is hardly necessary to add.

In due time Rabbi Horovitz found many to help him in the major task of re-uniting the various elements within Judaism. By the time of his death, the jealousy and hatred of the non-traditional groups had all but ceased, and his view had unquestionably prevailed among his own brethren within the traditional ranks of German Jewry. But at the outset he stood almost alone. What caused him to deviate from the opinions of most of his friends and associates? Rabbi Jacob Rosenheim, one of the most distinguished disciples of Rabbi S. R. Hirsch, wrote in his eulogy: "Rabbi Horovitz was able to sense the rise of a new area of greater centralization within Judaism, due to the constant attacks of anti-Semites."[8] Certainly this does not do justice to his real nature. As a truly religious man, the Ramah was shocked by the widespread bigotry; as a truly wise man, he was suspicious of the Prussian government which protected the freedom of the Jews (by allowing them to leave their communal assemblies) more than the freedom of their Protestant neighbors;[9] as a gifted organizer, he understood that the problem of welfare work could not be solved without the spiritual and material support of the entire community. Yet perhaps there is more than a grain of truth in the judgment of Rosenheim. For not only did Rabbi Horovitz "sense" the rise of a new era of centralization and brotherhood, but he was fully alive to this new spirit. He saw that

[8]Jacob Rosenheim, Gesammelte Aufsaetze, Vol. 11, page 451.

[9]From the days of Wilhelm of Humboldt, the Prussian government proceeded to strengthen all tendencies of disintegration within Jewish ranks in order to accelerate complete assimilation. However, only the zealots of emancipation followed this line.

this turning point would not come from outer pressures alone, but through a revival of the ancient communal ties of the people of Israel. Divergent approaches to Judaism caused Rabbis Horovitz and Hirsch to disagree intellectually, but even more so were they divided emotionally on this point.

Rabbi Hirsch believed in the "abridged" version of Judaism as simply a religious entity not because he, God forbid, wanted Jews to assimilate, but, on the contrary, to emphasize thereby their unique historical character. "In Israel, religion (Torah) is not just an added element. It is not just *part* of life, but *all* of life. Torah alone is the foundation of our people, its width and breadth. Torah is the spiritual home of the nation."[10]

Hirsch insisted upon retaining strict adherence to the use of Hebrew as the only proper language for religious services, because it would not be possible to offer exact translations.[11] He fasted on *Tisha'h be-Av,* "not because of the material loss—this indeed any foreign land could restore—but because simultaneously with this loss came the loss of the land upon which had flowered a people rooted in the spirit of the Eternal."[12] Only through the acceptance of the Torah could other Jewish values take on meaning. "All who turn from Torah have revolted against the Jewish people and all who return to the Torah become once again a part of the body which is Israel." In Rabbi Hirsch's view of Orthodoxy we cannot find a single trace of love or admiration for the Hebrew language or a Hebrew culture per se, similar to the sentiments which emanated from any of the generation of emancipation. Consequently, even in the final days of his life, Hirsch could find no common ground between himself and free-thinkers.

We can understand now not only why Hirsch insisted on "separation", but also the negative reaction in Eastern Europe.

---

[10]See *"Horev"*—714; page 561.

[11]Ibid., 688; page 534.

At the conclusion of this article he states: "By the time the leaders of the Great Assembly instituted the prayers, Hebrew had already ceased to be the language of our people." That is to say that, contrary to the opinion of the extreme reformists, the use of Hebrew does not give our prayers any particular nationalistic aspects. It is noteworthy that even among the Reformed, many rabbis retained the use of Hebrew "in order to protect the unity which binds the people of Israel," or "that Hebrew may remain a living language."

[12]Ibid., pages 150, 342.

The Russian and Polish Rabbis opposed separation even from a community which supported secular schools, because their deep feelings for the oneness of Israel dissuaded them from breaking the bond which joined them to their brethren. It was this view that motivated the Ramah's actions as well.

Rabbi Horovitz's sense of communal responsibility was expressed on various occasions, and particularly at the conference of the "Union of Orthodox Rabbis of Germany" during the discussion of Zionism. The leaders of this group, among them the Ramah, brought before the first Jewish Congress the well-known declaration censuring the "efforts of those people who call themselves Zionists and who wish to establish a national Jewish homeland in Israel". This declaration was delivered at a time when it was not as yet possible to judge Zionism except on the basis of Herzl's "Jewish State" and the discussions which the book aroused. Yet, as the first Congress progressed, Zionism began to take shape, and the various currents in the movement came to the fore. In particular one could note a distinct feeling of sympathy on the part of the religious masses towards the leaders of Zionism. Afterwards, the Ramah gave a direct report on the declaration to both his Orthodox and Reformed friends. While he spoke in guarded terms about the question of Judaism in general, his approach to the Zionist issue deserves careful study. In his report, he condemns the secular character of the new movement: "Are they not profaning God's name when they say that Zionism has no connection with religion?" Thus he supports the dissenting declaration. But while the declaration only criticized the negative aspects of Zionism, Ramah recognized its positive side as well. "In one matter the Zionists are completely in the right: in their critical evaluation of the present state of affairs. The disease of anti-Semitism is quite serious and cannot be cured with superficial treatment alone. The germ of Jewish hatred is found on every corner."

How different is this approach from that of most of the Ramah's friends who, as Jews and democrats, believed in the speedy and complete triumph of the forces of emancipation over the dread disease of anti-Semitism! Furthermore, many years before the advent of Zionism, Rabbi Horovitz had already evinced a pessimistic attitude. In a sermon, delivered almost 50 years earlier, he refers to the story of Rabbah Bar Bar Hana[13] about a group of travelers who were disembarking from a ship onto what they believed to be dry land. It turned out, however, that they had climbed onto the back of a whale, and had it not been for the fact that the ship was still nearby, they all would surely have perished. The Ramah felt that this story depicted the exact situation of the Jews in Germany. For these Jews had been fully convinced that they could live peacefully among the nations. But now the rude awakening by resurgent anti-Semitism called attention to the fact that they were standing on precarious ground. How fortunate are those who have not wandered too far from the ship of their faith!

"Diagnosis alone is not sufficient, and as strong as Zionism is in its critical evaluation of the disease, it is confused as to the cure". But even here the Ramah agrees to the important role of nationalism in the approach to that cure, and to that extent justifies the Zionist position. He writes, "A well known rabbi has circulated a book which attacks Jewish nationalism. In it he states that Judaism does not favor the idea of nationalism, but rather sees world citizenship as its ideal. We cannot accept this opinion nor see it as a true conception of our faith. No component part of the Messianic thought intends to minimize nationalism. To the contrary! It tells us that all the nations will serve one God, but they will always retain their individual identity".[14]

Undoubtedly the speaker composed these words very carefully in order to find a common ground for all his listeners. Yet the sharp opposition which the Ramah's declarations evoked clearly indicates that his listeners understood his thoughts and his overall attitude only too well. It could only be due to Max Nordau's nationalistic feelings that the Ramah would refer to him as a "repentant soul". "If he (Nordau) and his co-thinkers have become imbued with a new spirit of Judaism, then I give thanks to the Eternal for Zionism".

Yet, aside from this, "Zionism had positive effects. A morbid hatred of the Hebrew language existed among emancipated Jews,

[13]Baba Bathra 73 b.
[14]He refers here to "Jewish Nationalism" by Guedemann. The author answered Rabbi Horovitz in the "Jewish Press" (39. 14. 1898).

but now the Zionists have appeared on the scene and re-kindled a new love for the language of our fathers and for its literature. There prevailed extreme religious laxity combined with a spirit of courage and perseverance. The masses of Israel were indifferent when a few devoted leaders appeared and raised before all the persecuted and oppressed the vision of a new home in the land of our holy memories." In particular was the Ramah concerned about the fact that the modern Jewish youth, who possessed little knowledge of our faith and could hardly be expected to make sacrifices for it, had in numerous cases become fervent supporters of Zionism. Rabbi Horovitz couches his praise for Zionism in a religious setting and trusts that the revitalization of culture and nationalism will have its culmination in a rebirth of faith.[14a]

Nevertheless, in his addresses he constantly opposed secular Zionism, which he believed to be its usual form. "In Judaism it is not the security of the home but its spiritual content which is our goal on earth, and for that we must live and, at times, even die". Such sentiments perhaps Ahad ha-Am, too, could have expressed in his criticism of political Zionism, but of course Ramah's understanding of these "spiritual contents" went much deeper. He believed in the eternity of the Torah and its revival. He had faith that even those who had forsaken Judaism would return to be resurrected as were the bones in Ezekiel's deathless vision. "What is discarded first (viz. religion) is retaken last."[15] Thus in all Jewish institutions comprised of religious and non-religious membership, he urged adherence to the religious commandments.

The Ramah's personal relations with everyone were always kept on an extremely friendly basis. He despised quarrelling.[16] "I do

[14a]He took a moderate approach because he doubted the effectiveness of political Zionism. Furthermore he feared, as did many of the followers of "Hovevei Tsiyon", that it would harm the colonization movement.

[15]From his sermon on resurrection which appeared in 1892.—See also "Yalkut Shimoni" on Ezekiel, XXXVII.

[16]In his eulogy on Rabbi Ezriel Hildesheimer, the Ramah related a dialogue between the former and a Hungarian rabbi with whom he had spent a great deal of time. At the moment of departure, the rabbi turned to Rabbi Hildesheimer and asked: "All that I have seen is fine but there is one matter which all of us have debated for quite a while. Where do you find the time for secular studies?" To which Rabbi Hildesheimer slyly replied: "The time that you spend discussing the matter—I spend in those studies." That can be said of the Ramah as well as of his teacher.

not say that we have no courage for strong words.[17] I would rather say that we do not have the ability. Nor do the eyes of Providence require that ability in a place where truth is found." As to the attacks which arose from the camp of assimilationsists, these he did not answer with words but with actions. Yet, because his pleasant ways served to set an example for all, his arguments held sway even among those who did not agree with his basic attitudes. One example will suffice. The assembly of the Frankfort Jewish Community had decided to erect a Reform Synagogue. It handed over the contract to a non-Jewish builder, and, after consulting the rabbinic authorities of the congregation, the assembly gave the builder the right to continue his work on the Sabbath. When informed of this, Rabbi Horovitz notified the heads of the assembly that in truth there was no direct violation of the Sabbath involved, but that the community was responsible for sanctifying the Sabbath in public. The new synagogue, until such time as it was turned over to its own Board of Directors, remained a communal endeavor, and hence it would not be proper to have construction work done on the Sabbath. The assembly accepted his view with no further discussion.

In all such instances, the Ramah took into account the effect which those actions would have upon the non-Jews. They would not understand the exact nature of the Jewish law and would believe that the Jews were disrespectful of their own holy commandments. How different is this attitude from that of our weak-willed brethren who fear to observe the *Mitsvoth* because they might appear strange in the eyes of the Gentiles! The very fact that we live amongst non-Jews adds to our responsiblities, according to the Ramah, and imposes upon us a greater obligation to be particular in following not only the letter, but the spirit of our Law as well. Because of this perception of the laws of our Torah, the Ramah despised all devious devices by means of which some of his easy-going friends managed to justify keeping their

---

[17]When a suggestion was brought before his congregation's assembly that its high school be opened on Saturday rather than on Sunday (of course without any direct violations of the Sabbath), the Ramah compared this advice to that of the Hellenists in the Hasmonean period who attempted to slowly divert the Jewish people from the proper path.

places of business open on the Sabbath, and, on the other hand, re-emphasized the *Hovoth ha-Levavoth,* the obligations of the heart, as well as the actual performance of our religious commandments. He stressed both attitudes in his sermons and in his book on the rabbis of Frankfort, which is filled with a spirit of wisdom and awe.

Hence we may understand his approach towards mysticism. It reveals the intellectual differences between himself and the majority of his contemporaries.

The Ramah was acquainted with Hungarian Hassidism from youth. Indeed, when he was fourteen, one of his teachers belonged to a Hassidic group. Some of their outlandish customs caused him to leave them. His view of them in his first youthful work is not always one of admiration, though he has nothing but praise for their manner of praying and applies to them the saying "if only man could pray and pray all day long." But it was in particular the total opposition to modern life of some of their adherents in Germany which aroused his opposition.

Man judges the past according to its effects upon the present. For this reason it is important to appreciate the fact that because of many a Hassid's narrow outlook, almost all of the champions of "the Science of Judaism" were critical not only of Hassidism but of the Kabbalists as well. The Protestant philosophers and theologians of the time were not sympathetic to mysticism until later, when their psychological approach towards religion led them to religious experience in terms of man's deep yearnings for the Eternal, rather than of ethical concepts or dogmas alone.[18] While the Ramah was not a psychologist, he was a deeply religious man who zealously guarded his thinking from the popular currents of the day. This explains his attitude of friendly neutrality towards mysticism in his later, mature work, "The Rabbis of Frankfort". Although he rejects faith in amulets and *gematria,* time and again he emphasizes the beneficial influence which flowed from the Kabbalah. "One may differ in regard to the value of the Kabbalistic movement in general, but one cannot fail to acknowledge the direction followed by Rabbi Isaiah Horovitz

[18]See Wobberman in his introduction to the German version of William James' book, "The Varieties of Religious Experience".

(author of *Shnei Luhoth ha-Berith*) and his son Shabbatai. By emphasizing morality and piety, it brought to Judaism a renewed vigor, reaching the deepest wells of the human spirit and directing all of life towards the fulfillment of the commandments."

Ramah remained aloof from the Kabbalistic way because he differed with it in theory and because by nature he was inclined towards greater clarity. Yet, as an unbiased student of the trends in Judaism, he did not demand "one color for every leaf", and as a man of action, he welcomed with joy whatever might effect humanity in a beneficial fashion. He considered all of the positive movements within Judaism as worthy of support, though this did not prevent him from asserting his own particular views.[19]

In conclusion, we may say that Rosenheim's judgment that "Rabbi Horovitz sensed the arrival of a new era" was true to a far greater degree than one could have possibly envisioned at the time of his death. And precisely because the Ramah expressed his ideas in actions more than in words, is it necessary to state his conception of Judaism, comprehensive and many-sided as it was, not only in terms of his manifold achievements, but in terms of his philosophy as well. Indeed, one can understand these achievements only through understanding his philosophy.

He rejected the narrow horizon of his generation, which in its effort to overcome the attacks of the anti-Semites from without and the betrayal of "enlightenment" from within, attempted to force Judaism into a Sodomic bed of Confessionalism on the one hand, and on the other, surrounded the mystery of faith with the iron fence of rationalism. He hurled a bold challenge at this double motif. For, although the Ramah was considered a confirmed optimist, and although he managed somewhat to curb the activities of the anti-Semites and to allay the fears of his frightened brethren,[20] he did not believe that anti-Semitism could be destroyed by means of the usual protective measures, that is, the abrogation of a distinctive Jewish religious life. At the same time, while religion remained in his eyes the basis of Jewish existence, he understood that the national aspects of the Jewish people, its

[19]He was profuse in his praise of Graetz, for example, although in truth he did not agree with all of Graetz's analysis.

[20]His friendly relations with a leader of the Catholic party, a powerful force in Germany at the time, indirectly brought about a change in that party's anti-Semitic attitude first indicated during the '70's.

history and its achievements throughout the ages, coupled with a renewed love for Zion, would eventually bring "the hearts of the children back to their fathers." And though by nature a man of science, he was also able properly to measure the influence of mysticism upon religious life. His unique personality allowed him to weave together so many diverse strands and to see beyond the horizon of the day. It was derived from a broad conception of Judaism that was based not so much upon exacting research as on firm roots within the very matrix of Jewish existence itself— all of which served to protect him from the blindness of his generation, from what has been called "the greatest lack of historical consciousness ever experienced by man".

During the last twelve years of his life, a spirit of repentance had begun to animate German Jewry; the Ramah no longer stood alone. Indeed, he was responsible for this change in two ways: First, he succeeded in influencing wide circles of leaders and laymen who had rejected any change in habits or ideas despite the changed conditions of the period. And secondly, he clearly indicated a common ground of activity for the pious traditionalists and those who, though having strayed from the path of the Torah, managed to retain, whether in a religious or nationalist sense, a love for their people. For this the Ramah surely deserves a prominent place among the very few who succeeded in overcoming the prejudices of their generation and prepared the way for the new era.

Indeed, the last generation went much further along these lines than the Ramah would have desired. They turned largely towards communal secularization and the curtailment of the religious character of the community. For, just as in the eyes of the generation of emancipation Judaism was conceived merely as a religious community analogous to those of other religions, so the modern view regards the Jewish people as merely a nation "like all nations". Whether this conception will be granted a longer life than that of the period of emancipation, which died almost as soon as it had been born, or whether the forthcoming post-war generation will quickly find its way back to an all-embracing Judaism, religious as well as national, the Judaism of Rabbi Marcus Horovitz—only time will tell.

ISAAC JACOB REINES

By Hayyim Z. Reines

ISAAC JACOB REINES

By Hayyim Z. Reines

Isaac Jacob Reines was born on the ninth day of Mar-Heshvan in the year 5600 (1840) in the city of Karlin, Russia. He was a scion of a famous family, which counted among its ancestors such "Geonim" (Talmudic geniuses) as R. Moses Isserles of Cracow, Rabbi Meir of Padua and the famous Rabbi Loew of Prague.[1]

As a child, he received the traditional upbringing of that period. At the age of three, he was sent to Heder (Hebrew School). He advanced in his studies at a remarkable pace. At ten, he is said to have been proficient in the Talmud far beyond his age. His parents sent him to continue his studies with the incisive thinker, the Gaon Rabbi Yehiel ha-Levi of Karelitz. There he began to compose some novellae on the Talmud. By the time he was sixteen, he had completed several works which have been preserved in manuscript for posterity. He finally attended the famous Yeshivoth of Wolozin and Eishishock. He received his Semikhah (ordination) from the Geonim Samuel Avigdor and Eleazar Moshe Horowitz of Pinsk. His reputation as an outstanding prodigy having favored him, he became the son-in-law of the Gaon Joseph Rosen of Telz, Lithuania (and afterwards of Slonim, Poland). According to custom, he lived in the home of his father-in-law for several years, pursuing his studies. But because the visits of many people eager to discuss Torah would interrupt

[1]He was also a descendant of Rabbi Moses Rivkes, author of "Beer ha-Golah", and through him was related to the Gaon of Vilna. When his father, Rabbi Shlomo Naftali, was still a youth, he joined the movement "Back to Palestine", started among the disciples of the Gaon. He settled in Safed and founded there a Hebrew printing press. At the time of the unrest, in 1834, the Arabs attacked his home, destroyed his press, and impoverished him as well as the other Jewish settlers of Safed. Upon the plea of the leaders of the community of "Perushim", Rabbi Shlomo journeyed to Europe as a representative of the "Kolel" of the Ashkenazic Jews. In 1837, while in Warsaw, he received the report that all the members of his family had perished in Safed at the time of the earthquake. Rabbi Shlomo Naftali decided to settle in the city of Karlin, the place where he had been in business. He married a second wife, Gela, and from this union was born his son Isaac Jacob.

his studies there, he rented a room outside of the city and there burned the midnight oil.

When he was twenty-two he had completed the following works (as yet unpublished) : *"Reshith Bikkurim"*—on the four sections of the *"Shulhan Arukh"*, *"Shoel u-Meshiv"* (Responsa), and a collection of comments on the Talmud. Some of his writings were printed in Rabbi Rosen's book, *"Eduth be-Yosef."* In 1867 he was elected Rabbi of Shukian (Lithuania) and there he composed his *"Eduth be-Yaakov"* on the laws concerning testimony. In 1869 he was elected Rabbi of the city of Shwintzian (Lithuania), whence his reputation spread throughout the world of Jewish learning.

HIS APPROACH AND HIS BOOKS ON "HALAKHAH" (JEWISH LAW)

Both Rabbi Reines' keen mind and the contemporary method of study at first inclined him towards "pilpul" (dialectical study), his first book *"Eduth be-Yaakov"* and his other works of this period following that pattern. But he longed, even in the days of his youth, for a different method. The decisive event occurred when he was about 15 years old. He was studying in the *"Beth ha-Midrash"* of his native city. A maskil (cultured person) entered and suggested that the young lad study mathematics with him, and as a preparation, he offered the work *"Milloth ha-Higgayon"* (Logical Terms) by Maimonides. The book made a profound impression upon young Reines. He began to examine the logical roots of the Halakhah and perceived that different subjects in *Halakhah,* which at first glance seem unrelated, are actually built upon similar foundations in logic. This made it imperative for him to re-examine the principles of the *Halakhah* and to systematize its legal concepts in a logical manner. For this purpose he began his great work *"Derekh ha-Yam"* ("The Way in the Ocean" of the Talmud), a methodology of the Talmud for the most part still in manuscript. In writing it he had a specific purpose: to answer the detractors of the Talmud, who had become both numerous and vociferous. By that time the pilpulistic method had by some been carried to an extreme, leading to a type of dialectical exegesis, which invited defamers and of-

fended many loyal scholars. He set out to prove that the Talmud
is built on strong logical foundations and is subject to the laws
of scientific thinking. In a moving passage he describes how he was
aroused to action.[2] The Torah itself can be heard crying out:
"Hearken, O ye few lovers of mine, to the words of my mouth.
Listen ye remnant of my followers to the words that I utter
in the bitterness of my soul! . . . Save me from the hand of
enemies, stubborn and rebellious, who pursue me for naught . . .
Lay bare their blindness! . . . For, if it be true that they possess
eyes, they do not see the right path . . . My words will help one
who wishes to walk the straight path. The upright who have eyes
to see will perceive the truth of my words and will find precious
substance in my house. And now, my loved ones, make ready for
my plea. Lay my words to your heart. Have mercy upon me and
my faithful ones who gave their very lives for me, who endured
every cruelty, but did not offend me nor bring shame upon the
sanctity of my name. Turn ye also, I beseech you, to me. Lift up
your voices on high to strengthen me, for if you will keep silent at
this time, a great destruction will break loose, God forbid, upon you
and upon me. Build a tower of strength for my interpreters. Reveal to everyone my justice, and the wisdom that is stored within
me.

"This plea must stir everyone. I too have heard it and I
hear it still. It captured my heart, all my thoughts are encompassed by it.

"I have considered my past life and wonder if, perchance, I may
be deemed worthy by Divine Providence to bring this great subject
to light. At last I thought, 'If God had not wished to help me
in this, He would not have opened my eyes to perceive it.' In
awe and trepidation I began, in the name of the Lord of Hosts, to
seek the central pivot upon which revolve all the hinges of the
doors of the oral law. For, from the beginning I felt that there is
one central point, one theme that cements the holy writ and the
oral law, and unifies all of the component parts into one body."

Thus spoke Rabbi Reines, anguished by the scant honor shown
to Torah in his time, and moved to apply his logical method to

[2]Introduction to *"Hotham Tokhnith"* (Mainz 1880), pp. 8-10.

the examination of the Talmud. This method, which he presented in his book *Derekh ba-Yam,* encompassed the entire sea of the Talmud. When he found that it was impossible for him to publish a book of such wide scope at that time, he made a condensation of it, published in two parts under the name of *Hotham Tokhnith* (Mainz 1880/81). It contains the logical principles of the *Halakhah,* of which he offers examples from various sources, endeavoring to show that the ways of Halakhah were founded on the same logical basis as all sciences, that the Halakhah sought to derive comprehensive concepts from the maze of details, and that along this path of analysis would be found the yardsticks with which the sages measured their comments on Scripture.

Thus Rabbi Reines arrived at the following conclusion: "The ways of reasoning that are known as the methods of logic will reduce and ultimately make an end to pseudo-*Pilpul* which does not clarify obscure passages and is far from being realistic. Hence indulgence in it is at best a waste of time. On the other hand, the sound ways of reasoning make *Pilpul* worthy of its name and an instrument of truth."

Rabbi Reines was not opposed to dialectic reasoning per se, but only to its abuse. Before launching into *Pilpul* one must steel himself to the rigor of mental discipline and avoid pitfalls and blind alleys of thought. Rabbi Reines had no intention of disparaging the traditional method of studying the Torah which had provided food for Jewish minds and hearts throughout the generations, but he sought to place it on firmer foundations. In a sense, his aim was similar to that of some Lithuanian contemporaries, who also based their novellae and their "Shiurim" (lectures) on incisive logic and on systematic analysis of the basic concepts. But Rabbi Reines founded a new comprehensive method of the study of the Torah. His book *"Hotham Toknith"* was outstanding for its scientific organization.

In the text he presents the principles with a few basic illustrations and in the notes he adds examples from the entire literature of the Talmud. All this is greatly condensed to give, as he says, "the synopsis of things." Every note is truly a "minimum containing a maximum." When the book appeared, it made a great impression not only on scholars "whose Torah was their profession" but also on many writers in the East and West, and there appeared reviews in many European languages. Thus it fulfilled its purpose in showing how one can counteract indifference to, and irresponsible criticism of, our spiritual treasures. It should be emphasized that *"Hotham Toknith"* is by no means a popular work, but intended primarily for those who have a thorough knowledge of Talmud. Yet it made a great impression on the "Maskilim." (Hebrew students of general enlightenment). Rabbi Betzalel ha-Cohen, Dayan of Vilna, who was counted among the geonim of the generation, called on all rabbis "to strengthen the hands" of the author in order to enable him to publish all his books, for "through them a new light would be shed on rabbinic literature."

At that period, Rabbi Reines began thinking also about improving the Yeshivoth, not only because attendance had seriously declined, but also because some of the students had been attracted to "Haskalah," (the new enlightenment) and many of them spent their time poring over modern books that turned them away from Torah and from religion. The orthodox Jews complained about this, but Reines insisted that it was not enough to condemn it, but it was necessary to look for the root of this evil and seek a remedy. He found that the youth did not see a future for themselves in the exclusive study of the Torah. Life demanded also secular education, without which it would be impossible to assume one's proper place in society. Since the Yeshivoth did not provide general education as well as Talmudic training, it was no wonder that the young men went elsewhere.

Rabbi Reines suggested to the rabbinic convention assembled in St. Petersburg in 1882 that they include in the curriculum of the Yeshivoth the study of the language of the country (Russian) and secular sciences.[3] But the rabbis objected to this suggestion, and it was taken off the agenda. Rabbi Reines realized that as long as religious education ignored socio-economic realities, it would lose ground inevitably.

Now was the time to act "for the sake of the Lord," and he took it upon himself to found a Yeshivah in which the study of Torah

---

[3]"Shnei ha-M'oroth (The Two Lights) part 2, p. 8.

and Derekh Erets would be harmoniously blended. In 1882 he established such a school in the city of Shwenyan (Lithuania) where he was rabbi. He met with tribulations and persecutions. He writes that there rose up against him zealots, not, God forbid, zealots of the Lord of Hosts, but jealous men who attempted to undo his work by all manner of chicanery. Vicious letters against him appeared in the Hebrew Press. Others stooped so low as to denounce him to the government. In 1883 he happened to be in Moscow. The Czarist regime was always ready to exploit slanders by Jews against their fellow-Jews, and Rabbi Reines was put in the prison reserved for political criminals. But Jewish leaders came to his aid, proved the falsity of the accusation and in a day or so he was set free. He continued his work at the Yeshivah, but finally family pressure made him give it up. He had contracted debts on behalf of the Yeshivah, that he could not meet because of lack of financial assistance. The Yeshivah was closed but he only waited for a more propitious moment to reopen it.

Meanwhile he received calls to high rabbinic office from many cities of various Russian provinces and foreign lands. Among other offers came one from a prominent congregation in Manchester, England. After a good deal of persuasion he accepted the position in the hope of being able to adjust himself to the Western environment. But the state of Judaism in England dismayed him, and three months later he returned to Russia, which was then the center of Torah and orthodox Jewry. He then accepted the rabbinate of the city of Lida (Lithuania), settled there in the winter of 1884, and remained there till his death. There he continued his literary work, but not in his previous field, the "Halakhah" (the preceptive part of Rabbinic literature), but in "Aggadah" (the non-preceptive part).

The majority of the great Torah scholars were interested mainly in Halakhah, and only very few occupied themselves also with Aggadah. A poor rabbi in a small town or an impoverished scholarly layman would compose a book of "Drush" often full of devious arguments. The discerning belittled or scorned these writings. And just as the field of popular exposition lost ground in written form, so did the art of oral exposition also degenerate. The rabbis would address their congregations only rarely during the year; public speaking being relegated to "Maggidim" (itinerant preachers), who, while fulfilling an important function in bolstering the spirit of the masses, nevertheless fell short of their mission. Rabbi Reines recognized that the field of Aggadah was very important, since its purpose was to stimulate the spirit of the people and to elevate its moral level.

Popular addresses had to be improved both in form and content. The "Maggidim," he noted, had degenerated into little more than popular entertainers, and the people who flocked to hear them were neither informed nor uplifted by their discourses. It was necessary to train men who understood the spiritual need of the people and who knew how to help them, using the beautiful stories, parables and maxims of the Haggadah for that purpose. A new way had to be shown by concrete examples.

Rabbi Reines knew how to hold and inspire an audience large or small. Drawing on his own vast experience and learning, he published in 1890 his volume *"Nod shel Demaoth."* The book is outstanding not only for its wealth of ideas, but also for its superior literary style—a rare feature in popular sermons. Let me cite one short excerpt from a sermon of his on Tisha'h be-Av at the cemetery.

"My brethren, harken unto my words!

Our feet stand now in this eventual resting place for all the living. Thoughts of eternity are awakened in all of us here. The stillness of death prevails here, but this stillness is in truth a mighty voice from the sacred domain of eternity. Here, at the boundary of the finite world, thoughts of the finite world fade away, and thoughts of the soul and of the Holy Spirit and of eternity take their place. Here every mound, every tree, every blade of grass, every shrub, every leaf, awakes a most sacred feeling, a feeling of eternity."[4]

In many places in this book, as in his other homiletical writings, one may find such passages as these, outstanding for their deep feeling and sublime serenity. In truth, Rabbi Reines is a pioneer in the art of modern homiletics. For while oratory and public speaking assumed a place of honor in Western Europe and in America, and even became the major pre-occupation of the rabbis, they were of

[4]Foreword to "Nod Shel D'maoth", Jerusalem, 1934, p. 33.

lesser estimation in Eastern Europe. Reines raised their status by
giving them interesting content and pleasing form, above all through
a bold grasp on modern problems. Over a period of years he produced an entire series of homiletical works. They are weightier
than "Drushim" in the ordinary sense of the word. They contain
philosophical articles on the content and form of Judaism and the
mission of the Jewish people. Their central theme is: The goal
of the Torah is the ethical completeness of man. The following
passages fully exemplify this point:

> "And the deaf will hear on that day the words of a book."
> —This refers to the book of the 'generations of man.'[5] The
> historic mission of the Jewish people is to labor to the end that
> the Torah be disseminated throughout the world. For only by
> means of the Torah will nobility of soul and purity of heart
> come about in the world. Advancement in science and in
> technical skill has not succeeded in eradicating wickedness and
> cruelty."[6]
> "Only when the Book of Books will spread throughout the
> earth, will the world be saved from the tragedy of the sword."[7]
> "Our sacred Torah is not the Torah of one people alone,
> but the Torah of all humanity."[8] "The Torah is universal in
> its scope and mission, and not national." At another point,[9]
> he interprets the saying[10] "Whosoever observes the Torah in
> Truth is accounted by Scriptures as if he had created himself" to
> mean that man, being different from other living creatures, is a
> continually developing creation, and his existence becomes com-
> plete only through his ethical completeness. He did not recog-
> nize a distinction between "Judaism" and "civilization," and
> contended that the basis of Judaism is also the basis of universal
> civilization.[11]

His books abound in penetrating observation, supported by
quotations from the entire range of Rabbinic literature. His style
is simple and clear. He possessed a knowledge of general history,
which he seems to have acquired from Hebrew books. And
though he did not know any foreign language and never studied

[5]B'reshith Rabbah XXIV.
[6]"Orah Ve Simhah (Light and Joy). pg. 42.
[7]ibid, p. 42.
[8]ibid, p. 30.
[9]"Or Hadash al Tsiyon" (New Light on Zion), p. 131.
[10]Midrash Tanhuma, Ki Thavo.
[11]"Or Hadash al Tsiyon" p. 181.

general philosophy, ancient or modern, yet he knew Jewish philosophy as well as the book of the Zohar and the entire literature of Kabbalah. He was one of the most original thinkers of modern Jewry.

Isaac Jacob Reines was not only a thinker. The fact that he was deeply immersed in scholarly problems and abstract speculations did not deter him from a course of action. Plans that involved the Jewish people were always close to his heart. Therefore, when the movement for "Hibbath Tsiyon" (Love of Zion) was started, he joined it. After prolonged correspondence with Rabbis Eliyahu Gutmacher and Tsevi Hirsch Kalischer, who were among its founders, he presented in 1887, in conference with Rabbi Samuel Mohilever, a broad program for the colonization of Erets Yisrael. Theodor Herzl's idea of political Zionism made a profound impression upon Rabbi Reines. He investigated his background and accomplishments and only after convincing himself of Herzl's dependability did he join him. He took part in all Zionist Congresses, with the exception of the first one. He made a vivid impression on the leaders of that time, who said of him[12] "Rabbi Reines, who looked like one of the patriarchs, was a teacher of infinite patience and a wise leader who knew his people."

The news of his having joined the Zionists caused profound dismay among the orthodox, who at that time were opposed to the Zionist movement because of the irreligious persons who stood at its helm. They sent one of the greatest men of the generation, Rabbi Israel Meir ha-Kohen, author of "The Hafets Hayyim", to persuade him to sever his connection with the Zionists.

Unable to sway him on halakhic grounds, Rabbi Israel Meir hinted to him that he was causing himself harm by joining the Zionist movement, because religious Jews would no more accord him full recognition. He answered that since he was certain of the right course of his action, he did not worry as to what might happen to him as a result of it. He had known beforehand that his step would entail a measure of self-sacrifice and realizing this clearly he had joined the movement. (Even before the beginning

[12]Book of the Congress, p. 38.

of political Zionism, he expressed in a letter to a friend his anguish about the orthodox Jews, who stand aloof and do not join the movement of "Hibbath Tsiyon."[13] The argument against helping the movement because freethinkers belonged to it he overrode by saying: "Should one spurn a holy commandment if freethinkers choose to fulfill it?" His attitude towards Zionism springs from his view concerning "Geulath Yisrael" (the redemption of Israel). For he believed, as did Rabbi Alkalay and Rabbi Tsevi Hirsch Kalischer, that the beginning of the Geulah will come about once the nations resolve to right the 2,000-year-old injustice done to Israel and allow them to return to the land of their forefathers.[14]

And since political Zionism, founded by Herzl, had ostensibly been conceived for this very purpose, he saw in it the beginning of the "Geulah." He also saw the finger of God in the fact that such a movement became popular in circles which previously had been distant from traditional Judaism, in fact almost entirely cut off from it. In the book "Or Hadash al Tsiyon," written in 1903, he says that Zionism is the movement of repentance foretold by the prophets. He was convinced that it arrested the process of assimilation which had affected wide circles of the "Maskilim" in Eastern Europe; for it was at the very time when the Zionist movement appeared that the wave of assimilation had reached its peak. The Jewish youth that had been caught by the flame of the Haskalah began to deny their Jewishness. It seemed a miracle that many of those who had formerly been zealous assimilationists repented and joined the ranks of Zionists.[15]

Of course, he said, one may argue that "repentance" implies a return to the Torah and its commandments, not only to nationalism and to the land of Irael. But the answer hinges upon the words of the prophet[16] "And when ye say, we will be as the nations, the races of the lands, to serve wood and stone. As I live, saith the

---

[13]Published in the pamphlet "Netsah Israel" (Eternity of Israel) by his departed son, Moses Reines.

[14]"Shnei ha-Meoroth", Introduction (1913): "For I hope that before long civilization will progress still further and all the rulers of the earth will assemble to establish universal authority in the conduct of the various states; and at that time 'the remembrance of Israel will come up before them for good', and they will help to better our position and to settle us in our Holy Land."

[15]P. 71.

[16]Ezekiel XX, 32-33.

Lord God, surely with a mighty hand, and with an outstretched arm, and with outpoured fury will I be king over you."

"This means that the more Israel tries to become assimilated, the more violently will he be rejected by the nations.

"When the Jews finally realize that complete assimilation is impossible, they will come closer to their breathren and begin to feel that God rules over them and that 'It is a people that dwells alone.' This will be the first step towards repentance. The nationalistic feeling operates even in individuals who were almost ready to take the final step and sever completely their bond with Judaism, and it compels them to return to their fold."[17]

As we read these words of Rabbi Reines, we are reminded how other Hebrew writers of that era, for example "Ahad ha-Am" (pen name of Asher Ginzberg), wrote about the intenseness of nationalistic feeling. Rabbi Reines differs from them. Nationalism to Ahad ha-Am is an end in itself, whereas to Rabbi Reines national consciousness is a means to an end, a device to protect the existence of Judaism. Its main and final objective is the Torah. The experience of the last fifty years has shown that the recent awakening of the nationalistic movement among Jews was in large measure a consequence of the general rise of nationalism among many of the nations of Europe in the last century. But Rabbi Reines drew his inspiration from his deep faith in the Divine guidance of the Jewish people.

It is therefore not to be wondered at that he saw the finger of God in the rise of the Zionist movement even in those circles that had previously been distant from Judaism. He hoped that these individuals would return to embrace Judaism wholeheartedly. His slogan was that the orthodox should become Zionists and the Zionists orthodox. He appealed to the free-thinking Zionists to recognize "that with us nationalism and Judaism are two inseparable twins, and the true bond between individual and the nation is the bond of religion."[18]

At the fifth Congress "cultural Zionism" was included in the program of the movement. Cultural Zionism stressed only the

[17]"Or Hadash al Tsiyon," p. 89.
[18]Ibid., Introduction.

Hebrew language and literature and ignored historical Judaism.
Rabbi Reines realized the need of organizing a distinct group of
orthodox Zionists. On his way back from the Congress in the
winter of 1902 he stayed for several days in Frankfort (Germany),
and told his friends that he would endeavor to form such a wing
after his return home. He undertook this task with his usual
energy, and invited rabbis and laymen whom he knew to be
sympathetic to Zionism to attend a conference in Vilna. He had
no secretary and wrote hundreds of letters personally, in addition
to making the necessary preparations for the conference. The
assembly was finally convened in Vilna at the end of Adar 1, 1902,
and at that time the "Mizrachi" was founded amid much celebration and festivity. The conference issued a statement calling
upon orthodox Jews to help the new organization. In this proclamation[19] it was made clear that the Zionist ideal was not new,
but had been alive in Israel ever since the days of the prophets.
Confronted with the aloofness of Orthodox Jews from the Zionist
movement (they had noticed that many of the adherents of the
movement did not conduct themselves in accord with the spirit of
Judaism and had introduced western materialism), he appealed to
the orthodox Jews to aid the Zionist idea, since a special place had
been found for the orthodox in the Zionist movement.

After the delegates had agreed upon the wording of this
proclamation, Rabbi Reines supplemented it with the outline of an
educational program along the lines of traditional Judaism.

He was full of hope that the Mizrachi group would increase its numbers and also gain influence with the free-thinking
Zionists, inducing them eventually to return to a full, vibrant
Judaism. The Mizrachi developed remarkably well in the course
of a few years and succeeded in forming educational groups for
the study of Torah. In this way it accomplished much for the
strengthening of religion. Rabbi Reines expected the opposition
of the orthodox to Zionism to disappear gradually. This indeed
seemed to be the case with those whose opposition stemmed from
religious apprehensions. But there were some whose pretended
fears served merely as a subterfuge to spread false charges

[19]An abstract of this proclamation is given in "Shnei ha-Meoroth."

against the Mizrachi and its founders. These people became even more violent in their opposition, when they saw
the success of the new organization. They resorted to all kinds of
unfair means to discredit the Mizrachi. Rabbi Reines, as was his
wont, did not answer those who persecuted him, and did not
repay them in like coin. But he found it necessary to put one
experience on record for coming generations.[20]

When he was once invited to speak in the city of Kovno
(Lithuania) and the Beth Midrash was filled from end to end,
a man went over to him and told him that he would not allow
him to speak. Rabbi Reines was afraid that if the arrogance of
this man became known to the audience it might lead to violence,
God forbid. He pleaded with the man not to interfere. Several
persons who had noticed the incident pushed the man aside, but the
latter held on to the Rabbi's coat and tore it when forced to let
go of it. On the following day, when this unfortunate encounter
became known, important men of the city came to visit the Rabbi,
even those who were opposed to Zionism, and expressed their regret
over the incident. On their insistence he stayed several days longer
and addressed two additional meetings.

This recognition encouraged Rabbi Reines to continue his
work. In 1904 he decided to call a world-wide conference of
the Mizrachi in the city of Pressburg (Bratislava, Czechoslovakia), a famous and ancient community where there had once
served as rabbi the sainted scholar Moses Sofer, author of the
Responsa "Hatham Sofer." Rabbi Reines, mindful of the Kovno
incident and recoiling from strife and dissension, inquired first
through his friends whether the then Rabbi of the city (a grandson
of "Hatham Sofer") was opposed to the idea. They visited the
rabbi, who declared that he was not opposed to having the conference in his city, but that he personally would not take part
in it. Yet when the conference was formally announced, it was
put under a religious ban (Herem) which was widely publicized
through the rabbinical periodicals appearing in Hungary. Under
the circumstances, Rabbi Reines was ready to withdraw. His
friends in Pressburg, however, assured him that the ban was an

[20]Ibid., p. 30.

empty gesture, and that one of the rabbis who had signed the ban
had notified him that he had been compelled to do so. Rabbi Reines
journeyed to Pressburg with his heart full of misgivings.   He
arrived there on Erev Shabbos and attended the synagogue. To his
surprise, the congregation welcomed him and the other delegates
warmly. His fears were allayed. During the morning service in
the synagogue, an opponent distributed a libelous circular against
him in which was asserted that the Rabbi was an atheist, and that
ample evidence of the Rabbi's heretical views could be found in his
book "Or Hadash al Tsiyon." After Shabbos, when this became
known to Rabbi Reines, he asked his friends to obtain for him
a copy of his book. It was shown to one of the highly respected
Dayanim whose office was hereditary as far back as the days of the
Hatham Sofer. The dayan, upon studying the book, said that he
was in full agreement with its contents which were worthy of the
author. The book passed then from hand to hand among the
orthodox scholars in Pressburg, who expressed their amazement
at the shameless insinuations of the Rabbi's enemies.

As it happened, this incident aroused great sympathy for the
Mizrachi conference. At a special session devoted to ways and
means for the strengthening of religion there was a heated discussion. Several Hebrew writers criticized the Rabbi for dividing
Mizrachi's energies in espousing projects that were not directly
connected with Zionism. One of the attending rabbis denounced
the rabbis of Hungary from the rostrum for their hostility. Rabbi
Reines opposed him because he was convinced that the Rabbis of
Hungary harbored no ill will but acted from lack of knowledge.

There were other personal attacks and humiliations because of
his connections with the Mizrachi. What caused him extreme
mental anguish was the fact that he was gradually excluded from
rabbinical conferences. There were notable exceptions among the
Rabbis. One was the Gaon Rabbi Eliezer Gordon of Telz, who
differed with Rabbi Reines on Zionism yet, out of respect for his
scholarship and integrity, invited him to the assembly of the Rabbinical group "Knesseth Yisrael." Rabbi Reines acknowledged the
invitation in a long letter which among other things dealt with
the problems confronting Jewry at that time.

The main reason for the prevailing religious apathy, in his opinion,[21] was the widespread ignorance of our religious literature. When now many of those who had been estranged from Judaism began to come closer to our people, they should be drawn to Bible and Talmud with "ropes of love," in order that they realize their great task. He was chagrined by the fact that divisive and vituperative tendencies had penetrated the schools of the Zionists. In the book "Or Hadash al Tsiyon," he interprets feelingly the words of the Sages dealing with Israel's return and settlement in the Holy Land. His work on behalf of religious Zionism was an essential part of his intense efforts to bring the children of our people closer to the Torah. Zionism was for him not only a political but also a spiritual and ethical movement that marks the return to Judaism of those who had forsaken it.

At that time he again began to lay plans for founding a Yeshivah, where sacred studies would be combined with secular learning. The idea had fascinated him for decades, from the time that he had been forced to close his Yeshivah in Shwenzian (Lithuania). In 1905 he was given the opportunity to open such an institution in Lida. In the course of a few years it attracted hundreds of students from the length and breadth of Russia. The major part of the curriculum included the Talmud and its commentaries, but the students were also instructed in the Hebrew language and literature, the language of the country (Russian), and in general disciplines, as taught in the secondary schools.

For, says he, "if it was formerly possible for one to devote himself completely to the study of the Torah without allowing place for secular subjects, it is not possible today, when, for economic or other reasons, general knowledge is demanded from every one, layman and rabbi alike.[22]

His goal was a double one: (1) to train rabbis, who would be great Jewish scholars and who would, at the same time, have a keen appreciation of general knowledge; (2) to provide laymen with knowledge of the Torah in sufficient measure to counteract the spirit of the time from affecting their loyalty to Judaism. He was particularly anxious that the Yeshivah should raise the status of

[21]"Or Hadash al Tsiyon", Introd., p. 10.
[22]Ibid.

the rabbinate. The honor of the rabbinate had declined very largely because it had become fashionable to elect rabbis to office very much in the manner of political elections with their attendant evils of propaganda and wire-pulling. The establishment of a recognized Yeshivah would, he hoped, make communities turn to it for advice in the appointment of religious leaders, and this in turn would keep the "final" choice above communal factions.

Such a step was urgently necessary from the time that the "Haskalah" had undermined the foundation of Israel, the honor of the Torah. The "Maskilim," the rich, and a considerable section of the rest of the people, became estranged from the Torah, and looked at the students of the Yeshivoth, the "poor boys," with scorn and derision, and the latter, the few who gave their time for the study of the Torah, felt miserable and humiliated. Rabbi Reines admonished[23] the young men who give their years to the study of the Torah, not to bow down their heads in shame and despair but on the contrary to stand erect and feel a special pride in their calling.

The Yeshivah of Lida succeeded in raising the honor of the Torah. Many wealthy parents who would otherwise have sent their sons to secular schools sent them to this Yeshivah, and many more were turned away for lack of space. "Roshei Yeshivoth" and trained teachers taught in the Yeshivah, and individual care and interest was given to each student. The one who showed special promise was given the opportunity of specializing in Torah; he who wished to be a Hebrew teacher received the necessary preparation for that calling; and he who wished to remain a layman was equipped with sufficient knowledge and love for Judaism.

On the Sabbath Reines was wont to expound Halakhah and Aggadah before the student body, in order to implant in their hearts love for Torah and the love of God. The students, who were very closely attached to him, were wont to come to his home to hear words of Torah from his lips. He would interest himself in them even after they had left the Yeshivah and gone out into life.

But he was not free from worries. First, his budget far exceeded that of other Yeshivoth; secondly, his opponents again rose against him and spread false reports about the Yeshivah. Trouble

[23]"Shnei ha-Meoroth", article "Zikkaron ba-Sefer", p. 22.

arose also from unworthy students who were asked to leave, and who, to justify themselves, published letters of calumny in the Hebrew newspapers. Again, there were informers who slandered the Rabbi before the Russian government. Thus, with a view to having the charter of his school revoked, they accused him falsely of not conforming to government regulations.[24]

Undaunted by all this, he did not cease to work for the Zionist cause, and attended all the Congresses. When it was decided at the Tenth Zionist Congress in 1911 that Zionism espouse Western culture as would any of the European polities, he became keenly disappointed and depressed in spirit. He had fought against this contingency for many years and had warned the Zionist leaders that such a move might disrupt the unity of the movement. Nevertheless he decided not to leave the Zionist movement, knowing full well that this would result only in harm, but he endeavored to exert influence from within.

The Mizrachi activities, as all other Zionist work, had been curtailed in the latter years preceding World War I. In his last book (published during his lifetime), "Shnei ha-Meoroth", he included two chapters about the Yeshivah and his Zionist activity. Pre-occupation during the last twelve years of his life with the Yeshivah and the Mizrachi prevented the publishing of his other books, the great majority of which are still in manuscript—among them his great work on the methods of Halakhah and Aggadah, a commentary on Midrash Rabbah, Rabbinic Responsa, and others.

In the last years of his life, he thought of settling in Palestine, and turned to Rabbi Fishman (Maimon) with a suggestion to purchase property for him. But meanwhile the war had broken out. He was at the time in Germany and it was only with difficulty that he, as a Russian citizen, was allowed to return home. En route he fell prey to a disease that was within a year to put an end to his life. The Jewish doctors did not wish to disclose to him the nature of the disease. He appealed to a non-Jewish doctor to tell him the truth.

[24]But the Rabbi was undismayed. In his last book, published two years before his death, he writes: In spite of all this, whenever I enter the Yeshivah and see how hundreds of students sit and study the Torah of God, the sight satisfies me as reward for all the troubles and worries, for it is so uplifting and so wondrous to behold."

The Christian physician did disclose the truth to him, and when the relatives were angry with the doctor over this, he answered, "The man is a philosopher, and he may know the truth." He suffered tremendous pains and was no longer able to put his thoughts down on paper. But nevertheless, whenever he felt relieved, he would sit up and receive callers. The war had brought many refugees to his city, and they would come to take counsel with him. Then he would utter the "inconsequential talk of a Talmudic scholar, which deserves study." The present writer remembers how the leaders of the city came to visit him a few months before his death, shortly before the holiday of Passover, and he, knowing full well his condition, chatted in his pleasant way, offering withal a message which made a great impression on the audience. A few months later, he passed away, on the tenth of Elul 5675 (1915) in the midst of World War I, several months before his seventy-sixth birthday.

Rabbi Reines was one of the most outstanding and original types that the rabbinate has produced. His mastery of Talmudic and Midrashic literature was prodigious, and he also possessed knowledge of the other branches of Jewish literature. He was another link in the chain of brilliant men in Torah, men who were preeminent in research and profound thinking. But he was especially aware of the change that had come about in Jewry in the latter generations, and the dangers due to this change. He was not one of those who imagine that by blinding one's eyes to them they will disappear of themselves. He well knew that for this a clear understanding of the spirit of the time was necessary and therefore planned concerted action to fortify Judaism. He understood well the menace of assimilation in all its forms, particularly when it put on a mask of "nationalism" and "national culture" derived from foreign sources. All his efforts were centered around one goal: to protect Judaism from the currents that engulfed it.

But such a struggle can bear fruit only if there exists an appreciation of the ethical essence of Judaism, and the meaning of Jewish history.

"Nationalism" devoid of religious contents has no permanency. It is espoused only because the new generation does not comprehend the values of Judaism. The one goal of his fruitful literary labors, as well as his public activity, was to prepare the hearts of Jews for the Geulah, redemption, so that the quickening of the spirit of the people in its homeland should be in the Jewish tradition. He was a man of most profound understanding and showed great patience to people who had been misled. But at the same time he was zealous in his opposition to those that opposed the spirit of Judaism. He used to say that he could stand free-*thinkers* in Zionism but not free-*thinking*. People also quote him as saying: "The Zionists say that all Jews must be Zionists; and I say that all Zionists should be Jews."

His contributions came not only from his thoughts and ideas but also from his ethical personality. The persecutions which he endured because of his ideals did not embitter him. The honor which came to him did not affect his natural humility and simplicity.

He was possessed of warm feeling, and his heart was always open to everyone. Because of all this did he have such powerful influence on his generation—one which few of the latter-day-rabbis have achieved—for everyone realized that all of his actions were "for the sake of heaven" and all his energies were bent upon preserving the Jewish people.

MEIR TSEVI JUNG

By Gershom Bader and Moses Jung

MEIR TSEVI JUNG

BY GERSHOM BADER AND MOSES JUNG

"Once again we come to an anniversary, the fifteenth, of that day, when, in London, Rabbi Doctor Maurice Jung, of blessed memory, closed his eyes forever. More than twenty-five years it is since he left Ungarisch Brod (Moravia), until that time the seat of his blessed ministry. But his memory remains undimmed in the hearts of the Jews there. The greatest accomplishment of his life was the establishment of Jewish Secondary Schools that combined the teaching of secular knowledge with traditional Jewish training, *'Torah* and *Derekh Erets'*. To this end he devoted his great talents.

"Unforgettable was his appeal to a distinguished Jewish gathering in Vienna in May, 1900, on the occasion of the founding of the society for the promotion of such schools, with their motto, "Faith and Science," from which the new organization took its name.

"Referring to Ezekiel's vision of the dry bones that came together but lived only when the spirit of the Almighty infused them, Dr. Jung showed how, after the ordeal of the Middle Ages and the Dark Ages for the Jewish people that followed, our scattered and withered members were reassembled. But it was soon found that this body was without a living soul. The new emancipation that we so eagerly espoused, the schools to which we sent our children, where they imbibed the teachings of the non-Jewish world, what did all this contribute to Judaism? Nothing! The only salvation lay in our own Jewish High Schools.

"Many in those days thought of Traditional Judaism as being outmoded, buried, and on its gravestone written 'This grave must never be opened.' But hidden in this grave there was, unknown to them, a living seed. This put forth roots and branches.

" 'We must', said Dr. Jung, 'revive the dry bones, with the living spirit of Jewish knowledge. This is the task of the Jewish secondary School.'

"Now the seed that Rabbi Jung planted has grown into a mighty tree. Others followed his example. And when we see

297

today such schools in all countries whose Jewish population warrants it, we may look at each one as a monument to this great soul in Israel." Thus Jacob Schoen, in June 1936, in the "Allgemeine Juedische Zeitung" of Pressburg, Czechoslovakia.

I

The two major influences on Rabbi Jung's life were the Torah and the university, each strengthening and complementing the other. His father had to be won to the cause of secular education. He had good reason to fear the influence of the secular State High School, the Gymnasium, but Meir Tsevi insisted and completed the course of study at the Gymnasium in Budapest, before proceeding to the Yeshivah for intensive Jewish studies. In later years, due in part to various changes, both in the state schools and in the attitude of the Jewish populations towards them, Rabbi Meir Jung implacably opposed the sending of Jewish children to the Gymnasium. In his own case, difficulties were overcome by special private instruction, and permission to be absent on the Sabbath (by no means easy to arrange).

He remained devoted to study throughout his life, and one of the sweetest childhood memories of his children is the *niggun* of his Gemara study, early in the morning. He continually engaged in correspondence with other great scholars of his time, with whom he discussed interpretations and applications of Jewish law. He attended many Yeshivoth and among his teachers was the world renowned Maharam Schick of Huszt. He received Semikhoth at the hands of *Ba'al Shevet Sofer* in Pressburg, Rabbi Samuel Ehrenfeld, the *"Hathan Sopher"*, Rabbi Yitzhak Glick, the Gaon of Tolcsva, Rabbi Yehudah Leib Julius of Shebesh, and Rabbi Zalman Spitzer of Vienna.

At the universities he took up Philosophy, History and Semitics, attending in turn Marburg, Heidelberg and Leipzig. He took his Ph.D. at Leipzig, where, under Professor Franz Delitzsch, he chose for his dissertation: A Critique of all the Books *Aboth* (The Ethics of the Fathers).[1]

---

[1]The extent of the research problems for his dissertation can be appraised best by a consideration of what is included: a complete bibliographical study, encompassing all Talmudic writings that are found under the classi-

From his paternal home, Torah-true in theory and practice, and from the Yeshivoth, stemmed his great devotion to the sanctuaries of our faith, and a capacity for glorious stiff-neckedness that defied material handicaps and blithely persisted in the face of every type of adversary, be it an obtuse majority, a gang of obscurantists, or, equally difficult, the mentally inert and uninterested.

The universities were a second source of strength, the whole intellectual climate from the categorical imperative of Kant to Ibsen's Brandt, with his "Everything or Nothing" principle. From Kant he derived endorsement of the Jewish traditional adherence to principle, to intellectual conviction. The Germany that he knew was that of Goethe and Hermann Cohen, of order and system; but its blatant militarism never penetrated the consciousness of the eager brilliant student. (A generation later Count Baudissin and Hermann Cohen, his teachers in the early eighties, recalled his qualities to an awe-struck student, his son.)

He could not understand base conduct. A broken promise, any act of treachery amazed him. In the abstract he had a wholesome contempt for any form of falsehood, and in the concrete form, it appalled him.

fication of *Aboth* ("Fathers" or "Principles"), large as well as smaller volumes. And resolved to leave no stone unturned, he delved yet deeper until he found a vast number of data to be gleaned from many manuscripts in various libraries, and which dealt with the time when it was decided that the "Ethics of the Fathers" was to be studied on summer Sabbath afternoons.

It is a matter of common knowledge among scholars that in dealing with "Ethics of the Fathers," it is important to examine *Kinyan Torah*, the sixth chapter of the Ethics in the Mishnaic "Fathers", but which does not belong to the *Mishnah* proper. It is, in fact, a Baraitha. Many commentators interpret it to be a *Baraitha* of Rabbi Meir's. To substantiate this interpretation, they point to the opening of the *Baraitha* which begins with the statement: *"Rabbi Meir says."*

Meir Tsevi Jung, however, is of the opinion that this statement proves nothing of the kind. He maintains, moreover, that this is a *Baraitha* of *Eliezer Ben Horkinas*. To prove his point, he calls attention to the fact that on the one hand, that which follows the opening statement, "Rabbi Meir says," is inharmonious in spirit, and incompatible in thought, with other sayings of Rabbi Meir, while on the other, everything which follows the opening statement of that *Baraitha* is characteristic both in spirit and thought-content of *Eliezer Ben Horkinas'* writings. To leave no doubt of the authenticity of this interpretation, and to support it beyond question, he offers a full measure of documentary proof.

One of his sons recalls that he used to accompany his father for walks in the mornings, after *shaharith* services and before time for school. It was characteristic of these walks that they invariably left the beaten path, and took cuts-up, inclines, dodging overhanging branches. Sometimes it was hard for the youngster to follow. This pattern was symbolic of the man, his spirit, and method. He was enterprising, pioneering. An example was the case of the Cracow School. It was to be the first of its kind, an adventure in educational-religious-social endeavor. First there came the call for energy, hard work, ingenuity. But soon there arose a new need, that of courage! Those who had promised support withdrew it on the eve of the opening; he found that he was suddenly in "enemy territory." Before he had a chance for defense, a group of obscurantist opponents of modern education, an unholy alliance of assimilationists and misguided orthodox Jews, attempted to arouse the populace against him. There were posters "Ha-Mashhith Ba el ha-Ir" (the Destroyer has come to town), a violent press attack. His work was condemned without a hearing by a Beth Din. But he knew he was right. He refused to postpone the opening of the school and could not be intimidated; his example gave courage to a frightened faculty. His composure when, after a few months, his beloved Cracow venture was closed by the authorities on account of false charges of "political radicalism," impressed his children so much that they marvel to this day at the goodwill, optimism and undiminished vigor with which he started new schools in Storozynetz and Lemberg.

After the tumult had died down, and before the above-mentioned new schools were organized, he sent an open letter (*kol kore*) to all his rabbinic opponents in Poland and Galicia. In attempting to describe it one thinks of such words as: integrity, singleness of purpose, courage, consistency, good will. One of his grandchildren on reading it for the first time was moved to tears. But here we are a little ahead of our story.

II

Meir Tsevi Jung was born in the year 1858, in the little Hungarian town of Tisza Eszlar. His father, Abraham Jung, was a man of means, a landowner, scholar, an ordained rabbi in fact, who chose to engage in business. He was widely known for his generosity and constructive interest in communal affairs.

In Tisza Eszlar, there lived but a handful of Jews, twenty families, the rest of the population, Hungarian Christians, both in town and in the vicinity, consisting for the most part of illiterate, impoverished peasants. The Jews, on the other hand, were educated and, by dint of sobriety and hard work, men of substance and social standing. There seemed to exist a state of harmony between Jews and non-Jews, but this rested on flimsy foundations; the peasants were friendly but ignorant and easily swayed, the hierarchy fickle.

In this atmosphere, the child grew up nevertheless secure, finding that security, as our people always have found, in Torah and Avodah, faith and work, and all that these connote for family, school and community life.

He was a man of twenty-four, his studies at the Yeshivoth completed, just embarked on the long-anticipated life at the university, when there came a catastrophe that threatened not only his career at the university but the very life of his family and of the whole Jewish community in Hungary. It was a shock that affected Jewry everywhere—the infamous blood libel in his village—and one can imagine how Meir Tsevi must have felt! And yet, in later years, the only references that his children ever heard to the whole frightful experience were expressions of thankfulness to, and admiration of, the Hungarian Christian advocate, Baron Eötvös, the Clemenceau of Hungary, leader of a small band of Hungarian liberals, who exposed the falsehoods of the accusers and established the innocence of the Jews. He used to refer also to the valiant efforts of that almost legendary figure, the centenarian, Sir Moses Montefiore. This was but one example of that valiant composure in the face of adversity, that optimism based on trust in God and faith in man, that freedom from hostility that wastes the energies of those less well adjusted.

In the year 1886, at the age of 28, he accepted his first rabbinical position in Mannheim, Germany. In the same year he married Ernestine, the daughter of Jacob Silberman of Eperjes in Hungary. It was a happy union, and an ideal companionship, until, in 1915, in London, she passed away.

It was in Mannheim that their first child, a daughter, Lolla, was born.

The position of Klaus-Rabbiner in Mannheim had a special significance and a distinguished history. Established in 1708, and filled in turn by a succession of great scholars, it had for generations been the citadel of Torah-true Judaism in a sea of nonconformity and indifference. It represented moreover a high standard of *Torah im Derekh Erets* (Torah wedded to secular culture).

The official chief rabbi of the Mannheim Jewish community was a man very different in his attitude towards basic Jewish observance, from the scholarly and Torah-true Rabbi Jung. There resulted a battle of principles, the record of which is to be found in the "Allgemeine Zeitung des Judentums" and in the "Mainzer Israelit," which published most of Dr. Jung's sermons.

In 1890, after four years at his first post, he accepted a call to the ancient and famous Kehillah of Ung. Brod, in the province of Moravia. The records of the synagogue there showed an unbroken history of nearly eight hundred years and the list of its incumbents revealed that among those who ministered there were worldrenowned rabbis, the great *Ba'al Turei Zahav,* Reb David ben Shemuel ha-Levi in 1635, and in 1648, the distinguished author of *Yevein Metsulah,* Rabbi Nassau Hannover. (In 1663, this great tsaddik lost his life at the hands of a marauding band of soldiers who almost destroyed the whole city.)

In Brod were born his four sons, Moses, Leo, Julius, Gabriel and one daughter, Bertha. They all retain lively memories of the many-faceted life in that community. There was always something new and thrilling going on. Rabbi Jung strengthened existing organizations, and created new ones. Among them the re-organized *Bikkur Holim* (Visiting the Sick)—society for the support of a hospital—where, without discrimination as to rich or poor, those in need received the required care; the *Gemiluth Hassadim* society where those in need of financial assistance or in temporary difficulties could borrow money free of interest. New and most important proved the *"Horev"* which he organized for cultural purposes. This group attracted a continuous stream of famous speakers and artists such as Gustav Karpeles, the author of "A History of Jewish Literature," Dr. Leopold Kahn, a great leader in Zionism and personal collaborator of Theodor Herzl, and Heinrich Grun-feld, the cellist.

The festivals took on a new meaning for the whole commu-nity. To give a few examples: In the absence of the type of com-munity center that obtains today, Rabbi Jung set up a stage in a large room at his home and the festivals of Purim and Chanukah were graced with dramatic presentations that the boys and girls of Brod, now grown and scattered to the four corners of the earth, can never forget.

In Brod there came to his home great Jewish literary figures, luminaries of the Torah, statesmen. But his interest was not con-fined to his own people. One of his sons retains the picture in his mind's eye of the rabbi strolling around the city square, deep in talk, with his friend, the local Catholic priest. And not only did church dignitaries come to him with religious and social problems, but there was a never-ending stream of peasant folk who came to him for sympathy, counsel and help, with personal and family problems. They tried to show their gratitude by gifts of money and offerings of fruit and eggs. All these were placed in the keeping of the wife of the rabbi, and the poor of the district, Jew and non-Jew, received all of it at her hands.

Christian friends often availed themselves of the opportunity to come to the synagogue to listen to his sermons.

The Yom Kippur services were so beautiful and so impressive, that the officialdom of the district never failed to attend respect-fully, in all the splendor of their dress uniforms. The throng of local Jewish worshippers would be increased on these occasions by the Jews from surrounding villages, every one, men as well as women, all in white; outside stood the Jewish policemen in full uniform.

The Kehillah of Ung. Brod, one of the oldest in Moravia, had preserved rich old melodies, an atmosphere and setting that helped make the services unforgettable.

It is interesting to note that Ung. Brod was not only a central or "mother community" for other small congregations, but it also was one of some twenty-odd autonomous Jewish communities of the Austro-Hungarian Empire with an administration of its own— a Jewish mayor, Jewish police, Jewish hospital, Jewish school, a

closed Jewish settlement, though many individuals lived outside
the *Judenstadt*.

III

Recognizing the futility of further delay, Dr. Jung decided
to turn forthwith to the one sure bulwark of defense against the
deterioration of Judaism: the Jewish youth! The means must be
provided for Torah-true Jewish education, complemented by a
satisfactory program of secular education. Rabbi Jung began working for the *"Torah* and *Derekh Erets* School" which was to offer a
comprehensive curriculum, where the Jewish student could absorb
the religious cultural values of the Jewish people and have the
opportunity for a secular education.

Presently a political situation arose, which served to intensify
the rabbi's determination not only to establish a gymnasium (secondary school) but also to keep it entirely free of all political influence. At this particular time in the history of the province of
Moravia, there was bitter enmity between the Germans and the
Czechs. The Jews, the eternal scapegoat, caught between the
fires, were suspected and accused by the Czechs of being German
sympathizers, and by the Germans of being on the side of the
Czechs. Rabbi Jung knew full well that such suspicions and accusations were but the harbingers of tragic cataclysms for his people.
Hence his determination to steer clear of all entangling alliances
in his educational enterprise.

Dr. Solomon Frankfurter, Expert on Jewish Affairs in the
Austrian Ministry of Education, approved of Rabbi Jung's project
and helped with advice, guidance and, most important, with obtaining of the needed charter. (He was, by the way, an uncle of Felix
Frankfurter, Justice of the United States Supreme Court).
Dr. Armand Kaminka, Director of the Alliance Israelite Universelle in Vienna, obtained a grant-in-aid for the new school.
He proceeded with his plan, and established his school. Before the
year 1904/5, the school had opened five classes, with an enrollment of 45 pupils, a large number of whom—22 to be exact—had
come from Galicia, to avail themselves of what they considered an
educational boon. Every class offered the curriculum which Dr.
Jung had promised in his original plan. In the fifth, highest class,

the advanced students were subjected to a comprehensive training in Jewish history, and the introduction to Jewish literature, in *Humash* and *Rashi*, the weekly portion of the Torah, in *Mishnah*, abbreviated *Shulhan Arukh*, and in a tractate of the Talmud with commentaries, in the book of *Isaiah*, and in *Divrei Mussar* (ethical instruction) from the book *Pele Yoets*.

The original plan for the school was proving workable. David Wolfson, Herzl's follower in the Zionist movement, became interested in the school and he assigned to it a sum of money to assist with its budget. Wolfson's interest may have been induced by the fact that Theodore Herzl, in a warm encouraging letter, had expressed his approbation of the school.

Now we come to the strange, exciting Cracow venture. Since the enrollment indicated a preponderance of interest by Galician students, who came from their native cities to study under him, Rabbi Jung decided that it would be a constructive service to establish schools for them in Galicia. He knew that in Galicia there was an element of orthodox young people who craved secular learning, but were restrained by their Jewish principles from reaching out for it, since, to avail themselves of secular learning in Galicia, they were compelled to desecrate the Sabbath. Galicia then held out the promise of a fertile field for a school such as his.

Paradoxically enough, the people of Ung. Brod as well as the other Jews in the province of Moravia, with few exceptions, had little understanding of the implication of Rabbi Jung's school. This lack of appreciation of its potential values, and of the profound influence which such a school must come to have on Jewish life, doubtless had a reason. This school of Rabbi Jung was a generation ahead of its time.

Rabbi Jung journeyed to Cracow and lost no time in calling to a meeting several orthodox Jews of prominence to discuss the plan for a *Torah* and *Derekh Erets* school. Result: Cracow, apparently, would welcome him and his educational ideas. With buoyant energy he proceeded to establish the Cracow school. It was to combine the best features of Central European secondary schools with systematic training in Jewish disciplines. Its faculty was composed of men who combined in themselves Judaism with contemporary culture, its board of directors were loyal to the

Torah and aware of modern problems and techniques. But he was
to discover that his belief in Cracow was a mistaken one. It was
as if, blindfold, he had plunged his hand into a live beehive!!

The basic insecurity of the greater part of the Jewish population of Cracow rendered it naturally fearful of innovation. In the
case of the new school of Rabbi Jung, the opposition emerged as a
sort of unholy alliance between traditional Jews fearful of destructive change and assimilationist Jews fearful of constructive progress!

After a few months, in October, 1960, the benighted enemies
of the school succeeded in having it closed by government decree.
The rabbi saw to it however, that the teachers were paid for the
full period of the contract.

It looked like a closed chapter, and so it might have been, with
anyone less staunch, with anyone possessed of less positive optimism,
less faith in the ultimate good in all men, and less good will than
Meir Tsevi Jung.

His "Kol Koré"—an open letter, written in classic Hebrew, he
had printed in thousands, and sent everywhere. His children,
those old enough to help, still tell of the high excitement that was
theirs. They lived through the whole Cracow affair, sharing its
hopes and defeats. They worked like beavers, folding, inserting,
addressing envelopes. For every rabbi, teacher, and community
officer of every Jewish group, large and small, in Galicia received a
copy of that priceless "Kol Koré." It is here reproduced:

> "The opponents of the school which I established in Cracow
> have spread in the camp of Israel a number of warnings and
> prohibitions emanating from the rabbis of Galicia and Hungary
> who forbid their people to send their children to this school.
> "After the storm of protest has subsided, I wish to make
> clear my aim and purpose in establishing this school.
> "These rabbis thought that all parents in the province of
> Galicia sent their children to the 'Heder' or the 'Yeshivah'
> where the pupils study Torah and Talmud and are trained in
> the spirit of our traditional faith. Therefore, they complained
> bitterly about my school in which the students would spend
> part of their time in the pursuit of secular studies. The truth
> however is this: In every city in which there is a government
> school, hundreds of Jewish children attend.
> "In Cracow alone more than three thousand Jewish children
> attend the public high schools. Their parents are not defiant

sinners. They do not delight in their children's offences against the Torah; but they believe that general education is essential for their sons and they are unable to withstand the great temptation and thus they offer up their children. These parents with sore hearts see their sons, who on entering the high schools still were loyal to God and Israel, gradually becoming estranged from our Torah. These parents heard that in my own community I had established a high school in which the spirit of tradition pervades the secular as well as religious education and therefore they urged me to establish such a school in Cracow. They are afraid to send their children to Moravia, where according to reports there is little Torah and less faith. I acceded to their petition and devoted my time and strength to the founding in their community of such a school, not in order to discourage those whose purpose it is to dedicate their days to the study of the Torah, but in order to bring nearer those who are afar, who are anxious to obtain general enlightment. These latter students, who in the state schools are being lost to Judaism, I have come to save, in order that they might become loyal Jews.

"And now I address myself to those who are loyal to the word of the Lord: Is it not our duty to listen to the voice of these parents who fear that their children might become assimilated and turn their backs upon the Torah? Are we not disregarding the prohibition *'Neither shalt thou stand idly by the blood of thy neighbor'*, if we are standing aside indifferently, at a time when thousands of Jewish children are lost in chaos and confusion because there is none to guide their way? Not only do you yourself do nothing to prevent disaster, but you make a vehement outcry when you see others devoting their lives to save these young people. Do you not realize that a great many Jewish people do not listen to your voice and send their children to the state schools? They would be happy if they could send them to such a school as mine.

"Are you just in asking me what right I have to 'interfere in your country's affairs?' If you see a man drowning in a river and you are able to save him, would you ask him first from what country he comes?

"You have asked me how I could think of solving the problem of education in your province without consulting its rabbis. My reply is: I do not wish to solve the educational problem of the 'Heder'. That is your work. But the educational problem of the children in the state schools I am anxious to solve, because you have abandoned them, thrusting them away with both hands. I wish to preserve what you have given up, gather in what you have abandoned. Therefore, you are not entitled to complain.

"And now to you pious in Israel, let me make my appeal. Religious loyalty has seriously declined in your province of Galicia. The 'Batei Midrash' for the study of the Torah are empty and forsaken. The leaders of the Jewish communities throw off the yoke of the Torah. What are you doing to stem the evil tide? Do you believe you can improve matters by prohibiting the Jewish youth from attending schools of general education? If your children become estranged from our faith, the fault lies not with general education, for general education in itself does not oppose faith. If you keep away from all those who seek enlightenment and make a pariah of every student who holds fast to it, it is you who have thrust them away from the God of Israel, and who make them serve other gods and espouse alien ideals.

"See what was the state of this province of Moravia in olden times. Great teachers of the Torah once lived here, but now the gates of their famous schools are mourning. Do you know why this province has suffered such great losses? It is because general education was lacking here two generations ago as it is in your country today. But the rabbis derided it and paid no attention to the children who entered the public schools. The parents, on their part, paid no attention to the rabbis who prohibited attendance at such schools and, as time went on, the schools of Jewish learning became empty and the students at public school became transgressors. Take this to heart lest you become responsible for the religious deterioration of your province. Do something and do it soon! Have mercy on the many thousands of children who are being lost in confusion. Strengthen the weak hands and uphold the stumbling knees. Bring near those in whose hearts the Torah is still aflame. Offer them general education in the spirit of purity and you will understand how right our sages were, when they said 'How good is it to combine the Torah with secular education, for the occupation with both will make sin forgotten' . . .

"I am ready to help you with all my heart and soul if you will only have mercy upon our young people, even as a father has mercy on his children."

Soon afterwards, a number of Jews in Lemberg, Galicia, and in Storosynetz, Bukovina, approached him with the request to establish schools in their cities similar to the one in Cracow.

Toward that objective, each of these men pledged his unqualified support. Dr. Jung established schools in both cities, which flourished until 1915 when the War destroyed them.

Shortly after the storm concerning the Jung school in Cracow, a new political movement arose, which encompassed all sections of the population in the Austrian provinces. There was a change from the class-system which had obtained hitherto in the Austrian parliament. The Galician Jews, blindly optimistic, believed that the new parliamentary system, in its greater liberality, would prove to be advantageous to them.

At that time, many orthodox Jews in Kolomea, supported by a faction of Zionists, implored Dr. Jung to become a candidate for the Austrian Parliament. Unwilling to accept the conditions of the Zionist organization, however, or to obstruct the Zionist candidate's chances for election to that post, Dr. Jung declined to avail himself of the opportunity.

Four years later, before the election of 1911, in an address which Rabbi Jung delivered in Ung. Brod, he expressed an attitude of indifference toward all such elections. He emphasized that it is not important for Austrian Jews to sacrifice their religious integrity for a parliamentary election. He wanted Jews to hold to present Jewishness and Israel, rather than ephemeral, non-religious nationalism.

As if the rabbi of Ung. Brod did not have problems enough, there arose a new one, immediately after the Cracow debacle, that would have been a kind of comic anti-climax, if the mischief makers had not been so devoid of humor. The president of his congregation had, in the absence of the rabbi, conceived of what was to him a grandiose plan to increase his personal prestige and that of the Jewish community, involving changes in the synagogue service, adding a mixed choir, etc. These changes were presented to Rabbi Jung on his return from Cracow as a fait accompli. He, of course, withheld approval on grounds of sacred tradition. His opponent refused to give in and so the rabbi had no choice but to remain away from the synagogue. An archduke and other dignitaries had been invited as guests for the new "reformed" service, but when a matter of principle was involved Rabbi Jung was no respecter of persons. He remained firm and won his point since the rank and file felt his absence too keenly and rose as one man to call the rabbi back. It was not done overnight. In the meantime a new world was preparing a new field for the genius of the Rabbi of Ung. Brod.

In London, England, Samuel Montague, Lord Swaythling, had taken counsel with others who were interested in the maintenance of Jewish traditions and had concluded that the need of the hour was for a leader, a rabbi who would combine in one person the scholarship sufficient to gain him authority in the eyes of every established rabbi in England, the personality to impress, and ability to organize new organizations where needed and improve and consolidate others. Since no less than sixty-eight synagogues were involved in the project, there was need for a great leader indeed!

A committee, consisting of Mr. Joseph Blank, secretary of the Federation, Mr. Marks Moses, and Mr. Herman Landau, public spirited Jewish orthodox laymen, travelled to the continent in search of such a man. The mission took the better part of a year. Every Jewish community that might yield help was visited, and every known rabbi of note was interviewed and consulted. Finally, at the recommendation of Rabbi Guedemann, Chief Rabbi of Vienna, an invitation was extended to Doctor Jung of Ung. Brod to come to London to head the synagogue union.

He felt at once the challenge of the new field and accepted without delay. Thus began a new and brilliant chapter in the life work of this devoted servant of God and fellow man.

His transition to a new language was noteworthy. Within ten months he was able to preach a sermon in flawless English, making the change from the flowery German with its long-winded periods, to the severe, clipped simplicity of the English pattern. Remarkable, too, was his acquisition of Yiddish in order to be able to address in that language the several East Side congregations, and come close to the large Yiddish-speaking group. His family found this even more admirable than his facility in English, since Yiddish was, to the German-trained adolescents, most difficult, most strange, its similarities with German only serving to make the differences more confusing. The family later testified that when they heard their father speak what had formerly seemed a mere dialect, it took on a rich juicy warmth, and they came to recognize its strength and its beauty.

For the devoted wife and mother the adjustment was more difficult. She came to a strange city from the town where all knew and loved her, not only as the wife of the revered rabbi but for her own sweet spirit and capable mind. She tried valiantly to acquire a good English accent, and, the crowding household and social duties notwithstanding, worked away at the Langenscheidt letters, a masterly set of courses for the acquisition of English. She was making fine progress when a malignant disease carried her off in the first years of the war. Rabbi Jung was shaken to his depths. He never really recovered from his loss. A year later he was still to be found in a melancholy mood.

His son Leo records that, like many other idealists, he had taken Mother's infinite devotion for granted, and as he never spared himself, he had not stopped to spare her. Their relationship was always exceedingly fine; she spoke of him in veneration, and he referred to her, with few words, but in a tone that made his sons and daughters feel she was the essence of an *esheth hayyil* and the source of all blessing. "I do not remember having seen him kiss her, except at infrequent farewells and returns from trips. Only once did mother tell me that he had written her the most wonderful letters during her time of engagement and that he remained to her the same throughout the years of marriage." That was two weeks before she died, Shevat in 1915. Perhaps a presentiment of her death, two weeks later, made her speak thus freely to her son. All of the children shared actively and passively that love and affectionate respect, and "though, in the ways of adolescents, we had our quarrels with each other, a word from Father or a sight of Mother's unhappy face at our wrangling would make us stop, miserable for the pain we had caused them."

The newly appointed Chief Rabbi of the London Federation of Synagogues found that there were great differences in the character and consequently in the needs of the various member congregations. In the North, West, and Northwest, the membership consisted mainly of the Englishborn, socially and financially established. Their needs were primarily improved religious schools and social and cultural programs for the young generation.

In the East End, with its large masses of Jewish workmen, small retail merchants, a large proportion of them recent immigrants, the needs were, in addition to those just mentioned, a very complete orientation program. Rabbi Jung conceived such a program to require:

A basic broadening in the training of the already established Yeshivoth, that would include college training. This led ultimately to an arrangement that required future rabbis and teachers to obtain a University degree.

Adult Education for the working men: This included the provision of facilities within the synagogues, and later workingmen's halls, where every type of educational (popular lectures and discussions) and social activity could be carried on in the completely independent manner especially suitable to the temper of the workers. One notable result was the organization of 30,000 workingmen for the purpose of securing the right of Sabbath observance.

In this connection there came to Rabbi Jung's consciousness a new and pressing problem. This is best expressed in his own words. We feel that it is important to reproduce his outline for a Jewish Trade School.

THE JEWISH TRADE SCHOOL   (London, 1912)

The future of Judaism rests on the education of the Jewish youth. The most impressionable age for moral and religious influences is from fourteen to eighteen.

At this age, many thousands of Jewish boys live in the workshops and in the streets. They forget their little knowledge of Judaism received in the schools; they do not sanctify the Sabbath, and in their bad atmosphere lose their morality.

What can we do to rescue these thousands of Jewish boys, and to educate them as true Jews: Establish Hebrew Evening Schools? Surely after a long day's work the minds of the boys are not susceptible to the influence of religious teaching. Should boys attend Government Technical Schools? This is out of the question, as the parents require the boys' wages, and the government pays no wages.

There is only one way open to solve this problem, and that is this: The establishment of JEWISH TRADE SCHOOLS, where the boys receive Hebrew instruction, practical knowledge of Trade, and also wages.

Will the boys, by learning other things, neglect the trade? Count up the days in three years in which they learn nothing in the workshops; it will be found that this time will be sufficient for Hebrew instruction.

Will the number of workmen be increased by these schools? Certainly not. We only wish to teach those boys who would otherwise go to the ordinary workshops. It therefore is certain that advantages only can result from these schools.

These were my original convictions, which led me to the establishment of the Trade School, which is making satisfactory progress, and has already justified its existence.

1. The school provides, at present, for tailors' apprentices only. The Staff consists of 2 master-tailors and 1 Hebrew teacher. The number of boys on the books is 33.

2. The hours of instruction are as follows: From 9 a.m. to 1 p.m., and from 4 to 7 p. m. instruction in the trade is given, while two hours, from 2 to 4 p.m., are utilized for Hebrew and religious instruction.

3. Daily services are held at the school, and a special address is given on the Sabbath, so that at the most impressionable age, from 14 to 18, the boys are brought under the best moral and religious influence, and are assiduously kept away from bad surroundings.

4. Moreover, greater facilities are afforded in this school for acquiring a good practical knowledge of the trade than apprentices receive in the ordinary workshop, because here they are taught all the time, from the very beginning of their apprenticeship.

5. In the first six months the boys receive a small wage, but after that period they are paid at the same rate as in the ordinary workshops.

Our scheme is so planned as to be at once economical, religious and moral. It affords the Jewish youth a good start in life, possessing not only a thorough knowledge of his trade, but also a good knowledge of Hebrew, a deep sense of loyalty to the Jewish religion and community, and an ambition to be an honourable and worthy citizen.

But, in order to carry on this work efficiently and more practically, financial support must be forthcoming, and I am fully convinced that you will not stand aloof, but give your warm support towards the advancement of our worthy object.

In this important scheme you ought, as a loyal Jew, to assist us. By rendering us help you will be promoting the highest interests of Judaism.

M. Jung

Excerpts from First Annual Report

The Jewish Trade School was opened in December, 1912 with 20 boys and 2 tailoring teachers. This number has since increased to 30 boys and 3 technical instructors. In the first eight months the boys were learning the trade, and could earn nothing, though they were given pocket-money after the first month. The busy time approached, and the school became self-supporting, thanks to the excellent progress the boys had made. They now earn 7/6 per week, the hours of technical instruction being from 9 a.m. until 11:30 a.m. and from 2 p.m. until 7 p.m., an hour and a half during the midday interval being devoted to religious training (in English) by Mr. I. Kyansky—Head Master of the Great Garden Street Talmud Torah. We maintain that in all respects the school compares very favourably with ordinary workshops.

It was originally estimated that £1,000 would be required to cover the cost of starting the School and the first year's maintenance. We have succeeded in raising only the sum of about £750. The school has so far more than justified all expectations, and has become self-supporting; we earnestly hope the community will assist us to continue the worthy task we have taken in hand, by helping to defray the deficit in the funds so that the seed we have sown may not be in vain.

The first world war broke the continuity of this outstanding enterprise, but the pattern is there.

The Sinai League

In the interest of youth all over England, Rabbi Jung organized the Sinai League. "Sinai," he stated, "is synonymous with Jewish tradition. A Sinaist is a Jewish man or woman who knows this tradition and resolves to live up to it. The Sinai League aims at promoting Judaism among Jewish youth in the most encouraging and enjoyable manner, leading them to its sources in literature and history; to induce and to foster the feeling of brotherly love among its members through social gatherings."

The Sinai League achieved thirty-two branches in England. It issued a quarterly review, known as *The Sinaist,* the contributors to which, besides Meir Tsevi Jung, included Sails Daiches, Moses Gaster, Prof. Waldemar Haffkine, Rabbi Isaac Herzog, Rabbi A. I. Kook, Professor Norman Bentwich, Nina Salaman and Helena Frank. From the very inception of *The Sinaist's* publication, Rabbi Meir Tsevi Jung's sons, Leo and Moses, cooperated in the work.

With the assistance of Rabbi Abraham Isaac Kook of Palestine, then the rabbi of one of his constituent synagogues, Rabbi Jung established a *Vaad ha-Rabbanim* for all of England. Later, he organized the *Tomkhei Torah Society,* for the benefit of aged Jewish scholars in need. After that, he established what he termed "Sabbath Observance Halls", whose purpose it was to offer opportunity for *Oneg Shabbat,* discussions and lectures, and thus to foster the honor and observance of the holy day "in the most encouraging and enjoyable manner."

In the last years of his life, Rabbi Jung devoted himself to the interests of the *Agudath Israel.* A consistent, self-sacrificing worker for Erets Yisrael, he considered Agudah's insistence on the centrality of the Torah in Erets Yisrael, no less than in the Galuth, a vital necessity. As president of the *Agudath Israel,* he succeeded in bringing it to the front ranks of Jewish endeavor in England, and as lover of our homeland he helped to bring about the Balfour Declaration.

Rabbi Jung left several Hebrew manuscripts of works on *Halakhah* and *Aggadah,* besides a commentary in English on the *Siddur* and scores of essays on the Jewish religion.

His last years were to bring to successful fruition plans for the reorganization of the ritual and educational affairs of London Jewry.

The Jung family cherishes the following account, related by his father, Rabbi Abraham Jung, and quoted in his own words:

"I had unlimited trust in the character of Meir Tsevi and his uncompromising loyalty. Yet, when he had left the environment of Hungarian orthodoxy for the totally different climate of the University of Marburg, I could not control occasional misgivings. I began to wonder what temptations he might meet, alone in the non-Jewish college, and no matter how often I would upbraid myself for such unworthy lack of faith in this son I was so proud of, gnawing doubt haunted me. One day I decided to pay him a surprise visit.

"It took more than two days to travel from Eszlar to Marburg, where I left the train, overtired at three o'clock in the morning. The summer dawn had just come when I arrived in front of his house. I prepared to sit down on the stairs and await the hour when I could enter, when I heard the door open. A man came down, looking askance at me. But when I said 'I am the father of cand. phil. Maurice Jung,' he smiled and said: 'His room is on the top floor, to the left.' I climbed the stairs painfully and carefully so as not to make unnecessary noise.

"At last I reached the top. The door had a visiting card with Meir's name on it, and there was light in the room. The door proved unlocked, and as I opened it, I saw my Meir seated at the table, absorbed in the study of the *Gemara*, chanting the ancient *niggun*, though in a very low voice. He heard some sounds, and without looking up, (assuming the interruption to have come from the servant), said: 'Please just put the shoes into the corner!'

"I stood there, rooted to the spot, a psalm in my heart, unable to speak, until he looked up and rushed into my arms.

"That was the proudest, happiest moment of my life."

ELIYAHU KLATZKIN

By Jacob Klatzkin

ELIYAHU KLATZKIN

By Jacob Klatzkin

I

MY FATHER—Rabbi Eliyahu Klatzkin

In my father's personality were fused practical gifts of the highest order and an ever-flowing spring of creative power. He was endowed with a remarkable memory, truly "a cistern that never loses a drop," with the faculties of immediate, lucid comprehension and profound and acute logic. Such a combination of genius and erudition is vouchsafed only to a select few, for those who are blessed with such prodigious memories usually collect such quantities of factual data, that their cognitions are necessarily superficial in quality. (The task of collecting facts preoccupies them so that they have no time for creative use of their findings.)

He occupied himself industriously throughout his life not only with the Talmud, but also with secular studies, especially with the natural sciences, history, geography and mathematics (with emphasis on calculus, both differential and integral). Indeed, he discovered some important new formulae in this field. From his youth he was a zealous student of medicine, and he finally acquired such a broad understanding of the subject, at least in its theoretical aspects, that he was on occasion called in consultation together with professional physicians to discuss some critical case. For decades, he participated in the famous periodical "Medizinische Wochenschrift," and he expended relatively large sums out of his limited means for medical books in many languages. He never failed to buy the newest works immediately upon publication or to borrow them from some neighbor physician, for he wished to investigate every discovery in the diagnosis or cure of disease. For example, when he heard of the insulin cure, he did not rest until he had obtained the books of Nordman and all of the other basic works on diabetes.

He could recite by heart the chemical composition of every drug listed in the pharmacopoeia. I remember that one of the leading doctors of Lublin once asked me to suggest to my father that he refrain from public discussion of medical matters with him in order to spare him the exposure of his shortcomings: "Your father assumes very naively that we all have a complete understanding of the science of medicine. Therefore, he discusses details such as the preparation of various drugs, with which I am less familiar than he is. As a result, I must listen in silence as a student before his teacher, and my reputation is damaged before the public."

In his research into Shehitah, embodied in his book *Imrei Shefer,* he made use of the findings of the scientists regarding nerves, arteries, evidences of the presence of life, reflexes and vivisection.

My father became conversant with Greek, Latin, German, French, English, Russian and Polish with hardly any expenditure of time or effort. (For some years he read the London "Times" regularly.)

One perusal of a pocket dictionary, usually during the hours before retiring, was enough to engrave on his memory all the definitions it contained. Next day, he would ask my mother to test him if he really knew the dictionary by heart. If, as it sometimes happened, he made a mistake, he would become depressed and groan softly, "Oh, what a poor memory I have!" He disregarded completely the practical value of the vocabulary, making no distinction between basic words and those of little practical importance. Rather, he felt obliged to master the dictionary in its entirety, from beginning to end. The same applied to scientific encyclopedias, which he memorized article by article with no regard for their practical utility. When we read Zola's Germinal together (my first studies in French and English were under my father's tutelage), he never had to resort to a dictionary although the work is replete with unusual words. His favorite masters of belles-lettres were Victor Hugo, De Maupassant and Tolstoi.

One of my relatives, Mr. P. of Lodz, told me that when my father was appointed Rabbi of Lublin, he journeyed there from Merimpol by way of Brisk, in order to spend a few days with his brother-in-law, Rabbi Jacob Zalman Libschitz, son of the Gaon, Rabbi Baruch Mordecai Libschitz of Shedlitz. Until that time he had never studied the Polish language, but now that his duties in Lublin were to include those of "official" rabbi too, it became necessary for him to master it. He therefore asked Mr. P. to buy him a Polish dictionary and grammar. After a few days, he was supplied with a copy of the "Kurier Warszawski." He began to read, but broke off and exclaimed to Mr. P. in surprise: "I believe that there is a grammatical mistake here in the leading article." Mr. P., whose Polish was fluent, took a glance and was amazed to discover that my father was right.

My father's wide knowledge of geography was incredible. I doubt if there was anyone better acquainted with the subject even among the specialists in the field. No point on the globe was unfamiliar to him. Even small, remote settlements, wildernesses, streams, brooks, swamps, hills and valleys, were an open book to him with their details of boundaries, climate, lines of communication and population. The maps in general use were inadequate for him and he used to carp at their slightest inaccuracy. He tried as far as he was able to obtain the scientific and especially military maps which were issued by cartographic societies. His maps covered every region and province, every city and town, and he would spread them on the floor, examining them until he was familiar with every road in every land, including all auto highways and the streets of every large city.

He was conversant with most of the railroads of the world, their stations and schedules, and could recite all the timetables in effect in Russia, Germany, France and England. Once when I was telling him some incident of a trip from Moscow to Odessa, he stopped me to ask at what time I had left the former city. When I told him the day (which was a Thursday) and the hour, he mused for a moment and then exclaimed, "Then you travelled the last quarter of an hour like a 'Porits'—because all the Jews must have deserted the train, leaving ample room for you to sit in comfort. For it arrived at Odessa on Friday about a quarter of an hour after sunset." In my embarrassment, I tried to refute him and convince him that he might easily have erred in such a small matter. But he called off all the stops between Moscow and Odessa, giving the exact time of each. Then he brought out the time table from the closet to verify his information, and I was forced to acknowledge that it was completely accurate. Nothing remained for me but a shamefaced confession and the lame excuse, "I made a mistake in the time of sunset."

The writer, S. Stupnitzki, relates that many Jews of Lublin about to emigrate to America used to burden their rabbi with questions about the sailings from Hamburg and Bremen and similar details. He always drew on his fund of information and gave them precise and accurate answers. It was his habit to follow through with a list of all the sailings of the past ten years—for good measure.

This abundance of superfluous information is characteristic of his thirst for knowledge. Utilitarian considerations were secondary. Facts such as these were as precious to him as any theoretical speculation and lost nothing of their value because they fulfilled no practical function. It was as though the reward for knowledge was knowledge, and that of research—research itself.

This passion for knowledge for its own sake led him to accumulate information in fields which had no relation to his own immediate interests. Thus, he was familiar with the streets of many cities which he never visited and had no intention of visiting. I recall that I once told him of a visit I had made at the home of one of our relatives in New York. He asked me what means of transportation I had used to get there from my lodging. When I gave him the details, he smiled and said, "You took a roundabout way. You should have taken the B. M. T. to station X and transferred to the I. R. T. as far as station Y." And he went to the trouble of going through his stack of maps to find the chart of the New York subways and convince me of my mistake.

His memory seemed to be a sort of living camera which reproduced with precision everything that came its way without any selection of the worthwhile or rejection of the unimportant.

Such a memory functions without effort or exertion—almost automatically, and therefore does not take the trouble to distinguish between matters of major or minor significance.

It is less effort to absorb everything in one glance than to take the trouble to try to bring the important image into focus or to eliminate the superfluous.

This being his method, it is no cause for wonder that he knew by heart thousands of articles from various encyclopedias in many languages, or hundreds of maps, or lists of the formulae of drugs, just as he had at his fingertips thousands of pages of the two Talmuds and their classical and modern commentaries, not in a general manner, but literally word for word.

This also explains my father's chagrin at his occasional minor lapses of memory. Elsewhere I explained this thus:

"Imagine a camera endowed with consciousness and the ability to criticize its own workings. If it found, among its thousands of reproductions, one which was false to its subject and inexact in some contour, would it not feel futile and useless? It would, of necessity, be grieved and humbled, for its essential function is precision, and any lapse, however, slight, any excess or diminution, impairs its very essence. If the watertight cistern loses a drop—if the man of exceptional memory proves to be not quite infallible, it is enough to alarm him and cause him anxiety about a decline in the very faculty which others admire in him. To generalize, the nearer a gift approaches perfection, the more the possessor's self-esteem will be shaken at the mere suggestion of a blemish, and his very superiority compels him to be modest."

Indeed, my father's humility sprang from his underestimation of his own worth and his lack of confidence in his talents and learning. He did not humble himself deliberately as a religious or ethical discipline. Rather he found himself unworthy because of the rigorous yardstick by which he measured himself. Consequently he used to deliver involved discourses in Torah before quite commonplace people, or to carry on scientific conversations with undergraduates or neophyte physicians, because he was simply unable to imagine that they could not understand a discussion on such a lofty plane.

Sometimes my mother tried to make him realize how ludicrous these situations were and to prevent him from imposing his wisdom on those who could not assimilate it, "lest their ears be strained." He would reply with great naïveté, "Is it possible that these people do not understand a discussion of Rabbi Akiba Eger, or of the authors of the *Shaagath Aryeh* or the *K'tzoth?* And if they can do so, they must surely understand what I have to say."

Or, "Is it possible that university students, and even more certainly doctors, should not be familiar with the subject matter of higher mathematics, or the natural sciences, or medicine?" It was just as hard for him to understand that the world is full of people of limited background in sacred and secular scholarship, as it was for him to grasp the fact that men could be sinners or unbelievers.

Likewise, he never conceded that secular learning tends to undermine religious faith or to weaken piety. "On the contrary," he used to say, "the more we devote ourselves to mathematics and the natural sciences, the more aware we must become of the wonders of the Holy One's world, saying with the Psalmist, *"How manifold are thy works, O Lord."* For this reason he strongly opposed my ardent desire to study in one of the Yeshivoth. "They do not teach the sciences, and you will return a complete ignoramus in worldly scholarship. I did not study in a Yeshivah but in my father's house!"

He was certainly an exceptionally progressive member of the rabbinate of his generation, a modern incarnation of the type of leader typified by Maimonides.

Although his prodigious memory and his familiarity with the "sea of the Talmud" and the various sciences were his most spectacular qualities, the acuteness and profundity of his intellect were the real source of his greatness. He grasped any subject quickly, penetrating to its very core. Although he did not discard the husks of knowledge, especially since they were gathered and stored up without effort, his sharp intellect pierced them through with one thrust and laid bare the kernel. He was thus spared the fate of those who are hampered in the free exercise of their powers of reason by the sheer weight of their book-learning. He was delivered from the danger of mere encyclopedism because his keen intelligence always had his accumulated knowledge well in hand, forcing it to bow to, and be absorbed by, his genius.

Although he was never failing in original thought on Talmudic problems and had some creative comment to offer on practically every saying of the Sages, he never permitted himself any innovation in general approach. Instead, he followed the paths trod by the great classical commentators and some of the later authorities, striking a firm balance between practical and theoretical investigation. His style has some resemblance to that of Rabbi Akiba Eger, blending erudition and logic in an appealing manner.

By nature and training my father was an intellectual, but he was not completely divorced from the world of fantasy and poetry. He was keenly interested not only in literature but also in architecture. When he passed through Vienna on his way to Palestine, he visited the showplaces of that capital and nearby Schoenbrunn. But most of all he took delight in music in general and Jewish melodies in particular. When the outstanding Hazanim came to his city, they were always invited to call and they sang for him by the hour.

II

My father's extreme humility arose from his great naiveté regarding the worth of his own personality. Indeed, this naiveté reached the point where it became a detriment to his practical efficiency. Thus he was alert and interested in everything that was going on in social, economic and political life and appreciated the newest technical inventions, including even those which were designed for purely practical purposes, as automobiles, airplanes, phonographs, dictaphones, motion pictures, and the first glimpses of television. When he became aware of the invention of motion pictures, he urged me to obtain for him the necessary equipment, including projector and screen, so that he could carry out experiments in his own workroom. But he was also an impractical dreamer in relation to the daily events around him, withdrawn as he was into his studies and preoccupied with the life of the spirit. He did not mingle readily with others and lacked any flair for psychological insight. There was a big barrier between him and those who came to his door to discuss Torah, worldly learning or communal problems. My mother struggled for years to train him to observe the simple social amenities—to be courteous to the officials of the community and to ask them to be seated as soon as they entered. Even so, since he did not welcome such visitors nor their discussions which interfered with his studies, he would usually blurt out a gruff "Please be seated," without looking up from the books on his table and without noticing if there were enough chairs for the guests. The officials, hesitant to call their rabbi's attention to the fact, would remain standing until finally he would look up, order the shamash (beadle) to bring chairs, and begin the conversation. Actually, however, he was not fully aware of their presence even when listening to them or answering them. For that matter, he paid little attention to the members of his own family. Only on rare occasions would he go to the Rebbetzin's quarters and discuss the welfare of their children. Occasionally he would tell a humorous story to those seated around the table. He had much of the awkwardness of the man who has retreated from society and lacks psychological acuteness.

He believed everyone. It was easy to deceive him. He was wise but not clever. In this he was completely different from his contemporary, Rabbi Hayyim Soloveitchik, who was very astute, psychologically speaking, while naive in moral issues.

Although a delicate person, who had suffered since his youth from various ailments, especially stomach trouble and chronic headaches, he was untiring in his work, both in studying and writing. In his younger days my father permitted himself little sleep, and studied twenty hours a day. In his mature years he devoted eighteen hours, and in his old age fifteen hours, to learning. He would usually fall asleep at about three o'clock, seated in his chair, his head resting on an open book. At six he would be awake, and if he happened to sleep a little longer, he would scold my mother for not awakening him, saying, "You seem to want me to be a clod and an *Am ha-Arets.*"

At fourteen he was familiar with the entire Talmud, but because of the high standards he set for himself, he felt as though he had merely "sipped a drop of the great sea." He always directed his thoughts to the distance he had yet to travel to attain full mastery of Torah and science, rather than to what he had already accomplished.

He was careful never to waste even a few moments of his day. For this reason, he distinctly stipulated in drawing up the contract for his last rabbinate, that of Lublin, that he was obliged to render decisions only in weighty matters, and that all minor questions were to be referred to the Dayanim of the city.

Sometimes he would explain: "If everyday questions of Kashruth or family purity come before the Dayanim, they will not labor over them but will decide without delay or misgiving, either trusting to their memories or taking a quick glance at the Shulhan Arukh. But if the same questions are laid before me, I feel obliged to examine thoroughly all classical and later authorities who have devoted themselves to these or similar points and to consider all the minutiae derived from the general decisions until I have reached the crux of the problem of Halakhah. Actually such questions are not worth the time or the mental effort, in comparison with problems of Agunoth (deserted wives) and the like. So you see that the Dayanim, who can decide quickly along accepted and familiar lines, are more useful than I am."

III

As might be expected, he disliked all official posts and avoided all communal activities with which most rabbis are charged. He refused to join the lay leaders in administrative matters, and even left to them the management of religious activities so that he might have more time for his studies. From time to time my mother would permit herself to reprove him for this policy, reminding him of the teaching of the Sages, that no rabbi may neglect his duty of attending to the welfare of his community, but he would pay little attention to her words.

Because he was so anxious that nothing should distract him from his inner world of Torah and wisdom, he was careful not to be involved in any controversies or disputes. He would even ignore many injustices to himself, such as the community's failure to pay his salary in full. He paid even less regard to the collection of other fees due him. For the same reason, he took no action when the leaders of certain factions invoked his authority improperly or distorted his words for partisan ends.

He once told me confidentially that some zealots of Jerusalem had stolen his seal and affixed it to proclamations without consulting him. I asked him why he had not refuted them in the religious press, and he answered me, "I am afraid that if I protest against the forgery I shall arouse the anger of these troublemakers and shall be forced into controversial speeches and statements. In any case they will surely be bold enough to besmirch the motive behind my denial, and I shall be forced to issue a protest. As a result my time will be wasted in controversy and I shall be unable to spend it in studying the Torah."

IV

He had disliked the office of the rabbinate from his youth, trying to escape from it in many devious ways. When he was visited by guests from foreign countries, among them the writers Salomon Goldman and his son, Dr. Nahum Goldman, Dr. Samuel Weinberg (who then resided at Frankfurt-am-Main),* Dr. Moses Gliskin and others, he would plead with them to try, each in his own city, to find him a part-time position in the business of some pious Jew, whether as translator of commercial correspondence into French, English, Russian or Polish, or as bookkeeper, for which he thought he could fall back upon his mathematical training.

At last, when he had reached the age of seventy, he realized a hope which had lain dormant within him all his life. He suddenly abandoned his rabbinate in Lublin, leaving the city secretly, without farewells to any of the members of the community. Only his shamash (beadle) saw him off, accompanying him as far as Vienna, and he was commanded to keep the matter a secret. Thus he fled to Erets Yisrael, in spite of the fact that the rabbis of Jerusalem, among them his old friends Rabbi Kook and Rabbi Yeruham Diskin, had advised him verbally and by letter that it was almost inconceivable that he would make even a modest living there.

Two strong desires joined in causing this flight, the desire to be freed from the burden of the rabbinate and the call to the ancestral homeland.

He disregarded the warnings of his family, and concerned himself only with the expenses of the journey (which he gathered painfully, bit by bit, for two years) and not with the problems of the

---

*Parenthetically, Dr. Weinberg brought him as a gift the famous book, "Compendium der inneren Medizin." This my father returned to him immediately with a gentle smile, saying, "I am indeed very grateful, but this edition appeared two years ago, and in the field of medicine things become obsolete so quickly that I have already purchased a copy of the latest edition."

days to come. He forsook his position of honor in Lublin without hesitation or misgivings, with no thought for the income he left behind or the lack of prospects where he was going. In complete poverty, he left the city which had shown him such an unusual measure of love and respect, and, with full foreknowledge of what it implied, accepted the status of a poor, aged and unemployed person in Jerusalem.

He utterly despised bribery. In fact, he always lived in horror of money, and would tremble when he touched it, as though the slightest contact with it were capable of defiling the soul. He would refuse to accept any fees other than his fixed salary. This led to many disputes with my mother, who saw no reason to forego this income, which would have contributed more to the household budget than his meager stipend.

The rabbis of Lublin who preceded him, even the famous author of "Torath Hessed" and Rabbi Hillel Lipschitz, used to receive fixed sums from the shohatim as part of their regular income. But as soon as my father was appointed he abolished this practice and refused to accept any money from the shohatim, in order to avoid the slightest suggestion of corruption.

Although the fees collected from litigants constituted an important part of the rabbi's income, he tried his utmost to avoid all such cases, leaving them and their compensation to the Dayanim, whether the trials took place on their premises or his own. He used to give two reasons for this: first, the interruption that the conduct of such cases would cause in his studies. "And besides," he would say, "although I am well able to achieve equity and reconciliation for the theoretical Reuben and Simeon of the *Hoshen Mishpat* (for that is my main occupation), when it comes to doing the same thing for a real Reuben and Simeon in court, I have no talent at all."

He paid no special respect to the wealthy and influential members of the community, and never accepted the invitations to their weddings and other celebrations, yet he occasionally visited the poor Talmidei Hakhamim in order to lend them prestige by the attention he showed them.

When he had settled in Jerusalem, his tiny room became a crowded center for people of all classes and parties. Rich and poor

came, old-guard Zionists and some zealots taking a stand beyond
that of even Agudath Israel, pious rabbis (especially Rabbis Son-
nenfeld and Meltzer) and adherents of the wordly Haskalah
movement. There were authors and scholars, but there were also
many vagrants and miscellaneous hangers-on. Once I asked my
father why he permitted any and everyone to come to his house
without discriminating between the deserving and the worthless.
He answered me, "You must admit that it is logical to assume that
all who come here are decent people. Ask yourself—for what
purpose would anyone come to me? Certainly not for any material
benefit, for everyone knows that I am penniless and cannot give
them any help. Shall we say they come to be honored by me?
Everyone knows that I am far from flattery, that I am opposed to
the use of the honorary titles which have become a conventional
courtesy and that I am even sparing in words of praise when
phrasing endorsements of the works of our great leaders. Therefore you will be forced to admit that my visitors must come to
hear my words of Torah and that it is self-evident that they must
be men of some spiritual worth or at least of good intentions."

Parenthetically, my father once told me that, in his younger
days in Dublin (near Riga), he was once visited by two young men.
One of these was Rabbi Yeruham Diskin, who at that time was
active in trade and who came dressed in conventional European
clothing with his *Peoth* tucked behind his ears. He was very proud
of his secular culture and especially of his fluent French. With
him came Rabbi Abraham Kook, wearing, in striking contrast, a
threadbare "Kapote" and a broad girdle, with his *Peoth* hanging
down almost to his chin. Rabbi Yeruham teased his companion,
saying, "What will become of this Batlan? When will he become a
man of the world?"

"Fifty years later," my father continued with a slight smile,
"I journeyed to Palestine and found things quite reversed. Rabbi
Yeruham, the modernist, had become an extreme pietist, and
Rabbi Kook, the Batlan, was classed among the progressives."

Let me mention here that at my father's funeral, Rabbi Kook
was driven away from the bier by a gang of young extremists,
just as was reported by the Jerusalem newspapers.

Another note: The story that my father tried to get to Berlin
to study at the Hildesheimer Seminary, and was turned back

at the border by messengers sent by my grandfather, is apparently quite fictitious.

V

Throughout his life he never felt any thirst for glory. He was oblivious to the many manifestations of esteem and respect which came to him from near and far. He was actually as simple as a child in this respect. Because he had no objective conception of his own outstanding ability and did not consider himself in any way out of the ordinary in intellect or character, he moved among his fellow-men as though he were on their plane. He was gracious to those of inferior mentality as though they were his equals in Torah and wisdom. He was upset by any signs of subservience shown toward him and could not listen to any expressions of reverence addressed to him. In fact, he would reprove those who used them and turn away from them with displeasure. He disliked any sort of testimonial celebrations and in general any kind of pomp. Many of his enthusiastic followers in Lublin strove to set up a rabbinical court for him with a hierarchy of officials to determine who deserved an audience with their rabbi and who was unworthy of this privilege. They were never successful, because he refused to be shut off by a wall of servitors, preferring to sit alone in the tent of the Torah.

He also became very provoked when asked to pray for the sick, and would cry out in anger, "Do I stand in God's stead? Let them rather give alms to the poor!" (Actually, he would mention the names of the sick in the traditional portion of the Sh'moneh Esreh, but he did not wish this to be known, lest people come to think of him as a "Tsaddik" whose prayers are especially efficacious in Heaven). Sometimes he would answer the suppliants, "I am unworthy to pray for you. Go to Reb . . . . the cobbler—he is more God-fearing than I." At other times, he would sigh quietly to himself, "Who am I and by what virtue can I help them? Only by a sincere outcry from the depths of my heart—and this outcry I need for my own salvation! Alas, the Lord has not granted me anything I can share with others—not even groans of sorrow."

Though he lived all his life in poverty, he was never really aware of it. His wants were few and he was content that his lot

was among those dedicated to the Torah. Only when he had
created a great output of comments on the Talmud and did not
have the means to publish them did he feel distressed, especially
since he feared that his manuscripts might become lost in the
course of time. He had had the experience of losing two thousand
pages of manuscript in his youth—as he relates in his book "Even
ha-Roshah." He had taken them along to Warsaw in a tin casket,
over which he watched with such care that it attracted the attention
of some thieves on the train. Certain that it contained gold or
jewels, they waited for an opportune moment and seized it when my
father put it down to pay the coachman his fare. Through advertisements in the newspapers and announcements in the synagogues, sections of the manuscript were recovered in the shops of various
tradesmen who had bought them as wrapping papers for their wares.
For years my father mourned this loss and could not be consoled.
Once or twice he remarked, "I shall never again be able to write
anything as profound."

Among the manuscripts were also articles on mathematical and
medical research, and philosophical articles, including some on the
system of Kant. "And again lately I was robbed of about a
thousand sheets containing comments on the entire Talmud and the
later authorities, representing years of toil by day and by night.
When I think of this my soul is downcast. May the Almighty
restore them to me!" (Introduction to his book "Even ha-Roshah".)

Although he had no striking literary talent (and was indeed
surpassed in this by my mother, whose Hebrew was distinguished
by a rich vocabulary and a light, fluent style), my father had a great
urge to write and continued to do so diligently to the end of his
days. Similarly, although he was not a gifted speaker or preacher,
he would frequently deliver sermons on Halakhic or Haggadic
subjects. It was as though he had an inner compulsion to unburden
himself of his spiritual creations for his own well-being, to express
them in writing or speech in order to clarify them for himself.
Therefore he was even more anxious to speak than his audience was
to listen. As a result, he never stopped to consider the level of his
public, and would pour forth the fullness of his erudition and intellect without concern for the capacity of his barely literate
listeners to absorb his message. He had no ability to communicate

a thought lucidly either in writing or lecturing, and perhaps he had no desire to do so. When expounding Torah, he was content with fragmentary hints, with incomplete, disorganized and unclarified statements, as though he were talking to himself and repeating his discoveries in the form of condensed formulae as an aid to memory. Possibly these shortcomings were due to his psychological limitations, to the very nature of his personality, which retreated into its own inner world, oblivious to the other beings surrounding it. This is, of course, a phenomenon often to be found in men of genius.

VI

Although my father had a kind, noble and forgiving nature and never spoke of anyone with malice or mockery, he was occasionally carried away by a fit of anger and would use harsh expressions which were not at all typical of him. Afterwards he would regret his outbursts and apologize for them. He would not vent his anger at the moment of provocation. It would rather come to the surface slowly, and he would then direct it at people against whom he had no grievance, but who merely happened to be at hand. As an example, if someone would come to him with an unsavory proposal, such as the endorsement of his products in return for a large fee which suggested a bribe, he would blurt out a gruff refusal and return to his work. Then, hours later, some substantial merchants would come in and ask him to decide or arbitrate a dispute that had arisen between them, only to be greeted by an outburst of temper which, really caused by the earlier unethical proposal, now descended on the wrong victim.

For his last forty years he was very melancholy and would at times become upset even over trifles.

He was easily moved to tears by the sufferings of any Jewish community and the mishaps which visited anyone, near or far. When he preached about the desecration of the Sabbath or dishonesty in business practices, he would be so choked by sobs that his voice became inaudible to the members of the audience, who would themselves be deeply stirred by his grief.

Throughout most of his days he was enveloped in a mood of deep sadness, and had he not found happiness in the study of Torah and science, he would never have known any gladness in his life.

I have often wondered whether this melancholy was connected with the suffering caused by the many ailments which attacked his naturally frail and emaciated body and turned it into a skeleton. Certain it is that his sadness arose from his extreme humility, which became so ingrained in him that it developed into a spirit of abject self-abasement. I have mentioned already that this stemmed from the exacting standards he set for himself in Torah and other learning.

Obviously, a man of such a temperament is not cut out to be a militant leader even in matters of faith. Nor does he fit into any movement or group, for even if he inclines to its viewpoint, his scientific objectivity will interfere with his complete loyalty. For this reason he detested all theoretical or practical extremism and abhorred any exaggeration or inflation of the truth. Conversely, he loved accuracy and precision.

Above all, he was alienated by religious extremism. He had the utmost patience with those with whose views he was completely at variance. Many of those who frequented his house were non-observant or were ignorant of the fundamentals of Judaism, but he respected them because of their fine character or intellectual attainments. Sometimes he would be more gracious to them and devote more time to them than he did to rabbis who were not up to the highest standards in Torah and social responsibility. He regarded all who shared in any kind of spiritual quest as members of one family, an exalted fellowship destined to suffer here and to be repaid in the next world.

Once he said to me in a jesting spirit, "It is true that there are great barriers between us, between your world and mine. And still we share the same fate. I write books for which humanity has no use; you, too, write books which society ignores. Just as my works lie in a corner untouched, so yours are overlooked by those who might buy them. By ordinary standards we are both misfits and both need Divine compassion. Therefore, since we are fellow-sufferers, Heaven forbid that we should quarrel. Rather let us live in peace as befits two unwordly creatures."

VII

In spite of his usual moderation, he had one characteristic which drove him to an extreme of zealousness: his very objectivity and love of truth. He was completely sincere. This was the central feature of his whole personality, the wellspring of all his other qualities, an uncompromising, self-sacrificing love of truth, a complete objectivity in relation to himself and his family, stronger than his kindness of heart and his compassion, and carried to amazing extremes. He refused to give me an adequate recommendation when he wrote to one of the rabbis of Frankfort to assist me, omitting all the honorary titles which had been given me by many distinguished authorities. It made no difference to him that this might hurt my cause. More than this, when a match was proposed for my sister, and the groom's father stated that he would rely "only on the holy words of the Gaon of Lublin", he rejected my mother's entreaty that he say something in their daughter's behalf, answering, "Better that they do not ask me anything, for I might spoil the match, since our daughter is not really worthy of such a noble young man".

In external appearance he was thin and tall. His features were delicate; his eyes expressed simplicity and sweetness. Deep springs of goodness and benevolence gleamed within them. His whole presence was a manifestation of grace and nobility. These traits were revealed in his mannerisms as well, in his measured gestures, in his response to burdensome demands which he would try to fulfill inconspicuously without the knowledge of those he was serving. There was nobility in his manner of speech and of keeping silence, in his carriage, in his modesty. He was very meticulous about cleanliness and the tidiness of his rooms and their equipment. He would not stand on his dignity, but would bend down to pick up matches or scraps of paper tossed on the floor by visitors, rather than wait for his attendant to do this chore. It was difficult for him to spend even a few moments in a dirty, untidy room. In the cleanliness of his person and his clothing he was even more precise; likewise in the care of his books. His Talmud and Shulhan Arukh were as good as new after more than sixty years of use, unstained and uncreased as though they had not been touched.

In contrast to most of the rabbis of his generation, his discussions of Torah, even those involving controversial dialectics, were carried on in quiet and relaxation, gently and affably, without accompanying them by swaying the body, squinting or wrinkling the forehead, waving the hands or emphatic gestures of the thumb. His every movement was dignified, and therefore he was displeased with the outlandish mannerisms affected by the students of the Yeshivoth. In general, he stood for delicacy even in externals and was sensitive even in trifling matters.

"There is a very pernicious tendency which has become prevalent in most humans. It is difficult to explain it away as a type of moral insanity. It seems rather to be an unhealthy attitude which has been implanted in them by bad training and habit. They have a mis-guided and distorted feeling that their own national self-conscious-ness implies a disdain and dislike for every alien race or nationality. If, for example, the blood of the Teutons flows in a man's veins, he feels compelled to despise those of Gallic or Norman stock, although they are racially related. When authors wish to characterize those of other races, they take as examples and symbols the most debased elements, sketch them in the darkest colors and ascribe to them the most despicable traits. Their readers are misled into thinking that these strangers are really sinners, criminals and degenerates, forget-ting that all these undesirable characteristics are the products of the writer's imagination. A taint of 'national' hatred is to be seen among our Jewish brethren, for those who dwell on the banks of the Vistula are unsympathetic to the Lithuanians, and even to those who are very similar to them in outlook and customs. It is evident that the spirit of national pride, while it is useful when under control, becomes the scourge of the human race if it reaches the level of chauvinism" (Even Pinnah, 22).

VIII

BIOGRAPHICAL NOTE

My father was born in Ushpol, in the province of Kovno, in the year 5612 (1852). He was the son of Rabbi Naphtali Hirz, who served in Schimburg, Courland, for 37 years. He remained in this small community, in spite of invitations to take over the rab-binates of Moscow, St. Petersburg, and other large centers, because he feared that too much of his time would be absorbed by communal duties.

He was the author of the book *Ayalah Sh'luhah,* and a disciple of Rabbi Moses Sofer in Talmudic learning and of Rabbi Menahem Mendel of Lubovitch in the study of the mystics. (He was a grandson of Rabbi Jacob Reischer, whose works were *Hoq Ya'akov* and *Shvuth Yaakov,* and was related to Rabbi Mordecai Meltzer-Klatzko, who was rabbi in Kalvaria in the province of Suvalk, and in Lida. He was also a relative of Rabbi Mordecai Gimpel Jaffe (of Rizino and later Petah-Tikvah). On his mother's side, my father was a descendant of Rabbi Naphtali of Birz (province of Kovno), who was among the outstanding disciples of the Gaon of Vilna, and of Rabbi Moses Margolius, author of the *P'nei Moshe.*)

He had six brothers, all unusually gifted and noble personalities.*

His brother, Rabbi Abraham, was among the most saintly characters of his generation. His greatness lay not in his intellectual, but in his spiritual qualities. He possessed boundless faith, an overflowing love of life, purity and holiness in thought and deed, and a passionate love for humanity. He lived in daily expectation of the coming of the Messiah, fulfilling literally the command— "though he delay, wait for his arrival". This hope set its stamp upon his whole way of life. For example, on the six workdays

---

*Rabbi Israel Isser Jacob, who became rabbi of Lewenhof, near Riga; Rabbi Schneor Zalman, who served in Rogatchov (province of Mohilev); Rabbi Abraham, who was rabbi of Rumonoba, where he was succeeded by his brother, Rabbi Moses, when he moved to Luzna; Rabbi David, who, although a great authority in Torah, did not wish to take upon himself the burden of a rabbinate, and emigrated to America, where he settled in New York and assumed the family name of Friedman; Rabbi Reuben, also a learned layman, who entered business in Neval.

Comments on the Talmud by the sons of Rabbi Naphtali Hirz and by the two gifted sons of Rabbi Isser appeared in a book called 'Amudei Shesh'. The latter were Rabbi Joshua Mordecai Klatzkin, rabbi in Britzi, Rasein and Libau, and Rabbi Hayyim David Klatzkin, who was an outstanding Talmudic scholar even in comparison with the great personalities of the time, and the possessor of the broadest general culture. My father used to say of him that he was of the stature of the great historical authorities and that it would be hard to find his equal in erudition and profundity. Yet at an early age he severed ties with the world of Talmudic scholarship and turned to commerce, in which he was very successful. When he moved to Kovno he entered politics in the spirit of the Bundists and was a regular contributor to the *Volkszeitung.*

However, much as he tried to forget his rabbinical background, he never really succeeded, and even in his old age, his wide knowledge and deep understanding of "the sea of the Talmud" continued to impress the greatest scholars.

he would sleep half-clad so that he might not be detained for one moment in welcoming the Messiah. Consequently, he never worried about his livelihood even when he was in great need, for anxiety about the morrow seemed to him a sign of lack of faith and an evidence of folly. Because he was always filled with this intense anticipation of the Redemption, he was moved to such an inspired joy that the misfortunes of life and his physical sufferings had no power to embitter his spirit or depress him in any way. If his wife complained, "Tomorrow is the last day that we can delay the payment of our rent and we have not a penny to our name", he would reprove her, "Woe to my ears that they should hear such blasphemous talk! Messiah will certainly come before then—just as we have been told—when he is least expected".

I once heard my father tell how he had seen Rabbi Abraham slap his son's face as he sat going over a passage in the Gemara. My father asked his brother in amazement, "Why do you strike him? Is he not studying diligently as he always does?"

"Certainly he is diligent", my uncle retorted, "But from his intonation, I can tell that it is done so without sincerity and only to display his knowledge".

It is told that my paternal grandmother burned our genealogical records because she feared that her seven sons would rely on the tradition that "The Torah returns to her lodging", i. e. to families who have a tradition of learning, and would not devote their time, day and night, to its pursuit.

When my father was twelve years old he had achieved a reputation as a prodigy who had mastered the whole Talmud, and when he was thirteen he was married to the daughter of Nahum Jacobson of Shklov, then a girl of twelve. His father-in-law had won a fortune in a lottery, and his great ambition, which he shared with many of the wealthy Jews of his time, was to use his possessions to win one of the most promising and widely-acknowledged young intellects as son-in-law. Because of his great arrogance, he kept a watchman at the door of his son-in-law's study and would not permit the townspeople of Shklov the satisfaction of seeing the young genius, unless they peeked through the keyhole. This fantastic attitude is vouched for by witnesses, among them the sister of Dr. Yehiel Tschlenov. Only the great figures of those times, including the rabbi of the city, Joshua Leib Diskin, were permitted to spend some hours with the wonder-child.

By this, his first wife, my father had one son and two daughters. The son and the older daughter were very gifted. He became an authority on agriculture, while she studied medicine and married a fellow physician, Dr. Tager.

After a short residence in Shklov the Jacobson family moved to Petersburg. It was there that my father began to devote himself to various scientific pursuits, especially to the natural sciences, going so far as to set up a miniature chemical laboratory in his home in order to further his studies. The great scholar Dr. Hayim Heller told me that Tsevi Hirsch Rabinowitz (the author of *Ha-M'nuhah V'ha-T'nu'ah*) used to say to his comrades in Petersburg that they could learn much about higher mathematics from "the young prodigy of Shklov".

Life in the Russian capital lured the Jacobson family away from our ancestral tradition and they were caught in the current of assimilation. Soon "the prodigy of Shklov" had no place among them, and within a few years my father and his lovely wife were divorced. He went his way, and she continued to spend her days and nights playing cards in the company of army officers, as was the mode in those days.

His way led him to Eishishok and there he studied in a Beth ha-Midrash frequented by scholars who had gone into retreat to devote all their time to Torah. After two years he married the daughter of the famous master of Talmud, Rabbi Baruch Mordecai Lipshitz, who was successively rabbi in Semiatitz, Volkovisk, Novorodok and Eidlitz and who issued two books, *Brith Ya'akov* and *Beth Mordecai*. (He traced his ancestry back to Maharam of Lublin; Rabbi Simhah Rappaport of Hurodno, Lublin and Lvov; Rabbi Tsevi Hirsch of Lukasch in Volhynia, author of *Hemdath Tsevi;* and Rabbi Mordecai Jaffe, creator of the *L'vushim*). His second wife, my mother, Liebe Yente, was blessed in an unusual measure with both wisdom and practicality. In her, too, piety and love of general culture were harmoniously blended. She was a zealous student of both foreign languages and religious literature, such as the Mishnah, the Midrashim, and works on ethics. Yet she could not approach her distinguished sister, Reizel, in Talmudic erudition, for the latter had progressed so far that she was sometimes invited to examine the lads in the highest class in the Talmud Torah of Brisk. My mother was rather a specialist in the Bible and its commentaries and in Hebrew grammar. Her Hebrew style had unusual vitality, which emanated straight from the original sources. It was spiced with quotations from the Sages and had its touch of pointed humor. The most accomplished stylists, among them Ben Avigdor, had nothing but praise for her. I remember my father rehearsing his sermons in her presence so that he might benefit by her advice. Sometimes she would offer criticism or even contribute some ideas of her own.

They had four children, two daughters and two sons, myself and my younger brother, Moses, who excelled both in Torah and in the study of medicine. He passed away at the age of twenty-three, leaving some Talmudic comments which my father published in the twenty-first section of his book, *Even Pinnah*.

My father's whole family were followers of the Habad movement in Hassidism. In his youth he spent much time over Kabbalistic works, but under the influence of his father-in-law, Rabbi Baruch Mordecai, who was a convinced Mithnaged and had directed the Beth ha-Midrash of the Gaon of Vilna, he left the Hassidic ranks, never to return.

In 5641 (1881) my father was appointed rabbi in Kartuz-Biriza, province of Grodno; in 1894, to the rabbinate of Mariampol, province of Suvalk; in 5670 (1910), to Lublin. In Elul of 5688 (1928) he journeyed to Erets Yisrael, where he died on the 16th day of Iyar, 5692 (1932).

His literary output included the following works: *Even ha-Roshah, Imrei Shefer, D'var Eliyahu, D'var Halakhah, Miluim, Miluei Even, D'varim Ahadim, Hibbath ha-Kodesh, Even Pinnah.** He also issued a collection of "Lectures and Papers" in Russian. Some of his Responsa were published in the compilations of other writers, e.g. in the encyclopedia of Responsa, *S'dei Hemed*.

---

*The appendix to this work contains his criticism of a pamphlet, *Pirhei Aviv*, which I wrote when I was thirteen or fourteen (Frankfurt am Main, 5662 (1902)). In this I had attempted to show my analytical and dialectic skill in refuting the comments of my father and my grandfather in his *B'rith Ya'akov*.

IX

In matters of ritual law he was one of the most lenient of the authorities of his generation. During the World War he permitted the use of rice and other grains not actually leaven on Passover, without heeding the outcries of the more rigid rabbis. Most of all he strove to make possible the re-marriage of *Agunoth* (women whose husbands had disappeared), and in his last decision on this subject (printed in *D'var Halakhah*) he proposed a legal formula which in most cases would annul retroactively the marriage of these unfortunate women. In this connection he would quote the words of the *BAH* in the preface to his Responsa: "He who frees one *Agunah* is considered as though he had rebuilt the ruins of Jerusalem."

He was reluctant to cause any material loss to those who asked for his rulings. Often this consideration was the pivotal point in his decision on an ambiguous point in the laws of *Tarfuth*. On the other hand, in the application of the law for himself he was very stringent, never eating meat from an animal which he himself had examined and declared Kosher.

In general he was guided by the principle that "It is better to permit than to forbid". In this connection he used to say: "To ban requires no great scholarship—in fact, any ignoramus can do it. But to have a right to declare things permitted, one must really be learned and keen-minded".

When he was only twenty-three the MALBIM declared him to be without equal in his generation. This recognition as an authority in theoretical scholarship was followed in due time by his being accepted as a definitive authority in the practical application of the codes. Problems were passed on to him from every corner of the globe, although he was not as punctilious in answering them as Rabbi Isaac Elhanan Spektor and others of their calibre.

SARA BAYLA AND HER TIMES
(1816-1905)

By Nima H. Adlerblum

SARA BAYLA AND HER TIMES

(1816-1905)

By Nima H. Adlerblum

I

Sara Bayla and Rabbi Jacob Mordecai Hirschensohn, her husband, came to Palestine around the middle of the nineteenth century. The upheaval of the world at large at the beginning of that century had slowly filtered into Jewish life, even within the walls of Jerusalem. While the world had begun to emancipate itself from the influence of Voltaire and other antagonists of religion, some of the Jewish youth had become their belated victims. Even Ernest Renan, the source of inspiration for Ben Yehuda and other radicals, did not go as far as did his Jewish disciples. He wrote to St. Beuve: "No, I did not want to detach from the trunk a soul which was not ripe." The method of the Jewish "emancipators", on the other hand, was that of eradication. As a result, in Jewish life progress became associated with irreligion by both the anti-religionists and those who fought against them. It was not progress as such that the rabbis of Jerusalem opposed, but innovations foreign to the situation. Progress has been inherent in Jewish life from its very inception. It grew out of its own roots and not through attempts at uprooting; out of inner enlightenment, and not from alien illumination. It reveals lack of historical insight to stigmatize the rabbis as obscurantist, narrow-minded and ignorant.

These "obscurantists", whether in the time of Maimonides or in other transitory periods, represent the force of self-preservation. Self-preservation is a repelling of attacks from the outside by recoiling upon oneself.

It was a way of life that the rabbis of Jerusalem wanted to preserve, just as we today are defending our American democracy against fascism and communism. Their aim was to preserve Jerusalem as an invulnerable fortress, even at the cost of some

NOTE: The notes to the text are numbered. The supplementary notes are arranged alphabetically. They consist of a glossary of the Hebrew words, of short biographies, and of some pertinent remarks by Sara Bayla.

desirable acquisitions. Jerusalem fortified would reinforce Jewish life abroad and enable it to withstand damaging inroads.

Jacob Mordecai and Sara Bayla joined the rabbis of Jerusalem in stemming these outward tides with Jewish dikes. That Sara Bayla was given full freedom to exert her influence is one more proof that the rabbis lacked no liberality within the fence of the Law. It is recorded that whenever she entered a place where the great Rabbi Samuel Salant was present, he would rise and say, "Double respect should be paid to the wife of our revered colleague, highly regarded in her own right."

Sara Bayla belonged to a prominent family in Pinsk who were direct descendants of the author of *Seder ha-Doroth* and closely related to the Gaon of Vilna and to Rabbi Isaac Elhanan Spector. Her father, Yehudah Leib, a Talmudic scholar and man of affairs, was known for his private generosity and as trustee of the philanthropies of the two wealthiest men of his town, Sha'ul and Moshe Isaac. Yehudah Leib ardently desired to find an outstanding scholar to become the husband of his daughter. His attention was directed to a boy of nine, orphaned of both parents, whose unusual understanding of the Talmud marked him as a future *illui* (prodigy). He took the child under his care and gave him the best rabbinic training available. He engaged Rabbi Jacob Meir Padua as his teacher, sent him for a number of years to the Yeshivah of Brisk, and upon his return gave him Sara Bayla in marriage. A year later the young wife urged her husband to go back to Brisk to continue his studies, while she remained at home. When Jacob Mordecai returned, he was acclaimed a most distinguished scholar, and offers of rabbinic posts came to him from large cities in Russia. He preferred to accept that of *Rosh Yeshivah* of Pinsk, especially because he did not want to uproot his wife, who was active in charities and in her father's affairs. The Yeshivah under his leadership attracted wide attention, and his fame spread rapidly afar.

That Palestine should be a place to live and not merely to die in, was an unfamiliar thought in those days. Jacob Mordecai was haunted by it through a peculiar dream. Moreover, Sara Bayla nurtured a silent hope that through the *zekhuth* (merit) of the Holy Land she might be blessed with children. Those who had been born to her had not remained alive. Jacob Mordecai began showing signs of distraction and sadness, the cause of which he would not reveal to his wife or his father-in-law, but finally he confided to his master, Reb Jacob Meir Padua, that night after night in his dream he saw his father studying with him the *Moreh Nevukhim* (Maimonides' philosophical classic) with commentaries. One night, after their study period, as he went to escort his father to the door, he suddenly heard a loud voice saying, *"Barukh kevod adonai mi-mekomo,"* (Blessed be the glory of the Lord from His abode)—and his father vanished. He interpreted the verse as meaning that the place of God's glory was *Erets Yisrael* and the *Mikdash* (sanctuary) in Jerusalem. There he must go to establish a Yeshivah. But he was reluctant to require such a sacrifice from Sara Bayla, not knowing that such was her secret wish too. She was an expectant mother and wanted to hasten the trip so that her child might be born in Palestine. However, they had to wind up their affairs, and their little Yitzhak had reached his second year when finally, in 1847, they managed to leave. The journey, with stopovers in Germany, Austria, Turkey and other countries, consumed one year.

Their meeting in Germany and Austria with Jacob Ettlinger, Samson Raphael Hirsch, and others, made them feel the tremor which Reform had brought into the Jewish world. Their mission began to take the more definite shape of creating a center of learning in the Holy Land which would wield spiritual authority over the whole of Israel, and render Reform insignificant. Rabbi Eliyahu Gutmacher, the Rothschilds of Frankfort, the elder Hildesheimer, the Berliner family, and other Jewish leaders offered to augment Sara Bayla's funds for the contemplated Yeshivah settlement. A fortunate audience with Chancellor Bismarck secured them German citizenship and the surname Hirschensohn. In Turkey they obtained from the Sultan a permit for the publication of a newspaper and the assurance of his protection. On the other hand, their meeting in Austria with Dr. Ludwig Frankl was disappointing. He offered substantial support on condition that they introduce the teaching of the German language into the Yeshivah. They rejected the offer and pleaded with him not to interfere with the natural development of the country, which they felt should be unaffected by the revolutions that illusory emancipations were causing in Jewish life elsewhere.

As to the seat of the Yeshivah, the dream determined their choice of Safed, situated close to the grave of Maimonides in Tiberias. Jerusalem already had some famous rabbis, while Safed, the birthplace of Karo's *Shulhan Arukh,* Luria's *Kabbalah,* and the classic Sabbath song *Lekhah Dodi,* remained unrevived.

The sailing boat, rocking up and down for several days at the shore of Jaffa, could not land there; it had to return to Acco, where the passengers finally disembarked. There Jacob Mordecai wanted to remain for a while to search for some of the Kabbalastic manuscripts for which Acco and close-by Tirje were renowned. He believed that probably even a part of the *Zohar* was produced by the school of Acco. In its golden age, the whole community of Tirje was wont to rise regularly at midnight to study the Kabbala. They would be awakened by the sound of a bell attached to a wheel which was moved by a waterclock. Jacob Mordecai would have loved to dig into its past, now somewhat obscured, but he accepted Sara Bayla's objection: Would it be fitting to make Acco their first stop, since its Yeshivah, under the direction of Shlomo Petit, had waged the bitterest war against Maimonides? They left for Tiberias, where they visited his grave. Like all pilgrims throughout the centuries, they asked forgiveness for those who had sinned against him. They recalled that while Maimonides' grandson was still alive, Rabbi Moshe ben Yehudah ha-Cohen of Safed and his *beth din* had gathered solemnly around the grave, and ordered, under threat of excommunication, that all offensive pamphlets against the Master be surrendered to the grandson, Rabbi David, then head of the Yeshivah in Egypt.

From Tiberias they proceeded along the trail to Safed, on small burros with Arab guides with whom they could communicate only by means of gestures and ejaculations. The latter, by their motions of despair, were probably endeavoring to tell them of the recent plight of Safed. About ten years before, thousands had perished in the disastrous earthquake of 1837, and the city was deserted. When, a few years later, some people returned, a plague wiped them out. The only signs of life were a few men here and there who, profiting from the Turkish homestead law, had come to claim the deserted ruins as their own. Sara Bayla refused to take possession of any land until, after prolonged search, she had located the Arab owner and paid him for it.

The building of the Yeshivah started under almost inconceivable conditions. They had no shelter, and only such food as could be gathered from scattered villages. To the Yeshivah Jacob Mordecai added a *parushic* (non-Hassidic) synagogue, the first and only one in Safed, still in existence. Sara Bayal's family were ardent *Mithnaggedim* (anti-Hassidim), while Jacob Mordecai came from prominent *hassidic* stock. (Hassidism: a mystical movement dating from the 18th century, with emphasis on piety). He had become a *parush* at the age of nine, before he met his wife's family. A *minyan* for his newly built synagogue could not be secured. Sara Bayla went from village to village to search for Jews, offering them free dwellings and whatever food could be obtained from the outside. She ground the wheat which the Arabs brought from afar, baked the bread in an outdoor oven, raised some chickens, kept some goats, planted a vegetable garden on hard mountain soil—all this so that the scholars might go on learning. Jacob Mordecai's fame and Sara Bayla's efforts helped Safed to grow at a rapid pace. The Yeshivah overflowed with scholars, some coming even from Jerusalem, and also with a number of hassidim who gradually came back to Safed. Whoever visited the place was Sara Bayla's guest. It is related that on one occasion there were thirty pilgrims who, detained in Acco on account of the weather, had decided rather to wait in Safed. There they were housed and fed by her for a considerable time. She gathered blankets from everywhere, and continually traveled on burros to Arab settlements to obtain food.

When their son Yitzhak reached the age of five, his education became a matter of much concern. His parents, with the help of the rabbis of Jerusalem, chose a most competent teacher from the Holy City, who stayed with them for a number of years until driven out of town by the hassidim. They had caught him teaching the *luah ha-pe'alim* (table of verbs). Jacob Mordecai told them that he himself had studied grammar, that many of our scholars wrote on the subject, and that it even alluded to some mysteries of the Kabbalah. He cited to them the will of Judah Ibn Tibbon which recommends, among other instructions, the reading of grammatical works on Sabbaths and festivals. The teacher was soon accused of a still more unpardonable sin, that of speaking against the Ba'al Shem Tov.

As soon as her second son, Hayyim, was born (1856), she brought him to the *Heder* in his crib so that the first sounds reaching his ears should be those of Hebrew learning. The *melamed* was paid the full tuition for allowing the cradle to stay there while he was teaching. She made one condition: The teacher must not hit the children in the sight of the baby, so that he should not develop pugnacious habits, and that the idea of hatred should not enter his heart. As soon as the child began to talk, the teacher taught him the *aleph-beth*. Sara Bayla advocated the method of reward instead of punishment. She made candy for all the children. When little Hayyim was about three years old, the hassidim found it a diversion to dress him in a *tallith,* place him on a chair, and ask him to recite. His favorite response seems to have been, *Torah tsivvah lanu Mosheh Morashah Kehillath Ya'aqov* (The Torah which Moses commanded us in the heritage of the congregation of Jacob). At the age of seven the little boy astounded Rabbi Meir Auerbach by reciting and expounding passages of the Talmud.

Sara Bayla herself had received from her father a fuller education than was usual for girls at that time. Like other women she perused the current books of religious instruction: *Menorath ha-Maor, Tse'enah u-Re'enah, Nahalath Tsevi, Nofeth Tsufim* and similar works. In addition, she was taught the Bible, and thus acquired a competent knowledge of Hebrew. Throughout her life, she never missed her daily reading of the Bible. Much of the *Pirkei Avoth* (Ethics of the Fathers) she knew by heart; she understood the *piyyutim* (liturgical poems), and was able to quote numerous passages from the *Hovoth ha-Levavoth* (Bahya's *Duties of the Heart*). She cherished the poems of Yehudah Halevi, and she may have studied even the *Kuzari* (Yehudah Halevi's philosophical work). When Talmudic discussion went on in her presence, she became deeply absorbed, and would startle the scholars by pertinent questions. Between meals and at night time, when her chores were done, Sara Bayla would sit on the stoop of the Yeshivah and listen attentively. However, the report current among the hassidim of Safed that she knew the Talmud "like a man" is no doubt an exaggeration.

This happy life was suddenly perturbed. A stone was thrown into the peaceful waters of Jerusalem, and the ripples spread as far as the isolated town of Safed. On the surface, this commotion would appear to be a pathetic trembling over an innocent plan. Dr. Ludwig Frankl had come to Jerusalem in 1856 to establish a German school. But in those days the founding of a German school in a place which had been guarded for so many centuries, was like the first breach in a spiritual citadel. For it was just then that the Czar of Russia planned Russian schools to russify the Jews; and the *maskilim* (the secularists) were aping foreign culture and disdaining their own. Disciples of Moses Mendelssohn neglected the other half of his maxim,[1] that of being Jews in their own homes. The innocent translation of the Bible into German eventually led to the schools of extremists like Abraham Geiger; to intellectual servitude such as that of Lazarus in his *Jewish Ethics;* to a distorted philosophy of Jewish history like that of Krochmal; to mass assimilation and even to baptism.

The rabbis of Jerusalem themselves were not unaware of the scientific attitude or of the categories of systematic thinking. The *Tif'ereth Yerushalayim* by Yehudah Leib Kutna became an essential supplement to all the books of the *Mishnayoth;* his *Zayith Ra'anan* could be regarded as a classical work in the literature of the Talmud. The *Imrei Binah* of Chief Rabbi Meir Auerbach of Jerusalem shows a wide knowledge and world-understanding. Rabbi Joseph Schwartz's excellent, still very useful book on geography, *Tevuoth ha-Arets,* reveals not only Talmudic but also great scientific erudition. He has been called the "Second Farhi" because he resumed the studies of Palestine started by Estori Farhi. The *Shethilei Zayith* by Jacob Mordecai, the husband of Sara Bayla, became a text book on Halakhah in Yemen. His treatise on *Kedushath Erets Yisrael* (The Sanctity of Palestine), with a preface by his son Yitzhak, contains valuable historical investigations. His *Talpioth*—annotations and source references to the Zohar—

---

[1]Mendelssohn's artificial dualism of Jew and man became a basic philosophy of the Emancipation. It was best epitomized by Yehudah Leib Gordon: "Be a Jew in your tent, and a man outside."

sheds much light on this difficult work. The *Iggereth ha-Kodesh,* his correspondence with Eliyahu Gutmacher and Jacob Ettlinger on ways and means of raising the standard of Jewish learning in Palestine, contains profound pedagogical principles. These and other works[2] all reveal a scientific trend of thought. His articles in the *ha-Misderonah,* edited by his son Hayyim, dealing among other items with the *shmoth ha-nirdafim* (synonyms) in the halakhah, show a fine understanding of method. In the same magazine, the series of articles on *Kevod Nashim* (Dignity of Womanhood) by Hayyim can be regarded as a declaration of women's emancipation in the light of Halakhah[3]. Hayyim's *Mosedoth Torah she-b'al Peh* (Foundations of the Oral Law) was used as a text book for Talmudic beginners in rabbinical seminaries outside of Palestine. The manuscripts published by Sara Bayla's elder son Yitzhak— so pious was he that he fasted every Monday and Thursday— attracted the attention of outstanding European scholars.[4] He was requested to go to London to make copies of manuscripts in the British Museum. Mention should also be made of the book *Emek Berakhah* by Michael Pines, even though it was probably intended as an attack on the rabbis. It endeavored to prove from halakhic sources that the rabbis did not possess the right of excommunication. His interpretation may be questionable, but it was none the less written according to scholarly standards. Rabbi Samuel Salant, who succeeded Rabbi Auerbach as Chief Rabbi and head of the fighting camp, was known for his moderation and liberal-mindedness. The very periodical *ha-Misderonah* showed the wide progress that can be accomplished within the rabbinic field itself. In each issue there was a warning that while selected *kelalim* (rules or principles) would be accepted from everyone, innovations (*kelalim mehuddashim*) would be welcome only if either composed or endorsed by a famous rabbi. But the articles displayed scientific

[2]Among Jacob Mordecai's other words are *Ayenot Mayyim; Mei Be'er*—comments on the section *Orah Hayyim* of the *Shulhan Arukh; Kevod Torah; Even Shelemah; Ner Mitsvah; Devar Ha-Shemittah.*

[3]At the death of his wife, after fifty-eight years of blessed married life, Hayyim prayed that should his books earn for him some *Olam Habba* (a portion in the World to come), the larger part of it should be allotted to her who had made his writings possible.

[4]For a full list of the MSS edited by Yitzhak, see the Jewish Encyclopedia. The *Devar ha-Shemittah* is wrongly attributed to him.

treatment, logical method and fine standards of historical investigation. *Ha-Misderonah* was devoted to a study of basic principles of *halakhah* and *aggadah* (the preceptive and non-preceptive portions of the Talmud), the etymology and syntax of its Hebrew and Aramaic languages, to the Masorah (traditional text of the Bible), and to post-Talmudic literature. Among the contributors were such luminaries as Ezriel Hildesheimer, Abraham Berliner, Simon Horwitz, David Hoffmann, David Tsevi Schoenfeld, Abraham Bick of Pressburg, and numerous others who combined profound erudition with reverence for Talmudic knowledge.

Many of the medieval Talmudic scholars were men of science in their days, and the Jerusalem rabbis did not hold their secular knowledge against them. Maimonides' *Moreh Nevukhim* was studied with the same earnestness as was his code, the *Yad ha-Hazaqah*. Who among the rabbis did not know of the letter of Maimonides to Ibn Tibbon describing his secular activities? Their contemporaries abroad who had received German training, such as Gutmacher, Hoffmann, Berliner, Hildesheimer, were held in high esteem. However, the Jerusalem rabbis stood fast on a line of demarcation between the world outside, the *huts la-Arets,* and the land itself.

All this refutes the false notion that fanaticism motivated the bitter fight against the establishment of the first German school in Jerusalem. The culture of the rabbis was not lower than the foreign one which was to be introduced. The problem was not about the establishment of a school in a Jewish milieu, but of a *German* school in Jerusalem—the *Miklat* (refuge) for persons displaced by the rapidly changing environment abroad.

Frankl was sent to Jerusalem by the Jewish Committee of Vienna in order to execute the plan of Baroness Lippet Herz Laemel to found there in memory of her father a German school of the European type. Foreseeing the difficulties which he might encounter from both the Turkish government and the Jewish authorities, Frankl secured about one hundred and seventy recommendations from the highest officials of the Austrian government as well as from many prominent rabbis, among them Rabbi Eliezer Hurwitz, Rabbi Baruch of Vienna, and Rabbi Simon Schreiber, son of Moshe Sofer, the author of *Hatham Sofer*. These rabbis, great as they were, were none the less foreign to the land, and could not fathom the distress which their premature idea was bound to engender. As soon as the object of Frankl's visit became known, the whole Jewish community, men, women and children, gathered at midnight at the Kothel Ma'aravi (Wailing Wall) and spent the night in prayers and in reciting the lamentations of Jeremiah. The next morning, at a meeting of the rabbis in the Central Synagogue, the old Hurvah, this appeal to the people was promulgated: "We see a terrible menace for the House of Israel. The Torah is lamenting and covered with sackcloth, like one in mourning. For there are in the city of God some men who want to build a German school to teach the youth of Israel to write and speak a language not their own. The beginning may not appear as harmful as it really is. We are assured that the school will be under the direction of pious Jews and that the principles of the Torah will be taught, but we well know from experience how bitter the end will be. Science will become the fundamental teaching and the Torah will be put in the background. It will be the cause of a desertion of the Torah and of impiety in Israel. It will turn the youth from essential knowledge inherited through centuries to an alien culture and language incompatible with their life. Danger threatens Jerusalem. Why should we allow such profanity in the holy city of God? Therefore our heart aches that attempts should be made to blind the eyes of the pious and the followers of God. Woe that this should happen in our days! We have therefore decided to prohibit the inhabitants of Jerusalem from attending this institution." On the following Sabbath the appeal was renewed in all synagogues with the exception of those of Rabbis Joseph Schwartz, Moses Sachs and Nissim Bak. Through the support of these rabbis, Frankl succeeded in holding a meeting with them all to discuss the matter. His plan was defeated on the ground that nothing from the outside should be adopted in Jerusalem, and that needed innovations should come from within. Only two votes, those of Joseph Schwartz and of Nissim Bak of the Hassidic congregation, were in favor of Frankl. Rabbi Moses Sachs, who sided with him at first, refrained from voting because he was afraid of his moral responsibility should the proposed institution turn out to be harmful to religion.

Frankl turned the school over to the Sephardim, who accepted it willingly and very faithfully maintained it for three years, but it occupied an insignificant place and had very few pupils.

Dr. Frankl, in Sara Bayla's words (when she met him in Vienna), "showed sensitivity but not real Jewish understanding." A poet he was indeed, and a notable one in his time. Very touching is the scene he describes when he saw the Temple Mount for the first time. The sight of the ruins seems to have awakened in him a panoramic view of the whole history of Israel. When entering Jerusalem he exclaimed with joy that the greatest wish of his life had been fulfilled. His book *Toward Jerusalem* (1858), with his impressions of the Holy Land, was translated into several languages, including Hebrew. It abounds in poetical passages, but breathes no hope whatsoever. There is a complete lack of understanding for the people, of whom he speaks with undeserved contempt.

Dr. Frankl left behind him confusion and fear of the seed he had planted. Every one suspected that his neighbor might relent and yield, even as happened during the French Revolution. The arrival of rabbis from abroad, hitherto a cause for rejoicing, became a source of worry. Even the news that the famous Rabbi Sha'ul Benjamin ha-Cohen was planning to come to Jerusalem was received with mixed feelings, though his intense piety was of course not questioned. (He was a direct descendant of an uninterrupted line of sixteen generations of rabbis of great distinction).[5]

Upon his arrival in Jerusalem in 1858, Sha'ul Benjamin was received with all honors. He was immediately elected a trustee of the Va'ad ha-Kolelim (Committee of Communities), and much

---

[5]One of Sha'ul Benjamin's early ancestors, Yehudah ben Eliezer ha-Levi, the renowned rabbi and chief of the beth din of Mintz who fled to Padua during the German persecution in 1461, may have been in large measure responsible for the great Jewish learning that came out of Italy. He is highly praised by Rabbenu Eliyahu Mizrahi in the fifty-sixth of his *Teshuvoth*. He had a large following among the notables, and his eminence in philosophy was recognized even by the Gentiles. There was a close friendship between him and Don Isaac Abravanel; they died within five days of each other in 1509 and were buried in adjoining graves. Rabbi Joseph Javitz Ha-Sephardi wrote that he saw this Rabbi Jehudah blessing the sun at the age of one hundred years.

befriended by Rabbi Meir Auerbach. With the building of one more synagogue all were in full accord. Jacob Mordecai and Sara Bayla wrote to Auerbach and Sha'ul Benjamin suggesting that renewed attempts be made to regain the synagogue built by Nahmanides. But the Moslem family, in possession since 1475, persisted in refusing to sell, regardless of price. However, Sha'ul Benjamin obtained the property adjoining it, and there was much rejoicing when the beautiful synagogue, named Beth Jacob, was completed. He also renovated and built a new roof to the *Beth ha-Kneseth ha-gedolah,* which still exists under the name of *hurvah,* a complete rebuilding of the ancient *hurvah.*

His Yeshivah, *Ets Hayyim,* was also welcomed as a valuable addition. The project of substituting for the *Heder* of the old system a newly built Talmud Torah, with ten large, airy, sunny classrooms, and with systematic methods of teaching, was eventually accepted. Thanks to the harmonious cooperation, the institution developed at a rapid pace and became an outstanding center of Jewish learning. In an article in the ha-Maggid (Vol. 5, No. 27), Yehiel Brill cites this institution as the best refutation of Frankl's bitter criticism in his *Toward Jerusalem.* Says Brill: "Let all those who read the words of Frankl know that he has not spoken the truth about his unhappy brethren. Let Dr. Frankl himself now come to Jerusalem and let him see which has greater success, the Ets Hayyim schools beloved by God and men, or the school which he establishsed there. The former are flourishing and fruitful, while the latter will never succeed nor in any way answer the needs of Jerusalem."

But an unhappy incident interrupted the contentment with the healthy growth of this new institution which was progressing from within. *Bildung* (i.e., German Culture) was the pivot this time too. The Prussian consul wrote a report on the Talmud Torah to its European benefactors. He called it the *"Bildungsanstalt of Jerusalem."* Since "Bildung" denotes the German cultural view of life, there was a new alarm. At a meeting held by Rabbis Leib Kutna, Meier Auerbach, Nahum Beharama, Samuel Salant and all the trustees of the *Vaad ha-Kolelim,* it was decided to forbid the directors of the Talmud Torah to quote the consul's letter in their annual report. To make the prohibition more emphatic the letter was publicly condemned in the ha-Maggid (1863): "We saw last Wednesday some epistles signed by Rabbis Sha'ul Benjamin ha-Kohen, Leib Javitz and Leibush Cohen, which were to be sent to Europe to ask for the support of the Talmud Torah and Yeshivah Ets Hayyim. With our own eyes have we seen them, and we deplore them bitterly. These epistles contained a copy of the recommendation given to the institution by the Prussian consul, and they would have conveyed a false impression to our brethren of Europe, as if Prussian 'Bildung' were taught in Jerusalem. Oh what a shame it would have been for Jerusalem and for the whole world if this were true! No, there is no such attempt to teach 'Bildung' in the Holy Land. We therefore, in the name of the holy Torah, order that those letters should not be sent to Europe. And although those guilty of this sin be as great as the cedars, let them fall down from their heights if they do not abide by our command." What a deeply stirring event this was, can be seen from the exciting words in the ha-Maggid by Rabbi Eliyahu Gutmacher of Grodetz, Germany: "Hasten, brothers, hasten to remedy the evil which comes to blind the youth and bring thorns and poison into the streets of Jerusalem. Oh Jerusalem, Holy City, lift up thy eyes and see how strangers come to desecrate thy sanctity. Jerusalem our Mother, arise in the darkness of the night and pour out thy heart like water before God!" In another issue of the ha-Maggid, an open letter to Gutmacher by Rabbi Joseph Schwartz explained the whole situation and praised the founder of the institution very highly. Sha'ul Benjamin left immediately for Germany to see Gutmacher, whose friendship and support he promptly regained. The latter wrote another article in the ha-Maggid with apologies and high praise of the Talmud Torah. Before long, harmony was re-established in Jerusalem too. Sha'ul Benjamin undertook a long trip to European countries on behalf of those institutions. He also made a journey to Siberia and to the United States, where he remained six months.

Sha'ul Benjamin was a colorful and energetic personality. His house was ever overflowing with visitors, but they were never allowed to indulge in vain talk with him. He would turn to the pages of the Talmud as soon as the conversation began to lead to no purpose. When his young daughters indulged in careless merriment, he would point through the window to the Mosque of Omar, to remind them that until the time of the Messiah, when the Temple would replace it, laughter should be subdued. His grandson, also a rabbi, relates that he found among his papers a minute account of his earnings for the sake of balancing them with his charities, to which he allotted one fifth of his income. For over ten years in succession, when he studied under Yitzhak Volozhiner and in the Yeshivah of the Russian town of Ostrin, he never allowed himself more than four hours' sleep, in order to devote eighteen hours a day to study.

I came across an interesting incident relating to Rabbi Abraham Ezra of Ostrin, while Sha'ul Benjamin was a student there. A ruling by the former on a complicated question of *kashruth* was believed by Sha'ul Benjamin not to tally with the *din* (legal principle). When the rabbi heard of it, he felt it his duty to give up the rabbinate for the time being. Without extenuating explanations he left the town secretly and proceeded to the city of Reswitz near Minsk, where he studied continually for ten years, under great pecuniary stress. This was related in the *ha-Melits* of the year 1883, when the pious Rabbi Abraham passed away.

A touching letter from Rabbi Akiba Eger, in the possession of Jacob Mordecai, revealed his hesitancy about accepting a rabbinic post. He feared that as rabbi he would have to account for the sins of his community. How could he carry such a burden, how would he know of the secret sins, and how would he be able to stand before God and account for them?

One could easily understand how spiritual leaders of such calibre would be profoundly disturbed at the slightest signs of spiritual disintegration. While the agitation about Sha'ul Benjamin's Talmud Torah was quick to die down, Eliyahu Gutmacher felt that the presence in Jerusalem of Jacob Mordecai and his wife would help re-establish complete harmony. He urged them to move from Safed to Jerusalem, hoping that they might also contribute towards settling the grave disputes between the Ashkenazim and the Sephardim. Also, the fact that the Christian missionaries had built seventy houses to shelter Jewish newcomers pointed to the urgent need for the increase of Jewish settlements. Sara and Jacob were strongly swayed by this appeal and decided to move. The chances of a better education for their sons gave additional weight to their decision. It was not easy to part with their Yeshivah, which gave indications of entering upon a new constructive era, and with the people of Safed, with whom they had grown to be one large family. Sara Bayla promised that once she was settled she would find room for whoever might wish to follow, and quite a number of people did join them.

Their arrival in Jerusalem was warmly hailed by all the rabbis. They were able to heal the breach between Sha'ul Benjamin and his opponents, and they played a role in the negotiations with the Sephardim. Their own Yeshivah project was welcomed. It was not regarded as a strain on the community, since Sara Bayla did not find it necessary to be a recipient of *Halukah* (Philanthropic aid from abroad). With new immigrants steadily arriving and with the growing generation, there was need for another Yeshivah in addition to the five in existence. Rabbi Samuel Salant suggested a place in the very center of the city, not far from his residence and somewhat removed from the Arabs, but Sara Bayla persuaded him that, with the expansion of Jewish settlements, Arab surroundings could not be avoided, and neighborly relationships would have to be developed. A large tract of land with trees and rocks, on a hill offering a view of the Mosque of Omar and the panorama of the city, not too far from the *Kothel Ma'aravi*, was at last located by her. It was in the section leading towards the Gates of Shekhem. Some Arab houses adjoined it, but the contour of the hill made it completely secluded.

While Sara Bayla attended to the construction, to the buying of the materials, watching the Arab laborers and dealing with Arab officials from whom permission had to be obtained at every step, Jacob Mordecai was the honored guest at each Yeshivah, invited to lead the discussions. His fame spread throughout the city. His elder son, Yitzhak, accompanied him to the Yeshivoth, and the seven-year-old Hayyim was put under the care of a tutor recommended by Auerbach as his foremost student. Amidst her preoccupation Sara Bayla was disturbed that out of Hayyim's full day's curriculum the study of the Bible was limited to *Humash* (Pentateuch) alone. The tutor did not deem it necessary to teach him the rest of the Bible, as it could be acquired without instruction, except for the customary sing-song that goes with it; but Hayyim could not sing. Sara Bayla promised him ten cents for each chapter he would memorize. By the age of twelve, Hayyim knew most of the Prophets by heart, and would recite any of them without a flaw before the Hakham Bashi, Samuel Salant and others. With the accumulated coins he bought his first books, which became the nucleus of a large growing library. Hakham Bashi David Hazan wrote to Hakham Jacob Tsevi of Salonica[6]: "The Ashkenazim are way behind us in the study of the Bible, but recently they have received fresh stimulus from a noble woman of an honored family, who came here to build a Yeshivah with a number of innovations." Among these innovations was the one of marking the *siyyum* (conclusion of a Tractate) with an original dissertation by the head of the Yeshivah, to be published and circulated among the scholars abroad. To some *siyyums*, Eliyahu Gutmacher, Rabbi in Germany, would send a treatise which was studied and commented upon at the Yeshivah sessions. Jacob Mordecai's later treatises were accompanied with introductions by his sons—Yitzhak commenting on the interpretations, and Hayyim usually pointing to their pertinent bearing on some problem of the times.

The architectural layout of the Yeshivah settlement, planned by Sara Bayla alone, was also novel. There was a sense of beauty in it, and a love for sunlight. Instead of dark rooms with dark courts, there were windows in each room, with sills for flower pots. Extreme care was taken to preserve as far as possible whatever trees there were. One lone tree with tiny, velvety, yellow flowers interfered much with the plans of the building; but the tree remained, and later became the children's favorite companion. The first cornerstone laid was that of the *Beth ha-Midrash,* followed by the synagogue for women, then by a large hall to serve as a guest house and at the same time as the dining room for the communal meals of the Yeshivah on Sabbaths and festival days. The *divrei torah* (words of learning), the *zemiroth* (songs), the scholarly guests from town, no less than the palatable dishes and the little yellow

---

[6]Hayyim Tsevi, son of Hakham Tsevi of Salonika, a rabbi at Constantinople, had the Hakham Bashi's letter among his father's papers which were bequeathed to him.

flowers cut for the Sabbath, rendered it an unforgettable dining hall. Moses Montefiore and many other great men ate in it.

Little cottages of two and three rooms were continually added for the scholars and their families. The terrace of hewn stones, fenced with cactus and shrubs, and built especially for the congregation to bless the appearance of the moon, became the town's favorite place. The built-in succah was the first of its kind. The cistern was planned to provide sufficient water the whole year around, and did away with the need of buying it during the summer months out of the leathern pouches carried by the Arabs. A lot on the hill behind the cottages was set aside for a playground, so that the *Beth ha-Midrash* should not be disturbed by the children's noises, and that in turn they might have full freedom in their play.

The name of the Yeshivah, *Succath Shalom u-Me'or Yaaqov* (Tabernacle of Peace and the Light of Jacob) was to symbolize Jerusalem as a center of peace. One of Sara Bayla's ideals was unity not only between Sephardic-Ashkenazic groups, but also with the hassidim and especially with the Yemenite Jews. She wanted to prevent them from becoming assimilated with the Arabs.

The first scholars came from Safed. Because of Jacob Mordecai's reputation abroad and Sara Bayla's requests from her friends, the philanthropists of Pinsk agreed to finance the immigration of all who wished to come. Day after day Sara Bayla would dictate to Reb Shimeon the letter-writer, known for his artistic and clearcut handwriting. The letters were addressed not only to scholars, but also to business men about the transfer of their businesses, and even to carpenters, tailors, locksmiths, iron casters, and shoemakers of her native town. Labor was needed; there was in Jerusalem but one Jewish farmer, Dan Peretz, and a very small number of workmen. Her own settlement could keep some of them busy, and the town was growing. Her correspondence contained innumerable bulletins of information for Doctors Berliner, Hildesheimer, Hurwitz, Gutmacher, the Rothschilds of Frankfort, and others who helped in her work.[7]

[7]When I visited Frankfurt a.M. in my student days, I was told by Wilhelm Posen that both he and the Baron Wilhelm Wolf Rothschild were keeping on file Sara Bayla's "letters sparkling with current information and keen analysis." Wilhelm Posen was the son of Zalman, rabbi and Hebrew teacher of the Baron. When the father passed away, the son continued to teach the Baron Mishnah and Midrash several nights a week.

Sara Bayla's day started at dawn with the preparation of breakfast for the Yeshivah scholars, and ended with the midnight meal for the nightshift. Her wish that the Beth ha-Midrash be filled with study day and night uninterruptedly was being fulfilled. On Mondays and Thursdays, when the two shifts joined for the *mishmaroth,* she too stayed up all night, going up and down the stairs with trays of coffee and rolls she had baked herself. The responsibilities of the Yeshivah settlement were hers, and with its growth her tasks multiplied. The young children had to be trained, and as they grew older and ready for the customary early marriage—age twelve for girls and eighteen for boys—she took care of the preparations and provisions. New arrivals in the community spelt new problems. The rabbis turned to Sara Bayla when difficulties were caused by government officials, who became more and more exacting with the increase of the Jewish population. Sara Bayla, known to the officials and held in great esteem, was continually implored by the community to be their go-between. "Ask Sara Bayla" became the usual refrain whenever intervention was needed. The Pasha, other government officials, and representatives of foreign powers were her frequent guests. She kept special wine for them. She presented *matsoh* to every Arab she knew, and to the German, French and Russian consuls. She was the first and only Ashkenazic woman of her time who learned to speak Arabic, and was extremely popular with the Arabs. Each time she went to market—in those narrow alleys in which furniture, dry goods, live chickens, vegetables, fruits and spices were heterogeneously displayed—the Arab sellers seemed to be awakened from their slumber and rose from their low chairs in the back of their shops, where the customers would usually bring the chosen goods to them. At her appearance they would call her by name and point to the more attractive merchandise. There was no cheating in the scales for her purchases, nor the wonted overcharge. She never had to bargain with them.

The Arabs were known to be irritable during the thirty Ramadan days (fasting by day and feasting by night). As some violence occasionally occurred, it was thought safer to store food for that period and to keep away from them as much as possible. Sara Bayla needed their provisions and could not avoid them, but she met with the same friendly smile as usual. Some Arab neighbors below the hill would even inquire whether their loud chanting during the Ramadan nights interfered with the study at the "school house" as they called it. Across Sara Bayla's grounds, separated with cactus plants and shrubs, there was a long narrow terrace where some Arabs came every afternoon for their ablutions and prayers. In summer months when water was scarce, Sara Bayla lined the terrace with jugs of water for their use. This helped not a little to cement their friendship.

A synagogue under hassidic auspices on the other side of the courtyard also received her attention. The Hassidim found it hard to understand how Sara Bayla could possibly belong to the Mithnaggedim. One of them saw a ghost one midnight, which he interpreted as a warning to Jacob Mordecai for having renounced his hassidic birth. A gifted young Hassid, fifteen years old, who would never pass between two women, wrote a kabbalistic poem showing that Sara Bayla's soul stemmed from hassidim and that in the world to come she would join them.

Perhaps those who can best speak of Sara Bayla are the children who grew up in her courtyard. Some, who by force of circumstance were transplanted to Paris at a time when assimilation was rampant, came out unscathed from that anti-Jewish climate, because of the impetus of pious generations which she transmitted to them. These profound and abiding impressions directed their dynamic Jewishness throughout their life. A group of children reared in that courtyard would vie with each other to rise at dawn to perform the Mitsvah of carrying the trays of food to the *Beth ha-Midrash*. Before Succoth or at some other festive occasion, there seemed to be a Marathon race as to who would be the first to get up to earn the Mitsvah of cutting the yellow little flowers or some thick branches for the *Succah*. There were also races to carry meals to the helpless ones at the Magrib Hall—a dark building with hard boards for beds, without tables or chairs, crowded with infirm old people without means of livelihood who had come from Persia and Turkestan to die in the Holy Land. Each child would carefully count the number of mitsvoth won through such errands. In the midst of their most concentrated games they would run towards Sara Bayla as soon as they sighted her. A penny to each

child was Sara Bayla's daily greeting. But it was not the penny in
itself which attracted them. One of the children, less than four
years old, made a suggestion which was unanimously adopted, that
the pennies should not be spent on candy, but accumulated to purchase the Mosque of Omar and rebuild the Temple in its place. The
children would gather in a circle around her, clamoring for stories.
She yielded, adapting the Biblical tales to their youthful minds.
One little girl of deep sensitivity took Sara Bayla's Bible and sat on
the stoop of the Yeshivah, seizing and holding the hem of each
passerby until he would read and explain to her a page of the
Prophets. The child, not fully six years old, astonished the town by
her knowing numerous passages by heart, particularly from Isaiah,
which she rendered with profound emotion. It was also through Sara
Bayla's picturesque portrayal of Yehudah Halevi's recital of his
"Ode to Zion" at the Gates of David, that the same child searched
for Halevi's poems, learned the ode by heart, and one day mysteri-
ously disappeared from the playground. She was found at the Gates
of David reciting *"Tsiyon ha-lo tish'ali li-shelom assirayikh."* The
city was stirred, and the incident was recorded in the newspapers.

Another story whch impressed the children was about the old
man of seventy who long ago made a perilous journey to Jerusalem
to gather ten Jews who would greet the moon each 'month at its
reappearance. Sara Bayla had in mind Nahmanides, who actually
came for this very purpose to Jerusalem in 1267, and who died there
three years later. He had calculated that Hillel ha-Nasi in fixing
the calendar could have blessed the new moon for a definite number of years, but not for eternity. A perpetual Jewish community
in the Holy Land was therefore essential to give validity to the
Jewish calendar by proclaiming each new moon.

Sara Bayla's story of the moon evoked a vivid picture in the
minds of the children, who eagerly awaited its monthly appearance.
They would rush with their supper, run to the terrace, stretch
their necks towards the sky, and clap their hands cheerfully as soon
as a tiny luminous point would become visible. They would run
up the stairs to the *Beth ha-Midrash* announcing with joyous excitement that the *levanah* (moon) was there and that they should
hurry to greet her. They would form a large circle of their own
as if to surround the moon, jumping, dancing, and chanting in

unison with the tunes sung by the men. What a beautiful tale a Jewish Hans Andersen could have woven out of this picture!

An outsider observing the children at play would have wondered why they would suddenly interrupt it when they saw a heavy laundry bag ready to be taken to the cleaning and dyeing establishment patronized by Sara Bayla. Each wanted to carry it, heavy as it was, because she had told them that the originators of this establishment were the only two Jews, two brothers, whom Nahmanides found on his arrival there. The few remaining Jews from nearby villages would gather there on Sabbaths for their joint prayers. Nahmanides built a synagogue and a Yeshivah adjoining their place and brought over a *sefer torah* which had been hidden in Shekhem.

The annual excursions to holy places and to the countryside were unique events which Sara Bayla introduced into the life of the children. I have met grandmothers and great-grandmothers who during their childhood had participated in those outings and still retained vivid memories of them. They revisited those places several times, especially the section around Hebron, where several of the children insisted upon searching for "the Jewish shepherds who lived there long ago." There was indeed in the thirteenth century a community of Jewish shepherds around Hebron who lived in tents and held their services outdoors. Their rabbis too were shepherds and preached their sermons in open fields. During the Tartar invasion under Hulaku Khan in 1260 when all Jews fled, these nomads remained unmolested. There have been no traces of them for the last few centuries. Thy may have migrated to Yemen and merged with the Jewish group there. In all probability Nahmanides did not know of their existence, for we see that he makes no reference to them, and indeed, had he known of them, he would have endeavored to incorporate them into the community which he was so eager to enlarge. He even wanted to bring the Karaites back into the rabbinic fold. He encouraged them to join his Yeshivah, which attracted famous Jews from everywhere. Some Karaites who occasionally visited Sara Bayla's courtyard claimed their descent from these, and said that they were nearer to the General Jewish Community than to their own sect. They spoke with pride of Aaron ben Joseph of Constantinople, famous physician, scholar and philosopher, who had come especially to Jerusalem to stury in Nahmanides' Yeshivah.[8] He became such an admirer of the rabbinic authorities that he took the Talmud as a model for his *Sefer ha-Mivhar al ha-Torah,* and also incorporated in the Karaite prayer-book some medieval Hebrew poems.

Nahmanides may be rightly considered the first pioneer of the Jewish resettlement in Palestine. His impact was strongly felt throughout the centuries, and especially in the period here dealt with. His commentary on the Torah—completed in Jerusalem— and his *Torath ha-Adam,* written there, were much in vogue at that time. He was talked of with deepest reverence in every scholarly household. Some of Sara Bayla's projects may have been patterned after his. The idea of a *beth sefer li-melakhah* (industrial school) must have come to her from the example of the healthy, peaceful community which clustered around Nahmanides' Yeshivah. Many were dyers, tailors, shoemakers; others were engaged in commerce and shop-keeping. A few were busy with medicine, astronomy and mathematics, but all of them—from the scientist to the shoemaker— were students of the Torah.

Long before the colonization period, Sara Bayla began to realize that with the increase of the population there would be a growing number who might not devote themselves to Talmudic studies. To forestall the emergence of an *am ha-arets* (ignoramus) class, so rampant in Russia, she worked out a plan whereby the Laemel Schule would be converted into a *beth sefer li-melakhah* for those who could not be attracted ot the Yeshivah. The *Tanakh* (Bible) and Talmud should be taught as far as possible; some Arabic should be studied instead of the German language and culture. The project met with the rabbis' approval, but the Austrian sponsors of the Laemel Schule, influenced by German philosophy, regarded German culture as far more important than practical work. Had her idea been carried out, there might have developed in Palestine a unique labor class with a Jewish consciousness.

[8]Kohler doubts whether Aaron ben Joseph attended Nahmanides' Yeshivah, even though he shows careful study of his works. But there is far better ground for the views of the rabbis of Jerusalem and of the Karaites that Aaaron ben Joseph did attend the Yeshivah. Joseph Schwartz and many other scholars who were so concerned with the minutest details relating to the Yeshivah are bound to be nearer the truth.

The rabbis themselves came to see that with the continual arrivals from abroad, Jerusalem could no longer remain just a
rabbinical center, that there was a large periphery that could not
be absorbed by the inner circle. Contrary to common belief, they
wisely reckoned with the exigencies of the times. What was
premature ten years before, became a need in 1868. The very
rabbis who were the strongest adversaries of Dr. Frankl—Isaac
Prag, Jonah Mendelssohn and Moses Pressburger—accepted the
direction of the *Dorshei Tsiyon* school founded by Joseph Blumen-
feld of Paris. Only Nissim Bak, who formerly had given support to
Frankl, now led the opposition. The school of Nissim Behar, established by the Alliance Israelite Universelle, which met with but
little opposition, would also have been completely accepted, had it
not been so totally impregnated with the Franch language and
French culture.

Palestine would have fared better without the foreign schools
which turned out superficially prepared students with as little
knowledge of world culture as of Jewish learning. Had Jerusalem's
own school system been allowed to grow into the twentieth century,
undirected by alien dictation, we should have been in possession
of a rich culture grown out of the Jewish soil. In spite of frustra-
tions and energy consumed in fighting violent superimpositions from
without, progress in Palestine came out of the rabbinic camp,
achieved not through imitation, but through indigenous growth.
Journalism, literary research, historical and geographical investigations, philosophical studies, all these were Palestine's own fruit.
Even if one rabbi occasionally would clog the circulation, all his colleagues would immediately reopen the Jewish flow. It is out of
the interplay of inner forces that progress emanates.

The progressive movement, of which the year 1877 marks the
beginning, was not an anti-rabbinical eruption as is usually believed. It was not an offshoot of the *haskalah* abroad, but one of an
entirely different complexion with no seeds of irreligion in it. It
was a kind of renaissance, a rebirth of the fertile all-embracing
Jewish spirit, a return to the scholarship initiated by the great
medieval Jewish masters. It was an enlightenment from within
the Jewish body, and not an estrangement therefrom. The initiators
were connected with some of the Yeshivoth and Talmud Torahs,

and the idea of breaking down the barriers was farthest from their thoughts. Among them were Moses Salomon, for a short time editor of the paper *Yehudah vi-Yrushalayim,* altogether free from heterodox tendencies, and Hayyim Press, whose sole object was to introduce among the young Talmudists a modern way of learning, and also the study of Hebrew grammar. He was eager to teach it free of charge to whoever wished to learn it. The most outstanding of the group was Jacob Saphir, the son-in-law of the editor of *ha-Levanon,* and the grandfather of Eliyahu Saphir, the Arabic and Hebrew scholar. Jacob Saphir came to Jerusalem at the age of ten and obtained all his education there. His love for the Bible overcame the prevailing fear that death would overtake whoever would touch the manuscript containing the *masorah* of Ben Asher, kept secretly in Egypt. He succeeded in obtaining access to it, and edited and published it under the title of *Divrei Hefets me-ha-Tanakh shel Ben Asher,* with a comparative study of this Masorah and that of Ben Naphtali. His book *Even Sappir* is of much value, He was also a poet of no mean rank. He shattered the pretenses of the false Messiah of Yemen, Shukar al-Rahil. Before his contemplated long journey, he visited Safed, and it was Sara Bayla who suggested his trip to Yemen, when he was set on traveling as far as India and Australia. He went to those places also, and was among the first to write about the Jews there.

There seems to have been no hard line of demarcation between this newly-born *intelligentsia* and the rabbis, to whom many of them were related by family ties. The moderation of Samuel Salant, of the Hakham Bashis Abraham Ashkenazi and Elyashar, the broad vision of Joseph Schwartz, the magnetic personality of Sara Bayla, the profound scholarship and open-mindedness of Jacob Mordecai, the wit and vast knowledge of their elder son Yitzhak and the fertile mind of the younger one, Hayyim, were predominant factors in turning this fermentation into a Jewish effervescence. They helped direct this welling current into a normal channel by giving it a Talmudic trend. Sara Bayla's family, in discussion or writing, invariably pointed to the inexhaustble intellectual material within the Talmudic pages. Her son Yitzhak, in jest or in earnest, was wont to say that he was willing to debate heresies with any radical, provided *Rashi* was taken as the final reference.

But it was the fear, so little realized by the historian, that this newly-born restlessness might turn into centrifugal channels if diverted from Jewish learning towards alluring foreign books, that brought about the agitation against the founding of a public library, suggested in 1877 by Moses Luncz and Dob Frumkin, to bear the name of Moses Montefiore in honor of his ninetieth birth-day. Sir Moses, advised of it, provided the necessary funds, asked that his wife's name be added, and stipulated that every evening a portion of the Talmud should be studied jointly by the readers. But the rabbis explained their attitude to Montefiore, who saw their point and withdrew his name. The *Beth Moshe vi-Yhudith* Library became so deserted that it had to be closed. The books were stored in the office of the *Havatseleth* until 1884, when the time became ripe for a library. Again it was through the initiative and efforts of some of the younger rabbis that the library came into being, Baron Rothschild maintaining it.[9] There was no opposition now—merely the demand for a discriminating selection of books, in the choice of which many rabbis took part at the invitation of Sara Bayla's son Hayyim. Out of this nucleus has developed the National Library of the Hebrew University.

The rise of journalism, too, could be traced to rabbinic efforts. As early as 1863 appeared *Havatseleth, Ha-Levanon* and *Kevod ha-Levanon*. *Ha-Levanon* was originated for the purpose of taking sides with some rabbis against others on a few issues of modernism. This paper's circulation became so widespread that its central office was subsequently transferred to Paris and then to Mainz, Germany. *Ha-Tsefirah* and *Ha-Melits* came into being after the appearance of *Ha-Levanon* and most probably through its stimulation. Owing to lack of funds, the publication of *Havatseleth* was at first of short duration. It reappeared seven years later under the joint editorship of Israel Dov Frumkin, the son-in-law of Rabbi Israel Bak, and Michael Cohen. The latter severed his relations with it after the third year. During the joint editorship the paper enjoyed the

---

[9]The renewed efforts towards a library originated with Hayyim, who enlisted the interest of Jacob Meir, Jacob Elyashar, and the sons of several rabbis, who fully cooperated with him.

active participation of the Hakham Bashi Abraham Ashkenazi and of Hakham David ben Shim'on, the rabbi of the Magribs, and the sympathy of all the rabbis. But as soon as Frumkin assumed the full responsibility, relations became strained, partly on account of his difficult temperament, but especially after the publication of two articles by Simon Trachtman, *Mei ha-Yam* and *Messilath ha-Osher*. The rabbis felt that Frumkin showed lack of discrimination in accepting material of a heretical nature when the paper was so closely sponsored by them. They asked for a joint editorial board, which Frumkin refused. As a result of this friction the paper went out of existence for some time. When it reappeared in 1877, Frumkin, prompted more by a passion for vengeance than by discernment, concentrated his efforts on attacking the trustee system of the *kolelim,* and the leadership of the rabbis.

The several newspapers[10] that appeared, for longer or shorter periods, were primarily devoted to local color. The scientific reviews were also mostly devoted to Palestine, but the Monthly *ha-Misderonah* kept a close intellectual relation between Palestine and the scholars abroad. The exchange of thought broadened through a trip to Germany by its editor Hayyim at the invitation of Dr. Berliner.

Until then, the chief bond between Erets Yisrael and the other lands had been that of beneficiary and benefactor. Palestine was regarded by its sympathizers as a worthy object of philanthropy. There was now added to this an intellectual union, as witnessed by the numerous contributions to *ha-Misderonah* from outstanding scholars in Germany. It was Hayyim's hope that this relation would balance whatever loss Jewish life might have sustained through emancipation.

At the age of seventeen, Hayyim became engaged to the younger daughter of Sha'ul Benjamin. But while the community was hailing his forthcoming marriage, the couple themselves had no knowledge of it until the engagement ceremony. It was eleven o'clock

---

[10]In its early years Ben Yehudah's *ha-Tsevi* followed the orthodox line. *Yerushalayim* and *Luah ha-Shanah,* edited by Moses Luncz, were studies of Palestine. Other newspapers of that period were of short duration—as, for instance, *Ariel,* by Michael Cohen, *Sha'arei Tsiyon* by Hayyim Press, *Yehudah vi-Yrushalayim* by Moses Salomon, and one in Yiddish, *Beth Jacob,* by Sara Bayla's son Hayyim, under the editorial pseudonym of *Havah.* It was especially dedicated to raising the status of women.

one night when Sha'ul Benjamin, Jacob Mordecai, and the two witnesses Samuel Salant and Dan Eliezer Gabrilowitz knocked at the door of the bride, awakened her, and told her of her engagement. On the customary visit of the bride and family to the bridegroom's home shortly before the wedding day, it happened that the chickens in the yard broke loose. All those present rushed out to catch them. The bride and bridegroom remained alone in the living room, both of them deeply embarrassed and blushing. At last he took courage and addressed her with a few words. Bewildered, she ran out as fast as she could. During his stay in Germany, a few years after his marriage, whenever Hayyim went outdoors he wore dark glasses when away from his wife.

Aryeh Leib, the son of the prominent and highly revered Rabbi and *Av Beth Din* Dan Eliezer Gabrilowitz, married the elder daughter of Sha'ul Benjamin. After years of Talmudic studies he was allowed by his extremely pious father to become a pharmacist; so as to have a share in saving human life. He took turns with his brother so that each spent half of the day at the pharmacy and the other half at the Yeshivah. As the pharmacy yielded a comfortable income, part of it was dedicated to the maintenance of the newly built Talmud Torahs.

In 1884 the *Yeshivah Degel Torah* was established, and also four new Talmud Torahs. Sara Bayla was among those responsible for their being set up outside the gates of the City in the various suburbs, and with what was then considered modern equipment. The reorganization of the Laemel Schule, under happier auspices, also took place that year. The Jewish community of Vienna transferred its supervision to that of Frankfurt-am-Main. They combined it with the orphanage they had in Jerusalem since 1879, with only four pupils.

A chief concern of Sara Bayla's son Hayyim, with which she was fully in accord, was to do away with the philanthropies from abroad. She assisted in the various economic and industrial projects he undertook for that purpose. His first endeavor, some years before the *Hovevei Tsiyon* movement, was to form a corporation for the purchase of lands from the Arabs. Several sons of rabbinic families were among those who joined him in numerous trips through deserted regions, seeking for places which could become a nucleus for Jewish expansion. Sara Bayla not only prepared the food supply and the leather jugs of water, but also obtained for them the geographical work *Kaftor va-Ferah* by Estori ben Farhi, a famous scholar of the thirteenth century. She had seen that book in the hands of her husband while he was preparing for their trip to Palestine. He brought it with him, and it was circulated a great deal among the rabbis. The volume, written in the time of Nahmanides, gave detailed information about the mountains, valleys, rivers and villages, together with halakhic references to them. Hayyim, familiar with the book, was much impressed by the author's attempts to facilitate commercial and industrial relations with other lands through rulings deduced from halakhic principles.

The purchase of land by this small group of young rabbinic pioneers marks the first Jewish expansion before the founding of the colonies. Sara Bayla had her share in it, and many a time there was need of her persuasion with some Arab landlord unwilling to sell land to Jews. Legends accrued around her successful intervention with them. The following incident, however, is authentic. After suitable arrangements had been made with an Arab landlord for a large piece of land on the road to Hebron, he suddenly changed his mind and declined to close the deal. It dawned upon him that this group of people, who did not impress him as business men, were presumably making the purchase for the establishment of a Jewish village. He withdrew his offer without explanation, and no amount of persuasion and higher bids were of any avail. Sara Bayla was appealed to. "She knows him just a little, but she will try." The Arab landlord did not decline the invitation for a visit to her home. He frankly admitted to her that it would not be pleasing to Allah if he were to turn over his beautiful property for an exclusively Jewish population. As the sing-song of the Yeshivah was reaching their ears, Sara Bayla turned to Mustapha Pasha and asked him to listen to it attentively. Calmly she said, "Mustapha Pasha, such people mean no harm; they want to study peacefully and live in peace with you. The newcomers may not spend all their days in the synagogues, but whatever they do, they will not cease to be peaceful and law-abiding." A few days later Mustapha Pasha convened the members of the corporation and offered them the land. They were under the impression that the increase in price had some influence on his decision. Mustapha Pasha, however, adhered to his initial offer, with but these words: "Sara Bayla is a saintly woman; it would not be a sin in the eyes of Allah." He and his descendants retained a genuine friendship for the Jews. This story was related by those concerned with the purchase, and also by Aryeh Leib Gabrilowitz, the main pharmacist in town, who got the story from Mustapha Pasha himself.

Sara Bayla also cooperated with her son in his industrial endeavors. When he established a printing plant for the publication of his father's works, of his own, of the manuscripts discovered by his brother and of other rabbinic writings, she threw much of her strength into it. She and his wife helped turn the wheels and even set the type when labor was short. She hoped that his successive iron, soap, seltzer, bed and mattress factories would absorb the Yemenite population which began to immigrate in large numbers, most of them laborers. She tried all she could to find work for them wherever possible. The soap factory introduced a liquid soap for those who had scruples about using solid soap cakes on the Sabbath. Sara Bayla distributed it gratis to observant colonists.

These enterprises turned out to be financial losses, but they were the seed for industrial growth. The growing youth was able to integrate Jewish life with the industrial and scientific progress of the times, without losing any of its own characteristics. The progress from the older to the newer generation was transitional and not abrupt. The estrangement came only with the newcomers, who wanted to eliminate the old entirely.

The chasm became larger with each new immigration. Sara Bayla, however, hoped that the newly founded colonies Rishon le-Tsiyon, Zikhron Yaaqov and Pethah Tikvah could still be absorbed into the prevailing Jewish spirit of Jerusalem. "The sap of a healthy tree," she would say, "runs through the branches, the leaves, and allows nothing to wither." When these colonies, as well as En ha-Kore of the *Halutsei Yesud ha-Ma'alah,* were yet little huts in a desert with muddy, bumpy roads, she was a frequent visitor of them. She pleaded with the people, even with the young radicals of the *Bilu,* that since they had come to the Holy Land for the love of Zion, they should not desecrate it by doing violence to the observances which should remain intact: "They should not pluck the heart out of the organism." She offered to keep with her in Jerusalem those children who would be willing to pursue Talmudic studies. She invited the early colonists to her seder, sent them ethrogim and lulavim for succoth, hamantashen on Purim, and gifts to Bar Mitsvah children.

What Sara Bayla feared most was that a split in the community would jeopardize the role of Palestine in Jewish life everywhere. So anxious was she that the extremists should not form an isolationist segment of their own, that she counseled the young rabbinic element to settle beyond the gates of the City, mingle with the newcomers, debate with them, and lead them to constructive ways. Controversies seem to have been in vogue in the homes, in the courtyards, on the streets, on the terraces, in the pharmacy, in the tiny stationery stores—wherever the two antipodal forces encountered each other. A little girl about four years old, who probably overheard some controversy, asked Sara Bayla tremblingly whether, if she did not believe in the leviathan, she would still be given a portion in the world to come.

The natural course of progress was twisted and thwarted by the imported philosophical currents towards the end of the century. The influx of nihilistic and anarchistic philosophies, born on Russian soil, could not have been successfully grafted on Jewish life, which came into being not through slavery and tyranny but thorough its very rebellion against them. The exodus from Egypt had already accomplished the Revolution which these philosophies were aiming at. In their overzealousness, the Jewish adherents of the world movement for amelioration failed to grasp the very roots of it. The Jewish mind, with its fertile seeds for further development and construction, did not have to become a *tabula rasa*. (See Leo Jung's Essay, "The Jewish Foundations of the New World Order", where he traces the basic Jewish social ideas.) The chief battle between the centripetal and the centrifugal forces in Jewish life derives primarily from the keen discernment of the one, and the lack of it in the other, of what constitutes one's genuine need. Progress is desired by both fighting camps. The profounder outlook is no doubt that of those who believe that growth can be forthcoming only from one's own organic center.

This sums up the nature of the antagonistic forces in the second half of the nineteenth century in Palestine. The concluding years of the struggle belong to the twentieth, and are too near our times to be envisaged in proper perspective.

The last years of Sara Bayla's life were saddened by the loss of her husband, the departure, years later, from Jerusalem of her son Hayyim, and subsequently the premature death of her elder son Yitzhak while gathering manuscripts in Europe. For some years the Yeshivah continued on its momentum, with a grandson at its head, and with Yitzhak's family assisting Sara Bayla.

Perhaps a deeper sadness in Sara Bayla came with the awareness that the dikes that had been built with such heroism by a whole generation did not prevent an inimical current. The Yeshivah itself, the courtyard, the children, must have assumed a different complexion, and so did Palestine.

Through force of circumstances, and moved by the desire to bring improvements into Palestine, her son Hayyim decided to go temporarily abroad with his family. Sara Bayla's funds were exhausted through building extensions and maintenance, and most of the German sponsors had passed away. Hayyim would give to his five children and two adopted boys an adequate education, and they would bring back to Jerusalem their acquired skills and knowledge. This would be the beginning of an educated class growing from within, with a religious foundation. "If you think that your plan will work out for the good of the land and for the Yeshivah, go with God's blessings and follow what you deem best." These were Sara's parting words to him, without a tear in her eyes, keeping the pain within her. Times had changed and Jewishness abroad needed its pioneers too. Her son and his family remained in the United States with her full understanding of the situation. She wrote to him that as long as he was needed in his congregation and outside of it, he should remain there. "Jewish destiny is of a revolving kind," she wrote him; "when it diminishes at one end, it increases at the other." But she asked him to keep his eyes and his heart on Jerusalem, which would eventually triumph and become again the heart of the people. "One cannot continually mistake pebbles for precious stones. The quality of the diamond does not remain hidden for long. Your children or grandchildren will rediscover it. Meanwhile the pillars of the Law must be careful watchmen so that the scoffers should not rob our children of their ancient heritage." Great was her joy when Hayyim mailed her his first discourse before his congregation, which was studied by her Yeshivah scholars. It was a lengthy Talmudic thesis, as Rabbi Hayyim did not yet know the nature of the American audience. She replied that she thanked God to be alive at a time "when the Torah extends from one hemisphere to another, and the sun does not set on it." These were her last words to her son shortly before she passed away at the age of almost ninety, retaining her vitality to the very end. It was late in the evening, and it is related that on that same day she awoke at dawn, prepared the Beth ha-Midrash meals, and went to prayers. "The Yeshivah" was the last word on her lips. She did not die in loneliness; her dimming eyes beheld the numerous pious friends around her, blessing the one who so beautifully embodied the strength of the Torah and the deep-rooted hope with which every Jew is born.

The Yeshivah continued for some years. But with the changing times, with the widespread disasters the First World War, it began to fade away and it finally disappeared.

It is hard to believe that this enchanted courtyard of children who wanted to rebuild the *Beth ha-Miqdash,* a place so rich in Jewish association, is no more. But, like all that is immortal, the body ceases and the soul remains. The present State of Israel will eventually blossom out of the seeds planted by these rabbinic pioneers. Themselves unaware, the pioneers of our day draw their strength from those who consecrated their lives to fuse into one the Land and the soul thereof.

II

This section is devoted to intimate details, treated separately so as not to diffuse the picture on which our view is focused. But their local color, and the human element, give us a broader view of the background and a rich relief to the picture itself. The agitated spirit, the deep concerns, the modes of living cannot be reproduced in words, but the items here selected may help us touch the pulse of the times.

(a) *Shemittah* (Sabbatical Year): Jacob Mordecai's *Devar ha-Shemittah*—a research into the laws of the Talmud referring to the sabbatical and jubilee years—was written on account of the controversy regarding the cultivation of the land in the shemittah year 1888-89. The administrators of Zikhron Yaaqov, Ekron, Pethah Tikvah and Rishon-le-Tsiyon came to Jerusalem to talk the matter over with the rabbis, in the hope that they might find a way whereby the tilling of the soil would not be interrupted. Samuel Salant, in the name of his *Beth Din,* decreed that the laws of Shemittah must be strictly applied, and he appealed for financial assistance to Baron de Rothschild and other philanthropists. Jacob Mordecai, on the other hand, felt that a careful study of the Shemittah laws might point towards some *hetter* (permissive easement). The agitation is reflected in the introduction to his book, which I quote in literal translation: "I have been asked by the people of the colonies that since the *Shemittah* year 5649 is approaching, I look into the matter to see if it is not possible to find a permissive aspect as to plowing and sowing during the Sabbatical year.

"If there cannot be found a means for a *hetter* in accordance with the *din,* there will be untold loss, which would endanger the lives of hundreds of Jewish souls, who have no way whatever to sustain themselves during the year after the *Shemittah.* Besides, it is almost a certainty that this could cause, God forbid, the ruin and destruction of the whole *yishuv* project. For who could or would furnish the needs of the colonists for over a year? There is also some ground for apprehension that it might cause the philanthropists engaged in this great *mitsvah* to weaken and withdraw their aid, and all this holy endeavor might collapse. When I considered the importance of the *yishuv* of Erets Yisrael and the great damage that could result from the lapse of this great *mitsvah,* God forbid, I said to myself that it is right and proper to ponder and go to the heart and depth of this *halakhah.* Perhaps there really is a possibility of easing the situation by some system which would help maintain a number of people in Palestine and save the whole yishuv project. I was certain that because of the importance of this *mitsvah,* the Lord would enlighten me as to the truth about it. It is my advice that the colonists should issue a public call to all our rabbis, both in Palestine and outside Palestine, to point out the way in which they should walk, according to the law of our holy Torah. This would be a most proper approach, right in the eyes of God and man. As for myself, I am acceding to their request to look into the matter, without any intention of making a *halakhic* decision, but only to arouse and plead before the rabbis who know the statutes and the laws, that they may find what can be done in accordance with them. First of all, it is necessary to look into the matter of *shemittah* at this time as to plowing and sowing. If it is a Pentateuchal (*Mi-de-Oraytha*) prohibition, then there is no hope of a lenient way out; but if it is a rabbinical injunction (*mi-de-Rabbanan*) then a basis for leniency might be found in the argument that the Talmudic rabbis did not intend their decree to apply where it would cause such a great loss."

His son Yitzhak was so stirred that he sent letters to many rabbis in Palestine and abroad asking for their opinions and offering to publish them at his own expense. His letter was also published in the newspapers, and attached to Jacob Mordecai's book. It reads in part: "The administrators . . . came to Jerusalem . . . about the *shemittah,* and the great rabbi and *gaon* rendered a strict and final decision, as if this question were of the lightest import, as if the lives of hundreds of people did not depend on it and as if it could not result, God forbid, in the possible destruction of the *yishuv.* We therefore call the attention of the eminent rabbis to the *Devar ha-Shemittah* by the eminent Rabbi Jacob Mordecai. We hope that the great rabbis outside Palestine, on whom the whole house of Israel is leaning and who have the heart to appreciate the importance of this question for Palestine, will not hastily incline towards a prohibitive decision before well weighing the matter and examining it from every angle. It is a great question that confronts the rabbis, a question on which possibly hangs the entire hope of Israel. And we trust that in their wisdom and their love for their people and the Torah they will not treat the question lightly and render an offhand decision."

Jacob Saul Elyashar (subsequently Hakham Bashi), Isaac Elhanan Spector and other rabbis concurred with Jacob Mordecai's opinion.

(b) *Sephardic-Ashkenazic Relations*: The Sephardim filtered into Palestine after the expulsion from Spain. They—but not the Ashkenazim—were regarded by the Mussulmans as the "Sons of Abraham." Their chief rabbis were given the rank of Bashi, with all the privileges going with it. Auerbach appealed to Hakham Bashi David Hazan to intercede with the Ottoman government that the Ashkenazim too be regarded as the "sons of Abraham." In 1864, after some bitter strife, David Hazan advised the Ottoman authorities that there were no religious differences between Sephardim and Ashkenazim. Under the Chief Rabbinate of Samuel Salant their relations became peaceful. Sara Bayla and Jacob Mordecai strengthened them through personal friendships. Hakham Bashi Abraham Ashkenazi presented Sara Bayla with a Sephardic Festival prayer book, to acquaint her with the Sephardic liturgy composed by great medieval poets.

When the Prince of Wales (later Edward VII) was Ashkenazi's guest at the Seder, Sara Bayla sent them the tiny colorful flowers from her hill and a silk napkin for covering the matsoth, artistically embroidered by one of her young brides with the inscription *barukh habba*. The Sephardim were wont to call Sara Bayla Alma Querida (Dear Soul); the Yemenites, "Amma" (Mother). The rabbi of the Magribs, Hakham David, referred to her as Ahath me-Elef (one in a thousand). Hakham Jacob Elyashar, the Sephardic chief dayyan and subsequently Hakham Bashi, and Jacob Mordecai would often discuss with her philosophico-ethical questions in which Elyashar was particularly interested.

The story of Sara Bayla and the pearl was a current one in Jerusalem. It was probably embellished, as there are many versions of it. After several verifications I find the following authentic. A poor Sephardic family told of their despair to Sara Bayla. Their young son was already of age to get married; they knew of a nice girl. But how could they possibly approach her without some jewelry gift from her bridegroom, at least a pearl necklace? They considered selling their little fruitstand for that purchase, but this would cut off the only source of income for themselves and the young couple. Sara Bayla understood their psychology and their plight, but how could she possibly divert for jewelry money she had to spend on the Yeshivah? Her own jewelry she had gradually presented to her daughters-in-law and other kin. She told them to come back within a few days. In the meantime she gathered the young married women of her courtyard and from other places and asked whether each one of them would be willing to donate one single pearl. The pearl necklace was thus obtained and the couple got married. Since then it has become almost customary for rich families to add three pearls to every necklace given to a poor bride.

Some years later the young married man conceived the brilliant idea of building a large open oven to bake the individual doughs brought to him by each household. Sara Bayla was among his first customers, and even advised him to hire a porter to call for the dough and return it baked. Little by little the housewives became accustomed to utilizing his facilities. As a form of appreciation, he would artistically intertwine in Sara Bayla's *halloth* the words *barukh habba* (welcome) whenever she had a guest from abroad. Later, when he became a little more prosperous, he asked Sara Bayla whether her Beth ha-Midrash would accept a *Sefer Torah* from him. It was of course accepted, and the presentation was marked by an impressive ceremony. For the first time, Sephardic rabbis and laymen were present at a joint ceremony in an Ashkenazic synagogue.

But it seems that the rift was not completely bridged. The following is a passage from a letter (1928) to Sara Bayla's son Hayyim by a close friend of his youth, Jacob Meir, later Hakham Bashi of Salonika and of Palestine. It is in relation to some halakhic question and was written more than thirty years after their separation:

"Thank you deeply for the precious and delightful present you have sent me, the third and fourth parts of your sacred book *Malki ba-Kodesh*. My sincere friend, the loving words of your letter to me (printed in Part Four) touched me to the depths of my heart and brought tears to my eyes. For I remember former days when we both worked together in the fruitful task of promoting peace and bringing closer together the hearts of the Ashkenazim and Sephardim, and to spread the use of our holy tongue in the Talmud Torahs and Yeshivoth in the study of our true Torah. And now, on my return by God's grace to our Holy Land after a sojourn abroad, and on assuming the duties of my sacred calling in Erets Yisrael, I am turning right and left, making one search after another with searchlight and beam, to find a man like you who stands above others, with a pure heart and not seeking honor, to be at my side, to take counsel with him on how to prevent the ever-widening rift. I realize it is a vain search. I should have liked to detail to you the causes which have led to this, but I fear God and would not want to profane the Holy Name, so I have sealed my lips in the confident hope that the day will come when the vision of our Prophet will come to pass, 'And I shall give you a heart of flesh and a new spirit shall I give you' " (Halifath Mikhtavim, Malki ba-Kodesh, Volume VI).

(c) *Spiritualism*: There came from the United States a certain Mrs. Stafford who claimed prophetic powers and formed a community in Jerusalem, later known as the American colony. One hundred and seventy Swedish-Americans, Swedenborgians, mostly from Chicago, also arrived, as well as a number of English spiritualists, and of those kind, noble Englishmen who believed that the salvation of the world was interdependent with the destiny of Israel. They would all seek association with Jews to spread their spiritualist doctrines. The call of the spirit would haunt them even in the midst of a conversation, when they would suddenly retire and rush to their quarters to receive the messages.

The fear of and belief in ghosts were widespread among ·he non-Jews of Jerusalem. The story of one particular ghost was quite upsetting; some Hassidim saw it, and so did Hayyim one night. He was in the habit, after leaving the midnight shift of the Yeshivah, of retiring to a lonely corner to study Kabbalah, Saadya, Maimonides, and even the writings on geography by Joseph Schwartz. He was absorbed in the *Zohar* on the creation of Adam, and when he lifted up his head he saw a white, shaking ghost across the field moving nearer and nearer towards him. Tremblingly he went on studying, with his mind no longer on the pages. After some hesitation he decided to go over to it, and step by step he forced himself nearer. With courageous determination he finally made one dash, stretched out his arm, closed his eyes, and touched the ghost. A ray of light came from the stars on the moonless

night, and he beheld a huge water jug, half painted white with a
brown bottom, gently rocked by a mild breeze.

(d) Kabbalah was on the decline in that period; however, it
was studied by many rabbis and particularly by the Sephardim.
Jacob Mordecai was among the authorities; Joseph Schwartz belonged to the kabbalistic synagogue Beth El, and was a member of
the Vathikim (pious students). The young Hayyim at the age
of fifteen was invited to lead a kabbalistic discussion at that synagogue, out of which developed his first book, *Atereth Hakhamim,*
published two years later, primarily a kabbalistic explanation of
Rabbi Yehudah's saying *Kol mah she-bara he-Qadosh barukh Hu
be-olamo, zug bera'am.* (All that the Holy One created in His
world, he created in pairs). His second book, written at the age of
nineteen, *Neoth Yaakov,* presented to his father as a Purim gift,
was also written in a kabbalistic vein.

In the year 1877 there was a vehement controversy between
a prominent rabbi from Galicia and the head of the hassidic
beth din of Jerusalem on some interpretation of the *Sephiroth*
(Emanations). The head of the *beth din* requested Hayyim to take
part in the dispute, and he wrote the *Iggereth ha-Kabbalah.* This
was the beginning of a semi-critical attitude towards the Kabbalah,
and the search for a conciliation between Nahmanides' kabbalistic
philosophy and that of Maimonides. It attracted the attention of
David Halberstadt of Hungary, who greatly encouraged Hayyim
in his writings.

The blending of Kabbalah with rabbinic studies contributed,
I think, to the enrichment of the literature of that period. When
essentials are sifted from the non-essentials, there are deep thoughts
in the Kabbalah—a metaphysics of no lesser value than other
outstanding metaphysics by ancient and modern philosophers. One
could bring out points of similarity with the works of Henri
Bergson and of the present-day Existentialists. Sara Bayla made an
apt remark on the different approaches to the Kabbalah by the
Mithnaggedim and the *Hassidim*: "The former seek in the Kabbalah an explanation of the laws with which God governs the
world; the latter are more interested in that which transcends the
laws and makes for a supernatural world." Some of the hassidim

who lived near Sara Bayla's courtyard would actually practice certain physical stances which they thought would lead them to the mastery of the Kabbalah. At midnight they would move to a far-away corner on the hill and stand motionless with hands between their knees and their lips moving, absorbed in contemplation for a considerable time.

Sara Bayla feared that it was among such mystics that the spiritualists from abroad could make inroads. She remembered the stories about the Frankists which were current during her childhood. The missionaries, too, searched less among the rabbinists than among the mystics and Kabbalists. One was likely to discover some missionaries disguised as Jews around the *Beth El* synagogue.

The missionaries, especially some converted Jews from abroad, would also mingle with the Jewish crowd in the markets and cause panic each time they were discovered. Children would get scared for fear of having inadvertently talked with them or shaken hands. One little girl came home bewildered, fearing that she had met a *meshumad* in the house of her teacher. "How do you know it?" "I guessed it because he was dressed so beautifully and spoke Yiddish."

In 1879 Rabbi Joshua Loeb ben Benjamin Diskin (the Brisker Rav) engaged in a vigorous campaign against the missionaries, prohibiting the use of their hospitals and refusing Jewish burial to patients who died there. The children in Sara Bayla's courtyard were deeply concerned as to how these people would be gathered during the resurrection.

The wife of the Brisker Rav, an outstanding personality, asked Sara Bayla to join in the campaign, and she did. It is doubtful, however, whether the missionaries made any converts among the Jews, with all their offerings—hospitals, housing, employment, schools and subsidies. Sara Bayla wrote to Hildesheimer: "It is not exactly a question of conversion. The elderly Jews who came through journeys fraught with danger, and the young ones born here, would never abandon their Jewishness. But we must save from dishonesty and humiliating degradation those who are accepting services with the full intention of not repaying in the way they are expected to."

(e)   *Festival celebrations*:

The Seders in Jerusalem had a flavor of their own. Households would vie with each other as to which would go on latest into the night. Young children would sleep during the day so as to remain awake until the singing of the *Had Gadya*. The more intrepid ones participated even in the final chanting of Shir ha-Shirim.

Jacob Mordecai's comments on the Haggadah lent much distinction to his Seder. After midnight those who were through with their own Seders—among them several rabbis—would pour into Sara Bayla's house to listen to Jacob Mordecai's words. The Hassidim found particular delight in his interspersing some kabbalistic ideas in the Had Gadya song. Only the approaching dawn brought the seder to a conclusion.

An additional feature was the singing of certain passages of the Haggadah by one of Sara Bayla's guests endowed with a fine musical voice. He was a lonely pioneer living in a tiny hut with a sandy floor, and with little water or food, on a deserted beach which later became Tel-Aviv. Sara Bayla found that hut on one of her trips and discovered that pioneer, to whom she gave moral and financial support. She also engaged him to join her household on every festival so as to enhance with his music the beauty of the Jewish verses in the minds of the growing youth. His songs of the Seder were often repeated by the children while at play. But what seemed to have most strongly impressed one little girl was that at the Seder she was eating the same sandwich (korekh) which Hillel Ha-Nasi ate so long ago. With each bite she would murmur to herself, half aloud, "I am eating the same matsah as Hillel Ha-Nasi." At one seder, when the household caught some sleep before dawn, she awoke to touch with her lips the sacred glass of wine set for Eliyahu ha-Navi (the Prophet Elijah). Half asleep, she consumed its whole contents and slept again. On the following morning there was quite some consternation as to what happened to Eliyahu's glass of wine.

In my student days in Paris I met one of those Jerusalem youths who, dazzled by the outside world, became somehow estranged from the habits of his early years. He told me that invariably a sadness overcame him on seder nights as he recalled the fascinating ones at Sara Bayla's household when he was still a young child.

Hayyim's last book, published when he had reached the age of eighty, was the Haggadah with rich comments and interpretations, and tracing of the source of each passage.

(f) The event of the great solar cycle (*Mahzor ha-Gadol*), taking place at intervals of twenty-eight years, was celebrated almost like a festival. It was a momentous occasion especially in the eyes of children, who would consider it a mark of distinction to have been born in that year. Sara Bayla's terrace was the meeting place of the town for that great occasion, when all would gather to bless the sun as it rose. Hayyim refers to it in connection with the date of his birth. In an article thanking rabbis from abroad for celebrating his seventieth birthday, he asks how they knew it. "I must confess," he writes, "that I myself do not know the exact year of my birth. This I know, that the year I became *bar mitsvah* was the year of the great solar cycle. Chief Rabbi Auerbach came to the terrace in front of our house to bless the sun at the moment of sunrise. My father took me over to him to bless me. After his blessing he said to me, 'This will be to you a bright sign of long life, to know that in the year you become bar mitsvah we pronounce with you the benediction, "Blessed is the Creator of the lights."' Even though this will never be forgotten by me, I do not remember whether it was in the month of Nisan that preceded or followed Elul. My bar mitsvah celebration was on the eleventh of Elul."

(g) *Extension and Growth*: Sara Bayla sensed the vast potentialities of the colonies and was very much concerned that nothing Jewish be lost in the process of their growth. On numerous occasions she arranged with the colonies to have halakhic lectures delivered by the younger element of her Yeshivah on matters pertaining to land and cognate subjects. The lecturers were usually assisted by Jacob Mordecai, who would work out the material for them. Their own young gifted grandson, around thirteen years old (a prodigy), would sometimes accompany Sara Bayla on her trips and deliver a lecture of high talmudic merit, prepared by himself. A tiny little girl insisted on going with them so as to see "Jewish cows and Jewish goats." She saw some in Jerusalem when her mother fetched the milk, but those were "Arab ones."

When the railway from Jerusalem to Jaffa, built by a French company, opened in 1892, Sara Bayla, one of the first passengers, carried along with her a number of prayer books for the colonies.

In a letter to Baron Rothschild—not Edmond but Wilhelm of Frankfurt a. M. with whom she usually corresponded—she called attention to the urgent need of larger water supplies for the colonies.

It seems that Sara Bayla was ahead of her times in her awareness of the importance of abundant and pure water. She and Sha'ul Benjamin made several attempts to have the government provide a proper water supply for Jerusalem. During the cholera epidemic of 1865 she advocated boiling the drinking water, and exerted pressure upon the owner of the public bathhouse—the only one in town—adjoining the *hurvah,* to change the water more frequently and maintain sanitary conditions. On her own premises there were around the cistern under a covered roof a number of large tin tubs for bathing purposes.

(h) *Table Conversation*: Problems and scholarly works from abroad also entered into the discussions. The controversy over Zechariah Frankel's *Darkhei ha-Mishnah* (The Ways of the Mishnah, Leipzig, 1859; with a supplement and index, 1867) extended to Jerusalem too. Jacob Mordecai regarded his position as untenable. That it was discussed at his table is indicated by his son Yitzhak's quoting Sara Bayla's words to Wilhelm Posen of Frankfurt a. M., who had gathered a number of her pertinent remarks. More by intuition than from knowledge, Sara Bayla had concluded the table discussion by saying, "Samson Raphael Hirsch is an unshaken pillar, but Zechariah seems a little puzzling. His love for Judaism does not sound like *Ve-Ahavta bekhol levavkha uvekhol nafshekha.* He seems to separate the present from the past and then seeks to build a bridge between them." What she did not know was that some of Schelling's, Schlegel's and Schleiermacher's romantic ideas had seeped into his historical conception of Judaism, and led to misconceptions.

Frankel's Introduction, *Mevo ha-Yerushalmi* (Breslau, 1870), caused a fresh study of the Palestinian Talmud in Jacob Mordecai's Yeshivah. Jacob Mordecai's copy of Frankel's book was filled with notes, written in tiny letters on the margins of almost every page, pointing to some errors of interpretation. It caused him to give a number of discourses and to renew his insistence on the need of a better understanding through a more extensive study of the Palestinian Talmud, which had been somehow eclipsed by the Babylonian. Later on Jacob Mordecai's sons joined him in this effort.

Elijah ben Solomon, known as the Gaon of Vilna, was among those talked about at Sara Bayla's table as well as in other households. Speculations were numerous on his having abandoned his trip to Palestine after he had started out for it. On his Jahrzeit, Sara Bayla would light a little oil lamp to his blessed memory, praying that his intention to come to Erets Yisrael be considered fulfilled. She rejected the prevailing opinion that the hardship of poor food on board the ship may have been among the deterring causes. He certainly would have put up with it, as did other travelers. She inclined towards the belief held by Jacob Mordecai that it was probably due to his realization that he could neither tolerate nor successfully fight in his old age the predominance of Kabbalah and Hassidism. While he was attracted to the Kabbalah, he could not go as far as Luria and his successors.

From the letter he wrote from Berlin to his mother, wife and household, one may infer that not least of his apprehensions was that the growing youth in the family might not receive the proper moral discipline during his absence. Deep morality and pious mysticism permeate every line of this letter, which also reflects the genuine reverence in which the Holy Land was held by him. The family must spiritually prepare itself for the trip, should God grant them the privilege of going "where one must walk in the way of the Lord without the slightest deviation." (*Ki sham tsarikh lelekh meod bedarkhei ha-Shem*).

(i) *Overseers of the Chicken Fat*: It was customary with comfortable families to spare a little chicken fat each Friday and gather it in tight jars for distribution on Passover among the needy. For lack of refrigeration much of it would get rancid. Sara Bayla had a large hole dug out in the cave, adjoining the cistern, lined with solid salt on all sides and with a cover of a huge chunk of salt encased in cement. All the chicken fat gathered in Jerusalem was stored in that cave, every little bit brought there by each housekeeper. To facilitate matters, a group of six outstanding women appointed themselves overseers. Each in turn would go from house to house, collect the fat in an earthen jar and store it in Sara Bayla's "Pesah Cavern", as they called it.

Before Yom Kippur Sara Bayla would also donate the roosters that served for the *kaparoth* ceremony. Several housekeepers followed her example. This fowl was portioned out to poor, elderly people and served ready to eat, for kitchen utensils and charcoal were not easy to obtain. When a *She'elah* (kashruth question) would occur, a consultation would be arranged among the authoritative rabbis. One sickly, poor old man wanted to make sure that there was no consideration of leniency on account of his weak condition if a she'elah came up in connection with his portion.

(j) *Tsemah and the First Stationery Store*: Next to Arye Leib's pharmacy, the entrance-way to Tsemah's little stationery store (5x12 feet), on the road to the Kothel Ma'aravi, was the most popular gathering place. The neat little packages of paper, envelopes, quill-pens and other miscellanies filled every inch of space. But the center of attraction was the little newsstand at the door with copies of *Havatseleth* and sometimes of *Ha-Maggid* and *Ha-Melits*. Some came to buy the papers, others to skim them over or to get the gist from Tsemah when they could not afford to buy them. On his way down the long trail from the *Havatseleth* office to his store, with the heavy bundle of newspapers, he would read the newly published copy so that he might honestly advise whether it was worth spending the two pennies for. He would also warn his customers when the ink he sold happened to be watery. When one brought from him more than one bottle of soft drink at a time, he would gently remind him that a Jew should not indulge in excesses. Occasionally he would let the children choose the candy on the tempting little table at the door, and give their pennies back to them. There were a large circular string of rock candy, smaller rings of halvah (corn fudge), a dozen or so sugar coated almonds, sugar canes, heaps of toasted melon seeds, and, for festival occasions, candied orange peel too. When the sales grew in number, Tsemah donated refreshments for some of the Siyyums. On a Siyyum day, a note would be pinned to the door, "Closed for the Siyyum . . . Join us there." At sunset he would run up the hill to Sara Bayla's Yeshivah to join the first shift of the night session, which lasted till midnight.

Tsemah came from Hungary to Jerusalem because his parents, advanced in age, wanted to spend their last years there. His whole fortune amounted to fifty marks (about ten dollars) and his mother's long diamond earrings, a family heirloom, of which he hoped never to deprive her. He consulted Sara Bayla about opening a dry goods store, since the two others were prospering and also because the wholesale merchants at Damascus were not hard on credit. The total absence of ready-made clothes was an advantage to retailers. Sara Bayla felt that business conditions pointed towards expansion into new fields rather than duplication, and suggested a stationery store. She recalled a small back-entrance to a large house leased to Jewish tenants for ninety years (Hazakah) by an Arab landlord. If the inside door of that back entrance, which was never used, could be shut off, Tsemah would have his stationery store.

The children of Sara Bayla's courtyard would try to assist Tsemah in carrying his newspaper bundles. His repaying their kindness with candy put them in a dilemma which called forth several joint conferences of boys and girls. Usually boys would keep apart from girls, but the difficult choice between the candy and the mitsvah for the errand required much thinking. If the reward is accepted, would the good deed, which was not motivated by the expectation of candy, carry the mitsvah with it? There were many pros and cons. Those in favor of the candy argued that Tsemah being neither sick, nor old, nor a woman, the mitsvah might not be such a weighty one. They finally hit upon a compromise: The candy should be accepted, but eaten only during their reading lessons, so that the Torah should be sweet in their mouths.

The above details are like slices cut from a moving life whose faith and outlook are that of *sub specie aeternitatis*. Sara

Bayla paraphrased *Dor holekh vedor ba, One generation goeth and the other cometh,* "but the Jewish stream flows from one to the other." These were among her last words.

Rabbi Samuel Salant was among the first ones to be immediately notified when Sara Bayla's sudden end seemed in sight. He said that "She lived and died with the Torah in her heart; among the most outstanding escorts to her grave were her own great work and well-earned fame." In a letter of condolence to her son Hayyim, he recorded her words of a few days before her death when she happened to call on him. She expressed the hope and faith that the newcomers would be re-generated through their own offspring who would eventually be imbued with the holy spirit of the land. He also wrote that he echoed a loud "Amen" to the touching blessing of Hakham Bashi Saul Jacob Elyashar, who exclaimed at her death, "Blessed be God for having blessed us with such a great pious woman in our midst." This was a heroic generation, in which every individual sensed in the life of the comunity the essence of his own.

REFERENCES

It is regrettable that a period so vibrant with Jewish life and struggling so hard to keep it intact should remain an obscure chapter in the Jewish annals. Whatever is written about it is without the proper perspective of the people and the times. With lack of insight, events too are likely to be distorted. Even the *ha-Maggid* and *ha-Melits* did not always see them in their true light. I have therefore tried to gain direct contact with the personalities themselves through their own writings and through the contemporary periodicals of Palestine. I do not lay claim to a full study of their Talmudic writings, but a careful reading of the introductions, prefaces, concluding chapters, pros and cons of debates, and a familiarity with the trends of thought, brought me nearer to them in my observations. The very choice of subjects, their systematic or involved manner of treatment, whether in the light of Halakhah, Kabbalah, or a blending of both; the keen interest in Geography of some, in ancient manuscripts of others, the deep concern with philosophic-ethical writings, the vehement

public circulars, the large correspondence with leaders and philanthropists abroad, the form of authors' dedications, the funeral
eulogies, the items in the strictly orthodox *Havatseleth* and other
journals on the natural sciences and the translations in their col-
umns of German and French essays—all these are the background
of the picture. It was not my aim to unfold a complete panorama,
but to sketch a picturesque Jewish woman as one of the multi-
colored figures of that time.

I do not indicate volume and page references to the *Havatseleth*
and other papers from Palestine, because there is hardly an issue of
these papers which does not refer to one or another of the outstanding personalities, or contain a contribution by them. I specify, however, the *Havatseleth* of 1879-80, with a series of weekly articles
by Jacob Mordecai on *Avodath ha-Adamah* (tilling of the soil), because these reflect the transition between that period and the suc-
ceeding one, *via the halakhah*. These articles gather, discuss,
and interpret every halakhic item relating to the soil, with the
conclusion that the *mitsvah* of settling on the land is not necessarily restricted to *tsaddikim* (pietists) alone, but embraces all those
who in their daily life wish to observe the Torah.

Sara Bayla is given a prominent place in publications on outstanding Palestinian women of the nineteenth and twentieth
centuries. She figures in contemporary periodicals in relation to
events of the day, and is mentioned in the writings which treat of
her husband and family. I also drew from some of her correspondence with her son Hayyim, from letters by him, and from
talks in past years with him and particularly with his wife Eva
who came to the house of her mother-in-law at the age of twelve
and always cherished the memories of her relations with her.
My own impressions of Sara Bayla, in my early childhood, are still
vivid with me. They were confirmed by the many talks I had
in the course of the years with children who grew up in her
courtyard, with relatives and with a number of her friends, who
speak of those times with deep nostalgia.

THE GAON OF ROGATCHOV

By Saul Silber

THE GAON OF ROGATCHOV

By Saul Silber

"No mystery was too profound for him."

The famous Gaon, Joseph Rosen, of blessed memory, who was rabbi in Dvinsk, was an extraordinary person, who seemed to belong to the realm of legend rather than to reality. . . Only in fantasy could one envision that long, long ago might have lived such a person, for our time appears unequal to the development of so scintillating a mind. So thorough was his mastery of all the departments of Torah, so dynamic was his intellect, that it is unbelievable that a man who lived in the present generation could muster them for the highest abstractions of theoretical Torah lore. As a rule, even the greatest Talmudic scholars are concerned primarily with the usefulness and practicality of its concepts. To the Gaon of Rogatchov these values of our age were utterly valueless, even in the field of Torah; he dedicated his entire life to the essences of Talmudic principles. In the highest sense of the term, he studied Torah for its own sake, until he became an amazing phenomenon, towering above the scholars of many generations.

Even among men of his own type, the Gaon of Rogatchov was thoroughly original. He gave all of his brilliant talents to the study of Torah. He almost succeeded in liberating himself utterly from the world around him, even from inescapable human requirements, such as eating and sleeping, in order to live for his studies. The universe as a material body was erased from his consciousness. It was as though he had wrapped up the entire world in the pages of the law. The ancient tradition that the Creator looked at the words of the Torah and fashioned the earth in accordance with them, closely describes his philosophy.

It mattered not how one engaged him in conversation, the Gaon would draw him into his Torah-net. The only significance he would ascribe to medicine, astronomy, history, commerce, politics or sociology was the extent to which they figured in the Babylonian or Palestinian Talmud, in their commentaries or codes.

395

Whenever it was necessary to prove a point or to illustrate
a situation that arose in the common experience of those about him,
he instinctively drew material from a hundred sources in Talmudic
literature that others might never have noticed. All that he was
and all that he possessed, he invested in Torah, and everything
that could not be fitted into that framework was beneath his notice
and unworthy of his time.

Who can undertake to appraise the greatness of his spiritual
powers? In all history one will rarely find so remarkable a combination of the qualities of genius as were embodied in the person
of the Gaon of Rogatchov. I have not the temerity to describe all
of his gifts, but I propose to discuss four of them, any single one
of which would have earned for him the traditional description,
"The only one in a generation." The four are: A. Super-diligence.
B. Phenomenal memory. C. Swiftness of comprehension. D. Keen
sense of logic.

These four qualities transform him into a kind of genius
that soared high above our own age, even though his biography
identifies him with it, and even though one can daily meet
people who spoke with him and had the supreme privilege of
receiving his instruction.

A. *Super-Diligence*

To study—that is, to concentrate all of one's thoughts for
a number of hours upon one subject—is a highly difficult process.
This fact was as well known ages ago as it is today. As the
Jewish sages expressed it, "Torah weakens man's physical power."
Only men of superior intellect have the power to think, probe and
thoroughly analyze a situation without interruption, through many
hours; their intellectual energies are drawn upon for the heavy
work of the brain. Whenever that brain is called upon to be creative for a still greater period of time, they seek to refresh their
mental apparatus, in the interval between major objectives of attention, by turning to subjects and ideas of a lighter sort. But the
Gaon of Rogatchov had a brain that never could grow weary—a
divine gift, by which his understanding never knew fatigue. The

quality of being able to concentrate all thoughts for many hours without becoming worn out was present in an equally great measure in the Gaon of Vilna alone.

To study more than twenty hours each day, to permit oneself no other interest in the world, to eat less than is necessary for the health of a little child—this is application, indeed! He would write down his comments, but in a very brief form, in order to conserve time. Thus vast mountains of original interpretations would be condensed into a brief phrase, "Refer to such and such a passage." For the same reason that the Gaon of Vilna penned his insights in brief notes—in order to save time, which is too precious to be wasted—the Gaon of Rogatchov reduced pages of explanation to very few words. Every moment belongs to eternity, and we dare not waste it on anything other than the study of Torah. To sleep more than an absolute minimum is fatal to the soul. So tremendous was his diligence that he did not study sitting but throughout his life he studied standing. When seated at his study table, he might fall asleep; hence he was on his feet throughout the night, and he studied aloud, as an additional precaution.

It is reported that during his first years as the rabbi in Dvinsk, hundreds of people would assemble during the night near the windows of his home and remain there for hours in order to listen to the heavenly "Voice of Torah" that rang out as he stood in his room and studied. Often the entire night would pass by, the stars would slowly be extinguished in the heavens, the morning star would send its heralding rays to announce the approaching sunrise, and the Gaon of Rogatchov would still be standing and studying. His was an entire life of study, with the Torah as the entire soul of the man. He could not turn away from these holy studies even for a moment.

Intellectual qualities that never grow weary and never seem to be tapped to their utmost resources constitute a phenomenon that is encountered only once in a century, and such diligence could rarely be discovered even in the greatest rabbis of the ages. In his time the Gaon of Rogatchov was the unique personification of uninterrupted Torah study.

B. *Phenomenal Memory*

He was, furthermore, "The only one in a generation" by virtue of his remarkable memory. His phenomenal knowledge of all that went into the oral law, beginning with the Babylonian and Palestinian Talmuds down to the later Talmudic commentators—in other words his knowledge of all the Talmudic literature that was created in a span of fifteen hundred years—constitutes, when one considers how thoroughly he knew the material, a marvel that transcends the ordinary human understanding.

Our concept of knowing thoroughly the contents of any given volume differs entirely from the way in which the Gaon of Rogatchov, divinely blessed, interpreted the idea of knowledge. Ours is a poor and weak concept by comparison. It would seem that never in his entire career did he forget something that he had seen, if even no more than once. In truth he was what is described in the Ethics of Fathers "a cemented cistern that loses not a single drop." He knew by heart every Halakhic discussion, by sentence and phrase. He could quote complete texts from all departments of the Torah without the slightest error. And greater than the wonder of his remembering the text everywhere is our consciousness that within the mind of the Gaon his total knowledge was so exceptionally vivid that it constituted, as it were, a living organism.

All of the different discussions and debates, the inquiries and their conclusions, the perplexities and their solutions, all the ideas and the syllogisms that are found by the tens of thousands scattered through the volumes of halakhah—all of these constantly hovered before his eyes. "All were surveyed in a single glance." It was never necessary for him to search for a passage. In his hand, as it were, there was always to be found the key to the countless treasurehouses of Torah wisdom. "No secret was hidden from him."

In his amazing volume *"Tsofnath Paaneah"*, which deals with the Code of Maimonides, one can see factual knowledge of Talmudic literature which is startling. There is one subject he discusses in his volume in connection with which almost 2500 rabbinical quotations occur (The Complete Epistle, section 4), an achievement that probably has no parallel in all of rabbinical literature. We must not forget at this point that the Gaon wrote at great speed, without stopping to check his sources, because he drew upon his infallible memory.

One of the great scholars of his time once wittily observed about the Gaon of Rogatchov: "There is nothing remarkable about the clarity of his recollection, because every portion of the law is being reviewed by him in the immediate present, and he can thus easily review the entire law each day, because he remembers all of it by heart." So mighty was his memory that he was able, whenever a Talmudic subject was brought up for discussion, immediately to quote all the passages in the Talmud where this item is mentioned, immediately to indicate how the item is intertwined with, and related to, other matters of Talmudic discussion that have a bearing upon it; and if the item was one about which the early authorities expressed differences of opinion, he was able to list the various opinions and to indicate how these individual opinions of the authorities are an extension of their respective viewpoints in portions of the Talmud that affect the one in question. If, for example, somebody would mention to him the word "rental", he would tell him how many types of rental there could be of chattels, of personal service, of articles that were devoted to holy purposes, and he would proceed to describe the hundreds upon hundreds of laws that branch out from these initial concepts, mentioning the numerous differences of opinion that have arisen through the centuries among the authorities on this subject.

He was in his own person the complete library of the Talmud, and his knowledge was as accurately classified as that of an encyclopedia with the index to all the topics at his swift call. Whatever his eye saw was kept forever. The memory of the Gaon of Rogatchov was the memory of a genius who is "the only one in a generation".

C. Swiftness of Comprehension

God also blessed him with lightning-like comprehension.

Whoever has seen the Gaon of Rogatchov discussing a point in Talmud has seen what was probably the mightiest dynamic force in the Torah world. The Talmud describes one of the great sages with the phrase, "Every bird that flew over him while he studied was consumed in flames," and this remarkable expression applies also to this superior genius of our own time. Whenever the Gaon of Rogatchov debated matters of Torah—and that is precisely what he did all his life—he became transformed into a fiery Mt. Sinai, from which millions of Torah sparks were emitted with amazing speed and power.

Each spark was an insight into Torah understanding, and each flash of lightning revealed a new approach to the teachings of our sages. At such a moment there stood before us a phenomenon impossible to describe. Here is a shrunken individual, whose movements are extraordinarily swift, and he seems to be toppling mountains with his thin bony hands, uprooting them from their bases and rearranging them to suit his powers of reasoning. He does not need to leaf through volumes, he goes not to consult the writings of the Rambam, he merely waves his magic hand and releases a spark from his glowing eyes, and all the passages reveal themselves immediately. They do not come forward unruffled; one could see these thousands of quotations rushing forward and overtaking one another with the tremendous speed of the Niagara waterfalls, all of them demanding expression impatiently, with only the tardy organs of speech obstructing their immediate physical manifestation.

The Gaon of Rogatchov seemed helpless in such a moment, since he could not give utterance to even a small part of all that was stored in his brilliant mind.

Of many great scholars it is customary to say that they were "Marvelous swimmers in the sea of the Talmud," but about the Gaon of Rogatschov we should say more pointedly that "The Talmud was a stormy sea in his mind"; its waves were ever restless, rising one above the other, and dashing with terrific force from some secret source to the shores.

His comprehension was so lightning-like in its swiftness, that whenever anybody wanted to raise a new point or ask him a question pertaining to his studies, he would immediately anticipate what was coming and exclaim, "Aha! No doubt you are going to point out that Rashi in yonder passage seems to contradict my interpretation; well, there is really no difficulty involved," and he would proceed to show that the question that was about to be asked was not valid. His exceptional mental powers began to pile up with astonishing speed hundreds of passages to refute the questioner, until the latter felt he would grow dizzy with mere listening. To the observer it appeared as though his mind worked with so much dynamic force that he himself must have lost control over it.

A well-known sage of our time once told me the following about the comprehensive genius of the Gaon. This rabbi had been spending some time with him in a Talmudic discussion, and, in putting a question to him, had remarked that there was proof for this theory is a certain Tosafoth (Thirteenth-Century commentary on the Talmud). "A Tosafoth?" the Rogatchover muttered hastily. "Which Tosafoth?" And he began to review rapidly in his mind every volume in the Talmud, all the discussions of the 3000 folio pages in several moments, and finally saying with absolute conviction, "There is no such Tosafoth in the entire Talmud." The scholar then told the Gaon that he believed that one could prove the point from the Tosafoth in the tractate Arakhin. Before he could even mention the page, the Gaon swiftly told him "Oh, you mean chapter so and so, but I assure you that it really has no bearing on what we have been talking about," and he heaped up a number of quotations to establish that his own interpretation of the given Tosafoth was the proper and logical one.

The marvelous memory that he possessed was joined in a happy union with his lightning-like comprehension, and the latter was also justly characterized as "the only one in a generation."

D. *Keen Sense of Logic*

In his very early years the Gaon of Rogatchov was reputed to be an exceptional genius. When the Hassidic congregation of Dvinsk sought a spiritual leader who might stand on a par with the rabbi of the Mithnagdic group, the world-famous Gaon, Rabbi Meïr Simhah, they selected the twenty-nine-year-old genius of Rogatchov, as he was then known in the world of scholars. At the time of the appointment people marveled at his amazing diligence, but they had not yet learned to appreciate the boundless thoroughness of his knowledge, the swiftness of his thinking, or the exactitude of his logic.

Soon, however, those who entered into Torah discussions with him became conscious of the limitless familiarity he displayed in dealing with Talmudic passages, and many began to concede that they had difficulty in keeping up with the speed of his mentality and that consequently they were unable to grasp the novelty of his interpretations. He even created a new terminology that the scholars of the time described as heretofore unkown. There was a natural tendency (not unusual among intellectuals) to suspect these new concepts, difficult to comprehend, of being valueless; so that in scholarly spheres a considerable amount of whispering circulated to the effect that he was undeniably a high genius in the extensiveness of his knowledge, and his logic raced like an arrow from the bow, but his new interpretations were somewhat confused. By playing upon his family name, Rosen (meaning in Aramic "secrets") one of the famous rabbis of the period observed that the learning of the Rogatchover was in the class called, *"Rozin d'Rozin"*—that is, a mystery within an enigma. Thus the Rogatchover passed through the stages of suffering that are the lot of all exceptional geniuses. Indeed a long period of time must elapse before people become fair in judging their abilities.

However, recognition of his logic finally came. Although his type of analysis differed considerably from what was common in the field of Talmud it was acknowledged that in every page of his writings one could find a large number of brilliant ideas, whereas one was satisfied to find two or three such ingenuities in an entire chapter of the average famous scholar. On occasion he would inject into a single topic more than a hundred suggestions deeply rooted in compelling logic. (See Tsofnath Paaneah, Hilkhoth Terumoth, I.) He fashioned hundreds of new expressions, and into his distinctive terminology he introduced the new thoughts that came as the fruit of his analytical reasoning powers. His eye never failed to detect the distinctions that must be logically made between the different aspects of the same subject, while conversely he sought out the logical kinship between apparently widely unrelated topics. By seeking for the root of the Talmudic idea, he proved that many a passage that seemed independent was to be linked with other passages. (See Tsofnath Paaneah, section A: The Number of the Commandments according to the Rambam.) Whenever his distinctions were superfine, one would have to surpass himself mentally in order to grasp them.

Should anyone desire to investigate the psychological factors that account for the choice made by the Gaon of Rogatchov of pouring out the powers of his spirit primarily into logic, rather than into any other mental capacity, he will no doubt conclude that the Rogatchover was above all a thinker in abstractions. His ideal was what Kant described as "pure reason", that is, reason utterly divorced from every material concept. Such paths as wound up at practical goals and concrete results did not attract him. for they would not lead him to the things he sought. He was not looking for decisions applied to mundane life; his great mind would not occupy itself with applied law, since it represents practical value. His spiritual world was made of different stuff. His ideal was to get to the very bottom of the system in the tens of thousands of subjects that figure in the marvelous ramifications of our Oral Law. He searched the contents of the Torah to uncover the intellectual intimacy between disparate theses, and by virtue of his gigantic reasoning power he found what he sought. Frequently a note of reference in his writings seems to the superficial observer a mere display of thorough knowledge, but deeper study makes it clear that the reference is meant to add depth of comprehension to the matter under immediate analysis.

It was as though he believed that the Almighty had thrust upon him the special function of preserving the Torah from being forgotten in Israel through the application of his special method. Torah analysis in all its logical depth was his very soul, the pure reason of his thinking. He felt there was no other way in which man could liberate himself from the heavy practicality of human existence. The sum total of man's being is to involve his entire life in Torah, to know what the Torah says, and to enjoy the spiritual delight of finding out why it says so. That is the meaning of the verse, *"And thou shalt meditate in it day and night."*

Some years ago, when I was returning from Dvinsk after I visited him for the last time, I remarked to one of the great scholars of our day that God had given our generation a beautiful gift, only we were not prepared to accept it. My suggestion was at that time that the Jewish people ought to select two outstanding Talmudists and several scholars in the more general fields of Jewish knowledge, who would be appointed to live with the Rogatchover in his home. The Talmudists would be responsible for writing down his Torah ideas, for he had a very fascinating way of expounding his thoughts. Whoever could follow him, whether for a few moments or for an hour, would greedily swallow his spoken words and his analytic demonstrations. He would, so to speak, be refreshing a thirsty mind at a fountain of living waters. If we would thus precisely and thoroughly record at least some portion of his logical innovations, we would enrich Talmudic literature by tens of invaluable volumes.

The second group of scholars would draw from him various opinions about other spheres of Jewish learning. It would thus have been possible to record his significant words dealing with historical research.

We lost an opportunity which comes to a people perhaps once in a century, when we failed to do this. In his death we lost not only him but a chance that was unparalleled in our time. The only hope now is that some great scholar will arise to select from the writings of the Rogatchover the thousands of intellectual pearls scattered through them, whose luster derives from the logic of his genius and his marvelous mind.

There is but one accurate summary to be made in connection with all the Torah-glories gracing the Gaon of Rogatchov—"The only one in a generation."

SARA SCHENIERER

By JUDITH GRUNFELD-ROSENBAUM

SARA SCHENIERER

By Judith Grunfeld-Rosenbaum

SARA SCHENIERER—THE STORY OF
A GREAT MOVEMENT

I

When Sara Schenierer, the founder of the Beth Jacob Movement, left this world, she was fifty-two years old. She died after a short illness in a Vienna Hospital in the midst of her work, having led the movement since 1923. When the news of her passing spread, thousands upon thousands of girls and women who had been praying fervently for her recovery, felt that their own life cord had been cut and that they had personally received a paralyzing blow. Tens of thousands had known her personally, had clung to her as to a personal intimate friend and had been known to her. They were her children; they knew her teaching, her manner of speech and her personal ways of life. They had her picture imprinted upon their minds—a living picture, giving stimulus together with vision. Sara Schenierer died an hour before Shabbath. She had asked for the candles to be brought to her bedside, and for the last time she had lit them. They were still burning when her soul returned to God.

Tens of thousands of women and girls knew then that to the end of their days they would feel the eye of Sara Schenierer watching them, her wishes urging fulfillment; that her questions to them would for ever demand the right answer and that they would have to live their lives in such a manner as to be able to meet the eye of Sara Schenierer again in Eternity. This was the impact of Sara Schenierer upon the women of her generation. The vibration of this encounter between a great woman and her disciples still exists and can still be felt.

When I first met Sara Schenierer, she was a woman of forty-two. She wore a plain black dress and her very lively face was framed in black silk, in a motherly, old fashioned way. You would not think of her as a personality in her own right, but as someone's mother who had come to greet you. Liveliness, simplicity and motherliness were the first impressions.

We met on the green meadows of the Carpathian Hills in midsummer. I had come a long way by train and coach to meet her, and she was walking along the path that led from the tiniest hamlet I had ever seen. She was coming with a group of thirty girls to meet the coach that brought me. I was the young teacher from Western Europe who was willing to spend some weeks of the University vacations in the Polish mountains to help that singular woman of whom almost legendary reports had reached me. It was not really a coach, it was a cart and horse that brought me from the railway station into that remote village, never recorded on any map. There I was, travelling along fields and meadows under the blue sky on a very hot summer day, passing lonely gypsy cottages and caravans to find the forlorn village where Sara Schenierer spent the summer in primitive huts with some fifty pupils.

I had heard that Sara Schenierer was a remarkable woman who had formerly been a dressmaker, and had then studied, on her own initiative, by night, in order eventually to convey to others as a teacher by day her newly acquired knowledge; that she shared her own room and food with a group of young women while training them to be teachers for the coming generation. What would she be like and by what qualities would she rule and impress her charges?

These were the thoughts that had puzzled me ever since I had decided to travel to Poland to meet her. I knew that she had already gathered fifty girls who lived with her and were content with the very frugal meals which a dressmaker's savings could supply for them. I also had been told that they were entirely absorbed in the new life with their teacher. What was it that this woman possessed that made her such a compelling force?

I watched the black-clad round figure of a little mother walking along with a swarm of girls round her, all talking, all bustling with life. My cart stopped by the roadside; they came swarming round the cart. Friendly words of welcome and greeting were called out to me. I was lifted out of the rickety cart and the small figure of a mother in Israel embraced me and bid me welcome. The girls lifted my luggage, paid the driver and I found myself seated on a wooden bench under a tree, in front of a little cottage, the "Mother" sitting next to me and I already under her spell. Whilst I am writing now—twenty-five years later—I can still smell the fragrance of the summer afternoon that came from the freshly cut grass around us. I can almost feel the sensation—a very strong and pleasant one—of being drawn into Sara Schenierer's circle, and my heart infused me with the very strong desire to coöperate in the great work that was being revealed to me.

Sara Schenierer told me that she was indeed a dressmaker—that she had many customers, but that when they came to her for fittings she found herself philosophising about them. She watched them as they looked critically into the mirror. As to dress, they knew what they wanted. They were very particular as to every little detail of fashion or workmanship. But, the little dressmaker mused, after the fittings were over and the ladies had departed, did they know what they really needed? She envisioned them beautifully dressed in body but spiritually in rags and tatters. If she could only help them to see where their real happiness lay!

As she went about the little town, she found no kindred spirit among the women. The older women seemed to be withdrawing into a spiritual world of their own—the younger longed to be "modern," untutored in Torah, and with a smattering of modern "science." In the Polish gymnasium they seemed to feel that Judaism was merely a useless restraint, a fetter, a shell that obfuscated and that must be burst to let in the light.

She felt that only because of ignorance were they ready to lose their priceless heritage, to exchange pure gold for mere tinsel. "I felt I must help them," she said "to see that they were ready to give up, not a shell but the very substance without which they and their dear ones would perish. But I was without education. I lacked the gift of speech to convey my convictions."

"Coming home from work, I used to meet my brother returning home from the Yeshivah. He is discussing something with a friend; the discussion gets more lively and more heated. They enter the living room and my father joins in the discussion. They are now pitting argument against argument, knowledge against knowledge—and they understand the meaning of each other's phrases.   .

"My sister, who is a pupil in a Polish gymnasium, is reading a book. She seems very much interested. My mother's hands clasp the 'Ts'enah u-R'enah' (Special Bible Lessons for Women). I go to Mrs. G. across the road. She has six daughters. Of the eldest one she never speaks. She left the house two years ago. When she had gone they found a letter from her: 'Forgive me, Mammeshy, I cannot bear the narrow home any more. I have gone to live with my friends.' She married without *Huppah* and *Kiddushin*. The second daughter, the fourth and the fifth, are in constant touch with her. They worship their heroic sister. They wish they could follow her. Only love for the poor, shaken, heart-broken mother makes them pretend that they belong to her.

"But there is still the youngest, our Esciu. She is twelve. She is not yet aware of all the conflicts. And Sara Schenierer together with Mrs. G. look at the sleeping Esciu. This one we may be able to keep. Her eyes still shine with that glow when the Sabbath comes in. How can we preserve that glow? How can we open her maturing and searching mind to the truth and beauty of the Torah? Where is the magic key to open up our treasures for her and all the others of her age who are still their parents' true children, but will soon awake from childhood's sleep, will hear the trumpets that are blown in the streets and market-places?" Sara Schenierer returns home. Her thoughts are of Esciu. She knows there are thousands like her.

"And we pass through the Elul days. The trains which run to the little 'Shtedtlach' (towns) where the Rebbes live are crowded. Thousands of Hassidim are on their way to them to spend the Yamim Noraim (Solemn Holy Days) with the Rebbe. Every day sees new crowds of old men and young men in the hassidic garb, eager to secure a place in the train, eager to spend the holiest days in the year in the atmosphere of their Rebbe, to be able to extract from it as much holiness as possible. Fathers and sons travel and those who can afford it make this journey several times a year. Thus they are drawn to Ger, to Belz, to Alexander, to Bobo, to all these places that had been made citadels of concentrated religious life, dominated by the leading figure of a Rebbe's personality.

"And we stay at home, the wives, the daughters with the little ones. We have an empty Yomtov. It is bare of Jewish intellectual concentration. The women have never learned anything about the spiritual content that is concentrated within a Jewish festival. The mother goes to Shul. The service rings faintly into the fenced and boarded-off women's gallery. There is much crying by the elderly women. The young girls look on them as beings of a different century. Youth and desire to live a full life shoot up violently in the strong-willed young personalities. Outside the Shul, the young girls stand chattering; they walk away from Shul where their mothers pour out their vague and heavy feelings. They leave behind them the wailing of the older generation and follow the urge for freedom and self-expression. Further and further away from Shul they go, further away to the dancing, tempting light of a fleeting joy.

"And when the father comes home from the Rebbe, he is too dazzled to see what will come out one day into the glaring light, revealing a breach that has gone beyond repair. While the men bend and sway in the rhythm that tradition has created, and their heads are held aloft into almost visionary heights, the girls go dancing, skipping, dreaming on in their own way, along the path of a world which is wide open, unfenced and pitiless. Their paths and the parents' paths may never meet."

Sara Schenierer's mind is troubled by that picture. She sees how fathers and daughters are strangers, living in different worlds; how the happiness of family life is shattered by the breaking away of the maturing girls. And the thought is conceived in her mind to collect the little girls early enough, when they are still hiding their little curly tops behind mother's apron and still sit on their father's lap, when they are still tucked in snugly in the home atmosphere. She wants to call them together and open up a new world to them. The *Alef-Beth* is the key to wonderful reading, and reading is the key to wonderful ideas, and the ideas are bright and warm and clear so that they stand out in the mind, illuminating the horizon. She wants to collect the little ones who have still a laughter fresh from their hearts, with feelings untouched by con-

flicts and unspoiled by outside influences and the adversities of
life. She wants to bring them together in towns and villages and
hamlets that they may learn together, that they may discover the
treasures of which their parents are the trustees. She will round
them up in comradeship and make them all strong in that security
of companionship. There will have to be club rooms, summer
camps, holiday centres, day schools. It will all have to develop into
an army that links hands together, and everyone will feel proud of
its strength, will feel ready for implicit obedience and will rejoice
in the numbers, the swelling numbers that will have almost un-
dreamed-of power.

This was the vision of Sara Schenierer. She unfolded it to
me with all the enthusiasm of an inspired and determined mind.
She made me see the thousands of girls, small, sweet, still within
the sheltering folds of their homes, see them march in a big array
across the span of time. They stretch, they grow, they become
huge figures and each figure splits again into numerous smaller
figures and the array becomes gigantic and triumphant in its march.

It is a simple woman that dreams these dreams. Yet her mind
has an enormous capacity to fill itself with this vision, so that this
vision becomes a force that overshadows everything else.

Her soul seems to have travelled from afar. She is a simple
dressmaker in Cracow. She is known there, walking along the
streets of the Cracow Ghetto, a plainly dressed motherly person,
always cheerful, busy, a lively little woman. But the soul that
shines out of her eyes has come from afar. It is as if her soul had
emerged from contact with the holiness of the Jewish past, pointing towards a messianic future. In the night, while children
sleep, while she stitches away on her customers' dresses, she seeks
to find a way in hard reality to make of the slumbering children that mighty legion that her vision beheld.

II

Sara Schenierer would probably never have left her small home
in the Cracow Ghetto, had not the World War forced her to seek
refuge in Vienna. 1915 sees her, a woman of thirty-two, in the
Jewish quarters of Vienna, together with thousands of others who

had fled from Galicia, struggling to find a temporary home until the storm had abated.

On a Shabbath morning, in one of the Shuls in the 20th district, a Rabbi ascended the pulpit to address his congregation. It happened to be a Shabbath Hanukkah and he spoke of the Maccabees, their strength, steadfastness and loyalty to the name of God. His thoughts were clear and deep, his illustrations and examples convincing and fascinating. In the women's gallery a stranger listened spellbound. She experienced a revelation. What was it that was so new, so striking in this speech that made her breathless with inner excitement? Here were the words she had been longing to find, here was the truth of Jewish teaching. The beauty and the glory of Jewish History were laid clear before the listener in a manner that could not fail to interest. Here were words like sparks that could kindle. Until now she had been groping in the dark, not knowing how to set out to accomplish the task for which she felt the burning desire. Now listening to Rabbi Flesch of the Stumpergasse, she saw her way clear before her. It would be simple, she would only have to magnify his voice, to pass on his words, so clear, so convincing, to all the women back home who were unaware of the fact that such truth existed. Like her, they would be dazzled by the light and then be guided by it. Their desire for learning, that had until now driven them away from home, would then be satisfied, the idea presented to them could not fail to impress them deeply and thus they would be led to respect Jewish life and to cling to it.

So Sara Schenierer wrote down with painful loyalty every speech, every lesson she heard from Rabbi Flesch during the years in Vienna, when she became his constant and most regular and conscientious pupil. And the thicker the volume of her writings, the more impatient she grew to go back to Cracow to share the treasures she had gathered.

In 1917 she returned home; and for five years she struggled in vain to find a way of attracting the young ladies of Cracow permanently. She assembled them, it is true, but she failed to hold them. Her words seemed to come back to her empty, and in spite of the growing determination to acquire a circle of listeners and pupils, she found herself alone for a very long time.

But with every failure her determination increased. She kept her treasure close to her heart and her vision clearly before her eyes; she was certain that just as she had been granted the language to speak so she would find the hearts to speak to.

And she found those hearts, willing to listen and to learn, when finally she turned to the children of the town.

Now we have come to the part of her story that sounds rather like an old-fashioned fairy tale, when the dressmaker turns overnight into a teacher and the workshop into a schoolroom, and the customers, instead of sending in their orders, send their children to be pupils of this school. A curious school indeed, without blackboard, bell, utensils, or books; with a teacher whose main qualification is her single-minded aim, and her love of the Torah. Who called that teacher to her place? No one ever bothered to ask. The children were all eager to come and to stay as long as they were allowed to; the older ones begged to be allowed to help the younger ones. They all loved Sara Schenierer and quite forgot that she was their teacher; they spoke to her as to a mother who had always time and patience to listen.

In spite of the primitive setup of the school, the number of children grew rapidly, and soon there were so many in the small room that it was impossible to carry on. Sara Schenierer saw herself forced to refuse admission to any more children.

Of course here was something wrong. How can one person teach hundreds of pupils? The solution would be the training of teachers who would each be able to teach a group.

So in the year 1923 Sara Schenierer started on her own initiative with her own meager means and in her own magic way to train teachers.

There is a small side street in the Cracow Ghetto. We walk into one of the large tenement houses and go up the narrow stone steps that lead into the various flats inhabited by numerous families with numerous children. We stop at one of the doors in the hallway of the first floor. We are at "Catachina No. 1." in front of Frau Schenierer's door. We shall soon see her "College." The door opens and we first enter a very small kitchen; a curtain separates this kitchen from a large room which looks bright and pleasant in spite of its bareness. Here, in Sara Schenierer's own room,

twenty girls sit by the table and study; some are seated on boxes
in the middle of the room and write with their books on their
laps, as there is no more space at the table. They are all intent,
they all seem lively and eager. Frau Schenierer sits at the table;
when she starts speaking they all turn to her, fasten their attention on every word she says. While they look at her, their faces
seem lit from within. There seems no fatigue in this room, no
slow creeping of hours. Time in this room seems to be unmeas-
ured and the atmosphere is bright and vibrant with intellectual
activity. They seem to be confederates; you can almost detect a
triumphant look when they share the scanty frugal meals in the
ascetically furnished room. All these girls have responded to
Frau Schenierer's call and have come forward when she asked
for volunteers, to be trained as teachers.

Not many have seen "Catachina No. 1." It was a place
hidden from the eyes of the world; and of those who have seen
it not many are left to tell the story, to recall the heroic hours
that were spent in study and happy privation. Here, a real
pioneer was at work. She allowed nothing and no one to discourage her or belittle her plans; she marched on, and the harder
she had to fight, the brighter became the sparks that flew from
her eyes when she came to grips with the realities of life
and made them bend to her will. Twenty-five young girls, none
older than sixteen, were the first willing disciples who lived with
Sara Schenierer in her two-room flat, sharing every hour of the
day under her guidance for several months. They all copied from
the exercise books which their teacher had filled in Vienna and
they felt rich in the possession of the thoughts gathered from there.
They all copied out a guidebook for teachers that she had compiled.
Though it was simple, primitive and old-fashioned in its style,
it seemed to them a panacea of teaching problems. Here is a
dialogue between teacher and pupil as it appeared in her book:

Teacher—Wus bist du? (What are you?)

Pupil—Yach bin a Yiddish kind. (I am a Jewish child.)

Teacher—Mit wus bist du a Yiddish kind? (What makes
you a Jewish child?)

Pupil—Yach bin a Yiddish kind, weil ich hob die heilige Toire wus hot gegeben der heiliger Bescheffer. (I am a Jewish child, because I have the holy Torah, given by the Holy Creator.)

Teacher—Wus steit geschrieben in der heiliger Toire? (What is written in the Holy Torah?)

Pupil—In der heiliger Toire steit geschrieben az der heiliger Bescheffer hot beschaffen die Himlen un die Erd. (It is written in the Holy Torah that the Holy Creator created the heavens and earth.)

And so it goes on for pages and pages. It is enough material to keep curly tops gathered around you, and it can serve as a key to the first gates of knowledge, love and loyalty. Then, after a few months of this kind of training are over, Frau Schenierer herself charges into the arena and leads her students.

I recall one of these events. It was Gittel's turn. Gittel was fifteen years of age. She had a pair of bright black eyes that were set like jewels in her firm, round, and childish face. She had a melodious voice and a clear way of pronouncing her words. Every sentence she spoke had a ring that carried it about the room. Her movements were graceful and assured. All this when she was only fifteen years of age! But she had learned the use of hairpins. With hairpins you can put your plaits up in a grown-up fashion and if you also wear a longer skirt than usual, you can look older than yourself. Gittel is sitting in the train next to Frau Schenierer, travelling to a town some hours away from home; on her lap, from sheets of paper, she is memorizing a speech that she wrote or rather that they both worked out together. It is all about the Jewish woman, her part in our great history, her mission in our own days, her duties as the mother of the coming generations. And when they alight in the town of their destination, big posters on the walls of the Jewish quarters invite all women of the town into the large Town Hall to a mass meeting to hear the two speakers.

The hall is filled to capacity. This is an event in a *"Klein Stedtel."* They all come, those that are interested and those that are only curious to see, all those that welcome a break in the everyday monotony and all those that hope to be able to sneer at the old-fashioned talk of two unknown woman-speakers. The child on the platform hears her heart beat as loud as a drum. She sees hundreds of faces staring up at her and she hears herself delivering the speech she had memorized in the morning, and she faintly realizes that the multitude and the situation she has to master make her speak in a voice that is not her own, with a confidence and a fire that seem to have suddenly come to her from the unknown. Her eyes roam over the crowd, she seems to master them all, and when Frau Schenierer, after she has finished, asks the audience whether they are willing to start a school with this girl as a teacher, there is an enthusiastic response. They enroll their children, and contribute to the setting up of the school. Gittel remains behind to be the one and only teacher, while Frau Schenierer takes the next train to make her second and third trips to establish further schools.

And Gittel and Sure Leie and Esther, they all teach, each in her own school, each from the same source and guide book, each in the same style and manner. And after some months they have come to the guide-book's last page and all their knowledge has been exhausted. There is nothing left, they have no books to draw from and they have never been instructed to go to the sources themselves.

But the pupils are not aware of any spiritual famine threatening them; the schools are at work and they are set on a very sound foundation. Gittel and her colleagues have built on that foundation with all the young, fresh, unbroken strength that flows when pioneers go into action.

By the year 1939 there were in Poland hundreds of Beth Jacob Schools. The training of the teachers had become more methodical and thorough; more modern and, altogether, educationally sounder. Meanwhile Dr. Leo Deutschlander had set up in the place of Sara Schenierer's first College a "Teacher's Training Seminary" of which we shall write later. But the aim of the schools did not change.

A BETH JACOB SCHOOL

A Beth Jacob school was a school but it was also an organization and a club, brightened up by the constant power of love and romance, a hero worship and a discipline that was almost like the discipline of a secret cult. All these things wove an original pattern into the quiet regular routine of school life. The teachers were all young. They all lived away from their own homes, away from their parents, and were devoting themselves to one purpose only, consumed by a fire which had been kindled by Sara Schenierer. They fulfilled their task even beyond their abilities, they planned and schemed, spending that youthful and radiant vitality which seemed to be so particularly strong in Polish Jewish girls. Skillfully they would weave a web capable of attracting and holding all those young ones entrusted to them. No other interests would interfere with their work. They were dedicated to their mission, like high adventurers or great artists. Their school became the horizon against which they set up their Beth Jacob dream, compounded of vision and reality. To the children and young girls who flocked in numbers to these schools, the young teachers became friends as well as instructors. They were important personalities in the Polish town, vested with directing power over the young souls. Slowly it became obvious how the almost lost ground of Jewishness was being regained and gradually redeemed.

Every one who has seen Beth Jacob magazines knows the typical photo of a large group of girls round a teacher not very much older than themselves. In the very way of grouping is revealed a kind of fellowship. Thousands of such photos existed. Hundreds stood in frames on small mantlepieces, on little shelves, by the girls' beds, in homes all over the country. And hundreds were carried about in the handbags of Beth Jacob girls as their dearest possession, carried even to journey's end. They were recollections of radiant days and promises. When, on fine summer days, teachers and pupils went across the meadows, talking and singing, they did not know whether it was just the summer that made them feel so happy, or whether it was their own youth or the secure feeling that they were guided by one they could admire and at the same time identify with their own parental home. The link to parents and traditions grew stronger, and the schools stood like citadels fortified by the pupils and under the High Command of Gittel and her colleagues.

Here among the girls, the inspiration of the Hassidic life had found its way into the woman's world. It had formed its own style, softened and differently moulded, but it was of the same fibre that made the Hassidim crowd round their Rebbe, made them stand for hours to catch a glimpse of him, made them unfold all their latent powers in the elevated atmosphere of hassidic devotion. No longer was the life of the Jewish daughter empty at home. She too had her community life, her school, centre and club, where there were comradeship and studies and well-organized activities— an outlet and a spur for her eager ambitions.

III

The centre of the whole school organization and the pattern according to which the ever-increasing number of schools formed themselves was the

Beth Jacob Seminary in Cracow

There it was in Cracow, a huge building on the bank of the Vistula, a five-story house overlooking the river. This house was a world of activity; there 120 young women, aged between sixteen and eighteen, concentrated on their intensive studies, filling the day between early morning reveille and bedtime at night. These girls had come from all parts of Poland and Lithuania and had been selected from hundreds of applicants. They attended the Cracow Seminary in order to train under Frau Schenierer as future teachers and to share life with her for a period of two years.

The studying and training went on all day long and was rounded off in the evening and on Shabbath by activities leisurely and recreative in character. Teachers and students formed one large family. They all seemed to be closely linked to each other, welded into one great circle. There was a fire of youthful enthusiasm and a purity of purpose, a satisfaction of duty fulfilled. Hours of study stretch into one another without any fatigue, the elasticity of mind seems unlimited, understanding bursts open, the intellectual spark ignites the emotions, releases new energies that seem to give unending drive to pupils and teachers.

I was a teacher in the Beth Jacob Seminary for many years. Here I wish to set a memorial to all those shining lights most of whom now illumine the eternal path; a memorial to those shining eyes that questioned you, that searched for deeper and clearer truth, that claimed and acknowledged and showed their receptivity to understanding in a flash of the eye that was unmistakable. Here is a tribute to all those voices that were heard in the classrooms, saying words which were like shrines containing treasures, which they had gathered and wanted to preserve. Never since have I heard such young voices, caressing the contents of their words, voices so warm and so keen and so anxious to express thoughts adequately. I want to pay tribute to those Beth Jacob Girls of Cracow who gathered for years round Frau Schenierer, to their unflinching loyalty in face of the high demands that were made upon them, asking them to keep pace with the very exacting self-discipline that Sara Schenierer expected from all her followers.

She demanded much of them. Wrapped up in a happiness of perfect harmony with herself and drawing continuous strength from her ideals, she demanded, with the vigor of a general, implicit obedience from all her students. But she was loved like a mother, with a love that increased with the span of time and growing maturity of her pupils. As they all would feel the security of belonging to her family of children when crowding round her, they would submit and give in. Some would do it with a little sigh, some with a slight revolutionary "murmur" in their heart, others with subdued longing or good-humored resignation—but they all gave in, gave in as you give in to a mother whom you love too much to have her serenity clouded.

This was the greatest mystery, something almost magic, and quite inexplicable; something that will probably evade forever any attempt at psychological or analytical explanation. All the young girls, those from Poland and those from Lithuania, those with a revolutionary rebel spirit and those who were by nature inclined to accept dictatorial leadership, those who had a searching mind, and those who found all answers ready in their own piety, those that came from wealthy homes, and those who had always lived in the squalid basement-dwellings of the Ghetto, the vivacious and progressive as well as the humble types, they all loved Frau Schenierer.

When that love was expressed, quite an uproar could be created. I remember those summer afternoons. All the girls were bent over their studies in the large common room. Frau Schenierer had been absent for a week on a mission to the provinces. Suddenly you would hear a clattering of hooves on the pavement below, a carriage jolting along, and then stopping in front of the house. One girl who had run to the window would call out "Frau Schenierer, Frau Schenierer" and fifty, sixty, seventy others would echo this call. Then all pens are flung down, all books are pushed aside and all girls rush down the stairs, they all crowd round the carriage and Frau Schenierer is triumphantly led, almost carried upstairs, and everything else has stopped in a breathless, excited mood. And although Frau Schenierer had been travelling and lecturing through the night, perhaps through two or more nights, she would, following this reception, unpack the experiences of her journey. She would give a report in a way that was a mixture of seriousness and amusement. Later, only much later, every girl would find her place back in the interrupted work, happy for having had the privilege of listening to Sara Schenierer's report of her travels.

This was the spell of Frau Schenierer's personality. She was able to produce in every one of her thousands of disciples a unique feeling that was a composition of love and respect and childlike devotion.

She had a good sense of humor. She liked stories, jokes and riddles. To her, nature was an illustration of Tehillim (The Book of Psalms), psychology and science an application of God's wisdom. Nothing had a meaning for her unless it could be connected with the supreme purpose. Even the new coat we persuaded her to buy would mean the enhancing of her prestige for the purpose of being able better to disseminate her ideals among those who stood yet aside or afar. Never would she start the delicious Shabbath meal without exclaiming in a merry, almost chuckling voice *li-Kh'vod ha-Shabbath* (For the glory of the Shabbath), while dipping her spoon into the hot, golden soup.

Yom Kippur Katan (a day of penance on the eve of the new moon) was always a special day in the Cracow Seminary. Whatever Sara Schenierer's idea behind it was, whether it was her natural piety that clung to this custom or whether she was following a Kabbalistic line, it always became the occasion for a memorable unfolding of Jewish History to the young girls under her banner.

Followed by one hundred and twenty girls she walked on Yom Kippur Katan to "Remo's Shool" (named after the co-author of the Shulhan Arukh, Rabbi Moses Iserlis) in the Ghetto. After they had all said their prayers inside the small old Shool, they walked to the graves of the Remo, the "Bach" (the great R. Joel Sirkis), the author of "Tosefoth Yomtov" (Rabbi Yomtov Heller) and other giants of the Jewish past. With the book of Tehillim in their hands, they felt included in the circle that connects every loyal Jew with those great and holy luminaries of the Torah. And thus the names of these great men and all they stood for, became imprinted on the minds of the girls while they stood in front of the tombstones. They felt eternity and mortality at peace with each other. The tranquility around the graves of these immortals inspired the girls to make their own contributions towards a lasting effort. Sara Schenierer probably could sense that those walls drew the young generation into the living circle of pulsating Jewish history. And on Lag B'eomer which is the *"Jahrzeitstag"* of the "Remo," when thousands of Hassidim thronged the Beth Olam, making the place tremble with the vibration of their presence and creating an atmosphere aglow with religious fervor, then Jewish History became overwhelming to those very young and impressionable girls round Frau Schenierer. It is good to lean back against these ancient walls. They are pillars in a world to which we add our own bricks. And when the girls went home, they felt that their footsteps on the cobbled street of the Cracow Ghetto echoed the footsteps of those great and holy men that had walked there in the past. They resolved to make sure that their echo would still resound in the future.

IV

Thus "Stanislawa 10" was the citadel of the Beth Jacob Movement. This large building was set up to bring the Beth Jacob students into pleasant, adequate surroundings.* The girls would no longer have to share one large room that served as a

---

*The funds were provided by the American Beth Jacob Committee, composed of Cyrus Adler, Sue Golding, Leo Jung, Rebekah Kohut, and Frieda Warburg; the ultra-violet ray equipment was the gift of Jacob Michael of Frankfurt a.M.

study during the day, no longer would they have to climb narrow staircases which at the same time were used as a day-nursery for the many children of the overcrowded tenement houses, no longer would they have to study in rooms over backyards which resounded with the chatter of neighboring women. They saw a house being built on a broad fundament that would be their Residential College. There was quite a ceremony on the occasion of the setting of the foundation stone on a large site in the Stanislawa. On a decorated platform, erected for the occasion on the muddy, empty site, speeches were made by various notables, promising that one day, in the near future, a new building would stand on this site, complete and spacious; that the pioneer students would then be rewarded for all their present privations and move into beautiful rooms well arranged and equipped. The crowd assembled on the side (thousands had come in honor of the occasion), applauding the words; the eyes of the Beth Jacob students widened in this cheering vision of the forthcoming improvements. And Frau Schenierer, who stood with her disciples amongst the audience—shunning, as a pious woman of her type would do, glaring platform publicity—sent up a prayer to God. It was in joyful anticipation of her dreams fulfilled, as well as in trembling fear, lest comforts and the luxury of normal standards might stifle the heroic efforts that had brought this movement into being. The mother's heart desired the best for her children. But the founder of the movement, who had seen Beth Jacob pushing itself through with an elementary force of defiance against odds, was somewhat afraid of the debilitating influence of easy conditions. Although she loved and appreciated beauty, she was always alert against beauty's possible dangers. And so the wishes of a mother mingled with the fervent prayer of one who felt herself responsible to history and posterity, and prayed for strength to ward off slackness in a movement that had to continue in defiance of a world of opposition.

While Sara Schenierer stood amongst the crowd on the 16th of Elul, 1921, her mind wandered back to the days when they had all shared a morsel of bread, back to the days when they slept crowded in the dressmaker's workroom, back to the endless hours of study and spiritual delight they had enjoyed together like a taste of transcendent pleasures. She felt the surge of loyalty and devotion that had made those hours blessed in the midst of squalor, and she prepared herself to be the keeper of this new and modern home so that its soul should not depart from it, but dwell in this frame in the same way as it had in the old one.

And then came the day in June, 1931. The ground floor and the first floor of the house were finished, while the four other floors stood still raw and unfinished. One hundred and twenty pupils moved into this building, which was more of a builder's workplace than a place fit for habitation. Cement, dust, tools of the workmen all over the place, floors that were not boarded and entrances that were without doors; yet they moved in; and from the inside they watched the gradual completion that spread over years. The guiding hand of Frau Schenierer was strong over them and the spirit of the school prevailed. Those who visited the Seminary in the years between 1933 and 1939 saw a fine building, well equipped, large dormitories and study rooms and a beautiful dining hall, sunlit and well furnished. But the building was never fully completed. The outside decorations, which were the last thing on the plan, were never actually made. When the hostile wind of destruction howled over the Jewish quarters of Cracow, the Beth Jacob Seminary in Stanislawa 10 still displayed an unfinished facade, bare against the sky. The powers that wove a pattern of Jewish history inside never made themselves evident to the passer-by. Deep down in the earth, below the foundation stone, there rests a document. It tells of the lofty ideals this house stood for and embodies the record of valiant men who sponsored and supported Sara Schenierer's Beth Jacob throughout the years. It contains also a prayer for the success of this holy work. High up in heaven there is the record of the martyrdom, heroism, agony and incredible suffering of which the walls of this house will forever be silent witnesses. The name of Yehudah Leib Orlean, who was the trustee of Sara Schenierer's spiritual legacy after she left this world, dominates the last phase of the history of this building, the details of which we shall never know.

But let me go back to those brilliant, sunlit days when crisp Bagels were sold at every streetcorner in Cracow by busy little women who earned their pennies in restless toil so that their men-

folk should have time to study the Torah; when the smell of
pickled herrings and onions coming up from the basement shops
scented the air of the narrow cobbled street; when the Yeshivoth
were resounding with the vigorous young voices of learning, when
Beth Jacob was budding and bringing forth blooms, when six
hundred letters were filed in the secretary's office in Stanislawa 10
asking for teachers to be sent hurriedly to hundreds of towns for
the thousands of children whose parents impatiently clamoured for
their children's instruction in the Beth Jacob way. Let us talk of
those bright days when the girls' life was unclouded, when the
School changed face several times a day, from College to Club
and residential home; when the pendulum of their activities swung
between the gaiety of youth and thoughtful search for the true
essence of Jewish teaching.

July and August were unbearably hot days in the Cracow
Ghetto. The heat and stench of the factories and tanneries, right
next to the residential apartment houses, made the air exceedingly
dense. We left Cracow for two months every summer. We had
rented a number of lightly built houses in the country. Huge
wagons drew up in front of Stanislaw 10; hundreds of suitcases
were stored in them, bedding, kitchen and household goods, and
for the next two months our schoolrooms would be meadows and
woods and the fields of lonely country places. We marched out,
at 6 A. M., in the cool morning air for physical training, we
learned *Tehillim* in the rays of the rising sun, by the slope of the
hill, we learned Hebrew grammar while the bells of the cows
grazing by tingled to the conjugations of the verbs. We read
Messilath Yesharim, S. R. Hirsch's "19 Letters" and "Horev," as
well as Isaac Breuer's *"Messiasspuren"* (Traces of the Messiah)
and *"Judenproblem"*, whilst the scent of the Carpathian vegeta-
tion filled the air. We listened to lectures of learned men who
came to us after they had become used to the fact that there was
a colony of girls who were themselves already young scholars and
intelligent listeners. We would sit in the meadows and have
debates on education and there the students would discuss improvements in their own school units.

At the same time, these summer courses were attended by the
majority of those Beth Jacob teachers who had already found

teaching positions in various schools. They flocked to these camps, formed themselves into groups and thus, during their summer vacation, they became once more disciples of Frau Schenierer and her teaching staff, in order to increase their knowledge and to keep abreast of educational developments. Thus the spirit of Beth Jacob never grew stale in them and the personal bond that linked them with their tutors and comrades never weakened.

The summer continuation courses of Beth Jacob were the backbone of the movement, which gave strength and support to an ever-increasing number of girls. It stimulated the emotions while it strengthened the intellect.

V

These courses were the work of Dr. Leo Deutschlander. They were the manifestation of his educational genius that had lifted the Beth Jacob from the dream of a dressmaker, from the vision of an untrained enthusiast, to the level of a systematic, well-planned organization. Frau Schenierer's fervent desire to bring thousands of daughters lovingly back to their parents' tradition could only have found small ways and means and a limited response among a narrow circle of more or less simple-minded people. Sara Schenierer kindled the spark; the flame of enthusiasm came from her; but the first years, when she was on her own, meant no more than a romantic picture in a small frame; her voice could not reach wider circles and her schools could not stand the scrutinizing criticism of the modern expert who demanded more thoroughness, more scholarship and a well-graded system.

What would have become of Sara Schenierer's visionary fervour had it not been joined by Providence with Leo Deutschlander's genius of organization and education, we do not try to imagine. It might have been a fire doomed to extinction for want of fuel to sustain it.

But in 1924 he did come along. He saw the tender beginnings, he recognized the latent forces and he set himself to work. He reared the child he had found in its promising infancy. And he found scope for his foresight and educational talents. Leo Deutschlander made of Beth Jacob a well-organized movement. The syllabus, curriculum, examinations, continuation courses, as well as the financial foundation of the whole work, the building of the beautiful Seminary—all these were the result of his wisdom and effort.

The spark that was kindled by a daughter of the hassidic tradition was fanned by the methodical manner of a man who had been educated in the best schools of modern European training, who had picked up what was best in European culture, and had blended it with the Jewish stores of his mind. He was deliberate in his plans, there was nothing abrupt or impulsive about him. He was by nature a reconciler of contrasts and his guidebook was *Tehillim*. There was no harshness in his disposition. Wherever there was beauty or goodness, he discovered it and held it up to be admired. In the valuable achievements of modern culture he saw the reflection of the Torah's eternal truth and as such he acknowledged it and borrowed from it. Thus he could speak to youth. Thus he could rouse and satisfy all those who felt the Ghetto too confining. Thus he could fascinate thousands of intelligent Jewish girls in Poland, whose desire for intellectual freedom had grown to formidable dimensions, and who were in danger of being lured away from Judaism by the phantom of philosophical negations. He could understand their questions and difficulties, spoken or unspoken. He eased their problems by his blessed smile, he analyzed them in his academic manner, he threw a new light on them in his generous artistic vein. He solved riddles by the blend of his wisdom and his harmonious personality. There were many eager girls who had loved Sara Schenierer, but needed him to help clear their minds. They would never have found their way without him. He linked them to the intellectual world at large and made them stronger on their own ground. He himself radiated harmony. Discipline and order, system and method, were introduced by him. He enforced them in his own entirely undictatorial way. And while examinations were held in the Seminary in an atmosphere of awe and respect, he would leisurely walk along the corridor to the examination room and address pertinent questions to the candidates in a sociable, almost soothing, way.

Leo Deutschlander spent two or three months of every year in the Seminary. All of a sudden he would appear and walk into the study room like one who had never been away. He smiled his own smile, seemed to know everyone, everyone's troubles, came with ideas, suggestions, new ways, help, support, progress. He was always the same. Kindness came from deep within him. With the "Tanakh" in his hand, he went into the classroom. He unfolded his thoughts and appeared to grow while he spoke. He seemed to exchange the plane on which we live for a more worthy one. When he had finished, the spell endured. Jewish law had become one with the law of beauty and freedom for which these girls longed so much; there was no more conflict, there was harmony in the Universe. The "Thou shalt" that some had felt as a burden had become transformed into a triumphant "I will."

Thus he stayed for weeks and then he left again, to come back when weariness threatened to hamper everyday life in the Seminary. None of the students could have realized how hard he worked, how he had spent the months in between his visits; that he had been through the countries of Europe and had spoken before many organizations, visited fashionable drawing-rooms in order to make friends for the growing work in Poland and Lithuania. I often watched him in this field work. In his gait and deportment he was always the scholar, modest, yet sovereign, without pretense or disguise, with the slight touch of a Bohemian, copying no one, being himself. For years he had given up rest and repose and the comfort of his pleasant home, had written and dictated letters in strange hotel rooms in all the capitals of the world, telephoned and wired across the ocean—all to keep Beth Jacob and the Yeshivoth alive.

The banker whom he faced in his comfortable office, and approached for financial support, had perhaps not heard anything about Jews and Judaism for years, his ambitions being of quite a different nature. Yet he could not help feeling that the cause for which his visitor pleaded so warmly and eloquently and without any obvious effort, must be a worthy one. Leo Deutschlander's cultured and noble personality with the mischievous spark of humor, was guarantee for the cause. He felt that here truth was represented and to this truth he had to pay his tribute. Sometimes the work was hard. But never was Leo Deutschlander bitter or out of gear. Perhaps he felt a little weary or had a pang of grief. But then the cheerfulness of his blessed nature helped him to fight any discouragement.

VI

In Erets Yisrael, where the remnants of Israel found a home on holy ground, the Beth Jacob movement struck fresh roots and is now bringing forth fresh blossoms. From Cracow through the hell of Europe into the haven of our homeland, Beth Jacob has remained unimpaired in its strength and undiluted in its program.

In the new developing land of Israel, the Beth Jacob Schools are on duty to see that Jewish girls are taught the sanctity of Jewish home and family life, so that they will be, like the mothers of old, the guarantors that the Torah will continue to rule the life of our people. *"Thus shalt thou speak to the house of Jacob"* . . . The house of Jacob, our sages explain, are the women who in all nations and at all times have the greatest influence in the making of the coming generation.

There are two teachers' training colleges in Tel-Aviv and a larger one in Jerusalem; there are many schools and kindergartens too. Eva Landsberg, who worked for many years with Sara Schenierer and Leo Deutschlander in Cracow and in Vienna, accompanied Beth Jacob on its route from Europe to Israel and helped to transplant the Beth Jacob ideal to the Holy Land. She died in 1947. Also in other countries, wherever orthodox Jewish congregations are found, Beth Jacob Schools have been set up, and although the local coloring may bring variations, the fundamental principles are everywhere the same. The Beth Jacob movement is woven into the fabric of the great history of the Jewish people.

The figure of Sara Schenierer will become more and more legendary. The story of her life will not lose its spell and will grow more touching as the movement grows wider and branches out. As time passes on, the personal touch that is still lingering round her name will fade and she will become a historical personality, known as the founder of Beth Jacob. But no one will know of the many who worked with her and gave of their strength and devotion to breathe life and vigor into the movement. Alas, for those girls who passed untimely into the realm "beyond", for those *"who were lovely and pleasant in their lives and in death were not parted,"* alas, for those sweet young teachers, so wholehearted in their efforts, so generous in their love for the school children, so loyal unto death to Sara Schenierer and to their own mission. Will Beth Jacob ever again bring forth girls like Hanka Grossfield-Biegun, the brainy, gay-spirited young person who, schooled in the Beth Jacob since the age of 15, had passed through all the stages of self-discipline and had become Sara Schenierer's first assistant in the Seminary and the central figure for all the girls after Sara Schenierer's death? The blessing of God had rested upon her to find grace in the sight of all. And Lacia Szarainka Wasciac, who in those difficult years, when the Beth Jacob had to squeeze itself into the poor Ghetto of Cracow, saw to it that the young enthusiasts should not suffer for lack of health and care; and when in those first days fanatic concentration on studies found them all forgetful of essential needs, she went quietly about setting up kitchens, healthy dormitories and sickbeds providing for all needs. There were Esther Goldstoff, Gittel Teitelbaum-Pass, Bela Gross, Betty Rothschild-Baumgarten, Ida Bauminger, Ester Heitner, Rosa Heitner, those brilliant teachers, firstlings of the Beth Jacob movement, trained in the movement and later on becoming lecturers in the Seminary. There were Yehudah Leib Orlean, Alexander Sische Friedman, Gerson Friedenzon, Senator Moshe Deutscher, Reb Ascher Spira, Freilich and Meier Heitner. Their names are recorded here as they have no graves or tombstones. But their souls are woven in the loom of life because they contributed their lives to the success of the Beth Jacob long before any one could realize that by their work history was being made. They belong to the champions of the Beth Jacob movement together with the precious thousands whose names cannot be recorded in these fragmentary annals. The continuation of the Beth Jacob movement is their Kaddish.

I have tried in this sketch to describe the personality of Sara Schenierer and the movement created by her. But as her personality is a mystery and eludes description, I shall conclude by letting Sara Schenierer speak for herself, by reproducing in English translation the words of her last will, written on her death bed, to her thousands of pupils all over the country:

"What shall we say, what shall we speak, how shall we justify ourselves? *There are many thoughts in the heart of man, but only the counsel of the Lord prevaileth.* Whatever the Merciful doeth,

He doeth for our good. May His great Name be blessed for his manifold kindnesses.

All my life I complained about my inability to cry at the time of prayer. But now it is hard for me to keep back my tears. Only now do I feel how strong is the inner bond that ties me to my children. But spiritual ties are very strong. They last forever. Just as I cry as I am writing to you now, so will your tears flow as you read these my words. May it be the will of our Father in heaven that your tears and mine reach the throne of glory to pray for Israel's complete redemption.

I am turning to you, my dear daughters, going out into the great world to guide and train the daughters of Israel and to establish homes in Israel.

I am convinced that you understand well your great task. We have a good God in heaven and he aids every person to walk in the way that he desires. Throughout the years of my work, men were sent to me who were genuine helpers.

I should like to single out two grave dangers which threaten you, my daughters.

Beware of the feeling of pride, arrogance or cocksureness, that persuades one to think that he is great in achievements and deserving of honor. Secondly, keep away from the other extreme, the feeling of inferiority which whispers to man: 'you are nothing, without any value.' This exaggerated humility causes sadness to abide in man, introduces doubt into his heart as to whether his work will succeed.

If the feeling of sadness should overcome you, if doubt should arise in your heart whether you are worthy of the mission entrusted to you, whether you are fulfilling your tasks properly—then examine yourself whether you have done your duty or not. If your answer is positive, then remember what I told you every day after prayer, quoting the passage in Deuteronomy. *'And now, oh, Israel, what does the Lord thy God ask of you, except to revere the Lord, thy God, to walk in all His ways, to love him and to serve the Lord thy God with all thy heart and soul.'*

And now my dear daughters, you are standing before the severest test, that of life itself. For some time life is hard, but in your hands, by the blessing of the Lord, are strong weapons of defense. They are fear of God, reverence, love and service.

Your sainted teacher, Yehudah Leib Orlean, once said, at the time of a formal examination: 'The tests have shown that you know how to learn and to teach. The problem which troubles us is whether you will also understand how to *train* Jewish souls.'

Before the High Priest entered on the service in the Holy of Holies, he would be asked 'Is there any whisper of evil intention in your heart, have you forgotten or perhaps not even learned? One can remedy ignorance or forgetfulness, but if your intention has become impure you would desecrate the Holy of Holies.'

My dear girls, you are going out into the great world. Your task is to plant the holy seed in the souls of pure children. In a sense, the destiny of Israel of old is in your hands.

Be strong and of good courage. Don't tire. Don't slacken your efforts. You have heard of a Hassid who came to his rabbi and said joyfully, 'Rabbi, I have finished the whole Talmud.' 'What has the Talmud taught you?' asked the rabbi. 'Your learning is fine, but your practical task is the main thing.'

Let me complete these words with the verses you all know so well.

Serve the Lord with joy.

I keep the Lord before me continuously.

The beginning of wisdom is the fear of the Lord.

Teach us to number our days.

The Lord's Torah is perfect, it restoreth the soul.

May the Lord guard your going out and your coming in from now and forever more.

May He listen to our prayers and send us the true redeemer and true redemption.

Yours forever,

Sarah Schenierer

My beloved daughters, may God grant you long life."

Cracow, 1935.

HAYYIM OZER GRODZENSKI

BY J. L. KAGAN AND H. B. PERLMAN

HAYYIM OZER GRODZENSKI (1863-1940)

By J. L. Kagan and H. B. Perlman

I

His world, almost completely destroyed in the second World War, has been memorialized in a book by Dr. A. J. Heschel, entitled "The Earth is the Lord's." For the Jewish people, to whom Hayyim Ozer Grodzenski ministered for nearly sixty years, to whom plain living and high thinking were the order of the day, his life was an outstanding illustration of that lofty thesis.

There are two types of scholars in Israel. The first devotes himself entirely to the study of Torah, makes a genuine and valuable contribution to his people's heritage and his concern for its welfare is sincere. But he lives apart from the workday world of the average Jew; there is a gap that he cannot bridge.

The second type, more rare, possesses, besides the scholarly talents of the first, a kind of vitality and emotional insight that activates his humility. Not for him the ivory tower; he must roll up his sleeves, be in the midst of the struggle. To his fellows he is entirely accessible, he is active in every communal enterprise, seeks to shoulder a share of every burden. Such a man was Hayyim Ozer Grodzenski.

He was born August 24, 1863, in Ivia, a small town near Vilna, where his father had served as rabbi for almost half a century. His grandfather, Rabbi Moses Aryeh, an outstanding scholar of his day, had held the same post during his last years. This ancestor had studied in his youth with the celebrated sage and founder of the Mussar movement, Rabbi Israel Salanter. One of nine children, he was named for his maternal grandfather, Rabbi Hayyim Ozer Einhorn.

He showed unusual abilities at a very early age. His father thought that he was getting more attention than was good for him at home, and sent him away to study in Eishishok, where there was a Torah Academy for a small group of advanced youngsters.

435

There the "Illui (prodigy) of Ivia", as he came to be known, remained until he became Bar Mitsvah. On that occasion, the address which he delivered ex tempore, on a subject chosen by one of the learned guests, was so original and so brilliant that it became legend. Those who were present could never forget it.

He then was sent to the Yeshivah of Volozhin for advanced study. This was the golden period of that remarkable school, when it was headed by Rabbi Naphthali Tsevi Yehudah Berlin, and Rabbi Raphael Shapiro. To be accepted as a student was in itself a distinction.

Rabbi Hayyim Soloveichik was at that time one of the outstanding scholars at Volozhin. Later appointed its head, he became famous as the Gaon of Brisk. His disciples were especially well prepared for religious and communal leadership. He gave a selected group of students intensive training in his own methods and approach. He realized that the boy was destined for greatness, and gave him every help. Theirs was a lifelong friendship.

At the age of twenty, young Rabbi Hayyim Ozer married the grand-daughter of Rabbi Israel Salanter and settled in Vilna, where he collaborated with his father-in-law, Rabbi Elijah Eliezer, who was active in the affairs of that important community. With his passing five years later, his son-in-law was selected to fill the vacant place on the local rabbinical council. He was very young to become the colleague of the most eminent and venerable Rabbi Solomon and Rabbi Bezalel, but there was no dissenting voice.

His ministry in Vilna marked the beginning of a new epoch in the life of a community that had become known as "The Jerusalem of Lithuania." It had begun to lose some of its former prestige, due in part to the insidious influence of the maskilim, those often sincere, but sadly misled apostles of the "New Modernism." There was need of a man to show that the golden promise of the Haskalah movement would yield merely tinsel, unless constantly nourished by the great moral and spiritual teaching of Torah, within the framework of the Jewish way of life. Such a man was Rabbi Hayyim Ozer Grodzenski.

He established a school for advanced studies, which became known as the "Kibbuts of Rabbi Hayyim Ozer." Its work he supplemented with seminars in his home on Saturday evenings. He never allowed the pressure of other communal duties to interfere with his lectures. Among his distinguished alumni are Rabbi Isaac Halevy Herzog of Israel, Rabbi Reuben Katz of Petach Tikvah, and the late Rabbi Moses A. Amiel, chief rabbi of Tel Aviv.

Not only in Lithuania and East Europe, but throughout the entire Jewish world did the fame of his wisdom and scholarship spread. His mail brought daily from every corner of the globe questions touching on many aspects of Jewish life, and he answered in his own hand. He had a clear, sparkling style; he loved to write and had a talent for it. His responsa and Halakhic writings were later published under the title: "Ahiezer." The first volume came out in 1922, troubled, hard times for such an undertaking, but in his introduction the rabbi reminds us that the study of Torah in times of trial has always been to the Jew a source of strength, an act of faith. Another volume came out in 1939, actually under the shadow of the terrible World War II. The world of Torah scholarship was thrilled and amazed.

There was a well established tradition in Vilna of avoiding pilpul or casuistical subtlety in the study of the Talmud and of concentrating on the broad, deep understanding of the text.

The school of Volozhin, following another approach, believed in the method of rigid analysis. Every Halakhah was reduced to its component parts. This method was developed by Rabbi Hayyim Soloveitchik of Brisk. New horizons were opened to the student which gave him a clear understanding of the problems under discussion. Rabbi Grodzenski adopted this analytic method and combined it with his own.

II

In his responsa and legal decisions he reveals unusual ability to be both concise and exhaustive. He explains every subject fully, but avoids repetition and rhetorical language.

The Ahiezer volumes, an excellent guide for the elucidation of Talmudic subjects, have been widely accepted as classics by the Yeshivoth.

The following lines, taken from the introduction to the third volume, are characteristic of the man. "Today is the time to accomplish much for the Almighty and His Torah. Every Jew who has the means and the power to work for our sacred cause, has great responsibility on his shoulders. How tragic is the plight of our people! One cannot compare the upheaval of the current situation with those of the medieval period. Jewish settlements in Europe are going up in flames, synagogues and study houses containing the Holy Scrolls of the Law are being burnt. New evil decrees are announced daily. Our enemies have decided to annihilate us, together with our holy faith. Large, prominent communities are being uprooted. Free countries have closed their doors to refugees. Tens of thousands of Jewish families are in the lands of enemies and murderers. Oh, what shame and disgrace have come to us! How every one tramples upon our glory and prestige!

"Even the light which shone for us from the East, from the land of our venerable ancestors, has become obscured of late, and we do not know what tomorrow will bring. Distress, troubles, killing, murder, expulsion, evil decrees surround us on all sides. The entire Jewish people is sinking in the rivers of blood and oceans of tears of innocent victims of oppression. Oh, what has become of us!

"In the Middle Ages the Jews had a firm, abiding faith in God and in His Torah. They were confident that He would not forsake them. This gave them strength to resist and courage to bear affliction and humiliation. Then, there at least was enough power left in the Jewish refugees to establish centers of Torah and Judaism in the new communities in which they settled. They were a living proof of the truth of our Sages' remark: 'To every place whereto they were exiled the Shekhinah went with them' (Megillah 29a).

"Unfortunately, however, in our own day we have been weaker in our faith, in our loyalty to Judaism. In Western Europe the Reform movement has taken deep root and has led to assimilation. From these lands there came forth the first signs of the bitter hatred for the Jew. The poison soon spread, and in the East there is an increase in the number of people who have forsaken God, who devote much time and effort to turn our people away from Torah and Judaism. In many lands our fellow Jews do not have the will to resist temptation. They give up the most sacred principles of our faith—the holiness of the Sabbath, which is the foundation of the entire Torah. They do not observe the dietary laws; they contaminate Jewish souls with unclean, non-kosher foods about which the Torah warns us *'And ye shall be holy men unto Me; neither shall ye eat any flesh that is torn of beasts in the field'* (Exodus 22, 30). *'Ye shall be holy unto Me'*— Even family purity has, unfortunately, been neglected and well-nigh forgotten.

"In spite of all this, many of our people have not as yet reached the proper conclusions. They have not been able to see and to understand the causes of our tragic plight. We are afflicted with blindness; our hands have become paralyzed. We sigh and we groan under the heavy yoke of exile. Every day brings new curses and catastrophies.

"Nevertheless, we must not allow ourselves to be caught in this flood. We must return with all our heart and with all our soul; we must repent. As the Torah puts it (Deut. 4,30) : *'In thy distress, when all these things are come upon thee, in the end of days, thou wilt return to the Lord thy God and hearken unto His voice.'* "

This prophetic note was written just before the terrible destruction of the Jews of Poland and Lithuania.

The three books of Responsa are a small fraction of Rabbi Grodzenski's writings; the rest—memoirs, responsa, correspondence, essays—were destroyed by the war.

III

His philanthropic work was of such great scope and variety that one short article can hardly do more than indicate in a general way the fields served by this great-hearted, tireless servant of humanity. The oppressions of the Czarist regime, the revolution with its special problems, and the hardships of the two world wars, all came during the period of his ministry.

His reputation for integrity and absolute accuracy in allocating funds according to the wishes of the donors brought in his mail large sums of money for institutions, families, or individuals. When there was not enough money for his many causes, he could be very persuasive, and his personal appeals were seldom without success. He could be ingratiating, insistent, very patient in seeking help for others, but when the needy came to him, demanding, impatient, often rude and unreasonable, he gave without rebuke. He was scrupulously careful not to hurt the feelings of the poor. He never forgot that "The gift without the giver is bare." They left his presence with a lighter heart, encouraged to remember that in him they had a friend.

Let us visit his home in Vilna on an average day. Long before 11 A. M., the official time for receiving visitors, the anteroom is crowded with people from all walks of life: rabbis, teachers, students, business men, with their problems, needs, and misfortunes. If there happens to be a delegation from the Vilna Beth Din, it is taken care of earlier, since the affairs of the city come first on his calendar.

All day the work goes on. His eyes are clear, his face is radiant with happiness and understanding, and he has a warm smile for everyone. As one caller gratefully expressed it: "It is as if a stone were lifted from my heart."

Between one interview and another, he works away at the piles of mail on his desk. That which requires further thought he sets aside for later; the rest he answers at once. He seems able to do several things at once: Write, listen and conduct the interview. He felt best when working at top speed. In a free moment he yields to his wife's insistence and sips a cup of tea, but sets the cup down unfinished. One visitor is a widow who is deeply troubled because she can no longer contribute to certain causes. The rabbi shows her how she can give help in other ways, minister to many social and charitable needs without actually having money to give. She leaves the rabbi's study jubilant, with a new knowledge and a higher goal.

Insight into Rabbi Grodzenski's personality may be gained from the following story: A Yeshivah student and his fiancee came to him for his blessing before their wedding. During the conversation he learned that the couple had no parents and relatives. "Are you acquainted with the laws of family purity?" he asked the bride. She indicated that she did not know the laws. The rabbi said: "This is no time for false modesty. The laws of family purity are basic in Judaism. In your home, your mother or older sister would have taught you. Now you are alone. I will explain." His office was full of people—but at the moment he was not

concerned with them. He was busy teaching the laws of family
purity to a daughter of Israel. After the explanation, he blessed
the couple, presented them with a gift, and asked his wife to attend
their wedding ceremony. Direct service to humanity seemed
always most important to him.

Mr. David Solomon Kossovsky, a nephew of his and a lawyer in
Tel Aviv, visited him a short while before the outbreak of World
War. The third volume of "Ahiezer" had just been published. Mr.
Kossovsky said to Rabbi Grodzenski: "Uncle, if you were to publish your books which are still in manuscript or if you were to collect
your widely scattered responsa, you would enrich our Torah literature." The Rabbi replied: "Years ago I thought that writing
books was the most desirable and honorable occupation. As I advanced in years, I began to realize that such work is insignificant
in comparison with the job of helping Torah scholars, orphans,
widows, and other unfortunates."

When Rabbi Grodzenski was at Druskenik, a well-known health
resort near Grodno, one of the residents offered to find him a suitable cottage. Of the two available Rabbi Grodzenski and his friends
liked one, and were about to rent it, when the rabbi hesitated and
said: "The cottage is very beautiful, but there is one shortcoming.
The living rooms are very far from the kitchen. It is the maid who
will be affected by the problem. Let us, therefore, ask her opinion."

Once, while the rabbi was walking with his friends, a man
who stuttered passed by and asked for the residence of the local
physician. One of the men told him how to reach the house, but
then Rabbi Grodzenski turned to him and said, "I want to ask a
favor of you. Please accompany him to the physician's house.
He stutters. Perhaps he will be ashamed to ask other people for
directions and thus he may not reach the right place."

Rabbi Hezekiah Mishkowsky tells this story: After Vilna had
been annexed to Lithuania, a delegation from Kovno came to Rabbi
Grodzenski to consult him about several problems. They asked if
he needed anything from Kovno. He replied: "I have two requests,
one minor, one major. The minor one is that I need some medicine which cannot be obtained in Vilna. The major one is that
our maid needs new shoes, and we can't purchase them here. I also
need shoes, but not as urgently as she does, for I live a sedentary

life. She must walk in the street every day and at this time of the year she may, God forbid, catch cold."

He would turn the pages of the Vilna edition of the Talmud, or the Torah volumes which he received in the mail, would run through scores of letters and newspapers, and would prepare a responsum while a learned visitor asked him a Halakhic question, and the head of a Yeshivah told him the substance of his last lecture. All spoke at the same time, and when they would stop, thinking that Rabbi Grodzenski was not listening, Rabbi Grodzenski, would say: "Please continue to speak; I am listening."

It was in such an atmosphere, when working at top speed, that he felt best. When he took ill, and was forbidden to receive visitors, he complained about the enforced idleness, the only thing he ever complained of.

Fond of children, he had only one child, a daughter. He had hoped for grandchildren who would continue the great Torah tradition of his family. Jewish mothers in Vilna would bless their daughters by saying "May you be like the daughter of Reb Hayyim Ozer." Her beauty, the goodness of her heart, her simple ways and her modesty, were widely known. But alas, at the age of sixteen she was afflicted with a dread disease. Her father called in physicians from Lithuania as well as from abroad. They tried many treatments but without success. "A decree had gone out from Heaven that could not be revoked." The girl was bed-ridden for four years and when she died the whole community was stunned. The only one who did not despair, nor protest Heaven's decree, was Rabbi Grodzenski. He comforted others, continued his communal work, his studies, and his fruitful activities.

IV

During the last days of her life, he took comfort in Torah. He delved into the most difficult and abstract passages of the Talmud. He might have said with the Psalmist, *"Unless Thy law had been my delight, I should then have perished in mine affliction"* (Psalms, CXIX, 92).

During the fifty-six years that Rabbi Grodzenski served in Vilna, he rarely left the city for an extended period. He felt a keen sense of responsibility towards his great town and the Torah world there. In 1915, during the first World War, special circumstances forced him to leave Vilna for two years.

The first losses of the Russians at the hands of the Germans had catastrophic effects upon the Jewish population. Expulsions, pogroms, plunder and confusion were their daily lot. The Chief Commander of the Russian Army, General Nicholai Nicolovitz, a notorious anti-Semite, placed the blame for the defeat upon the Jews. He maintained that the Jews were spies, that they had secret agreements with the Germans. This theme was reiterated by newspapers and public speakers. The lives and property of the Jews were left unprotected. It was announced that they were enemies of Russia and traitors to their country.

The rabbis (the Russian government suddenly realized that the spiritual leaders chosen by the Jews, not the rabbis appointed by the government, were the true leaders), heads of the Jewish settlements, communal workers, and other men of influence, were taken as hostages and exiled to Poltava, Yekaterinoslav, Tchernigov, Ukraine, and even to Rostov and Siberia. These hostages underwent great hardships, and many died in exile.

A Russian official informed the heads of the Vilna Jewish community that Rabbi Grodzenski was among those to be taken as hostage. He advised escape, but it was not easy to convince Rabbi Grodzenski. He finally yielded to the urgent appeals, particularly of his distinguished colleague and intimate friend, Rabbi Israel Meir ha-Kohen Kagan, the "Hafets Hayyim", who prevailed upon him to leave his beloved Vilna and settle in Homel.

Rabbi Grodzenski's departure was a source of grief to the Jews of Vilna. The city, however, became headquarters for the rescue of Jews. In exile he headed the Rescue Committee, which aided hundreds of thousands of starving refugees from Russia, Poland and Galicia, who were scattered throughout the Russian Jewish communities. Funds collected by him supported rabbis and Yeshivah students for several years.

The reputation of Rabbi Grodzenski was great even in distant Jewish settlements. His appeals for help were well received. Russian Jewry poured large sums of money into his relief projects. He visited Kiev, Moscow and St. Petersburg, contacting the men of affluence and influence. The charm and magnetic quality of his personality secured esteem, love, and cordial receptions for his appeal. Special committees were formed to help the Yeshivoth, and the rabbis of the different cities stayed in close contact with him and sent him the money they collected. Again the voice of Torah was heard in places where the tunes of the Gemara had been silenced. Yeshivah students, concerned with the education of local Jewish children, established Talmud Torahs and Jewish day schools. These students exposed themselves to great danger by crossing the borders between Poland and Russia to continue their studies.

One of the refugee rabbis who accompanied Rabbi Grodzenski and witnessed his heroic rescue efforts was Rabbi Judah L. Graubart, who served as rabbi in Satchov and later in Toronto, Canada. He describes the selfless devotion and sacrifice which characterized Rabbi Grodzenski. The exhausting program sapped his physical strength but the results of his work brought him great happiness.

After the overthrow of the Czarist regime by the Kerenski government, Rabbi Grodzenski went to Moscow and St. Petersburg to confer with the leaders of religious Jewry. He hoped to build the foundation for the organization of religious Jewry, and formulated plans to publish a daily newspaper which would serve as the mouthpiece for Torah-true Judaism. It seemed as if the proper time had come, as if it were now possible to translate the dream into reality! But it was not to be. After the October revolution, Kerenski was out, and with him disappeared the chance for the ambitious program. The new regime had other plans.

Rabbi Grodzenski left Russia and returned to Vilna, from which he had been absent for three years. Although ill and exhausted, he started forthwith the new chapter, a period of twenty years, the most fruitful of his life. It was, then, too, that he began to arrange his responsa for publication.

The city seemed headed for spiritual ruin, the irreligious elements having taken control of communal institutions. Funds contributed by American Jewry had often been distributed by the Joint Distribution Committee to leaders of the irreligious parties, enabling them to dominate the Jewish scene.

Havoc was greater in the field education. Yeshivoth ceased to exist. Some moved to interior Russia. The rest scattered and were without leadership. Elementary schools and the Talmud Torahs were closed. In their place, secular schools were established.

Rabbi Grodzenski devoted himself to the task of spiritual rehabilitation with such vigor that his associates were amazed to see such power in so weak a body.

A great task confronted him. He had to rebuild everything. It was necessary to gather large sums of money to reopen the religious schools. Moreover, food and clothing had to be provided for the children. The secular Jewish schools offered free meals and clothing to attract children of the poor. It was necessary to compete with them on every level. Rabbi Grodzenski contacted his many friends and colleagues in the United States and the Central Relief Organization. Under his influence ten organizations known as "Ezrath Torah" were established, which collected money to save Torah education from ruin and rabbis, scholars and communal endeavours from starving to death.

Torah schools were opened in Vilna and throughout Lithuania. Yeshivoth also opened their doors, attracting thousands of students. The voice of Torah, silent during the years of the war, was again heard. The Lithuanian Yeshivoth established branches in the district of Volhgo as well as certain sections of greater Poland.

A few months elapsed between Rabbi Grodzenski's return to Vilna and the arrival of Dr. Kantor and Dr. Friedlander, American representatives of a Relief Organization. As the harvest of his work in Poland, they found scores of preparatory academies and Yeshivoth, already re-established, and a system of elementary schools and Talmud Torahs, housing tens of thousands of Jewish children.

The moneys from America were substantial, but not enough to cover all needs. There were large numbers of individual rabbis and laymen, homeless on account of the war. To help them, the rabbi asked for and received funds from the non-orthodox Jews of Vilna as well as from the communities of England and South Africa.

To further carry out his plan, Rabbi Grodzenski appointed a committee of distinguished scholars—Rabbi Simon Shkop of

Brisk, Rabbi Abraham Gelbard of Grodno, Rabbi Judah Leib of Slonim, Rabbi Hezekiah Joseph Mishkowsky of Krynki and Rabbi Moses Shatzkes of Lomza. Rabbi Grodzenski headed the committee, which also included three members of the Vilna rabbinate. In 1919 they met in session for one week. Most of the resolutions adopted were translated into action. A committee for the assistance of religious institutions was appointed to aid 119 congregations in the region of Vilna, Grodno, Bialystok, Brisk and Kovno. Three months later, a second meeting was held. It was decided to open elementary schools in every Jewish settlement and to establish a Teachers' Institute. The committee supported more than 300 rabbis.

Rabbi Grodzenski's influence and prestige increased during this period. Under the Treaty of Versailles, Poland became a nation, with a total population of thirty-five million. There were three million Jews who had common problems and they looked to Vilna, to the distinguished rabbi and leader of Israel, whose mind was already occupied with plans for new assistance and rehabilitation. The Jews of Poland, separated during the course of a century, united themselves, once the political boundaries were removed. After the pogroms in Lvov and the murder of Jews in Pinsk, Polish Jewry saw its salvation in Rabbi Grodzenski's work for Torah and Jewish tradition. His home served as a center for Polish Torah-true Jewry, whose representatives spoke in the legislature chambers of the land and advanced the cause and prestige of Torah among Jews and non-Jews.

Rabbi Grodzenski's dream of a strong united Torah Jewry was now a reality! He had begun to organize for it under the Czar. Since his youth, he had entertained the idea of uniting religious Jewry to advance the ideals of Torah and Orthodoxy. Laxity and lawlessness were increasing because positions of leadership in Israel were occupied by men completely divorced from Torah, who spoke in the name of the Jewish people, represented Jewry before the government, and consistently attempted to remove the influence of the great rabbis from communal affairs. These men established schools devoid of the principles of Judaism, published newspapers and periodicals for the purpose of lowering the prestige of Torah, and disseminated attitudes and viewpoints

contrary to Jewish faith. Religious Jews felt discouraged and almost desperate. But there were a few who battled for our holy
traditions, some writing, some lecturing, others exerting personal
efforts with government officials. Rabbi Grodzenski threw his
support and influence with these defenders of Torah. In 1909,
with his backing, there had appeared a brochure entitled *"Elbonah
shel Torah*—The Humiliation of the Torah." Devoted to the
problems of secular education which were beginning to enter the
Jewish community, it contained letters from outstanding rabbinical
leaders of the day. But temporary efforts were not enough. Rabbi
Grodzenski conceived of an organization which would include all
Torah-true Jews throughout the world.

The first meeting was held at Vilna in 1909 and was attended
by the greatest Jewish leaders of the day. Those present had one
goal. Understanding and mutual sympathy permeated all sessions.
Rabbi David Friedman was elected Honorary President and Rabbi
Grodzenski President. This meeting was indeed historic and its
influence was felt throughout the Jewish world. After a century
of struggles and quarrels this was the first time that leaders of
Hassidim and Mithnaggedim became partners in working for
a common objective. Differences of opinion were forgotten; the
foundation for united efforts was laid. Rabbi Grodzenski's wisdom
and tact were largely responsible for the success of the conference.

It resulted in the founding of the religious organization—
"Knesseth Yisrael". Prospects for its success seemed good. It
could count on a following of hundreds of thousands, for the
vast majority of Jews in Russia and in Poland were religious.
The great rabbinical leaders who supported the organization helped
to attract many, but the Russian government ordered the Vilna
office of Knesseth Israel to close its branches. This edict did not
discourage Rabbi Grodzenski's efforts. He remained firm in his
determination to organize. He established schools, preparatory
academies and Talmud Torahs. To head these he appointed competent men who might also be of help in communal endeavors.
The entire project was organized quietly and functioned well.
Vilna, or, to be more correct, Rabbi Grodzenski's home, was the
unofficial center of religious Jewry, in Russia as well as outside
of Russia.

He participated in the organizational meeting of the Agudath Yisrael in Kattowitz in 1912. Here he met the religious leaders of Germany, and the efforts of the East and the West were combined.

He helped organize the Agudath Yisrael in Poland and Lithuania after World War I, and participated in the first two Agudah Congresses which were held in Vienna. As President of the Rabbinical Council, he was the spiritual head of the Agudath Yisrael.

He played an important role in reconciling differences. It was his habit to listen attentively to others, never expressing his point of view until all had the opportunity to make their opinions known. Then he would give his decision in clear, pointed language that could not be interpreted in two ways.

There came a steady decline in the amount of money coming from America for the support of the Yeshivoth, while at the same time their financial needs grew from day to day. The leaders of the Joint Distribution Committee maintained that Polish Jews ought to contribute to the support of their own institutions. The Jews of Poland lived amidst such unfortunate economic conditions that it was difficult for a family to support its own members, let alone to aid educational institutions and communal organizations.

To cope with the situation, a conference for the support of Yeshivoth was held in July, 1924. The main speaker was Rabbi Israel Meir ha-Kohen Kagan, the Hafets Hayyim of sainted memory, whose address inspired the establishment of the Va'ad ha-Yeshivoth (Council of Yeshivoth). Upon every Jew in Eastern Poland a minimum tax was imposed of one dollar every six months for the support of the Va'ad ha-Yeshivoth. The decree was announced by the Hafets Hayyim in the presence of hundreds of rabbis and thousands of Jews; the rabbis present agreed to visit various cities for the purpose of establishing branches of the Va'ad ha-Yeshivoth.

A meeting of the Va'ad ha-Yeshivoth and representatives of the Central Organization, held in Vilna in 1930, decided that it would be of great value to have Rabbi Grodzenski visit the United States of America. The Hafets Hayyim communicated this to Rabbi Grodzenski, who replied that he had already thought about such a trip, but that unfortunately, his physicians would not permit him to undertake it. Upon hearing the reply, the Hafets Hayyim apologized to Rabbi Grodzenski and said: "Had I known that the trip would in any way affect your health, I never would have suggested it. In my opinion you are the greatest asset the Jewish people have today."

The greatest scholars and saints had deep affection and admiration for Rabbi Grodzenski. The heads of the great Yeshivoth (Rabbi Barukh Ber Leibowitz of Kaminetz, Rabbi Simon Shkop of Grodno, Rabbi Elhanan Wasserman of Baranowitz, Rabbi Aaron Kotler of Kletzk, and Rabbi Eliezer Judah Finkel of Mir, were always ready to carry out his suggestions and projects.

The Va'ad ha-Yeshivoth developed. It had hundreds of Torah institutions and scores of Yeshivoth under its supervision. About five thousand students studied in the higher institutions of learning which it sponsored. The Va'ad supported also other schools, published textbooks and a special newspaper, "Das Wort."

To raise funds, the Va'ad decided to have a Sefer Torah written and to dedicate it to the memory of the sainted Hafets Hayyim. Men and women could purchase the privilege of writing one letter of the Sefer Torah, which was to be placed in the Hafets Hayyim's Beth Midrash in Radin. Special memorial meetings were held to publicize the project, which was favorably received. Rabbi Grodzenski purchased the first sentence of the Torah in the name of his wife and himself.

The great importance of the Va'ad ha-Yeshivoth was proven in the early days of World War II. Vilna became the center of Yeshivah life. In the winter of 1940, hundreds of Yeshivah men reached Vilna destitute. The Va'ad ha-Yeshivoth welcomed them, established special kitchens, gave financial aid, clothed and assisted them in every way.

The second World War broke out in Poland in September, 1939. The Nazis' invasion of Western Poland brought terror. Jews of Eastern Poland welcomed the Soviet Army with relief. At least they saved their lives. Like Abraham of old, they pleaded *"Give me the persons, and the goods take to thyself"* (Gen. XIV, 21).

Yeshivoth had to be saved again. As Maimonides expressed it, "The life of scholars and students without the study of Torah is considered a living death."

The problem facing the Yeshivoth was how to escape. Soviet Russia was on one side and Nazi Germany on the other. Rail connections between Vilna and other sections conquered by the Russians enabled many Yeshivah students to reach Vilna. The border was soon closed but the flow of students continued. Rabbi Grodzenski sent word to the Yeshivoth that they be moved to Vilna. The academies of Mir, Kletzk, Radin, Kaminetz, Baranowitz, Bialystok, were transferred. Only parts of the other Yeshivoth were rescued. The number of students who reached Vilna was two thousand five hundred. Torah was heard in all the streets of Vilna, the Jersualem of Lithuania.

The Va'ad ha-Yeshivoth arranged to support Yeshivah men who arrived in Vilna. Rabbi Grodzenski appealed to the United States and England, and within a short time shipments of clothing arrived.

During these days of horror, the glory of Rabbi Grodzenski emerged brighter than ever. His heart grieved over the calamities, he became the spokesman for his people. Two leaders of Israel passed away, Rabbi Simon Shkop, head of the Grodno Yeshivah, and Rabbi Ber Leibowitz, head of the Kaminetz Yeshivah, at a time when their Yeshivoth were in ruin. Their students mourned. Even the average Jew could sense the greatness of the loss. Rabbi Grodzenski had special reasons for grief. The great scholars and rabbis were passing away, leaving him additional duties and responsibilities.

He sought to re-establish in Lithuania all the institutions of Polish Jewry now destroyed by the war; to reorganize the Agudath Yisrael; to publish a daily newspaper, religious in outlook. Conditions make it impossible. In the winter of 1939-40 a meeting of the Agudath Yisrael was held. Delegates from Lithuania, Latvia and Poland were present. Jews of Poland and Latvia worked together for mutal benefit. This was the last meeting in which Rabbi Grodzenski participated. The head of the Telzer Yeshiva and President of Agudath Yisrael in Lithuania, Rabbi Eliyahu M.

Bloch, and Mr. Leib Muntzberg, went over the details with Rabbi Grodzenski.

He was anxious about the fate of great scholars who were left behind in Poland, particularly Rabbi Abraham Mordecai Alter, the Gerrer Rebbe, and was elated to hear that Rabbi Alter had left Poland and had reached Trieste on his way to the Holy Land. He was also concerned about the fate of the rabbis of Lodz and Warsaw, particularly Rabbi Menahem Zemba. It grieved him that they would not come to Vilna. He tried unsuccessfully to rescue Rabbi Aaron Levin of Reisha and Rabbi Halberstam of Bobov.

The basic thing, he maintained throughout, was to devote oneself to diligent study. "The world exists through the merits and virtues of Torah. In this time, when great Jewish communities have been destroyed, the voice of the Torah has become weak. Those who have the opportunity to continue their studies must double their efforts."

V

Rabbi Grodzenski suffered much pain from an incurable ailment. But, continuing cheerfully, he did not stop his devoted work until his last day, August 9, 1940 (Av 5, 5700).

On July 17, the Soviet Army entered Lithuania and the Baltic countries, annexing them to Soviet Russia. This caused alarm and confusion among Jews, for it meant the confiscation and destruction of their homes and stores. Yeshivah men who had just escaped from the Red Army were caught again.

Rabbi Grodzenski was greatly affected by these events. His was the responsibility for the preservation of Torah and the support of scholars who, on his advice, had escaped to Lithuania. The grave problems sapped the little strength left in his body. He no longer left his bed. Only a few intimate associates were allowed to enter his room.

He was persuaded to go to a summer resort near Vilna, in Magistratska, and there he continued to direct his activities. He remained in full possession of his faculties until his last moment.

Refugees stormed the consular offices, searching for entry permits that would allow them to live in free countries. Permits were obtained for Curacao, Japan and China, but the journey would be expensive, and the refugees were despondent. It was suggested that Rabbi Grodzenski obtain a permit to Palestine for himself. His reply was: "I'm only looking for a visa to the world of life." In spite of his condition, he would not rest. He sent cables to Palestine and asked for certificates to America and for entry permits. He insisted that everyone work hard and always continue the study of Torah.

The Soviet officials made their influence felt in Jewish life. Religious and communal institutions were closed. Ritual slaughter was interfered with, and this led to a decline in the observance of Kashruth. Jewish children were forced to attend Communist schools. Religious Jews remained firm in their refusal to send their children to the new Red schools, in spite of all penalties imposed. Students in the Yeshivoth studied with increased diligence. The Communists themselves, paradoxically, sometimes admired these lovers of the spirit and were suspicious of those who changed loyalty and ideology too easily!

The last few days of his life were full of activity. He himself wrote a letter to the President of the Agudath ha-Rabbanim in the United States concerning plans to rescue the Yeshivoth. Upon learning that writing tired him, his friends suggested that someone write the letters and that he merely add his signature. He refused, saying: "Perhaps when Rabbi Eliezer Silver sees the letter in my own handwriting, he will realize the seriousness of the situation, and will seek additional means of helping the Yeshivoth."

He worked incessantly for the relief of refugee rabbis and Yeshivoth. Upon leaving him, one of his associates remarked that we need not give up hope about the Torah, for the Almighty gave us a specific assurance that "it shall not be forgotten out of the mouths of their seed." Rabbi Grodzenski replied enthusiastically: "I am relying on that declaration."

Rabbi Zalman Sorotzkin visited Rabbi Grodzenski a few days before his demise. The latter told him, "I have received an inquiry from Switzerland concerning the administration of a shock-producing injection to an animal before slaughter. It is a well-known fact that the kosher slaughtering of animals is prohibited in Switzerland. The Jews of that land used to obtain kosher meat from Germany, France and Denmark. Since the Nazis came to power in these countries, the Jews of Switzerland have been left without meat. They therefore turned to me, stressing that the injection does not cause the animal to die.

"I replied: 'The Jews are a very ancient people, in spite of all the decrees which their enemies have put into effect to destroy them. Israel's enemies have passed on to oblivion, while the Jewish people has continued to exist. In the period in which we are living, we must make every sacrifice to observe Rabbinical enactments, particularly when there is cause to fear that by ignoring them we may violate the law of the Torah.' I decided to prohibit the use of injection, for we must not yield one iota. *'The grass withereth, the flower fadeth, but the word of God shall stand forever'* (Isa. XL, 8)."

He was concerned to the last for refugee rabbis and Yeshivoth, and the problem of a haven for them became very urgent. Eighty refugee rabbis wanted to go to the United States or to Palestine. Only a certain number of entry permits were available. The question was asked: "Who is to receive priority—the older men or the younger ones?" Rabbi Grodzenski replied that the older men ought to be given preference, for, upon their arrival in the United States, they could be of great help to the Jews left in Europe.

The last evening of his life arrived. Rabbi Grodzenski set his affairs in order and upon finishing said: "In spite of everything, there is no reason to give up hope."

The following morning (Friday, August 9, 1940— Av 5, 5740), everyone realized that death was at the door.

At 11:00 A. M. Rabbi Mosheh Shatzkes and Rabbi Michael Kossovsky, his sister's grandson, sat at his bedside. They spoke and he listened, for he lacked the strength to answer. Suddenly he closed his eyes as if he wanted to slumber, and it was thus that he returned his soul to its Creator.

The sad news spread rapidly throughout Vilna and threw that entire Jewish community into deep mourning. A meeting was held at the office of the Vaad-ha-Yeshivoth to make the necessary arrangements for the funeral, and to send the news to Jewish communities throughout the world.

The road from Magistratska in Vilna was lined with multitudes of people who cried out bitterly, "Our Rabbi and Teacher, you left us in a period of great darkness. Upon whom can we rely? The world gives us but gloom, persecution and darkness. *The godly man has perished from the earth*" (Micah 7, 2).

As the coffin was removed from the house, no special permit was received from the Soviet authorities for the funeral. Nevertheless, the officials did not interfere, and sent several officers and guards to keep order. All stores, even those of non-Jews, were closed during the funeral.*

Memorial meetings in honor of Rabbi Grodzenski were held in Jewish communities throughout the world. Jews everywhere mourned their irreplaceable loss and devised means to perpetuate his name.

A street was named after him in Tel-Aviv, a Yeshivah in Old Jerusalem adopted his name. Many circles and groups in Palestine adopted the name Ahiezer.

A Yeshivah in Tel-Aviv and Rabbi Abramski of London issued memorial volumes which contain many Torah essays as well as the story of his life.

---

*In the eyes of religious Jewry, not only in Vilna and Lithuania but the world over, no one but Rabbi Hayyim Ozer was ever considered as the real chief of the rabbinate of Vilna, but in this connection it is interesting to recall the incident of Rabbi Rubinstein and the position of Chief Rabbi there. In every Jewish community, the government required a "chief rabbi" who registered births, marriages, deaths, and acted as a sort of liaison officer. This man was regarded by the Jewish communities as merely a political appointee and had no real religious jurisdiction. When such a post became vacant in Vilna, in 1910, Rabbi Grodzenski actively supported the candidacy of the above-mentioned Rabbi Rubinstein who bade fair to maintain a helpful attitude towards the traditional group. One never knew when the need might arise to placate a fickle government.

All went smoothly for a time, but, in the absence of Rabbi Grodzenski, after the outbreak of World War I, Rabbi Rubinstein fell prey to an over-weening ambition to become, indeed, Chief Rabbi of Vilna, and he managed to get himself so elected by the Kehillah.

This action caused some pain to Rabbi Grodzenski. The humiliation of being forced by governmental decree to defer in some important decisions to the upstart "Chief Rabbi," did not trouble him so much as the betrayal of a promise, and the violation of an unwritten law. For over a hundred years that post had been left unfilled, out of respect to the memory of the illustrious Elijah Gaon of Vilna. The Vilna Kehillah had finally offered it to Rabbi Grodzenski, but he had refused to break the time-honored precedent, and had continued to serve as a member of the rabbinical board, refusing even to accept an increase in salary, unless a similar increase be given to his colleagues.

The Board of Rabbis in the United States proclaimed a month of mourning and urged all members to arrange memorial meetings. A special fund in memory of Rabbi Grodzenski was established whose purpose it was to support distinguished Torah scholars.

The great sages of the day revered him. Rabbi Barukh Ber Leibowitz, head of the Yeshivah of Kaminetz, said, "Since the passing of my teacher, Rabbi Hayyim Soloveitchik, I've made Rabbi Grodzenski my teacher and my guide." Rabbi Yeruham Leibowitz, the spiritual counsellor of the Mirer Yeshivah, used to say, "Rabbi Grodzenski is the greatest treasure of our generation. Would that we knew how to honor and appreciate the great gift which the Almighty has graciously given to our generation."

"Rabbi Hayyim Ozer is not only a distinguished personality," declared the Hafets Hayyim, "he is an institution—which we must guard very carefully."

World Jewry must continue to carry the load which was on his shoulders—the responsibility for the preservation of Torah and Yeshivoth!

Among the papers found after his departure were the following resolutions, dated the eve of Yom Kippur, 1934. They really form a spiritual testament. Therein he urges all Jews:

(1) To spend some time each day in the study of Jewish ethical literature—to read books like "The Gates of Repentance" by Rabbi Jonah Gerundi and "The Path of the Upright" by Rabbi Moses Hayyim Luzatto, and similar works, and to take a daily spiritual inventory.

(2) To refrain from worthless, vain talk, and to engage only in worthwhile, meaningful conversation.

(3) To set regular periods for the study of Torah every day, even on the busiest days, so that not one day will pass without reflection and meditation.

(4) To pray with devotion.

(5) To stop writing on Friday afternoon at least one hour before sunset, unless there is something very urgent at hand.

(6) To urge rabbis to do their full share in stressing the importance of the Sabbath, kosher food, and family purity.

(7) To encourage classes and lectures in the Beth Midrash for laymen and young Jews.

(8) To do everything possible to avoid anger.

(9) To systematize philanthropic activities.

ISRAEL MEIR ha-KOHEN, THE HAFETS HAYYIM

BY MOSES M. YOSHOR

ISRAEL MEIR ha-KOHEN, THE HAFETS HAYYIM

By Moses M. Yoshor

There is a story in the Midrash of a remarkable peddler who went from place to place crying "Buy my elixir of life." He met with scorn and skepticism and was denounced as a fake or a fool. But Rabbi Yannai approached him one day and offered to buy this preparation. The peddler refused him, saying, "This is neither for you, nor for any man like you." He then opened the book of the Psalms and pointed to verses 13-14 of chapter thirty-four: *"Who is the man that desireth life and loveth to enjoy happiness for many days? Keep thy tongue from evil, and thy lips from speaking guile."* "Indeed," the rabbi replied, "this elixir is for me, for your dramatic interpretation has given the passage a new meaning for me."

On February 6th, 1838, there was born in Zhetel, Poland, a child named Israel Meir, who, as he grew up, came to identify himself with the peddler of the story. He proposed to devote the energies of a whole lifetime to revitalizing for his fellow-men the message of that passage in the Psalm. His father was a teacher, his mother a pious woman who always had at hand a well-thumbed book of the Psalms.

For almost a century (he lived until 1933) he served his ideal. It is by the title of his first published work (1873) "Hafets Hayyim", "He Who Desires Life", that he came to be lovingly known. The title page bore no author's name. He had modestly omitted it.

In the beginning, R. Israel Meir was his own salesman. He published his own books, and wandered from town to town to sell them. When he approached people, he did not tell them that he was the author. He enjoyed his humble incognito. All through life, when fame chased him, he scurried away.

That he was called "The Hafets Hayyim" was no mere gesture. There was a close tie between the author and his work. In a real sense the author lived according to the principles he expounded.

What were these principles of the "desirer-of-life?" Speech is said to be the most precious gift bestowed on man; if properly cultivated, this faculty raises him to pre-eminence over the beast, but when degraded to the vulgarities of calumny it lowers him to brutishness.

Throughout Jewish history, Israel's leading thinkers had warned against defilement of the tongue. "Very often," says R. Israel Meir, "an evil statement injurious to one's neighbor might easily lead to a violation of other laws . . ." He enumerated fourteen positive and seventeen prohibitive commandments of the Torah that were related to the prohibition concerning the evil tongue. And, further, he cites the Talmud's comparison of slander to the most grievous sins of idolatry, adultery and murder. The serious consequences of evil talk could not be too much emphasized. They could destroy innocent lives.

Moreover, a talebearing tongue convicts itself, the slandered one and him who listens to the slander. It kills three with a single blow. Gossip, he further asserts, is a sin, not only when false, but even if true; not only when spread against and among our own kinsmen but even among strangers. A stranger may be more apt to give credence to the evil tale than a kinsman.

The solution: One should train himself to think before he opens his mouth to speak, and to maintain silence if his utterance would in any manner cause the least suffering to others.

This writer recalls an incident which he witnessed: Once a disciple complained to the Hafets Hayyim that his own two-hour preaching seemed to have no noticeable effect on his congregation. With whimsical humor the sage replied, "Remember the Midrash: 'For each and every second that a man keeps silent, abstaining from evil talk, he will enjoy the rays of mystic light in the Hereafter.'

"If such a treasure," he continued, "is promised for only one second's silence, reflect on the reward you will have for regularly keeping your congregation in silence—in silent abstinence from evil talk—for two whole hours!"

Even if someone tells a story about himself, it would not be well for his friend to repeat it in his absence. This admonishment from the sage came about as follows:

One of his household mentioned that he had heard something interesting about Mr. M., who had recently visited them. From the story, the "something interesting" turned out to be unfavorable to Mr. M.

"Please stop talking evil about others," the Hafets Hayyim protested, "we have enough of our own defects to talk about."

"But Mr. M. told the story about himself, and in front of everybody."

"Nevertheless, you must not repeat it. One may very well like to reproach himself, yet not like to be reproached by others. It is like a slap which one may playfully administer to himself, but not allow others to do so."

It is told that as a very young child he evidenced those traits which were to endear him to all. Once his schoolmates snatched up some apples that were falling off an old lady's pushcart. Israel Meir beseeched his mother to spare a few pennies, and with these he replaced the poor peddler's loss.

At the age of ten he lost his father. His mother made every possible sacrifice to have her beloved Israel Meir continue his studies uninterruptedly. She went to Vilna, the intellectual center of European Jewry, where he studied for several years till his marriage. Meanwhile his mother re-married and moved to Radun. In Vilna, Israel Meir came into contact with the secularizing *Haskalists* ("enlighteners"). A. D. Lebensohn, one of the founders of the *Haskalah* movement, heard about the brilliant young Talmudist from Radun, and made a friendly effort to entice him to his own circle. Israel Meir rejected the flattering attention paid to him and the offers of a moneyed future; he determined to proceed with the course of pure Torah. Already then he saw envisioned his true destiny.

He returned once from a vacation visit to his mother, and was summoned by his dean, the great Rabbi Jacob Barit. There was the problem of filling the rabbinical vacancy in the town of Radun. Two parties were contending for the position. Rabbi Barit asked Israel Meir for information on the matter. The boy humbly asked to be excused from making any statement because he had taken it upon himself not to speak the slightest evil of others.

When he was seventeen he married Frieda, the daughter of his step-father. He refused the customary dowry. He settled with his bride in Radun. He was to make this little muddy village between Grodno and Vilna famous throughout the world. It would be his home for the rest of his life. Invitations to high rabbinical posts would come to Radun, but he would decline all offers and evade all honors.

At first he acceded to the request of the townspeople of Radun and accepted their rabbinic office, but without remuneration. The venture lasted only a few months. When someone refused to accept his decision in a case of religious law, he resigned his position and indeed never again accepted public office. He preferred to remain a layman.

To make a living, his wife opened a small grocery shop, but as a result of his endeavors to offer the finest merchandise at the smallest profit, and his over-scrupulousness in not expanding his group of customers, he could not long flourish in the competitive realm of business. He turned to teaching, and served as a Talmud instructor in Minsk and Washilishok from 1864 to 1869.

In 1869 (when he was 31), a cherished dream of his life came true. He brought into existence in his little Radun a Yeshivah. The "Yeshivath Hafets Hayyim of Radun," as it was later known, grew into one of the most prominent centers of Talmudic learning.

He labored hard at soliciting funds for the Yeshivah, keeping nothing to himself. He always lived very simply. After becoming an author, he eked out a livelihood from the sale of his books, allowing himself only a meager profit and refusing to accept anything above the price he had set. Even when one of the Rothschilds sent him three hundred francs for a set of his works, the Hafets Hayyim deducted thirty francs for the cost of the books and returned the remainder with a note of thanks for the generous offer and with a suggestion that if the donor were willing, he could send the balance to his Yeshivah. To Rothschild the experience was entirely novel. He sent back a considerably increased remittance to the Hafets Hayyim's institution.

* * * *

He believed that the Torah constituted the essential *raison d'être* of Israel, and that its spirit should be infused into Jewish daily living.

"The scroll of the Law is considered by every Jew as a most sacred object. Obviously the parchment itself does not constitute the reason for its sanctity. It is rather by virtue of the holy contents inscribed therein that the scroll is hallowed and endeared. How much more sanctified does a man become when the living words of the Torah have been absorbed in his blood and indelibly imprinted on his heart."

The Hafets Hayyim deplored those who had gone astray from the path of rectitude. He deeply grieved over those who were recklessly drifting away from the religion of their fathers. To illustrate the grave consequences involved in such drifting, he cited the pitiful spiritual state in which he found German Jewry (during a visit at the end of the nineteenth century). "It was heartbreaking how they had sold their birthright for an illusory mess of pottage. . . . The Reform movement which they originated has wrought calamity in Israel."

In the lectures he gave at his Yeshivah he sought to emphasize the essentiality of good deeds, *maassim tovim*. "The performance of good deeds is the ultimate goal of Jewish ethics. Devotion—*kavanah*—may be an important element in the realization of a mitsvah, but it is devoid of merit when not accompanied by action. Should one spend the whole day in solemn meditation and concentrate all his thoughts on a good deed without actually performing it, he will reap no reward. The Torah consists primarily of 'Thou shalt do' and 'Thou shalt not do'. Doing, action, is indicated. The only time a person may get credit for a deed he has not performed is when he has been actually prevented from carrying out his intention."

A stranger who visited the Hafets Hayyim soon found out that his host took the action-part of the mitsvah quite seriously. He was astonished to see the revered sage making up his bed. He vehemently protested against this menial service. The saint should not trouble himself. At least he must permit him, the guest, to help.

"No, no, dear sir, you must not help me," said the Hafets Hayyim. "It is my mitsvah, not yours. I am your host, not you mine." And he illustrated his argument: "When you saw me don *tefillin* this morning at the synagogue, did you then also offer me your help? Just as you cannot substitute your person for mine in the performance of the mitsvah of *tefillin,* so too must you not substitute your person for mine in the performance of the mitsvah of *hakhnassath orhim* (hospitality)."

HIS BOOKS

Three years after the appearance of *Hafets Hayyim,* that is to say in 1876, he wrote a complementary treatise, *Shemirath ha-Lashon* ("The Guarding of the Tongue"). *Hafets Hayyim* treats of the righteous tongue in the light of halakhah (precepts); *Shemirath ha-Lashon*—in the light of haggadah (non-preceptive principles and attitudes). In 1888 he set forth the legal and moral principles of love and kindness in *Ahavath Hessed* ("Loving Kindness"). It covers the field of human relations from general exhortation to sympathy with others, to specific prescriptions on the relation between employer and employee. The author stressed the need of a healthy society that would guard the rights of labor as well as of capital.

Though his was the traditional Jewish way of life, according to the tenets and principles of the Torah; though he instructed others to follow them, he did not become a personality desiccated by overpiety. He passed Judaism's supreme test; he did not let his personal inclination—no matter how loftily significant—interfere with the fulfilling of his duties toward his fellow men.

One afternoon, while vacationing in the country village of Zhermon, the Hafets Hayyim and his coterie were worrying about the absence of a tenth man to complete the *minyan* (prayer quorum) for the *Minhah* service. Dinner must wait on the *Minhah.* One of the disciples suddenly beheld a man approaching the master's domicile. "Now, Rebbi, we shall have a minyan!"

"Do not say that, my son," Israel Meir admonished. "Nowhere in the Torah is it stated that when a visitor comes to your home you must offer him prayer; it is stated that you must offer him food, drink and a bed to rest in."

As the man crossed the threshold, the Hafets Hayyim rose to welcome him, to offer him shelter and to invite him to his table.

He did not believe in an ill-timed rush to perform the devotions. He could sense when it would be right to postpone, when it would be right to proceed, when service to man preceded service to God.

At a rabbinical convocation in Warsaw a certain problem led to prolonged discussion. When someone moved for a recess to pray *Minhah,* the weary rabbis were eager to disperse. They were startled to hear the nonagenarian Hafets Hayyim object: "Did we gather from all the corners of Poland to pray Minhah? Let us settle this problem here and now, first."

Later on the Gaon Hayyim Ozer Grodzenski of Vilna facetiously observed: "The Hafets Hayyim and the other rabbis were both right. The Hafets Hayyim was right because he meant it entirely *lishmah* (all for the sake of Heaven), so that his discussion was a pure mitsvah; and he who engages in one mitsvah is free from a concurrent mitsvah. The other rabbis were right, too, because they did not mean all for the sake of Heaven, so that their discussion was not a pure mitsvah; hence they were not free from the mitsvah of *Minhah."*

Concerned with the lot of the Jewish soldier away from home and thrown into a strange environment often hostile to Judaism, he wrote *Mahaneh Yisrael* ("The Camp of Israel") in 1881.

In the eighties a wave of savage Jew-baiting swept through Russia, resulting in a mass emigration of Jews to distant lands. The Hafets Hayyim felt intense anxiety over the lot of these wandering Jews who faced the difficulties of readjustment in alien lands. To help in their adjustment, he wrote in 1893 a special book for the Jewish emigrant, *Nidhei Yisrael* ("The Dispersed of Israel"). It contains a selection of all the laws whose observance might be challenged by the changed conditions and strange surroundings. His exhortations breathe a spirit of love and sympathy for his distant brethren. His concern for their spiritual welfare, as well as for their material well-being, is evident throughout. He lays particular emphasis on the importance of keeping the Sabbath.

> "By calling the Sabbath a 'sign', the Torah impressed on us its supreme importance. An artisan hangs out a sign indicating his occupation so that all may come to him for his wares. As long as the shingle remains on his house, all can see that the artisan still dwells and works there. He may leave his home from time to time, yet the sign remains to indicate that he maintains his permanent residence there. How-

ever, as soon as he removes the sign, the passers-by assume that he has departed and is no longer to be found at his old address.

Similar is the case with the Sabbath. It is a sign that the Almighty created heaven and earth in six days and rested on the seventh. The Jew who holds aloft this glorious standard demonstrates explicitly that he believes in the Creator and Master of all, and acknowledges that it is his duty to be obedient to Him with all his heart and soul, since He is Lord over all possessions. It serves as a symbol of the Almighty's presence in the Jew's life and heart, inspiring and filling his soul with serenity and holiness."

Faith was the incentive of his task. A pure and serene faith prompted his every move. He was unswerving in his devotion to God, permeated with a most passionate love for his Maker. Faith to him meant much more than a theological profession. It was a pervading reality. He felt it in every fibre of his being.

In 1893 he wrote *Shem Olam* ("The Everlasting Memorial"), which title he derived from the verse in Isaiah (LVI) concerning the reward of the childless man who pleases God. Reason, he stated, is not in opposition to faith, but is rather its complement. He was convinced of the absolute truth of Judaism. What seems to have been beyond his comprehension was the agnostic. How could the agnostic fail to see what was so inwardly clear?

Faith attains sublime heights when all human powers and faculties are dedicated to the divine service. According to the Hafets Hayyim's teaching in *Shem Olam,* Torah in its entirety is like a living organism. The six hundred and thirteen mitsvoth comprise its vital members. Hence, just as one cannot handle a single isolated organ of a living entity as though it possessed life independent of the rest, so one must not judge any single mitsvah independently of the rest. Every law, beside having its own interpretation, helps to explain the other laws. Only when *"the teaching of the Lord is perfect,"* that is to say, *complete,* says the Psalmist, does it *"restore the soul."*

The late Ephraim Kaplan, an American Jewish journalist, on visiting the sage in Radun, asked him what one must observe in order to be a good Jew.

"Observe the *Shulhan Arukh,* and that means all the mitsvoth expounded therein," was the rejoinder.

"If so, you exclude ninety percent of the people from that privilege," argued Mr. Kaplan.

"True," retorted the Hafets Hayyim, "but if you buy a bottle of pure alcohol and reduce its strength and adulterate it, the shop-keeper who sold it to you is not to be blamed for the changed strength. You asked me to define pure, unadulterated Jewishness, which I did."

And he wrote:

"The knowledge of the Torah is the noblest yearning of human aspiration and its possession the greatest of man's treasures. There is no joy loftier, no contentment deeper than an understanding of its principles."

The code of Rabbi Joseph Karo and Rabbi Moses Isserles, as continually brought up to date by the decisions of modern Torah authorities, derives its authority from the Talmudic halakhah. The Hafets Hayyim in his day realized the need for a more extensive and more explicit definition of Jewish laws. He felt the lack of a popular edition of the Shulhan Aruch, with notes about the original motive and significance of each law. Since Halakhah represents a living plan, it required an expression of vivid experience. He gave it such expression.

Probably he had long felt the urge to create such a work. Once he had made up his mind, he lost no time in his attempt to realize his ambition. He worked indefatigably. He certainly knew how to use his time to full advantage. He deplored people who did not appreciate the value of time. Indulging in paradox he would say, "Money is Time." And he would add, "The possession of too much money represents an over-expenditure of time. He who squanders his time squanders his life, for killing time is equivalent to killing life."

Israel Meir named his most important work *Mishnah Berurah* ("Lucid Learning"). It brilliantly recapitulated Orah Hayyim, the first section of the *Shulham Arukh,* in a style under-standable to the layman. He defined the original laws and customs, offering his own decisions and opinions, derived from Talmudic literature. The author divided the *Mishnah Berurah* into six volumes, consisting of more than eighteen hundred pages. The first volume saw the light in 1884, and the sixth in 1907. The *Mishnah*

Berurah quickly became the most popular, unabridged code of Jewish law.

As the body needs food for its sustenance (he writes in the introduction to the first volume), so does the soul need Torah as its spiritual food. The most important part of the Torah is that which deals with everyday conduct, which the *Mishnah Berurah* seeks to elucidate. Upright daily life implies daily study. One reinforces the other, and together they spell (Olam ha-Ba) a man's salvation.

Realizing that the sanctity of the Jewish people depended on the happiness of family life, the Hafets Hayyim felt deeply pained to see many women ignore the observance of the ritual of Taharah, a fundamental law in Judaism. He wrote books—*Geder Olam* in 1890 and *Taharath Yisrael* in 1910—and pamphlets urging conformity to this basic mitsvah. He travelled to many Jewish communities, admonishing them to maintain family purity.

In the radiance of his faith there was no shadow of doubt. He looked confidently to the fulfillment of the divine promise. Under no circumstances would he write off one iota of the prophecies envisaged for Israel. If an earthly lord deems it a matter of principle to keep his pledge, how much more so the Lord of Heaven.

He prayed for Israel's total rehabilitation, not a homeland in reduced territory or mere political independence. It was not worthwhile, he said, to become another Albania or even another Belgium after nineteen centuries of suffering. A state must be re-established on Torah foundations. It must be a reign of justice and godliness, with the Holy Temple restored and sacrificial offerings reinstated.

Messiah could come any day! As a *Kohen,* he might be summoned at once to the Temple service. To prepare for the possible call, he must learn thoroughly all the neglected laws of Temple and sacrifice. And he did. If he had been called to the Third Temple he would have been ready.

To others he communicated this urgent duty to revive the study of *Kodashim,* Temple law. Hitherto only the rare scholar had ever looked at *Kodashim;* now, at the Hafets Hayyim's urging, it became the fashion in the Yeshivoth and is still popular today.

But the ultimate achievement of his efforts to revive *Kodashim* was his massive *Likkutei Halakhoth.* It is not his most popular work, but it is his most scholarly. The first volume appeared in 1900, and the concluding fifth volume appeared in 1925.

Rabbi Isaac ben Jacob Alfasi (1013-1103) had condensed the halakhic parts of the Talmud. Styled "The Little Talmud," his work had omitted all those laws not applicable to the Diaspora, notably *Kodashim*. The Hafets Hayyim, convinced by his deep faith of the nearness of Israel's restoration to the Holy Land, supplied what Alfasi had left out. *Likkutei Halakhoth* is a halakhic condensation of *Kodashim,* adorned by many scholarly footnotes.

In conjunction with the *Likkutei* he wrote an exhaustive commentary on *Torath Kohanim,* a halakhic Midrash on Leviticus. Here, too, he made the laws of *Kodashim* understandable to moderns.

THE FATHER OF HIS PEOPLE

In 1914, after the First World War broke out, the Czarist Russians increased their harassment of the Jews. They became so hysterical in their phobias and suspicions that they interpreted the solemn calls of the *Shofar* as secret signals to the enemy.

Acting on false information, the Russians arrested a young boy from Memel, Germany, who was studying at the Yeshivah in Radun. The Hafets Hayyim took up his defense, and never deserted him as the case dragged on. Finally a military court sentenced the boy to ten years of imprisonment. The Hafets Hayyim remarked: "Fools, they sentenced him to imprisonment for ten years; it never occurred to them that their corrupt system may not last ten months, or perhaps ten weeks!" March 1917, which saw the fall of Czarism, was less than ten weeks off!

In 1916, while a refugee in the city of Smilowitz, Russia, he was asked to make an appeal from the pulpit for *Maoth Hittim* (Relief Fund for Passover). He said, in part: "Brethren, I want your advice. I am growing old, as you see, and, before long, expect to be summoned before the heavenly tribunal of justice. Suppose I should be asked, 'Israel Meir, you were in Smilowitz. Tell us something about your brethren there.' What should I then reply? To say that you are charitable would not be the truth; and all my life I have never lied. To tell the truth, that you are not charitable, would, on the other hand, involve evil speech, which, as you know, I also guard myself against. What should I do?" This brought a response of lavish contributions.

More and more the stature of the Hafets Hayyim had grown. He occupied the forefront as religious guide of the Jews of Eastern Europe. He commanded the respect of the non-Jewish world as well.

He was one of the very few religious leaders treated with deference by the early Bolsheviks. They admired his extremely simple mode of life, and his never-wavering kindness to others. Yet his efforts to achieve a measure of tolerance by Soviet officials toward Jewish religious practice proved futile. With the aid of General Wladyslaw Sikorski—who died in 1944 while Premier of the Pro-Western Polish Government-in-exile—the Hafets Hayyim was able to get out of Russia, back to his native Radun, in the summer of 1921.

The Hafets Hayyim in his personal outlook followed the method of the Gaon of Vilna. Unlike the Gaon, he had no quarrel with Hassidism. He became a sought-after conciliator of Hassidic disputes, a "neutral" whom all Hassidim esteemed. Always he strove for unity, for a reconciliation of contending factions.

The finest moment of his closing years came in August, 1923, when he opened the world convocation of traditional Judaism (Agudath Yisrael) in Vienna. None of the rabbinic dignitaries—of which there were a multitude—attracted as much attention as the plainly-clothed, retiring Hafets Hayyim. All turned to him. Yet he was genuinely surprised at having been chosen to open the assembly. His brief address commenced thus: "Why did you bestow upon me the privilege of opening this Torah Parliament? Surely not because you think I am a scholar. For, in truth, I am an ignoramus. Nor because I am of priestly descent. Some sages hold that priestly genealogy is somewhat suspect.

"The only reason for this great honor is my old age. On that basis let me address you, my beloved brethren."

To the very end of his life he continued his untiring efforts to alleviate the effects of a fearful anti-Semitism which had sprung up and spread like wildfire through Europe. He petitioned President Moscicki and other officials of Poland on behalf of the Jews. In 1930 the Hafets Hayyim headed a delegation of rabbis and laymen to Dr. Bartel, the Polish Prime Minister. He insisted on the elementary right of the Jewish citizens to arrange their religious life in their own way and vigorously protested against the economic restrictions and social discriminations imposed on his coreligionists.

"Our sages declare" (he argued) "that Cyrus of Persia deserved to be instrumental in the rebuilding of the Temple because he shed tears upon hearing of the destruction of the First Temple. I recall the horrors of about seventy years ago when the Russian cossacks dragged in shackles those Polish patriots who rebelled against the Czarist yoke, banishing them to Siberia and to other isolated sections. I remember how heartbroken I felt. In tears, I retired to my room and prayed to the Almighty, saying: 'O, Father of mercy and justice, have not these Poles a right to live their own lives as freely and as independently as their oppressors? . . .' So God granted me the privilege of seeing a resurrected and independent Poland. Do you wish to cause me to shed tears again? Remember that God always intervenes in favor of the oppressed! Then why be oppressors?"

THE LAST YEARS

During the final decade of his life, the Hafets Hayyim attempted again and again to carry out his yearning to settle in the Holy Land. His disciples in Zion anxiously awaited his coming. They built a house for him in Pethah Tikvah and kept it furnished for his coming. It was in vain. The earnest pleas of his flock in Poland determined him to stay.

In 1928, for example, he quietly set afoot preparations to leave. When this became known, a worried delegation of leading rabbis and deans of Yeshivoth begged him to postpone his departure. The existence of the Yeshivoth was at stake. He had helped found the Committee of the Yeshivoth (*Vaad ha-Yeshivoth*) which now collected a Yeshivah-support tax from the Jews, and his authority was still needed to maintain the project. He argued that he was too old to count for much. One of the rabbis replied, "The mere presence of a father at the table, though old and broken by age, induces a different quality of respect in his children." The "father" yielded on condition that his "children" would not hinder his going later.

There was no "later." His physical condition worsened to such an extent that another attempt to make the trip would have been fatal.

After the First World War, the Hafets Hayyim did not share the elation of others. He spoke of evil to come. Rabbi Mendel Zaks, his son-in-law, asked him why the master was sad, and he answered that there would be another war and greater evil, that he saw it in certain Biblical passages.

Rabbi Elhanan Wasserman, the Hafets Hayyim's greatest disciple, stated that during one of the High Holy Days of 1923, after finishing his silent *Mussaf* prayer, the Hafets Hayyim turned to the worshippers around him and wept. "A time is approaching during which we together with our families will be exposed to the severest dangers."

These premonitions of doom gave him no rest. But his voice was now too weak. The Jews would not listen to the alarms of an ailing old man.

After two years of invalidism, he died at the age of ninety-five. He was laid to rest in the little cemetery of Radun. His funeral evoked scenes of pathetic grief. Thousands came from all over Poland to the town on which he had bestowed his glory, to pay respect to their beloved master.

The life of the Hafets Hayyim represented a long unbroken continuity of study and saintliness, of devotion to his people. His death marks the close of an era. We may call it the Era of Learning and Piety (or perhaps the Polish Talmudic Era), marked by simultaneous physical impoverishment and spiritual opulence, outer harassment and inner serenity, earthly abasement and heavenly ennoblement.

That period lasted over four hundred years. It began with Rabbi Jacob Polak, who founded a Yeshivah in Cracow in 1506. It produced such luminaries as Solomon Luria, Moshe Isserles and Mordecai Jaffe. It reached its zenith with the appearance of the

Gaon of Vilna in the eighteenth century, and saw its end with the death of the Hafets Hayyim in 1933.

"The sun ariseth and the sun goeth down".

While the sun sets in one part of the globe, it rises in another. Before the sun of Israel's spirituality set in Babylonia it rose in Spain. Before setting in Spain it rose in France and Germany. Before setting in France and Germany, it rose in Poland.

The Hafets Hayyim has passed away but the unquenchable spirit of his teaching, the heartening example of his life, lives on and the sun will rise again in a new place and in our day.

BRITAIN'S THREE CHIEF RABBIS

BY CECIL ROTH

BRITAIN'S THREE CHIEF RABBIS

By Cecil Roth

On Monday, October 31st, 1842, Rabbi Solomon Hirschell passed away in London, and with him an era in Anglo-Jewish history ended. He had been brought to the country just forty years before to act as Rabbi of the Great Synagogue—the premier Ashkenazi community in the capital, and indeed in the country as whole, which had been established at the close of the seventeenth century. When he came over, it had been essentially a 'foreign' congregation, composed for the most part of persons born outside England and speaking Yiddish as their normal means of intercourse: persons, too, of a relatively low social status, mainly peddlers and old clothes men, with a sprinkling of petty shopkeepers and the like. But, in the course of his long years of office, the face of the community had changed. The Napoleonic Wars had led to a cessation, if not suspension, of immigration, much as the First World War a century later was to do in America, so that now the community was preponderantly English-born and English-speaking. The process of the past years had greatly enhanced their economic status, and now families such as that of Rothschild, which played a foremost role in Synagogal affairs, were outstanding in the life of the City and of the nation. On the Continent, the emancipation-movement had made such progress during the past half-century that a new standard had been set in Jewish intellectual life, secular culture coming into its own, sometimes indeed to the detriment of traditional values; and this development could not fail to be noticed in England too. Moreover, the same process that had been going on in the capital had begun to affect the provincial communities as well, such as Portsmouth, Liverpool, Birmingham, where the little 'foreign' groups had developed during these last years into well-established Anglicized congregations. All of these looked to the Great Synagogue in London under the auspices of

which many of them had come into existence as the premier community of the country and to its Rabbi as their own spiritual and
intellectual guide, to whom they would submit any of their problems
for decision.[1] (In many cases, indeed, they did not have any Rabbi
of their own.) Moreover, the other Ashkenazi communities of the
capital—the Hambro' Synagogue, founded in 1707, and the New
Synagogue, founded in 1761, as well as the smaller congregations
that had come into existence more recently in Westminster—by
now recognized the superior authority of the Great Synagogue's
Rabbi, notwithstanding the fierce jealousies that had formerly prevailed between them; there had in fact been a single Beth Din
for the London communities for some time past.

Solomon Hirschell's commanding personality and force of
character, regarding which many stories were still current down to
the beginning of the present century (as the present writer can
well recall from his boyhood days) set the seal on this supremacy.
He had been elected Rabbi of the Great Synagogue; his death was
generally mourned, as that of the principal, or Chief, Rabbi of
the Jews—the Ashkenazi Jews, at least: and they were the overwhelming majority—of Great Britain, and indeed of the British
Empire.

I

The appointment of his successor was therefore a great responsibility. In view of the altered circumstances, something other
than the old type of 'Rav' was needed to fill Hirschell's place.
The spiritual leader who was to succeed him had to combine something of the qualities of the English pastor with those of a Jewish
teacher; and he would have to be able to preach in English—an
attainment that Hirschell, notwithstanding his long incumbency,
had never mastered. Moreover, the office of Chief Rabbi had as
it were come into being spontaneously, de facto. It was necessary
to recognize it de jure; and the Great Synagogue determined to
associate in the election all of those other communities, metro-

---

[1]It may be mentioned that the same applied even to the newly-
established communities of the British colonies—South Africa and Australia—and even to some of those in which English-born Jews were active
in the United States of America.

politan or provincial, which were prepared to take a nominal share, however small, in the upkeep of the office. The new Chief Rabbi was therefore elected by a Committee of Delegates representing not only the four metropolitan communities but also those of nineteen provincial cities. There was at this time—a phenomenon more than once repeated in Anglo-Jewish life—no possible candidate in England, and the vacancy was advertised abroad. No fewer than fifteen candidates presented themselves, one of them being Samson Raphael Hirsch, then Provincial Rabbi of the Province of East Friesland, later to be known as the great pillar of German orthodoxy. It is interesting to speculate what differences might have resulted in English Jewry had he been appointed, and whether the Duke's Place Synagogue in London might then have become the centre of the neo-orthodox movement in Europe. At one time, indeed, Hirsch was actually agreed upon, at an informal meeting of the champions of the rival paladins, as compromise candidate. But the arrangement did not get carried into effect; and the choice of the conference actually fell, by an overwhelming majority, on Dr. Nathan Marcus Adler.

He had been born on December 11th, 1803 and was now just over forty years of age. His father, Marcus Baer Adler, member of a Frankfort family long distinguished for its learning, had been Rabbi of Hanover at the time of his birth, and he had therefore come into the world as a subject of George III of England—a fact that carried some weight, it is said, at the time of his election. He had moreover other English connections, for his grandmother had been a sister of David Tevele Schiff, Solomon Hirschell's predecessor in the Rabbinate of the Great Synagogue. A child of the post-emancipation era, he had studied at the Universities of Göttingen, Erlangen, Würzburg and Heidelberg; had qualified almost simultaneously in 1828 for the degree of Doctor of Philosophy at the University of Erlangen, and the Rabbinical diploma from Rabbi Abraham Bing of that same city, had been given him at his first appointment as Rabbi of Oldenburg in 1829; and within a few years received a call to his native city of Hanover in the same city (His seal of office, showing an Eagle ('Adler') with outstretched wings, is in the collection of the present writer). The recommendations that he had presented were of the most cordial nature; it was said that they were backed by private communications from Queen Victoria's uncle, the Duke of Cambridge, who, as Viceroy of Hanover, had come into contact with him. Because of his German origin and upbringing, the Prince Consort found him congenial company; and family legend tells how he, expert in the problems of nationality, warned the Queen on an historic occasion of the legal complications that might ensue to any of her children born in Germany. He had lived in his youth through historic times, and had stirring recollections; he recalled seeing Napoleon's troops as they marched through the streets of Frankfort in retreat after the Battle of Leipzig. (This was told to the present writer by his son, Elkan Nathan Adler, who died only in 1946).

Nathan Marcus Adler's period of office (1844-1890) was of tremendous importance in the history of Anglo-Jewry, which during this period was converted from a roughly-organized Pre-Emancipation Kehillah into a community similar in essentials to that of today. In all the important developments of the time Adler played an outstanding part. The fact that he was a University-trained scholar was in itself of very great significance; it meant that, from the point of view of Western culture, he was on the same level (at least) as the intelligentsia of his community or the spiritual leaders of Christian bodies with whom he came into contact. But this did not imply that his allegiances to traditional Jewish values were in any way impaired. No religious innovations or reforms were permitted to invade the congregations over which he presided, though he certainly exerted himself unstintingly to bring about an improvement in congregational decorum and discipline. He combined with his European scholarship a considerable degree of Rabbinic learning of the traditional type, conducted Talmudic lessons and gave Talmudic discourses in the customary fashion; presided over the deliberation of the Beth Din and responded learnedly to enquiries regarding ritual law. Of his publications, his *Nethinah la-Ger*, or 'Gift to the Proselyte'—a commentary to the Targum of Onkelos on the Pentateuch—established his name as a scholar even among the critical Eastern European intellectuals; while his various volumes of Discourses (Derashoth) and one of Novellae (Hiddushim) were sufficient to establish his competence in the purely Talmudic field.

Besides all this, in the tradition of his predecessors, he was expected to inspire his flock in a fashion considered more consistent with the standards of the nineteenth century, and he did not disappoint these hopes. He was, it may be said, the father of the Anglo-Jewish pulpit. In eighteenth century England, the Rabbi had given regular Talmudic discourses—of course in Yiddish—and visiting Darshanim (preachers) had occasionally delivered highly-emotional ethical harangues of great length in the same language. (The Sephardic communities had approximated even more closely to these European standards, but had made use of Spanish or Portuguese for the purpose.) With the beginning of the nineteenth century, a few devoted scholars or enterprising laymen had very occasionally given discourses in the Synagogue in English, to the delight of their audiences; and even Solomon Hirschell had made use of the vernacular on some special occasions. It was Nathan Adler, however, who acclimatised the vernacular sermon in the country. His inaugural address was delivered in German, which was understood (if only because of its affinities with Yiddish) by a good part of his audience. But before long he mastered English, and the homiletical style that he introduced set the standard for the English pulpit from that time onward. Today, it seems to us natural; then, it was a drastic, almost revolutionary, step.

His ministrations were not of course confined to the Great Synagogue, though it continued to be his official seat, for the balance of English Jewry—not the foreign element only—was at his time and for long after still concentrated in the East End. He gave occasional sermons in the other synagogues in the Metropolis, and set the example of going on occasional pastoral tours throughout the country, where his arrival would be considered an important public event. He was in touch with the new congregations that were established in rapid succession at this time in the British overseas dominions. He issued a Code of regulations 'for all the Synagogues of the British Empire'. In 1866, he gave evidence before the Royal Commission on the Marriage Laws, presenting an important memorandum on the subject as it affected the Jews of England. He worked strenuously to further free religious education in the community, and he was largely responsible for the introduction into the English synagogues of the institution of Hospital Saturday, when collections were made for hospitals, as a counterpart to the Hospital Sunday in the Churches. He was the channel of communication between oppressed or distressed communities abroad and those institutions in Anglo-Jewry which attempted to ameliorate their conditions.

One institution in Anglo-Jewry after the other received its present form owing to his efforts. If new qualifications were now necessary in the Anglo-Jewish spiritual leader, and if the Synagogue pulpit was to become effective, clearly it was necessary to establish an institution for the training of Anglo-Jewish ministers, similar to the Rabbinical Seminaries in the new tradition that had existed on the Continent for the past generation. (The earliest, that of Padua, in Italy, the presiding figure in which was Samuel David Luzzatto, was opened in 1828.) Accordingly, owing to the Chief Rabbi's earnest efforts, Jews' College for the education and training of Rabbis, Ministers, Preachers, Readers and Teachers of Religion for Jewish Congregations (as it is now officially described) was opened in 1855; Dr. Adler remained its leading spirit and ever since, the Chief Rabbi has been Chairman of the Council.

His name was associated with much more than this.

One of his first achievements was the reorganization of the old Beth ha-Midrash and its provision with a proper Library and Librarian, which made it into an intellectual centre for the old-type Jews of the East End thereafter. He was in the background at the time of the organization of the Board of Guardians for the Relief of the Jewish Poor in 1858—still after nearly a century the premier Anglo-Jewish charity.

On the first day of the feast of Tabernacles, in the autumn of 1866, the Chief Rabbi invited the Wardens of the Great Synagogue as usual to take breakfast with him in his Succah after Service. In the course of conversation, he impressed upon them how important he considered it that the London congregations to which he administered should be united into a single organization, eliminating wasteful overlapping of functions and avoiding such dispute between them as had punctuated the past. They were profoundly impressed, and promised to do what was possible. As a result, in 1870 there came into being the United Synagogue—

then a union of three congregations comprising five places of
worship, now perhaps one of the important and best organized
inter-synagogal organizations in the world, comprising twenty-two
Constituent Synagogues all over London, with a total membership
of about 15,000, with some thirty-four communities numbering
8,500 members in looser affiliation. It is this organization which
takes the principal share in maintaining the office of the Chief
Rabbinate and has the preponderant voice in the election to it.
It is perhaps Dr. Nathan Adler's greatest monument.

II

Nathan Adler established a new clan in Anglo-Jewry, which
continued to play a prominent part in communal life for a century. One of his sons, Marcus Adler, an actuary by profession,
is memorable for a number of important contributions to Jewish
scholarship, including the standard edition of the Travels of
Benjamin of Tudela; his son, Herbert Adler, was co-editor, with
Arthur Davis, of one of the most magnificent editions of the Jewish liturgy that has appeared in any language. Another son of
Nathan Adler's was Elkan Nathan Adler, a lovable bibliophile and
indefatigable globe-trotter, who produced many learned works and
above all built up the finest collection of Hebrew manuscripts
that has ever been owned by a private individual in recent generations; it is now in the Library of the Jewish Theological Seminary
of America, which has thereby become one of the world's greatest
collections of Hebraica. It was, however, Nathan Adler's second
son, Hermann, who was of greatest importance in Anglo-Jewish history, for he followed closely on his father's steps. A child when
his father came over to take up his office, he received secular education in England, and was then sent abroad to complete his
studies. In 1862, he received his doctorate at the University of
Leipzig; in the following year, the *hattarath horaah* (rabbinical
diploma) was conferred upon him by Solomon Judah Loeb Rapo-
port, Chief Rabbi of Prague, one of the founders of the 'Jüdische
Wissenschaft'. On returning to England, he became for a time
Principal of Jews' College, and was then appointed Minister of
the newly-founded Bayswater Synagogue—at that time the most
fashionable of London synagogues, with a highly distinguished

membership. Here he occupied the pulpit for many years, and
established a considerable reputation within the community and
beyond it. In the later eighteen-seventies, his father, now an old
man, began to find the burden of office too great, and was compelled
to delegate some of his onerous duties to his son. The latter thus
came to fill as his father's deputy more and more of the functions of
the Chief Rabbi. When, in 1890, the other died in his 87th year, he
was thus the invitable choice as his successor: all the more so, indeed, since, although Anglo-Jewry had produced in the past generation a number of gifted, eloquent and learned Ministers, it was
thought superfluous at that time for them to qualify as rabbis. He
was to remain in office for just twenty years.

Strongly Conservative by nature, as his father had been;
scholarly, as evidenced by a number of articles, though by no major
work; a highly effective preacher, in the restrained style of his
day; extremely conscientious, and devoted to the cause of his
people, Hermann Adler's outstanding characteristic was perhaps
his dignity. He belonged to the generation of Emancipation in
the fullest sense, and was in many ways its most typical son. He
was not yet twenty years of age when the first Jew was admitted
to sit in the House of Commons, and the legal discrimination
against English Jews virtually disappeared. He had been familiar
from his youth with such leaders of Anglo-Jewry as the Rothschilds, who on the one hand presided in more than one generation
over the affairs of the United Synagogue, and on the other were
among the intimates of the Prince of Wales—the future Edward
VII.—who treated Hermann Adler, too, with great cordiality.
The Anglo-Jewish community was at the height of its influence and
consideration in the outside world, and Adler was its representative. He represented it, indeed, superbly well. He elevated the
institution to a dignity and position almost unequalled in the
history of the Diaspora. On all public occasions when it was
called for, the Chief Rabbi would figure on the platform, by the
side of the Archibishop of Canterbury and the Cardinal of West-
minister, and would be heard with the utmost deference; at state
services in Westminster Abbey, at times of national mourning or
celebration, his impressive figure would be seen in a seat of honor.
There was therefore an inevitable tendency for him to reinterpret

his position almost in Anglican terms. He was, as it were, the Bishop of Anglo-Jewry. He dressed the part, wearing a quasi-episcopal rosette in the ribbon of his top-hat as an addition to the clerical garb which had become the conventional wear in the Anglo-Jewish ministry; and I have been told (I do not know whether this is authentic) that at one time he even enclosed his calves in episcopal gaiters. One can understand, in view of this, how little sympathy Theodore Herzl found in him when he came over to England when the new Zionist movement was launched; and how the Eastern European immigrants who came to the country in such large numbers from 1881 onwards, could not fail to look at him and at the Anglo-Jewish community with a certain degree of diffidence. But this does not imply that he was in any way out of sympathy with them; it would have been impossible for any man to have championed their cause more warmly.

III

He died in 1911. His successor, appointed in 1913, was a man whom it is no exaggeration to term one of the outstanding Jews of our generation. He was a very different type from his predecessor. Hermann Adler had been a typical product of the placid Victorian era in Western Europe. Joseph Herman Hertz was a child of the dynamic, vital, much-travailed Eastern European Jewry, with all of its warmth, enthusiasms, and yearnings. He was elected to his position largely on the strength of his great oratorical powers, which made it certain that he would worthily represent his community on formal occasions. But even then he had already had an unecclesiastically adventurous career, and was a citizen of the world in the most literal sense. He had started his wanderings early. Born in Slovakia, in 1872, of a Rabbinical family, he was taken at the age of twelve to the United States, where he was educated at Columbia University and the Jewish Theological Seminary of America, of which he was the first graduate. His first appointment was at Syracuse, N. Y. In 1898 he received a call to the principal synagogue of the rising, exciting community of Johannesburg, South Africa. It was in the days of Boer rule, which, however picturesque it may appear in retrospect, bore harshly in many ways on minority groups, as 'uitlanders' and religious dissidents knew only too painfully. The young rabbi already displayed, however, the qualities which above all others distinguished him in after-life—a boundless courage and an inability to maintain a tactful silence in the face of wrongdoing. He soon began to lead the protests against the religious disabilities from which Jews and Catholics suffered in the Transvaal, which deprived them of some elementary rights. As a result, he was suspected of pro-British sympathies, and shortly after the outbreak of the Boer War President Kruger ordered his expulsion from the country. The official document was signed by the State Attorney, a young lawyer named Jan Christian Smuts, who subsequently, as Prime Minister of the Union of South Africa, must have chuckled over the episode when he met the Chief Rabbi of the British Empire. At the Portuguese port of Lourenco Marques the exile embarked on a 300-ton cutter which took him to Cape Town. Among his fellow-passengers was a young ex-officer-journalist with a gift of language and a cherubic face named Winston Churchill, who had recently escaped from a prisoner-of-war camp.

When settled conditions were restored in the Transvaal, Rabbi Hertz returned to his congregation, which he served with distinction for some years, among the institutions which in great measure owed their existence to him being the South African Board of Deputies. In 1911 he returned to New York as Rabbi of the Orach Chayim congregation, with which, however, he was destined to remain for only a very short while. His election to the office of Chief Rabbi attracted a great deal of attention, and his inauguration at the Great Synagogue in April, 1913 was a great public event. The old Lord Rothschild, as president of the United Synagogue, took out a Sefer Torah from the Ark and handed it to him, with the words (as Dr. Hertz afterwards recounted) 'I give the Torah into your keeping, to bring up the congregations of Israel in accordance with the Din Torah (the Law of the Torah).'

It was not long before he began to show his mettle, in a manner which from the beginning was almost disconcerting for those brought up in the placid Victorian tradition. That summer the International Congress for the Suppression of the White Slave Traffic met in London, and Dr. Hertz, as Chief Rabbi, represented the Jewish community, in the manner that had become conventional, at the inaugural meeting. He took the opportunity, in the presence of the representatives of the Churches and of the outstanding members of the Diplomatic corps—including the Russian Ambassador— to denounce publicly the infamous 'Yellow Ticket' system which the Czars imposed on Jewesses who wished to enter the universities in cities otherwise barred to Jews, which was possible for them only if they were formally enrolled as prostitutes. It was obvious that Rabbi Joseph Hermann Hertz did not have quite the same conception of the functions of the Chief Rabbinate as his predecessors.

He continued in the same tradition throughout his thirty-two years' incumbency of office. The recently-established Eastern European Jews found in him one who understood their outlook, sympathized with their yearnings, and spoke, both figuratively and literally, the same language. Indeed, it is probably true to say that this realization was responsible to a large extent for the fact that they began to feel themselves at one with the old-established Anglo-Jewish commmunity, and in due course helped to revitalize it. The outstanding exemplification of this was at the time when the Government was contemplating the issue of the famous statement (the Balfour Declaration) expressing its sympathy with the reconstitution of a National Home for the Jewish People in Palestine. During the preliminary conversations, the feelings of a number of prominent members of the Anglo-Jewish community were sounded. Many of them, belonging to the older-established element or adhering to Reform Judaism, were outspokenly antagonistic, and had there been a lack of sympathy on the part of the ecclesiastical leader of Anglo-Jewry there can be little doubt that no more would have been done. Dr. Hertz used to recount how the Cabinet Messenger reached his house when he was in Synagogue on Simhath Torah, and if I am not mistaken, the same happened on a second occasion. But at last he received the communication, which thrilled him to his inmost being. 'I must as Chief Rabbi thank . . . the members of the War Cabinet', he wrote in his reply, 'for their striking sympathy with Jewish aspirations, and assure them that the overwhelming majority of Anglo-Jewry . . . will rejoice with me at this broad humanity and

fair-sighted statesmanship of the men who guide the destinies of
the Empire'. There can be no doubt that this clear-cut expression
of opinion proved of vital importance at a vital moment; a hesitant or a flaccid reply might well have helped the anti-Zionists to
gain the day.

Two more historic episodes in his career as Chief Rabbi must
be mentioned. In 1920-1, shortly after the conclusion of the First
World War, he went on a Pastoral Tour on behalf of the Jewish
War Memorial Appeal round the far-flung communities of the
of the British Empire: to South Africa, Australia, New Zealand,
Canada, visting and speaking in every Jewish community of note,
and arousing a great degree of interest and even enthusiasm in the
general population. Even in the days of Solomon Hirschell, a hundred years before, the Jews in the British Colonies had looked for
inspiration and guidance to the Chief Rabbi in London. Under
the two Adlers, by which time they had increased in number and
importance, a more intimate and regular relationship had developed. This, however, was the first time that the Chief Rabbinate
had become a reality as far as the Empire was concerned. Dr.
Hertz's dynamic force made his tour an outstanding success, and
elevated his office to its peak.

A few years later the British Chief Rabbi took the lead in
another matter which vitally affected the interests of Jewry as a
whole. Proposals had been set on foot, backed by large amounts
of American money, for the reform of the Calendar, by adopting
a symmetrical system (highly useful for bookkeeping, but with no
other particular advantage) based upon a year of 364 days. This
entailed the interposition between one year and another of a 'blank
day', which should not belong to any week: with the result that
the seventh-day Sabbath would fall on a different day of the week
every year. Obviously, this would entail an unendurable economic burden for the observant Jew, as well as the conscientious
Sabbatarian of other faiths; but the peril was not apparent, and
there was a considerable danger that the new system might be
adopted by the League of Nations without realization of what it
implied. Hertz, with his exceptional mental alertness and his tremendous vigor, realized from the outset what was at stake, and
threw himself heart and soul into what he termed 'the battle for

the Sabbath', stirring up interest among Jews and making non-Jewish bodies as well realize the issue. The climax came when in 1931 he headed a Jewish deputation which went to Geneva to be present when a Committee of the League of Nations debated the matter, gave a stirring speech before its members, and presented a petition of protest signed by hundreds of thousands of Jews all over the world. He was certainly instrumental in part in securing the rejection of the proposals. Yet the agitation continues, and it will be necessary to marshal the Jewish forces again and again in the future—always, however, along the lines that Joseph Hermann Hertz laid down, and making use to a large extent of the material that he prepared.

It is impossible to speak of Joseph Hermann Hertz without making mention of his literary productions. He had an astonishing power of quotation and a memory of incredible range, but he was not a great scholar; he produced many books, but he was not a great writer. On the other hand, there were among his books several which have had an influence hardly paralleled in Jewish literary life since the Middle Ages. His *Book of Jewish Thoughts* —an anthology first produced during the first World War for distribution to the troops, which has since circulated in at least a quarter of a million copies—is one of the most remarkable collections of material of the sort that has even been brought together, and has done a vast amount to enchance respect for Judaism among the Gentiles, and self-respect among the Jews. (The author has never tired of recounting how he produced it in the first instance at the suggestion of his wife, who while they were on their honeymoon complained to him, when they visited a London book-shop, that nothing of the sort existed for Jewish use.) Later his Commentary on the Pentateuch, and his Commentary on the Prayer-Book, brought Jewish learning down to the masses, and made the Synagogue service a living, palpitating reality for the simple worshipper.

The last years of his life were clouded by the appalling persecution on the Continent of Europe, the destruction of the seats of traditional Jewish learning, and finally the Nazi extermination of so great a proportion of European Jewry. Time after time, Dr. Hertz's voice was raised in warning and in protest. Time after time, he appeared on the public platform and made one of those dynamic speeches which stirred his audiences to their depths. Time after time, he organized services of prayer and intercession in the Synagogues. Time after time, he sent to the British Press those immensely telling letters, which circulated round the world in twenty-four hours, in the writing of which he had such mastery. There would not be a word too much; there would not be a word too little; the phrasing was so perfect that it appeared easy and inevitable; and only those who were nearest to him knew how much work and thought had gone into the preparation, and how many drafts had been discarded before the final form was reached. In these years, he came to transcend his office. Throughout the world, Jews looked to him as their champion and representative. In public sentiment, he was more than the Chief Rabbi of the British Empire; he was, one might almost say, the Chief Rabbi for the whole of Europe. It was only after his death, which took place on January 14th, 1946, that the measure of what he had meant to the community became apparent; in the following months, with the brutal closing of the 'Door of Hope' of Palestine in the face of helpless Jewish refugees, and the crowning horror of their deportation back into Germany and the abominable reaction to which this gave rise, Anglo-Jewry realized how much it had lost, and that there was no one else who could take his place. He was perhaps one of the men who wore his faults such as they were upon his sleeve; his qualities, on the other hand, were deep and abiding. There can have been in our generation few persons with the same devotion, the same courage, and the same dynamic force.

THREE SEPHARDIC LEADERS

By Abraham Ben-Jacob

THREE SEPHARDIC LEADERS

By Abraham Ben-Jacob

In the course of the centuries there arose many men among the Sephardic Jews of the Middle East, great personalities whose influence extended far beyond their own generation: in the ages of the Talmud, of the Geonim and of the Golden period in Spain. We need but recall the illustrious names of Maimonides, Yehudah ha-Levi, Yitzhak al-Fassi, etc.

But even in the last centuries, in the Eastern countries, the Jews have been blessed with great teachers who were famous as men of thought, of scholarship, and especially because of their work for the common good.

These rabbis created a spiritual revolution wherever they dwelt, and uplifted their people through Torah and wisdom of life. Among them three were outstanding. In different ways, each created a golden period, which was named in his honor. For they benefited many thousands in Israel, and to this day the results of their accomplishments are felt. They were Rabbi Judah ben Solomon Hai Alkalai, the herald of the national revival; Rabbi Abdallah Somekh, founder of the Bagdad Rabbinical College; and Rabbi David Sassoon, the prince of the Jews in Babylonia and India.

I

Rabbi Judah Ben Solomon Hai Alkalai

In the nineteenth century, Jews were subjected to deadly persecution, both in the East and West. The frequent pogroms and blood-libels shook Israel in all its scattered communities and imperilled the very lives of our people almost everywhere. Jewish leaders, by diplomatic and philanthropic action in behalf of their oppressed brethren, endeavored to obtain civil rights for them, and financial aid for those who had lost their wealth or their chances of earning a living. Thus they hoped to achieve a final solution. They were unaware of the fact that such diplomatic and charitable work would produce but a temporary remedy, since it did not attack the evil at its roots, nor prevent new growth of anti-Semitism that would again place in jeopardy the very existence of Israel in the lands of his exile.

This attitude, sterile both religiously and politically, resulted only in weakening the principles of traditional Judaism. For it made many Jews aim to become citizens in the lands of the diaspora and to remain there permanently. To this end, they began to advocate Reform Judaism, and even erased the word "Zion" from their prayer-books. Many of our brethren from the so-called higher classes, who could have done much to attain the legitimate aspirations of our people, became a curse rather than a blessing. Against them arose rabbis who preached about redemption from heaven, in a miraculous fashion, because "only the Messiah will have the power to save the people from their afflictions, and the third Temple will not be built in a natural way but rather in a spiritual manner (*be-derekh ha-ruah*)." They prayed day and night: "May our eyes behold Thy return to Zion", but they did nothing practical or natural to accelerate that return. They preached a spiritual *Teshuvah*—a turning from evil ways, but not a tangible return to the homeland. For "until the Messiah will come, we are compelled to accept our fate and continue to bear affliction." The majority of the Jewish people, who never followed the pernicious tenets of Reform, were reduced to contenting themselves with the hope in the Messiah, who, at a day not too distant, would bring them complete redemption. So they struggled on for their physical existence whilst remaining loyal to Torah and *Mitsvoth*. The futility that encompassed them gradually made them indifferent both to themselves and to the fate of their nation. Thus they undertook not one practical step to hasten the general redemption.

In such atmosphere there appeared on the Jewish scene in the first half of the nineteenth century a noble Sephardic rabbi who preached a new idea, buttressing it by countless proofs from sacred texts: "Israel cannot survive except through the establishment of a political state in Palestine. No other solution can stop the pogroms and other persecutions of the Jews in the Diaspora. If Israel return not to its own country, then even the Messianic redemption will not come about. Whoever delays the realization of this thought, delays the Redemption."

This idea was expressed by Rabbi Alkalai more than fifty years before Herzl expressed it in "The Jewish State." Alkalai was the first individual to propose a detailed plan for the establishment of a Jewish state in Erets Yisrael. All writers who followed, including Herzl, merely re-affirmed this plan without adding anything to it. All the positive realities that Zionists have accomplished up to this day, are set forth plainly in Alkalai's many pamphlets and books. He was also the first to suggest the ideas of a Zionist Congress, Jewish Agency, National Fund, and mass immigration to Palestine.

To us who by now are completely adjusted to the teachings of Alkalai, his ideas appear self-evident. But a hundred years ago, when the horizon of the Jewish people was very limited, few men had the foresight that he manifested.

Rabbi Judah Alkalai was born in Sarayevo, Serbia, in 1798, the fourth son of his father, who was a teacher of Hebrew and also a communal worker.

Not much is known of Judah's early youth, except that his parents left Sarayevo for Palestine, where he enjoyed the teaching of many rabbis,[1] but was especially influenced by Rabbi Yehudah Samuel Bibas, whom he called his "holy teacher", and who inspired him by his ideas about the return of Israel to the Holy Land. Bibas, even in those days, preached of mass immigration and the establishment of a Jewish State in Palestine. Alkalai mentions him often. On one occasion he writes: "I must not hold back the moral teachings that I heard from the mouth of this holy man of God. I must let his ideas be known. He said that Israel sinned against God, that we turned our back on Him. Did not our Sages, in the Talmud, say long ago that he who lives outside of Erets Yisrael is like one who has no God? And what do

---

[1]Among the teachers who influenced him were Rabbi Eliezer Papo, Rabbi Jacob Sikhli, Rabbi Jacob Pintzi, Rabbi Jose Pintzi, and Rabbi Abraham Hai Mussafia.

we do in all our scattered places in the Diaspora? We wander
from city to city to look for our livelihood, but we do not go to
Erets Yisrael, 'about which the Lord, your God, is concerned continually'. It would be better for us to eat bread and drink water
in scarcity in Palestine; we would at least know that we have a
God! Israel should return to His land; this is also the meaning
of the prophetic passage: God said, *'Return unto Me* (to the Holy
Land) *and I shall return unto you!'* Many such expressions made
my heart tremble and my feet stumble . . . oh that I had wings
like a dove that I could fly and dwell there!"

In 1825, at the age of twenty-seven, Alkalai was chosen rabbi
of the Sephardic congregation in the City of Semlin, near Sarayevo.
He kept this position until 1876, when he left for Palestine. No
sooner had he come to Semlin than he worked out a plan for
the education of the younger generation and the dissemination
of the Torah among all the ranks of the people. He gave special
attention to Hebrew language and grammar. No appropriate textbooks of Hebrew grammar being available, he published in 1839
his first book, entitled *"Darkhei Noam"* ("The Pleasant Paths"),
a brief text written in Ladino, the lingua franca of Sephardic
Jews, and containing "all the paths and bypaths of Hebrew,
written in a clear Sephardic manner for the needs of students." In
the introduction he chided those who neglected the systematic study
of Hebrew, criticized the educational system of his time, and
called for improvements in method. With profound observations
on this subject, he expounds the idea of the redemption and the
necessity of living in Palestine. As early as in this book he states
that the redemption of the Jewish people must take place by physical effort: "We must take the bread away from our own mouths in
order to aid our nobility who dwell in Jerusalem. It is because of
our sins that they suffer; because of the transgressions of us who do
not live there—they are afflicted. The *Geulah* will come through
Torah, *Tsedakah,* and *Tefillah,* all of which can be practised best
in Palestine. We must make up our mind to return to Jerusalem
and to accept the yoke of His Kingdom!"

Idealism of such a high nature evoked a negative reaction among
some of the Jews in his environment, because their hearts were

impervious to an understanding of his great vision. They mocked him both secretly and openly.

A year later (in 1840), he published his second book, *"Shelom Yerushalayim"* ("The Peace of Jerusalem"), which served as "an answer to the mockers." It deals with the special laws obligatory only upon those who dwell in Erets Yisrael, with the Messianic idea, and with the return to Zion as the first requisite of redemption. He writes: "We will watch our claim to receive the rights of government for our homeland. There we shall be considered as its citizens, nor shall we lose our presumptive rights (to Israel) even if we live in foreign lands. Rabbi Bibas had this in mind when he interpreted *'Shuvu elai veashuvah aleikhem'*—thus: 'We must return first to Palestine before God will make His *Shekhinah* rest upon our people there!' Let us consider ourselves like unto the merchant who goes to the market, but whose main thought is to return to his home." Alkalai concludes the introduction to his second book with these words: "Whosoever has a heart, to him these my words will be sufficient, and him whose heart is not with him, my words will not help. He who loves the truth will find good sense in them. He who wants to hearken will do so, he who refuses to comprehend will cease to do so. Nor is it upon myself to complete the work."

In the same year a turning point came in the development of his vision, when the "blood-libel" of Damascus made Israel tremble throughout the Diaspora, serving as a bitter lesson concerning the fate of his people. Alkalai saw it as a strong warning to those Jews who live serenely in strange lands, while Palestine lies in ruins, forsaken and longing to be rebuilt. "There is no safe haven for Jews in foreign countries. The only solution is to leave the Diaspora and to settle permanently in Palestine." To realize this idea we must have general unity upon a common ground. Alkalai desired to exploit the universal Jewish interest aroused by the Damascus libel, for his Zionist ideas. Therefore, in 1843, he published in Hebrew his *"Minhath Yehudah"* ("The Offering of Judah"). Here he unfolded all his scheme—nationalist and Zionist. His main ideas were afterwards expounded and clarified in many pamphlets and books published during the next thirty-five years.

Whosoever reads the works of Alkalai will be greatly impressed by his practical, sound ideas as manifested in the presentation of his plans. The reader becomes aware of a noble personality, a powerful and consistent fighter for his revolutionary thought, far above the feeble thinking of contemporary Jewry. This rabbi, deep in the lore of Kabbalah, unwordly and humble, reveals himself as a great statesman, who foresees the future with crystal clearness and discovers a sure cure for the wounds of his people. He is not satisfied with any temporary solution of our people's problem. No small thought pleases him! No ephemeral device will he accept! No personal motive invades his mind! No defective formulae, however ancient, will he brook! For the idea of redemption, he wages a bold, proud battle in an unprecedented way, unacceptable in those days. He is not terrified by those who malign him, pays no attention to personal insults, but fights those who dare oppose his faith, and whose animosity he sees directed against Redemption itself. Nor does he limit his propaganda to his own small circle, but spreads his scores of essays and books all over the dispersion of Israel.

The lengthy preface to his book *"Minhath Yehudah"* contains his principal teachings: At the beginning of the redemption, Israel will unite with a single aim into one society, and appoint a leader who will go to Palestine. Since no group can exist without the counsel of the elders, as a first step elders should be chosen from every district, men of ability who fear God, men of truth, of counsel and efficiency, to supervise the affairs of the total group. The activity of these elders corresponds to the function of the Messiah, son of Joseph, destined for us. These elders must be appointed by our great and powerful princes. After all the exiles will have gathered in one group and the elders will have been appointed, they should beseech all kings for permission to return to our land, the heritage of our forefathers. They should appoint a leader over us and give us permission to rebuild the house of the Lord our God.

This plan and program Alkalai develops in greater detail in his other works. The *Geulah,* according to him, will come about through these main agencies:

1) *General return unto God*—"Teshuvah" (both return and repentance). There are two types of *Teshuvah*:

    a. A personal one—each individual repents his sins in accord with the ancient rules governing repentance.

    b. A general *Teshuvah*—all Israel returns to the Lord our God, and to the land of our fathers.

Israel will be redeemed only by the second kind of *Teshuvah*. All redemption is based on the condition that we return to Palestine. The redemption will not come if we lie supine on our couches. But if we open the door, even as little as the eye of the needle, He will open it for us as wide as a great hall!

We must return to Palestine in order that God should be justly called "King" (*"Melekh"*) of the Holy Land. Every day do we pray: "May our eyes behold Thee when Thou returnest to Zion with mercy." Over whom shall He cause His *Shekhinah* to hover? Over wood and stone? To commence the work of the redemption of our soul, twenty-two thousand Jews must return to our land, so that God may make His *Shekhinah* rest on them. If Israel will not return to the land, it will not be redeemed. If Israel will not return to its land, God will raise a King over them whose decrees will be as severe as those of Haman. The people of the land will be jealous of them, eye their possessions to plunder them, and the Jews will cry out but will not be answered. (How prophetic these words must sound to the survivors of Hitler's fury!)

Those who survive this persecution will migrate to Palestine, but God will not fill their homes with gold and silver, nor will they die of starvation. Every year, people leave our land for the Holy Land, yet not one of them dies of hunger; some of them succeed and they dwell in security and in peace. We must needs discourage people from spreading tales about the poverty of our land, for even in Europe the manna does not come down into the houses of study, but the friends of Torah support the students. How much more should they aid those who study the Torah in the courts of the house of our Lord! In short: The redemption will come not only through a miracle, but also in a natural way.

2) *Little by little. . . .*

The Aliyah to Palestine must come slowly and gradually, not all at one time, but by degrees. "Our country is desolate, ruined. We must build homes, drill wells, and plant vineyards and olive trees. God adjured us that we do not go up all at once for two reasons:

   a. In order that our brothers in the Diaspora should help those who are going to Palestine, for, needless to say, the first immigrants will be of the poorer class.

   b. In order that we should not be left to live in the open fields, like Bedouin tent-dwellers, but build little by little, until our land be built and prepared. May that come true, soon, in our days!"

3) *One Band.*

There is to be one society. The first condition for redemption is genuine brotherly love, for Jerusalem was destroyed only because of causeless hatred and disunited hearts. And Israel will not be shown an auspicious omen until we all join into one group. When the Exiles are gathered, Israel must form one band, composed of both the righteous and the wicked, the former obtaining forgiveness for the latter.

4) *A Meeting of the Elders.*

There must be a Council of Elders, to avoid separation and division of opinion. We must have spiritual leaders great enough to impress the people, so that all things performed by them will be generally approved. For this reason, we must call a General Assembly (i.e., a Zionist Congress), appointed by the Council of Elders (i.e., the Zionist Executive), that will begin action immediately. "For from Zion shall direction come forth and the word of the Lord from Jerusalem." They should have a seat in Jerusalem, and we all must obey them. To avoid endless disputations in Israel, whoever agitates against them should be subject to penalties.

The functions of the Assembly of the Elders are:

   a. They shall declare that we have but one language, one script, and one Torah. They shall make us one nation in the land, without any division into Sephardic, Ashkenazic, Polish, French, or other groups. "Israel" shall be our common name.

b. They shall provide the students of the Torah with all their needs. These should no longer suffer the affliction of hunger. There should be named a teacher of righteousness (a judge or rabbi), a cantor, a *Shohet,* a *Melamed,* and a Scribe for every village and settlement.

c. They shall bring trustworthy, capable men from Europe to supervise the settlement in Palestine.

d. They shall import from Europe expert farmers and wine-growers, for in Europe are to be found many craftsmen and merchants of great ability.

e. They are to influence our brethren in the Diaspora to immigrate to Palestine and to provide them there with homes at a minimum price. If the number of buyers for the houses prove insufficient, the homes should be offered in a lottery throughout Europe, in order that building in Palestine shall not stop, and that work with mortar and bricks shall be provided for those among the poor who are incapable of being farmers.

f. The Executives shall supervise all the details which a community requires. They shall make rules about all the *Mitsvoth* dependent on Israel's living in the Land, and provide the older scholars with a livelihood, so that they may raise many disciples and regulate standards of conduct and good behavior.

g. To recapitulate: they should build homes and highways, plant vineyards, arrange for trade and industry—all for the common good, for the promotion of business. Little by little should they gather the scattered poor of our people, attract them to the land, so that they shall be farmers and wine-growers.

5) *The success of the heads of the people* will depend on the wealthy and influential men to whom God gave knowledge, understanding, and common sense. Theirs is the responsibility to care for our remnant, for *"we have had our fill of contemptuous treat-*

ment by those who are at ease." In their wisdom they shall gather our dispersed people from the four corners of the earth, to unite them for one great purpose. The leaders of the people shall supervise and provide for the community, awaken those who slumber, promote enlightenment and righteous living for all Israel, united in a common cause.

6) *Intervention with Temporal Powers.*

The heads of the communities should be united in one body to submit their united plea to the governments and to the kings on behalf of our people, that they permit us to return to our homeland. Such intercession will be the special *Mitsvah* of our brethren who live in free countries, such as Britain, France, America, where they have access to men in the highest positions. These men should also implore the Sultan of Turkey to sell us the heritage of our fathers piecemeal, on an installment basis, year by year. "When our land and inheritance will again be called by the name of Israel, every Israelite will be aroused to help the homeland and its community with his body and his money for the salvation of Israel, imploring the kings of the world on our behalf to enable us to go back penitently to the house of our Mother. We must beseech the world's kings, for they are kindly, and God will inspire them to proclaim freedom unto us, and let us go home."

Seventy years before the Balfour Declaration of 1917, Alkalai foresaw that the help will come from Great Britain: "They will say to the daughter of Zion: 'Behold thy salvation'. The Kingdom of Britain will be the first to bestow their close attention upon us; afterwards France, too, will guide us. If the kings of the nations will deal justly with us and restore unto us the inheritance of our fathers, then the three of us, Israel, Rome, and Ishmael, will bring blessing to the land."

7) *The government.*

There will be a democratic government in the Jewish State. The representatives of the people will make the Holy Land a land of liberty, which will be extended to all its inhabitants without religious discrimination; for *"All the peoples shall walk each in the name of their god, and we shall walk in the name of the Lord our God for ever."*

8) *National Funds.*

In order to realize the return to Palestine, even to commence the rehabilitation, we must have enormous funds. Alkalai, consequently, suggests that a tax be imposed upon all members of the nation, in the form of a tithe. A fund should be established, to be known as *"Shelom Yerushalayim"*, to which each person should contribute one-tenth of his income "sacred unto the Lord". We must accept graciously whatever a poor man will contribute, however small his mite. These funds are to defray the cost of immigration to Palestine after permission is granted by the home government of the foreign country. Furthermore, all synagogues, all societies in every city should accept the figure of one tenth of their incomes as a legal tax, to aid in the rehabilitation of Palestine.

The society should be called *"Hevrath Kol Yisrael Haverim"*, with the right to coin the holy Half-Shekel, which is to be purchased by all Jewish communities and to be made an official unit of their currency. In the month of Adar, when in days of old proclamation was made concerning the Shekel, every Jew should obtain his Shekel from the treasurer of his community.

Sixty years before the establishment of the Jewish National Fund (*Keren Kayemeth*), Alkalai suggested that land be bought with the money of the *Maasser* fund, as he termed it. He called on the rich to redeem the land, lest it be said concerning them "Their money went to Baal". He wrote that the redemption would come about either through war or through purchase. Since we cannot use force, we must hope to reach our goal through munificent expenditure of money. Since "the redeemer must be a man of wealth", Alkalai applied to the Rothschild family and to others, *"to return, seek the Lord, and David, His King,"* so that through them *"the Lord will again claim the remnant of His people."*

9) *About a Shareholders' Company.*

If the settlers of the land are to be supported by charity, their settlement will be of no solid value, for it cannot endure. Therefore the Holy Society (*Kol Yisrael Haverim*) must settle the land as others do it, making the settlers sharers in a commercial enterprise. Homes should be built, vineyards planted, a fleet established, trades and professions developed, all likely to succeed with the help of God, because the land is fruitful and the people are energetic. The poor in Israel will be able to earn their living by the labor of their hands and by the sweat of their brow.

10) *Sources of Income from Agriculture, the Building Trades, Commerce, and Industry.*

"As long as there will be no means of earning a livelihood in Palestine, Israel will not return to the land." Hence, Alkalai pleads with our brethren in the exile to create such conditions in Palestine as will allow its inhabitants to earn a living. He prayerfully hopes that the Holy One, blessed be He, may inspire our rich men to build homes for themselves in Palestine. "Others will imitate them; thus the poor and unemployed will be encouraged, all Israel will promote Palestine's welfare, and it will become a land great in commerce and trade."

The work of redemption will commence with the growth of agriculture. *"When you come to the land, plant ye every type of fruit-tree."* He condemned those super-pious rabbis who had dissuaded Sir Moses Montefiore from sowing and planting in Palestine. "Through preventing agricultural pursuits, they prevent mass immigration", he thundered. Those rabbis who claimed that Jerusalem was built only for the constant study of Torah, even if they be right in theory, are wrong from the practical viewpoint, for in this material world we must not act as if we lived in the world to come, "where there will be no eating or drinking." This does not imply, perish the thought, that we should forsake the Torah! The farmers, the workers in the vineyards, the craftsmen, and the merchants, they all will support those who study the Torah and supply them with all their wants.

"Agriculture will cause the return to the land, for it is a source of livelihood for the poor. The first *Mitsvah* incumbent upon those who enter Palestine is to work on the land. The first newcomers from Europe should be chosen for their expert knowledge of agriculture; after them may come the artisans and the merchants. It is the duty of every Jew worthy of the name to help those who settle in Palestine, by getting them jobs."

11) *Abolition of Sects and Customs.*

It is the function of the Elders to equalize all the sects in the community by abolishing different types of congregations and customs.* All should maintain the same script, language, Torah, and customs. All the decrees of the Elders shall have legal validity, and they shall decide on the type of service that shall be observed. All shall conduct themselves in a spirit of love and brotherhood.

12) *The Revival of Hebrew as the National Language.*

"The spirit of the times demands the establishment of a country together with its language. So is it with Palestine and Hebrew. It is essential to gather our scattered people from all corners of the earth into one society. Every country has its own language and its own folkways. The Jews, living among many nations, thus speak different languages and adopt various customs; that makes for diversity, separation, division, and delays our redemption. The Talmud maintains that there were three things that helped Israel's deliverance from the bondage of Egypt: Israelites did not change their names; they did not change their language; and they did not change their manner of dress.

"But all these things were lost during our period of Galuth. All my life I was deeply grieved over the fact that our fathers permitted our tongue to be forgotten and our nation to become a melting pot of seventy different nations and languages, according to the lands in which we were scattered. But let us not despair; let us rather with might and main bend all our efforts toward the establishment of one common language, as a main goal for our people. Does not the Talmud say: *'If someone tells you "I tried hard and succeeded", believe him!'* "

13) *One Pronunciation.*

Alkalai complains about differences in pronunciation. The Sephardim pronounce the *Kamets* like the *Patah*. The Ashkenazim read the *Kamets* like the *Holom*. Undoubtedly it is not correct that we should be so divided as to be unable to read the same passage of our Scriptures in the same manner, or to pray together

---

*Some of us would abhor every type, however well-intentioned, of co-ordination, esp. recalling the horrors of *Gleichschaltung*.—Ed.

with the same accent. This divergence is not a law of the Torah that we would not be permitted to change. However, one individual cannot correct such a condition, and "when the crown will return to its old glory," when the Masoretic experts will go back to Palestine, they will decide upon a uniform system of pronunciation, and the Elders will carry out their recommendation.

14) *All Israel should use but one Script.*

Why should every country harboring Jews have a different manner of writing? Consider for example the Rashi script with which every Jew is familiar! One such script for all Israel is a self-evident desideratum.

These are the fourteen principles upon which the future Jewish State should be established.

In the General Assembly, Alkalai sees symbolized the Messiah ben Joseph. This Assembly will choose as its head one to be called the Messiah ben David. Thus the Messiah ben David will not come flying through the sky, with fiery chariots and horses, but will be a man whom Israel will choose to be its head, and who, perchance, may be a lineal descendant of King David. God's spirit will rest upon his head and he will perform wonders and signs so that all the world will turn to one faith and proclaim the name of our Lord. Do not think that the end of *Galuth,* the *Geulah,* the *Yeshuah,* the *Nehamah,* and the coming of the Messiah are synonymous, that they will all come to pass simultaneously! Each has its prescribed time and limit. The arrival of the Messiah is the last of these, and the most wonderful of all before the resurrection of the dead. And even while, according to some teachers, we are not permitted to speak about the Messiah ben David, we are obliged to talk about Messiah ben Joseph, the General Assembly, because that depends on ourselves alone. "As soon as Jerusalem is rebuilt by order of the General Assembly, the Messiah ben David will come. The arousal of spirit must originate from us, but the actual achievement will come about through God, blessed be His Name."

By recourse to combinations of the numerical values of letters and words, Alkalai found the year 1840 auspicious for the beginning of the *Geulah*. From this year, he began to count the number of years that passed without any concrete results. At the time when famous men made attempts to heal the wounds of Israel sustained in the Damascus affair by philanthropic means, by helping the poor, by laboring for equality of civil rights, when even religious reform in the Diaspora was assayed as a panacea, Alkalai, ignoring all palliatives, came upon the scene to declare that the only solution was the return to the homeland. He did not believe that the final answer lay in philanthrophy. "Instead of milk and honey, welfare and blessing, on which we would have fed in our Holy Land, we are being fed on blood, murder and evil decrees in the lands of the other nations." In the Damascus incident Alkalai heard the voice of the Shofar, summoning all our hearts to consider the plight of Jerusalem.

"Now, it is the duty of every Jew to plant a tree in Palestine, to send one of his children to settle on the land. From Damascus and its evil we should return to find shelter under the wings of our God in the Home Land." Alkalai in his pamphlet *"Minhath Yehudah"* addresses Israel's sages: "I adjure you, holy rabbis, who form the Supreme Court, by the power of the universal Tithe, on which I have based my whole message! Within ten days after you receive this pamphlet, appoint ten Elders, capable men, who should consider my suggestion, discuss it in accordance with the mental faculties God bestowed upon them, and help bring to light this doctrine for the sake of the Holy One, of Israel, and the House of the Lord, our God. Thus, pray, stop the mouths of those who are talking vanity and falsehood, men of blood and deceit, who prevent the sons of Israel from going to the land which God promised them; who have so little faith as to say: 'Perchance the inhabitants of the land will rise against us.' "

As with many other great thinkers, so with Alkalai; his book *"Minhath Yehudah"* only helped to increase the number of those who mocked him. Rabbi Ignatz Einhorn, who wrote a review of his book in German, came to the conclusion that its author was out of his mind, and its purchase a waste of money.

In 1848, Alkalai proclaimed in a public message that since Israel had not aroused itself to return to the land of our Fathers,

the decrees of expulsion and destruction had commenced, for salvation depends on *Teshuvah* (*Teshuvah* means both "repentence"
and "return", ingeniously combined by our author), the return
of Israel to the Land, having repented of voluntary exile.

"Ever since I began to reflect upon this matter the situation
has become clearer to me. The solution lies in an appeal to the
governments of the world. I do not ask that my opinion be
accepted, but only that you discuss it in the light of day, including
every unfavorable aspect, until 'the truth will come out of the
earth'." To the rabbis who opposed his design, he said: "Give
glory to the Lord your God, and do not prevent the redemption
of Israel. We are exiles from Palestine, and they who live there
are in constant jeopardy. How can we expect peace, when each
day sees evils enhanced and causeless hatred increased? Our eyes
look forward to the building of the Third Temple. I adjure
every wise man in Israel that if he find contradictions in my words,
he should inform me at once; and if his heart prompt him to sanctify
the name of God, he should strengthen our hands."

In 1849 Alkalai published a book entitled *"Pethah ke-Huddah
Shel Mahat,"* wherein he wrote that the sages of Israel will have
to give account for their failure to inform our leaders that the
redemption rests with their appeal to the governments of the world,
and condemns them for not arousing our brothers for a general
repentance and return. In deep affliction he cries out: "Why do
not the influential men beseech the mercy of humane governments
for our nation and for the cities of our God? I have adjured
them to testify if there is truth in my words. Although truth
speaks for itself, I still need their testimony, because the world
is being led by fools, *'the small foxes who destroy the vineyards
of the Lord of Hosts'*. They ridicule my message before the people
and prevent them from returning.

"Whosoever habitually and without reason would ignore my
words, no matter how great he be, by my life, I shall not deign to
look at him. Truth must not be afraid! My words are based on a
solid foundation, and even if all the world's winds were to attempt
to blow them away, they could not move them from their place."

What Alkalai preached, he also practised. He began a journey through the lands of Europe in an attempt to awake people from their slumber, to make them accept his plan and gird for action. Not one attentive ear did he find in France or in Germany! In 1852 he arrived in London, where he founded a society for the settlement of Palestine, which he named *"Shelom Yerushalayim."* Non-Jews also joined the organization, but as soon as the rabbi left the city, it disbanded.

That year Alkalai came to Leipzig. "There," he writes, "the great scholar and defender of his people, Dr. Fuerst, showed me a signed contract with the Lloyd steamship company catering to Mediterranean passengers, which agreed to transport persons to Palestine at a third of the regular rate. Had only the rabbinic authorities endorsed the plan, all Israel would have acted upon it."

But Alkalai did not despair. He got in touch with important non-Jews, who promised him definite aid if and when the Jews commenced to leave for the Holy Land. However, the Jews argued, "England is our homeland. We want to participate in the Parliament." This was their main concern.

In 1852, Alkalai published his sixth work, *"Mevasser Tov"* ("Harbinger of Good Tidings") in Hebrew, with an English translation. It is a brief digest of the ideas expressed in his other works. He kept on publishing and mailing numerous letters, articles, and books to strengthen his cause. Between 1842 and 1870 he published nine additional volumes and nine more pamphlets, all of them containing a concise analysis of the state of our people. By this time his prophetic sense had grown much keener. He knew what was going to happen in the course of time and he was deeply grieved that we were neglecting the golden opportunity. His plans were very complete and detailed, the result of thorough knowledge and profound grasp of reality. He not only sought a general programme, but had outlined the methods for realizing every detail, every particular. His was a masterly, clear, complete work of statesmanship. He documented his thesis with hundreds of quotations from our sages, omitting not a single relevant passage in Biblical and Talmudic literature, and citing even the works of Rabbi Isaac Abarbanel, the book "The Two Tables of the Covenant", and others.

In 1857, when his book *"Goral l'Adonai"* ("A Lot for the Lord") came from the press, Samuel Schwartz, in the introduction to his book *"Die Messias-Zeit"*, wrote that he agreed with the courageous author that the wealthy Jews ought to support the poor in Palestine, and enable them to acquire property there and improve their condition. But as far as the establishment of a Jewish colony was concerned, if, indeed, money were offered for this purpose, "America, and not Turkey, is the country to turn to!" Such were the thoughts of the intelligentsia in those days!

The book "A Lot for the Lord" went through three editions. Alkalai succeeded in obtaining the endorsement of the great men of his time.* However, he was not satisfied with endorsements alone; he demanded action.

In 1860, Alkalai expected a good deal of the society *"Kol Yisrael Haverim"* (I. C. A.), founded in Paris under the auspices of Baron Hirsch, for the purpose of directing immigration to Argentina. At once he communicated with the leaders, sending them pamphlets and letters in an attempt to direct the movement toward Palestine. But it was all in vain. His hope rose again when the agricultural school *"Mikveh Yisrael"* was founded. He implored this society to buy large tracts of land in Palestine through an issue of shares, and to aid the farmers through the importation of trained experts. He implied that the real solution lay in the salvation of the whole nation; in this way individuals too would be saved. "Complete redemption could come only in the land, the inheritance of our fathers". He suggested that the heads of the Alliance issue shares of stock; in the name of the organization, with the money realized, tracts of land might be acquired for Jewish and non-Jewish farmers to settle upon them. "It is not necessary

---

*Rabbis like Ruben Barukh of Vienna, Isaac Yitzhak Levi Barditchever, Jacob Meir of Bucharest, Eliezer Horovitz of Vienna, Jacob J. Ettlinger (Berlin), Samuel J. Rabinowitz (Sapotkin), J. J. Reines (Lida), P. Razovsky (Sventzian), Nahum Greenhaus (Troki), Gedaliah Titkin of Breslau, and scholars like Dr. Julius Fuerst of Leipzig, Dr. Tulens, M. E. Stern of Vienna, Dr. Michael Sachs, Dr. Leopold Zunz of Berlin, and Dr. Adolf Jellinek of Vienna, endorsed Alkalai's book.

to reward with gold those who desire to take plow in hand.
A proclamation should be issued that any person wanting to dwell
in Palestine could go with the blessings and material support of
the society, which would find him work and sustenance. Thousands of Jews, living in misery, and especially the victims of Polish,
Persian, Yemenite, Moroccan, and general Danubian hatred, are
anxious to flee to God's land, many of them having a good
knowledge of the soil. With the money obtained by the sale of
shares the company shall build houses in Palestine, which many
persons, Jews and non-Jews, will flock to buy. The man who buys
a home for a thousand dollars will reap a tenfold profit in a
decade, and there will be ample sustenance even for porters and
builders of roads."

With similar demands Alkalai approached other societies, such
as *Hevrath Yishuv Erets Yisrael,* founded in Russia in 1860 by
Hayyim Lurie; *Hevrath Mekitsei Nirdamin,* established in 1861;
and others, imploring them all to unite into one society, whose sole
aim would be the redemption of Palestine. He appealed to the
people to join them and to lend their help to the leaders.

Alkalai found much satisfaction in the Zionist activities
of Rabbi Hirsch Kalischer, whom he mentions often in his writings.
Ever since their first meeting in 1863, Kalischer had been greatly
influenced by Alkalai, accepting the new ideas, and using his
very terms.

In 1865, Rabbi Hayyim Tsevi Schneierson, also a prominent
rabbi, was sent to Austria under the auspices of the "Houses of
Shelter" (*Batei Mahseh*), and there began to disseminate the idea
that redemption would come about in a natural way. In 1869,
Schneierson traveled to the United States, where he was very active
for the rehabilitation of Palestine and for settling there the Jews of
Roumania, who were mercilessly abused. As a basic solution of
the problem of the Jews persecuted throughout the Galuth, he
suggested the establishment of a Jewish State in Palestine. He
published all details in a book called *"Erets Yisrael and Roumania",*
which appeared in English in New York City during 1872. On
the same topic Schneierson wrote in the newspaper *"Ivri Anokhi".*

With all this Alkalai was most happy. He praised Schneierson generously in a letter to the paper, saying that he gave joy to God and man, that the spirit of the Lord spoke through him, and he emphasized again the duty of influential men to prod the governments into action.

In the periodical *"Levanon"* (5th Year, 34th Issue), Kalischer wrote a letter demanding that people support the Palestinian settlement. Against this there appeared in the same paper a letter from Jerusalem, signed by a certain "Ben David". In an article, also in *"Levanon"*, Alkalai did his utmost to support Kalischer, stating that "Ben David's" letter was but the verbiage of a man without sense, a desecration of God's Name, deserving sharpest censure. He called on that letter-writer to stay home, for "Palestine will be rebuilt without him and without his cowardly associates in Zion!"

With great bitterness, Alkalai attacked those who despaired of the *Geulah* and who began to settle in their native lands, regarding them as their national homes. Especially did he assail those reformed rabbis who had changed the prayer-book, erasing the name of Zion. He made an onslaught on the rabbinical assembly in Braunschweig, and again in Kassel, reiterating that all our troubles stem from our despair of the *Geulah*. These sinners, he declared, have become messengers of destruction, laying impious hands on our prayer-book, omitting all words recalling the promise that God would restore us joyfully to our land.

Alkalai lashed out against Rabbi Nahman Nathan Kornel, who, in the preface to his "Five Pamphlets", had contradicted him; he wondered why not even one of them dealt with the redemption of Israel and the restoration of the Shekhinah to Zion, since it befits every Israelite to compose books on the *Geulah, "for this is our very life and the span of our days"*, that we dwell in our own land. When appealing to the masses, Alkalai warned them not to heed those who exaggerate the difficulty of the task, for, indeed, it was impossible that all Israel should agree on one idea. We ought to be ashamed of ourselves for having wasted so many years that might have been profitably spent to redeem our nation. "We must serve the Lord not only with pious thought and reverent prayer, but with concrete work!"

About 78 years ago, when Rabbi Moses Sachs wrote against resettlement in the *"Maggid"*, Alkalai attacked him keenly. "One quarrel", he said, "may destroy a hundred means of livelihood, and this unhappy dispute, in its fury, dims the glory of Israel. Woe unto the generation in which such things come to pass! It is because of such things that our folk lose hope in *Geulah,* divert their ideas toward other matters, and bring about the blindness and grotesqueness of the reform movement. I can see all this only as the result of despair in the *Geulah,* which these pious men, unthinkingly, keep delaying. I cannot endure the thought of our Homeland being destroyed, yea, the Torah and our heritage. I cry out in an agony of grief, but no one listens. I plead with those in power, and with the common folk, to honor the Lord before the darkness encompasses all."

His appeal unheeded, like a voice crying in the wilderness, he lost faith in the prominent personages, in the leaders of the society of *"Kol Yisrael Haverim",* and even in Moses Montefiore. So, at the age of seventy-seven, he decided to go to Palestine to organize, with the meager forces at his command, the *Yishuv,* or settlement of Erets Yisrael.

Arriving at Jaffa, in Sivan of 1871, Alkalai published an article of thanksgiving in the newspaper *"Havatseleth",* wherein he prayed that the Almighty stir up the hearts of the powerful leaders of Israel to establish colonies, and to build up the Holy Land. He visited Karl Netter in *Mikveh Yisrael,* and pronounced the blessing: *She-heheyanu.* Visiting Jerusalem next, he published in *"Ha-Maggid"* a very discouraging article about the plight of the Jews in the Holy City, who had visited him en masse and urged him to aid them. After weary conferences with the Sephardim and the Ashkenazim, he wrote in *"Havatseleth"* that he was a life-long servant of those who feared the Lord, dedicating his life to the Holiness of His Name. Having arrived at that place which God had chosen, he but lived to work for the rehabilitation of the Holy Land. For this privilege he would offer his thanks to God, the Lord, for being so greatly favored to be able to do so.

On the 29th day of the month of Sivan, 1871, the elite of Jerusalem met with him and agreed to establish the society called

"Kol Yisrael Haverim". Both Sephardim and Ashkenazim joined to help the society accomplish its aim: to cultivate the land, so as to provide for the poor. "In truth any Jewish heart must be grieved to see the great poverty in Jerusalem. Who could be deaf to the cry of the lowly?"

The headquarters of this society was in Jerusalem, with a branch in Jaffa. The great rabbis and leaders of Jerusalem participated in both administrative committees. For a short time all signs pointed to a movement in the right direction, but soon the Halukah people, under the leadership of Akivah Lehren, became aroused against it. In the prophetic design of Alkalai, they saw a danger to their power, a possible reduction of their incomes, despite the assurance of Alkalai that their Halukah would not be touched, even to the extent of a hairbreadth, that the society would only help them, and that agriculture would supply an income and sustenance to those who spend their time studying the Torah. All this notwithstanding, the Halukah people were adamant.

When Alkalai left Palestine to visit the European countries to obtain sympathy and material assistance for the society, it was dissolved because of the threats of the men of the Halukah.

Embittered by these obstacles to his plan, Alkalai wrote a forceful article in the *"Ha-Maggid"*, in which he expressed the hope that God would silence the mouths of those who spoke contemptuously and arrogantly against the righteous members of the righteous society. Akivah Lehren published a letter in *"Levanon"* against Alkalai, saying that it was foolish to hope for vain aid, and to make labor in the field a basis for redemption. The land will not give us its strength until we first offer our religious repentance in full.

Out of fear of the heads of the Halukah and of Akiva Lehren, before whom all those receiving the moneys of Halukah trembled, many rabbis who at first had sided with Alkalai and joined his society, now opposed him, and signed a public declaration against him. At a large gathering held in Jerusalem, they decided not to endorse his theories, read his letters, or have any further contact with him. All newspapers were requested not to publish any more of his articles concerning the Holy Land.

Old Rabbi Alkalai was embittered, but not dismayed. He waged war openly, like any heroic figure who is certain of the truth of his cause. In a letter published in *"Havatseleth"*, he vehemently attacked Akiva Lehren and all his other opponents, saying that it would be tragic if all the false complaints were not publicly exposed and the good work of the noble society made widely known in Israel. "There are more people with us, thank God, than with them. Our society's flag is the Lord. About insults to myself I have remained silent, but for the sake of Zion I must not hold my peace until they confess their iniquity and their blasphemy!"

He attacked Rabbi Meir Auerbach, spiritual head of the Ashkenazim in Palestine, for having urged the editor of *"Havatseleth"* to reject any further articles from him on the ground that "they cause dissension in Israel, and estrange the people from their Father in heaven." Alkalai averred that Rabbi Auerbach spread evil tales about our Holy Land, and about those who love it, to make the land hateful in the eyes of the children of Israel. He felt doubly aggrieved because it was from Jerusalem that these words of abuse had come, and he begged all who love Zion to pay no heed to such sinister talk. Jerusalem will never be a city rejected . . .

From 1871 until 1878, the year of his death, he published twenty-six letters and articles, describing his ideas in detail— seventeen in the newspaper *"Havatseleth"*, six in *"Ha-Maggid"* and three in *"Ivri Anokhi"*.

Alkalai returned to Semlin and commenced to interest the wealthy men in buying land in Palestine. When he read in *"Havatseleth"* that the government wanted to sell land between Jaffa and Ramleh, he tried to influence the rich family of Russo, and was happy to be able to wire to the editor of *"Havatseleth"* that he had succeeded to the extent of getting them to buy some of this land. Again he asked the I.C.A., the Paris society, *Kol Israel Haverim,* to establish colonies in Palestine, but as their report of 1873 shows, their answer was in the negative.

In the summer of 1874, Alkalai again returned to Palestine to settle there with his wife Esther, and, despite his advanced age, continued his work of encouraging immigration and settlement.

In the same year there was founded in London a society called *Mazkereth Moshe,* whose purpose was to perpetuate the name of Moses Montefiore through some definite work in Palestine. Alkalai urged this new organization to unite with the Society *Kol Israel Haverim,* and to beseech the Sultan, "who will not turn you away empty handed."

When Samuel Montague and Dr. Asher, as representatives of the society, came to examine the conditions of the *Yishuv* in Palestine, Alkalai pleaded with them that if they really and truly wanted to benefit Israel and Erets Yisrael, they should make the start in Jaffa, and that this small beginning would develop into a large enterprise. But if they insisted on beginning their work in Jerusalem, such effort would be the punishment for our great guilt, for it would lead to a new disaster arising from the quarrels with the Halukah people and involving endless hatreds and jealousies.

Of Montefiore, Alkalai wrote that he greatly respected this Prince, who had power to advance the Jewish cause, but whose retinue was misleading him, and making him lose his chance for eternal glory. He wrote many papers in honor of Montefiore. "For thirty-five years, with bated breath, have I waited for him. At the end of his life he showed his love for the ruined land. And if this prince of ours has failed, God will send us friends from another place."

Alkalai pleaded often for the Jews of Poland. In 1870 he wrote that settlement in Palestine would cure the ills of our stricken brethren there. They would be happier with a piece of dry bread at the table of our heavenly Father, than with houses replete with all good things in another land. Unlike the merchant, the farmer does not have to fear going to a place where he is not known. When we shall have settlements, farms and vineyards, then, little by little, will come craftsmen and merchants from among the scattered sheep of Israel, returning like pigeons to their nest.

In 1875, he sent a public call to our brethren in Poland, saying that all the troubles that befell them were designed to arouse them to return to Zion, for the *Geulah* depended upon themselves. The next year he reiterated that the Jews of Poland, among whom there were many expert farmers, should not hesitate to send their best men to Erets Yisrael to establish the first colony.

When Rabbi Tsevi Hirsch Kalischer died, on the fifth day of Heshvan, 1875, Alkalai suggested in *"Havatseleth"* that a colony be established in his memory, to be called *"Nahalath Tsevi"*, but unfortunately there was no response.

To his dying day, Rabbi Alkalai fought bravely for the settlement of Erets Yisrael, but, alas, he found no attentive ear during his lifetime. Full of grief and completely exhausted, he died in Jerusalem on the fourth day of Tishri, 1878.

His teachings were realized at a later date, though not in the manner he desired. Had we but hearkened to his voice, a hundred years ago, it is almost a certainty that the cruel disaster of our time would not have come upon us, and the Jews of Poland would have been safe in our own Homeland.

II

RABBI ABDALLAH SOMEKH

(Founder of the School for Rabbis in Bagdad)

In the past two centuries there have lived in Babylon many rabbis who have excelled in keenness of mind and in profound familiarity with Jewish law, and who were considered among the great Torah authorities of their time. Many of them published valuable works on halakhah, homiletics, Biblical commentaries, and responsa. Some of their writings were printed; others remained as manuscripts in the possession of private persons or in libraries.

The study of the Torah in Babylon in that era blossomed through the efforts of four great men who founded Hebrew schools, opened Yeshivoth, introduced improved academic customs, and served as shining examples to all the people.

They were Tsedakah Hutzin, Moses Hayyim, Abdallah Somekh, and Joseph Hayyim. Each of them created a glorious period which was named after him in his honor. To this day these men exert a profound influence not only because of their learning, but because of their communal work and the impact of their personalities on Babylonian Jews, as well as those in other lands. At that time Babylon had many scholars, but these four surpassed them all.

At the beginning of the year 1742, a plague broke out in Babylon, from which many perished, among them a large number of its rabbis. The Jews fled to near-by places. When the plague had spent itself, they returned and began to organize new communities. Since the Chief Rabbi of Bagdad and all the members of the Beth Din had died in the plague, the Jewish community of Bagdad was forced to ask succor from Aleppo, and extended an invitation to one of its greatest rabbis, Tsedakah Hutzin, to come to Bagdad, where he served for 30 years, spreading the Torah and raising Jewish scholarship to a great height.

Once again, in 1773, a severe epidemic struck Bagdad, in which Rabbi Hutzin and his three sons perished. Of the prominent rabbis who succeded him are to be mentioned Rabbi Tsalah ben Joseph Matsliah and his son, Rabbi Nissim, who are considered the greatest poets of ritual liturgy of that period.

The blossoming of Torah learning, begun in Hutzin's time, increased sevenfold in the time of Rabbi Moses Hayyim. The latter was a great authority on Jewish law, and was gifted with unusual talents. At that time there lived in Bagdad the Kabbalistic poet, Rabbi Sassoon Bar Mordecai Shindukh, who published many books.*

This revival of learning increased even more in the era of Rabbi Abdallah Somekh. Thanks to him, the famous millionaire Ezekiel ben Reuben Menasheh and his sons established a Rabbinical School (Yeshivah) in Bagdad, that educated many great rabbis who officiated in all Babylon and its surroundings.

*Among the great disciples of Rabbi Moses Hayyim were Rabbi Reuben David Navee, Rabbi Jacob Path-hi, Rabbi David Babah, Rabbi Eliyah Bar Shlomoh Cohen, Rabbi Eliyah Bar Joshua Ovadiah, Rabbi Shalom Nurial, Rabbi Jacob Bar Joseph Harofs, the poet Rabbi Adbullah Bar Katzirson of Solomon Hanin, and Rabbi Moses Bar Solomon ha-Levi.

The family of Somekh is one of the most prominent ones in Babylon, with a record of rabbis, leaders, merchants, scholars, and men of great repute. According to tradition, they are descendants of the Gaon Rabbi Nissim, who is the composer of the great *"Viduy"* (Confession) recited on Yom Kippur, and included in all the prayerbooks of the Sephardim.

Somekh was born in Bagdad in 1813. His genealogy up to his sixth ancestor is as follows: Rabbi Abdallah ben Abraham ben Joseph ben Ezekiel Somekh, ben Eliyahu ben Abraham ben Nissim. From his early youth he dedicated himself to the study of the Torah, and especially to the Talmud and the literature of the rabbinic authorities. He was the pupil of Rabbi Jacob Bar Joseph ha-Rofei. Since his father was a successful jeweler, the young lad did not have to worry about his livelihood. His wonderful mind enabled Somekh to advance rapidly in all his studies. Before many years had passed, he was winning fame as one of the great scholars of his generation.

At first he engaged in business ventures, trying to combine the study of Torah with a wordly occupation, but when he noticed that the study of the Holy Law in Babylon was diminishing because of the lack of a Rabbinical College, he was influenced by a holy love of Torah to gather ten young men about him whom he taught free of charge.

In those days there lived in Bagdad a wealthy and generous leader, Ezekiel ben Reuben Menasheh. When he saw the efforts of Rabbi Abdallah to strengthen Torah in Babylon, he became deeply attached to him and agreed to aid the young men financially.

In 1840, Menasheh purchased a large courtyard, whereon he erected a Rabbinical Seminary called "Seminary of Abu Menasheh". It was designed for Abdallah's pupils, for whom he established a large endowment to assure them a sufficient monthly income.

At that time there existed in Bagdad an educational institution called "Midrash Talmud Torah", whose students were mostly orphans or children of the poor. Rabbi Abdallah and Ezekiel transferred its more industrious and intelligent students to the new building. Here they were taught Gemara, commentaries, and decisions of Jewish Law. The philanthropist saw to it that they were fed and clothed, and, later on, provided them with wife and home, and permanent support for their families for the rest of their lives.

The efforts of Rabbi Abdallah bore fine fruit. The students increased in number and became prominent in the sphere of learning, receiving the titles of *"Hakham"* and "Rabbi". Each in turn founded a Talmudic school for a few students of his own to teach them Gemara and its commentaries, so that there arose small colleges under the shadow of the great academy.

The traveler Benjamin the Second, who visited Bagdad in 1848, wrote: "The religious instruction among the Jews of Bagdad is admirable, for there is a large Yeshivah (Rabbinical School) in which 60 young rabbis study theology. This school is under the direction of the learned Rabbi Abdallah ben Abraham Somekh, who performs the duties of his office gratuitously. He is a very rich man, and at one time headed one of the principal commercial houses. But he has given over the management of his business to a partner, in order to devote himself entirely to his pious office."

The philanthropist Menasheh died on the 14th day of Tammuz, 1851. He was survived by two sons, Menasheh and Sassoon, both socially-minded like their sire. They not only continued, but increased the support that their worthy father was wont to give to the disciples, to enable them to study in peace and free from financial worry. They gave awards to many new young men who had not been lucky enough to obtain scholarships while the older Menasheh was alive.

In 1854, the philanthropist Menasheh ben Ezekiel demolished the Seminary that his father had built, bought three buildings on this lot, and also erected a large synagogue called *"Midrash Abu Menasheh"*. Adjoining the synagogue he built a two-story Yeshivah, naming it *"Midrash Beth Zilkah"* in honor of the philanthropist Ezra Zilkah, who had owned the lot before. In the same year Menasheh bought more than 1,000 volumes for the library of the Yeshivah.

This new seminary was even larger than its earlier counterpart, and its fame spread in many lands. From all the cities of Babylon came students seeking knowledge under the great teacher Abdallah Somekh, to graduate as rabbis and scholars of the law.

The traveler Rabbi Yehiel Fischel bar Jacob Kastelman, who came to Bagdad in 1860, wrote on the 14th day of Sivan: "Thank God that in Babylon there are Yeshivoth and scholars who sit all day occupied with Torah and worship, especially in the Yeshivah named after the philanthropist Menasheh, who supports it and provides for all its needs, spending some fifty gold pieces in its behalf every week in accord with the testament of his father who had left money for this purpose."

In 1863, under the supervision of Somekh, there were thirty prominent rabbis in that Yeshivah, each the head of a small group of his own pupils, a *"Yeshivah Ketanah"*, in which Gemara and its commentaries were studied.

Rabbi Shneur Zalman Menahem Mendel, a messenger of Jerusalem who visited Bagdad in 1869, wrote: "There are in Bagdad Yeshivoth supported by the philanthropists Menasheh and his brothers, where scholars study Gemara and its commentaries, under the direction of the *Hassid* (saint) Rabbi Abdallah Somekh." He was greatly impressed by their beautiful customs and ceremonies on Simhath Torah and on Hoshanah Rabbah.

The traveler Ephraim Neumark, who was in Bagdad in 1884, wrote that some very great scholars sat in the big Yeshivah called *"Midrash Beth Zilkah"*, a two-story building. The "Dayanim" (judges; here, faculty members) lived on the upper story. There were about fifteen scholars, and the old Rabbi Abdallah Somekh was their leader. From this *Beth Torah* there were ordained rabbis and *shohatim* for all the surrounding places of Bagdad, yea even as far as East India and Persia. Sages from distant places appeared with their questions, to be answered by the scholars of this Yeshivah. Rabbi Somekh was highly respected by the people of these regions, where he was addressed, not by his name, but by the revered title of "Rabbenu" (Our Master).

The traveler M. Edelman, who visited Bagdad in 1889, reported: "Of all the rabbis who were in this city in the last decades, the most honored one was Rabbi Abdallah Somekh, who served as rabbi and as 'Hakham Bashi' (Supreme Religious Leader). For many years, without accepting any compensation, he did great things, introducing important improvements in the community, and—his life's major task—spreading Torah among the people. Besides this renowned 'Hakham Bashi', there were many other sages who for many years had received their knowledge from him."

Rabbi Solomon Bekhor Hitzin of Bagdad, who was his pupil, wrote in 1899 in the *"Ha-Tsefirah"*, that Abdallah was great in learning, in worship, and in the practice of loving kindness, and that he had restored to Babylon her former glory, the glory of the study of Torah that had been taken from her for many hundreds of years. For he established an institute of higher learning, raising many disciples, and spreading Torah in Israel. Almost all the rabbis, judges, and other sages of Babylon, Persia, Media, and India had sat at his feet and imbibed his wisdom. Most of the Jews in these lands called him *"Istayi"*, which means "My Teacher and Master", even as the editor of the Mishnah, our holy Teacher, was called "Rabbi".

The traveler Rabbi Jacob Sapir, who visited Yemen in 1864, relates: "In the city of Anezi there are about seventy families, who in all matters of Torah obey the rabbis of Babylon (i.e. Bagdad), and do not turn aside from whatever they teach them. They live eighty days' journey away from Babylon. Yet when they need a *Shohet* or a teacher or a rabbi, they come to ask Rabbi Abdallah Somekh for such dignitaries."

Rabbi Abdallah possessed a logical mind and a phenomenal memory. His wisdom was pure, his approach not that of a sophistical dialectician; he fought the battles of the Torah with probity and faultless logic. He was regarded as one of the chief authorities of Jewish law in his generation, and the founder of the institutions of learning in Babylonia which function to this very day.

The personality of Abdallah was exalted above all the wise men of his time in the Middle Eastern countries. His name was greatly revered, even sanctified, and never did any mortal dare oppose his word. Even the Gentiles respected him and kissed his hands in humility. Through his endeavor, money came streaming to the institutions of charity in Bagdad, and especially from such philanthropic families as Sassoon, Gabbai, Yehudah, and Bahir.

In the year of 1849, Somekh approved the book "The Voice of Sassoon", written by Rabbi Sassoon ben Mordecai. On the

11th day of Tebeth 1877, he was asked to approve the work *"Sidrei Taharoth"*, on the tractate *"Ohaloth"*, written by the learned Rabbi Gershon Hanokh Henikh of Radzin, Poland. This endorsement is described as "The Approval of the Rabbi, the Gaon, the famous Tsaddik, the hoary scholar who resides in the Yeshivah, the glory of Israel and his Saints, a thorough sage who can uproot mountains, our eminent teacher, servant of the Lord, Abraham Joseph Somekh, head of the Yeshivah in Babylonia, in the city of Bagdad." His pupil, Rabbi Solomon Bekhor Hitzin, added his mite, stating: "I, the humble and the insignificant one, just one of the group who studied under our great teacher in the Yeshivah in Babylonia, taking hold of the fringe of his garment, also approve this work."

In the year of 1899, many fell victim to an epidemic in Bagdad, among them, on the 18th of Elul, the great Abdallah.

In 1904, in the same city, his book *"Zivhei Tsedek"* was published, containing legal decisions and responsa concerning the four volumes of the *"Shulhan Arukh."* Some of his novellae were printed in the journal *"ha-Meassef"* in Jerusalem (1897), and in the book *"Nofeth Tsufim"* of Rabbi Salomon Tevinah.*

The river Tigris, as is well known, bisects Bagdad into two parts. The Jewish settlement is centralized in the eastern part of the city, the Moslem settlement being located in the western portion. There, within a fortified wall, is the grave of the High Priest, Joshua ben Yehotsedek. The Bagdad Jews were anxious to bury their saintly Abdallah in the court of Joshua's burial place, but Vahli Mustafah Azim Pasha, an enemy of Israel, opposed their wish. In consequence, riotous quarrels broke out between Jews and Moslems, which alarmed world Jewry in general and our people in Bagdad, Constantinople, and London in particular.

*He left also the following manuscripts:
1. *"Ets ha-Sadeh"*, a commentary on tractate Betsah, written at age 17, and kept in the Synagogue called *"Beth Zilkah"*.
2. *"Kibbuts Hakhamim"*, a commentary on the Haggadah of Passover.
3. Another commentary on the Haggadah of Passover, 1846.
4. Book on the Hebrew Calendar (Intercalation), written in 1846.
5. Novellae on most of the tractates of the Talmud, for a long time kept in the Beth Zilkah Synagogue, but destroyed when the building burned down.

As a result of the whole affair, most of the leading rabbis in Bagdad were arrested, and Vahli was dismissed from his position. These events have an important place in the history of the Babylonian Jews.

III

Rabbi David Sassoon

(Nassi of the Jews in Babylon and in India)

It was a custom in Bagdad for the Mayor who ruled the city to select a weathly, influential Jew as Treasurer, with the title of *"Tsaraf Bashi."* Through such an appointment this Jew automatically became the leader of his own people, possessing all the authority that the *"Roshei ha-Golah"* (exilarchs) enjoyed.

At first, custom decreed that this leader be a lineal descendant of King David, this incumbency passing down from father to son. Originally, when the Nassi rode his horse down the streets of the city, the masses would shout: "People, pay homage to the son of David!" They would even term him "King of Israel." But this feature was abolished at the beginning of the 18th century, for the Mayor appointed as Nassi even men who were not direct descendants of King David. The Nessiim had great power and acted imperiously. They acted as mediators between the Jewish community and the government. The Nassi of Bagdad, also called Nassi of the Country, was considered the head of the entire Jewish community, and exerted great influence upon the government. He had the authority to punish people with fines, even with whippings, according to what appeared right to him. Nessiim were also appointed in various other towns of Babylon, but highest of all was the Nassi of Bagdad.

He possessed much power, which, if abused, might have caused serious consequences for Jews and Moslems, for as he depended only on the Pasha, he could purchase indulgence for all his actions and caprices, regardless of whom he injured.

The first Nessiim were all noble men, greatly concerned with the welfare of their brethren. But not all the later leaders were fit for this great task. Some acquired the coveted honor through slander or bribery. Thus many Nessiim were murdered without cause. In 1849, this office was abolished and replaced by that of the Chief Rabbi, called *"Hakham Bashi."*

Among the Nessiim was Sheikh Sassoon ben Tsalah ben David ben Jacob ben Tsalah ben David, who was the sire of the family of Sassoon, famous in Babylon, China, Japan, India and England in the fields of commerce and philanthropy. Born in Bagdad in 1750, he served as Nassi and Treasurer of the province for forty years (1781-1821), acquitting himself of his task in probity and righteousness, and often standing in the breach to benefit his fellow Jews. He practised much charity, and his name is mentioned with reverence by the Jews of Babylon up to this day.

Rabbi Nissim ben Tsalah Matsliah, the Jewish poet of Babylon, wrote a poem in 1797 in his honor, which expressed this sentiment: "Every day praises and thanks are offered to Sassoon, great prince and head of the Diaspora, the Nassi who helped with his wealth. Indeed he is the crown of the Exile, and all his wealth and all his power are spent in works of grace and mercy."

Sheikh Sassoon married Aman, daughter of the philanthropist Abraham bar David Joshua Gabbai. She died in 1827, after bearing many children; most famous among them was David, born in Bagdad in Heshvan, 1792. In his youth he received a considerable Jewish training. He possessed nobility of character, a brilliant intellect and great practical ability. He knew several languages: Hebrew, his religious tongue; Arabic, the tongue of the locality; Turkish, the official language; and Persian, the language of commerce. At a later time he also studied the Hindu language. He had a talent for business, and was a genius in finance.

The task of the Sheikh as a Nassi of his people and *"Tsaraf Bashi"* of the Mayor, was not an easy one. He served in the interregnum between one administration and the other. The quarrels in this corner of the Turkish Empire never ceased. During the forty years of his incumbency as Nassi, there were six different governors in Bagdad, who were extremely jealous of the personality and influence of Sassoon and persecuted him without let up. Even in 1776, we find that Sassoon, for fear of the governor, could not show himself in public. More than all others, it was the governor Daoud Pasha who, in the fourteen years of his rule, constantly assailed the Nassi, and earned a reputation for cruelty and tyranny. His persecutions forced Sassoon to flee Bagdad just in time to escape death.

By then, Sassoon was 67 years of age. His son David, then twenty-five years old, took his father's place in all communal matters. When the Jews saw that Daoud Pasha was attempting to steal all their money and to take their lives too, and particularly to ruin their leaders, they escaped with their wives and children in 1822 to Basrah and from there to Abu Shihir, living in the new region for many years.

The patriarchs of Bagdad tell of this flight in various versions, most of them untrue, for Rabbi Jacob Sapir, who visited David Sassoon in Bombay in 1860, wrote expressly concerning the Nassi and pious Rabbi Sassoon Tsalah that "he had been an honorable prince in Bagdad, the scion of a noble family in that city. He stood by the Jews even in those days when the hands of Turkish governors imposed heavy and cruel burdens on them. Thirty years ago, a tyrannical governor had taken over the reins in Bagdad, who oppressed the Jews severely, and, jealous of the Nassi's great repute even among the Gentiles, plotted to hang him on trumped-up charges, as he had done with other Nessiim. The old prince and his son escaped miraculously by night, just in the nick of time, to Basrah, where a benevolent ruler was in power. Their wives and children followed them, all staying for a short time in a Persian port. There, in 1829, the father died of old age, and David with his family journeyed to India."

Soon after arriving there, in 1832, David opened in Bombay a large firm called the David Sassoon Company, with many branches in India, China, Japan, in the cities of Calcutta, Shanghai, Canton, Hongkong, Yokohama, Nagasaki, and other places. Later he opened branches in England, and after the death of the founder, his main office was transferred to London. Obtaining the monopoly for the import of textiles, he erected large factories in many cities like London, Liverpool, and Manchester, organized insurance enterprises, and built ports for trade ships. In this way, he promoted trade and industry in many cities, conferring blessings and prosperity upon their inhabitants.

Sassoon suceeded in business through his common sense, courage, and intelligence, and not merely because of inherited wealth. He attributed his success to two factors: that his sons were his agents in various cities, conscientiously attending to the firm's interest; and that he contributed one-tenth of his earnings to the charities of all countries wherein his business had ramifications, among them India, Palestine, Persia, Turkey and England.

David's activities in behalf of his own people were very important. You will hardly find any institution in the East or West with which his name is not associated. He established many communal organizations, schools, houses of learning, hospitals, orphanages, and supported hundreds of rabbis in the publication of their books.

Rabbi Shneur Zalman bar Menahem Mendel, who lived in Jerusalem and Hebron, after a stay in Sassoon's home, wrote in 1858: "I shall remember David's kindness all my days. Thank God, I found what I wanted. He is Sir David, the Prince, the son of Princes, the Pious One, of the famous Sassoon family. He received me in a very friendly way, and gave me a donation for the family organization of the Ashkenazim in Jerusalem. I stayed in his house twice, where they treated me with great respect, and I came out of his house delighted and satisfied."

Rabbi Jacob Sapir, who went to Bombay in 1860, praised Rabbi David Sassoon thus: "He is a Prince, the main leader, a fine, pious man, a philanthropist. Even the trees of Gan Eden cannot compare to him for fragrance. This house of David Sassoon should be called the Uppermost House of all the Princes of Israel, for they all know Torah, and fear God, and follow scrupulously in the footsteps of our Fathers. His great wealth was no obstacle to his attachment to Jewish learning. The high position of his children did not prevent them from pursuing the right path. As great as his riches were, so were his charity, the reputation of his firm, and his humaneness. The table of his house was like the table of a king; the entire courtyard was filled with poor people who came every day from all countries and got food in plenty there.

For the worthy poor who remained in the yard of the Synagogue, or in their homes, nourishment was also provided. On the holy Sabbath, after the *Seudah Shlishith,* all the prominent men in the city and other guests came to his home. The learned men would sit at the head of the table, and discuss words of Torah. They would chant the Psalms until it was time for the evening prayer, which they would recite there. In his courtyard, there was also a kosher Mikvah. Kashruth, purity, and cleanliness shone in every corner."

When David was an old man of seventy, he still presented a fine, upright appearance, with a long beard coming down over his clothes. He wore a tall hat, just as people used to dress in old Bagdad. Purity and honor were his badge. This extraordinary man was honored also by men of other nations and creeds. All the rich men of the city, the merchants, visited him eagerly, and his name was mentioned with respect by the officials and the princes of the State. It was on everyone's lips. He served as member of Parliament and of the Judiciary with such prestige that when Jews came to trial before Gentile judges, the latter would say: "Go to Sassoon, and do as he will tell you." All Jewish lawsuits were decided by him.

Most of the citizens of the city derived their livelihood from the House of Sassoon, benefiting from his gracious kindness. The bookkeepers, salesmen, and clerks in his enterprise were all Jews, to whom he paid wages beyond the usual scale. "Always the poor came to him from such distant places as Bagdad, Persia, Bukhara, Aleppo, and Damascus, including delegations from our Holy Land, and never was a soul disappointed. To each he used to give a handsome donation of money and provisions for the way so that they might travel whithersoever they desired; all this besides the contributions that he sent to scholars, to Yeshivoth in Bagdad, and to his near and distant kin. None departed empty-handed." Thus reports the eye witness, Rabbi Jacob Sapir.

Rabbi Asher Amshe Javits, in a sorrowful eulogy included in his book *"Shoshanim le-David",* had this to say about him: "David excelled all in charity. There was none like him in his philanthropy. The goodness of his heart reached to the ends of the world; he dealt righteously and kindly with all people, opening his gracious hands to every man of every nation and tongue. He built synagogues and schools and homes of shelter for the poor and the sick; he bought cemeteries in many cities, in India and China. Even to the Holy Land did his loving kindness extend. Even there he gave to the poor and to scholars who studied and practised Torah. As the Psalmist put it: *'And David was successful in all his ways and God was with him.'* "

Others who had heard of him or knew him well said that in ability Rabbi David Sassoon was superior to his European competitors: He knew the ways of all the lands in which he did business. He appointed his eight sons as agents of the business in various places. He brought many young men from Bagdad to India, training them gratuitously in his school, and then appointing them in his enterprises in various cities with magnificient salaries. In this way he benefited both others and himself.

When David came to Bombay in 1832, there were 2,242 Jews in a population of a half million natives, a very colorful Jewish group, recruited from many places. He encouraged a steady stream of immigrants from Bagdad and Basrah to the city. In 1855, he organized a Jewish congregation in Bombay, founding the society *"Hevrath Beth David"*, that became a blessing to Indian Jews in general, and to the Jews of Bombay in particular. David was president of the society, his sons assisting him in its management. This society published various booklets concerning the constitution of the congregation. Most important among them was the newspaper *"Doresh Tov le-Amo"*, which for eleven years, from 1855 to 1866, was published in Bombay.

It was the personality and the business activity of Sassoon upon which all Bombay depended, from the Governor of the city and the influential non-Jews down to the helpless poor. A great portion of the population was permanently supported by him. Many came from Bagdad and from Basrah to receive his support and work in his offices or factories, while their children were trained in his schools and, later, earned a livelihood in his firms. His branches in China, in Japan, and in other countries served as cultural and educational agencies, and as sources of charitable work for the whole district. Having a good command of the Hebrew language, he knew every precept and adhered to every Mitsvah, large or small. In 1859, he wrote the preface to the book *"Davar be-Itto"* by Rabbi Sassoon ben Rav Mordecai, and published it at his own expense.

Sassoon's contributions are estimated to have amounted to many million Pounds Sterling. We cannot enumerate them all, but mention may be made of some outstanding ones:

1. In 1858, he erected the building around the grave of *Ezekiel ha-Navi* (the Prophet Ezekiel) in the City of Bagdad.

2. He constructed a synagogue in the ctiy of Heelah in Iraq.

3. In Bombay, he founded schools for boys to obtain Torah and secular knowledge without charge; the outstanding students he employed in his business until they became men of wealth in their own right.

4. He established a school for girls in Bombay.

5. He built in Bombay a Trade School for the poor and insisted that it be non-sectarian, assuming all expenses of both school and students.

6. He established a large hospital in Bombay with the most modern equipment.

7. In 1861, he built in Bombay a large beautiful Synagogue named *"Magen David"* (Star of David), and adjacent to it a Talmud Torah and a Shelter (*Beth Hakhnassath Orhim*) for transient poor.

8. In the city of Punah, the place of his summer residence, he established many charitable organizations, a splendid synagogue in 1863, and a large general hospital named "the David Sassoon General Hospital", noteworthy for being non-sectarian. All patients were provided, free of any charge, with medicine and food.

9. He contributed huge sums for the building of a Hospital for Mental Diseases, in addition to gifts for leprosariums, and homes for delinquent youths. He built homes for aged sailors in Bombay and in Hongkong. The hungry, the orphans, the widows of soldiers slain in the Indian Revolution of 1857, received

his lavish support, and to the Nakshir Foundation he presented an annuity. Palestinian institutions were very grateful for his numerous gifts.

10. In the hall of the Museum of Bombay stands a beautiful monument, six meters high, in memory of Prince Albert, husband of Queen Victoria, who died rather young. On this memorial is a Hebrew inscription: "Prince Albert, husband of her Majesty Queen Victoria, great in counsel and great in action, who sowed wisdom, and caused understanding to blossom forth, beloved by all his people. His memory will not depart from his land! Erected by David Sassoon in the year 5624 of creation and in the twenty-seventh year of Queen Victoria." This tremendous and very expensive monument, built by Sassoon, is the only one in the world erected for a European prince that bears a Hebrew inscription.

11. A short time before his death, he made a great contribution towards the establishment in Bombay of the "Sassoon Mechanics Institution", containing also a Reading Room, Library, and Educational Museum.

In the gorgeous Museum, built by Sassoon, stands to this day a statue of an elderly Jew, wearing an oriental hat. It represents Rabbi Sassoon. Thomas Woolner, R. A., executed this work of art.

On the sixth day of Heshvan (November 7th), 1864, Rabbi David Sassoon passed away in the City of Punah and was buried in the Synagogue Ohel Moed which he had built during his lifetime.

His many sons followed in the steps of their father, each deserving a special encomium for his good deeds.

THE LEADERS OF THE JEWS OF BOKHARA

By Walter J. Fischel

THE LEADERS OF THE JEWS OF BOKHARA

By Walter J. Fischel

I

The twelfth-century "Travels" of Benjamin of Tudela is usually cited as a source for the descriptions of the various "Remnants of Israel" in Asia. Yet this important travelogue leaves us entirely uninformed on the subject of the Jews of Bokhara, that central city between the rivers Oxus and Jaxartes. While Benjamin of Tudela mentions the Jewish communities in Central Asia, Chiva and Samarkand, he remains silent about Bokhara; not even its name is mentioned. Yet the Jewish diaspora in Asia, which at an early date spread all over Khorasan, Trans-Oxania, Khwarizm and other Central Asiatic territories, could hardly have by-passed that great center of Islamic civilization, that meeting-place of scholars and merchants, Bokhara. The earliest documentary evidence pertaining to a Jewish settlement in Bokhara is derived from Ibn al-Futi, an Arab chronicler of the thirteenth century who, by his report that a fanatical Muslim mystic and magician threatened in 1240 to exterminate the Jews and Christians in Bokhara, gave us definite data pertaining to a Jewish community there. We may assume that the Jews who were at that time living in Bokhara had survived this threat, as also that of the various Mongol invasions under Genghis Khan, Hulagu, and later, in the fourteenth century, under Tamerlane. Like Samarkand, the residence of Tamerlane, Bokhara had in all probability regained some of its former splendor and must have received new Jewish settlers, skilled artisans and laborers. Because of meager sources about the life of the Jews of Bokhara from the fourteenth century on, many centuries of Jewish history in Asia remain entirely unrecorded.

The existence of Jews in Bokhara remained unknown to the outside world and Jewish historical research did not place Bokhara on the map of the Jewish diaspora in Asia. An entirely new light was shed on this unknown remnant of Israel, however, when, half a century ago, through newly discovered literary remains, they entered the arena of Jewish history.

535

II

These documents, brought to Europe mainly by Elkan N. Adler, constitute a part of the lost and hitherto unknown literary heritage of Bokharian Jewry. They reveal a most amazing story, telling us that in the seventeenth century Bokharian Jews, remote from the dynastic quarrels and civil wars on Persian soil, untouched by the persecution which swept over their brethren in Persia, enjoyed a great degree of leisure and devoted it to literary activities. Not only have we confirmation of the physical existence in the 17th and 18th centuries of this almost forgotten branch of Oriental Jewry, but we know now that they produced scholars and poets who explored the field of Jewish literature, especially poetry, and made translations into "Tajiki," their own particular dialect. The Bokharian Jews represent in culture and language an offshoot of Persian Jewry.

More than any other group of Oriental Jews, those of Persia were constantly searching for a haven that would offer political and religious freedom and economic opportunity. Throughout the ages, Persia seemed to serve as a reservoir for the Jewish diaspora of Central Asia, dispatching continuously droves of wanderers into almost every corner of the Islamic and Oriental world.

The most outstanding Jewish scholar of Bokhara was a certain Yusuf Yahudi (1688-1755). He was the author of a famous ode, "Mukhammas," devoted to the praise and glory of Moses, and of "Haft Braderan" (The Seven Brothers), based on the Midrash of the martyrdom of the seven brothers and their mother. These works, together with his "Tafsir" (commentary) to "Megillath Antioch" and his hymns in honor of Biblical heroes such as Elijah, as well as other poems bearing his name in acrosticon (some of which are bilingual and trilingual), form, to our own day, an integral part of the spiritual heritage of the Persian-speaking Jews of Bokhara.

Yusuf Yahudi was not less famous and fruitful as a translator of medieval Jewish poetry. Many of the "Zemiroth" of Israel Najara, incorporated in the collection of Judaeo-Persian song books, such as "Yismah Yisrael," were introduced by him into Judaeo-Persian literature. In his time, a "School of Jewish Poets" was established in Bokhara whose members, following his example, composed Judaeo-Persian poetry.

Among them was Benjamin ben Mishal, known also as Amina, who not only published "Megillath Esther" in Judaeo-Persian translation in metric form, but also translated into that tongue some poems of Solomon ibn Gabirol, such as "Azharoth" and "Yigdal." A Daniel Apocalypse, "Daniel Hameh", of a Khodja Bokhari (1705), is also ascribed to this Amina.

Special mention should be made of Elisha ben Samuel, also known as Mulla Raghib, who translated the romantic popular story of "Balsam and Joseph" (after the Hebrew version of Abraham ben Hisdai) into Judaeo-Persian under the title "Shah-Zadeh and the Sufi" (The Prince and the Dervish).

One of the finest poems in the Bokharian Jewish dialect is Ibraham ibn Abjil Gheir's famous "Khodaidad." It narrates the tragic story of a Jewish merchant Nathaniel (Khodaidad) who, despite all the alluring promises of the Mohammedan ruler and his neighbors, refused to embrace Islam and died a martyr. The author in his moving work presents a very interesting picture of the religious and political conditions in which the Jews of Bokhara lived in the second part of the eighteenth century. The poem also furnishes an authentic specimen of the linguistic peculiarities of the Persian poetry of Bokharian Jews.

III

This Bokharian-Jewish school of poets, together with their Persian brethren, also had a great share in the popularization of classical Persian poetry, and cultivated it with particular eagerness. Whilst devoted to their own Jewish heritage, as manifested in their translation into Judaeo-Persian of the poems of Yehudah Halevi, Solomon ibn Gabirol, Israel Najara and others, they had a special interest in the poetry of non-Jewish authors.

Inspired by their cultural atmosphere, the Jews in Persia and Bokhara shared with their neighbors a deep admiration for the great masters of Persian poetry. Some talented persons tried to make outstanding literary productions of their Persian environment accessible to Jewish circles, not only through translations from

Persian into Hebrew, but especially through transliterations from the Persian script into the Hebrew script. Some of the most important works of Persian authors such as Nizami, Sa'adi, Hafiz, Jami and others, were put into Hebrew dress, into Hebrew characters, with strict and exact retention of the Persian language, the rhyme and meter of the poetry. Thus they bridged the graphic separation between Mohammedans and Jews in Central Asia. These remarkable efforts represent a new branch of Persian literature in Hebrew characters.

The literary activities of Bokharian Jews must have come to a standstill towards the end of the eighteenth century; at least no further documents have been found. Interesting as these Judaeo-Persian products are, their authors do not seem to have affected Jewish life in Bokhara in general or to have penetrated to the masses very deeply. They appear to have been limited to certain upper strata of Jews who were assimilated into the culture and literature of their surroundings. This seems to be proven by the spiritual exhaustion, the lack of creativeness and the ignorance which marked the Bokharian Jews from the middle of the eighteenth century and which must have brought them to the brink of complete religious dissolution. Cut off from the rest of Jewish world, in the heart of Asia, they would have suffered the fate of the Jews in China had Providence not led to their re-discovery through a "Messenger from Zion."

IV

The redeemer of Bokharian Jews from ignorance, isolation and disappearance was a rabbi from Morocco, who came to visit Bokhara and, moved by the deplorable condition of his brethren, decided to stay to ameliorate their lot. The earliest reference to this rabbi, until now entirely overlooked, is found in Baron de Meyendorff's famous "Voyage d'Orenbourg à Boukhara fait en 1820", (Paris, 1826). The author states (p. 174 ff):

> "The rabbi of Bokhara, a native of Algiers, who still knows a little Spanish, told me that upon his arrival in Bokhara he found his co-religionists in a state of the greatest ignorance; only a very small number of them knew how to read. They

possessed only two copies of the Holy Bible, and their manuscript copy contained only the first three books of the Pentateuch. The Rabbi assured me that this manuscript was not older than a hundred years, and that its text did not differ from the standard text. This old Algerian Jew, full of spirit, who almost wept for joy on seeing Europeans again, has neglected nothing to spread education among his brethren. He established a school, ordered books from Russia, Baghdad and Constantinople, and now all the Jews of Bokhara know how to read and write and they study the Talmud. The rabbi showed extraordinary pleasure when I quoted from the book of Benjamin of Tudela, which was in his possession."

Interesting as this reference is, Meyendorff did not mention the rabbi's name. Other contemporary sources, however, which confirm and supplement this report, supply it. According to the first Jewish source, he was Rabbi Joseph Ma'man al-Maghrebi. In his book, entitled "The Travels of Rabbi David d'Beth Hillel, from Jerusalem through Arabia, Koordistan, part of Persia and India to Madras" (1828), a mine of information on the Jewish communities in the Orient in the first quarter of the nineteenth century, Rabbi David d'Beth Hillel inserted an account of a conversation with two Bokharian Jews, whom he had met in Baghdad in the year 1827. "I was told by them," said Rabbi David, "that in Bokhara there are three thousand families of Israelites, who are very rich, and speak broken Persian. They were formerly ignorant of the Hebrew language and customs, having no Hebrew books nor manuscripts nor anything relating to Hebrew law, but only a few prayers in manuscript which they had inherited from their forefathers. But about thirty-five years ago, there passed there a traveller, a North African Israelite named Rabbi Joseph Marobi (Maghrebi). This man found them so ignorant that he would not even eat with them. They, however, were able to keep him as their rabbi and teacher of the Torah. After some time, not being able to get any Hebrew books nor anything relating to the law except texts which he had brought along with him, he sent a letter through Astracan to Sklow to the Israelites there. . . ."

The importance of this account is enhanced by the fact that it represents the first reference from a Jewish source to that distinguished "African Israelite" to whom Bokharian Jewry is so immeasurably indebted and about whom, until the time of its author, nothing was known in Europe. This Rabbi Joseph Marobi (Maghrebi) is Rabbi Joseph Ma'man al-Maghrebi, a native of Tetuan, Morocco, who settled in Safed towards the end of the 18th century and who, in 1793, became the official emissary (shaliah) of that community to the Jews of Bokhara. Rarely has a visit of a messenger had such far-reaching repercussions. Rabbi Joseph brought about a radical transformation in the religious life of Bokharian Jewry. He impressed upon them—his purely subjective belief—that they, the Bokharian Jews, were the scions of the Sephardic Jews exiled from Spain, and as a result he succeeded in replacing the Persian rite by the Sephardic one. Under his spiritual leadership, the scattered remnants of the Jews of Bokhara were reclaimed for the House of Israel.

Another visitor to Bokhara, Joseph Wolff, also stressed the situation which confronted the new "Messenger from Morocco" upon his arrival. Rabbi Joseph is said to have preached: "Woe is me! Oh, my brethren, to find you in such condition, that you have forgotten the Law of Moses and the Prophets and the words of the wise men!" For six months he refused to eat their meat, and during that time he taught them to slaughter animals according to Jewish law, ordered them to perform ablutions and induced them to send men to Constantinople, Vilna, Leghorn, and Capusts to purchase Talmudical books. He sent for a Sofer (scribe) who wrote for them the Law of Moses upon parchment. He took under his instruction several young men, and thus made of Bokhara, as they used to say, "a little Jerusalem." He married (a second time) at Bokhara, spent sixty-one years there, lived to the age of eighty-one, and died lamented by every Jew there. They called him "the Light of Israel."

This account in its main part is also confirmed by the Jewish traveller Ephraim Neumark in his *"Massa l'Erets ha-Kedem"* (1859). He reports: "These Bokharian Jews, formerly so remote from their brethren, were also remote from the Torah. But eighty years ago there arrived one of the scholars from the West, by the name of Joseph Ma'man. When the people realized that he was a distinguished man they urged him to stay. He agreed, and settled in Bokhara, and began to teach Torah to the children, until they themselves became teachers. They possessed very rare books; one of the prominent people showed me the Zohar. With the coming of the Russians to Bokhara from across Turkestan, a way was opened for the Bokharians to Russia. They began to come to Moscow for trade purposes and they brought back from there all kinds of Hebrew books. Bokharian Jews also started to study Talmud in Moscow, until their community became an important one in Israel."

During his sixty-one years' stay in Bokhara, Rabbi Joseph's leadership was once contested by a Rabbi who came from Sana'a, in Yemen, a certain Rabbi Joseph ben Zechariah ben Matsliah. He, it seems, intended to introduce the Yemenite ritual into Bokhara and clashed with Rabbi Joseph ben Ma'man, who insisted on the Sephardic one.

V

From all these reports three main achievements of Rabbi Joseph Ma'man emerge: (1) the establishment of Jewish schools in Bokhara; (2) the introduction of the Sephardic rite; and (3) the importation of books from abroad. These measures helped to take the Bokharian Jews out of their isolation, to re-establish their contact with other Jewish communities, and to integrate their religious life with that of the whole Jewish people.

The supply of books is particularly stressed by J. Wolff, who states: "This Joseph Maarabee (Maghrebi) actually reformed the Jewish nation at Bokhara, Samarcand, and Balkh; for they all came to see the great Joseph Mooghrebee, i.e., 'Joseph Maarabee, the African'; and ever since his time, they have got their Bibles and Talmudical writings from the Jews of Orenburg, in Siberia, and from the great market-places in Russia, called Makariev."

The supply of books from Russia had been the object of a correspondence with the Jewish community of Shklow. The letter of Rabbi Maghrebi, transmitted to "all parts of Poland and Turkey," reads as follows:

"To our Brethren in Russia!

In the course of my travels I have arrived in Bokhara and have there come upon certain of our brethren who have attended upon me for instruction. We are not eager after gold, or silver, or jewels, or any worldly pleasures, but to hear the word of our Lord. We have, however, no manuscripts, no books nor anything pertaining to the Law. Therefore I beseech you to mail us as soon as possible, manuscripts, Bibles, prayer-books, and other religious requisites, whose price and cost of transportation we shall defray with great pleasure.

Your obedient servant,
Joseph Marobi."

VI

The Bokharian Jews, awakened through Rabbi Joseph, received additional stimulus through a wave of immigrants from Persia, Jews from Meshed, who, after the forced conversion of their community in 1838, looked for a new haven among the Jewish communities in Central Asia. From that time on, a steady stream of refugees poured into the neighboring Jewish communities, to Afghanistan, Turkestan and Bokhara. These refugees from the Marrano life revitalized Jewish life and, with their devotion to, and deeper knowledge of, Judaism, gave solidarity to the various remnants of Israel in Asia and particularly in Bokhara.

Another link between the Jews of Bokhara and Jews abroad was forged by the "messengers of Zion," Shelihim, who, at various intervals, left Palestine to visit their brethren in remote places. European travellers to Bokhara, from the beginning of the nineteenth century and on, made repeated reference to the Jewish community there. The reports of Russian scholars such as G. de Meyendorff (1821), Ehanikoff (1845) and others, the account of the Jewish missionary, Joseph Wolff, the information furnished by Rabbi David d'Beth Hillel, and, above all, the eye-witness accounts in Hebrew by the "Messenger from Safed" (1859), Ephraim Neumark (1883), E. N. Adler (1897-98) and others, convey a picture of the social and political conditions under which the Jews in Bokhara had to live.

VII

The influence of Rabbi Joseph and his work left an impression that is felt to this day. He implanted in them not only love of Torah, but also of Zion. He became the spiritual father of that *Hibbath-Tsiyon* movement in Asia, which, towards the end of the nineteenth century, led hundreds of Bokharian Jews to Palestine and to settlement in Jerusalem. As early as 1827 some left for the Holy Land. Rabbi David d'Beth Hillel reports having met in Baghdad two Bokharian Jews, en route to Jerusalem, with whom he conversed in Hebrew. He found them to be zealous adherents of Rabbi Joseph's teachings: "They were men of good talents, having a good knowledge of the Hebrew books and customs, and more pious and God-fearing than any other Israelites I have come across . . ." They seem to have been, indeed, the forerunners of that great wave of migration of Jews from Bokhara to Jerusalem, which introduced a new chapter in the relation between Oriental Jews and Zion.

Although there was probably no direct contact, the "Hovevei Tsiyon" movement from Russia to Palestine had its parallel in a similar movement of Persian-speaking Jews from Bokhara, Turkestan, Afghanistan and Persia. In a continuous stream they came from Teheran and Shiraz, from Hamadan, Yezd and Isfahan, from Kashan and Meshhed, from Herat and Kabul, from Bokhara, Samarkand and many other centers of Jewish settlement in the Middle East. They settled in Tiberias and Safed, in Haifa and Jaffa; but the bulk went to Jerusalem and established there a colony of Persian-speaking Jews. It was particularly the Jews of Bokhara who went exclusively to Jerusalem; in 1889 they established a "Society of the Lovers of Zion", and in 1893 they built a "Shekhunah," called "Rehovoth," which in the course of time became the focal point of the settlement of Persian-speaking Jews of Bokhara.

The establishment of this Bokharian colony in Jerusalem therefore not only opened a new chapter in the history of the urban colonization of Jerusalem, but inaugurated a new epoch in the history of Judaeo-Persian literary activities. The leaders of the Persian-speaking colony in Jerusalem, not content with having attained the realization of their long hoped-for return to the Holy Land, were very eager to help both spiritually and physically their brethren still in the lands of their origin. To create stronger ties between "Zion and Iran," between Jerusalem and the "Remnants of Israel" in the remote Oriental diaspora, they offered religious education and inspiration. With this in mind, they embarked on a unique enterprise.

This was the establishment in Jerusalem of a publishing center, a printing press for Judaeo-Persian literature, to issue the literary treasures they possessed in the manuscripts they had brought with them. Books were to be printed and distributed among all Persian-speaking Jews, in Palestine and abroad. The press was established as a formal token of their gratitude for having reached the land of their hopes, and to honor the memory of their fore-fathers. It was destined ultimately to bring about a decisive and far-reaching change in the educational history of Persian-speaking Jews. Jerusalem now became the exclusive center of Judaeo-Persian printing; henceforth all the liturgical and literary needs of Persian-speaking Jews were taken care of by the Jerusalem Judaeo-Persian press. The Bible, Bible Commentaries, Prayer-Books for every occasion, Rabbinical writings, Mishnah and Zohar, Religious Philosophy, Medieval Jewish Poetry, Piyutim, Selihoth, Pizmonim, Midrashim, Historical Narratives, Anthologies of Songs and Stories, were translated into Judaeo-Persian, printed and distributed. Secular literature from non-Jewish sources, such as parts of the "Arabian Nights," and of Shakespeare's "Comedy of Errors," which appealed greatly to the imagination of the Oriental Jew, found its way to the translators and printers.

VIII

Very significantly, these Judaeo-Persian publishing activities represented a cooperative endeavor on the part of all the various groups of Persian-speaking Jewry: Jews of Bokhara joined hands with the Jews of Persia and Afghanistan and participated in the greatest common cultural enterprise in the history of Oriental Jewry. Of the many outstanding figures who took part therein only two can be mentioned here: one from Samarkand, the other from Bokhara.

Solomon Babajan b. Pinchasoff of Samarkand, editor, author, translator and publisher, entered the field of Judaeo-Persian publications with his translation of "Job," which was followed by Judaeo-Persian translations of Yehudah Halevy's *"Mi Kamokha,"* Solomon ibn Gabriol's *"Kether Malkhuth"* and other liturgical and religious poetry. His greatest service, however, was closely connected with the "Hibbath Tsiyon" movement of Oriental Jews. A great part of the literary output in Jerusalem was clearly aimed at the furthering of the ideals of Zion and at promoting the knowledge of the Hebrew language among Jews who remained in Central Asia. A typical expression of this tendency was the Judaeo-Persian translation of *"Ahavath Tsiyon,"* with all its romantic Biblical background, and the translation of the "Hatikvah" into Judaeo-Persian which was appended to many of the publications.

He also put forth "Sefer Millim Shishah" (Jerusalem, 1909), a dictionary in six languages (all in Hebrew characters), a linguistic compendium for all the Jews of Central Asia who intended to come to Palestine. In the brief Hebrew preface the author says: "I have composed it for the use of our Jewish brethren who intend to go to Jerusalem, to enable them to learn all the languages necessary, without too much trouble and effort."

Among the lexicographical and linguistic treatises should be mentioned the Hebrew-Persian-Russian dictionary, *"Sefer Kitsur ha-Millim,"* by David b. Jakob Chwailoff, published in 1907 in Jerusalem; it contained about 5000 words in Persian, with their Russian and Hebrew equivalents in Hebrew transcription. The whole edition of this linguistic guide was sent to Bokhara for distribution among its Jews, who were familiar with the Russian language.

In addition to Persian, there appeared guides in Russian, French (later, in the second edition, Ladino), Arabic, Turkish and Hebrew. This "philological Baedeker" was in great demand.

IX

The second outstanding figure is Simon Hakham. Born in 1843 in Bokhara, to which city his father, Eliahu Hakham, had emigrated from Baghdad, he received a thorough Jewish education and became deeply rooted in Jewish tradition. He emigrated in 1890 to Jerusalem and died there in 1910. It was in Jerusalem that he began his manifold activities as author, translator, editor and publisher.

With the establishment of the Judaeo-Persian printing center in Jerusalem, he brought there for publication not only his own literary compositions and translations, but also many manuscripts of his countrymen, Jews and non-Jews. Special mention should be made of his Judaeo-Persian translation of the Biblical novel "Ahavath Tsiyon" by Abraham Mapu. It appeared in Jerusalem in 1908, and immediately became such a popular book among Oriental Jews that a second edition was printed in 1912. Simon Hakham was so enthusiastic about the novel that he concluded his translation with the following words: "Whoever reads this book only once, has certainly not yet comprehended it; he who reads it twice, has only slightly understood its contents; only he who reads it thrice will fully grasp its meaning and penetrate into the depth of its ideas; but even he who reads it a hundred times until he knows it by heart will certainly wish to read it a hundred and one times."

He rendered a special service in publishing part of the *"Epos of the Jewish Past"* by Maulana Shahin of Shiraz of the fourteenth century, to which he added his own poetical compositions. Of great value was his publication of the Judaeo-Persian translation of the Shulhan Arukh, under the title of "Likkutei Dinim," prepared by his countryman Abraham Aminoff, the leading Rabbi of the Bokharian colony of Jerusalem.

The crowning glory of his literary contributions, however, is his translation of the Hebrew Bible into the Judaeo-Persian dialect of the Bokharian Jews. It was a custom among the Jews of Bokhara to have the Bible explained, in the schools and especially in the synagogue, orally, by a *methurgeman* or translator, on the basis of a commentary which had been orally transmitted. This oral method created, in the course of centuries, variants and explanations departing from the traditionally accepted interpretation, and not always faithful to the text of the Bible. To eliminate further confusion, Simon Hakham wished to create "a fixed coin" —a written text of the Tafsir (commentary) in the dialect of his fellow Jews.

He was, however, also motivated by another factor. He saw in Jerusalem the "Remnants of Israel" from the four corners of the earth, each using the prayer book and the Bible in his own language and dialect. The Ashkenazim had their Yiddish, the Sefardim their Spaniolish, the Yemenites and Maghrebim their Arabic; "Why is it that we, Persian-speaking Jews of Bokhara, do not possess a translation in our own dialect as well?"

Proud of the culture and language of his country of origin, Simon Hakham desired to make the Bible again a popular work by creating a written, standard, authorized Judaeo-Persian translation. He knew, of course, of the existence of the Pentateuch translation of Jacob B. Tawus (1546), but this version could hardly be used for his educational purposes; no copies were available and the version differed from the specific Bokharian dialect; nor could the Bible edition of the Christian missionaries be used—for obvious reasons. Translations of some parts of the Bible, such as the Psalms (1883), Proverbs (1885), Job (1895) and Shir ha-Shirim (1896 and 1904) into Judaeo-Persian did exist. But a complete Bible translation for the daily use of Bokharian Jews was lacking, and it was this consideration which prompted Simon Hakham to embark on his great enterprise. His "Tafsir," started in 1906, appeared in successive volumes, along with the Hebrew text, Targum Onkelos and Rashi, and had it not been for his untimely death in 1910, the whole translation would have been accomplished. He completed the Pentateuch and the Prophets, up to Isaiah XLI 9, but it was left for his collaborators to complete the translation of the whole Bible.

With this monumental achievement Simon Hakham entered the ranks of the great Jewish Bible translators. What Saadia Gaon did for the Arabic-speaking Jews, what Moses Mendelssohn did for the German-speaking Jews, Simon Hakham did for the Persian-speaking Jews of Bokhara. Editor, author and promoter, it is his Bible translation which made him pre-eminent. He continued the chain of Jewish learning which was implanted in the hearts of his fellow Jews in Bokhara by Joseph Ma'man al-Maghrebi, and became the undisputed leader of that group of the "Remnants of Israel" which, forgotten for centuries, emerged from oblivion revitalized and enabled to play its part in the reconstruction of Israel in our days.

THE CONTRIBUTORS

Leo Jung. The Editor is the rabbi of The New York Jewish Center, former President of the Rabbinical Council of The Union of Orthodox Jewish Congregations of America, Prof. of Ethics and Jewish Philosophy, Yeshiva University, Chairman of the J. D. C.'s Cultural and Religious Committee, translator (Soncino Edition) of two tractates of The Talmud, and author of "Fallen Angels, an Essay on Comparative Folklore;" "Mistranslations as Source of Lore," "Living Judaism," "Crumbs and Character," "The Rhythm of Life," and other books, pamphlets and articles on Judaism and Jewish Law.

Moses M. Yoshor, Rabbi of The New Brighton Jewish Center, Brooklyn, N. Y., President of Rabbinical Board of the Shore Front Jewish Communities, contributor to various publications, and author of "Saint and Sage," "Israel in the Ranks," and "Das Leben un Shafen fun Hafetz Hayyim." He received his rabbinical education at the Yeshivoth of Lomza and Hafetz Hayyim of Radun, and his secular knowledge at the College of the City of New York.

Charles P. Chavel. Ordained as Rabbi by Beth Medrash LeTorah of Chicago, 1928; Ph.B. University of Chicago; M.A., LL.B. University of Louisville. Served Congregation Anshe Sfard, Louisville, Ky., from 1929 to 1945, since then, Congregation Shaare Zedek, Edgemere, L. I. Author: "The Book of Divine Commandments of Maimonides" (Soncino Press, London, 1940); "A Companion for Jews in Armed Forces" (Rabbinical Council of America, 1944); "Sefer Ha-Hinukh" (Mosad Horav Kuk, Jerusalem, 1952); contributor to new edition of "Minhath Hinukh" New York, 1952 and to the rabbinic periodicals, "Hapardes" and "Talpioth."

Solomon Wind. Born in Galicia, studied in early youth at Ujhel, Hungary, entered Yeshivath Rabbi Isaac Elchanan in 1922, was ordained in 1929, graduated from CCNY in 1930, pursued graduate work in Semitics at Dropsie College and at

549

Columbia, received D.H.L. from Bernard Revel Graduate School in 1942, served as Rabbi at Nathan Straus Jewish Center and at Congregation Etz Chaim of the Bronx. At present, he is instructor at the Teachers' Institute of Yeshiva University and at the Hebrew Teachers' Training School for Girls.

Author of "Responsa Noda BeYehudah as source material for Jewish History;" "On the Relations between Rabbi Jonathan Eibeshutz and Rabbi Ezekiel Landau"; "Rabbi Landau's Rabbinate," "The Hebrew Calendar—its structure and function," and *"Miknesseth ad Knesseth"*—a Survey of Jewish History from the Babylonian Exile to the Present.

HAROLD I. LEIMAN studied at the Mesifta Torah Vodaath, at New York and Columbia Universities. He is Superintendent of Yeshivoth, and Principal of the Hebrew Institute of Long Island. He has written for the National Education Association and is co-author of "Science and Judaism."

SOLOMON EHRMANN, (Ph.D., D.D.S.) studied at the Yeshivah of Frankfurt, where he received his semikhah at the hand of the sainted Rabbi Solomon Breuer. He obtained his secular education at the Universities of Munich, Berlin, Giessen, Kiel and Frankfurt. He was honorary lecturer at the Yeshivah of Frankfurt, member of the Supreme Council of Agudath Israel and Director of its Palestine Office. One of the founders of the interdominational Kepler Society, a member of the *Kant-Gesellschaft,* he served (1938-42) as rabbi in Paris and since has resided in Switzerland. There he developed a fruitful activity as rabbi in charge of refugees, as writer, lecturer and director of the world organization of Agudah. He edited *"Unser Weg"* (1908-10) of *The Bund Juedischer Akademiker,* the monthly *"Nachalath Zvi"* (1930-37) and contributed many essays and articles to the "Israelit," "Die Juedische Presse," "Der Tag" (Warsaw), "Unser Wort," (Vilna), "Kol Israel" and "Hamodia" (Jerusalem).

JOSHUA FINKEL was born in Warsaw in 1897 and came to the United States in 1913; was graduated from New York University (B.A.) in 1919, and from the Dropsie College (Ph.D.) in 1929. From 1924 to 1926 did research work in Egypt, in the field of Judaeo-Arabic and Islamic civilization. In 1937, he was appointed Professor of Semitic Languages and Literatures at Yeshiva University. He wrote a number of studies in various scientific periodicals published both here and abroad; published two books: In 1926—*The Three Rasail of Jahiz* (Cairo) and in 1939—the critical edition of Maimonides *Treaties of Resurrection* (Introduction, Notes, Arabic text and Ibn Tibbon's Hebrew translation).

ISAAC BREUER of blessed memory—scholar of the Talmud, brilliant jurist, and President of Poale Agudath Israel in the Holy Land, was the author of half a dozen profound works among which the "New Kuzari," "Moriyah" and "Nahaliel," are most significant. He is one of the most seminal influences on Torah-true thought in our days.

M. L. BAMBERGER is a graduate of the famous Yeshiva of Slobodka and of Wuerzburg University; was rabbi of Mainz (Germany) and is now associated with the great Torah Academy in Gateshead, England.

JOSEPH ELIAS. Born in Germany, 1919; studied at various European Yeshivoth and universities, received "Semikhah" from Rabbi Elia Chazan ("Merkaz Hatorah," Montreal); B.A. (Toronto); M.A. (Chicago); in 1943 he received the Isserman Peace Prize (Toronto) for a study on international cooperation. Has held various educational positions and presently is Principal of Yeshivath Beth Yehudah, Detroit, Mich. Editor of the "Jewish Books" series, author of "The Spirit of Jewish History," "Social Order—The Jewish View" and other books. Contributor to various Jewish periodicals.

The sainted DR. ISAAC UNNA, formerly Chief Rabbi of Mannheim (Germany), completed his life's work at the head of a synagogue in Jerusalem. He was the author of a number of books and essays on Jewish life and law and a leader in the World Mizrachi movement.

ISAAC HEINEMANN, Ph.D., now in Jerusalem, is a world-famous scholar, author of standard works on Greek and Jewish philosophy, and from 1920-38 editor of the *Monatschrift fuer die Geschichte und Wissenschaft des Judentums.*

JOSUE JEHOUDA, of Geneva, a disciple of Elie Benamozegh, has done very significant work as transmitter of important aspects of the Jewish tradition to French-speaking Jews. His publications have aroused widespread interest.

HAYYIM Z. REINES. Born in Preny (Lithuania), educated at the Yeshivah of Lida, (founded by his grandfather Rabbi Isaac Jacob Reines), studied Semitic languages and Philosophy at the University of Berlin, where he received his Ph.D. Was a lecturer on Jewish History at the Duquesne University of Pittsburgh. Published—"Labor in the Bible and Talmud," "Individual and Community," "Prolegomena to a Philosophy of Judaism," "Priests and Prophets," "Bibilical Studies," "Labor in Rabbinical Responsa" (Jewish Library vol. V), "The Support of the Scholars in the Talmudic Period." An essay on the Philosophy of Jewish History "Tradition and Ideal in Judaism," a book on the import of "Torah in rabbinical thought," and "Torah and Musar," are scheduled for publication by *Mossad Harav Kook.*

GERSHOM BADER, journalist, playwright; born August 21, 1868, Cracow, Poland; son of Isaac Moses Bader; self-educated. Teacher, public schools, Lemberg, Galicia, 1893-1912. Contributed to foremost Hebrew dailies in Petersburg and Warsaw. Editor, *Hashemesh,* 1899, in Kolomea; *Hasharon* in Lemberg, 1893-95; also *Haeth* (Lemberg), 1907; edited 18 volumes of a Yiddish year book, "Gershon Bader's Folks Calendar," 1896-1912. Founded "Tagblatt," first Yiddish daily in Austria, 1904; editor, "Neues Lemberger Tagblatt," 1906 and "Der Strahl," also in Yiddish. Author of plays: "In Keller" (produced in Liptzin's Theatre, 1910); "Near the Fire," "Israel Bal Shemtov" (produced in Lemberg, 1911); "The Rabbi in Fire" (produced N. Y. 1912); " 'Twixt Love and Death" (produced N. Y. 1913); "The American Doctor" (produced in N. Y. 1913); "The Golden Rose" (produced in N. Y. 1920). In 1919 wrote libretto to Rumshinsky's operetta, "The Rabbi's Melody." Since 1914, a member of editorial staff, Jewish Daily News. Since 1927, with the editorial staff of the Jewish Morning Journal.

MOSES JUNG, LL.B., Ph.D., Lecturer in Comparative Religion, Columbia University and Consultant in Jewish-Catholic Relations, American Jewish Committee; Consultant in Research to White House Conference on Children and Youth; formerly, Lecturer in Sociology, New York University and Professor of Religion, State University of Iowa. Author: "The Jewish Law of Theft," a study in comparative law; "Modern Marriage," a symposium (editor and contributor); "Source Book of Jewish History and Literature" (Co-Author).

The late DR. JACOB KLATZKIN, a world-renowned philosopher, wrote a dozen books in several languages; edited the ten-volume Jewish encyclopedia in German, wrote four-volume *Otzar Ha-Munahim—Ha-Philosophiyim"* and translated "Spinoza's Ethics" into Hebrew.

NIMA H. ADLERBLUM, Ph.D. Columbia University; Lecturer on contemporary philosophy. Member of the American Philosophical Association and of the Inter-American Congress of Philosophy. Elected by the Inter-American Congress of Philosophy of 1950 as editor of a contemplated edition of contemporary philosophical tendencies throughout the world. Active member of the American Committee (chairman, Professor Kilpatrick) for the translation and dissemination of John Dewey's and American philosophy through Latin America. Founder of the Hadassah National cultural work; its national cultural chairman and member of its National Board from 1920-1933.

Research Work: 1934-1936 on problems and conflicts of minority nationalities in Central Europe and in Soviet Russia, on Nazism during the Hitler regime.

Immigration to Mexico: In 1938 she obtained concessions from former Mexican President Avila Camacho for the immigration of European refugees; in 1940 she took an active part in fighting Anti-Semitism in Mexico.

Author: *A Study of Gersonides in his proper Perspective,* Columbia University Press 1927, aiming at the vindication of Jewish philosophy which had hitherto been regarded as a mere branch of scholasticism. Among her other contributions (in the

Journal of Philosophy and other magazines) : "A Reinterpretation of Jewish Philosophy;" "A Perspective for the study of Jewish Philosophy;" "The Emotional Content of Jewish Philosophy;" "Jewish Philosophical Romanticism;" "Medieval Jewish Philosophy" Jewish Ethics; Bachya Ibn Pakuda, Creative History; "The Role of History;" "Main Currents and Thoughts of the 19th Century;" "Pragmatic Aspects of Jewish Philosophy," etc.

Her book "A Perspective of Jewish Life through its Festivals" has been transcribed in Braille.

SAUL SILBER.   The sainted President of the Hebrew Theological College of Chicago was a leader in American Mizrachi, a great orator and bold pedagogue.

JUDITH GRUNFELD-ROSENBAUM, Ph.D., a disciple and chief lieutenant of the sainted Sara Schenierer is Principal of the famed Jewish Secondary School of London and one of the outstanding Torah-true pedagogues in today's Jewry.

J. L. KAGAN, grandson of the author of "Panim Meiroth" (on the Yerushalmi) and son-in-law of the sainted Chief Rabbi Kossovsky of Johannesburg, was trained in the Yeshivoth of Mir, Radun and Kelm, received his semikhah from the sainted Gaonim Rabbi Hayyim Ozer Grodzensky, the head of the Mirrer Yeshiva, the Gaon Kamai, the Chief Rabbi of Tel Aviv, Rabbi Amiel, and from the present Rosh Yeshiva, Rabbi A. Finkel, and the Gaon Dr. Hayyim Heller.   Rabbi Kagan was dayan of the Jewish Community of Antwerp, rabbi of Kehillath Yeshurun of Lyon, Professor at the Yeshiva Jacob Joseph at the Beth Hamidrash Latorah in Chicago, and is at present head of the Yeshivath Rabbi Israel Salanter in the Bronx.   He has contributed learned papers to rabbinic and talmudic journals.

HAROLD B. PERLMAN.   A graduate of Yeshiva University, he has occupied pulpits in New York and New Jersey, served on the faculties of the Hebrew Teachers' Training School for Girls, the Rabbinical College of Telshe (Cleveland) and the Yeshivah of Hudson County.   He is a member of the Executive Board of "Moriah," sponsored by Torah U'Mesorah.   His writings have appeared in "Jewish Life," "Jewish Parents' Magazine" and the Publications of the American Jewish Historical Society.

CECIL ROTH. Historian: Reader in Jewish Studies at the University of Oxford, author of over thirty books and hundreds of scholarly articles. His works have been translated into six languages. His latest book, THE JEWS OF MEDIEVAL OXFORD (1951) is the most detailed study of a medieval group, Jewish or non-Jewish, ever written. Born London, March 5, '99. Fought World War I: returned to Oxford, where he studied history: his first book, THE LAST FLORENTINE REPUBLIC (1925) received compliment of translation into Italian, earned honorary membership of Italian learned societies, and is still regarded a standard work. After other contributions to Italian and general history, he began to turn to Jewish. His JEWISH CONTRIBUTION TO CIVILISATION was translated into several languages and denounced on the German radio!

Greatest title to distinction—that he was included (with Churchill and Eden) in list of first 500 to be arrested by Nazis when they arrived in England.

ABRAHAM BEN JACOB. Born in Baghdad, his family emigrated to Israel in his youth, and made Jerusalem their permanent home. A graduate (1935) of the Teachers' Seminary, Ben Jacob acquired a fine reputation as a teacher and author of approved text books. He specialized in Judaism and Jewish history, and published hundreds of essays and researches in 35 publications all over the world dealing with education, folklore and philology. He contributed to Margoliuth's Encyclopedia Biography of Leading Israelis," to the "Hebrew Encyclopedia" (Massadah) and to Tidhor's "Encyclopedia of the Pioneers and Builders of Israel." He was associate editor of the weekly *"Hed Hamizrach,"* from 1942 to 1951. Presently he is engaged in writing a monumental work on the Jews of Iraq in the last thousand years, their history, customs, poetry, folklore and maxims, with philological animadversions. His article in the present volume is a fair example of his learning and excellent style. Abraham Ben Jacob is a communal worker of note. His activities concern the spiritual welfare of Sephardic Jews in Israel, the proposed great Teachers' Training College and Rabbinical Seminary and the Sephardic cultural center, which is to serve them in Israel and in Galut.

Dr. Walter J. Fischel is Professor of Semitic Languages and Literature and Chairman of the Department of Near Eastern Languages at the University of California, Berkeley. For many years he was a member of the faculty of the Hebrew University, Jerusalem. One of the principal fields of his investigation has been the cultural and sociological aspects of medieval Islamic and Hebrew civilization. He is the author of many books and studies on the subject. Recently he edited "Semitic and Oriental Studies presented to William Popper," (University of California Press, 1951). He is now preparing a translation of the entire text of Ibn Khaldun's "Autobiography" with a commentary based on the several manuscripts. His major writings include, "Jews in the Economic and Political Life of Medieval Islam," London, 1937; "Jews and Judaism at the Court of the Moghul Emperors in India" (Proceeding of Jew. Acad.) New York, 1950; "Israel in Iran, a Survey of Judea-Persian Literature," New York, 1949; "History of the Marrano Community in Central Asia (Hebrew) Zion, 1936; "Jews in Persia under the Kajar Dynasty" (1795-1940) Jew. Soc., New York, 1950; "A Journey to Kurdistan, Persia and Babylonia (Hebrew), Sinai, Jerusalem, 1940; "Khorosan in Medieval Hebrew and Islamic Literature" (Historia Judaica) (New York, 1945); "New Sources to the Diaspora in the 16th Century" (J. O. R. 1950); "Ibn Khaldun and Tamerlane" (Berkeley 1952); "Ibn Khaldun's Activities in Egypt" (Berkeley 1952); "Ibn Khaldun and Tamerlane"—Their Historic Meeting in Damascus in 1401 A. D. Translated into English with a Commentary by Walter J. Fischel, Univ. of California Press, 1952.

THE JEWISH LIBRARY

Edited by LEO JUNG

CONTENTS

VOLUME I (1928; second revised edition, 1943)

---

*Omitted in second edition.

**Only in the first edition.

Volume II (1930)

1. The Romance of the Hebrew Alphabet, by the Very Rev. Haham Moses Gaster.

2. Faith and Science, by Moses Legis Isaacs, Ph. D.

3. Fundamental Ideals and Proclamations of Judaism, by the Very Rev. Chief Rabbi Dr. Joseph H. Hertz.

4. Worship as a Mode of Study, by Edwin Collins.

5. What is Orthodox Judaism? by Rabbi Leo Jung, Ph. D.

6. The Centrality of Palestine in Jewish Life, by Rabbi David de Sola Pool, Ph. D.

7. Shehitah, by S. Lieben, M. D.

8. Bahya's "Duties of the Heart," by Edwin Collins.

9. Scientific Aspects of the Jewish Dietary Laws, by David L. Macht, D. H. L., M. D., Phar. D., LL. B.

10. The Great Preamble—A Rereading of Genesis, by Prof. Nathan Isaacs, S. J. D., Ph. D.

11. Dogma in Judaism, by Rabbi Salis Daiches, Ph. D.

12. The Jews at the Close of the Middle Ages, by Cecil Roth, Ph. D., F. R. H. S.

Volume III (1934)

"The Jewish Woman"

1. The Jewish Woman in the Bible, by Rev. Dr. B. Jacob, Ph. D., Dortmund (Germany). Translated by Armand Lowinger, B. A.

2. Some Stories about Jewish Women, by the Very Rev. Dr. Moses Gaster, Ph. D., London (England).

3. Modern Marriage Problems, by Rabbi Leo Jung, Ph. D., New York.

4. The Jewish Woman in the Home, by Irene R. Wolff, Montreal, P. Q.

5. The "Women's Branch" of the "Union of Orthodox Jewish Congregations of America," by Betty F. Goldstein, New York.

6. The "National Council of Jewish Women," by Hannah G. Solomon and Nannie A. Reis, Chicago.

7. The Jewish Woman in the Responsa, by Prof. I. Epstein, D. Lit., London (England).

8. The Grande Dame in Jewish History, by Rabbi Felix Aber, Ph. D., Bremen (Germany). Translated by Hugo Mantel, B. A.

9. Literature for Jewish Women in Medieval and Later Times, by Rabbi Arthur Posner, Ph. D., Anvers (Belgium). Translated by Rabbi A. Burnstein, M. A.

10. Outstanding Jewish Women in Western Europe, by Dr. Cecil Roth, Ph. D., London (England).

11. Jewish Women in Social Service in Germany, by Dr. Else Rabin, Ph. D., Breslau (Germany). Translated by Rebecca Latz and I. S. Adlerblum.

12. The Jewish Lullaby, by Rabbi Israel Goldfarb, Brooklyn (N. Y.).

13. Art and the Jewish Woman, by Hebe Rahel Bentwich Mayer, Frankfurt am Main (Germany).

14. Taharah—A Way to Married Happiness, by Rivka Levi Jung, B. A., Iowa City (Ia.).

15. Neurosis and the Modern Jewess, by Dr. W. M. Feldman, M. D., London (England).

16. The Jewish Woman in Eastern Europe, by Studienrat Ari Wohlgemuth, Riga (Latvia). Translated by I. S. Alderblum.

17. The Jewish Woman of Palestine, by Lotta Levensohn, Jerusalem.

18. The World Organization of Jewish Women, by Rebekah Kohut, New York.

VOLUME V (1946; second revised edition, 1949)

ISRAEL OF TOMORROW

RELIGION

1. Jewish Foundations of the New World Order, by Rabbi Leo Jung, Ph. D., New York.

2. Religion and the World of Tomorrow, by Siegmund Forst, New York. (Translated by Eugenie A. Propp).

3. Judaism and the World of Tomorrow, by the late Isaac Breuer, LL. D. (Translated by I. S. Adlerblum).

RELIEF AND RECONSTRUCTION

4. J. D. C. In World Jewry—Past, Present, and Future, by Leon Shapiro, and Boris Sapir, New York.**

LAW

5. Labor in Rabbinical Responsa, by Dr. Ch. W. Reines, New York.

6. Judaism and International Law, by Rabbi Philip Biberfeld, Ph. D., New York.

7. The Jewish Attitude Towards Peace and War, by Rabbi David S. Shapiro, Indianapolis.

8. Jewry-Law—Past, Present, and Future, by Professor Guido Kisch, New York.

8A. Anti-Semitism in the World of Tomorrow, by Professor M. L. Isaacs, New York.*

8B. The Attitude of the Hafetz Hayyim Toward Labor, by Rabbi Oscar Z. Fasman, Chicago.*

THE ARTS

9. The Halakhah and Aesthetics (Judaism of Tomorrow and the World of Art and Beauty), by Rabbi H. Raphael Gold, M. D., New York.

**Only in the first edition.

10. Some Directives for Jewish Music of Tomorrow, by Rabbi Milton Feist, New York.**

11. Jewish Literature in the World of Tomorrow, by Professor Meyer Waxman, Chicago.

12. Gersonides in Jewish Thinking of Tomorrow, by Dr. Nima H. Adlerblum, New York.

SCIENCE

13. Natural Science and Problems of Judaism, by Professor Bruno Kisch, M. D., New York.

14. The Economic Prospects of American Jewry, by Professor Nathan Reich, New York.**

PALESTINE

15. The State of Israel and the United Nations, by Tamar de Sola Pool, New York.**

15A. Palestine in the Post-War World, by Tamar de Sola Pool, New York.*

16. The High Court of Justice in the Past and in the Future, by the late Rabbi Isaac Unna, Ph. D.

POLAND

17. Polish Jewry—Yesterday, Today and Tomorrow, by Dr. Wolf Blattberg, New York.

18. Religious Judaism in Independent Poland, by Dr. Isaac Lewin, New York. (Translated by Rabbi Abraham Burstein).

AMERICA

19. The Jewish Communal Organization of Tomorrow, by the late Rabbi Bernard Drachman, Ph. D.

20. America and Israel of Tomorrow, by Elisha M. Friedman, New York.

21. Yeshivah Education in America, by Professor Jacob I. Hartstein, New York.

22. The Role of the Talmud Torah in Jewish Education in America, by Morris B. Benathen, St. Louis.

---

*Omitted in second edition.
**Only in the second edition.

Volume VI

1. The Rabbis and the Ethics of Business, by Rabbi Leo Jung, Ph. D.

2. Eliyahu of Vilna, by Rabbi Moses M. Yoshor.

3. Shneyur Zalman of Liady, by Rabbi Charles B. Chavel.

4. Ezekiel Landau, by Rabbi Solomon Wind, D. H. L.

5. Akiba Eger, by Rabbi Harold I. Leiman, Ph. D.

6. Moses Sofer, by S. Ehrmann, D. D. S. (Translated by Eugenie A. Propp, from the German).

7. Menahem Morgenstern of Kotzk, by Professor Joshua Finkel, Ph. D.

8. Samson Raphael Hirsch, by the late Isaac Breuer, LL. D.

9. Seligman Baer Bamberger, by Rabbi M. L. Bamberger, Ph. D.

10. Israel Salanter, by Rabbi Joseph Elias, M. A.

11. Ezriel (Israel) Hildesheimer, by the late Rabbi Isaac Unna, Ph. D.

12. Elie Benamozegh, by Josue Jehouda. (Translated by Eugenie A. Propp, from the French).

13. Marcus Horovitz by the late Rabbi Isaac Unna, Ph. D.

14. Marcus Horovitz, by Isaac Heinemann, Ph. D. (Translated by Rabbis Eliezer Horovitz and Samuel Dresner, from the Hebrew).

15. Isaac Jacob Reines, by Hayyim Z. Reines, Ph. D. (Translated by Rabbi Theodore J. Adams, from the Hebrew).

16. Meir Tsevi Jung, by Gershom Bader, and Moses Jung, LL. B., Ph. D.

17. Eliyahu Klatzkin, by the late Jacob Klatzkin, Ph. D. (Translated from the Hebrew by Rabbi Milton Feist).

18. Sara Bayla and Her Times, by Nima H. Adlerblum, Ph. D.

19. The Gaon of Rogatchov, by the late Rabbi Saul Silver. (Translated by Rabbi Oscar Z. Fasman, from the Yiddish).

20. Sara Schenierer, by Dr. Judith Grunfeld-Rosenbaum, Ph. D.

VOLUME VII

"STUDY AS A MODE OF WORSHIP"
AND OTHER ESSAYS by
NATHAN ISAACS

(in the press)